STANDARDS OF ARCHAEOLOGICAL EXCAVATION

Controlled excavation and recovery is the essence of good archaeological practice. Field notes, reports, drawings and photographs are the embodiment of the site; once excavated, many of the contexts are destroyed forever, and the records are the only evidence they ever existed. The graphic and textual reconstruction of the site enables repeatable comparisons to be made, allowing re-evaluation and re-interpretation as necessary.

With more than 250 checklists, diagrams, photographs and tables, this fieldguide takes the archaeologist from site evaluation through to grid systems, methods of excavation for different context types, archiving, report writing and post-excavation assessment. All these activities comprise the holistic archaeological practice which is advocated throughout this work. Using the prescribed methodology, the excavator can gather data in an ordered, logical manner, presenting it in layered form to enable further interpretation. This fieldguide is a comprehensive resource for anyone conducting excavation fieldwork anywhere in the world. From Palaeolithic campsites to historic buildings, Standards gives practical advice to guide the archaeologist towards best practice in any excavation context. It is thus an invaluable resource for lecturers, students, field directors, excavators, consultants and specialist, in the classroom or on site.

Geoffrey J. Tassie is the Managing Director of the Egyptian Cultural Heritage Organisation. Lawrence S. Owens is a lecturer in bioarchaeology, Birkbeck College, University of London.

E C H O

Actively making archaeology work to protect Egypt's heritage

The Egyptian Cultural Heritage Organisation

Standards of Archaeological Excavation; a Fieldguide to the Methodology, Recording Techniques and Conventions

Geoffrey John Tassie
Egyptian Cultural Heritage Organisation

Lawrence Stewart Owens
Birkbeck College, University of London

Golden House Publications
First edition – 2010

Egyptian Cultural Heritage Organisation Monograph Series No. 1

This title is published by

Golden House Publications

Written by G. J. Tassie and L. S. Owens

Artwork by G. J. Tassie, with additional drawings by Colette Standish

Edited by Tim Stevens & Lawrence S. Owens

Originally devised by G. J. Tassie & F. A. Hassan

For more information on how to become a member of ECHO and other ECHO projects and promotions visit our website on: www.e-c-h-o.org

A catalogue record of this publication is available from the British Library

ISBN 978-1-906137-17-5

Printed in the United Kingdom
By

PrintonDemand
9 Culley Court, Bakewell Road, Orton Southgate,
Peterborough, P
E2 6XD

London 2010

To Vera Janet Tassie

The much-loved and missed matriarch of the Tassie family, who encouraged my studies every step of the way. I hope this work justifies her pride and expectations.

...and Charles Stewart Owens

for being the rock around which his family has revolved, and being the man I one day wish to become

ACKNOWLEDGEMENTS

The writing of this book has been greatly enriched by contributions, skills and advice from the following ECHO members, interlocutors and other archaeologists: Ceri Ashley, Andie Byrne, Bram Calcoen, Louise Cave, Natalie Cohen, Kaz Czerwinski, Niall Finneran, Maybeline Gormley, Kate Griffiths, Cordelia Hall, Fiona Handley, Diccon Hart, Anies Hassan, Fekri A. Hassan, Janet Johnstone, Cornelia Kleintz, Mona Korolnik, Mark Landymore, Duncan Lees, Mary Ann Murray, Dominic Perrins, Peter Popkin, Joanne M. Rowland, Ian Shaw, Colette Standish, Tim Stevens, Kris Strutt, Amanda Sutherland, Dan Swift, Aloisa de Trafford, Claire F. Venables, Ken Walton, Joris van Wetering, Penny Wilson, Richard Woolley, Melissa Zabecki and Cyril. We would like to express our thanks to all the SCA inspectors and other personnel that we have worked with in Egypt at various sites; their thoughts, wishes and ideas have helped greatly in formulating this book. A huge debt of gratitude and many thanks is owed to Professor Dr. Gaballa A. Gaballa, former Secretary General of the Supreme Council of Antiquities (SCA), Egypt, for his encouragement in writing this book. Professor Gaballa's vision that there be made available to young archaeologists - especially Egyptian archaeologists - a fieldguide of excavation methodology in both English and Arabic was the catalyst for this book. This book would not have been possible without the work of the pioneers of Egyptian archaeology, such James H. Breasted, Howard Carter, Gertrude Caton-Thompson, Selim Hassan, Said A. Huzayyin, Hermann Junker, Ahmed Bey Kamal, Georges Legrain, Karl Richard Lepsius, Auguste Mariette, Gaston Maspero, Jacques de Morgan, Margret Murray, William M. F. Petrie, George A. Reisner, Herbert E. Winlock, and the many others who made serious advancements in archaeological practice, to whom all the present practitioners of archaeology owe a huge debt of gratitude.

TABLE OF CONTENTS

LIST OF FIGURES

LIST OF TABLES

Recording of the historic city of Wakra, Qatar.

The partially restored Step Pyramid of King Netjerikhet Djoser, Saqqara, Egypt.

Open-area excavation of the pits outside the city walls of Wakra, Qatar.

PREFACE

This fieldguide was first conceived in 1998, and was prompted by the scarcity of excavation textbooks designed for the somewhat specific demands of Egyptian archaeology. Professor Gaballa A. Gaballa, former Secretary General of the Supreme Council of Antiquities (SCA), noted in conversation[1] that young Egyptian archaeologists urgently needed a fieldguide on excavation methodology. Archaeological fieldwork has been carried out in Egypt by Egyptologists and archaeologists from different countries for many centuries, each conducting fieldwork according to their traditional national manner or school of archaeological thought, without any real debate as to the advantages and disadvantages of different archaeological techniques. Although excavation manuals have been available in Egypt, these were produced by large expeditions specifically for use on their own sites. Rather than assessing and setting standards in method and practice and creating coherent conventions for the larger Egyptology community, these actions have resulted in a plethora of recording systems and approaches. For an academic discipline that is two hundred years old, this lack of standardisation and common archaeological practice is both surprising and deplorable (the last two published 'manuals' on Egyptian archaeology were by Maspero [1895] and Petrie [1904]). However, it also reflects the international – not to say imperialist – manner in which the field has developed. Another reason for the scarcity of comprehensive text books on Egyptian archaeological methods and practice is the fact that traditional Egyptology is based on monumental archaeology and epigraphy. These problems are not restricted to Egypt, but permeate archaeology worldwide and within many countries there is no common standard of archaeological methodology or documentation (Ucko *et al.* 2007). In some countries there is greater emphasis placed on the correct registration of finds than the site itself, although there is no consensus as to what constitutes an artefact, with some country's including Egypt, only registering complete or most significant finds in the register, and although provenience is recorded, no specific documentation or procedure is advocated for the context (Luciani 2007: 152).

When Jean-François Champollion announced his decipherment of hieroglyphs in 1822 with his *Lettre à Monsieur Dacier*, and subsequent *Précis du système hiéroglyphique*, the birth of a new academic discipline was born - Egyptology.[2] Further advances were made by Karl Richard Lepsius (*Denkmäler aus Aegypten und Nubien*), John Gardner Wilkinson (*Manners and Customs*

---

[1] A much smaller, site specific version of this book was being used at the UNESCO sponsored fieldschool being run at Kafr Hassan Dawood (KHD), East Delta, Egypt from December 1998 to January 1999, where Egyptian students were being taught methods of archaeological excavation. Professor Gaballa on seeing this book in action commented on how useful this book was. At two conferences in 2000 Professor Gaballa specifically stated to G. J. Tassie (the site supervisor of KHD) that it was his vision that an excavation manual, such as the one being used at KHD, should be made available to all archaeologists working in Egypt, particularly young Egyptian students. Both authors were at that time engaged in doctoral studies, but the background research for the book began in earnest, with the methodology being tested on many different types of sites in various countries: Egypt, Peru, Qatar, and the UK, developing and refining it over the next few years.

[2] Although the Napoleonic Expedition of 1798 produced a very influential scientific work – *Description de l'Égypte*, and others such as Belzoni were conducting exploration, and even before them, many Arabic scholars (El Daly 2005) and European travellers showed interest in ancient Egypt (even conducting excavations), it cannot be demonstrated that it was an academic discipline in its own right before Champollion (see Reid 2002).

of the Ancient Egyptians) and Alexander Henry Rhind (who in the 1850s advocated meticulous written, drawn and photographic recording *in situ* [leaving the monuments intact in the country], and highlighted the importance of stratigraphy for dating). One of the biggest advances in the discipline was the founding of the *Service d'Antiquités* in 1858, with Auguste Mariette as its first director; the establishment by Mariette of the Cairo Museum of Egyptian Antiquities closely followed this in 1863. The aim of the subject at this point, with few exceptions, was the uncovering of monumental buildings and beautiful artefacts, but this was closely related to the reading of texts and the filling of museums with objects to marvel at. In 1892 the Edwards Chair of Egyptology was founded at University College London (UCL), and with this recognition by one of the world's foremost universities Egyptology was given more credence. Petrie, often regarded as the father of modern Egyptology, pioneered systematic excavation practices, advanced surveying techniques, strict record keeping, and devised the sequence dating of potsherds to help date the site's stratigraphy. Petrie was not only interested in the large monuments of Egypt, but was fascinated by the small every day objects and the minutia and detritus of antiquity. Although Petrie, as the first Edwards Professor taught archaeological methods and practice to his students, this was not a practice that was to continue.

Egyptology as a taught subject started to become detached from archaeology during the late 1920s, when the amount of artefacts that were permitted to be retained by excavators was drastically reduced (Reid 1989: 237-9). The ruling by the Egyptian courts was made in response to the discovery of King Tutankhamun's tomb and the debacle over ownership of the bust of Nefertiti, now in the Berlin Museum (Reid 1989: 237-9). Due to the fact that the major funding bodies (museums and universities) could no longer export large amounts of finds, the number of surveys and excavations in Egypt declined (Reid 1989: 237-9), resulting in Egyptology focusing on history and philology. At this period, and even still amongst some classically trained Egyptologists, archaeology was practiced within the theoretical framework of cultural history. This is essentially a descriptive method to reconstruct the past in relation to a time sequence (Bard 2008: 18). Although many excavations continued up to World War II, it was not until the UNESCO Nubian Rescue Campaign of the 1960s that large-scale international archaeology was again conducted in Egypt. The building of the Aswan High Dam caused new archaeological incentives, those of rescue archaeology, and brought a multidisciplinary approach to Egyptian archaeology, drawing on the skills of architects, anthropologists, engineers, technicians, geologists, conservators, Egyptologists and archaeologists (Midant-Reynes 2000: 1-11). As this campaign was conducted in the period that processual archaeological theory emerged (a framework for explaining processes of cultural change and advocating scientific methods), several of the missions adopted this new theoretical approach, particularly those engaged in prehistoric archaeology. Out of this campaign came new archaeological developments that stimulated scientific advances throughout the 1970s and 1980s. The heightened concern with conservation, preservation and cultural heritage management of the 1990s and 2000s can also be attributed to the UNESCO campaign, for many legal instruments were drawn up as a result, not least *The Convention Concerning the Protection of the World Cultural and Natural Heritage*.

Due to the fact that classical archaeology has always been dominant in Egyptian studies, research has usually been conducted by art historians or philologists focused on retrieving inscribed art and architecture. Some excavations conducted in the modern era have resulted in the majority of information on past societies being thrown on the spoil heap. At several sites human remains, potsherds, and environmental remains have been ignored and discarded as rubbish whilst the excavators look for whole artefacts or inscribed blocks. As Sauneron (1968: 41) has noted: 'More than any other ancient people, the Egyptians have produced a huge multiplicity of texts, therefore, whatever the importance of the strictly archaeological evidence uncovered up till now, the study and interpretation of Egyptian texts still forms the basis of most of the research that Egyptologists undertake'. As a result, most of our knowledge of Egyptian society was focused upon the elites' material culture, thus ignoring other, less dramatic evidence that is of equal if not greater worth for elucidating past cultures. Unlike historical texts that may contain propaganda, the archaeological remains are a physical record of what actually happened, not what was said to have happened (Wenke 2009: 99). Iconographic and textual data need to be compared with and explicated by other types of archaeological remains to understand past human societies and individuals and the dynamic processes of the past.

However, the rigid practices of classical archaeology are at last relaxing, so that it is now possible to employ all the techniques and practices of mainstream archaeology to obtain a more holistic understanding of ancient Egyptian culture (Davies & Friedman 1998). Egyptology is wholeheartedly embracing many of the different areas of modern technology, such as information technology (IT), geographic information system (GIS), remote sensing using satellites, geophysical prospecting, and computer generated graphics and animation, making many advances in these fields. Some of the recent text books synthesising the results of modern archaeological investigations in Egypt (i.e. Bard 2008; Kemp 1991; Wengrow 2006) reflect this move away from classical archaeology and demonstrate the new theoretical models (post-processual methods investigating gender, ideology, belief-systems, aesthetics, individual agency and other aspects of human behaviour) driving current archaeological practice, and the use of statistical analyses of archaeological data, and scientific analyses of materials. Whereas, Wilkinson (2008) has highlighted the various components of modern Egyptology, a work that illustrates that unlike in de Morgan, Petrie and Reisner's day, it is now impossible for any one person to be able to be fully competent in every aspect of the subject, and that it is vital that fieldwork and research is undertaken by multidisciplinary teams of specialists.

Although the methods and practices used in fieldwork in Egypt are gradually changing, this is largely due to the individual agency of the practitioners who have actively sought professional archaeological training to compliment that of purely Egyptological. Unfortunately, the academic institutions have generally been slow to adapt, with the majority of universities offering Egyptology, teaching concentrates on philology and history, without a specific degree focusing on Egyptian archaeology (Bietak 1979; Giddy 1999; Tassie 2007). The teaching of Egyptian archaeology as an academic discipline was not introduced into a British university until 1991, when David Jeffreys founded a degree course at UCL (Tassie, Rowland & de Trafford 2000: 99). Although mainstream archaeological practice (including anthropological, historiographical, sociological theory and practice) has been conducted in the study of prehistoric and Early Dynastic Egypt for many years, the study of events before the Pharaonic era still lies outside of mainstream Egyptology (Guksch 1991: 38-9; Midant-Reynes 2000: 1) and these methods and practices have been slow to be taken up by traditional Egyptologists (Giddy 1999; Weeks 2008). Even today, the specialised techniques and methodology involved in archaeology are still largely expected to be learnt in the field, by the majority of those Egyptologists wishing to conduct fieldwork (Bietak 1979: 159-60). Egyptology, as taught in many universities worldwide, is not a preparation for archaeological fieldwork; history and philology do not help you to distinguish between contexts and neither do they teach you how to compile a site matrix, conduct a stratified random survey or the methods to excavate intercutting pits. However, this is not to say that history and philology are unimportant, but that there needs to be more balance, with archaeological method and practice being given as much weight as learning history and philology. It is essential that the world's universities offering undergraduate Egyptology degrees include archaeological elements, and that at post-graduate level students can specialise in one of the following as they pertain to Egypt: 1. archaeological method, practice and theory, 2. cultural heritage management and public archaeology, or 3. history and philology.

The funding bodies also need to adjust their agendas to provide more funding for the needs of the archaeological remains. Many archaeological sites, not just in Egypt, but throughout the world are threatened by urban sprawl, development projects, agricultural expansion, pollution and looting (Tassie 2005). Although development-led archaeology in Europe and the USA means that sites in danger of imminent destruction usually have their excavation paid for by the developers, this is not the case in many countries throughout the world, particularly in Asia and Africa. Many of these are developing countries trying to encourage multi-national companies to invest in their economies and so do not have legislation in place to enforce developers to pay for archaeological investigations. The governments of these countries do not have the resources to pay for the excavation of all these endangered sites, which results in hundreds of sites being lost every year. The acquiring of funds from the large funding bodies to pay for a site that is being destroyed by various means is extremely difficult unless the project is run by university or museum personnel and couched in a larger undertaking examining some aspect of the environment, landscape or culture. Emergency funds must be made available by the funding bodies for rescue archaeology or emergency conservation if we are not to loose these valuable, finite resources (Luciani 2007: 160). It is our duty to protect and preserve this heritage so that we, and future generations, can share in this historical legacy of our predecessors.

Standards of Archaeological Excavation

The authors conducted extensive reviews of the various methods used by foreign missions working in Egypt and around the world, in order to garner the very best methodologies currently being used. The original aims of this fieldguide were to establish standards and conventions that can be used (and, if wished, adapted and built upon) on any site in Egypt, Western Asia and Africa. As financial considerations are often a major brake on archaeological development, care was taken to not only provide the most modern, appropriate and efficient methods, but also to make them as cost-effective as possible. Attention was focused on best practice rather than invariably promoting high-technology for data retrieval, recording, presentation and dissemination. However, as the manuscript developed, it became apparent that many of the techniques and approaches used are essentially universal and can be used anywhere in the world, merely requiring contextualisation into the cultural setting of the country/region in question. As every archaeological site presents its own challenges and problems, it is always best to be flexible. There are however, basic methods and principles that should be followed, and where appropriate adapted to fit the specific situations independent from the different schools of thought. By deliberately increasing the parameters of the original, brief, therefore, we believe this volume to be one of the most comprehensive and flexible excavation fieldguide currently available – promoting generally accepted protocols and standards. These standards can be modified to conform to the cultural and technical requirements of an individual country, but the basic principles outlined are for best practice in excavation methodology and documentation. The ECHO Code of Ethics (**Appendix 1**) provides an ethical framework in which to conduct not only field investigations, but general archaeological conduct. This book, therefore, is neither a review of all archaeological techniques nor a general book on archaeology (see Renfrew & Bahn 1991), but a guide to the best practice for archaeological fieldwork.

Due to the objectives of this fieldguide, various areas of archaeology had to be omitted. These include the general introductions to archaeological surveying, dating methods and advanced theoretical interpretation. The book is structured as follows: Chapter 1 introduces the concepts of archaeological excavation, focusing on the use of single-context recording. Chapters 2 and 3 cover the setting-up of an archaeological excavation, while Chapters 4 to 6 cover the actual process of excavation from conducting evaluation fieldwork and formulating a research design to constructing the end of project assessment. Chapters 7 to 9 are concerned with recording methods - written, drawn and photographic. Chapter 10 covers the construction of a stratigraphic matrix, to aid in full site visualisation. Chapter 11 is concerned with the processing and cataloguing of data retrieved during fieldwork.

Controlled, organised excavation and recovery is the essence of good archaeological practice. Field notes, site reports, drawings and photographs are the post-excavational embodiment of the site; once excavated, many of the contexts are destroyed forever, and these records stand for the features that were found there (Lucas 2001: 214). The graphic and textual reconstruction of the site enables repeatable comparisons to be made, allowing re-evaluation and re-interpretation as necessary. Therefore, the core of this guide deals in great detail with the various methods used to record and organise observations of the various contexts, features, artefacts and ecofacts. This fieldguide is not a text on advanced analytical techniques and interpretation (see Balme & Paterson 2006; Banning 2000; Renfrew & Bahn 2004), but permits the excavator to gather data in an ordered, logical manner, presenting it in layered forms of interpretation to aid further interpretation. The bibliography lists numerous references that can take the reader further along any desired line of investigation.

CHAPTER ONE

Introduction to Excavation Conventions, Concepts and Methodology

"Scholarship is by no means all that is wanted; the engineering training of mind and the senses … will really fit an archaeologist better for excavating than bookwork alone"

(Sir William Matthew Flinders Petrie 1904).

Excavation is an essential part of archaeology, the main process by which data is gathered. Archaeology has many different facets and consists of many sub-disciplines (see Renfrew & Bahn 1991), necessitating the adoption of a multidisciplinary approach. Fieldwork usually constitutes only a small percentage of an archaeologist's time, for even during the fieldwork phase of a project an inordinate amount of time is spent doing paperwork. The majority of an archaeologist's time is spent behind a desk, in the library or laboratory doing research, analysis and interpretation.

What is archaeology? Archaeology is one of the four main branches of anthropology: 1. archaeology, 2. social/cultural anthropology, 3. physical anthropology, and 4. linguistics. Archaeology constitutes the study of past human societies through what they left behind, the study of how they behaved and reacted with one another and the world around them: a diachronic examination of human existentiality. At the heart of archaeology is the long-term preservation of the past for the present and future benefit of humanity: this preservation can occur *in situ* as structural remains, or as an archive of finds and records stored in an archive repository (Cohen in press). While fieldwork is central to archaeology, it is just one small part of the process. Fieldwork, whether survey or excavation, is the gathering of raw data upon which theoretical models are based. Excavation is a programme of controlled, intrusive fieldwork that has defined research objectives involving the recording and interpretation of archaeological deposits, features and structures, and the retrieval of artefacts, ecofacts and other remains within a specified area or site. "The aim of excavation is to identify, define, uncover, date, and – by understanding transformation processes – interpret each archaeological context on a site" (Drewett 1999: 107). The records compiled and objects gathered during this fieldwork are studied, written-up and published in accordance with the research design (IFA 1999e: 2). Excavation can be undertaken as a response to development or planning projects, as part of site management projects, to mitigate against plans for land redevelopment (agricultural, land-reclamation, building or other potentially destructive activities) or as part of a research programme developed through academic intention rather than as a response to a specific threat. While many sites identified through survey and evaluation may not be threatened directly and are technically protected by national heritage legislation, they are often at risk from looters, agricultural practices or unscrupulous developers, and therefore need to be targeted for excavation. A number of individuals or organisations can instigate or commission excavations, including local planning authorities, national advisory bodies, developers (or their agents), private landowners, governmental bodies, non-governmental organisations, international organisations, archaeological bodies, museums, universities and archaeological researchers.

Like all academic subjects, archaeology is constructed upon a theoretical foundation. However, within archaeology there is a considerable divide between those who use theory as a heuristic device to interpret their findings, and those for whom 'pure' theory is the main aim of the discipline. While carrying out an epistemological examination of archaeology's basic assumptions, the current text is by no means a theoretical work. Archaeology can therefore exist as a 'pure' theory subject, a science, an experiment and an academic exercise – the processes of survey/excavation, compilation, analysis, interpretation and publication should be viewed as a continuum, each process inextricably linked to all the others. Even after the final publication of a project, the process is not ended as it will influence future academic research and other projects' research designs; the knowledge thus gained will constitute a part of the engine that drives the discipline.

Archaeologists can be either purely fieldworkers or theorists, although many are both, which gives them a better understanding of archaeological processes and allows for better synthesis of all the facts. Their theoretical viewpoints, technological expertise and organisational capacity will affect the way in which the data is gathered (Roskams 2001: 7-29). The debate on subjectivism verses objectivism is in some ways an irrelevant debate; from the modern standpoint (even using empirical evidence) we are inevitably influenced by our own social context, however much we try and escape it, each successive era produces its own disparate frameworks of interpretation. Archaeologists should aim to reconstruct the past, not construct it (Shanks & Tilley 1987: 103; Tilley 1993: 8; Wylie 1992: 19). In all cases, theoretical viewpoints have had a profound influence over the way in which the past was excavated, assessed and interpreted. W. M. Flinders Petrie, who was inspired by the evolutionist thinking of the period, developed seriation (which he termed Sequence Dating) as a means of dating features. Petrie's meticulous collection and description of everything he found, and the recording of their placements in graves allowed him to carefully order his data-sets. His dating method (which still forms the basis for a relative chronology of Predynastic pottery) was based on the fluctuating frequencies of certain types of pottery and other objects in graves (Petrie 1920). Cultural historians such as Mortimer Wheeler (1954) and Kathleen Kenyon (1952) viewed sites as a fossilised history, and stratigraphy as a series of building, repair, rebuild and destruction phases, separating and numbering finds accordingly. This was reflected in their approach to the sites, as they targeted vertical stratification by excavating in a series of square boxes. Processual archaeologists of the 1960s and 70s (i.e. Lewis Binford) saw sites as parts of buried systems, and, therefore attempted to understand past societies by sampling their behaviour. In the field, this translated as excavating in a series of small, rectangular sondages; the assumption was that the sample can represent the whole, and therefore that the more randomly these sondages were put in, the less likelihood of bias. Open-area excavation – which aims to examine activity areas and the manner in which humans used tracts of space – was introduced in the 1930s in the Near East and Scandinavia (see **Chapter 4**), and has now become the dominant technique.

Archaeologists have a dialectical relationship with the material they study, and their accounts of the past move within hermeneutic frameworks (Hodder 1992: 188-193; Shanks and Tilley 1987: 107-108). "Contexts include both the interpreting archaeologist(s) and the questions asked and entities existing in the archaeological record. These are always sliding and changing, never fixed or given since the context is decided upon by future or prior analytic intentional structures. In inserting artefacts into contexts we find ourselves in a hermeneutic circle which can never be completely described. Context is not just a matter of the artefact and its associations on a site, within a region, etc; it is also a matter of history - of interpretative context, of a dialectical relationship between the archaeologist and that studied. Archaeological contexts are always changing temporally in accordance with how they are framed by disciplinary codes for producing knowledge" (Tilley 1993: 9). The biggest current debate is when and how much interpretation should be done in the field; the relationship between archaeologists, the material they study and the ways in which this material is interrogated and presented. Steve Roskams (2001) discourages interpretation on-site and prefers to reserve all interpretation until the stratigraphic matrix has been interrogated. However, post-processual archaeologists such as Hodder (1999) and Lucas (2001) encourage interpretation on-site, even recording the excavators' thoughts on video. Both approaches have their merits; the best of each have been incorporated into the approach advocated in this fieldguide.

Due to humanity's enormous diversity, there are – technically speaking – as many different site 'types' as there are sites. In general terms, however, all archaeological sites are built up of strata, features (formed of cuts and deposits), artefacts and ecofacts. The job of the archaeologist is to examine the sediments and debris, and to try to make sense of this accumulation of construction, occupation and destruction. This accumulation of various elements is often termed the archaeological *record*, although this concept has been challenged, preferring the term archaeological *text*, as it is open to differing interpretations by different groups or individuals, and as such can be written from a biased perspective, so selectivity and bias can influence the presentation and materiality of archaeological sites (Patrik 1985). However, the term 'record' is retained here for reasons of clarity, while acknowledging the inherent problems of this term.

This fieldguide is organised as logically as possible, taking the archaeologist from site evaluation, through laying out the site grid to archiving, report writing and the final post-excavation assessment. However, fieldwork is not a uni-directional process that moves from excavation to finds processing to analysis and finally synthesis; all these activities combine to comprise the holistic archaeological practice which is advocated throughout this work. Analysts should take care to constantly feed information back to the excavators, thus assisting with the interpretation of contexts and features; equally, excavators should ensure that the analysts are kept appraised of stratigraphic information, thus contextualising the artefacts during the process of analysis (Lucas 2001: 14). The deposition and types of pottery and other artefacts are not independent of site formation processes, and it is therefore important to know the nature of the context when analysing the artefact so that it can be more fully understood (Lucas 2001: 14). This multivocality is essential, for it feeds into the research design, thus potentially changing hypotheses and fieldwork strategies. The archaeologists themselves must be aware of what they are doing and why they are doing it, in what Hodder (1999) and Lucas (2001) term 'reflexivity'. The holistic approach combines interpretation within the site records but also allows for the data to be presented in an objective manner, using the various levels of interpretation inherent within the system.

Archaeologists use various terms to classify the archaeological deposits and units of excavation, such as locus, lot, spit, context, stratigraphic unit, level, feature, layer, etc (for a full list see the glossary). Lots, levels and spits are different terms for arbitrary or metric units of excavation that are sometimes used to supplement the context or locus systems of excavation. The two major systems used for excavating and recording archaeological units are dubbed the 'American-Israeli locus' and the 'British context', which are geographical or cultural units of stratification (see Lucas 2001: 47-51 for a discussion of differences between US and UK terminology). The locus is only used for describing the **positive record** or stratigraphic unit – namely deposits and sedimentary accumulations. The **negative record** refers to the cuts that are incised into sedimentary deposits. The term 'context' is more general. It can be used to describe all discrete archaeological entities and their interfaces with other contexts (both the positive and negative records) - what is added as well as what is taken away. However, these terms are somewhat fluid, and have changed slightly in meaning according to the requirements of archaeologists. For example, the term 'context' originally only referred to layers and features, but was redefined by archaeologists working in urban settings where numerous building and re-building phases created extremely complex, deep and stratified sites. The locus recording system, which was originally developed for recording shallow, stratified indigenous American sites, and was later transformed for recording deep stratified sites at *tell* excavations in Palestine - has seen the term 'locus' used to define walls and the lining of pits as well as other discrete deposits (Dever & Darrel Lance 1978: 76-8). The problem is really one of language and labels of convenience; the ancients did not talk in either contexts or loci, did not think about cutting a context or depositing a locus. However, if you do not contextualise cuts/interfaces, you will lose data. This flexibility should always be borne in mind when designing recording systems and planning excavation campaigns.

One of the biggest methodological improvements for archaeological recording of the past 40 years is the widespread use of **single-context planning** (complemented by **single-context recording sheets**), both of which are fully explained below. It was first developed by Max Foster in 1972 in order to make sense of complicated multi-phase urban sites where stratification is sometimes only found in discrete 'islands' that cannot be interrelated. This system was first adopted in York and London, particularly by the Museum of London's Department of Urban Archaeology. It is an 'objective' system that records evidence without colouring it with interpretation, is easy to use when there are large numbers of workers on the site, and allows for the delegation of routine drawing tasks to those not specialised in draughting (Barker 1993: 168-70). This system is now used by the majority of archaeological units working in both urban and rural sites across the UK, and has recently been employed by the *Giza Plateau Mapping Project* (GPMP) in its excavation of the pyramid builders' settlement, and the *American Research Center in Egypt* (ARCE) on many sites across Egypt. The single-context recording system is ideal for complex *tell* sites as it helps to make sense of the different stratigraphic layers encountered, permitting the various phases of building and re-building to be easily understood and reconstructed. Although the term 'context' and 'locus' may sometimes be seen as interchangeable (as the latter has generally not yet evolved to include cuts) it seems better to use the term 'context' to describe discrete archaeological entities. As standardisation in terminology and recording is desirable, it may be better if the term 'locus' was expanded to take in the negative record, and also the methodology modified to include 'single locus planning'. The single locus recording system was successfully introduced into Palestine/Israel by the *British School of Archaeology* working at Jezreel, but the terminology has not yet been implemented throughout the Levant. Therefore, for those wishing to modify the locus system, where the word 'context' appears in this work, simply substitute the word 'locus'. As the conventions of single-context recording are now well delineated and the terminology generally accepted by not only the British but the larger archaeological community, it seemed an obvious methodology and terminology to use in this work.

Although there are many different strategies, techniques and methodologies used around the world, those advocated in this work should cover most situations. However, there is a major difference between the way archaeology is conducted in Europe and the Americas and the way in which it is conducted in much of Africa and Western Asia. In the former, the actual physical act of excavation is carried out by trained archaeologists from beginning to end, aided by specialists where necessary. By contrast, African and Western Asian archaeological excavation is usually carried out by a locally-hired workforce, supervised by trained archaeologists. This goes back to Petrie and Kenyon's days when recording was confined to annotations on drawings and site notebooks, recorded by the site director or a few select supervisors. Some of these paid labourers may be very experienced, especially the Quftis and Qurnawis; they are often very familiar with local sedimentary matrices and are fully cognisant of archaeological field techniques. These labourers are often controlled by a *reis* who will shout directions for them to follow. However, paid labourers are not academically-trained archaeologists and it is not their responsibility to record the data or describe the contexts that they excavate. The recording of the contexts and data is the responsibility of the trained archaeologists who supervise these paid labourers, and who should maintain frequent contact with the archaeological surface, clarify contextual relationships and identify features. This is essential if the archaeological site is to be recorded thoroughly. It is fine to have people assisting, but the archaeologists themselves must excavate the more sensitive groups of contexts, such as graves with finer tools such as trowels and brushes. The archaeologist should constantly discuss the process of excavation with the paid labourers, permitting both parties to a gain a greater knowledge of the site. Only constant liaison between the archaeologist, the excavator and the context sequence will permit a full understanding of the construction, occupation and destruction debris and sediments.

All archaeologists undertaking work of whatever type – be it survey, evaluation, watching briefs, excavation, or artefact assessment – should adhere to the basic principles outlined in the ECHO *Code of Ethics* (**Appendix One**) or similar codes of conduct such as those produced by the Institute of Field Archaeologists (IFA) or the Society for American Archaeology (SAA). The ECHO *Code of Ethics* was designed to be used with this fieldguide and to help guide appropriate conduct in all archaeological work.

THE CONCEPTS, CONVENTIONS AND METHODOLOGY OF SINGLE-CONTEXT RECORDING

For the purposes of single-context recording, a context is a single geologically- or culturally-formed unit of stratigraphic activity, and its' interfaces with other contexts. The basic assumption is that ancient actions will leave either a positive or a negative record on the archaeological site. Cultural processes tend to emulate natural geological processes: the cultural equivalent of erosion is a cut, grave or ditch, where material has been taken away. This is referred to as a negative record. The cultural version of deposition is a wall or a fill, where material has been added. This is referred to as a positive record. Therefore, a grave cut is a negative record, while the grave fill, substructure, superstructure, grave goods and body are all positive records. The cut of a foundation wall is a negative record, whereas the wall is a positive record as is the fill of the foundation trench. Each scenario presents two separate and distinguishable activities, thus requiring two separate records. The activities may have occurred in close succession (i.e. the cutting and filling of a grave) or they may have been separated by a significant time lapse (i.e. the burning of a structure many years after it was constructed). The detailed recording of each activity will help to elucidate its temporal, spatial and cultural relationships with all the other contexts on site. A context can be large or small, from the cut of a post-hole to the base of a pyramid. A group of contexts may constitute a feature, and a context that spreads across a large area – such as a floor – may also constitute a feature (Wass 1992: 114). Regardless of size, if it has occurred in one distinct phase of activity/deposition, it is still a defined, singular 'context'. The medium in which archaeological artefacts, ecofacts, contexts and features are found – and which immediately surrounds archaeological data – is called the matrix (usually sediments such as gravel, sand or clay).

The terms 'layers' and 'features', which go back to the early 20th century, are still often used on archaeological sites. These are used to describe a type of context or a group of related contexts, respectively. A feature can be the product of a number of actions that have occurred over a short or long period of time. In the context system of recording, deposits and cuts are treated as equals, whereas the layer-feature system recognises that a higher level of interpretation is required for cuts (Roskams 2001: 210). However, the two types of terminology do not compromise one another, as the term 'layer' correlates with a stratum, and is just another word for an extensive deposit. A feature is a group of related multiple contexts (such as a pit, ditch, grave, wall, etc) and is more descriptive than 'a group of multiple contexts', but less interpretative than a 'mud-brick wall'. Therefore, while the terms are concerned with different degrees of description, they do not compromise the interpretation of the material and can therefore easily be used together. However, features, until they are found to be either a grave or structure should not be given a feature number, this will usually entail careful consultaion of the area or site matrix.

If a grave or structure has been assigned an alphanumeric code, this can be highlighted in the site matrix, thus making it easier to understand which group of contexts represent a grave or structure and with which phase a particular structure or grave is associated. However, structures often have several rebuilding phases; as such the assignation of the contexts that constitute each phase is best done during the post-excavation analysis phase (see the **Stratigraphic Record**). Certain sites have a long history of excavation, such as Abydos, Amarna, Buto, Hierakonpolis, Merv, Naqada, Pompeii, Stonehenge, Tell Brak or Troy. At sites with a long history of excavation there can be a well established numbering system in place, such as that for the Valley of the Kings in Thebes where tombs are given a KV prefix followed by the sequential number, e.g. KV62 for Tutankhamun's tomb. Although modern excavations will probably not follow the methodology used in the past, the numbering system given to the various features, such as tombs, is often best kept to avoid confusing people.

A feature such as a grave will usually consist of many distinct contexts: one for the cut, several for different layers of the fill and various contexts for the various building phases of any identified substructure or superstructure. A deposit will either be above or below specific contexts or otherwise in direct association with other contexts (i.e. the fills of cuts).

A context can either cut – or be cut or truncated by – one or more contexts. Deposits and cuts can postdate, predate or be contemporary with other cuts and deposits (contexts). In situations where two (or more) contexts that were originally believed to be separate turn out to be the same context, then 'equivalent' or 'equal to' should be used to describe their relationship.

Normally only strata, cuts and deposits receive context numbers, which enables the true stratigraphy of the site to be reconstructed on paper or computer by means of the Harris Matrix system. However, in rare cases where large artefacts (such as coffins) or ecofacts (such as shell middens) are encountered, they too receive a context number. Groups of artefacts may also sometimes receive a context number. If artefacts are given a context number, however, they are not placed in the Harris Matrix as they do not normally count towards the stratigraphy of the site. The assignation of context numbers is the responsibility of the site supervisor, and it is their responsibility to decide whether an object should be recorded as a context or merely given an artefact number.

The single-context recording system is flexible enough to accommodate the recording of all various site types, from deeply stratified urban sites to a cemetery or a Palaeolithic campsite. However, it is particularly useful on settlement and *tell* sites. The two most important media used for recording are the 'context recording form' and the 'single-context planning sheet'. While there is considerable flexibility in terms of approach, urban and *tell* sites will require each context to be planned separately on a single-context planning sheet, whereas camp sites and cemeteries (being generally simpler) may have their features planned on a multi-context planning sheet. Contexts are always recorded separately on the single-context recording form regardless of the type of site: this is done to show their stratigraphic relationship to one another. A post-hole will have context numbers for the cut of the post-pit, while the fills (including the post/pipe) will also have their own context numbers. The associated contexts may be planned on a multi context planning sheet with other associated post-holes, post pits and hearths. The single context recording system is employed as the main method to record and keep a tight control over the archaeological record, and the stratigraphic relationships of which it is comprised. Examination of stratigraphic relationships and sequences are the primary route to understanding what actions have gone into forming the archaeological record.

The archaeological record is formed by a series of deposition and removal processes. Sometimes there is a truncation or hiatus on a site that isolates one or more contexts from the main sequence; these separated contexts will therefore constitute their own matrix (Westman 1994: 7). Within the stratified sequence, the earlier chronological context will always be sealed or cut by later contexts (Westman 1994: 7). This accretion of contexts is built into the running matrix, so a site stratigraphy can be established by isolating the interfaces of specific contexts. However, irregularities of redeposition can confuse the interpretation of the sequence. For example, slumping episodes can partially refill cut features, or pits may be partially refilled with the same material that was excavated from it, resulting in the mingling of older and younger artefacts. Just because there is a physical relationship between one context and another, therefore, it does not necessarily follow that they are chronologically related. For example, a pit may physically cut several earlier stratigraphic layers, but the only relevant stratum is that from which the pit was dug (i.e. the living surface from which the pit was cut – Westman 1994: 7). The fill of a pit may be built up of many different stratified deposits that pertain to different periods or activity phases. These may be natural or anthropogenic, and may have accumulated over large stretches of time or through prompt refilling directly after the pit was dug.

All contexts within the site must be given equal consideration in the stratigraphic sequence (Westman 1994: 7). The vast majority of contexts will probably be deposits and cuts, although a number of contexts will be made up of structures or large artefacts such as coffins (Westman 1994: 7). The full stratigraphic sequence **must** be recorded, with each context being given a separate context number. In the case of grave goods, the cache may be given one context number and each individual artefact given a grave good number. In the case of a larger tomb, there may be several caches of artefacts; each of these will be given a separate number, and each artefact given an individual 'grave good number' and recorded on the 'grave good recording form'. In the case of a grave, up to four distinct context numbers must be used: numbers for the grave cut, the body itself (in addition to the burial number), the grave fill and the tumulus or other structure over the grave (if present). Although giving the body a context number may seem strange, the placement of the body is one action that is both socially significant and archaeologically visible. When dealing with multiple burials, the recording of bodies as single-contexts helps greatly with the reconstruction of chronology. Only if this method is strictly adhered to can the full stratigraphic sequence be properly understood.

A vast number of separate data sheets are generated by use of the single-context recording method, and these must be inter-related if the archaeologist hopes to achieve a full understanding of the site's chronological and stratigraphic sequence (Westman 1994: 7). The running matrix (an adaptation of the Harris Matrix) is used to relate these contexts to one another according to their stratigraphic positions, thus graphically compiling the stratigraphic sequence. Where possible, each context should be drawn on a separate piece of tracing film once all overlying contexts have been removed. This is then removed to expose the next layer, where the process should be repeated (Westman 1994: 7). This will allow inter-contextual relationships to be ascertained. These relationships can then be checked against the running area matrix and a site matrix may then be compiled (see 'planning'). However, the matrices must be completed as soon as possible during fieldwork so that the information can be fed back into – and thus help guide – the excavation process. To complement the single-context plans, phase plans are also drawn. The draughting record therefore has varying levels of interpretation inherent within it. All the recovered artefacts and ecofacts are numbered and their exact provenience recorded, so that they can be traced to their exact 2D position and depth (chronological stratigraphic layer) within the archaeological matrix. Sediment samples are taken from each context and are graded by texture, Munsell colour number and consistency. The use of the embedded interpretation sections in the *pro forma* recording sheets and utilisation of notebooks for recording the archaeologists' thoughts help give the recording system further layers of interpretation. This layering of interpretation based on objective recording allows more flexibility for future reassessment, and also reduces the risk of erroneous (and irreversible) assignation of contexts and features.

As already pointed out, a 'context' may be a patch of gravel, a layer of dust or a large wall: each context is different, and must be approached in a different way (Drewett 1999: 107). A crucial element in excavation is context definition. Sometimes it is easy (as in the cases of walls or pits), and other times it may be very difficult (such as isolating the excavated sediment from a post-hole). It is essential that the limits of each context be defined before the recording (and excavation) of the context, making sure it is not overlapped by any other context. They are differentiated visually and texturally in order to identify variability in colour, texture and consistency, as well as the interfaces of these differences. As mentioned above, the last vestiges of later contexts must be excavated before the chronologically earlier contexts. If the limits of a context are not defined on all sides in the horizontal plane, mistakes can be made in assembling the master stratigraphy of the site. If one end of a context is left undefined, it may later transpire that it continues below a second context that is then cut by a stratigraphically earlier pit, which is earlier than a mud-brick wall, which is abutted by all the extant stratigraphy on site (Roskams 2001: 111). It is therefore very easy to completely undo the perceived stratigraphic network. The excavator is then left with an incompletely-recorded context, the full extent of which may not become clear for weeks or months. Always ensure, therefore, that attention is paid to interface recognition and isolation, and to recording them in both the drawn and written records. These differences are easy to define in temperate areas, but an experienced and skilled excavator can discern these differences even in sandy desert conditions.

Horizontal and Vertical Control

LOCATING THE SITE

The site grid and datum are the basis of any recording system, and must therefore be precisely and accurately positioned within the landscape. The datum can be arbitrary or tied into height above sea level; the grid, however, should be tied into the local landscape. If possible, the site grid should be located to the national or world grid. This control will prove invaluable to future archaeologists if they wish to re-assess the exact position of your site.

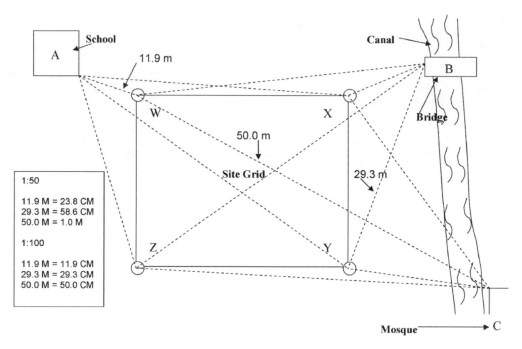

Figure 1: Locating the site grid to the national grid.

Locating your site's position within the national or world UTM grid is a relatively simple process that can be carried out using a total station or tape measures and a compass. Firstly, create a drawing of your site grid with its dimensions and orientation, then select at least three permanent local landmarks that are easily recognisable on a national map of the region, such as a river, canal, road, church, mosque or school. These local landmarks must then be located on the ground and measurements of length and angle taken to the corners of your grid by means of triangulation, plane table, sighting compass or total station (see section on **Measuring, Recording and Surveying**). These measurements must be recorded on the drawing of the site grid, citing and showing the landmarks to which the measurements were made. These measurements must then be transferred to a 'base map' of the region at a 1:50 or 1:100 scale (although smaller scale maps can also be used). The scaling-down and transfer of measurements on to the base map should be done using a scale rule, protractor, and a beam compass or pair of spreading compasses (Hawker 1999: 11). Therefore, the grid is not only related to the modern landscape, but also the ancient landscape. A plan of the site giving its exact position on the national grid can now be made at 1:50, 1:100 or whatever scale you chose. Once the trenches are opened-up within the operational areas, their position must be plotted on the grid outline on the base map. However, if no local landmark is available - as may be the case in open desert - then a Global Positioning System (GPS) can be used to establish the position of the site grid and level of datum to within 5.0 metres. A Differential Global Positioning System (DGPS) is the most accurate instrument, giving centimetre accuracy of both longitude and latitude as well as height above sea level (a.s.l.).

THE SITE GRID

The site grid enables all contexts, artefacts and ecofacts to be placed within a controlled horizontal framework, and related to the landscape of the region. The establishing of the ambit – from which the site grid is hung – is the first step in any excavation after the initial survey has been completed. Without the coordinates afforded by a site grid, all artefacts and contexts recorded are without exact provenience. The point of origin of the site grid must be selected carefully, for this will be the site datum, a fixed area outside of the area of excavation that may be in use for many years. The proposed and expected area of excavation must be defined through geophysical sub-surface survey (see **Chapter 4**).

Grid Size

The size of the grid is determined by the extent, complexity and stratification of the site. For most sites a grid of 5.0 metre squares will usually be sufficient, although large sites may use 10.0, 20.0 or even 50.0 metre grid squares. Using a 5.0 m grid planning at 1:20 allows the plan of the grid square to easily fit on a manageable size sheet of draughting film and drawing board, for 5.0 x 5.0 m grid unit at 1:20 equals 0.25 x 0.25 m. Strings can be easily put across a 5.0 or 10.0 metre grid square in order to divide it up. Smaller gauge excavation grids may be placed over important features within the main site grid; it should also be noted that it may not always be expedient or financially viable to excavate the entire area of the site. Therefore, only archaeologically significant areas, as identified through geophysical surveying methods, are usually excavated. If this is the case, then the operational areas and trenches must still be placed within an overall site grid (see **Fig. 7**) and tied into its coordinates. In special cases such as a Palaeolithic camp floor, a much smaller scale grid may be used (i.e. 1 metre square).

Orientation

It is often convenient to orientate the grid in a north-south direction, as this helps in referencing the grid and in locating the grid on existing maps (Drewett 1999: 64), although it should be placed at a tangent to any extant archaeological structures so they become more clearly defined. If you align your grid in a north-south direction, the southern edge of the grid is the baseline and the south-west corner is your point of origin termed the site datum. However, if a cardinal point grid is being used, the centre of your grid is its point of origin and acts as the grid reference point and should also be the site datum (see **Fig. 6**). The north-south line of the cross lines is then termed the 'meridian line' (or 'datum line') and the east-west line termed the 'baseline'. This latter type of grid is useful when excavating extremely large settlements.

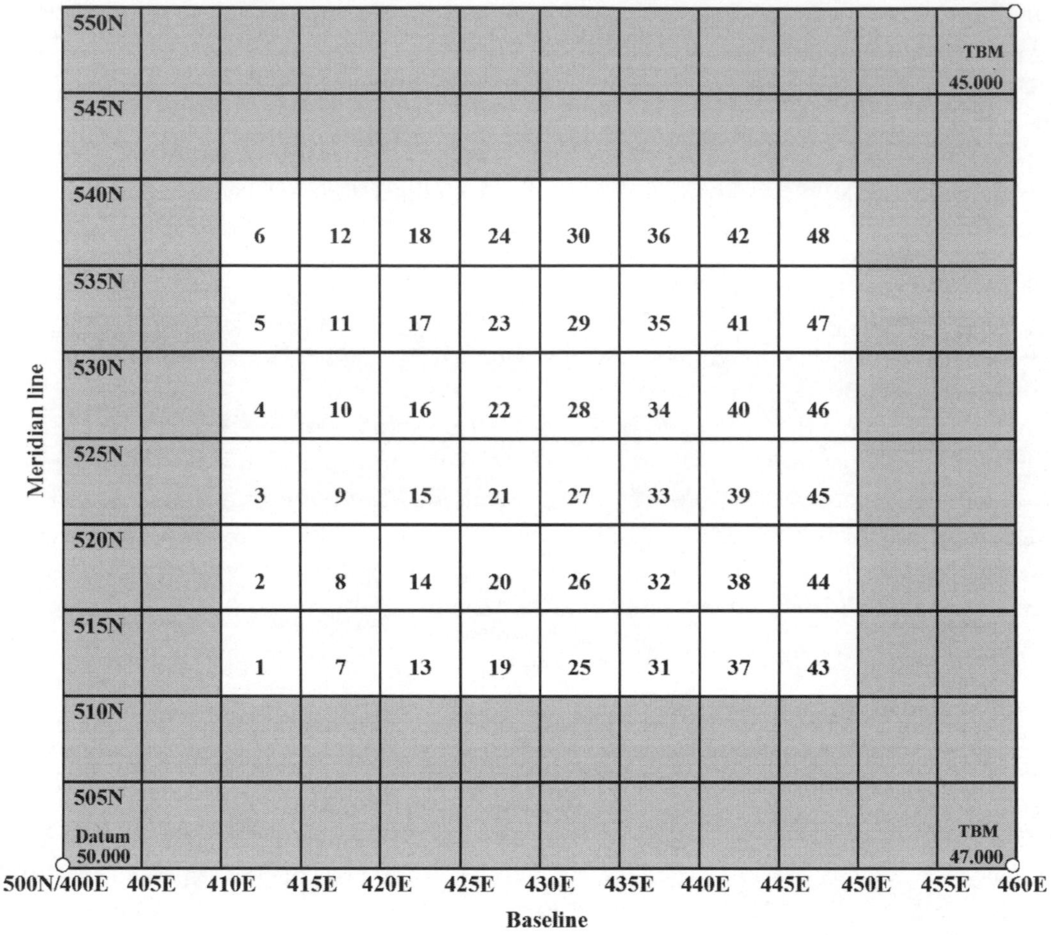

550N												TBM 45.000
545N												
540N	6	12	18	24	30	36	42	48				
535N	5	11	17	23	29	35	41	47				
530N	4	10	16	22	28	34	40	46				
525N	3	9	15	21	27	33	39	45				
520N	2	8	14	20	26	32	38	44				
515N	1	7	13	19	25	31	37	43				
510N												
505N Datum 50.000												TBM 47.000

Meridian line (vertical label, left)

500N/400E 405E 410E 415E 420E 425E 430E 435E 440E 445E 450E 455E 460E

Baseline

Figure 2: The site grid is laid out in 5.0 metre squares. Each of these grid squares may then be numbered either along the northings (horizontally) or along the eastings (vertically) as shown in the diagram. Although a 10.0 metre border is shown (shaded in grey) left outside the excavation area, this is for diagrammatic clarity, and in reality the datum (500N/400E) should be set much further away, between 20.0 and 30.0 metres outside the area to be excavated.

When using a compass, it must be remembered that there is a difference between magnetic north and true north, caused by the effect of magnetic declination (deviation). This difference is not constant, and differs temporally and spatially depending on the pull of the earth's magnetic field. The north shown on maps is true north; however, due to the fact that this changes each year, it is likely to be slightly out. Unless you have a very modern map or your compass has the capability of compensating, therefore, you must make the required adjustments yourself. The current declination can be acquired from www.geolab.nrcan.gc.ca/geomag/e-cgrf.html. However, a rough guide is that magnetic

12

north in Egypt is 3° east of true north, so 3° east should be added to your calculations for true north. If you are transferring a bearing from a compass (that does not have magnetic declination adjustment) to a map, then add 3°. If you are transferring a bearing from a map to a compass, subtract 3° (Hawker 1999: 15). However, if the site grid is not being aligned with the national grid, then magnetic north should be sufficient for the orientating of the site grid. The fact that magnetic rather than true north has been used to align the grid should be clearly stated on all relevant documents. The declination at various key locations around Egypt at present is: Alexandria 3·0 degrees east, Aswan 2·6 degrees east, Cairo 2·9 degrees east, Ismailia 3·1 degrees east, Marsa Alam 2·7 degrees east and Luxor 2·7 degrees east.

Setting Out a Grid

Grids can be laid out on the ground using sophisticated surveying equipment such as theodolites and total stations, or simple equipment such as 30 or 50 m tape measures, ranging poles and a Brunton or sighting compass. The baseline should be laid out first; this should be aligned on an east-west axis. A ranging rod is placed at the starting point, the site datum, and another pole is sighted by the compass to the termination point of the grid; if they are too far apart to sight, use an intermediary point. The intended size of the grid determines the placing of further ranging rods; if a 5.0 m grid is required then if a 100.0 m baseline is measured out an associate takes a ranging rod along the baseline and measures out 50.0 m. To ensure the pole is correctly aligned, a sighter must look through a sighting compass at the three poles and align them all by moving the middle pole until the poles are all directly in line with one another (see **Fig. 3**). This process should be repeated until all the grid points are established along the baseline, filling in the 25.0 m and 75.0 m ones first, then the other intermediate points. The terminal pegs of the grid baseline should be cemented into position. This baseline should be placed outside the intended area of excavation. A third peg should be cemented in to form a line at a right angle to this horizontal baseline (also outside the area to be excavated) to form the 'meridian line'. The right angle can be calculated using Pythagoras' theorem, optical square or any of the other means described in the section on measuring and surveying. The grid points should then be marked out on the meridian line in the same manner as those on the baseline.

The site coordinate or grid system is centred upon these two lines, with subsidiary metal or wooden pegs at 5.0 metre intervals (**Fig. 2**) dividing up the site into individual grid units. To establish the ambit points, perpendicular lines must be marked out from either the 5.0 m points on the meridian line or baseline, pegs being placed at 5.0 metre intervals. To check that the points of the ambit are placed square to one another, the length of the hypotenuse should be checked (see section on measuring and surveying). The pegs that mark out the intersection of the gridlines (usually the bottom left hand or south-western peg of an individual square) should be flagged with their grid coordinates. It may help to paint these pegs a bright colour so that they can be easily seen if the 5.0 metre grid squares are to be divided up into smaller excavation units, or if you intend to use trenches that do not follow the grid. Use brightly coloured string to distinguish the grid squares, although only the actual trenches or squares to be excavated actually need to be strung-up. It may help to have slightly elasticised string (or springs attached to each of the pegs, and the string tied to the springs), so that anyone tripping over the string does not cause movement of the pegs. If using a total station, then only the baseline and meridian line need actually be put in. Grids need only be used over certain features, while the rest of the grid can be planned with the total station as necessary; however, with inexperienced excavators it is always best to physically label the grid pegs.

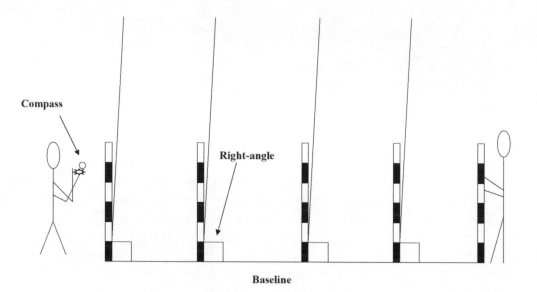

Figure 3: Establishing the site grid.

Whatever type of grid is used, the type of grid pegs used and their placement is very important. Either metre-long wooden stakes or 30 cm long angle irons or hooked metal rods can be used, although polyvinyl chloride plastic survey stakes are often more durable and do not rust. When marking out the actual excavation units, it is advisable to place 15 cm nails (longer if excavating in loose sediment) at least 0.10 – 0.15 m past the corner of the excavation unit. Make sure that the string crosses at the corner of the unit, thereby eliminating the problem of peg disturbance when excavating into the corner (see **Fig. 4**).

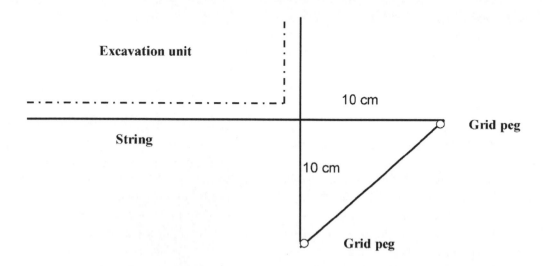

Figure 4: The stringing up of a trench corner.

Labelling a Grid

The labelling of the site grid can take various forms, using a combination of letters and numbers (**Fig. 5**), or referring to cardinal points of the compass (**Fig. 6**). These two types of grid systems are often used for gridding large city sites, where the individual grid units can be from 5-500 metres square, and the large grid squares are then subdivided into smaller excavation units or have trenches placed within them. The most convenient type of grid is the coordinate grid system. The origin of the site grid should start with high numbers: 1000 metres East by 2000 meters North on large sites, and 400E by 500N on smaller sites, thereby ensuring that negative numbers are never used. This is done to facilitate the growth of the site grid if further archaeological remains are unexpectedly discovered, and also to prevent confusion and facilitate recording of measurements. The grid coordinate system makes the recording of the site much easier, as any point within the grid can be named by a single reference using 'eastings' (measurements taken along the west-east axis) and 'northings' (those taken along the north-south axis). The 00/00 point from which the grid emanates is not actually marked or laid out. The first grid peg is the point of origin in the south-west corner of your grid (numbered 400E/500N), which is placed outside the area of excavation and can also serve as the datum. The next peg in the northern direction in a 5.0 metre grid would be 400E/505N (as shown in **Fig. 2**). The individual grid units are identified by their south-west grid peg.

If a central point of origin is used for the grid, then the cardinal points of the compass can be used to label your grid in a similar fashion to eastings and northings; the main difference is that southings and westings are used as well. The archaeological remains found to the west of the north axis, are recorded as so many metres west by so many metres north. The archaeological remains found to the south of the east axis, are then recorded as so many metres east by so many metres south. This system allows for unlimited expansion of the grid. If coordinates other than east and north are used, the fact must be clearly indicated: 123.90W/257.67S, etc. However, using southings and westings are generally avoided.

Many sites now employ a floating grid, sometimes referred to as an electronic grid. The grid is usually laid out using a total station, so the only solid part of this grid is the baseline and the meridian line (apart from the trench pegs), although not even these need to be actually laid out on the ground. The total station is reoriented daily by using its point of origin (Hawker 1999: 24). The floating grid uses the same grid coordinates each day; the only difference from a traditional grid system is that only a few grid pegs can be seen on the ground as the coordinates are stored in the total station's memory (datalogger). Each time the instrument is used it must be checked for alignment with the site grid (Hawker 1999: 24). The total station can then be used to locate individual contexts and features in relation to the site grid, by taking key points on the context or feature and relating them to the plan (see the drawn record). Total stations can also locate points directly to a national or world grid. Once a national or UTM grid point has been located on a map of the area, three recognisable points on the map must also be located; the coordinates of these recognisable points should then be programmed into the total station. Readings must then be taken on each of these points; once you have 'told' the total station which points it is taking readings from, it will be able to orientate itself to the national or UTM grid (Hawker 1999: 13). To insure the greatest accuracy in establishing the site grid, an archaeological surveyor should be included in the site personnel.

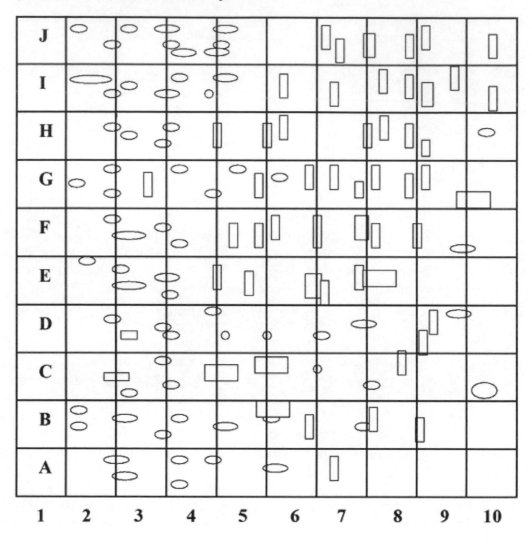

Figure 5: A cemetery site with a grid system using numbers and letters; the squares are then recorded as A2 or J 6. The rectangles and ovals represent graves.

The coordinate system makes it easy to locate your finds and deposits within your excavation units (see **Chapter 6**). To simplify the recording process and for ease of identification the excavation units are usually given a name or number in addition to their grid coordinates. On large sites where there are discrete zones (i.e. where both settlement and cemetery areas are known to exist) it is best to label each locale as a distinct area of operation. At Hierakonpolis they have labelled these areas of operation as localities, i.e. HK6, HK11, and HK43. These areas of operation can just as easily be labelled Tell Abu Dawood, Operation 1, Operation 2, etc. Within these areas of operation are placed the excavation units, and just as the areas of operation need to be labelled, so to do these excavation units (see **Fig. 7**). On smaller sites where there is just one locale being excavated the use of areas of operation can be abandoned, and just the actual trenches need to be labelled.

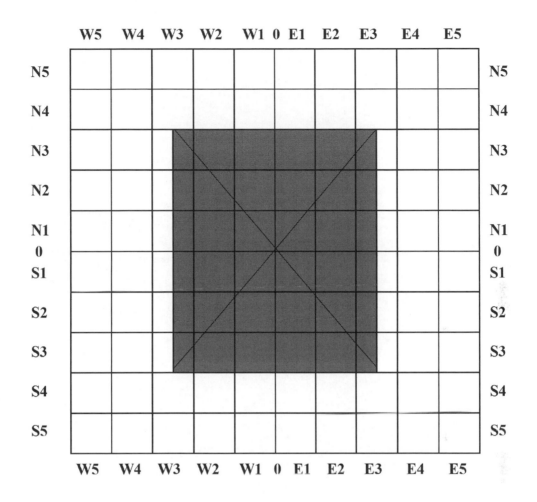

Figure 6: A monument with a grid system using the cardinal points of the compass, with a central datum point. The squares are recorded as E4/N1 or E2/S3, etc.

A simple means of labelling the excavation units is by naming them Trench 1, Trench 2, etc. However, if the whole area is to be excavated, the individual grid units are often given an alphanumeric code (see **Figs. 5-7**), and the 5.0 m or 10.0 m grid units serve as the basis for the excavation units. These units can also be sub-divided, usually quadranted, for example Square 97, which is 10.0 x 10.0 m, divided into four would be 97A, 97B, 97C and 97D, each measuring 5.0 x 5.0 m. This sub-dividing of the site means that every object, deposit or cut can be precisely pinpointed to its point of origin and makes the labelling of bags quicker and easier (Burke & Smith 2004: 125-7). The labelling of the excavation units is usually dependant on the type of site and sampling strategy to be employed, as such the grid size and labelling system should be part of the research design, and must be decided upon before any excavation is undertaken. Whichever labelling system is chosen it must be logical so that no confusion arises.

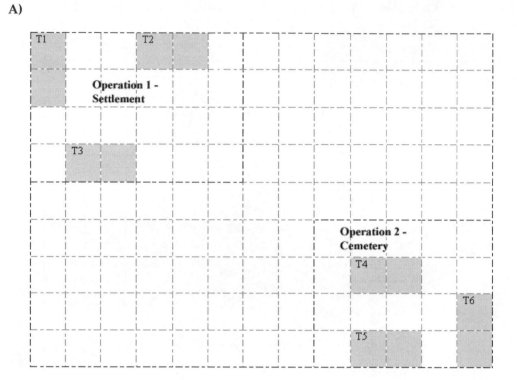

A)

B)

Figure 7: A) The operational areas of the site showing the excavation trenches located within, and the 5.0 x 5.0 m grid covering the whole site; B) The operational areas shown with each 5.0 x 5.0 m grid square numbered.

THE SITE DATUM AND TEMPORARY BENCH MARK

A datum is a known fixed point. The site datum enables all contexts, artefacts and ecofacts to be placed within a controlled horizontal framework, and to be related to the social and physical landscape. The site datum should also be the main elevation (vertical) control point of the site, relating the site's vertical framework to the landscape as well (Fryer 1971: 19). When locating a site datum, it is best to use an unchanging point at the highest level of the site - a fixed point outside the area of excavation. Both the grid baseline and meridian line emanate from this point, and as such it must be the first point established on the site grid. However, if it is not practical to use the site datum point for the vertical control of the site a separate temporary bench mark (TBM) must be established at the highest point of the site outside the area to be excavated (Hester *et al.* 1997: 224). Ideally, it is best to use actual metres above or below sea level (a.s.l./b.s.l.) for the site datum but it is often more convenient to use an arbitrary level for keeping vertical control of the site. This can later be related to the nearest national bench mark. The site datum serves as a reference point for all TBMs and control points. If creating a Geographic Information System (GIS) or conventional map of the site and surrounding region, it is essential that the site be tied into the actual landscape using national or global vertical and horizontal measurements. The terms temporary bench mark and datum are to some degree interchangeable (with datum and local datum being used more in the USA), although the TBM does not necessarily relate to the site grid; there can also be several TBMs around the site, but only one site datum. If excavating a large site, several TBMs should be located at convenient positions for taking elevations of the archaeology.

The universal height adopted by most national surveys as the national datum plane is the mean sea level (Fryer 1971: 19). In Britain the Ordnance Survey has marked certain known heights above sea level on churches and other public buildings which are known as 'bench marks', their elevations calculated in terms of height in metres Above Ordinance Datum (AOD). In the USA, these bench marks are on government survey control stations. In Egypt, bench marks and control points are shown on both the 1:50,000 and 1:25,000 scale Map of Egypt series. The height a.s.l. of the site datum (and thus the TBMs) can be ascertained and tied into the bench mark by carrying out a simple running levels survey. If there are no national height markers available, as is often the case in the desert, then the site datum's height a.s.l. can be ascertained by taking a minimum of three measurements with an altimeter or one with a DGPS on the site datum. However, if a DGPS is not available and the site datum cannot be related to a bench mark, its arbitrary height must be recorded in all reports and also in the field notebooks. Levels a.s.l. may become available for the region at a later date, so that the site datum and the points to which it refers can be spatially contextualised within the landscape.

If using an arbitrary site datum, an assumed elevation of either +100.000 or +50.000 metres is useful. Although this datum will be used as the reference point for all other levels taken on the site, it is not the zero point. The actual datum (the 0.000 point) is in reality 50.000 or 100.000 metres below the surface of the ground. The 0.000 point must be at the lowest point of the site, below the deepest level of any archaeology likely to be encountered, obviating the need to use minus (negative) figures. The assumed elevation (+50.000 or +100.000) is therefore dependent upon the likely elevations to be encountered on the site – the deeper the stratified sequence, the higher the value used. All levels are thereafter recorded as so many metres above site datum (SD).

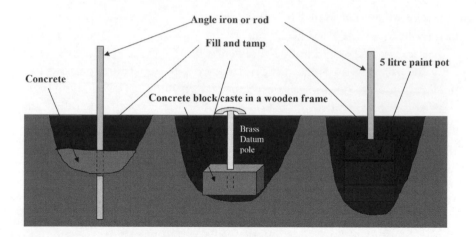

Figure 8: Methods of cementing-in datum and terminal grid pegs (after Dever & Darrel Lance 1978: 143).

The site datum and temporary bench marks should be marked using a brass rod or mushroom-shaped disc set in concrete, with the elevation engraved or painted on it for easy reference. The concrete must be set deep enough for the TBM not to move, as it may be in use for many years. The missions name and contact details should also be marked on the datum, so that other people know the reasons for its existence and can check if it is still in use. Other points along the baseline can also be cemented in position so that the grid can be easily orientated.

Site Management and Logistics

The human and technical resources required on an excavation should be specified during the research design and site evaluation (see **Chapter 4**), although the finances secured tend to dictate what can be done (Roskams 2001: 68). Any archaeological project should employ a logistical approach from the outset, to generate and assess the required finances, staff and legal permits. The smooth running of a site is dependent upon numerous elements coming together. The site **must** be maintained in terms of tidiness, accessibility for the workers and public, the supply and maintenance of correct tools and equipment, and – above all – the safety of both the workers and the public. The hazards that may be encountered must be identified and then minimised by conducting a risk assessment exercise, therefore making the site as safe as possible. The size and character of the site, the likely artefact assemblage and the preservation rate should all be assessed during the site evaluation. Equally, the amount of sediment that is likely to be removed during the excavation should be calculated to help plan spoil disposal, while the nature of the site should be fully evaluated before hiring supervisors, specialists and other personnel. The site evaluation report should also specify the amount of space and type of facilities needed for conservation, environmental and finds processing and storage (see **Chapter 11**).

PERSONNEL

Like most professions, archaeology can be distinguished by the way that it enforces rules and norms of conduct among members of its professional group. Certain types of people are more apt at conforming to these activities than others; this is not dependent on gender or age, but on the ability to learn academic as well as relevant practical and social skills. .It is wise to become familiar with what might be described as the discipline's own ideology, which is typically built up of heroic myths and legends. As such the archaeological community is bound by a sense of identity, and through social control over the selection of professional trainees passes on social skills and knowledge to the next generation of archaeologists. This professionalisation incorporates notions of what it means to participate in the life of the discipline. Fieldwork is absolutely integral to archaeology, and might be considered to be a form of proving ground for archaeologists, where people are judged worthy members of the profession (Moser 2007: 240).

Fieldwork is a highly social experience, as people have to live together in an unfamiliar environment and cooperate as part of a team. Many people make life-long friends, indeed partners, whilst on archaeological fieldwork due to the group bonding processes that are a key element of the enterprise. As well as making bonds with one another it is the arena through which professional identity is transmitted; skills that are socially learnt rather than formally taught. The ability to work and communicate well as part of the team, coping with working in often harsh outdoors conditions, enduring the physicality of the work, the ordeals and hardships associated with living in remote regions, and participating in the spirit of the whole endeavour is profoundly important in assessing the potential of employees and trainees (Moser 2007: 247). Therefore, while technical skills and cognitive understanding are important, social skills and behavioural attributes are also valuable assets of an archaeologist. The role of fieldwork can thus be seen as central in the construction and maintenance of the disciplinary identity; as the arena in which practitioners acquire a 'sense' of what it is to be an archaeologist and learn the necessary skills of professional practice (Moser 2007: 258). As such, it is essential that not only are individual attributes but that group dynamics are considered when recruiting archaeological personnel.

On a practical level the minimum personnel needed on site are three, so that if one person gets injured or sick, one person can stay with them whilst the other goes for help. However, in this age of mobile phones, the absolute minimum can be reduced to two people. However, for most sites the sheer volume of work entailed demands a much larger team, with each individual playing their specific role within the system. Archaeology is a multi-disciplinary subject, and the number of disciplines necessary to properly excavate and understand a site are too numerous to reside with one person alone. Every site has different requirements regarding the approaches and specialists needed, and the archaeological team should be tailored accordingly. For example, it would be unnecessary to have a full-time bioarchaeologist on-site if excavating a non-cemetery settlement. One of the most efficient uses of personnel is if some of the excavators are also specialists in a particular field, particularly if their specialisation can be conducted during post-excavation or when they are not required in the field. The best compromise – and the most commonly used – is a project core team including all relevant specialists (e.g. head archaeologist, environmentalist, artefact specialist, surveyor, conservator, geoarchaeologist, documentary historian) whose expertise and experience is essential to the smooth running of the project, supplemented where necessary with other specialists or excavators according to the requirements of the season.

On a large site the indispensable personnel are headed by the *principal investigator* (site director) who plans and oversees all field operations, logistical/academic policies and strategies in accordance with the research design. The director may be assisted by an *assistant director* if the site is very large, while the *archaeological/logistics manager* is responsible for the day-to-day running of the site, including management of local labourers, procurement of food and other supplies. There should then be a series of people dealing with specific aspects of the project, such as the *site supervisor* who is directly responsible for the day-to-day implementation of the strategic plans and all field procedures. The next level of authority lies with the *area supervisors*, who are responsible for the excavation and recording of their assigned operational areas. They are assisted by the *area finds recorders* and *trench assistants* who are responsible for the excavation of their trenches and the recording of finds. The supervisors participate and oversee the excavation together with other archaeologists, assistants and workers. The trench and area supervisors usually oversee the hired labourers as they remove the overburden and sterile layers, and begin excavation of archaeological horizons. The excavation team is assisted by the *conservator, photographer* and *draughtsperson*. Finally, the specialist workers – including *bioarchaeologists, geoarchaeologists, surveyors, archaeobotanists, zooarchaeologists, ceramicists, lithicists, philologists* (for scripts), and *architects* (for standing buildings), amongst others – should be standing by to assist where required (while working as finds processors, excavators or supervisors when not thus employed). The finds processing is usually carried out by the area supervisors and excavators, under the supervision of the *finds manager* and relevant specialists who will later analyse the finds. As laptop computers are now a common piece of archaeological equipment – especially using programmes such as *Access, Excel* and *ArcView* (Richards 1998; Rains 1995) – it may be necessary to train core team members to work the systems, unless the excavation budget can stretch to specially trained computer-literate staff to maintain databases and Geographic Information System (GIS) programmes. A locally hired cook who can create good food under normal field conditions is invaluable to any team, and helps not only to sustain a high morale among the fieldworkers, but more importantly helps maintain their health and well-being (Hafford 2006).

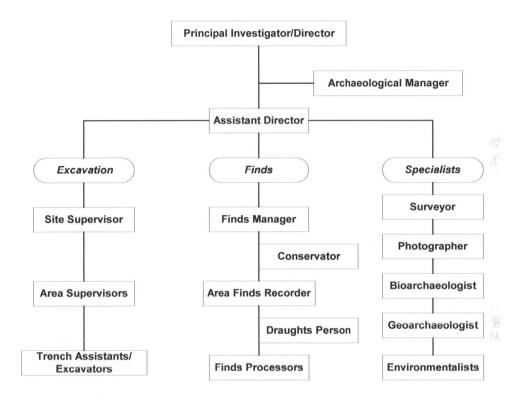

Figure 9: Flow chart showing archaeological management system (after Drewett 1999: 88).

Communication between site personnel is essential if the site is to run as smoothly and efficiently as possible and to make full use of the resources, including time, personnel and data. Particular attention should be paid to the following areas as outlined by Drewett (1999: 88) and the Centre for Archaeological Guidelines (1991: 10-12):

- All records must be double-checked by the area or site supervisor to ensure that all data is correct. This ensures that any errors found can be rectified as soon as possible.

- Everyone must know their job and responsibilities, and must take pains to establish clear lines of communication and referral.

- There must be a common understanding of the objectives of the fieldwork, and each individual's role in achieving them.

23

- The project management must ensure that all team members fully understand recording/recovery policy and on-site procedures, and, where necessary, provide collective or individual training.

- It is very important to establish good site morale and a light, friendly ambience; if anyone evinces dissatisfaction with the project, it is the management's responsibility to find out why. Therefore, although a hierarchy is in place, the management personnel must talk to all those involved in the project in a friendly and concerned way.

- It must be instilled in all personnel that despite the 'summer vacation timing' of many excavation seasons, the excavation process is a serious and potentially hazardous business. It is therefore vital that they act responsibly when working on site, and that any illness or accidents are reported so that appropriate action can be taken.

ORGANISATION OF AN ARCHAEOLOGICAL SITE

The efficient running of an excavation is partially defined by the overall organisation of the site. Regardless of the excavation methodology used, it is essential to carefully situate spoil heaps, wheelbarrow/dumper truck runs, living quarters, laboratories and other amenities. It is also important to be aware of national or local legislation relating to archaeology (O'Keefe & Prott 1984), and to work with all necessary authorities to ensure the smooth running of the project.

The research centre, campsite and other amenities should be placed so as to be easily reached from both the site itself and the roadway. These points are mainly logical: for example, the equipment shed should not be placed far from the site. The same is also true of toilet facilities and the drinking water supply, which should naturally be kept well away from one another. If vehicles need to access the site, the routes in and out should be carefully planned and marked. There should also be areas of cover for rest breaks and for shelter in case of thunderstorms, sandstorms or oppressive heat. If working in a very open area, it may be advisable to erect tarpaulin sheets on metal or wooden pole frames over the area being excavated. This protects the workers from the sun, and also protects the deposits from drying out and helps provide a monotonal lighting environment for improved photography.

As a lot of wasted time and effort can go into the relocation of spoil heaps, their placement should be carefully thought out in the planning stages. There are various points to consider, the most important of which is the safety aspect. Spoil heaps must not be placed where their unexpected collapse may be a danger to fieldworkers or the general public; they should therefore be placed well away from the edges of the excavation. The excavation area's potential growth should also be considered, as should the necessity for backfilling. If the site is destined to become an open-air museum or have a visitor's centre, or if further analysis of an area is likely to be required, then the spoil heaps should be placed well outside the excavation area and must not be allowed to impede access to the site. If backfilling is being practised, then the spoil heaps should be placed as near as is safely possible (at least 2 m away) to the trench they are to refill. 'Rolling excavation' is a good way of managing spoil – this involves backfilling the trench that has just finished being excavated with the spoil from the new trench. The last excavation unit to be excavated is then filled in with the spoil from the first.

The wheelbarrow runs should be as short as possible up the sides of the spoil heap. The maximum gradient should be no more than 1:6, unless the run is spiralled, and must be of sufficient width for the amount of traffic they are going to receive. Boards can be a help with grip on the barrow runs, with batons across them for added purchase in wet conditions (Roskams 2001: 88). If dumper trucks are also being used, then the run should be spiralled at a low gradient and placed far away from the wheelbarrow runs and any path that any workers might take. If any heavy machinery is to be used, very brightly coloured string needs to be used, or a metre trench needs to be dug around the area to be excavated. High-visibility vests should also be considered (although this may only be necessary in more northern latitudes or in inclement weather). Dumper truck runs should also be clearly marked for everyone's safety. Sieving or screening is usually done on or by the side of the spoil heap; the prevailing wind direction should be taken into account in order to prevent the sieved sediment from blowing back into the excavation area.

Because archaeology benefits from the mixed blessing of an elevated public profile, it is likely that visitors and the press may come to view the site. The archaeological team should not only take pains to foster positive public relations, but must also appreciate that they are spokespeople for the entire subject and should therefore act accordingly. A well-run and organised site will look scientific and professional to visitors, and reflects an appropriate concern for the safety of both workers and guests. The strategic placing of signs explaining the dangers of visiting the site may be useful as is the erecting of orange barrier fencing around the excavations; in some countries these are a legal requirement. To help avoid unauthorised visits, site tours should be arranged for the public and press; these should be led by a responsible site worker or, preferably, the director. It may also be useful to provide multilingual leaflets on the work at the site (particularly the local language); these can then be distributed to the visitors, the press and the local community. Exhibitions of finds and a lecture on the work at the site are also good for public relations, while the truly enthused may be permitted to volunteer for duties such as sieving or washing of potsherds, or perhaps to trowel a relatively robust part of the site under the watchful eye of an area supervisor. The director should ensure that the guides and other public-contact personnel are fully briefed about progress at the site, to ensure consistency in communication of such facts to visitors and the press (Roskams 2001: 69-73). On certain sites where highly valuable artefacts are being found, it is necessary to employ guards to protect the site around the clock in order to prevent looters from plundering archaeological material. If the valuable material is still being worked on and its examination would be hampered by it being placed with a regional magazine or museum, an on-site magazine should be erected with no windows and the entrance sealed by a reinforced steel door secured with anti-theft locks.

The drawing-power of a site as a tourist attraction is reliant upon where it is situated, the types of finds being made and how much media attention it has received. A Palaeolithic campsite in the Western Desert is unlikely to attract any visitors, whereas a monumental building near to a major city or on the tourist trail is very likely to receive considerable attention. These facts should be taken into account at all times, because the amount of attention a site receives can make a profound difference to potential academic development, funding opportunities and media coverage. The importance of fostering good public relations cannot be overstated – it is perhaps most appropriate to prepare for the maximum potential level of attention and then sculpt your approach in order to cater for local requirements.

TOOLS AND EQUIPMENT

The selection and maintenance of appropriate tools is essential if the excavation and recording is to be done well. Badly made, blunt, old tools with bad fittings (such as loose handles) should be avoided as they are both unsafe and unprofessional. It is vitally important to choose the right materials for the job in hand. The tools must be carefully looked after, and always cleaned (and oiled if necessary) at the end of the days work. Mechanical, electronic and digital capture devices are particularly susceptible to harsh environments, such as water, wind and sand (see McPherron & Dibble 2003) Cameras are particularly prone to damage; keeping them in plastic bags with ventilation holes is a good means of protecting them. Special rugged forms of equipment are also available, such as tough computers (e.g. Panasonic's *ToughBook* laptop range and water/shock proof cameras). All site equipment **must** be returned to its place of storage after use. One of the first things that must be done at the beginning of any field season is the site inventory of all the tools and equipment. Personal tools should have the owner's initials inscribed on them, therefore preventing confusion or arguments over ownership. Tools pertaining to different areas can be colour coded in order to prevent equipment getting mixed up, as this is often a cause of great stress on excavations. Tools may also be colour coded according function, such as surveying equipment, excavating equipment, recording equipment, conservation supplies, draughting equipment, finds processing equipment and general site equipment. The inventory is kept by the site director; at the end of the season the tools must be checked against the original inventory, so the site director knows what needs to be purchased for the next season.

Table 1a: Personal Excavation Equipment:

Essential:

3 or 4-inch Welded Solid Handle (WHS) or Marshalltown trowel (US equivalent)

3-inch wall paper brush or paintbrush

1-inch paint brush, toothbrush, make-up brush

Dental tools, orange sticks, bamboo skewers, lolly sticks, toffee-apple sticks, teaspoon

Clipboard and ring-bind folder

2h, 4h and 6h pencils

Pens, coloured pencils, pencil sharpener, eraser

Triangular scale ruler

Notebooks

Rulers, protractor

Reflecting compass

Recommended:

Camera & film (or digital media equivalent)

30 metre fibron or glass fibre tape measure

Swiss Army knife

Contour or profile gauge

Sliding callipers, spreading callipers

Set-squares

Scientific calculator

Torch (flashlight)

Small rucksack for daily use on site and a bum bag

Laptop computer, mobile phone

'Standards of Archaeological Excavation' by Tassie and Owens

Water canteen (ideally with in-built cooling system)

Waterproof or indelible marker pens (e.g. Sharpie ®)

Plumb-bob, masonry string, and line-level

5-meter metal tape-measure (with power lock)

1-meter folding measure

Sunglasses, bandana, hat, sunscreen and insect repellent

Gardening gloves

Tweezers

Steel capped boots (if working with heavy digging equipment), sandals or canvas shoes for working in caves or rock-shelters

Personal first-aid kit

Hand held Global Position System (GPS)

Hand lens (small, folding magnifying glass)

Table 1b: Site Equipment:

Essential:

Levelling equipment or Total Station, surveyor's staff

Ranging poles

50 metre fibron tape measures

Long-handled *fases* (hoe)

Small *fases* (hand hoe)

Shovels (with long handles) and spades

Pick-axes or mattocks

Wheelbarrows

Buckets or baskets, seed trays

Dustpan & brushes, broom

A variety of nested sieves with different mesh gages (2 mm, 5 mm and 10 mm)

Munsell Soil Colour Chart

Photographic equipment (including scales, North arrow and black- or letter board)

Drawing frame

Zip-seal plastic bags, and cloth bags (assorted sizes)

Steel rods, wooden stakes or angle irons, string, flagging tape, tags

6-inch Nails

First-aid kit

Recording sheets, note books

Draughting film, graph paper

Microscope / magnifying glass

Cling-film or / and aluminium foil

UHU-Glue

Gypsum or plaster of Paris

Crepe bandages

Plastic basins, drying trays

pH testing kit

Gaffer and duct tape, wire

Batteries (AA and others)

Recommended:

Hard hats and other personal protective equipment

Kneeling mats

Draughting table, tables and chairs

Angle poise lamps

Rotring pens & ink

Magnifying glass

Storage boxes and cartons, air tight plastic containers

Silica gel

Acid-free tissue

Primal, Paraloid

Disposable dust masks

Syringe

Pulley, rope

Sandbags, planks of wood

Ladder (for deep trenches), step ladder for photography

Saws, axes, sledgehammer (for breaking rocks)

Machete (for cutting bushes and other large plants)

Pruning shears, secateurs

Cement

Flotation unit

Paper clips, hole punch, stapler

Large water containers (for group water)

Water hand sprays (to wet down surfaces), hose

Dumper truck

Canopies or tents

Spikes, angle irons, tent pegs or chaining arrows (for marking out the trenches)

Car battery and adaptors, solar panels

Connection leads for all electronic equipment

Walkie talkies

With the increased use of electronic equipment, it is essential that proper provision is made for the supply of power. Although the research centre should be fitted with a mains supply of electricity, this is not always possible when working in remote areas. Therefore, a combination of solar panels and car batteries should be used and connected to the equipment via a car's cigarette lighter (McPherron & Dibble 2003: 30). An excellent range of portable rugged solar chargers called Power Monkey Explorer is produced by *PowerTraveller*. Rechargeable batteries require that they must be regularly recharged, sometimes for up to 12 hours. Other equipment with internal batteries (such as Total Stations and mobile phones) may also need to be recharged. This recharging of batteries must become a ritual, although sets of non-rechargeables must be available on site in case of failure to recharge. Ideally two sets of rechargeable batteries per device should be on site, so one can be used while the other is recharging. Whatever equipment is being used in the field, it is essential that proper provision is made for the supply of power. Larger-scale excavations should consider the use of an on-site generator.

HEALTH AND SAFETY

Health and safety is the responsibility of the site director, who must take every precaution to safeguard of the workers, press and public. All personnel have a duty to take reasonable care of their own health and safety, and to promote safe working practices for themselves, their colleagues and visitors. However, anyone setting foot on an archaeological site must be made aware of the dangers that an archaeological site can pose. If a danger is identified, all work should immediately cease until the hazard as been dealt with. Many of the potential dangers can be avoided if common sense safeguards are observed. A well-managed and organised site poses fewer dangers than a badly managed, untidy site, as outlined in the section above. However, a full risk assessment of the potential hazards likely to be encountered on site **must** be made. All recommendations arising from such an assessment must be taken, and remain valid for the duration of the work. A COSHH (Control of Substances Hazardous to Health) risk assessment – which concerns the handling, storage and disposal of substances hazardous to health – **must** also be conducted. It is advisable to become acquainted with the flora and fauna of the region you are working in, and to ensure that you are briefed about emergency procedures regarding any poisonous plants or animals.

Health and Hygiene

One or two individuals trained in First Aid must be present on site at all times. It is the director's responsibility to ensure that if no members of the team are already qualified first aiders, then one or two members of the team receive the necessary training before the expedition begins. An Accident Book should always be kept on site to log all accidents, to record when an incident happened and how, so that future similar situations can be recognised in advance and their causes eliminated (Roskams 2001: 89). This should be carried out by the first aider who should also look after the first aid kit and ensure that it is well stocked and maintained.

It is essential that at least one first-aid kit is present on site (or vehicle). It must contain the following elements: plasters, gauze bandages, adhesive/micropore tape, a tourniquet, sterile syringes, iodine, eye-bath and solution, butterfly sutures, thermometer, tweezers, salt rehydration tablets (*Diorite, Gatoracle {w}*), antihistamine cream, antiseptic cream, painkillers, burns cream, insect repellent, pills for diarrhoea and related disorders and a first-aid book. However, all workers should be advised to have an anti-tetanus injection and to bring their own personal first-aid kit, containing syringes, aspirin/paracetamol, codeine and antiseptic. A full survey of volunteers and workers is necessary to ensure that you can address any allergies and specific medical requirements. Depending on where you are excavating, it is also advisable to have an anti-snake bite kit; the model produced by *Behring* includes a disposable syringe, a tourniquet, 4 x 10 cc ampoules of anti-venom, and alcohol swabs, all packed in a box (Melville 1981: 99). The anti-venom in these kits is of the polyvalent sera (a mixture of anti-venoms for various snakes, sculpted for the area in mind), further details on snake bites are provided below. If acid or a strong alkaline is splashed into the eyes or skin, the affected area should be cleansed immediately with clean water before taking the patient to the hospital. If a patient needs stitches, these must be done within 24 hours of receiving the wound.

Good sanitary conditions are essential on-site if the workforce is to stay healthy. This includes clean toilets and a supply of fresh drinking water. If there is no research centre available, and tents are being used, then proper camping provisions should be supplied. Everyone must wash their hands regularly, especially before eating, drinking or smoking (and after going to the toilet), as numerous diseases can be contracted from sediments, animals and general rural environments. Personal water canteens should be clearly marked and must *not* be shared with other personnel. This so that if someone on site contracts dysentery or another communicable disease, it will be more easily contained and not be spread throughout the personnel. All personnel working in extreme heat must drink plenty of water at regular intervals to avoid dehydration; at least half a litre per hour. The rule is to drink enough water to keep you passing urine as frequently as is your normal practice. It should be a pale straw colour; if it is any darker you need to drink more water (Melville 1981: 77). As well as increasing your water intake, you must also increase your salt intake; 1 salt supplement table per day combined with the normal salt taken with meals should be sufficient. However, if you only have access to a limited amount of water, then do not increase your salt intake (Melville 1981: 77). If you do not have access to rehydration salts, a teaspoon of sugar and half a teaspoon of salt dissolved in a pint of water can act as an alternative. If someone shows signs of heat exhaustion they should sit down in the shade and take frequent small drinks of cool water and loosen any tight clothing. If someone is vomiting and appearing to be suffering heat stroke (pale skin, progressing to reddened skin, nausea, dizziness, exhaustion, perspiring) seek urgent medical attention (Burke & Smith 2004: 55). Sun-screen of at least SPF 15, wide-brimmed hats and protective neck wear such as a bandanna are advisable to protect your skin from the effects of the sun. Suitable loose long sleeved clothing forms a barrier to the sun's harmful rays, especially tightly-woven fabrics. Check skin regularly for any unusual spots, and see a doctor if moles or birthmarks change shape, size or colour, or start to itch or bleed.

Snakes and scorpions should never be approached. If a coiled snake is encountered detour slowly around it, giving it a wide berth and inform the site director of its whereabouts. If a moving snake is encountered, stand still, do not run away. Keep quiet and watch in case the snake intends to strike. Most snakes are not aggressive and prefer flight to fight, although some highly aggressive species (i.e. king cobra) are less shy (Burke

& Smith 2004: 54; Johnson *et al.* 2008). When the snake has moved to a safe distance, move slowly away. If working near a village, it is worth finding out if they have a local snake handler who can remove any potentially harmful reptiles to a safe distance from the site. If bitten by a snake, immediate action is necessary as the venom can spread very rapidly. Firstly immobilise the victim by laying them down, preferably on a bed. Clean the bitten area and keep it as cold and still as possible; seek specialist medical assistance as a matter of urgency. A freeze kit is ideal for keeping the bitten area cold. Pressure immobilisation should then be applied between the bite and the trunk, this involves tightly bandaging the limb, preferably with a splint if available (Johnson *et al.* 2008). Try and ascertain the species of snake that delivered the bite. The pressure should be as tight as the patient can bear. For some very poisonous species, the snake venom must be sucked out within seven seconds (Melville 1981: 97-8).

Scorpion and spider bites are not normally as serious as snake bites, and those that occur are unlikely to be fatal. For scorpion bites apply prompt local suction to the affected area and pack the area with ice or cold water. Treat the patient for shock, and administer scorpion anti-venom. In addition, local anaesthetic should be administered, and the patient should be treated for shock (Melville 1981: 100). If the patient is bitten by a spider, local anaesthetic should be applied to the bitten area, and the patient should be kept warm and lying down. If spasms occur calm the patient down and administer pain-relief tablets (Melville 1981: 101-2). Always seek professional medical treatment if bitten by a scorpion of spider as soon as possible. Ticks can also be a problem in certain areas of the world and can be transmitters of various diseases; be especially careful in livestock-rich areas and consult a local doctor for advice. Wearing boots that cover the ankle and tucking your trousers into your socks is a good defence. However, if a tick does attach itself, leaver it out gently with a pair of tweezers or apply DEET; do not try and pull, squeeze or cut the tick out (Burke & Smith 2004: 54). Many local populations remove ticks using a lighted cigarette. The ocean holds a number of threats that could constitute a problem for coastal excavations. Sharks, jellyfish, stingrays, scorpion fish and a host of other species can all wound and even kill an unwary swimmer. Freshwater is often home to parasitic worms, as well as crocodiles and numerous other potentially harmful species. Avoid swimming in sluggish water and always keep a careful eye on your surroundings and your companions. In all cases, seek specialist knowledge (consult a local doctor for advice on what to avoid, and how to treat any animal injury) of the area in which the excavation will be held, and tailor your safety policy accordingly.

Risks and Safety on Site

Many potentially dangerous situations may arise on archaeological sites, although the two areas that are most likely to cause accident are deep holes and machinery. Personal Protective Equipment (PPE) should be supplied by the director, to include masks, hard hats and protective earphones (where necessary). When digging holes, care must be taken to ensure the safety of the people working in them. The central question, of course, is defining what a 'deep' hole is. If a person is working on their hands and knees, a hole of 1.2 metres might be considered deep. Each situation must therefore be assessed on its own merits, specifically the type of work being carried out and the nature of the sediments involved. Sand and gravel are not very cohesive, and may even need support or battering at a depth of 1.0 metre or less. It must be remembered that every cubic metre of sediment weighs a tonne, more than enough weight to kill. The decision as to when shoring should be used must take into account the level of moisture in the sediment (also groundwater sources), the time of year (weather conditions), the type of excavation and the processes being carried out. Sources of vibration such as underground transport (e.g. the Tube [in London]) and adjacent roads should also be considered (Drewett 1999: 82). However, a good guide is that if the depth of the trench exceeds half the width, then shoring should be seriously considered and hard hats worn. If the depth of the trench exceeds the width, then shoring **must** be used. Most archaeological field units insist on shoring when the depth exceeds 1.2 m deep (Roskams 2001: 104).

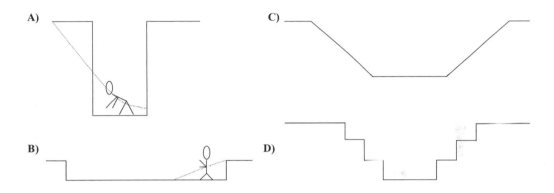

Figure 10: The types of trenches, A) Narrow trench, B) Open-area excavation unit, C) Battered unit D) Stepped unit. Dotted line shows collapsed baulk (after Drewett 1999: 83-4).

Open-area excavation is much safer than digging in deep, narrow trenches; if the sides of a deep narrow trench collapse they can bury the workers within, whereas if the sides of a large open-area excavation collapse they are more likely to spread over a wide area. When working on a monumental building or a rock-cut tomb, it is always best to bring in a civil engineer to assess the integrity of the structure and employ specialist contractors to erect scaffolding and shoring where necessary. On more open sites it may also be advisable to employ specialist contractors. Shoring usually consists of strong wooden planks set against the section faces and – if in a trench, tomb or monument – internal braces of steel or wood with acroprops attached to them. However, it is difficult to extend this type of shoring downwards and it may be preferable to insert a vertical framework held in place by cross-members (Roskams 2001: 104). This type of shoring arrangement is extendable downwards, and both metal sheets and timber boards can be utilised for the shoring. This can obviously present some problems for section drawing. Cumulative sections are probably the best type of sections to draw if you are using this form of shoring. Another reasonably cheap method for shoring-up holes 2.5 metres or less is chicken wire and sheeting placed over the profiles of the excavation unit. The chicken wire should be firmly anchored at the top and into the face of the profiles, clamping the sheeting directly against the face of the profile. A vertical frame is then used to keep this in place, supported by cross-members. The pieces of chicken wire used must be of one length, reaching from the top of the section to the bottom in one span, and with enough spare to match the deepening excavation. This type of shoring is not recommended for very deep excavations. If large open areas are to be shored, you should use interlocking sheet piling driven into the ground by a piling rig (Roskams 2001: 105). If work proceeds to any great depth, additional cross-members may be required. This type of shoring is the most expensive and needs to be erected by specialist contractors. It is better to ask professional advice when installing this or any other type of shoring. A ladder or other suitable means of access/egress must be provided in trenches of more than 0.50 m deep.

An inexpensive method of securing an excavation area is 'battering' - sloping the sides of the excavation area to an angle of 45⁰ or less. This will necessitate the use of cumulative section drawings to keep a record of the stratification in the baulks. This type of safety precaution is particularly useful in loose sandy sites. If the mechanical removal of the overburden of sterile aeolian sand is beyond the budget of the excavation, then the overburden could be dug with battered sides whilst the archaeological layers are excavated with straight sides. Another type of excavation is stepped-trenching, where the sides of a large open area are cut in 1.0 metre steps, getting narrower as it descends (Renfrew & Bahn 1991: 93). This allows the stratigraphic profiles to be read, whilst also keeping the excavation unit safe (see **Fig. 10**). In a sandy matrix, where the sides easily crumble into the excavation area, the stepped increments may need to be 0.50 m to prevent baulk collapse. It is much easier to step a trench in than to step it out, therefore, to achieve a 10.0 x 10.0 m trench at a depth of 3.0 metres below surface a 14.0 x 14.0 m trench will initially have to be laid out on the surface.

To protect the vulnerable top edges of the excavation area from being damaged, sandbags filled with spoil should be placed around the edge of the excavation unit(s). This should be done as the first lot of spoil is removed, as it not only helps to stabilise baulks and profiles but also helps to delineate the area of excavation. The sandbags must be placed end-to-end all around the top edge of the excavation unit, and any bags that subsequently split must be replaced immediately. This kind of shoring is particularly useful when excavating in areas characterised by loose sediments, such as deserts. As well as helping to prevent profile collapse, the sandbags also help prevent tools and other objects from being kicked into the excavation area. However, these sandbags *must not* be used as seats, as this can cause trench collapse. The areas around the edge of excavation unit must be kept clear of tools and spoil for at least 1.5 metres back from the section face. To help prevent objects and tools from being kicked, tripped over or falling into the excavation areas, all tools *must* be placed face-down when not being used.

When working in rock-cut tombs, monumental buildings or in deep excavations it is **essential** that the workforce wear general-purpose industrial safety helmets to protect their heads from falling objects or rubble. A specific health and safety issue when working in enclosed dry and dusty environments such as caves or rock-cut-tombs (particularly when just opened) is the presence of mould, fungi, or organic dust, which can cause serious lung congestion or allergic alveolitis. It is advisable when working in such conditions to wear a respirator or filtered dust-mask that can filter out particles as small as 2 microns (Hester *et al.* 1997: 111). Steel-capped boots should be worn when working with plant or heavy hand tools, such as pick-axes, mattocks or forks. It is also advisable to wear strong boots when working in monumental buildings or rock-cut tombs. Wheelbarrows *must* be held by one crew member while they are being filled if the trench is more than 1.0 m deep; never overfill the wheelbarrow. In trenches over 1.0 m in depth, spoil and tools should be taken out of the trench via winch and pulley system. Hoists for lifting spoil out of deep trenches can be either manual or mechanical, depending on the amount of spoil being moved. The secure positioning and maintenance of such equipment is essential. If removing tough or thorny plants, tough gardening gloves *must* be worn. Be aware that many innocent-looking plants may be poisonous, or may provoke allergic reactions (seek expert local knowledge in order to identify potential hazards).

All premises (including the site itself), machinery and associated fixtures, vehicles and tools must be fully maintained, and a safe and efficient working system enforced. All equipment must be securely tethered within a vehicle prior to the outset of a journey. If a vehicle is being taken on a long journey, it *must* have a full service before commencement of the trip, and must have a tool kit, fire extinguisher, first aid kit and ideally a mobile phone on board.

If digging equipment such as a tractor or JCB 3c with a back actor (hydraulic arm with hoe) is used on site, it is important that a proper work pattern is established. The driver must be able to see the people working on site, so high-visibility bright clothes – such as flash-vests – are advisable. Ideally, all machine excavation should take place before the main workforce arrives on site. However, if the workforce is present, then the heavy machine digging should take place well away from them. The most dangerous part of the machine is the radius of the back actor, and workers should stay well away from this part of the machinery. If a worker wishes to enter this zone, then the driver of the machine *must* be informed first, and the machine should be switched off.

In urban areas there may be utility pipes and conduits buried beneath ground, such as electric, gas and water pipes. On certain sites these may be dead, but on others they may still be live. Finding out their location is essential. The local authorities may be able to provide you with a utilities map, although a CAT scan can also be used to locate their location.

The site should be covered by indemnity and health and accident insurance to cover not only the workers but third parties such as visitors and tourists. This is to not only to protect the people on the site, but also protects the site director or organising institution from being sued in the event of an accident.

CHAPTER FOUR

The Process of Excavation

The layout and form of archaeological sites reflects the ancient inhabitants' lifestyle, ecology, limitations and social/environmental context. If any object or feature is carelessly excavated without due attention as to its exact provenience, it becomes archaeologically useless. As beautiful as it might be, therefore, its significance has been destroyed because it conveys no information about the time, place, and situation in which it was made or used (Joukowsky 1980: 159). It is only by recording the matrix, provenience and contextual associations of a feature or artefact that it achieves archaeological value.

Site excavation is the most costly and destructive process undertaken in archaeology, and should only be undertaken after the potential of non-destructive (and cheaper) methods have been exhausted (see **Fig. 12**). However, although remote sensing and geophysical techniques are capable of answering many questions, they cannot address all aspects of ancient human activity. At present, therefore, excavation is the only viable means of capturing much of the archaeological data, and must be combined with geophysical survey so as to be both informed and precisely targeted (David 2001: 525; Pusch 2000: 145-6). The aims of excavation are to identify, define, uncover, record, date and interpret each archaeological context, and to understand the formation processes that went into making them - establish sequence and event (Drewett 1999: 107-8). Each archaeological context is a potential source of cultural or ecological information, whether it is a cut or a deposit, or if it contains artefacts or ecofacts (Miller-Rosen 1986: 8), but, it is only in the process of making observations about the appearance and configuration of deposits that they are turned into data. Once data has been gathered, it is possible to analyse them and turn scattered observations into the hard evidence of past societies (Roskams 2001: 35), thus realising the true aim of archaeology.

Archaeology employs interpretation not only during the post-excavation phase, but also during excavation itself (Barker 1993: 147; Hodder 1999: 80-4). The archaeologist inevitably uses interpretation to decide what to excavate and record, while choices and interpretation are made at the edge of a trowel in deciding what changes in sediment texture and colour to follow and which to ignore. The recording forms have separate spaces for description and interpretation, for while both are technically interpretation, it is useful to make a distinction between what is observed on the basis of knowledge (description) and a *post hoc* 'reading' of what the context may actually signify (interpretation *sensu stricto*). This allows for greater ease in handling large amounts of data, and refining or reinterpreting the site archive at a later date.

The method of excavation is often decided upon by an initial assessment of a context or group of contexts. For example, possible hearths should be wet-sieved as they may contain charred seeds, whereas a layer that is likely to be sterile will receive much less rigorous examination. We should, however be aware that we are always making judgement calls, as only after these contexts have been excavated can they be properly interpreted (Hodder 1999: 92). To mitigate these problems we may use exploratory excavation and sampling to help ascertain which excavation procedures should be used, although it cannot always be assumed that all the sampled parts of a cultural deposit, site or groups of sites are similar

(Hodder 1999: 82). Previous research of other sites and exploratory investigation of a site should therefore guide the project, while careful excavation should be accompanied by continual reappraisal and sampling. Before a group of contexts is designated as a 'feature' or 'structure', careful stratigraphic analysis of the matrix should be conducted. Some features may be obvious (such as graves or tombs) whereas the significance of more nebulous finds - such as a group of pits or post-holes - may only become clear after reconstruction of the matrix. Therefore, although the method of excavation and sampling of certain groups of contexts may be used on initial assessment, they should not be named as features in the recording process until the matrix has been carefully consulted (*contra* Carver 2005: 109). Feature numbers are not required to make the matrix work; it is the matrix that should inform your interpretation (see **Chapter 10**).

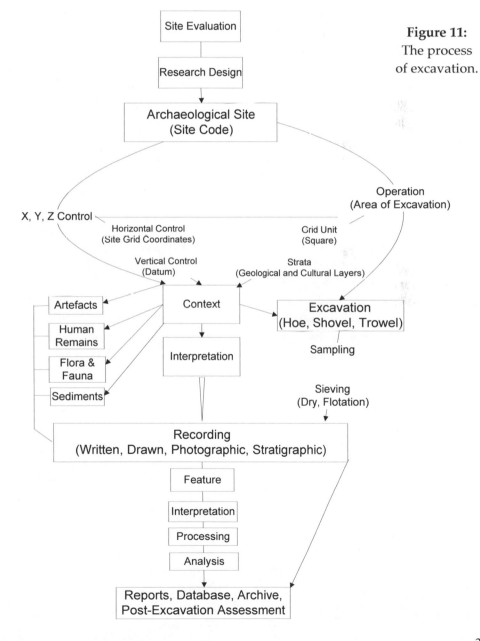

Figure 11: The process of excavation.

35

RESEARCH DESIGN AND APPROACHES TO EXCAVATION

Archaeological excavations can be split into two broad categories: 1) research and 2) rescue, and the three main approaches: 1) problem-orientated excavation, 2) value-led excavation and 3) total excavation. While these are not necessarily mutually exclusive, research archaeology is often associated with universities, museums and similar institutions, whereas rescue archaeology is usually linked with developer-led contract projects. Egypt sees a fusion of rescue and research aims, as demonstrated by the interdisciplinary and international nature of the UNESCO Nubian Rescue Campaign. Although many research concession licences have and still are being granted, concessions to excavate in certain areas of Egypt are usually only granted where archaeological remains are under threat from factors such as urban sprawl or agricultural practices. However, while this may technically qualify it as rescue archaeology, the manner in which the projects are allocated and executed differ from the majority of developer-funded Western rescue excavations.

Modern pressures on archaeological remains are particularly high in the developing world, and are especially notable in Egypt. The destructive forces of salinisation, mechanical farming practices, agricultural intensification, fish farming, land reclamation (flooding of vast areas of land), pollution, a high water table, *Sebakhin* (diggers for ancient mud-brick and mud-brick wash, to use as fertiliser or in manufacturing new mud-bricks), looters, demolition, development projects and general urban sprawl are all gradually eroding away vital archaeological sites. The increasing need for arable land is pressuring archaeological sites ever more, and even sites that are protected under law are gradually being eaten away. Therefore, to effectively protect the archaeology it is important to know the extent, whereabouts and quantity of cultural heritage present. National Sites and Monuments Records (SMRs), also termed Heritage Environment Records (HERs), are an excellent means of recording known cultural heritage. Regional and national surveys (cartographic, remote sensing and fieldwalking) are a good means of locating and assessing sites in the rural (including desert and forest) and semi-urban landscape (see the **Survey Recording Form: Sheet 49**). Urban environments are more problematic. Unless ancient buildings are standing, the only way to access archaeological remains is exploratory excavation when an area is being redeveloped, or possibly by the use of aerial and land-based remote sensing techniques such as satellite imagery and ground penetrating radar (GPR).

Site selection should take place on the basis of 1) whether the site is in imminent or direct danger of being destroyed, or 2) if such a project can answer a specific research question. If the former, all should naturally be done to save the site. Sites that are chosen to answer a specific research question should ideally be part of a regional or national research strategy. The location of sites through remote sensing from the air and investigation of individual sites on the ground through geophysical and surface survey can give background information for assessing the significance of sites. Archaeologists collaborating with the national archaeological body are then better able to target sites with the potential to answer research questions. The keeping of SMRs is of invaluable assistance in this process. Sites under direct danger of being destroyed (those where legal permission has been granted for development of other planning processes) should be evaluated immediately for further investigation.

Development-led rescue archaeology is often – and incorrectly – thought of as merely comprising the collection of raw data, unlike the more theoretically-based paradigm of research archaeology (Roskams 2001: 31). The major differences are the manner in which the archaeology is presented in the reports and multivocality during fieldwork. It is also a common error to assume that total excavation is objective, whereas problem orientated excavation is subjective. Whether rescue or research-based, a certain process should be followed: assessment, evaluation, and establishing whether further research is required. This further research can take the form of trenching or open-area excavation, depending upon the amount of time and money allocated to the project. The dynamic, complex interaction of stratigraphy, past human actions and present archaeological excavations **must** be recognised on any project. The techniques of excavation used are not mutually exclusive to either of the categories or approaches and the different types of archaeological research must inform one another and drive developments in best practice (Tilley 1993).

Every excavation must possess a research design, sometimes also called a 'method statement', 'project design' or 'written scheme of investigation'. Even if a site is about to be destroyed, the planners must agree upon a research design to determine what can be effectively excavated, how to obtain answers to specific questions, and how much can be excavated in the time and resources allotted. The research design should be based upon extant knowledge of other sites, but should not directly copy other designs as each site is individual. The research design should anticipate the types of data likely to be encountered, identify those which may help resolve or evaluate a particular hypothesis, and then implement or develop methods and a team to acquire and analyse those kinds of data (Banning 2000: 91). In certain circumstances it may not be possible to fully outline the research design for the post-excavation and publication phase of the project until the fieldwork has been started or even completed. In this case, you must provide a post-excavation research design detailing the methodology for data procurement, the analytical methodology and archiving of the site and materials, and a detailed structure of the report.

The research design is the starting point for any project and should explicitly state the aims and objectives and how the project will address/achieve them to internationally accepted standards. The strategy is based upon the research design, and is shaped to provide answers to the objectives within the constraints of logistical issues (i.e. material survival, technology, bureaucratic negotiations, budget, etc). Research designs are based on previous research (usually desk-based assessments or field evaluations) for their formulation, and should be multi-stage, multi-vocal, cyclical or reflexive, allowing feedback from fieldwork for an appraisal of progress, to refine methods and hypotheses, to define new kinds of data with which to test them, and to introduce new hypotheses to account for unexpected results (Banning 2000: 91). A cyclical approach requires all types of data to be gathered, analysed and fed back into the hypothesis, which is only feasible if information from the specialists (ceramicists, bioarchaeologists, geoarchaeologists, etc) is continually fed back into the excavation process. This requires the specialists to conduct initial analysis and interpretation while excavation is taking place, necessitating their presence on the excavation to consult with field staff as to optimum excavation methods, and defining and adapting the sampling strategy to answer specific questions (Hodder 1999: 96-8, 189). Although not essential, the use of computers permits rapid analysis of the data retrieved from the site, and will increase the speed with which information is fed back for interpretation. Excavation, sampling and interpretation therefore progress together, leading to dynamic and ever-changing interpretations of the site and its contexts (see **Fig.**

17).

The aims of archaeological investigation should be wide-ranging explanations of human activity: 1) the consideration of the *form* of archaeological evidence and its temporo-spatial distribution, 2) the determination of the past *function* - based on form and function - to construct models of ancient behaviour, 3) to define the *processes* of culture and why cultures changed, and 4) to comprehend cultural *meaning* through the context of symbols, values, and world view (Hester *et al.* 1997: 18-9). In every case, however, the initial research question must be appropriate for the type of site to be excavated. For example, if investigating an entire settlement, it is not sufficient for a research design to focus on the economy (storage pits or crop processing areas) if intra-site spatial patterning and other phenomena are not included. The research question must address all the aspects of society that a certain type of site can answer, and the research design must be developed to answer them. The Institute of Field Archaeologists (1999d; 2001b) gives the following guidance for the structure of a research or project design, which has been modified for a more global audience:

The Contents of a Research Design Should Include:

1. A non-technical summary of the project (which must be intelligible to a non-specialist).
2. Site location including map(s) and a description (GPS location of the SW corner of the site, national grid reference, known size of site, geology, land use and any physical constraints).
3. The context of the project. State whether it is research-driven, if there are any planning policies, if it is a World Heritage Site, national scheduled monument or other protected site. Note proposed development if relevant, necessary legislation and any environmental issues.
4. The geological, environmental and topological background.
5. A summary of the archaeological and historical importance of the site or area, including built and landscape. What is the site status? Is it a registered archaeological site and, if so, what is its national classification? Is it included in the national Sites and Monuments Records (SMRs)? What are the views of other stakeholders?
6. A summary of any previous archaeological investigations of the site or area (including any plans, sections and photos), and how the proposed project relates to them and other research.
7. Aims, objectives and purpose of the fieldwork (these should be clearly stated in both general and specific terms).
8. The field methodology (detail all the approaches, techniques and methods selected. Justify any selections made. State artefact collection and discard policies, environmental collection strategy and implementation, the procedures for dealing with human remains, recording techniques and any measures for conservation, preservation and protection of the site).
9. Resources (structure and size of project team with their specialities. Information about any materials and equipment required to fulfil the identified tasks, details of any premises to be built or rented).
10. Post-fieldwork methodologies (cleaning, conservation, cataloguing, packaging, dating techniques, archive preparation, artefact analysis and site management).

11. How the report will be prepared, with a list of contents.
12. The intellectual copyright clause of the person undertaking the fieldwork and/or report writing. The copyright pertains to both the written and graphic material produced during the fieldwork project, and unless this has been varied in the 'contract' for the work, the copyright remains with that person. The copyright should clearly state the circumstances under which other parties may use the report or records.
13. Archive deposition (including finds ownership and the name of the recipient museum/repository)
14. Outline of dissemination proposals, to include publication plan.
15. The timetable of the whole project shown on a cascade chart.
16. Health and safety policies and implementation, including risk assessment.
17. Details of insurance cover.
18. Monitoring and reporting structure (to maintain the standard and timetable of work).
19. Budget (the projected costs of the individual stages and of the complete project).

The majority of excavations define the remains of a cemetery, temple, building, tomb or some other area where people have done things in the past as a 'site', but these are only ever components of a complete ancient living space. Strictly speaking, a site is a complete living environment and all the factors that influence it. A complete living area may include the remains of a settlement with its activity areas, a cemetery, areas for agriculture or foraging and other material resources that are set within the surrounding – and socially constructed – landscape. Tell el-Amarna is one of the few Egyptian sites where the term 'site' is met to its fullest extent, having its agricultural fields, necropolis, and settlement all investigated within the landscape (Kemp 1989: 261-317). Inevitably, the majority of excavation area selections are based upon a subjective choice, choosing a part of the ancient living space or landscape to excavate on the assumption that the results will answer the questions being asked. The oft-forgotten fact about archaeological landscapes is that they are constantly in a state of flux. There are many questions that must be addressed if your data are to be significant. What was the life use of this tomb? How did this settlement grow and change through time? Was this accompanied by the emergence of elites and social stratification, and if so, did this affect diet and health conditions between strata? Is this likely to be archaeologically visible? The total excavation of - for example - one temple does not constitute a complete living space, while the excavation of an entire settlement hardly ever includes the associated catchment area. While certain nodes within urban landscapes are treated as sites in their own right, this usually reflects resource restraints or the erratic way in which rescue digs are situated as these are only small areas of the ancient cities that lie below and do not constitute the entirety of any ancient living space. In urban archaeology a mosaic excavation strategy must therefore be deployed, building up a picture of the ancient city as and when archaeological investigation is allowed to proceed. In this context, 'total excavation' is therefore something of a misnomer (Roskams 2001: 33). Equally, trenching sites in order to answer specific archaeological questions is of questionable value. A combination of both approaches should be employed in excavating a site, as well as conducting off-site sampling of the local landscape. You must also be prepared for unforeseen eventualities; while you may aim to examine on-site cultural transitions and ecology at the Neolithic/Bronze Age boundary, for example, you must nonetheless meticulously excavate and record the Iron Age cemetery that unexpectedly overlays it.

Although site directors may favour one approach over another, there is no 'right' way to excavate a site. There are as many approaches and methods throughout the world as there are sites on which to employ them (Drewett 1999: 92), which may in turn range from camps and caves, to permanent settlements (both secular and religious), cemeteries and ship wrecks. *Tell* sites, deeply stratified urban sites, complex structures containing thousands of artefacts cannot be excavated in the same way as an open Palaeolithic campsite or cemetery site. The conditions must always dictate the approach and strategy used, while the type of contexts, structures and materials expected must dictate the recovery methods employed. Finally, time and financial restraints always determine what can and cannot be carried out at a given site. It is therefore best to be flexible in your approach to excavation, adapting your methodology to fit the nature of the site, being able to change direction or emphasis to accommodate the changes encountered in the archaeological record (Roskams 2001: 36). To this end, a multi-disciplinary approach should be taken, involving the social, biological and physical sciences as well as humanities such as history and philology (Roskams 2001: 36-9).

Appropriate sampling strategies should be chosen on the basis of the size and form of the entities to be sampled, and the profusion or pattern of their distribution (Roskams 2001: 41). Even if the investigation focuses on urban spatial structure (an area of archaeology that is not amenable to random sampling - Shennan 1988: 28), cluster sampling may be conducted to reduce costs. Large 'representative' areas of the site will usually be exposed in open-area excavation, with other areas excavated with trenches and yet others investigated by sub-surface survey and cluster sampling. Orton (2000) covers a wide range of sampling strategies, and how and where to employ them. Ultimately, the decision on which methodological approach is to be used may depend not only on the archaeology, but the available time and finances (Drewett 1999: 92) and even political considerations.

SITE EVALUATION: DESK-BASED ASSESSMENT, WATCHING BRIEFS AND FIELD EVALUATION

Before an excavation takes place it is essential to conduct extensive background research. This is done in three phases: appraisal, assessment and evaluation. The more information that is amassed, the easier it is to draw up a detailed project design for further research and excavation.

An archaeological assessment can involve a detailed appraisal, desk-based assessment, field evaluation and watching brief, and may occur as a response to a development project that threatens the archaeological deposits, as part of an environmental impact assessment or in response to destructive natural (i.e. coastal erosion) or anthropogenic (i.e. agricultural intensification, forestry development or works by public utilities) forces. They may also be conducted on a site or area not under specific threat, or in connection with the management plans for a site or area by private, local, regional, national or international bodies. Desk-based assessments, site evaluation and watching briefs may be commissioned by developers, local planning authorities, national advisory bodies, private landowners, government agencies, archaeological bodies or archaeological researchers.

They may be a legal requirement for the preservation of archaeological remains, particularly in the planning stage of a development project.

An appraisal usually involves checking the sites and monuments records, local knowledge and other sources to determine whether there may or may not be an archaeological aspect to a proposed development project. If an archaeological dimension is indicated further stages of site evaluation are then required (see those listed below).

Desk-based Assessments

Desk-based assessments are to determine the known or potential archaeological deposits within a specified area or site (land-based, inter-tidal or marine). This is accomplished by examining and collating archaeological databases, archival records, reports and library resources (written, graphic, photographic, cartographic and electronic) in order to identify the likely characteristics (preservation, quality, quantity) of the actual or potential archaeological entity in its local, regional, national or international context. An assessment is also conducted to assess the presence or absence, character and extent, date, integrity, state of preservation and relative quantity/quality of the potential archaeological deposits within a given area or site, in order to make an assessment of its merits in context (IFA 1999b: 2).

Desk-based assessments will usually lead to: 1) the formulation of a strategy to ensure the recording, preservation or management of the cultural heritage, 2) the formulation of a strategy for further investigation if the archaeological deposits were not sufficiently defined to allow a mitigation strategy, or 3) the formulation of a proposal for further archaeological research (IFA 1999b: 2).

Besides planning or development-induced desk-based assessments, the area for potential investigation or study will have been selected by an archaeologist based upon: 1) specific aspects or themes relating to their own defined research interests, 2) threats of a general or specific nature, or 3) the intensity of previous archaeological investigations (see **page 35-39**). This work may be conducted through universities, central government archaeological agencies, international bodies (such as UNESCO), local authorities, museums, independent trusts, non-governmental organisations, private companies, groups or individuals. Site visits are usually necessary to ascertain the nature of the site and the use of land upon which it stands, as this may affect the survival of archaeological deposits. After the desk-based assessment is completed, all data should be included in the project archive. A report addressing the aims of the project must then be written around the results of any site visits, and submitted to the local and regional archaeological agencies and SMRs office as well as the developers or planners. A report should also be submitted to a national digest of fieldwork (in Egypt, this is the Annals du Service des Antiquités de l'Egypte [*ASAE*]).

Evaluations

After a desk-based assessment has been conducted, further site evaluation will usually be required. Site evaluation should be used to test whether an area contains significant archaeological remains, to assess the suitability of the research design and to determine how the excavation strategy should be structured. This takes the form of restricted non-intrusive and/or intrusive fieldwork to determine the presence or absence of archaeological features, structures, deposits, artefacts and ecofacts within a specified area. If archaeological remains are found, the evaluation should define their character and extent, relative quality, date, integrity and state of preservation. The report arising from the evaluation enables the sites' worth to be assessed in a local, regional, national or international context. The field evaluation is often the first step in the formulation of a proposal for further archaeological investigations - set a strategy for recording, preservation and management of archaeological deposits or to formulate a plan to mitigate a threat to the archaeological deposits. It is important to fully evaluate the nature of the evidence, create deposit models to suggest areas for fuller excavation and set a more detailed agenda, including the personnel and resources required for specific tasks (Roskams 2001). The field evaluation should be minimally intrusive and destructive of the archaeological remains in both design and execution (IFA 1999d: 2-4).

The evaluation design must reflect the nature of the archaeological remains likely to be encountered, and involves the use of a combination of sampling procedures and other techniques; although non-intrusive methods should be the first option, this may not be sufficient to produce reliable results. Although a sampling fraction of 2% is often regarded as a 'standard' to evaluate a site, there is no statistical rationale for this figure whatever (Orton 2000: 120-1). Evaluations can vary from 2% to 20% of a site and their effectiveness is determined by the overall size of the site, density of the contexts, size of the contexts or features, the required probability of detection, the visibility of the various contexts and the sampling strategy and methods (Orton 2000: 121). Limited use of intrusive methods should therefore be employed to obtain the necessary data; many of these are listed below (IFA 1999d: 8) and are expanded upon in the next section.

Non-Destructive Methods of Field Evaluation

- Geophysical survey

- Topographical survey

- Remote sensing

- Geochemical survey

- Earthwork survey

- Field scanning (mapping of artefact distributions, but not the collection of artefacts)

- Standing building survey

Destructive Methods of Field Evaluation

- Coring

- Shovel test-pits

- Hand-excavated test pits

- Hand-excavated trenches

- Machine-stripped and manually excavated test pits

- Machine-stripped and manually excavated trenches

- Probing (usually used underwater)

- Fieldwalking and surface artefact collection

After the field evaluation has been completed a report should be written and disseminated to all stakeholders (as outlined above for desk-based assessments).

Watching Briefs

Archaeological watching briefs involve the observation and investigation of anthropogenic or natural forces (i.e. developers) that could potentially harm suspected or actual archaeological deposits. Watching briefs are usually conducted as part of 1) the planning process, 2) an environmental impact assessment or 3) forces outside the planning process (any other potentially destructive natural or anthropogenic force). The watching brief will be within a specified area or site on land, inter-tidal zone or underwater where there is the possibility that archaeological deposits will be disturbed or destroyed. Watching briefs are usually conducted when a building is demolished as part of redevelopment planning or a highway or pipeline is to be laid. These activities cause the ground to be disturbed allowing archaeologists to 1) observe, investigate and record the nature of any archaeological deposits, and 2) signal to all interested parties that an archaeological find has been made and that resources should be allocated accordingly. The objective of a watching brief is to establish and make available information about any archaeological deposits existing on a site. They are not intended to reduce the requirement for excavation and preservation of deposits, and are meant to guide (not replace) further and more comprehensive excavation and preservation measures as deemed appropriate under the circumstances (IFA 1999c: 2)

In many countries the preservation of archaeological deposits is a material consideration, and as such developers and local authorities are obliged to take archaeological considerations into account in their planning process (in Egypt this is Law 117, a rendering is available at www.e-c-h-o.org). Watching briefs therefore fulfil part of the obligation of developmental and planning legislation, which must be conducted in accordance with the law and may be instigated by developers (or their agents), local planning authorities, national advisory bodies, private landowners or non-archaeological government agencies. However, the national archaeological agency may also be legally required to conduct watching briefs as part of their obligation to cultural heritage management, and will in that case supply the archaeologists to conduct the programme. Monitors may also be employed to ensure that the watching brief is being conducted in compliance with the agreed specifications and project design.

After an initial appraisal a research design should be compiled and submitted to the relevant stakeholders. Various intrusive and non-intrusive methods may be employed during a watching brief, although the archaeologist's direct involvement must be negotiated with the contractors. Samples may need to be sent away for further investigation and analysis. The majority of the work will involve non-intrusive observation as the foundations of the old building or structure are demolished or an area is prepared for redevelopment (see Empereur 2000; Stapp & Longenecker 2009). Full and proper records (written, graphic, electronic and photographic) must be kept using *pro forma* recording forms and sheets as applicable (IFA 1999c: 5), including the measuring and planning of *in situ* archaeological deposits. After the watching brief is completed, all data generated should be added to the project archive. A report addressing the aims of the project must then be written and submitted to relevant archaeological agencies and the SMRs office, as well as to the developers or planners. A report should also be submitted to a national digest of fieldwork. If substantial archaeological deposits are found at the site, a programme of rescue excavation may then be instigated after negotiations between the developers and appropriate archaeological agencies. A specified time may then be allocated to complete these excavations before development continues. In addition to academic and social value, construction companies or their clients are also benefited through good public relations, and may even be able (or persuaded) to preserve archaeological remains in the subterranean areas of their buildings.

EXPLORATORY EXCAVATION: CORING, TEST PITTING, TRENCHING AND FIELDWALKING

Many of the sampling methods used to evaluate an existing site can also be employed to find new sites (see above), including satellite imagery, aerial photography (Cox 1992; Parcak 2009; Riley 1987), documentary evidence, local knowledge, previous excavations (Roskams 2001) and ground-based remote sensing using magnetometry, resistivity or ground penetrating radar (English Heritage 1985; Gaffney *et al.* 1991 & 1998). Two of the most important methods of locating new sites are fieldwalking and aerial photography (Corbishley 2004; Léva 1990). Fieldwalking involves the collecting of artefacts and is therefore a destructive technique as it removes part of the archaeological remains (Dunnel & Simek 1995; Shott 1995). The selective collection of artefacts will bias both the collected and remaining artefact assemblage, and should therefore always be coupled with a carefully selected sampling strategy. Coring can also be used to locate new sites in the landscape, or to provide more detailed stratigraphic evidence about sites that have already been pinpointed.

Exploratory Excavation and Non-destructive Sampling Strategies

Excavation projects can only hope to be successful once the archaeologist knows what deposits are likely to be encountered on-site, using a variety of non-destructive and minimal intervention techniques (Roskams 2001: 62). This section deals with methods of exploratory excavation, and its interplay with non-destructive site sampling strategies. The two types of site sampling (non-destructive and destructive) are complementary, shallow test pits being used to check the results of the geophysical survey. However, key-hole or 'telephone booth' archaeology, where a narrow deep pit is dug, is of limited archaeological value (Flannery 1976: 3), and is particularly hard to use on stratigraphically complex sites (Drewett 1999: 93; Shott 1987). However, the use of at least one deep *sondage* (control pit) can be of great value to the archaeologist in providing a preview of what they are likely to encounter (depth of stratification, information on the sedimentary, geological, chemical and environmental composition), especially on *tell* sites (Miller-Rosen 1986: 19). Coring can also be used to this end, as geoarchaeological studies of drill cores can reveal site formation processes, occupational fluctuations, landscape changes and climatic anomalies (Miller-Rosen 1986: 19).

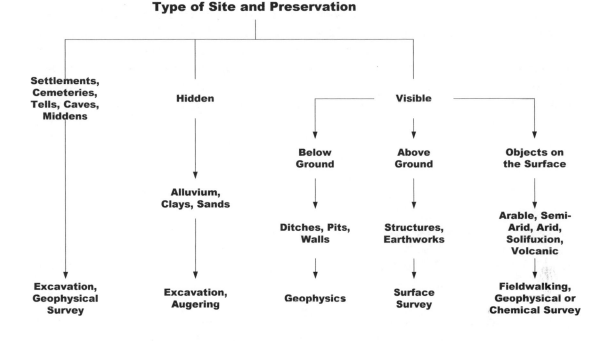

Type of Site and Preservation

Settlements, Cemeteries, Tells, Caves, Middens → Excavation, Geophysical Survey

Hidden → Alluvium, Clays, Sands → Excavation, Augering

Visible

Below Ground → Ditches, Pits, Walls → Geophysics

Above Ground → Structures, Earthworks → Surface Survey

Objects on the Surface → Arable, Semi-Arid, Arid, Solifuxion, Volcanic → Fieldwalking, Geophysical or Chemical Survey

Figure 12: Initial archaeological investigative methods best suited to various types of sites and contexts (after Evans & O'Connor 1999: 113).

Exploratory or trial excavation is usually used to assess the potential of a site for further excavation, to ascertain the extent of the site or to answer specific questions about certain features. However, it should be noted that the exploratory trench is not an end unto itself (as it might be in rescue operations), but is purely a means to enable the archaeologist to make informed decisions regarding the future investigations of the site (Joukowsky 1980: 146). Systematic sampling strategies may be employed to ascertain the horizontal spread of the site, and will usually be carried out in a grid system. Random sampling can result in clustering of test holes. Systematic sampling is a better method, as long as the test holes are always placed at the same point in each square. Another method is stratified systematic unaligned sampling, which involves placing the test hole at different locations within each grid square (Drewett 1999: 44). Another method of sampling is to study the landscape of the site and combine this with knowledge of cultural behaviour to guide the sampling pattern. However, this technique carries a certain risk of cultural bias.

Fieldwalking

Fieldwalking involves walking over areas of land, usually ploughed fields, observing minor fluctuations in the form or character of the ground surface, searching for architectural features and collecting artefacts. If features are found or artefacts collected, the grid square is registered accordingly on special recording forms. The area to be investigated is 'walked' in lines (transects) or as a grid. In the transect method each walker can be placed at 5.0, 10.0 or 20.0 metre intervals. The walkers then walk in a line noting features and collecting any artefacts that they see. If team members are placed at 10.0 m intervals, it will take about 60 person-hours to cover 1.0 square kilometre. In the grid system, the grid units can be 5.0, 10.0 or 20.0 m square and the collection time in each grid unit can be stipulated (i.e. 10 minutes per grid unit.) The artefacts collected from each unit are placed in pre-labelled finds bags. To increase the efficiency of fieldwalking various kinds of sampling strategies may be employed, such as the vacuum method, where a 5 m diameter circle is placed within the 10.0 m square. Within the 5.0 m circle all artefacts found are recovered whereas in the areas outside the circle only diagnostic artefacts are retrieved. Again, a time limit can be imposed; a suggested interval is 5 minutes for collection within the circle and 10 minutes outside the circle. If large areas are to be covered the quadrates or grid squares may be 1.0 or 1.5 square kilometres in size. Various random and stratified sampling strategies may then be employed to cover whole regions (see Orton 1999: 67-111). The collection of artefacts, identification of archaeological features and building debris will suggest foci of human activity, as well as the dates at which it took place. Once identified, the amount and type of artefacts from each period should be plotted on a distribution map of the survey area, thus showing patterns and concentrations. Phase maps or a series of overlays can be used to display the data for each period or type of artefact. GIS is ideal for analysing this kind of spatial data, particularly if the grids or transects are tied into the world UTM or national grids.

However, there are certain limitations in using fieldwalking to evaluate complex sites such as *tells*, particularly when surveying for the earlier phases. Studies have shown that surface collections of potsherds on mound sites are significantly biased in favour of the later periods, by as much as 10 to 1 (Miller-Rosen 1986), due to stratigraphic replacement and the erosion of earlier materials. This bias in favour of the later periods is also true of off-mound potsherd distribution. This can be slightly mitigated by scraping the surface by 50 mm before collecting potsherds. However, very early (i.e. Neolithic and Bronze Age) sherds may only appear on the surface of certain sites if the level of these occupations is less than 5.0 m from the surface (Miller-Rosen 1986; Boismier 1997). Equally, a lack of obvious concentrations does not necessarily mean lack of occupation, as agricultural exploitation (see Dunnel & Simek 1995 for the effects of the ploughzone) or geological weathering of the land may affect the results in various ways (Orton 1999: 119). It is therefore essential that fieldwalking be complemented by exploratory excavation techniques, otherwise the site and its stratigraphic sequence cannot be assessed for its full archaeological potential.

Coring and Augering

Coring, which covers all types of subsurface examination using mechanical devices (hand auger, power auger, cable percussion drill-coring rig) drilled into the strata from above is one of the most useful and least invasive methods for assessing the makeup of deep stratified sites. The corer extracts a core of sediment from the site, ideally from the surface down to bedrock (Canti & Meddens 1998). This is then examined to ascertain stratigraphic, cultural, sedimentary, chemical and environmental composition.

A borehole survey can map stratigraphic sequences over a large area, whereas (single) spot coring is useful in collecting palaeoenvironmental samples. Borehole surveys do not replace trench evaluation, but should be seen as a first phase in establishing the sedimentary sequence and help guide trench locations. One instance where borehole surveys may be used in isolation is when the deposits are extremely deep, or the water table is very high (English Heritage 2004: 15).

If using a grid system, the cores are usually taken at the grid intersections in a systematic sampling strategy (Drewett 1999: 93) although other sampling strategies are also used (Bailey & Thomas 1987). This method can establish both the horizontal and vertical extent of the site, although vertical distortion (usually compression) of sediments may preclude exact levelling. The spacing of the boreholes is critical in developing an accurate understanding of the stratification processes, and should be determined by the nature of the entity being examined. If an intra-site survey is being conducted the boreholes should be close together, no farther apart than the entity's minimum dimensions. However, when conducting landscape surveys in order to examine changes in stratification, the first boreholes can be placed far apart (predicting the intervening strata), then testing the hypothesis with further boreholes between the preliminary outliers (English Heritage 2004: 16). Coring surveys should be recorded on the **Drill Core Recording Form - Sheet 48**.

Drill Type	Advantages	Disadvantages
Drill Coring Rig	• Depth penetration • Sleeved holes • Intact sample recovery	• Relatively expensive • A loss of 50-150 mm sediment between samples • Depth measurements can be imprecise
Power Auger	• Portable • Continual sampling ability • Relatively cheap	• Unsleeved holes • Relatively unwieldy
Hand Auger	• Portable • Quick • Cheap	• Relatively shallow penetration • Difficult to collect intact samples • Attrition rate on equipment

Table 2: Advantages and disadvantages of the various coring methods (after English Heritage 2004: 16).

The hand auger, being manually operated, is not to be used for taking cores at more than 6.0 m unless the sediments are extremely soft. The hand auger is pushed into the ground (use a gouge attachment or screw head for dense sediments) then pulled up and the sediment block logged. Metre long extension rods are added to permit deeper sampling, although the amount of sediment collected in the head is still only about 0.20 m at a time. Power augers use an engine to drive various metal probes and sampling devices into the ground (Canti & Meddens 1998) and can obtain a continuous core of sediment. However, although more substantial than hand augers, it is not advisable to use these devices on deposits more than 10.0 m deep.

Cable percussion drill coring rigs are used by commercial engineers to locate and characterise deposits, and must be operated by professional drillers. These are the largest and most powerful coring machines, capable of depths of over 50.0 m. For archaeological purposes a team of professional drillers can be employed to conduct a survey, or access may be granted to examine cores already extracted for geotechnical purposes. If professional drillers are employed it is important to have a geoarchaeologist observing the procedure, logging borehole location, the depths of the deposits and labelling the cores with sample number, depth and sample orientation. Drilling rigs usually produce metre-long plastic sleeved samples ('U4/100 samples') with melted wax poured into each end to contain the moisture. A disadvantage of these commercial rigs is that they use a cutting shoe to collect samples, thereby leading to a loss of 50-150 mm of sediment between cores. The sediment from the cutting shoe can be cut out and gathered in plastic bags, but this hinders the collection of the full stratigraphic sequence (English Heritage 2004: 16).

Shovel Tests and Test Pits

The horizontal spread of a site can be assessed using a shovel test survey. This involves shovel-wide holes being dug at the intersections of a grid down to the top of the *in situ* archaeological remains. These are then recorded and plotted on the map of the site (see Kintigh 1988). This type of site sampling is only really useful on shallow sites, and even then should be used in moderation for the resulting series of holes may obliterate important relationships between uncovered features. If used carefully, this kind of sampling can produce very good results and at a very cost-effective rate (McManamon 1984).

While coring and shovel tests have their uses, more destructive sampling procedures such as test pits (also called quadrates or *sondages*) and evaluation trenches are normally required to finalise a full excavation strategy (Roskams 2001: 58). Test pits usually measure 1.0 x 1.0 m or 1.0 x 2.0 m, but for safety reasons width should be directly proportional to depth; therefore, if the test pit is 3.0 metres deep, then it should be 3.0 m square (Joukowsky 1980: 146). These are designed to give a clearer picture of the stratigraphic sequence, and should be excavated respecting the stratigraphic layers; the deposits and objects from each stratum should be treated and recorded separately, for otherwise you may seriously damage relationships between features. Different strategies should be used according to your research plan. If you aim to ascertain the horizontal extent of the site, then they should only be dug to the top of the *in situ* archaeological remains (following the grid system so that they can easily be plotted on the site plan and enlarged into a proper excavation unit if appropriate). However, if you aim to understand the vertical stratigraphic sequence of the site, then only one or two strategically placed *sondages* should be sunk in order to limit the amount of damage caused to the site. If test pits are being dug to understand the natural stratification of the landscape then they should be placed outside the area where archaeological remains are likely to be found.

Long narrow trenches or transects can also be used to ascertain the extent of archaeological remains, and to determine relationships between linear features such as ditches, roads, earthworks and banks. By placing a transect across and at a right-angle to the feature, information can be gained about the shape and size of the cut, the sequence of the fills and any recutting sequences. However, transects only shows the sequence of events of the feature in that particular area, the sequence may differ markedly in others. Trenches can also be used to obtain information about defensive works such as moats and ramparts, roads, earthworks and banks. However, if deep transects are dug without prior knowledge of what is likely to emerge (i.e. aerial photography or geophysical survey has not been carried out), they can cause great damage to the site. Deep transects are best used only when adequate data about what lies below the surface has already been gathered (Sundstrom 1993). However, shallow transects can help elucidate the extent of the site, being used like a series of shovel test pits. To elucidate the nature of certain areas of the site, you should machine-excavate transects or strips between 1.0 and 2.0 metres wide and an equal distance apart, in order to expose the archaeological deposits before they are excavated by hand.

Whatever form of exploratory excavation is used, it must be remembered that archaeological sites are full of inconsistencies and even sites that might be expected to be formulaic may contain unanticipated or unique features. The stratigraphic layers of a site can be truncated or appear only in patches, and even the best systematic or random sampling can totally miss major archaeological features. Features in sites identified by artefact scatter that are covered by windblown sand are unlikely to be discovered by test pitting, and will probably require the use of augers (Orton 2000: 139-140). The choice of test pits or trenches can be dictated by the period and type of remains likely to be encountered. Test pits are more appropriate for periods that generate scatters of finds, such as Epi-Palaeolithic sites, whereas trenches are more appropriate for periods that generate large and particularly linear features (Orton 2000: 120). As any type of sampling strategy can only ever cover a small percentage of the site, never assume your test pits to be representative of the entire site as inaccurate interpretations are otherwise likely to ensue. Adaptive sampling, where the test pit or trench in the selected sample unit is expanded to the neighbouring units to uncover any contexts of features discovered has much to offering in making sampling strategies more effective.

SYSTEMS OF EXCAVATION

The site grid can be established either before or after the site has been evaluated, but is essential before full excavation. However, if you aim to use the sampling techniques and strategies outlined above, it is essential to establish the site grid and datum first. While many excavation systems have been developed over the years (see Barker 1983), only the two most important are summarised here. These are the Wheeler-Kenyon box-grid system, and the Hatt-Giffen area plan (open-area) excavation. Since their introduction in the early to mid 20th century, these two systems have been extensively modified, redefined and renamed. In the US, for example, the box-grid method equates to the unit-level method, a method Joukowsky (1980: 139) recommends as though it were the only legitimate option, whereas, the US equivalent of open-area excavation is stripping (Hester *et al.* 1997: 85-7). Both types of excavation have their faults and advantages, and their un/suitability is determined primarily by the nature of the site in question.

The box-grid system uses excavation units of 5.0 x 5.0 metres in a trench formation that retains walls (or baulks) between the units of the grid. While all excavation units will have **primary baulks** (the four sides of the trench), the box-grid method also has **secondary baulks** - sediment walls usually a metre thick - between the excavation units. Recording of vertical stratigraphic sequence is carried out by examining the section drawings of the vertical profiles and then correlating them across the site. The bias is naturally towards the section faces, which take precedent over the recording of information on the horizontal plane. Excavation can either proceed by removing individual layers, each of which receives a context number or in spits. Once the section drawing has been completed and the general layout of the site ascertained, the secondary baulks **must** be taken down to reveal additional features and to define stratigraphic links between physically dislocated features exposed in the first excavation phase. The process is then repeated, building up new baulks and the trench eventually turns into a large open-area. The main drawbacks of this system are that it is relatively easy for the excavation of various strata to get out of phase or to be mis-matched, increasing the potential for misattribution of objects collected from them (Lapp 1975: 27-28), and that the baulks must be read and removed on a regular basis, or else they may become hard to read as well as very unstable and dangerous. This has the effect of reducing the accuracy of section drawings, and may obscure context relationships (Drewett 1999: 94). If this system is not used on a grand-scale, as done by Wheeler, and only a few small box-grids are used to sample a site, the horizontal extent is rarely understood, and generalised statements arise about the whole site on too small a sample (Barker 1983: 15).

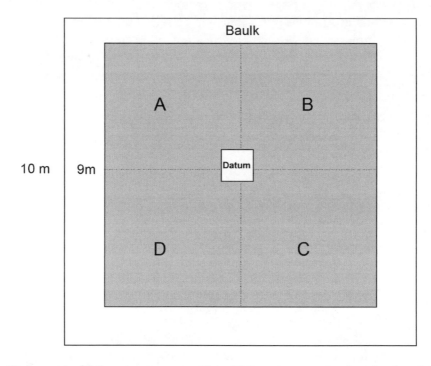

Figure 13: Layout of 9.0 metre square within 10.0 metre square, showing local datum in the centre.

In an adaptation of the box-grid system, a central or local datum is added to each 10.0 x 10.0 metre box-grid excavation unit. The local datum consists of a 1.0 m square block of sediment laid out in the centre of the excavation unit, which is left standing as the surrounding sedimentary matrix is taken down. This allows manual vertical measurements to be taken by means of a line-level, steel tape and a plumb bob. The square is subdivided into units or quads A, B, C and D, and a metre baulk is left between adjacent

10.0 metre squares (**Fig. 13**). These central data are then levelled into the site datum by automatic levelling equipment if available (see **Chapter 6**).

The part of the operational area being investigated must then be turned into open-area excavation once clear contexts become visible, only retaining secondary axis control baulks that show the typical stratigraphy of the area. If continuing excavation from a previous season, an old axis baulk may be re-utilised. Where possible, utilise a primary operational area baulk as this allows one to anticipate the stratigraphic layers likely to be encountered in the excavation units. Secondary non-control baulks should never be allowed to build up. The sections should be read and drawn at every 0.20 m level, thus building up a cumulative section drawing. Unless a special feature is present in the baulk, they should be removed before they reach a metre in height.

The main problem with this system of excavation is that the central datum cannot be removed until after the excavation is finished in that area, thus potentially blurring relational associations of contexts. This system is therefore best suited to shallow open-sites, as manual measurements are only effective to depths of about 1.70 metres. Although the datum can be reduced, shoring will be required if the squares go deeper than 2.0 metres. This system is therefore of limited use on deep stratified urban and *tell* sites. Note, however, that if open-area excavation is not practiced once discrete contexts have been identified the problems of the standard box-grid method will recur.

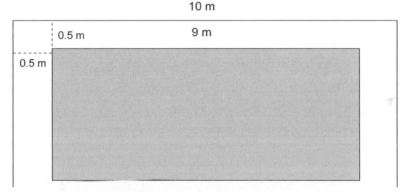

Figure 14: How to create a 9.0 metre square within the 10.0 metre square, therefore creating a metre-wide baulk between two adjacent squares.

The area plan system, developed in the 1920s and 30s was originally used on sites of limited depth lying on flat alluvial land in southern Scandinavia, northern Germany, the Netherlands and on the Giza Plateau in Egypt (Hatt 1957; Reisner 1942; Steensberg 1974), and focuses upon the stratum plan while recording archaeological features in vertical view. The aims of this technique are to examine activity areas and the manner in which humans used tracts of space.

Each excavation area was given a number, after the removal of the overburden, revealing various features for individual study, artefacts were recorded by the layer in which they were found. Each layer was removed after it had been recorded and individual features excavated (Lapp 1975: 27). This system was developed into true open-area excavation by exponents such as Barker (1983: 68-115), and has been extended to sites with deep stratigraphy using single context recording of the extent, contours, depth and consistency of each context before it is removed. It is now generally agreed to be the best system for excavating sites as diverse as settlements and cemeteries (Drewett 1999: 96-7).

The size and shape of the area to be excavated is dictated by the size and shape of the archaeological site, and is defined by a grid with the edges kept straight and vertical. The whole area is taken down by first removing the overburden (stripping), usually by mechanical means, and then excavating the matrix to reveal the various contexts beneath (see **Fig. 15**). Vertical sections or baulks are kept to read the vertical stratigraphic sequence, and trenches are only cut so particularly complex stratigraphic relationships can be more easily understood (such as those of intercutting ditches). In practice, open-area excavation involves a group of excavators hoeing or trowelling back from one side of the trench to the other, recording context relationships with grid units and keeping at the same vertical level of excavation. Some contexts may expand outside the excavation unit, and it is the job of the area supervisor to decide whether the unopened area should be excavated. Once a new context or feature has been observed, it is usually best to expand the excavation area to establish its extent.

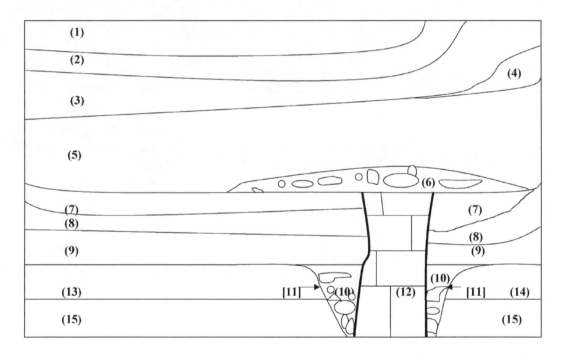

Figure 15: A section showing the order in which the contexts should be excavated using standard rules of stratification.

The three-dimensional recording of the stratigraphic sequence is of the utmost importance if the site is to be accurately reconstructed. For this reason it is important to keep a running matrix of the excavated contexts, a process that has been facilitated by the introduction of on-site computer systems and recording system databases. However, this method is more demanding on the excavators for they not only have to dig, but also record meticulously, be aware of numerous stratigraphic relationships and be highly critical and intuitive (Renfrew & Bahn 1991: 92-93). However, this disadvantage is counterbalanced by the direct engagement of the excavator with the archaeology and the prompt recording and interpretation of data as it becomes available. It is not practical to open up the whole of a very large site at once, as the team would have to be immense. It is therefore far better to open controllable and workable open-area trenches that can be 'fully' excavated in the time allotted, for if a site is totally stripped of its overburden but the area is not fully excavated, it is then far more prone to environmental degradation and looting. Therefore, the size of area opened must be dictated by the size of the team, the complexity of the archaeology and the duration of the excavation season. On large sites with distinct regions more than one part may need to be investigated concurrently, such as the settlement and cemetery, therefore these are termed operational areas (active excavation areas). The placement of the operational areas and trenches within will be determined by the research questions, the results of the remote sensing techniques and the contents of the exploratory excavation units.

METHODS OF EXCAVATION

The objective of excavation is to recognise the individual actions – construction, occupation, and destruction – that go to form the site (Roskams 2001: 213). This is done by recognising differences in the physical nature of the strata or contexts. Once the standard early stages of the excavation have been carried out (removal of overburden, selection of archaeological techniques), the team should start to remove each natural or cultural context (or layer) separately; each of these contexts should be recorded on the **Context Recording Form: Sheet 1**. This process is usually carried out in the reverse order of construction, deposition or cutting, with the most recent material being removed first, gradually revealing each earlier stage in the history of the site (Drewett 1999: 107; Joukowsky 1980: 159; Wass 1992: 111). In addition to uncovering artefacts and floral/faunal remains, it is important to accurately define contexts, and to recognise how groups of contexts, in turn, constitute features. The system is by necessity highly flexible, as a context may take the form of a wall or just a difference in the colour, consistency, texture and size of the sediments (Drewett 1999: 107; Lapp 1975: 30). Identifying slight changes in texture, consistency, etc are not skills that can be easily learnt from books, for it takes experience to distinguish the outline of a grave cut from the surrounding matrix, or the cut of a foundation trench through earlier levels of occupation (Drewett 1999: 107; Lapp 1975: 30). If the light is too strong, it is better to wait until the sun is at a more oblique angle so that the limits of the context can be more easily distinguished. One of the most difficult features to distinguish on a settlement or *tell* site is a mud-brick wall from the mud-brick wash up against it; often the only way to tell them apart is the difference in compaction (Lapp 1975: 30). Familiarity with the different types of sedimentary matrices is beneficial. In order to enhance the difference between contexts, wear polarised sunglasses or spray the area with water. First thing in the morning or after a light rain is a good time to identify various contexts, as the differential drying of various materials and sediments helps to bring out walls or graves from the surrounding matrix (Petrie 1904). More complex methods of identifying different contexts include special photographic techniques and chemical treatments (Roskams 2001: 111). Once a context has been identified and defined, decisions have to be made as to how to excavate it. This will depend on the level of recovery required and the nature of the context (see below). On sites with complex stratification, it may be useful to flag each context with a context number.

Certain deposits are more archaeologically important than others, such as primary and secondary fills of a pit. Deposits or features that are deemed to be of importance are

53

excavated with great care to stratigraphic distinctions, whereas less evidently fruitful strata are demoted noting general tendencies for change within the deposit (Roskams 2001: 230). Before excavation of the archaeological deposits begin, it is important that the excavators be able to excavate reliably and to make stratigraphic distinctions. Excavators should only remove one deposit at a time, to ensure that the stratigraphic integrity of the site is respected. Or, as Roskams has succinctly put it:

"remove unit A until you get to anything that is not like unit A"

(Roskams 2001: 231).

Earlier contexts should never be excavated before later contexts; the only exceptions are motivated by safety reasons, or if the later context is to receive specialist treatment or be preserved *in situ* as part of a permanent display (Roskams 2001: 111). Excavating in arbitrary unit levels or lots is not recommended (Drewett 1999: 93), as they may cut several contexts at once, obscuring their relationships and missing much of the evidence. However, under certain circumstances digging in spits may be the only alternative, such as when the matrix is devoid of visible strata, or has only limited stratigraphic distinctions in the horizontal plane (Roskams 2001: 221; Sharer & Ashmore 1987: 262). While these strata have internally imperceptible interfaces and boundaries in the horizontal plan, they cannot be differentiated by eye alone. In these instances, rather than excavating the entire deposit in one block, arbitrary spits or lots of 5, 10 or 20 cm may be used to excavate the site (Sharer & Ashmore 1987: 262), and should be recorded on the **Lot Recording Form: Sheet 2**. To keep a tighter stratigraphic control it may be advisable to excavate in smaller excavation units (as digging in small units gives greater control of object provenience and stratigraphic relationships [Sharer & Ashmore 1987: 262]). The levels are taken down in 5 or 10 cm spits until a feature – such as a grave – is found. In this event, the feature would be excavated within its own outline and context numbers will be given to the contexts within that feature (i.e. the general context of an area may be 1021, the cut of a grave will then be 1022, and the grave fill 1023, etc). In cases where the sedimentary matrix seems devoid of visible strata in the horizontal plane, carry out exploratory excavation to assess vertical stratigraphic organisation.

When an evaluation indicates homogenous deposits are likely to be encountered and excavation in spits is undertaken and well defined stratigraphic contexts are meet, it would be irresponsible not to change to single-context excavation (Roskams 2001: 230). Therefore, it may be appropriate to combine arbitrary lots and single-context excavation (Hester *et al.* 1997: 92) as demonstrated in **Figure 16**. In this example context 1069 was excavated using the lot system because it is a very thick layer. The base of the last lot (lot 5) follows the natural form of the top of context 1070, and marks the boundary between the lot system and the excavation of contexts 1070 to 1076 (which uses the standard rules of stratification). If a context is broken up into arbitrary lots, use a single-context recording form and separate lot recording forms. Log the numbers of the lots on **Context Register: Sheet 15.**

Each level within a layer should be given its own unique number, and be recorded on the **Lot Recording Form: Sheet 2** (the context number should also be recorded on this form). The **Context Recording Form: Sheet 1** should only be used when discrete contexts become visible. The **Level Recording Form: Sheet 3** should be used to record the top of each new context or level. All artefacts found must be recorded on the appropriate forms.

If they are bulk finds (*ex situ* secondary discard) they must be recorded on the back of the **Context Form: Sheet 1**, or if of specific interest logged in the **Finds Register: Sheet 5**; if the finds are primary discard (*in situ,* such as found in a grave or hoard) they should be recorded on the **Special Finds Recording Form: Sheet 9** and logged in the **Finds Register: Sheet 5**. A sediment sample must be taken from each context excavated, and recorded on the **Sediment Sampling Form: Sheet 6**. Record the context and lot number on each bag containing finds from a sub-division of a context or lot, to permit patterning distribution of material to be detected (Roskams 2001: 214).

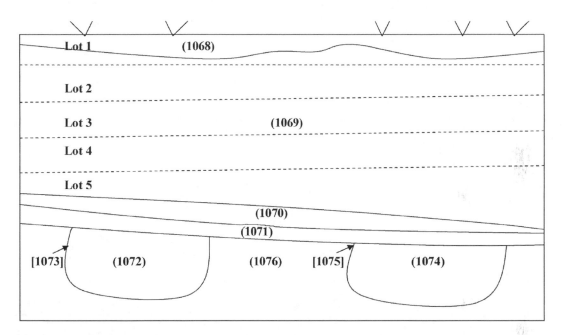

Figure 16: Profile of an excavation showing the use of arbitrary spits and stratigraphic units. The dotted lines indicate the lots and the solid lines outline the contexts.

The Excavation Procedure – Further Details

Irrespective of whether you are digging by lots or stratigraphic units, the recording process remains the same. Before excavation begins, the exploratory excavation records, site archive and database should be consulted. If it is the first season, results of research at similar sites should be consulted. The overburden should be removed mechanically, followed by manual removal of matrix over the excavation area until a change in sedimentary material is observed. Do not excavate into the new context until the remains of all previous contexts have been cleared away. The extent of this new context or layer should then be defined, all levels being recorded on the appropriate sheets. For each context or layer, the characteristics of the sedimentary matrix (texture, colour, consolidation and sedimentary structures) must be recorded on the context recording form. The site photographer should take a photograph of the context or feature, and a plan must be drawn (usually at a 1:20 scale), stratigraphic relationships calculated and all measurements (and coordinates) recorded on the recording forms. Finds bags and context baskets should be labelled for the context. On a settlement, each context is assigned a pottery basket (or bucket or tray) and a separate basket for other types of objects. These pottery baskets are labelled with the context number and then a sequential number for each successive basket relating to that context (see **page 74-8**).

Figure 17: The cyclical process of excavation for excavating a single-context/unit.

It is essential that all materials are cross-referenced, so that all the materials from individual contexts can be considered during their analysis. Consult the specialists and area supervisor to assess the need for special sampling (^{14}C, faunal, floral, etc) and the best excavation strategy, assessed on the merits of that context. The unit should then be excavated, with any special features and artefacts being recorded on the context recording form and mapped onto the single-context plan. Each deposit or cut is excavated separately once identified, and the description modified as necessary on the context recording sheets and plans. Only then can the surrounding matrix be taken down. All contexts and objects are given their own unique numbers, and described in the field record sheets. The reference numbers for samples, photos and drawings associated with a context must be recorded on the recording forms and registers. Context tags should be placed in the primary and secondary baulks to mark the position of contexts. After a context has been completely excavated, recheck that all the finds and samples are labelled correctly then remove all finds bags and containers back to the field and research centre for processing, and prevent them being confused with the new context's material. The relationships of the various contexts should also be recorded on the recording forms and the multi-context plans. If multiple contexts are visible in the horizontal plane, they should be tagged with their context number. Each context must be fully recorded, the recording forms finalised, and plans and sections drawn before the next context is excavated. Before excavating the next context or layer, all baulks should be trimmed to stop later sediment and artefacts from falling into the new context (Joukowsky 1980: 177). The individual excavators' note book should be updated and the excavation process fully described. The process is then repeated from the first step again for the new context (see **Fig. 17**). The information generated by the specialists and supervisor will then be entered into the site archive and database.

Further Considerations

It is essential that close contact be maintained between the specialists, excavators and supervisors, as this facilitates the transfer of ideas and information. The specialists should be consulted on excavation strategies and regularly visit the trenches to help contextualise their data (Hodder 1999: 96). If the excavators are made aware of what certain categories of finds and features look like, this will allow better interpretation of what they are seeing and excavating; teaching excavators to identify ceramics from different periods so they can detect context interfaces is a good example of specialist/excavator cooperation. On a highly stratified *tell* site with thousands of contexts, it is all the more important that specialist evidence be available immediately so as to enable the development of local excavation strategies. The specialists also benefit from excavator consultation as this gives them greater information about the exact context of the material they are analysing. This integrated and multidisciplinary approach is vital for a full understanding of artefacts, ecofacts and contexts.

PROCEDURES FOR RECOVERING THE EVIDENCE

When artefacts, ecofacts and features are revealed, work should be halted in that context until the situation has been re-evaluated, and tools and excavation method adjusted. The main tools used will be a trowel and a brush, although other, more delicate implements may also be required for specialist jobs (Joukowsky 1980: 161). A summary of major context types and the excavation methods best used for each is presented below (see **Tab. 3**).

The levels of recovery on an archaeological site vary with the different sampling strategies, methodologies and tools used. For example, hand retrieval can miss up to 85%

of certain finds categories (Roskams 2001: 221). The amount of evidence that can be processed and stored must also be considered. It is usual to uncover, record and analyse all the walls, floors or graves on an archaeological site, but it is not practical to collect and analyse all the sediment or pollen grains. Therefore, archaeology inevitably consists of formal and informal sampling strategies, ranging from coarse to fine, from mechanical to microscopic, from manual to chemical.

Type of Context	Retrieval Method
Floor surface, occupation levels	Take a total bulk sample and 3-D plot any *in situ* finds before hand retrieval.
Laid floor surfaces	Hand retrieval of tiles or tesserae. Use metal detectors *in situ*.
Walls, destruction layers	Hand retrieval. Metal detect foundation trenches for metal objects.
Roads, pavements	Hand retrieval. Metal detect *in situ* for dropped metal objects such as coins.
Industrial deposits	Bulk sample industrial residues, such as slag. Use metal detector *in situ*.
Coffins	Lift by hand, in consultation with a conservator.
Grave fills	Total bulk sample of fill and dry sieve; hand retrieval of grave goods after 3-D plotting.
Hearths	Bulk sample and dry sieve. Flotation may be appropriate.
Wells, drains and cesspits	Bulk sample, dry sieve and flotation.
Pit fills	Hand retrieval and bulk sample (if remains are plentiful); dry sieve.
Waterfront and foreshore deposits	Hand retrieval and bulk sample; metal-detect *in situ*.
Marsh deposits	Hand retrieval; possible wet sieving.
Middens	Hand retrieval and bulk sample.
Any layer or fill	Look for scatterings and concentrations of objects; hand retrieval.
Natural deposits	Look for any signs of cultural activity.

Table 3: Retrieval methods for different types of contexts and features (Westman 1994:102-3).

Machine Excavation

Earth-moving machinery (also called plant) is the coarsest level of recovery, but have earned their place on archaeological sites. The best types are those with back actors; it is important that they are used to pull the sand or soil off the site rather than pushing it off and have the vehicle drive over the freshly-revealed surface (top marques include JCB 3c's, Case 1835B Uni-loader, Hymac and Poclain, or tractors with a back-hoe or hydraulic arm and bucket). Front-end loaders can be used to scrape or blade the surface to reveal the archaeological deposits before manual excavation (Hester *et al.* 1997: 74-7). However, heavy machinery is better at uncovering than recovering, and should only be used to remove over-burden. Displaced potsherds and other artefacts found in a machined-out context are only useful in ascertaining that there is archaeological material of a certain type and date on the site; beyond this, the sample is of no archaeological use. The stripping of aeolian (wind blown) sand dunes is usually best done by machinery, as is the removal of concrete floors (on an urban site), or plough soil that has moved down a slope to cover a rural site (Drewett 1999: 98). In all cases, exploratory excavation should be carried out in order to determine the amount of overburden (also termed plus) overlying the archaeological layers.

Large Hand-Held Tools

Heavy hand-held tools such as pick-axes, mattocks, sledgehammers, forks, hoes (*fas* in Egypt), spades and shovels c an all be used for excavating make-up deposits, secondary fills, slumped deposits or any context where limited refinement is required. These tools should be used efficiently, expending the minimum effort for the maximum effect, making sure to bend the legs and thus avoid back strain. The tool should not be swung above head height. Let the weight of the tool do as much of the work as possible, as this reduces the likelihood of damaging objects and disturbing relationships between contexts. Certain heavy tools, such as hoes, can be used for chopping or scrapping, and if used gently can be quite a delicate tool. On most Egyptian and Western Asian sites, local workers are employed to do this heavy work, usually with the *fas* and the shovel. In all cases, the *fas* users should receive guidance as to where and what to dig, what to look for, and when to stop. Heavy tools should not be used to excavate an *in situ* floor or a grave, as their use will lead to a bias towards the recovery of large artefacts, the destruction of fragile ones, and toward the identification of strong, contrasting colours of sediment rather than subtle shades (Drewett 1999: 98). It is also harder to feel slight changes in the sedimentary matrix of the contexts.

Smaller Hand-Held Tools

Small hand-held hoes and picks are more controllable than larger tools, although they are not sufficiently robust to excavate indurated sediments. They are generally similar to the large tools described above; both tools have a flared, flattened end, while the picks have a spike as well. These tools can be used in a chopping or scraping motion, and are particularly useful on compacted sediments. If used carefully, they can be just as precise and delicate as a (pointing) trowel, which is the main tool of the archaeologist and is used for excavating deposits where high levels of control and definition are required. While trowel model is largely a matter of preference, a welded (rather than riveted) handle is required. The standard lengths are 4" and 6", and the two major manufacturers are WHS (UK) and Marshalltown [USA]. The wider and thinner Marshalltown is useful for cutting sections and excavating looser sediments (i.e. sands), whereas the more angular WHS is more suitable for firmer, harder sediments. Their mode of use also varies, the Marshalltown being used to 'cut' sediments, the WHS for scrapping. Further information about small tools and their use in the recovery of artefacts is provided below.

Trowelling and Recovery Techniques

The trowel is used both for defining a deposit and to remove it in order to expose underlying strata (Roskams 2001: 227). The trowel can be used in a hacking/digging motion (using the point), a scraping motion (using the length of the blade) or a cutting motion (blade parallel to sediment surface). Using the point of the trowel increases the rate of retrieval of artefacts and ecofacts, while scraping with the side of the trowel may damage delicate finds but gives more stratigraphic control (Roskams 2001: 229). The type of trowelling action is therefore chosen to match the types of sediment and deposit, with a scraping or cutting movement being used on shallow deposits of loose sediments. Scraping movements are done with the blade held at either a 45 ° or 30 ° angle to the surface. When trowelling deep deposits with compact sediments, the point may be pushed into the surface and the blade turned to loosen the material, although the base of the deposit should be cleaned away with the side of the trowel to allow more control at the point at which the underlying strata appears (Roskams 2001: 229). If differences have been observed in the deposit, a decision must be taken whether to trowel across or along the line of interface. When trowelling fine sediments (such as Nile mud or clay-rich, sticky deposits) it is usually best to trowel across the proposed line of intersection of two separate contexts. Although this smears the sediments slightly, different layers will often break away from each other to give a clear distinction (Roskams 2001: 227). This is particularly useful when trowelling merged mud contexts, although is also useful for mud contexts dug into a sandy matrix. Working along the line of sticky sediments will easily merge it with one below, thus suggesting a limit to the deposit that merely follows the direction of the trowelling. For sandier sediments or less cohesive deposits, trowelling down the line produces the best results (Roskams 2001: 227). Do not produce false edges, and always work from the known edges to the unknown ones in a methodical manner. Trowel towards yourself, then gradually move back.

The spoil generated by trowelling ('loose') should be broken up and pulled back into a pile, brushed into a dustpan and put into a bucket or wheelbarrow. When the loose has been cleared up and any artefacts and ecofacts collected, a critical re-evaluation of the surface **must** be made. Ensure this is done just after it has been freshly trowelled and the loose cleared away, as dry sediments show much less contrast in colour, and establish the relationships between the freshly-removed deposit and the underlying strata. This is the reason for trowelling back the individual deposits, thus keeping the freshly trowelled surface clean of knee- or footprints. The trowelling surface should be kept as even as possible, while following the natural contours of the context as they become apparent. If objects occur in the freshly trowelled surface, they must be left *in situ* until the next layer is trowelled off and their correct context can be identified. Holes must **never** be dug and partially concealed objects must **never** be pulled out, as their provenience and relationship with other associated artefacts may be lost.

To help keep confusion to a minimum, trowelling should all be in the same direction; if trowelling a hill, it is always best to trowel downhill (Barker 1982: 75-77). Where rows of excavators are trowelling across a large context or excavation unit, it is important that they all trowel in the same direction so that the contexts can be clearly seen and their relationships understood. When trowelling compacted sediments, the weight of the body should be kept over the trowel to create the force necessary to remove the sediments effectively. The excavator is very close to the archaeological surface when trowelling, being either in the kneeling or crouching position (never sitting), thus ensuring that the rate of recovery is kept high (Drewett 1999; Roskams 2001). Whisk brooms and stiff brushes are good for cleaning areas of brickwork or (on certain types of contexts) increasing the contrast of colour discontinuities or defining interfaces between contexts.

Trowels can also be used for cleaning masonry and sections. This sweeping of surfaces (called *rabotage*) should be avoided on sandy contexts as it tends to blur the interfaces.

Fine Tools and Cleaning

For finer work, smaller tools such as bamboo skewers may be used, aided by a 1-2" fine brush. Dental tools may also be used for excavating compacted sediments, and can be used for excavating skeletal material and fragile artefacts. Slightly more unorthodox tools can also be used, such as porcupine quills (especially good for excavating fragile items such as bones). The edges of the exposed object are followed by removing the sedimentary matrix, making sure that the outer layer of the object is not damaged. Once the sediment is loosened, soft brushes are used to remove the sediment surrounding the object; the sedimentary matrix of the surrounding context must be taken down at the same rate, thus gradually revealing the object. An even level must be maintained, excavating methodically until the entire object has been exposed. Do not dig holes around the object, nor remove the contents of vessels. In practice, this means that the matrix directly surrounding the fragile object is removed by bamboo skewers and soft brushes, whereas the rest of the context can be removed by trowel. Brushes should be used sparingly, as they can blur the outlines of the contexts, especially those with a high sand content. Use a trowel or similar to prepare an area for photography, to ensure a smooth, un-blurred surface.

While constituting a serious threat to archaeological sites in the hands of unprincipled thieves, metal detectors can be of considerable value to a comprehensive recovery plan. Responsible enthusiasts from the detectors clubs are often enlisted to assist in this way. Detecting – especially if using staff not directly attached to the excavation – should be done under strict supervision of the director or supervisor. If metal artefacts are likely to be found on your site, careful use of a metal detector can alert the excavator of the presence of metal in their context. Do not dig holes retrieve the artefact; mark the approximate position so that special care can be taken when excavating that area. The contents of the context should also be screened.

Sieving

Sieving or screening will improve levels of artefact/ecofact recovery. The sieve mesh is usually 10 mm or 5 mm, which will be sufficient to catch most coins, potsherds, beads, bones, lithics and other artefact fragments. However, it is important to realise that there are biases inherent in sieving (Shaffer 1992). Smaller meshes will increase recovery level, but will slow down the screening rate. A 10 mm screen can be set over a 5 mm one in order to separate out larger objects (Hester *et al.* 1997: 93-7). Although an object's exact provenience cannot be ascertained this way, limiting the amount of spoil to be sieved at a time to that from one context or lot will permit their approximate position to be assigned. These objects must then be bagged by their separate context or lot.

If using the lot method of excavation, sieving will usually be necessary (Joukowsky 1980; Roskams 2001; Sharer & Ashmore 1987). The percentage of each lot sieved will depend upon the overall research design, quality of preservation, formation processes and whether the lot is a primary or secondary context. Some archaeologists propose that the whole matrix of each lot be sieved (Joukowsky 1980), but this is very time consuming and is unnecessary for most lots. Exceptions to this rule include very important or ancient sites, such as a Palaeolithic campsite where the rarity and value of any artefact recovered justifies the time and expense involved. It should be noted however, that the sieving of complete lots from less valuable sites will not improve knowledge of the sites temporo-spatial spread, and will only provide background information.

Screening in the field is usually done in large rectangular sieves (usually 1 m by 0.6 m) with handles at each end, to be agitated by two people. Sometimes these are hung like a swing or a hammock, so that the job is made easier and can be done by one person. The contents of a sieve should be turned out onto a sorting table covered in light coloured (not white) plywood faced with Formica. The table should have retaining walls on three sides and a hinged board on the other, to prevent spillage. Inspection of the sediment should proceed by pushing the majority of the sediment into a pile, and then selecting a small amount of sediment for inspection. This makes it easy to see at a glance if there is anything of interest to collect. Once finds have been removed, the sediment is brushed away and another section selected from the pile on the table. Seven inch gauging trowels may be useful for this work, and stiff brushes can be used for sweeping away the inspected sediment. The use of a sorting table helps reduce eye strain and minimises damage to delicate objects that may be aversely affected by the wire mesh of a sieve (Joukowsky 1980: 165-70).

As a rule, all the sediment from features (graves, pits, *in-situ* floors) should be screened, as well as any additional contexts deemed to be important. If in doubt, screen. The only time at which all the sediment from the site should be sieved is a site where very high recovery levels are required, such as a Palaeolithic camp site. If large amounts of sediment are to be screened, it is advisable to use a dump sifter – a large screen, up to 3 metres long and 1 metre wide. Three sides are surrounded by sideboards, and the bottom covered in 5 mm mesh hot dipped in zinc to stop the wires from coming loose. The sifter is set at an incline of 45° with the bottom edge resting on a sorting table, and is agitated by means of a rope. Once the sediment is on the sorting table, the sideboard is released and the work of sorting the matrix can begin (Joukowsky 1980: 165-70). Smaller round sieves may be used in the lab to recover objects from sampled contexts lifted *en bloc.*

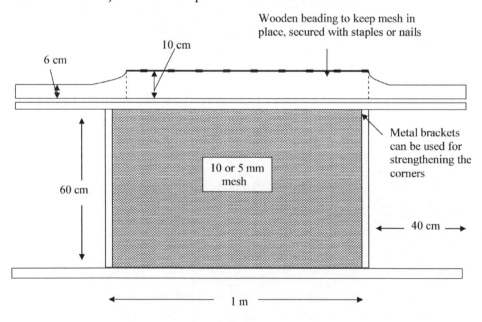

Figure 18: Plan of a hand sieve (Joukowsky 1980: 166).

Flotation

Wet sieving with fine mesh sieves is essential to recover plant remains, tiny shells and other minute objects. Bucket floatation is the simplest method, and involves a sieve (mesh <1 mm) being placed in a bucket of water until the water level reaches just below the top of the sieve's rim, and then agitated gently. Light objects such as carbonised seeds, charcoal and other organic matter will float to the surface and can be skimmed off, whereas heavier objects such as pottery fragments, bones or lithics will be caught in the mesh.

A more elaborate wet sieving method involves the use of a flotation unit (**Fig. 19**). This consists of a tank of water (the tank can be made out of an old oil drum, 90 cm high) with a 1 mm mesh for holding the sediment at the top of the tank. These flotation tanks can usually be made up by a local blacksmith or plumber (see **Fig. 20**). The tank is filled with running water, either mains water or recycled with a pump, which then bubbles up through the mesh and sediment, making the organic material floats to the surface. This light fraction (flot) flows over the lip of the tank, over the weir and is caught in a nest of 30 cm sieves (a 4 mm or 3.5 mm and a 1 mm) placed below the lip (Drewett 1999: 102). The flot (which must be numbered) is then collected and hung out to dry in a coffee filter or fine netting before being sorted. Ensure that the flot number is kept with it all times. Alternatively, a netting bag can be made with a fine mesh sieve at the bottom, and used instead of the nest of sieves; this can then be hung out to dry without transferring the contents to another container. Gumerman & Umemoto (1987) have suggested the addition of a siphon to help retrieve charcoal from the heavy fraction. Lack of wet-sieving equipment does not militate against taking samples, as these can be processed at a later date.

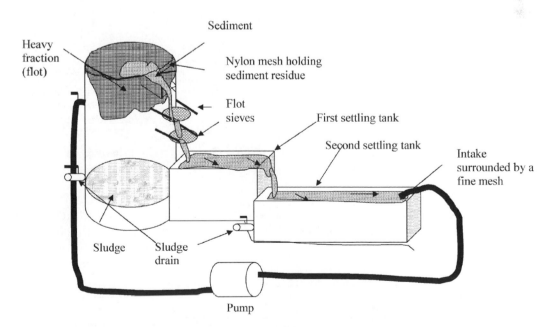

Figure 19: A recycling flotation tank unit (after Renfrew & Bahn 1991: 251).

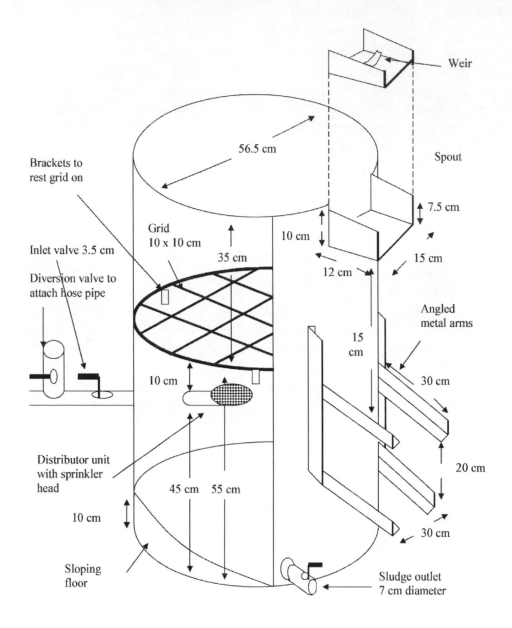

Figure 20: Isodiametric view of a flotation tank (adapted from original designs by Gordon Hillman and Mark Nesbitt).

Desiccated material is not always suitable for wet sieving as it may explode from expansion on contact with water, as such a small sample should be tried first. If the material is not suitable or there is a doubt it should be dry sieved and picked out with tweezers.

Microscopic, Analytical and Chemical Methods

Microscopy and chemical analysis are very useful in recovering traces of objects or identifying microstratigraphy. Environmental sampling can produce information on palaeo-environment, human economy and behaviour through the analysis of phytoliths, molluscs, pollen, fish and bird bones and diatoms (for further details see below). Sedimentological analyses, including such fields as micromorphology, mineralogy, granulometry, calcium carbonate and organic matter examination can all elucidate cultural and natural processes (see Huckleberry 2006: 338-361). A number of analytical methods are referred to in **Tab. 4**.

Analytical Method	Scale of Investigation	Sample Type	Archaeological Application
Particle Size Analysis	Site specific and regional survey	Bulk sample	• Identification of sediment source areas • An understanding of sedimentary and pedological processes
Loss on Ignition	Site-specific and occasionally regional survey	Bulk sample	• Identifying soil development sequences • Tracking fluctuations between sediment accretion and peat growth in sea-level studies
Magnetic Susceptibility	Site and structure scale	Bulk sample	• Geophysical prospecting • Identification of human activity in weakly defined sequences
pH	Site and structure scale; occasionally regional scale	Bulk sample	• Understanding sediment history • Taphonomy: artefact and ecofact preservation
Mineralogy	Site and regional scale	Bulk sample	• Identification of sediment origins • Biominerals that assist in identification of soil or sediment use and history
X-Radiography	Site scale	Intact block	• An understanding of depositional phases and environments
Micromorphology	Site, structure and feature scale	Intact block	• Aid to archaeological interpretation of features, structures and sites
Multi-Element Survey	Regional, site, structure and feature scale	Bulk sample	• Prospection and survey to identify and delimit sites • Determination of activity areas within settlements and sites • Interpretation of individual features or contexts
Phosphorus Survey	Regional, site, structure and feature scale	Bulk sample	• Prospection and survey to identify and delimit sites • Determination of activity areas within settlements and sites • Interpretation of individual features or contexts • Interpretation of past land-use practices

Table 4: Summary of analytical methods and their archaeological implications (English Heritage 2004: 23).

Micromorphology involves taking columns of sediment extracted from stratigraphic layers and impregnating it with resin. A slice is then cut from the block and ground to a uniform 30 μm (a procedure that can take several months in the laboratory). A petrological microscope with various controlled light sources is then used to examine elemental composition (English Heritage 2004: 20).

Other common methods of examining microstratigraphy and micromorphology (on a sediment core or monolith) in the field are X-radiography and magnetic susceptibility, which use electro-magnetic radiation wavelengths to detect changes in sediment stratification (Barham 1995; Matthews *et al.* 1996). Chemical analysis can help detect degraded artefacts or bones that may only exist as chemical traces in the sedimentary matrix. Multi-element geochemical analysis examines between 10 and 30 elements (including phosphorus, lead, zinc, copper, nickel, calcium, strontium, chromium, manganese, cobalt and cadmium) deposited by human activities such as agriculture, settlement and industry. Multi-element analysis surveys can aid in the identification and delineation of sites, and also the interpretation of features and structures. Granulometry involves the examination of sediment particle sizes. Dividing these into grain-size population grades through sieves and settling (or laser diffraction) can provide information on the origin of the sediment, mode of deposition, depositional environment, post-depositional processes and environment and aid assess the potential for studies in palaeomagnetism, microbotanical preservation and reworking of archaeological materials (Huckleberry 2006: 340-343).

Other analytical methods employed include mineralogy, particle size analysis, loss on ignition and pH (*potenz* [power] of hydrogen-ion) analysis (see **Tab. 4**). Mineralogy examines the mineral content of sediments (mainly quartz and clays, with lesser amounts of feldspars and calcium carbonate and other minerals), and involves carrying out counts of particles with a polarising microscope to show different trends in origin. This method is valuable for provenancing sediments, building materials, wind-blown material, biological processes or wastes (English Heritage 2004: 21). Particle size analysis is based upon an accurate account of all sizes categories, which are sorted using analytical sieves for the coarse grains (sands or larger) and sedimentation/diffraction systems to analyse silts and clays. This process is valuable for examining sediment source areas, and aspects of sedimentary or pedological processes. In many cases the finger test (see **Fig. 84**) is all that is required to assess the character of sediments. Loss on ignition is a laboratory process used to measure the organic matter content of soils and sediments, and is valuable for examining topsoil development sequences. The process works on the basis that the weight lost on heating of a sediment sample is closely correlated with the organic matter content. Measuring the pH of a sample indicates its acidity or alkalinity, helping to understand its depositional history and thus to explain aspects of taphonomy and preservation and can indicate different cultural activities, including farming (see **Tab. 9**). The pH scale goes from 0 (most acid) to 14 (most alkaline), with 7 being neutral. The human body has a pH value of 5.5. In general, well-drained siliceous deposits will have acidified over the millennia pH >7, whereas calcareous ones will remain alkaline, close to that of calcite or 8.0. Soils in humid environments tend to be more neutral to acidic pH values. However, a wide variety of possibilities exist between these two extremes. Factors such as waterlogging and redox characteristics produce conditions that differ between sites and even within the area of a single site. The pH is measured either using an electrometer and probe in a suspension of sediment (sample) in distilled water or by a colorimeter, strips of paper (litmus paper) impregnated with a solution of phenolphthalein or methyl orange (English Heritage 2004: 21-2).

Phosphorus Sampling

Organic matter (principally plant and animal remains) constantly recycle phosphorus into the sedimentary matrix in which they are buried (Herz & Garrison 1998:181). In addition to this background recycling, phosphorus can be introduced into settlement areas from animal and human excreta, garbage, food processing or storage, animal/human carcasses or organic building materials Therefore, a higher level of phosphorus (in addition to nitrogen and carbon) characterises areas of human occupation (Eidt 1984). Phosphorus becomes fixed upon deposition in most sediments, and is relatively stable and resistant to leaching. Phosphorus surveys can be used to identify features or activity areas on a site, and should be combined with other techniques, such as fieldwalking, borehole survey, geophysical or aerial reconnaissance.

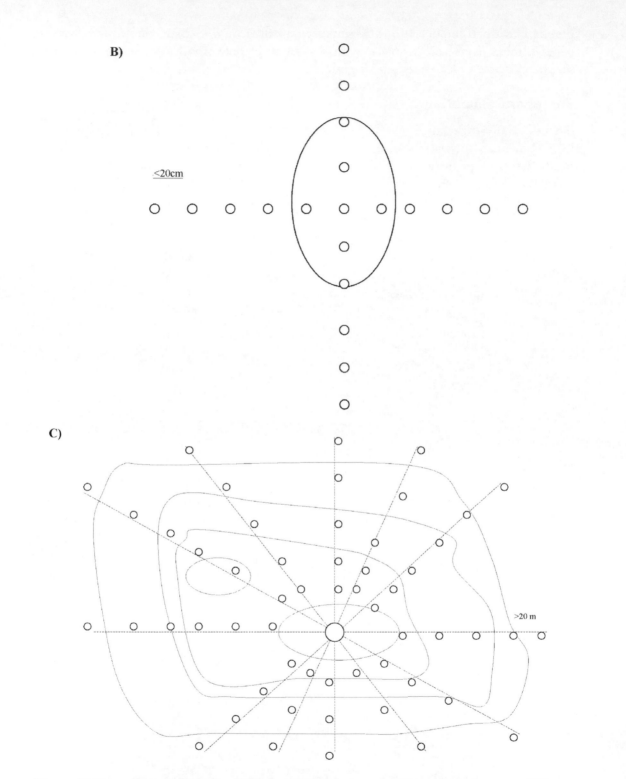

Figure 21: Sampling strategy for A) large rectangular graves; B) small oval graves; C) large feature radial survey.

Before sampling for phosphorus, you need to make a colorimeter of known percentages of phosphorus from the same sediment types that are likely to be encountered on-site. It is best to make a colorimeter with water colours on card, with their percentages written beneath them expressed as milligrams (mg) of Phosphate (P_2O_5) per 100 grams (g) of sediment, thereby producing a graded shade depth chart or colorimeter on paper or card. Before testing the site for phosphorus, control samples should be taken from the same type of sediments that are found on-site, to give you an undisturbed phosphorus baseline. An individual concentration (e.g. 3500 ppm) has no inherent interpretive value and can only be understood in relation to the surrounding concentrations. These reference samples will act as a standard for the naturally-occurring background variations. Do not sample near trees or in freshly manured fields, as this will give biased results. The retention capacity of sediments is determined by texture and pH, so deposits with comparable values will allow the most secure interpretations of enhanced levels created through human activity (English Heritage 2004: 17). Phosphorus levels tend to be higher near the surface and then decrease with depth; both the reference and study samples should therefore be taken at the same depth. This sampling regime can be very useful in determining whether a body was originally present in a seemingly empty grave. For this reason, control samples should be taken from inside and outside graves that hold human remains, and the strategy should be the same for the control samples as for the apparently empty graves (**Fig. 21**). This taking of control samples from inside and outside a targeted entity is essential when attempting to assess the function of other areas of human activity such as fields, enclosures, floors or fills.

Phosphorus surveys are usually conducted on a grid system (**Fig. 21B**) with the intervals being determined by the size of the area of interest (usually between 1 and 20 m for site surveys and 0.2 and 0.5 m within individual features). A radial survey - with transects radiating out from a focal point of known archaeological significance - can be very effective, particularly for large features.

A number of methods can be used to assess the concentration of phosphorus in the sediment samples, and the type of phosphorus (available, organic, inorganic or total phosphorus) detected. Most of the methods rely on the extraction of phosphorus using acids or alkalis, with or without the addition of a reagent. This is then added to develop a colour (usually blue), the intensity of which can be assessed visually (in the spot test) or measured against the colorimeter. To extract the total phosphate from the sediment a strong acid or alkaline should be used to make a soluble orthophosphate. A 100-g sample of sediment should be taken and boiled in hydrochloric acid (HCl), followed by adding 10 ml of Mo blue reagent to reduce the solution. The intensity of the colour is proportional to the amount of total phosphate present: the higher the amount of phosphate, the more intense the colour. This should then be compared to the colour standards (Herz & Garrison 1998: 187). This experiment must be done in the field laboratory using protective clothing and goggles. To extract the available phosphorus, the quickest and safest method is the spot test. Two solutions must be prepared: Solution A, which remains stable for a month, and Solution B, which must be prepared daily:

Solution A: Dissolve 5g ammonium molybdate in 100 ml distilled cold water then acidify by adding 20 ml of 5N hydrochloric acid

Solution B: Dissolve 1g ascorbic acid in 200 ml cold distilled water

Method	What it Measures	Advantages	Disadvantages
Spot Test	Proportion of available phosphorus	• Cheap, quick and easy to use • No sample preparation needed • Rapid availability of results means quick feedback to survey/excavation strategy • Easy to learn; can be taught in brief training session	• Qualitative data • Results can be difficult to interpret and can be misleading • Easy to create artefacts in data set if strict protocol is not followed • Only suitable for prospection and site delimitation
Available Phosphorus	Phosphorus available to plants (labile fraction)	• Quantitative data set • Simple analysis • Data can be formally analysed using statistical methods to identify areas with significant concentrations of sediment 'P'	• Amount can fluctuate over short periods of time • Slow feed-back of results as samples must be processed in the laboratory • Strict protocol must be followed as even slight variations in temperature can affect the amount of sediment 'P' extracted by reagents • The relationship between available phosphorus and phosphorus added through archaeological activity over time is poorly understood
Inorganic Phosphorus	Inorganic component of phosphorus	• Relatively quick and can be adapted for use in the field or laboratory • Mineral sample preparation (air-dry and screen) • Yields quantitative data	
Total Phosphorus	Organic plus inorganic components (nonlabile fraction)	• Quantitative data set • Data can be formally analysed using statistical methods to identify areas with significant concentrations of sediment 'P' • All fractions of phosphorus in the sediment sample are extracted and measured, therefore obviating the need to understand the relationship between available phosphorus and that incorporated through archaeological activity	• Relatively expensive, labour intensive and with slow feedback of results as samples must be processed in the laboratory regardless of protocol for conversion of organic to inorganic phosphorus and subsequent extraction methods • All phosphorus in the soil is extracted and measured, including fractions that are not archaeologically meaningful

Table 5: A comparison of different methods for detecting phosphorus in archaeological sediment (after English Heritage 2004: 19).

Value	Descriptor	Observations
0	Negative	No blue tint visible
1	Trace	Blue tint develops up to 2 mm from sample with discrete blue rays
2	Weak	Blue tint develops a circle around sample with individual blue rays bleeding together
3	Positive	Distinct blue band forms around sample with a diameter of 10 – 15 mm
4	Strong	Large blue spot of 20 mm or greater develops

Table 6: Relative grading for degree of colour development and interpretive meaning in a spot test (after English Heritage 2004: 28).

Once the solutions are prepared, place 5g of sediment onto ash-free filter paper and add two drops of Solution A with a pipette. Wait 30 seconds then add two drops of Solution B via another pipette. If phosphorus is present, a blue ring will have developed on the filter paper around the sediment sample after two minutes. The intensity of the colouration is representative of the amount of available phosphorus. The reaction can be stopped by immersing the filter paper in a solution of sodium citrate (a ration of 1:2 with water). The filter papers can be stored and labelled for archive records (English Heritage 2004: 28). For the full list of methods for analysing the various phosphorus fractions see Gurney (1985).

SAMPLING STRATEGIES (OBJECT BIOGRAPHIES AND RECOVERY)

As Orton (2000: 1) points out, almost all archaeology is sampling, as the material recovered on an archaeological site is not the total of what was lost or discarded in that location. A good example of this is the ubiquitous potsherd which, while found everywhere on the majority of archaeological sites, do not represent the true proportions of the pots from which they come (Orton 2000: 2). A valid sample is supposed to be representative of the whole; it is therefore essential that the correct sample collection strategy be chosen for the different types of features and strata. The preservation rate, transformation processes, excavation methods and research design will all affect the sampling strategy as will available time, money and resources (Roskams 2001: 219; Orton 2000: 2). The site sampling strategy should be developed in advance of excavation, and modified if the need arises (Orton 2000). Samples may be taken from a region, a site, an on-site feature and even from an assemblage or from an individual object (Orton 2000: 3). However, even after the site evaluation has been conducted, it is impossible to know all the localised preservation conditions that exist on a site. Therefore, the sampling strategy must be flexible enough to accommodate the unexpected, and to react if preliminary flotation and sieving produce unpredicted results from sampled contexts. What - and how much - to sample are important questions, as is the diversity of the sample. Samples that are too small or too big are useless, for small samples may not be representative of the whole, whereas too large a sample cannot be processed in the time allotted.

Archaeological sampling can be 1) random, 2) stratified, 3) systematic and 4) clustered. The former two types are usually best combined into random stratified sampling (see **Fig. 25**); systematic sampling consists of samples being taken at equal spacing, whereas cluster sampling consists of taking more than one sample from a randomised position in the context. Cochran (1977: 5-8) outlined an overall sampling process in eleven stages. Orton (2000: 28-9 & 159-169) modified these stages and added the initial 'assimilation of existing knowledge'. His stages are outlined below.

0.   **Assimilation of Existing Knowledge:** Any project should start with a clear summary of existing knowledge, and its implications for future work. As much background reading as possible should be done on other similar sites. It is also useful to read up on the procedures employed by others in sampling certain types of features; for example, what mesh sizes were used for sampling? What types of material were retrieved?

1.   **Objectives:** Unless the project has clear objectives, the project will lack focus and is unlikely to succeed. If a multi-disciplinary project is being conducted, the different objectives must be stated from the start. Recommendations as to various sample sizes to be taken should be given from the outset (standard sample sizes for various materials are given in this handbook).

2.   **Population:** The term 'population' describes the fields that are being surveyed or studied, and these must be clearly defined from the outset. To this end, it is often prudent to define that which is **not** being studied. Samples taken from a feature should be compared to contexts that lie above and below it, so that the specifics of a particular feature can be distinguished from the background. This is a type of cluster sampling. The samples from the various deposits must be no larger than necessary.

3.   **Data to be Collected:** It is often tempting to collect as much data as possible. However, this will impair efficiency, so a selective sampling strategy – linked to the objectives of the research design – must be implemented. The sampling strategy must designate the units to be sampled and the data sets to be collected. The type of site, state of preservation and the research design will normally dictate the type of data available. At the base level, the data will comprise counts of specific object types in each sample, such as the number of shells of different species, potsherds of different fabrics or seeds of different species. Artefact/ecofact measurements and descriptions are also required, as a note of their condition, as statistical analysis will be hampered if finds are fragmentary or data is missing (see Orton 2000: 51-7).

4.   **Degree of Precision Required:** Defining the required precision of the samples and the acceptable degree of error will determine the resources required. How much of a deposit needs to be sampled for a representative sample to be taken, and what margin of error is permissible? Discussions must be held to determine what constitutes a significant sample, and the probability of its analysis answering the research questions.

5.   **Method of Measurement:** How the remains are to be measured or recorded; setting definitions as to what is or is not a significant finding; determining if samples should be counted or weighed. The choice depends on the questions being asked, the resources available and the time allotted.

6.   **The Frame:** The site will already have been split into grid units. The sampling unit, however, will usually be a division of a feature (such as a context or arbitrary spit) from which a sub-sample can be taken. The choice of the method of sampling (hand collection, site riddled, bulk sampling) all constitute the sampling frame. The aim is usually to compare assemblages. If two similar features are sampled, this should be done in a standardised manner, and to the same degree of intensity, so that they can be compared on equal terms.

7.   **Selection of the Sample:** The main issues are project design and sample size - how much has to be sampled in order to acquire a representative sample? Cluster sampling methods are most commonly employed on archaeological sites, even if sub-sampling from an assemblage. It is preferable to take several smaller samples across a feature rather than a single large sample, thus ensuring a more representative spread. These samples should be stored and sorted separately. A simple random (or, preferably, systematic) sampling strategy should be employed, to ensure that every element has the same chance of selection.

8.   **The Pre-test (Pilot) Survey:** A pilot survey is designed to assess variability in the population, and therefore allow the sampling design to be developed and adjusted for the main project. This can be done on a site-wide basis in the assessment phase, before the main excavation begins. Pilot surveys of individual features can also be conducted, time permitting.

9.   **Organisation:** The pilot survey can help in assessing how many people it will take to complete the task, what specialists might be needed and what equipment should be purchased.

10.   **Summary and Analysis:** There must always be sufficient time left to process the data; 1 month's worth of analysis per week in the field is the general rule (Renfrew & Bahn 1991: 481).

11.   **Information Gained for Future Work:** Be self-critical when compiling the final report, so that your experiences and mistakes can help others in the future. State how your project could have been improved, and provide alternative interpretations of your results. The knowledge gained about distribution densities, artefact variation in various context and feature types can be very useful to other archaeologists planning work in the future.

Archaeological Formation Processes

Ancient structures and artefacts will deteriorate at various rates in the ambient environment, leading to collapse and eventual burial through the natural action of paedogenesis (soil formation), deposition, cataclysmic events or human activity. Once interred, however, most archaeological objects will not remain unchanged and all are more-or-less affected by archaeological formation processes. This term refers to all the chemical, mechanical and biological processes that have modified an object from the time it was originally made and then discarded to the time of its excavation and analysis (Lamotta & Schiffer 2005:121). Some formation processes modify or obliterate traces of past human behaviour, while others will move objects from their original position and place them in spurious association with unconnected objects. Selective destructive processes will create a bias in the preservation of certain types of objects, creating an imbalance. For instance, organic remains are generally less likely to survive than inorganic remains (see **Tab. 9**), while lithics and pottery, being almost indestructible, are likely to survive with their fabric virtually unchanged. Some objects are more breakable than others and some, because of the context of their use, are more often lost than others, whereas others are more quickly used up than others (Hurcombe 2007: 45). Also, some object may have been used for a short time, a day or few weeks, while others may have been in use for a hundred years or more. It is therefore important to ascertain how formation processes have affected the various portions of the archaeological record, as this dictates what questions can be asked, the choice of analytical tools and quality of the conclusions that can be drawn from the results (Lamotta & Schiffer 2005:122).

The study of archaeological formation processes has various sub-disciplines, of which taphonomy (literally "laws of burial": Gk.) and object biographies are the most important. Taphonomy, once defined as transforming objects from the biosphere to the lithosphere is the study of the chemical and physical processes that modify an organism after its death and through which the remains are incorporated into geological deposits (Lamotta & Schiffer 2005; Lyman 1994; Miksicek 1987). This can in turn be divided into two broad categories: natural and human formation activities:

a) **Natural Formation Processes:** These include bioturbation (root action; earthworm and insect action; natural earth movement such as earthquakes; soil slumping) and the effects of wind, water, chemical reaction, bacterial action, climatic flux, decay, gnawing and disturbance by animals of all sizes.

b) **Human Formation Processes:** Less difficult to predict than natural processes, these include tomb robbing, re-use or desecration, robbing of building material (brick or stone), ploughing, flooding, burning and the (re-)building of structures, ditches and pits.

Object biography (Allison 1999; Hurcombe 2007, Schiffer 1995; Schiffer 1996; Skibo 1992; Walker 1995; Wood & Johnson 1978) is concerned with the procurement, manufacture, use, discard and possible reuse of objects (see **Tab. 7**). In general, all portable objects go through a similar set of processes, and may enter the archaeological record at any one of these. In order to accurately reconstruct the original activity, it is essential to identify the nature of the object when it entered the archaeological record (raw material vs. finished product; cereal vs. bread, flint pebble vs. lithic tool, etc). This area of study is not without its problems, however: reuse can obliterate traces of original use, or move the object far from its original archaeological context. This makes the examination of the original residues and abrasion marks very difficult to interpret with certainty.

Geological formation and transformation processes are also a major consideration (Barich *et al*. 1991), as sedimentation and erosion can change an archaeological site beyond recognition by eroding the surface or burying it under metres of sediment. These processes can also erode or deflate sediments, thus exposing buried artefacts that may then become damaged through exposure and erosion (Barich *et al*. 1991). Artefacts deposited in colluvium are likely to have been reworked by surface run-off whereas, objects on a surface may represent a lag or residual accumulation as a result of the erosion of the sedimentary matrix in which they were once held (Hassan 1987: 6).

Activity - Artefact	Activity - Food
1. Acquisition of the raw material	Harvested
2. Manufacture	Processing*
3. Use	Consumption
4. Discard (although the object may be reworked, reused and recycled, repeating phases 2., 3. & 4.)	Digested and excreted
5. Decay	Decay

Table 7: The biographies of two categories of objects (after Renfrew & Bahn 1991: 46). * Before processing another stage of storage can be added for some foodstuffs.

Artefactual Sampling

Archaeologists must accurately identify the relationship between deposits and the material found within them (Roskams 2001: 219). Objects fall into two categories: inadvertently discarded or lost and deliberately disposed or placed. Within these two categories are various classes of disposal: chance loss and de facto discard come under inadvertent discard, and primary discard, secondary discard, structured deposition and structured deposition in an altered physical state come under deliberate disposal (see **Fig. 22**). A coin dropped out of someone's pocket or purse in the past constitutes a chance loss, whereas de facto discard is the incidental leaving of objects or the trimmings of objects. The whittling of bone tools or knapping of flint leaves debris in the place that the manufacture activity took place. Another form of de facto discard is when an object that had a short use life was left behind where it was last used (Hurcombe 2007: 38). Deliberate disposal includes primary discard, objects that might have been associated together in a task or in life and deposited deliberately in one place, and secondary discard where objects were transported some distance to be disposed in a special place (Hurcombe 2007: 38). Two other categories of deliberate discard also exist, structured deposition, which is deliberate placement outside the living context temporarily or permanently, e.g. in a grave or hoard, and structured deposition in an altered physical state, which consists of the breaking, burning or bending of an object prior to their placement outside the living context (Hurcombe 2007: 47).

Although archaeologists use terms such as rubbish and refuse, the processes by which artefacts enter the archaeological record are a complex mixture of chance loss, the deliberate leaving of an object where it was last used (or placed), the enforced leaving of an object due to a disaster such as a volcano, the deliberate accumulation and then deposition of objects as a conscious act of disposal, and the deliberate placing of objects outside their normal interaction with people (Hurcombe 2007: 39). Try to avoid the use of generic words such as rubbish or refuse (Hill 1995; Needham & Spence 1997); more specific descriptive terms should be used. If excavating a settlement, secondary occupational debris is likely to be encountered, artefacts and building material that have been moved from their original position by site formation processes (*ex situ*). However, if excavating a hoard or grave, deliberately placed goods are likely to be found where they were generated (*in situ*) in a primary context.

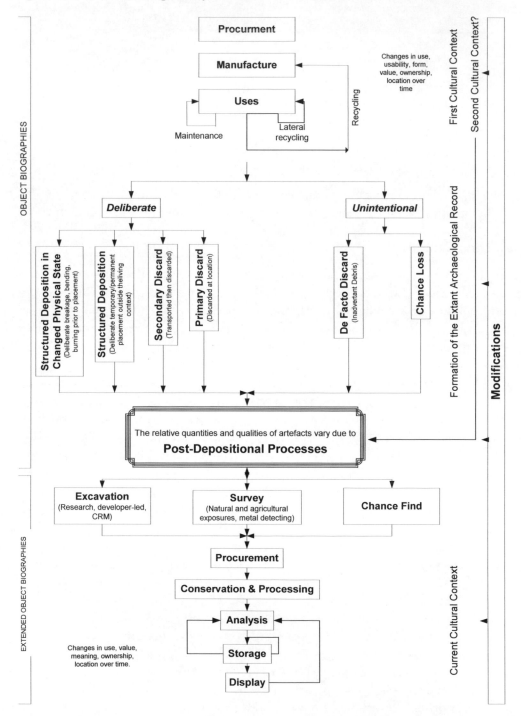

Figure 22: The key issues and concepts surrounding the formation and recovery of the material culture of past societies (after Hurcombe 2007: 40).

A primary rubbish fill is likely to be found in a rubbish pit, although it was probably accumulated elsewhere. Primary (*in situ*) deposits should receive preferential treatment in retrieval and recording procedures whereas, material found in secondary deposits (while providing general evidence of site activities) are usually bulk sampled. However, the term *in situ* can be interpreted in different ways, firstly that an object has not been reworked by secondary natural formation processes. However, the term has also been used to imply that an object is in its original cultural context, where it was first used (Hurcombe 2007: 52). Given the many complex object biographies that exist (see **Fig. 22**), the term *in situ* without further explanation should be used carefully. There can be reuse and recutting of stone; when these older stones have been incorporated into a later building they are *in situ* in their secondary cultural context but *ex situ* of their first cultural context. Therefore, *in situ* should only be used to denote that an object is in the place where it was last deployed or deposited and has not been disturbed by natural process, or the anthropogenic ones of ploughing, flooding, burning, demolition or cutting of ditches and pits - human actions that have inadvertently moved the object. It must always be stated in the written record if an object is known or suspected of being in a secondary cultural context (reused), even if it is in a primary deposit.

Most sites of Neolithic date and later will have potsherds scattered throughout the various stratigraphic layers. These fragments are far too numerous to plot individually and are therefore grouped by their context or lot number, bagged and labelled. The total amount of sherds found on the site is governed by 1) original rate of discard which is related to the type of site and context within site, settlement sites usually producing the most potsherds; 2) the type of pottery; 3) the number of breakage events, and 4) the sampling strategy. These potsherds have usually been reworked by site formation processes and are in a secondary deposit, not found in their original place of deposition. When excavating a settlement site the sheer number of these potsherds can be quite overwhelming and it may be appropriate to just collect and weigh the non-diagnostic sherds (see Orton 2000: 51-66). Rather than putting the pottery in a plastic bag the potsherds should be collected in a bucket or basket. The information that is normally written on the finds bag label should be written on the pottery basket label. If the pottery in the basket is found to date to various periods, the basket is split by the ceramicist. The excavator is then asked to re-evaluate the context, as the errant pottery may indicate an intrusive feature (such as a pit) that the excavator has missed. The place from whence the pottery came is then assigned a new context number; if a context error has been made, the basket must then be corrected during post-excavation. However, if it is only a small amount of pottery from a later period, it may have travelled down from the context above by natural means (animal burrows, sediment collapse, etc). If the exact provenience of an object is in doubt, then it **must** be assigned to the stratigraphically later context. Certain objects may remain in general debris or come up through plough soil and be deposited much more recent features such as pit fills during backfilling by chance, these much earlier objects are termed residual. However, certain objects may be heirlooms or ancient artefacts picked up as curiosities or talisman. Objects from a past distant to their own may have been picked up and used within a past society. The finding of Predynastic ceramic vessels and other objects in a Ptolemaic grave in a cemetery containing both periods of graves, such as Kafr Hassan Dawood, indicates that the later grave probably cut the earlier and the ancient objects were incorporated into the Ptolemaic grave assemblage as talisman. The ancient and current Pueblo people collect ancient arrowheads for use in various rituals (Hurcombe 2007: 51). Therefore, not all older objects found in a later deposit are residual and may have been treasured artefacts by past societies.

Many other classes of finds are also found scattered through the site, including bone and shell fragments, building material, stone vessel fragments, lithics, glass shards, metalwork, etc. These are usually also bagged by context, although different materials are kept in separate bags (or finds baskets). New bags and baskets **must** be assigned each time a new context is opened. However, another category of bulk finds also exists, those of specific importance that are found *ex situ*, such as figurines, coins, crucibles, lamps, potsherds with writing or dates on, stamps and seals, leather shoe uppers, decorated leather, mosaics, complete decorated tiles, carved wood, decorated bone and ivory. Such finds must be given a sequential finds number taken from the **Finds Register: Sheet 5** or allocated by the finds manager. It is not always possible to distinguish between primary and secondary contexts until the underlying configuration of strata and features have been uncovered (Roskams 2001: 220). Therefore, if in doubt as to whether a bulk find is *in* or *ex situ* it should be three-dimensional plotted. This is also the case if the *ex situ* context of the find is likely to provide valuable information about its lifecycle, although this is at the discretion of the excavator.

Artefacts found in their primary context can provide information about what happened in that locale (Drewett 1999: 120). If an object is found in a primary context (even if it has been reused) it **should** be three-dimensionally recorded *in situ* using written, drawn and photographic media. An artefact's primary importance on-site is for its context and association; the artefactual and aesthetic value is secondary (Drewett 1999: 120), hence academic archaeology's disapprobation towards looting. Artefacts must be revealed by the careful stripping away of the matrix as part of the normal excavation process. Artefacts must **never** be pulled from their matrix and should only be left on a pedestal for purposes of *in situ* conservation or block-lifting. If an artefact is likely to be exposed for some time whilst the rest of the context is taken down, it should be recovered with its sedimentary matrix, maintaining the conditions of its original micro environment as closely as possible (Joukowsky 1980: 177). This is because, once exposed, an object undergoes certain structural changes. Many artefacts are very friable (such as low-fired pottery, which is liable to crumble if not allowed to dry slowly); therefore, whole objects and/or pieces of an artefact found in their primary context may need specialist treatment or lifting procedures (see below). Some ceramics may need to be consolidated before lifting, using consolidants such as Paraloid B72, polyvinyl acetate (PVA) dissolved with acetone, and Primal WS24 dissolved with water (see **page 125** for methods of application). It is always best to consult the conservator as to the best method of lifting, and any first aid that the object may require. Objects requiring restoration are submitted to a team of conservators in the field laboratory, and then undergo finds processing. Objects that are too delicate to move must be thoroughly recorded *in situ*; scale drawings and photographs must be made. Once this is done, they can be safely removed to the conservation laboratory. Any discoloration found around an object must be recorded and sampled for later chemical analysis.

It is better to over-sample from a context as unneeded samples can be discarded during the processing phase. Admixed artefacts will not alter the dating of that context, which will be dated to the latest pottery found within it unless obviously modern/intrusive (Dever & Darrel Lance 1978: 79). The latest artefacts in a sealed deposit provide the context with a *terminus post quem* (literally 'time after which'), meaning that the deposit can be no earlier than the date of the latest artefact. The deposit can have been created after that time, but not before. Features that may constitute primary contexts for finds include graves, ovens, hearths, burnt floors, threshing floors, cesspits, middens, wells and drains. Secondary ditch fills, open-areas, make-up dumps, construction features and walls are less likely to produce primary finds. Occupation or living surfaces may contain both primary and secondary discard. Gé *et al.* (1993) have developed a model for the formation, preservation and recognition of occupation surfaces, but this model's use must be based on objective observations. The type of feature or context will itself indicate what type of material is likely to survive and what method of sampling is required (see **Tabs. 3 & 10**). Cesspits should be sampled for coprolites and foodstuffs, while hearths may yield charcoal. Upper Egyptian tombs and graves are good at preserving organic material through desiccation, whereas Delta sites may have waterlogged deposits with preserved organic material (this is also a characteristic of some Northern European archaeology).

The finding of export and import objects can provide a means of cross-dating. If pottery of Canaanite origin is found below a well-dated Egyptian context, it gives a *terminus ante quem* (literally 'time before which'); which means that the Canaanite artefacts cannot be later than the well-dated Egyptian context. Scientific dating of deposits can also help in the dating of artefacts. If an ash layer is discovered and scientifically dated it gives a *terminus ante quem* - an ending point - for the contexts below, and a *terminus post quem* (a starting point) for the layer above.

Environmental Sampling

One of archaeology's greatest aims is to understand how human populations interacted with and modified their worlds in the past, and how they adapted to fluctuating environmental challenges and opportunities. The human 'environment' can be divided into: the modified environment (settlement, cemetery, fields), the operational environment (direct natural environment in which individuals lived) and the geographical environment (the perceived greater landscape), all of which had an impact on humans in the past as today (Evans & O'Connor 1999: 15-16). As outlined below, environmental study is structured in terms of local climatic information, long-term environmental change, local eco-systems and the consumption and/or domestication of plants and animals. Sampling can also provide behavioural data about what activities took place where, including cereal crop processing, butchery or the functions of individual rooms within a structure (or structures within a settlement).

The preservation of plant and animal remains on an archaeological site provides tangible data for environmental reconstructions, and is dependent upon the physical, chemical and hydrological conditions of the deposits. Unless the sediments are waterlogged or desiccated, organic remains are unlikely to survive or will be poorly preserved. The sampling strategies used on-site will vary with the available environmental data, and it is always best to seek the advice of an environmental archaeologist to assess the degree of preservation on-site. Sampling should be carried out in contexts that can be securely dated and well stratified, and where risk of contamination is low. However, if in doubt, take a sample; unsuitable specimens can always be discarded later.

Microscopic and macroscopic floral and faunal remains are direct evidence of past biotic taxa, and indirect evidence of past climate. Certain types of biota are more sensitive to climatic and environmental change (terrestrial and aquatic invertebrates) whereas others are more resilient and can better withstand local or global changes (larger animals and trees). Humans and their commensals (domesticated and human-reliant animals) tend to have a dramatic impact on local habitats, leading to changes in the original biota through environmental destruction or competitive exclusion (Evans & O'Connor 1999: 133).

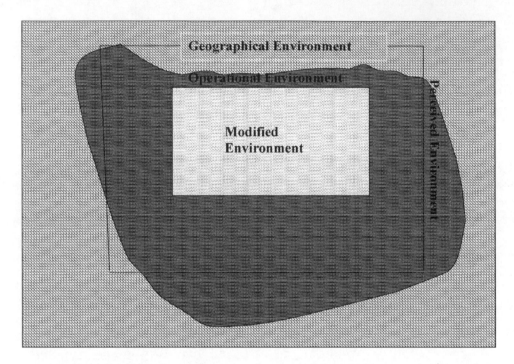

Figure 23: The environmental categories in relation to people. The modified and operational areas generally constitute the 'site catchment area' from which most of the objects found on the site are derived (after Evans & O'Connor 1999: 16).

Microscopic Floral Remains. Plant microfossils include pollen and spores, phytoliths, diatoms, starches, raphides, resins, gums, waxes, and cereal bran. Pollen is produced by all spermatophyte plants, and is dispersed via air currents or insect vectors. Different taxa produce differing sizes and shapes of pollen, which can be identified using a microscope. The outer shell of the pollen (the exine tissues) are resistant to decay and can survive for millions of years certain environments (especially acidic, anoxic matrices such as floodplain deposits). Palynology allows the ancient vegetation of a region or site to be identified, leading to ecological reconstructions of the area at different points through its history. This can be substantiated with the use of phytoliths and diatoms. Phytoliths are silica cells produced by many genera of grasses, and are morphologically diagnostic. They are resistant to decay and can survive in many sediment types, notably river gravels. Diatoms are unicellular algae that occupy frustules (silica chambers), which survive after the algae die. They occur in the hydrosphere, with various species producing highly individual and easily-identifiable frustules. Diatoms can be found in most aquatic sediments, and in oligothrophic lakes (such as ancient Lake Moeris [Qarun] in the Faiyum) they can be so abundant that they form a major component of sedimentary layers called diatomite. The study of species turnover in diatomites can help identify changes in water oxygenation, temperature and chemistry, which in turn indicate changes in their direct environment. Raphides are needle-shaped crystals of an irritant substance such as oxalic acid formed in plants. Cereal bran and cuticles are microscopic plant parts, which can be collected by laboratory sampling and used to reconstruct ancient diet. Microscopic floral remains are usually collected by means of laboratory sampling (see below) before being examined under a microscope.

Macroscopic Floral Remains. Plant macrofossils are produced by most types of plants and consist mainly of cellulose with a minor element of lignin. Seeds, fruits, nuts and woods may all be preserved, and are most likely to enter the archaeological record if charred, or deposited in desiccated or waterlogged conditions. Plant macrofossils are usually collected by bulk sampling, site-riddled sampling or hand collection, and are identified with the naked eye or under the microscope. Like pollen, macrofossils can be used to reconstruct past plant communities and their utilisation, manipulation and transformation by humans. They are invaluable for reconstructing human economy, behaviour (i.e. boat/bridge/house building; tools, arts and crafts) and diet, while charred remains can also be used for radiocarbon dating. The identification of tree species can identify the types of woodland cover in a region, as well as the types of wood utilised by humans.

Microscopic Faunal Remains. Molluscs and insects are particularly useful in environmental analysis (Evans & O'Connor 1999: 140), as arthropod exoskeletons and mollusc shells are both durable and highly diagnostic. Because they have short life-spans and are intolerant of climatic change, they are also a sensitive indicator of ecological circumstances. Beetle remains survive well in acidic, anoxic environments, and are collected by bulk sampling, site-riddled sampling or hand collection. The various taxa can be categorised by ecology to permit accurate interpretation of the local and regional environment. At an intra-site level, information can be obtained about ground surface conditions, vegetation, stored products and utilisation of plant material (Evans & O'Connor 1999: 140). On a regional level, they can be used to assess major trends in past climate and climatic change. The sediment obtained by deep sea-cores contains foraminifera (tiny one-celled marine organisms). Changing environmental conditions are observed by the presence, absence and fluctuations of various foraminiferan species, as well as fluctuating ratios of stable oxygen isotopes 18 and 16 in the calcium carbonate of their shells (Miller-Rosen 2007; Renfrew & Bahn 2004: 233). These differences reflect not only changes in temperature, but also oscillations in the continental glaciers.

Macroscopic Faunal Remains. The shells of molluscs are highly durable, survive well in alkaline deposits and can usually be collected by hand (or flotation for very small species). While they are not as highly adapted to their environmental niches as beetles, and cannot therefore be used to the same level of refinement, the analysis of molluscs can provide information about ecology and long-term environmental change. Ostracods can also be used to interpret past environments; these mainly freshwater crustaceans have highly specific water and substrate requirements and can help in the interpretation of the hydrosphere. Mammals, birds, reptiles and fish are usually represented as bones, which are collected by bulk sampling, site-riddled sampling or hand collection, and can be identified with the naked eye or under the microscope. The study of vertebrate remains - particularly the larger birds and mammals - indicate which animals co-habited with human populations as domesticates or as prey (Evans & O'Connor 1999: 146). The types of domesticates may indicate how the past environment was modified through clearance or grazing, while wild species can indicate the wider environment and habitats. On a larger scale, small vertebrates such as rodents are sensitive to ecology and have risen to prominence as indicators of climate and ecology in various periods of human and early hominid history (i.e. the Middle Pleistocene 'vole-clock').

Procedures for Recovering the Evidence

When considering faunal or floral analysis, samples can be taken to answer specific questions ("what was this beaten earth floor used for?") or general questions ("what farming system was used by this population?" or "what was the nature of local eco-systems?"). The usual questions asked of environmental samples concern long-term environmental change, spatial analysis of on-site activities and economy. Methods and practice of each of these is summarised below:

1. **Long Term Environmental Change:** To assess environmental change over long periods of time, it is necessary to sample long sequences of deposits. This should be done with a Kubiena or monolith box (see **Fig. 24**), or with coring equipment. Palaeochannels are good sources of data, often yielding pollen, plant macrofossils and insect remains which can give information on economy as well as long-term vegetational change (Murphy & Wiltshire 1994: 2).

2. **Spatial Analysis:** If the research design aims to locate different types of activities on-site, horizontal sampling will be necessary. This can take the form of sampling of linear features at regular intervals or using a grid pattern for buried deposits, in order to give a balanced indication of spatial variability (Orton 2000). Systematic sampling may be scaled-up for the surrounding landscape (Murphy & Wiltshire 1994: 2).

3. **Economy:** Because it is not practical to sample all deposit types for crop residues, a stratified random sampling strategy should be employed alongside sampling from contexts that are deemed to be significant (see **Fig. 25**).

There are four main ways of collecting environmental samples: laboratory sample (LS), bulk sample (BS), site-riddled sample (SRS) and hand-collected samples (HCS). For further details on these processes see below. The method of sampling and the size of the sample will be dependent on whether it is macro- or micro-fossils that are to be sampled (Murphy & Wiltshire 1994: 3-6).

1.   Laboratory Samples

These samples are relatively small, ranging from a few grams to a few kilograms, and are processed in the laboratory. These samples are usually collected by an environmental archaeologist. The methods of sampling include:

a. Monolith sampling: intact blocks of sediment removed with a metal box from the face of a section (e.g. by Kubiena boxes).

b. Pollen spot sampling: a vertical series of spot samples taken with a spatula or scalpel at 20 mm intervals to a depth of 10 mm into the face of a section (used when monolith boxes cannot be inserted).

c. Deep coring: drill cores taken with a Russian corer (Jowsey), piston corer or percussion corer from the surface (used when sections cannot be cut).

d. Contiguous column sampling: samples are between 1-10 kg and spaced contiguously (touching) at 50-100 mm intervals, although never straddling context interfaces (layer boundaries). Each sub-sample is bagged and labelled separately, and all sub-samples are placed in one large bag.

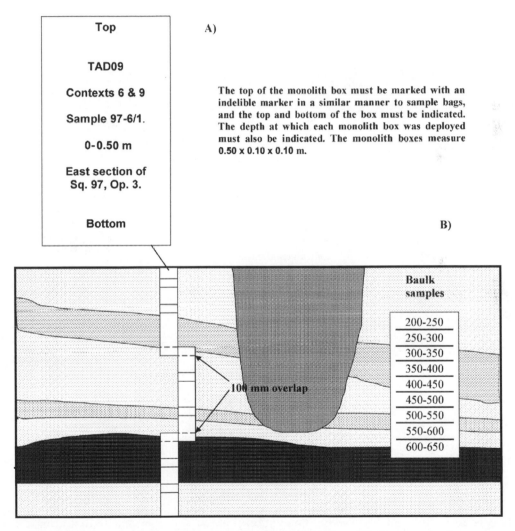

Figure 24: Sampling a sequence of deposits using monolith boxes. The boxes must be staggered, overlapping by 100 mm. Once the monolith boxes have been pressed into the face of the section, they must be cut out by removing the matrix around them, slipping the trowel behind them and easing them free from the section. The monolith box must then be wrapped in a heavy-duty plastic sack and secured with elastic bands. The information written on the box must then be transferred to a label and stuck to the bag (after Murphy & Wiltshire 1994: Fig.3).

2. Bulk Samples

These samples constitute 1-4 buckets (15-60 litres) collected by the excavators with trowels and spades, usually from dry deposits. These samples are processed by dry sieving or flotation at the excavation centre prior to being sorted. Before processing, the samples may be stored in heavy-duty plastic sacks or sealable **plastic buckets.**

3. Site-Riddled Samples

These samples are entire or high proportions of the fill of a feature (usually 100-200 litres). They are collected by the excavator, using a trowel and shovel, and are usually bulk sieved using 4 mm mesh sieves. Sand sediments are usually dry sieved, whereas clay and mud may have to be broken down with a water-hose. The remaining artefacts, ecofacts and other materials are then picked over by the archaeologist. This procedure should be carried out on-site as part of the excavation process unless water is required, in which case the sample should be taken back to the excavation centre.

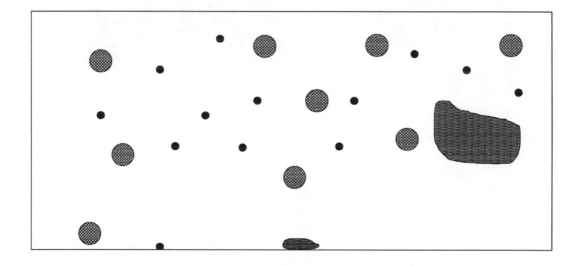

Figure 25: Stratified random sampling. Divide the types of features to be sampled into their type. Here there are 8 pits, 12 postholes and 1 hearth. If the site sampling strategy is to sample 50% of pits, 25% of post holes and all hearths, then 4 pits, 3 post holes and the hearth would be sampled. The context number is then randomly selected for each type of feature, thus avoiding sampling bias (after Murphy & Wiltshire 1994: Fig. 2).

4. Hand-Collection Sampling

This type of sampling is part of the excavation process, whereby individual artefacts and ecofacts are manually extracted from the surrounding matrix. However, single mollusc shells are of limited value unless they are part of a larger assemblage collected by one of the other methods. Large bones should only be lifted after consultation with a zooarchaeologist or physical anthropologist (if human). Likewise, wood and charcoal should only be lifted after consultation with an archaeobotanist. If a specialist is not present, the object should be lifted carefully along with its sedimentary matrix.

All samples should be stored in conditions that resemble as closely as possible those of the context from which they come (generally dark and chilled with the air excluded), thus preventing fungal, bacterial and algal growth (Murphy & Wiltshire 1994). Damp or waterlogged samples should be kept in a fridge in a sealed container to prevent them drying out. Dry samples must first be kept in open bags to ensure they are fully dry, at which time the bags may be sealed. The samples should then be stored in a dry, cool, dark section of the excavation centre. The sites from which samples were taken must be plotted on plans and sections. Photographs of sampling taking place can also be useful in providing a complete record of sample location and orientation.

Sampling Method	Description	Advantages	Disadvantages
Simple Random	A statistically random method of selecting contexts to be sampled	Mathematically rigorous, eliminates potential sources of bias, and deposits have an equal chance of being selected	Could miss important deposits if used on its own
Stratified Random	Area divided into geographic or activity zones, then randomly selected within these zones	Takes into account the geography or cultural activity	Poses a risk of personal bias of the archaeologist
Judgement	Samples selected from obviously 'rich' deposits	Cost and time effective, as only the 'good' samples are targeted	Highly subjective: 'good' contexts are not always apparent to the archaeologist
Systematic Random	Samples selected by an agreed strategy, with samples collected from same place in each deposit or area	Ensures that whole site is considered: can be easily re-evaluated and changed during excavation	Can miss unusual contexts, or sample inappropriate contexts if poorly planned
Systematic Unaligned	Samples selected by an agreed strategy, with samples taken from a different place in each deposit or area	Covers whole site, but maintains a random element, giving relatively even coverage	Can miss unusual contexts, or sample inappropriate contexts if poorly planned

Table 8: Sampling methodologies. This demonstrates the strength of using a combination of methods in order to gain the widest coverage (after English Heritage 2002 a: 19).

All environmental samples should be double-bagged in strong plastic bags and clearly labelled with their context number, context type, sample type and sample number (see

Filling Out of Labels for Finds Bags). The context information should be written on a spun-bonded polythene (Tyvek) label using an indelible marker, and placed in the outer bag with the information facing out. If the sample is large, it should be placed in a plastic bucket (preferably with a sealable lid), with a Tyvek label bearing all the information tied to the bucket handle. All tools used to take a sample must be cleaned directly afterwards to prevent contamination of future samples. Once a sample has been taken, it must be logged on the relevant recording form (for general samples, **Sediment Sampling Form: Sheet 6** should be used). The recording form must state the volume of sediment, the percentage of the context sampled and all provenience details, and must accompany the sample to the specialist. A general guide to depositional environments, sediments and preservation is presented in **Tab.9.**

Depositional Environment	Main Soil and Sediment Types	Typical Situations	Environmental Indicators
Acid, pH usually <5.5, oxic	Podsols and other leached soils	Heathlands, upland moors, some river gravels	Soil pollen, charcoal and other charred plant remains, phytoliths, pollen & spores, diatoms
Basic, pH usually >7.0, oxic	Rendsinas, lake marls, tufa, alluvium, shell-sand	Chalk and limestone areas, valley bottoms, karst, machair	Molluscs, bones, ostracods, foraminifera, parasite eggs, pollen & spores
Neutral, pH 5.5-7.0, aerobic	Brownearths and gleys, river gravels, alluvium	Clay vales and other lowland plains	Charcoal, pollen & spores and sometimes bone and shell
Acid or basic, anoxic	Peats and organic deposits, e.g. lake sediments and alluvial gleys	Well sealed strata such as organic urban deposits, wetlands, river floodplains, wells, wet ditches	Insects, macroscopic plant remains, bone, wood, charcoal, molluscs, ostracods, foraminifera, parasite eggs, pollen & spores, diatoms

Table 9: Physico-chemical conditions for the preservation of organic remains (after Evans & O'Connor 1999: 80).

Type of remains	Sediment type	Information to be gained	Extraction/examination	Volume
Plant Remains				
Charred (cereals)	All	Vegetation, diet, crafts, technology, fuel, behaviour	Dry sieve, flotation to 300 microns (μm)	75 ltr.
Uncharred (fruits, seeds and leaves)	Wet or desiccated	Vegetation, diet, crafts, technology, fuel, behaviour	Laboratory sieving to 300 μm	10-20 ltr.
Wood	Wet or desiccated	Dating, climate, building materials and technology	Hand collection, dry sieving, flotation, and microscopy x 10	Hand collection
Diatoms	Waterlain	Salinity/acidity of deposit and water levels	Laboratory extraction, and microscopy x 400	0.10 ltr.
Pollen, microbial remains, plant spores	Buried soils, waterlogging	Vegetation, land use history, climate	Laboratory extraction, and microscopy x 400	0.05 ltr. or by column sample
Phytoliths	All	Vegetation, land use	Laboratory extraction, and microscopy x 400	0.05 ltr. or by column sample
Animals				
Large mammal	All but very acidic	*	Hand, trowel and sieve	All
Small mammal	All but very acidic	Fauna, ecology	Sieving to 1 mm	75 ltr.
Bird bone	All but very acidic	Wildfowling, domesticates	Sieving to 1 mm	75 ltr.
Fish bone, scales, otoliths	All but very acidic	Diet, subsistence, trade, seasonality	Sieving to 1 mm	75 ltr.
Foraminifera	Alkaline and neutral	Salinity and elevation of intertidal depositional environments	Laboratory extraction, and microscopy x 400	0.10 ltr.
Marine and freshwater molluscs	Alkaline and neutral	Diet, subsistence, trade, seasonality, salinity	Hand, trowel, sieve	75 ltr.
Land molluscs	Alkaline	Sedimentation, environment,	Laboratory extraction, and sieving to 500 μm	10 ltr.
Insect remains (charred)	All	Environment, climate, pests	Laboratory extraction, and flotation to 300 μm	10-20 ltr.
Insect remains (uncharred)	Wet or desiccated	Environment, climate, pests	Laboratory Extraction, and flotation to 300 μm	10-20 ltr.

Parasite eggs	Wet or desiccated	Disease, sanitation, pathology	Laboratory Extraction, and microscopy x 400	0.25 ltr.
Soils/Sediments				
Micromorphology	All	Pedogenesis, sedimentary structure and the human impact, function of features, alluviation, nature of husbandry.	Hand, trowel, sieve, laboratory sampling	0.25 ltr.
Chemistry	All	Pedogenesis and climatic impact. Nutritional status and acidity of palaeosoils, impact of arable and pastoral husbandry, evidence of human occupation	Hand, trowel, sieve, laboratory sampling	0.25 ltr.
Particle size	All	Sedimentary sequences. Evidence of water flow	Hand, trowel, sieve, laboratory sampling	0.25 ltr.

Table 10: Chart of methods and rationale for sampling environmental remains (after Murphy & Wiltshire 1994: Table 1; Westman 1994: 42-4). *The range of information to be derived from large mammal remains is far too great to cover here, but includes animal husbandry, domestication practices, butchery practices, diet, disease, social status, cultic practices, wealth, human/animal behaviour, craft techniques, environmental and climatic data.

The above table (**Tab. 10**) is a basic guide to the sorts of information that can be gained from the different categories of data and the amount of material required. Analysis of the environmental samples should be carried out by an archaeobotanist (flora) and/or zooarchaeologist (fauna). It is important that the individual environments found on-site be taken into account, and to distinguish between acidic/alkaline sedimentary matrices. However, some fossil remains (such as charred grains) are fairly resistant to a wide range of preservational environments (Murphy & Wiltshire 1994).

Collection of Samples for Absolute Dating

Absolute dating methods require the sampling of various types of materials found on archaeological sites. These are then sent to a scientific laboratory for processing. However, each method has its limitations in terms of accuracy, the types of material it can date, and the time range in which it is useful. Radiocarbon (^{14}C) and luminescence (TL and OSL) are two of the most common absolute dating methods used in Quaternary and archaeological science.

		Dating Method	Description	Examples and Range
Annual cycles and calendars		Sidereal Methods	Calendar dates or count of annual events	Dendrochronology (0 – 10 kyr), varve chronologies (0 – 12 kyr), historical records (0 – 5 kyr)
	Radioactive clocks	Isotopic Methods	Radioactive decay changes in isotopic composition	Radiocarbon (1 kyr - 60 kyr), potassium-argon (100 kyr – 5 myr), U-series (1 kyr-500 kyr)
		Radiogenic Methods	The cumulative nonisotopic effects of radioactive decay	Electron energy trap and crystal damage methods – OSL, TL (0 -400 kyr), electron spin resonance (5 kyr – 1 myr), fission-track (100 kyr – 500 kyr)
Calibrated Relative Methods		Chemical and Biological Methods	The measure of time-dependent chemical or biological processes	Amino acid racemisation (1 kyr -100 kyr), Obsidian hydration (0 -500 kyr), cation-ratio (0 – 12 kyr)
		Correlation Methods	The establishment of age equivalence using time-dependent properties	Tephrachronology (1 kyr – 5 myr), palaeomagnetism (200 kyr – 5 myr)

Table 11: Various dating methods available to archaeologists grouped by type and showing time-range applicable (after Holdaway 2005: 121 and Renfrew & Bahn 2004: 132).

Other radioactive clock methods can be used for dating extremely ancient deposits. These include electron spin resonance (which is used to date bone and shell) potassium-argon (volcanic rocks), uranium series (rock rich in calcium carbonates) and fission-track (obsidian and other volcanic glasses). Method and sample selection is of critical importance, and hinges on the aims of the project and the materials available. There are several factors to consider when selecting a sample for dating: will the material be able give a date in the expected time range of the site/deposit? What are the dating methods available for that sample? Is the dating method likely to provide sufficient precision to answer the research questions? What is the danger of contamination? What is actually being dated by using the chosen material? Is it the actual artefact or deposit or is it from the context above or below (see **Tabs. 11 and 12**)?

Radiocarbon Dating (^{14}C/AMS)	
Charcoal, wood, reed, twigs and seeds	Basketry
Bone	Dung
Marine, estuarine and riverine shell	Macrofossils
(carbonates)	Plant material
Leather	Mud-brick
Pollen	Metal casting ores
Hair	Wall paintings and rock art works
Organic temper in pottery	Iron and meteorites
Bird eggshell	Coprolites (samples of preserved faeces)
Corals and foraminifera	Coral
Blood residues	Lake muds (gyttja) and sediments
Textiles and fabrics	Soil
Paper and parchment	Peat
Fish remains	Organic sediment
Insect remains	Water: $BaCO_3$, $SrCO_3$ (ice cores)
Resins and glues	Water (as liquid)
Antler and horn	CO_2 Gas

Optically Stimulated Luminescence (OSL) and Associated Luminescence	
Pottery	Fluvial systems
Faience	Glacial sediments
Artificial glass*	Fluvial sediments
Terracotta	Aeolian sediments, dune sands
Baked clay	Lacustrine sediments
Kilns	Shallow marine sediments
Wasp nests	Soil Horizon A
Burnt/fired mud-brick	Soil Horizon C
Ceramic bricks	Glacial deposits*
Vitrified forts or earth mounds*	Loess
Marine sands	

Thermoluminescence (TL)	
Pottery	Travertine
Faience	Stalagmites
Artificial glass*	Burnt/fired mud-brick
Terracotta	Ceramic bricks
Burned flint and stone	'Dirty' pedogenic carbonates
Baked clay	Vitrified forts or earth mounds*
Kilns	Slags*
Marine sands	Tephra
Volcanites	Mollusc shells
Colluvial and alluvial silts	Loess
Dune sands	Fluvial sediments

Table 12: Types of absolute dating, and the materials upon which they rely. * Although dates have been obtained on these materials, they are either felt unreliable or have greater than 10% accuracy.

1. Radiocarbon Dating

Radiocarbon dating is used on organic materials and uses the decay rate of the radioactive carbon atom ^{14}C. All living organisms uptake carbon. When they die they cease to uptake carbon and the amount of ^{14}C starts to decline through radioactive decay. This carbon atom has a half-life of 5730 years, which means that the amount of ^{14}C atoms halves every 5730 years. As the amount of carbon in the atmosphere has varied over time, the ^{14}C dates received back from the laboratory (e.g. 5369 ± 60 bp) need to be calibrated against the calibration curve based on dendrochronology (uranium-thorium dated corals and varve-counted marine sediment). The second set of numbers (± 60 bp) in the dates received back from the laboratory is the probable error known as the standard deviation, which has a .68 probability (a ± 16 year accuracy is now possible with the high-precision technique). Computerised calibration programmes such as OxCal, PALCAL and CALIB will then be able to give Cal BC/AD or Cal BP dates for the samples with a .95 accuracy (two standard deviations, .68 is a single deviation). Radiocarbon dating takes two forms: radiometric and accelerator mass spectrometry (AMS). Although AMS dates are more expensive than radiometric dates, they directly date the sample and require much smaller samples. However, radiocarbon age measurements are to be regarded as what they are - probabilistic estimates with a margin of error thus requiring multiple measurements for each target event (Hassan *et al.* 2007).

2. Luminescence Dating

Luminescence dating measures the energy of photons released when a sample is exposed to radiation (heat or light). Materials with a crystalline structure (such as minerals and pottery) contain small amounts of radioactive uranium, thorium and potassium, which decay at a steady rate, emitting alpha, beta, and gamma radiation. This radiation bombards the crystalline structure and displaces electrons, which then become trapped at points of imperfection in the crystal lattice. A steady flow of electrons becomes trapped over time, and only when the material is heated to at least between 350-500° C (or, in the case of sediments, exposed to sufficient sunlight immediately prior to deposition) can the electrons escape, resetting the radioactive 'clock' to zero (Renfrew & Bahn 2004: 154-8). Once this has taken place, they immediately start to accrue luminescence which can be measured in order to establish when the firing (or exposure) took place. There are various forms of luminescence techniques: Thermal (TL), Optically Stimulated (OSL), Photo-Transferred (PTTL), Green Light (GSL) - Feldspar & Quartz, Infrared (IRSL) - K-Spar, Blue Light (BSL) – Quartz, and Red Light (RSL) - Volcanic Feldspar & Quartz. TL can be used on samples exposed to heat (e.g. pottery) whereas the other techniques can be used on samples exposed to light. The most commonly used in archaeology are thermoluminescence (TL) and optically stimulated luminescence (OSL), which can date a variety of materials (see **Tabs. 11 & 12**). The principal minerals used in luminescence dating are quartz and potassium feldspar, thus permitting the dating of certain sediments. OSL techniques produce ages from 100 to 400,000 years with an error of around 10%, although the single-aliquot method of OSL pottery dating allows a 1-2% error margin.

The careful collection of the correct size of samples for scientific dating is important if errors are to be avoided. The **Environmental Sampling Form – Sheet 28** and other contextual information showing the locations of samples (along with the **Chronometric**

Recording Form – Sheet 25) should be sent to the dating laboratory with the samples. At least one photograph should be taken of the sample's location, showing the stratigraphic context, and one further close-up to show the texture of the sediment sample. If submitting shell samples, provide the laboratory with the name of the species in question and do not mix different species in the sample (Burke & Smith 2004: 156). When collecting OSL and TL samples it is especially important that the depth of sample below ground level is recorded, as this is needed for a calculation of cosmic ray component of the D_R. Also provide data on the level of the water table and seasonal variations in rainfall.

Collection of Luminescence Samples:

During fieldwork, a member of the luminescence dating laboratory staff should visit the site to collect samples or to advise on sample collection, and to measure the environmental contribution to the annual radiation dose using a portable gamma spectrometer. This can significantly improve the dating precision and sample turn-around time. However, if this is not possible contact the laboratory staff who may be able to provide sampling equipment.

When gathering samples try to avoid sediments that show any post-depositional disturbances such as root penetration, animal burrows, krotavinia (bioturbation), carbonates, ground-water leaching, unusual soil formations or large stones. The procedure for sampling is provided below:

OSL Collection

• Excavate back 0.30 m to expose a fresh face, then push a 0.25 m long by 50 mm diameter steel or PVC sampling tube into the back of the hole to collect the luminescence sample. PVC tubes often benefit from a sharpened or bevelled edge on the back of the tube to be driven into the sediment. Tubes should be driven in by sledgehammer; a metal or wood plate should be used against the end being hammered to prevent shattering or collapse. If the only exposure that is available is one in which cracks, roots or krotavinia may be encountered at depth (or the sediment is so hard that it will be difficult to remove the tube once driven in) then a cube block sample should be cut. The sample tube should be carefully pried or dug out from the hole by pushing a knife or chisel alongside the tube and levering it sideways.

• If the sample is being collected during daylight hours, a black or opaque cloth **must** be used to shield the sample collection and the immediate site from light and moisture. Do **not** remove the sample from the hole or black cloth until the open end is closed with a black cap or duct tape. If the sample is collected at dusk or night, a red-filter light can be employed. Both ends of the tube should then be sealed with black electrical tape to prevent displacement during sample shipment. Mark the end of the sample that was exposed to the surface. Wrap it in aluminium foil, a black bag (several layers if being shipped) and tape tightly to prevent disintegration. Write the sample name on both tube and bag.

• A second sample must be collected from the back or sides of the same hole and from the layer above, layer below and the same stratigraphic layer as the OSL sample, but not too close to the original sample. This 'bulk sample' does not need protection from light, and should be placed in a double zip-seal 1-quartz size bag to inhibit loss of moisture, so that the gross moisture content can be measured in the laboratory. This sample can also be used to obtain a D_R if field analysis is not possible, in which case at least 600 grms is needed.

TL Collection

- The samples of ceramics, burned flint or stone must be sufficiently large to ensure that adequate material is available for dating after the removal of the outer 2 mm thick layer over the entire surface. You should aim to acquire a sample with a minimum volume of 5 mm x 20 mm x 20 mm.

- As well as the artefactual sample, it is essential to provide a minimum bulk sample of 100 grms of the soil or sediment in which the pottery, flint or other material was buried. This bulk sediment sample must be representative of the surrounding deposits up to a distance of 0.20 – 0.30 m. The sediments from which you take all samples should be as uniform as possible – do not collect the artefact from an area near to a pit interface or similar feature, or from a depth of less than 0.30 m from the present ground surface.

Deposit	Age Range (years)
Glass / Volcanic Ash	10 - 250,000
Loess	8,000 - 416,000
Fluvial	Modern - 400,000
Colluvium / Alluvium	100 - 150,000
Aeolian	10 - 70,000
Paleodischarge - A&C Horizons	3,000 - 190,000

Table 13: Typical dating ranges of different materials using OSL.

Collection of Carbon-14 Samples

Material for carbon-14 dating is usually retrieved through hand collection, during sieving or flotation. Parts of an artefact, ecofact or human bone (those parts that are not useful for morphological and pathological examinations) may be selected as a dating sample. Special attention must be paid to the problem of old wood and settlement debris (Hassan *et al.* 2007). It is better to select an object with a short life-cycle and biography – one that is not likely to have been reused, such as reeds, seeds or dung from a secure or sealed context. When collecting samples for carbon-14 dating, it is important to remove possible carbon contaminants as age estimates can be skewed by any intrusive organic material (Holdaway 2006: 119). Artificial contaminants include ash from tobacco, hair and fibres, paper from packing material and oil or grease (Higham 1999). Therefore, the sample collector should wear rubber gloves, and a hairnet/hat if they have long hair; it is **essential** not to smoke nearby when the sample is being collected. Do **not** put the samples in paper bags; pack with cotton wool or tissues, and never place paper or cardboard provenience labels near the samples. Collect the sample with metal or plastic implements, such as tweezers, nylon brushes or a trowel, and **not** wooden tools or bristle brushes (Burke & Smith 2004: 153-6). To help protect the sample from contamination it should be wrapped in aluminium foil before placing it in a plastic container or zip-seal bag (which should be pierced to let out any moisture in the sample) and stored in a dark place to avoid any continuing photosynthesis.

Material	Radiometric	AMS	OSL & TL
Wood	7 -100 grms	10 – 100 mgs	-
Seeds	7 – 100 grms	10 – 100 mgs	-
Charcoal	2 – 30 grms	5 – 50 mgs	-
Thin charcoal scatter	1 kg	10 – 100 mgs	-
Shell	7 – 100 grms	15 – 100 mgs	-
Forams	7 – 100 grms	15 – 100 mgs	-
Peat	15 – 100 grms	15 – 100 mgs	-
Cloth, paper, papyrus	3 – 100 grms	5 – 50 mgs	-
Organic Sediment	20 grms – 1 kg	5 - 10 mgs	-
Bone	200 – 500 grms	2 – 30 mgs	-
Flesh, skin or hair	5 – 45 grms	5 – 30 mgs	-
Dung	7 – 30 grms	5 – 50 mgs	-
Plant material	5 – 50 grms	10 – 50 mgs	-
Water as ice	7 – 50 grms	15 -50 mgs	-
Water	2 litres	1 litre	-
CO_2 Gas	-	0.5 – 1 cc	-
Textiles, cloth	7 – 100 grms	2 – 5 mg	-
Pottery	-	-	100 - 200 mgs
Bricks	-	-	100 - 200 mgs
Fine Sediment (silt)	-	-	100 - 500 grms
Medium Sediment (sand)	-	-	100 - 500 grms
Burned lithics	-	-	12 - 15 grms.

Table 14: Size of sample required for various methods of absolute dating; the first weight is minimum size, the second is recommended sample size. TL dating usually requires a larger sample than OSL (after Burke & Smith 2004: 157).

Although most laboratories will conduct physical pretreatment and chemical pretreatment, it is advisable to carry out an initial physical pretreatment on-site (usually by the site conservator). Natural carbon contaminates such as rootlets, pieces of wood, lumps of soil and dead insects can all occur in the post-depositional environment, and can make any samples in which they are found appear either too old or too young. Organic samples such as wood, charcoal, soil and bone are especially prone to this and should be examined closely before, and after collection, for evidence of root penetration. Contamination may also be caused by humic acids (decayed remnants of dead plants) circulating throughout the soil, especially in peats and soils (Higham 1999). Degraded and oxidized plant fragments in charcoal, or powdery/chalky shells (indicating recrystallisation) can also ruin the accuracy of dating methods. Dating laboratories have means of mitigating these contaminations, with the exterior of lumps of charcoal often being carved off to remove the contaminants absorbed into the surface and dating the fractions removed as a control. However, the site conservator should remove any contaminants or obviously contaminated exterior layers using a scalpel, tweezers and magnification (Higham 1999).

When submitting the sample to the radiocarbon dating laboratory the relationship between the material and the geological (or archaeological) context should be described graphically (section drawing) and textually (context sheets). Information detailing the type of environment from which the sample was obtained and the likelihood of rootlet intrusion or other contaminants should also be supplied (Higham 1999). Any processes conducted on the sample - such as physical pre-treatment - and the degree of accuracy required must be noted in the **Chronometric Recording Form – Sheet 25**, which should accompany the sample to the dating laboratory. It is also important to know the size of sample required (see **Tab. 14**).

END-OF-PROJECT ASSESSMENT

The end-of-project assessment (EPA) should be conducted at the end of the last fieldwork season, after the archiving process but before the final report is written (this is above and beyond the interim reports, which are written at the end of each season). In contract archaeology there is often a stage of post-excavation assessment to consider whether full analysis, interpretation and publication is needed, or if further excavation is required. The EPA has developed out of these original initiatives but has a wider scope and is applicable to all archaeological fieldwork projects. The main factors to consider are the potential for further investigation, analysis, publication, conservation and site management, and/or to detail recommendations for site reclassification. This involves comparing the results of the project against the original research design to determine the extent to which the aims and objectives have been met, to identify any new research questions that need to be addressed during post-excavation, and to propose recommendations for further research (IFA 1999e: 5).

The pressing need for agricultural and development land means that archaeological sites are rarely safe unless known to be of local, regional or (inter)national importance, or incorporate notable standing structures. Following evaluation or fuller investigation (excavation), therefore, an EPA is usually required to determine the site's local, regional or national importance, and whether it needs further investigation or preservation for future generations. It also permits archaeological or governmental bodies to plan management programmes and target research projects more effectively. For example, if a site seemingly showed great promise but actually contained very little of archaeological value, the EPA will allow authorities to reclassify the site. Equally, planners can use the information acquired to design cultivation or development plans that respect the archaeological remains (i.e. not allowing buildings with deep foundations, or deep ploughing). If a site has been 'totally' excavated, there may be no need for further investigations, although the site will need to be re-evaluated before it can be returned to landowners or developers.

If the site has not been fully investigated, for whatever reason, recommendations for future research are essential. The EPA should be conducted by experienced archaeologists and monitors (from the local museum or archaeological body). This assessment entails an evaluation of the site and an examination of the records and materials. The final result is a report that fully details the work done, includes recommendations for future work, and details what further research needs to be conducted.

The end-of-project assessment report should contain:

1. Introduction
    a. Scope of project, including a base plan of the site(s).
    b. General details and dates for fieldwork, and those of any previous investigations.
    c. Details of all management team, contact and individual institutions.
    d. General comments on report organisation.

2. Original research aims and objectives.

3. Summary of the documental history of the site(s).

4. A complete list of all work conducted at the site: the location of operational areas and trenches, the scope and type of work conducted, and the types and results of scientific analysis.

5. Synopsis of the fieldwork results.

6. Interpretation of the fieldwork results.

7. A digest of the site archive: site records (plans, sections, drawings, photographs and digital media, site matrix), finds, environmental material and other research documents.

8. Assessment of the data.
    a. An appraisal of how the recovered data was used to address the aims and objectives laid out in the research design. The various classes of data should be discussed in an integrated manner, sub-divided according to the project aims.
    b. A statement about the data's potential for developing new research aims at the current site and other projects.

9. An assessment of the data and site in terms of local, regional, national and international importance.

10. Statement on the project's scope for developing further research and on the probable amount, variety, quantity, quality and range of archaeological material remaining at the site. Provide an evaluation of any anthropogenic or environmental threats to the site.

11. Recommendations for site management, further conservation or reclassification of the site for minimal, medium or full protection. Provide a summary of the potential effects of agricultural or construction development upon the remains in the event that the site was returned directly to the landowner.

12. Appendices of supporting illustrations and data-sets, noting any and all reports or published articles on the site or data derived there from. Provide an index, references and any relevant disclaimers.

The report should then be submitted to the local and regional archaeological agencies and SMR office as well as the developers or planners. A report should also be submitted to a national digest of fieldwork.

CHAPTER FIVE

Specific Archaeological Excavation Methodology

Whichever approaches, methods and procedures are used, flexibility and creative thought are absolutely essential at all level, from the director to the supervisors and other personnel. Methodologies have been developed to guide the archaeologist, not to constrict their approaches; when unexpected problems arise, creative solutions should be sought. Different types of objects and features - and the varying contexts in which they are found, - present their own excavation problems. While every site is, of course, unique, certain trends can be assumed to generate a **general** approach, be it a cemetery, settlement, monumental structure or campsite. Features ranging from graves to pits, walls or buildings must therefore be anticipated. Preservation can be very good, or very poor, with differential survivorship of artefacts and ecofacts. When archaeologists excavate, they must be constantly alert to the possibility of discovering unexpected features, although it should be noted that many of the actual floors and levels occupied by humans cannot be recognised even by the most careful excavation (Drewett 1999: 108). Exercise all the controls that are necessary to tie in strata with features, and features within horizons: this can be done using a small gauge (i.e. 1 x 1 m) grid laid out over the feature such as a floor to enable the more precise plotting of the provenience of artefacts, particularly on important sites, such as low-visibility Palaeolithic campsites. The recording of features and objects in the horizontal and vertical planes locates them three-dimensionally on the site plans, permitting the development of the site's chronological sequence (Joukowsky 1980: 178). The development of computer aided design (CAD) and geographic information systems (GIS) have permitted increasingly complex temporo-spatial site analysis over recent years. However, while these modern technological developments can improve the visual presentation of a site, they do not lessen the need for precise manual recording, which can then be entered into an archaeological recording system (database), such as ARK (Eve & Hunt In press).

ARTEFACT RECOVERY AND LIFTING IN THE FIELD

Each artefact/ecofact class brings its own problems. Some standard practices are outlined below.

Filling Out of Labels for Finds Bags

Special finds, those found *in situ*, **must** have their position accurately plotted in three-dimensions on the plans and carefully recorded on the **Special Finds Recording Form: Sheet 9**. If there is a specialist finds processor on site, they should assist in the recording process. While special or fragile finds are usually lifted in the field by one of the means listed below, general bulk finds (those found *ex situ*) are usually collected by hand. Each type of bulk material - pottery, shell, bone, building material, glass, etc - should be separately bagged by context (or lot if being used). This not only facilitates speedier processing but also ensures that the more fragile bulk materials are not crushed by the

97

heavier, i.e. brick and tile (Grey 2006).

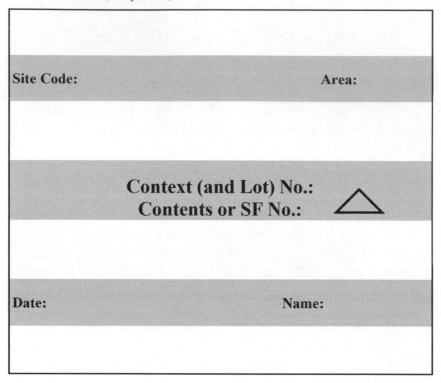

Figure 26: A sample of a finds bag label.

Robust finds should initially be placed in plastic bags, either zip-seal or normal closed with a single staple. These bags should be pierced to allow moisture held within the objects to escape into the atmosphere and prevent them from going mouldy. Some objects should be double bagged to ensure that the objects are not lost (see **Tab. 47**). These bags can then be boxed by object type within, and then sub-divided into contexts. Fragile or unstable finds should be stored in individual plastic or cardboard containers. Certain categories of finds (such as metal) should be placed in a box with silica gel to extract the moisture. Other finds may need to be kept damp, and these should be kept in wet boxes until the conservator is ready to treat them. A special water tank may need to be constructed for immersion of large pieces of waterlogged timber. Caution must be exercised regarding chemical additives in storage contexts, as gasoline paraffin used to stabilise charcoal can affect tree ring counts for dendrochronology, while fungicide used to stabilise organic remains can affect the object's suitability for ^{14}C dating (Roskams 2001: 226). The main aim of storing finds in containers is to keep them safe from crushing, in a stable condition and ensure that their provenience information stays with them until they go through finds processing.

It is vitally important that – no matter what type of find is recovered - its provenience information is kept with it. It is important to fill out the finds bags labels clearly, stating exactly where the artefacts or ecofacts were found, and what they are believed to be. In the larger bags place two Tyvek labels with their provenience information written in indelible ink, one placed loose inside the bag and the other stapled inside at the top of the bag (Grey 2006; see **Chapter 11**). Smaller bags only require one label, placed so that the information can be read. This allows the bags to be reused, rather than writing on the outside of the actual bag. The information required on the label includes: the site code, the excavation unit number, the context number (and lot if being used), the type of object(s), special finds number, the date, and the initials of excavator (**Fig. 26**). Ecological samples such as sediments may also be bagged in plastic bags; these again must be clearly labelled. Sample numbers are written in a diamond, and special finds numbers written in a triangle. When a context (or lot) has been fully excavated, all finds bags pertaining to it must be entered on the back of the context form in the relevant fields. The bags should then be given to the finds processor for entry in the unit and site inventories, **sheets 43** and **44**.

Lifting in the Field

Although lifting objects in the field is ideally done by a conservator, it can be done by the archaeologist if one is not available. The basic principle of lifting is to fully support the object being lifted, ensuring equilibrium between the internal and external pressure of the object, as laid out in the following guidelines. You must always remember to:

1. Establish the extent and depth of the deposit *before* clearing around the object or excavating down.

2. Always ensure that the upright sides of a soil block are *completely vertical*, properly wrapped (see diagrams) and supported before undercutting and sliding a rigid support underneath.

3. Protect the top of the object, preferably with some more sedimentary matrix followed by some padding acting as a separating layer (such as acid-free tissue [which must be crumpled up and stretched out before use otherwise it tears], cling-film or aluminium foil).

4. Keep the lifting supplies all in one place/box so they are always to hand when needed.

Basic Lifting Supplies

The basic equipment required for lifting objects in the field includes:

Flat steel baking trays to act as rigid supports for sliding underneath blocks.

Woven gauze bandage of various widths. This should be non-stretch, although elasticised bandage can be used if not stretched tightly over the objects.

Plaster of Paris or gypsum, to be mixed into a slurry with water and applied to the bandage. Gypsona, bandage already impregnated with Plaster of Paris, is a quick, easy-to-use alternative.

Mixing bowls and cups. Rubber mixing bowls are especially useful for Plaster of Paris, as they are easy to clean.

An ordinary kitchen knife for undercutting sediment blocks before sliding in the rigid support. Trays and cardboard boxes, safety pins, bamboo skewers, soft sable brushes and flat ended metal plaster's tools in various sizes are all required for cutting and lifting blocks.

Aluminium foil, cling-film, acid-free tissue paper, webbing (for large objects), polyether or polythene foam, terylene cord, pallets, scissors, tape measure and a torch.

Methods of Lifting Archaeological Objects in the Field

1. *Lifting on a Pallet*: This method can be used for both small and large objects which possess little intrinsic strength, such as crumbly bone, waterlogged wood or leather. First the object is slightly pedestalled (keeping waterlogged objects wet), it is then gently undercut using a knife or palette knife, packing the trench with acid-free tissue paper for support. Once a quarter of the object has been undercut, the rigid support (tray or pallet) is slid underneath; the rest of the block is then undercut and the tray pushed underneath until the whole of the object is on the tray. The object should then be secured to the tray with inert ties (with wet polyether foam between them and the waterlogged object), cling-film or polythene sheeting, and tagged with a provenience label.

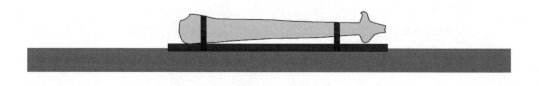

Figure 27: Lifting on a pallet or tray.

2. *Lifting Using Aluminium Foil*: This method is used for lifting fragile or fragmented skeletal material that requires a medium amount of support. The edges of the exposed bone are followed by gently removing the sedimentary matrix, making sure that the periosteal layer (outer layer of the bone) is not damaged. The matrix below the bone must be undercut to allow a strip of heavy-duty aluminium foil to be placed around it. This strip should be about 5 cm wide and four to six times as long as the diameter of the bone. If wrapping a skull, then the foil should be about 15 cm wide. The two ends of the foil strip are gently pulled (making sure not to disturb the bone) and then folded together, making several revolutions until that segment of the long bone is wrapped more or less tightly. Additional aluminium foil is placed beneath the bone for support. The entire process is repeated until the whole bone is wrapped in 5 cm wide segments of aluminium foil, overlapped to provide constant support and protection. When the entire bone is wrapped in two or three layers of foil, lift it, and place it in a container filled with fine sand or padding. The bone can be lifted with the help of another person from its two ends with the other person holding the middle part of the bone for support. It is very important to attach a label with the grave number, provenience data, date, and initials of excavator written on it, and the identity/side of the bone should be written on the aluminium foil. Robust skulls can also be lifted in this manner, covering it with two layers of foil before carefully lifting it and placing it in a container filled with sand or polyether foam. Once excavated, do not leave the sediment inside the skull; carefully remove it as the differential drying rates of the bone and sediment may cause the skull bones to fracture.

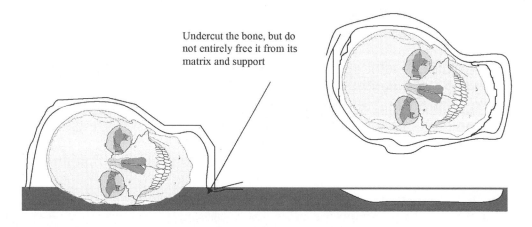

Undercut the bone, but do not entirely free it from its matrix and support

Figure 28: Lifting using aluminium foil.

3. *Lifting Using Dry Bandage*: This method is particularly useful for intact or nearly intact ceramic or stone vessels which - due to having hairline or actual cracking - cannot be lifted without support. Crepe or gauze bandage is wrapped around the vessel, overlapping the bandage first in one direction then the other. If full, the contents of the pot must **not** be removed; if the pot is empty, it must be stabilised by filling it with sand or finds bags filled with air. The wrapping process proceeds as the pot is exposed from its matrix in the course of excavation, the vessel must **not** be pedestalled or have a trough dug around it. The completion of the vessel's bandaging is therefore achieved only when the whole vessel is free of its matrix. Cling-film can be added beneath the bandage as a release agent.

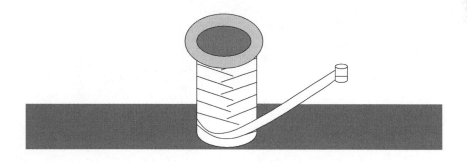

Figure 29: Lifting with a dry bandage.

4. *Block lifting Method Using a Box for Support*: This method of lifting is ideal for small, single objects held within a cohesive matrix. On uncovering the surface of the object, a box-shaped block of the matrix is left around it, with sufficient sediment to protect the object during lifting. The box should be placed over the block of sediment. The block should then be gently undercut using a knife, and a tray slid underneath the block to support it. String or cling film can be added around the box and tray to prevent slipping whilst transferring it to the conservation laboratory.

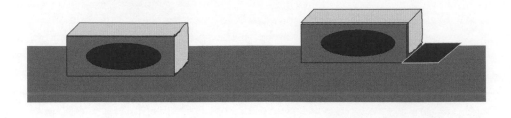

Figure 30: Lifting using a box for support.

5. *Block Lifting Using Plaster Bandage*: This is a slightly more complicated lifting process, but one that is extremely effective for lifting single objects, complex objects and small assemblages. It may be the only option for extremely fragile and/or important objects, and it is regularly used in palaeontology. On uncovering the surface of the object, a block of the matrix is left around it, sufficient to protect the object during lifting. A release agent is placed over this block of sediment, such as cling-film and/or aluminium foil. The gauze bandage is wrapped around this, having been first dipped in Plaster of Paris (Gypsona can also be used). This method can also be used without the sediment. In both methods, a tray is slid underneath to support the block after the plaster has set.

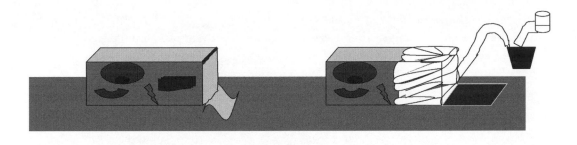

Figure 31: Block lifting using plaster and bandage.

Other methods include block lifting using a plaster collar and caps, polyurethane foam, and the use of consolidants and facing material. The latter method is usually used for mosaics and wall paintings, the former two for larger objects. However, these methods are best left to a qualified conservator, for if they are not carried out with the utmost skill and care, they are liable to cause more harm than good (see Watkinson & Neal 1998). When lifting large statues or stone blocks, employ a winch (such as used for lifting car engines) in conjunction with appropriate basket slings and blankets wrapped around the object for protection.

SPECIAL METHODOLOGICAL PROBLEMS

It might be said that while there is no overall right way to excavate, there are many wrong ways to excavate. Certain features and situations require particular methods of excavation. The following is a guide on excavating some of the most common or potentially problematic features that may be encountered. While these are based upon Egyptian sites, they also have applicability elsewhere. Many of the features need to be carefully 'dissected' so as to obtain both a horizontal and vertical profile. The method chosen should be flexible enough to cope with the unexpected, whilst maximising the amount of data retrieved. Most people lived on surfaces, not on walls, down pits, or post-holes and trenches, but it is important to ascertain when these features were first dug, their size, shape and what happened to them during their life-history.

1. Hearths: Hearths commonly produce artefactual or environmental evidence, and are particularly important on prehistoric sites where they stand as foci for activities such as flint knapping or bone carving. Hearths often have evidence of several burning episodes (reuse) indicated by vitrified sediment interspaced with non-vitrified sediment. On Neolithic or later sites, charred grain is likely to have fallen on the fire during cooking activities, while remains of food and other domestic refuse will often be preserved around the edge. Therefore, this entire area must be very carefully excavated.

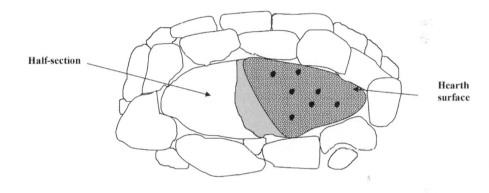

Figure 32: Excavating a hearth.

Once the hearth has been fully exposed, drawn and photographed, the sedimentary matrix and wider area around the hearth must be investigated for human activity. The hearth will probably be composed of a ring of stones around the actual area where the fire was; these stones may display fire cracks. The area within the hearth may contain charcoal, which is useful for carbon dating purposes and must be sampled, after which the remaining fill must be bulk sampled and dry sieved or flotated. To understand the construction of the hearth it should be half-sectioned (see below), remembering to follow the natural layers and keeping all the spoil for sampling purposes.

2. Pits: Pits are defined as any hole cut from the living surface, and may serve as ovens, grain silos (and other storage pits), quarry pits, cesspits, artefact caches, refuse dumps or for ritual purposes. They are extremely important archaeologically as they may contain a great deal of socioeconomic information, and must be dug with care. It is important to establish the layer from which the pit was first dug, its size and shape, if it has any lining, the sequence of events of its construction and eventual filling and how it relates to other features on the site. Once the top of the pit has been defined, it is best to half-section the pit, marking the line with two nails and a piece of string. The half-section should be aligned to the cardinal points, and the direction of the sun should be taken into account for photographic purposes. One half of the pit should then be excavated following the natural layers of its fill, taking note of the direction of the tip lines. Arbitrary spits should only be used if no clear layers are visible. Each layer must be given a separate context number, as must the cut of the pit itself. There are problems with preservation of pits owing to instability of the cut, fills or both. For instance, the top edges of a pit may be squeezed over because of pressure from above, or the edges may be eroded. The top fills of pits often consist of loose material derived from sunken pit fill. There may be a thin dark-brown crust outlining the pit. This is dubbed the 'iron-pan effect', caused through precipitation of iron compounds from water percolated through organic material (e.g. matting that once lined the pit). Sometimes pits are cut through many layers of earlier material. In instances where no clear pit cut can be discerned the only indication may be later material mixed with the bulk of earlier material.

Procedure for Pit Excavation and Interpretation: The pit must be half-sectioned, the outline discerned, the layers excavated in one half of the pit, the section drawn and photographed, the written record correlated with the vertical view, and photographs taken. If two inter-cutting pits are encountered, the half-section line should dissect both of them; both pits need to be defined in the horizontal plan so that their relationships can be calculated. Remember that the objects found in a pit do not date the pit's initial creation; the action of pit filling postdates the pit creation but can be with earlier sediment, and may provide information on general activities onsite rather than those pertaining to the pit itself. Pits are best dated by objects found in sealed deposits above and below them. As pits often promote good preservation, it is usually worthwhile to sieve/analyse the pit's contents to retrieve organic remains.

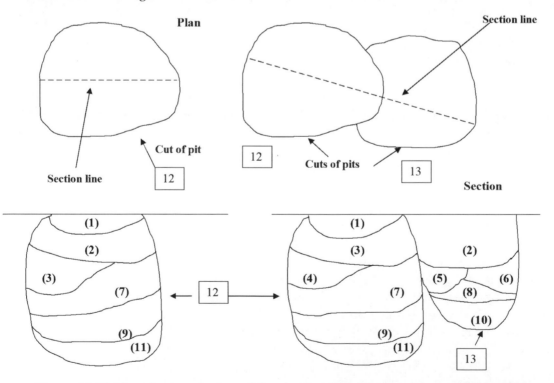

Figure 33: Half-sectioning single and intercutting pits. The layers' contexts should be written inside circles or brackets (after Drewett 1999: 110).

104

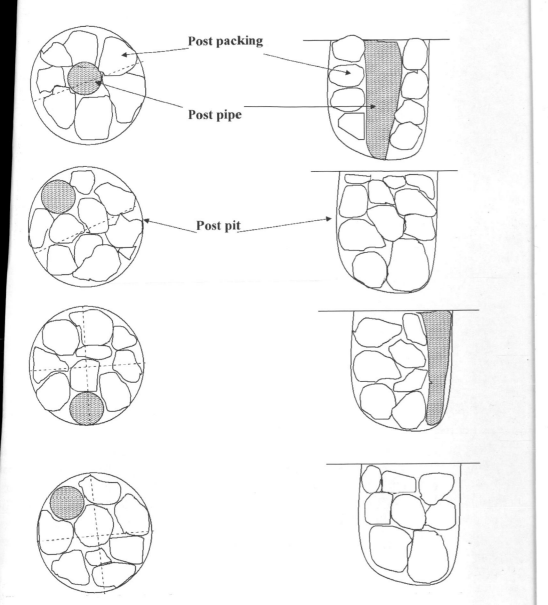

Figure 37: The plan and section of a post-hole, and the problems involved in half-[section]ioning and quadranting. It the post-pipe is located in certain areas quadranting may [los]s it, although an erosion cone may be visible even if the pipe has disintegrated (after Drewett 1999: 112)

[M]ounds and Tumuli: The usual method of excavating raised circular features, such as [mou]nds and tumuli, is to use the quadrant excavation plan. The mound is divided up into [four] sections with a staggered 1 m baulk in between. Each of the four sections is then [exca]vated sequentially in an alternating manner. The baulks provide a complete transverse [strat]igraphic section across the mound. The baulks are left standing until eventually being [rem]oved to reveal the contexts and features within and beneath them. If a burial, it is [likel]y to be in the centre of the mound. If the burial has been positively located, a rectangle [sho]uld be left around it, and this should only be excavated after all the other quadrants

If a pit-fill contains clear stratigraphic layers, it may be excavated by sequentially removing the layers in their totality, thereby not leaving an upstanding section. The advantage of this method is that the whole surface of each context may be seen at once. Special attention should be paid to the sides and bottom of the pit, as these may give indications of the pit's original use. This gives a clearer view of the activities and processes that went into the construction and filling of the pit.

3. Ditches: Ditches vary enormously in terms of size, form and function, and may include defence, irrigation, boundary demarcation or ritual behaviour. Ditches can have square, curved or V-shaped bottoms, all of which can be indicative of its date and cultural associations. Their linear form presents various problems to the archaeologist, for a single cross-section across the ditch will only provide data on size, shape and sequence of events in that particular area. If the ditch is small, however, it can be sectioned length-wise and in a series of full transverse sections, therefore enabling a series of cumulative section drawings to be taken across the length and width.

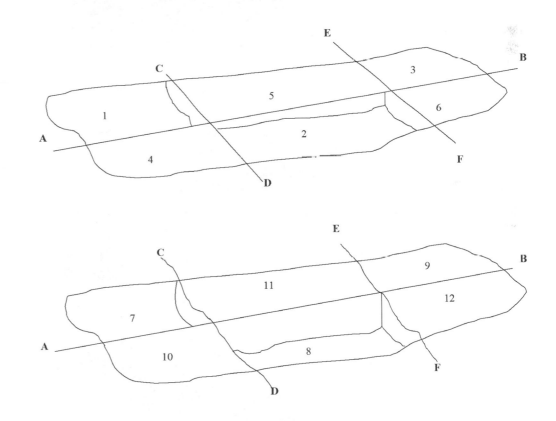

Figure 34: Cumulative sections are drawn, 1 longitudinal and 2 transverse, the sections are removed sequentially, and then the relevant sections drawn (after Barker 1993: 93).

Large defensive ditches and earthworks are usually investigated by a series of trenches cut at right angles through them (see **Fig. 36**), for while it is preferable to fully excavate defensive ditches in the horizontal plan it is a very time-consuming method. Once the profile of the ditch (and earthwork system) has been revealed, it may be possible to

excavate some of the ditch system with plant equipment (as long as sensitive areas, such as gate networks, are avoided). If a mechanical digger is used, the spoil should be screened. Although any artefacts thus found will probably postdate the ditches creation, they will provide at least some information about the ditch's life history. Ditches, like pits, are best dated by the sealed layers above and below them.

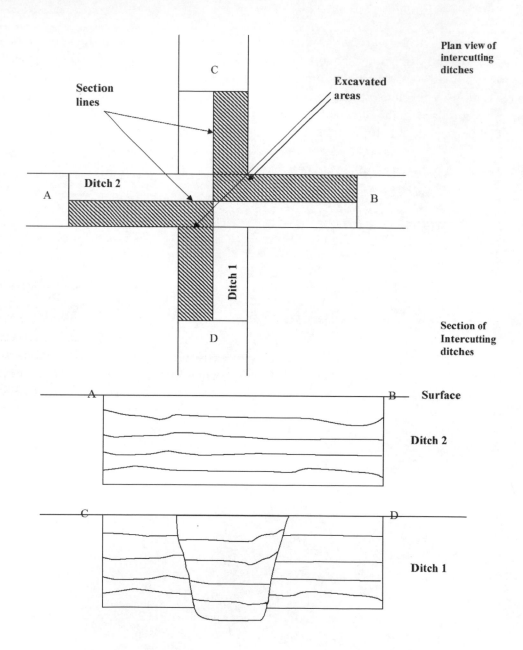

Figure 35: Box-sectioning intercutting ditches (after Drewett 1999: 115).

If addressing a series of intercutting ditches, it may be impossible to assess the digging sequence from the plan view. It may therefore be better to box-section the ditches and analyse their profiles. This involves placing sections across both ditches, as shown in **Fig. 35**.

106

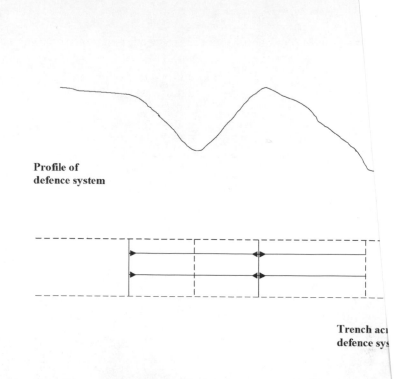

Figure 36: Trenching defensive earthworks.

4. Post-holes: A post-hole consists of the post pit and the post p[...] pit dug to hold the post and its packing material, while the post pi[...] where the post once stood (and may, in some circumstances, be pres[...] normally detectable on the basis of colour and texture diff[...] surrounding matrix. Once discovered, the surrounding area should [...] scraped (with a mattock or *fas*) to establish whether there are any as[...] the post-hole is part of a larger feature, all the elements should be pl[...] and recorded in writing before being individually excavated. If the [...] plan, place a half-section through the post-pipe and packing to the [...] across the diameter of post-hole. The post-hole should then be [...] Excavate the post-pipe fill first and keep the finds and material separ[...] the post packing. Once the post-hole is half-sectioned it must then b[...] written and photographed), before the other half is excavated. If no po[...] in plan, then the post-hole can either be quadranted or excavated in pla[...] reconstructed from the series of plans made at every 5 cm. See **Figure 37**[...]

The dating of post-holes is best done by the layer from which they w[...] for this will give a *terminus post quem*, while the layer directly above w[...] *ante quem*. This is because the objects found in the packing material [...] earlier layer than that which the post-hole was dug into. Materials in [...] only provide a *terminus ante quem* if the original post was pulled out, wh[...] latest object will give a *terminus ante quem* for the removal of the post (Dre[...]

108

have been completed. If there are no artefacts or useful stratigraphic evidence in the first two quadrants to be excavated, it may be appropriate to excavate the central rectangle and leave the other two quadrants unexcavated.

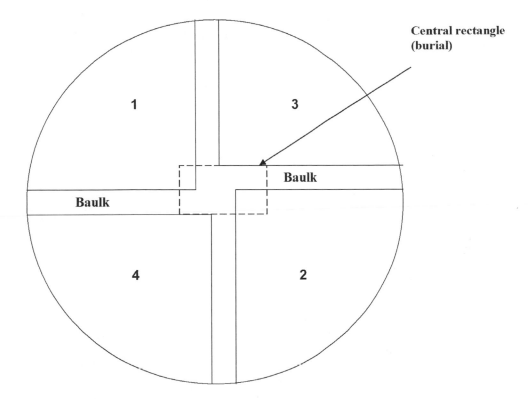

Figure 38: The quadrant excavation plan. The quadrants should be sequentially excavated in the numerical order shown (after Joukowsky 1980: 146).

6. Walls, Foundation and Robbers Trenches: There is a suite of methods designed for recording standing structures (Hutton 1986; Smith 1985). Some of these can be applied to more traditional archaeological contexts below the surface, such as largely standing buildings, grave or pit linings, in horizontal layers (i.e. a floor) or irregularly heaped. Owing to humankind's rapacial appetite for building materials, masonry walls may only be represented by foundation or robber trenches (see below). Walls are usually either built on bedrock, have footings set in a foundation trench or on a platform. The foundation trench can either be dug the width of the footings and the footings lowered into the trench from above, or the foundation trench is dug about two metres wider (1 metre each side) than the footings, to accommodate the workers laying the footings. The remainder of the trench is then backfilled. Any objects found in the trench, unless it has been robbed, are likely to be older than the wall itself as they probably pertain to the levels the trench was dug into, although contemporary and may also have fallen in the trench. It is important, as with all other pits and trenches, to establish the layer from which the foundation trench was dug, as this will give you the earliest date for the laying of the foundation. Although it is often tempting to follow the walls by excavating alongside them, this must be resisted as it will destroy relationships between the walls and any accompanying floor levels. Once detected, walls should be cleaned with a stiff brush, and a plan made once the outline has been uncovered. An excavation grid should then be laid out to reflect the building's groundplan, and this should be tied into the main site grid. Each room should be treated as a distinct archaeological entity, and excavated separately. If the contexts are clear, each room should be excavated in the horizontal plan. However, if the contexts are indistinct, then a 1.0 m wide trench should be dug at a right-angle to the wall, cutting right through the flooring layers and foundation trench (see **Fig. 39**). This will illuminate the relationship of the walls to the floors, the stratigraphic sequence, the construction of the foundation trench and the building/re-building phases. The point where walls meet is a good location to determine the construction sequence, for if one wall abuts another with a straight join, it will usually suggest different periods of construction. This can be confirmed if there is a difference in building material, mortar and depth of foundation trench. The use of underpinning and rebuilds means that the stratigraphic relationships of walls often mean that they have to be worked out or amended in the process of excavation.

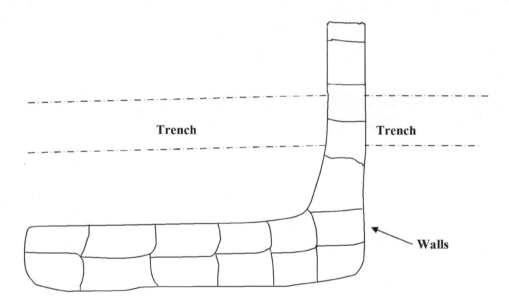

Figure 39: Placing a trench across a wall (after Joukowsky 1980: 181).

Sometimes walls can only be traced by the presence of robber trenches, which may contain lumps of plaster, mortar and unwanted or missed stones. The robber trenches were often left open to fill with rubbish and other debris, the contents of the fill may then enable you to ascertain the date at which the robber trench was dug. Care must be taken when excavating the robber trench to establish its relationship to the original foundation trench; robber trenches usually follow the actual width of the original wall or are slightly wider (see **Fig. 40).** Consequently, robber acts are often 'ghost' contexts and can only be inferred by the presence of robber fill.

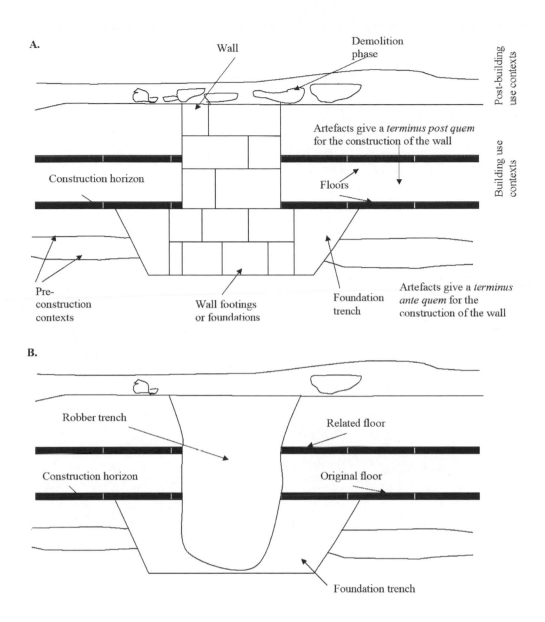

A.

Wall

Demolition phase

Post-building use contexts

Artefacts give a *terminus post quem* for the construction of the wall

Construction horizon

Building use contexts

Floors

Pre-construction contexts

Wall footings or foundations

Foundation trench

Artefacts give a *terminus ante quem* for the construction of the wall

B.

Robber trench

Related floor

Construction horizon

Original floor

Foundation trench

Figure 40: Excavating walls and robber trenches (after Drewett 1999:116 & Webster 1974: 95).

7. Floors: Floors can be of hard packed beaten earth, and may be covered with plaster, or consist of lime-based mortar, tesserae (mosaic), stone slabs or tiles, and are usually associated with walls. It is very important that construction techniques and physical relationships with surrounding features are ascertained before excavation continues to the next context. Floors were often re-laid, and may therefore consist of multiple layers associated with the same building phase. It is therefore important to assess how the floors connect with the walls. Floors were usually living surfaces, and as such debris from human or animal activity accumulated on these surfaces, leaving observable traces in the archaeological record. Floors are sometimes hard to detect with the naked eye and need techniques such as soil micromorphology to understand their nature (Goldberg &

111

Macphail 2006: 244-6). Each floor layer and the artefacts embedded therein must be individually recorded using the photographic, drawn and written media. Once recorded, the actual floor should be excavated removing the upper floor level so that earlier floor levels are revealed. All the flooring material and associated debris should be peeled off then sieved or flotated. Samples must be taken for geoarchaeological analysis so that the various floor layers and activities conducted on them can be ascertained (Goldberg & Macphail 2006: 247-67). If it is possible to distinguish between occupational debris and the floor itself, they should be flotated separately and given separate context numbers. The stratigraphic sequence and relationships of the floor layers with the building and re-building phases should have been revealed in the baulks of the trench, and this will aid in the excavation of the floors themselves. Artefacts found on the surface of the floor will give a *terminus ante quem* for the laying of the floor, whereas material found in or under the floor will give a *terminus post quem*. However, beaten earth floor deposits are characterised by trampled in layers varying in thickness from 200 μm to 1 mm, which although not representing different floor laying episodes, may represent trampling in from different environments (Goldberg & Macphail 2006: 246). Bulk analysis of these trampling episodes will average out these various episodes and the best results come from micromorphological analysis, such as thin section studies of the floor deposits.

Floor Type	Characteristics
Stable Floors	Typically homogeneous, where high concentrations of organic matter, phosphate, and pollen grains may be preserved. Plant remains are often preserved in layered fragments, which may be cemented or stained by phosphate. The pollen may be highly anomalous with the surrounding area. Fragments of animal dung, insect worked dung, grass and cereal stems may all be present in the deposit.
Domestic Floors	Typically heterogeneous and comparatively mineralogenic, massive structured, and contain abundant anthropogenic and allocthonous inclusions, including burned sediment, charcoal and ash. Plant fragments are less common, although may exist in layers of mat remains or charred food waste. A few pollen spores may exist, including diverse weed assemblages that reflect settlement flora. Dung, earthworm granules, and human coprolites can be trafficked in from outside. Metal slag, leather, and other substances can be trampled in from the industrial areas.

Table 15: Deposits likely to be encountered in archaeological floor deposits (after Goldberg & Macphail 2006: 264).

6. *Tells and Settlements*: *Tells* (or *koms* in colloquial Egyptian Arabic) are the long-term effect of repeated human occupation on a single site, with composite occupation strata, destruction levels and some naturally-deposited sediment. *Tells* occur from Hungary and Greece, through the Levant, North Africa, to Iran and Central Asia as well as the Americas. They are extremely complex, with multiple (partly) superimposed settlement phases, partial or complete levelling of previous structures, pit-digging through older layers and irregular rebuilding phases over some or all the mound surface, which becomes smaller as

the *tell* gets taller. Mounds are mainly comprised of mud-brick (although stone structures are sometimes found), and are mixed in with redeposited fill, stratified settlement deposits and the debris of their own collapse and decay (Spencer 1994: 315). Fieldwalking is of mixed utility in the evaluation of *kom* sites, as studies have shown that surface collections of sherds on mound sites are significantly biased (<10/1) in favour of the later periods, as a result of stratigraphic replacement and the erosion of earlier materials (Miller-Rosen 1986: 52). It should be noted that this bias in favour of later periods is also true of off-mound sherd distribution. The under representation of the earlier periods and overrepresentation of the later periods can be slightly mitigated by scraping the surface by 50 mm to collect potsherds (Miller-Rosen 1986: 51), although the early sherds will only be expected if the level of the early occupations is less than 5.0 m from the surface (Miller-Rosen 1986: 51). To demonstrate, at Tell el-Fara'in in the West Nile Delta, the Neolithic layers are located at up to 10.0 metres below surface, and not a single Neolithic potsherd has been recovered during fieldwalking. Moreover, when it comes to interpreting site signature from disturbed contexts, such as ploughzones (where the top 0.30 m of archaeology is destroyed, by turning, mixing, breaking and spreading out of artefacts and contexts), certain biases must be borne in mind (Steinberg 1996). Those found in ploughed soil will only represent between 0.3% and 15% (usually about 5-6%) of the artefacts present at a site. The artefacts are also spread over a much wider area than the actual site itself (for more on the ploughzone paradox see Steinberg 1996: 368-75). Therefore, when conducting fieldwalking, it is essential that it is complemented by exploratory excavation techniques if the site is to be assessed for its archaeological potential, especially the site stratigraphy.

Mound Development: *Koms* will usually contain two main sediment types: those that form the matrix of the site (mud-brick wash and sediment), and those that form structural features (mud-brick, stone, and lime or gypsum plaster). Walls are not always constructed just from mud-bricks, but can be made from mud mortar bricks, mortared bricks, rammed earth, or clunch (hand paddled mud). Other elements include organic matter such as beams, thatch, other structural elements and cultural material, such as floors, storerooms, courtyards, streets, stock management areas, and latrines. To fully understand mound development, detailed sedimentological, chemical and botanical studies need to be made (Goldberg & Macphail 2006: 226-7; Miller-Rosen 1986). The mud-brick walls and structures if not maintained, or are abandoned will decay, erode and the debris can be redeposited as colluvium. The destruction of these buildings will be quickened by the effects of rainfall, rising groundwater, and reprecipitation of salts (Miller-Rosen 1986: 11). New occupation phases were often begun by levelling the old mound summit to produce a flat, stable surface on which to build their new settlement. This levelling was often accomplished by fully demolishing old buildings and dumping and spreading basket loads of sediment, followed by compaction of this surface (Goldberg & Macphail 2006: 232-3).

Mound Erosion: *Koms* are subject to biological, chemical and mechanical destruction, prompted by both human activity and the climate. The post-depositional erosion processes that affect the *kom*, and are responsible for the breaking down of the mud-brick material, can be divided into three main categories of variables: climate, structure and stage of evolution. These forces produce various patterns of mound erosion, which affect stratigraphic preservation. The upper levels of the mound are then smoothed over by erosion and redeposition. Those *koms* that have a large amount of stone structures will take longer to erode than those with predominantly mud-brick structures. The climate of the region will affect the form of the *kom*, especially water (rainfall, groundwater and humidity), which is the most destructive single element for mud-brick (Miller-Rosen 1986). Most slopes are affected by both slope decline and parallel retreat (backwearing), where the base of the mound lengthens as in parallel retreat, with some loss of height (downwearing) as the slope declines (Miller-Rosen 1986:27-37). The orientation of the mound is one of the biggest factors in determining the type of mound evolution; those slopes facing the direction of the rain will be affected more strongly than those that do not. *Kom* size can vary greatly, from 100 m to 1500+ m in length, and from 5 m to 30+ m in height, covering from 0.5 to 200 acres (average size is around 7-20 acres). The mounds in Egypt tend to be smaller than those in the Near East. However, in Egypt as most *koms* are located in the dynamic environment of the Delta, rapid wind and rain erosion tends to contour the mounds so the mud-brick walls are flush with ground level. It is therefore rare to discover large brick walls standing above the ground, as are found in the less turbulent environment of Upper Egypt (Spencer 1994: 318).

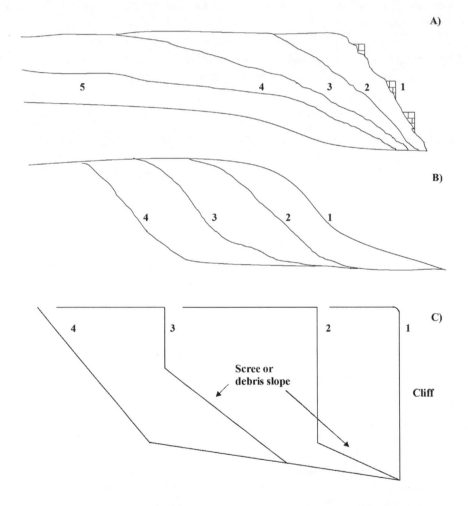

Figure 41: The three forms of slope erosion A) downwearing (slope decline, B) backwearing (parallel retreat and C) Slope replacement. 1 equals the first stages and 4 the latter stages of erosion (after Miller-Rosen 1986: 26).

Excavation methodology: The type of *kom* will dictate the type of sherd distribution, and

114

also the approach to excavation. The potsherds found on the different shelves of shelved *koms* will **generally** indicate the period of that layer of occupation. However, this cannot be said of sealed *koms* (Miller-Rosen 1986: 46).

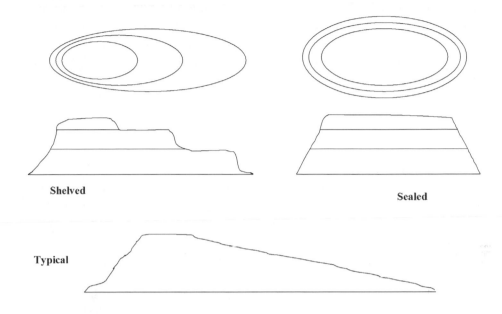

Figure 42: Typical Tell profiles (after Miller-Rosen 1986: 34, 47).

Sondages and trenches are of limited use when excavating a *kom*, as the settlement will have oscillated backwards and forwards across the area of the mound. Therefore, what you find in a single trench and area is very unlikely to be an accurate reflection of sedimentological or artefactual actualities elsewhere on the site. This is of course true of any site, but is particularly acute in the case of mounds where the sediments and the archaeology are essentially the same thing. Drill cores can be used to assess the general sedimentological, chemical and botanical compositions of the mound, as long as these considerations are borne in mind. *Koms* should always be recorded using single-context planning, as this will greatly aid the reading and interpretation of the complex stratigraphy. Where possible, the open-area approach should be used, although the leaving of some baulks may be preferential in certain circumstances; any and all devices must be used to accurately identify the varying construction methods, levelling of past structures, building of retaining walls, digging of foundation trenches, robbing of ancient building materials and pit/channel digging that collude to complicate *kom* stratigraphy. If the excavation is to be seasonal rather than continuous, a limited area should be opened, which can be easily completed in the time allotted (e.g. 50 m x 50 m). Although the different layers of occupation often intercut and truncate one another, each context should be stripped off separately. The single-context recording system elucidates cultural and natural processes and will perform well on *kom* sites and urban settlements, for which it was originally designed.

Mud-brick poses certain problems for the archaeologist, as it often merges with the surrounding matrix, itself usually comprised of mud-brick wash (sediment derived from disintegrated mud-brick). The situation is further complicated by *Sebakhin*, who crater sites in search of mud-brick (and mud-brick wash) to use for fertiliser or manufacture of new bricks. When excavating *tell* sites, mud-brick may only be distinguishable from the surrounding wash (also called mud flow) by the sound it makes when tapped with a trowel: the bricks make a sharper sound, than mud-brick wash as they are more compact. By careful excavation with a trowel, therefore, the difference can be easily felt and heard. Tools heavier than a *fas* should not be used, as the mud-bricks can easily be damaged. The different types of mud-brick bonding are shown in the mud-brick bonding corpus (**Fig. 93**). The brickwork should be carefully scraped to reveal the joins; having identified the brickwork, trowel along the joins rather than across them, to avoid blurring the features. The size of the bricks should gradually become apparent, thus making it easier to predict where the next joint should appear and thus target trowelling more effectively (Spencer 1994: 316). Once an area of brickwork has been identified, its area can be determined by working outwards to define its limits (Spencer 1994: 316). An area of brickwork that is difficult to define can sometimes be made clearer if allowed to dry out for a few days (Spencer 1994: 318). In areas of high salinity such as the Nile Delta, the clarity of the joints may sometimes be enhanced as the salt usually crystallizes along joint lines, thus making them easy to identify (Spencer 1994: 318). Ordinary mud-brick is greyish and sandy mud-bricks a pale yellow colour; these are comparatively easy to differentiate from the surrounding wash (Spencer 1994: 316). However, a lot of bricks destined for domestic architecture tended to be made from mud and soil with small bits of pottery and stone mixed in; identifying courses in this material is extremely difficult, as the joins do not show up well (Spencer 1994: 316). The edges of brickwork made from better-made mud and sandy mud-bricks are often delineated by an accumulation of potsherds and stones that have gathered along the face, forming a linear pattern (Spencer 1994: 317).

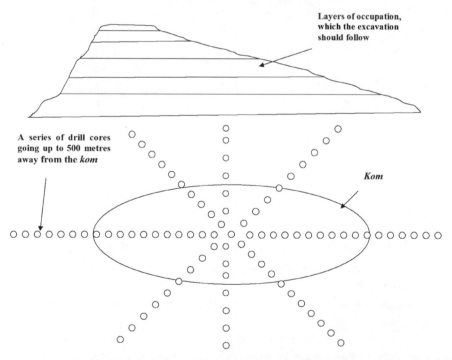

Figure 43: *Kom* excavation approaches A) Showing the different layers of excavation and B) on-*kom* and off-*kom* sampling strategies.

Context	Prepared or Unprepared surface	Accumulated Deposits	Postdepositional Modifications
Roofed Structures			
Food preparation	Loam covered surfaces	Discrete strong parallel orientated lenses of organo-mineral deposits, often with grindstone fragments; vegetal pseudomorphs and siliceous graminae plant fragments	Organic staining, bioturbation and salt formation immediately below surface
Food cooking adjacent to hearths and ovens	Plastered and compacted surfaces	Multiple layers of moderate parallel orientated loam with organo-mineral matter, burnt fuel, hearth fragments, bone, flint fragments, charred grain, tubers, phytoliths.	Sub-horizontal cracking in plastered floors, bioturbation, salts, organic staining
Storage in small rooms or silos	Clayey plaster with organic matter inclusions, lime plaster	Charred cereal grain often mixed within building debris	Bioturbation
Reception and 'clean' activities	Well made and finished plasters often with matting impressions	Thin lenses of charred and siliceous plant material, sterile silty clay with strong parallel orientation	Horizontal cracks and organic staining
Rituals associated with alters, sculptures and wall-paintings	Multiple, often fine plaster layers, occasionally painted matting impressions	Burnt remains, waterlain crusts, red or yellow ochre remains	Organic staining, bioturbation and salts
Probably Roofed			
Stables	Undulating surface, very few prepared	Interbedded lenses of dung fragments	Organic staining, bioturbation and salts
Unroofed			
Domestic courtyards and streets	A few pieces of plaster, aggregate hard core surfaces, bitumen pathways	Layers or unorientated deposits with cultural references, reworked and undisturbed wind- and water-lain deposits, dung, loose refuse deposits	Bioturbation, salts, wind and water reworking
Civic, administrative, and ritual courtyards	Mud-brick foundations, lime plastered surfaces, few unprepared surfaces	Mineral rich deposits with some burnt and cultural refuse, thin layers of ash	Bioturbation, salts, wind and water reworking
Middens	Few prepared surfaces, unprepared surfaces with many depositional episodes, *in situ* burning	Unorientated massive deposits, some wind and water laid deposits and *in situ* burning	Bioturbation, settling and compaction, organic staining

Table 16: Micromorphological and macromorphological attributes found on tell sites (Goldberg & Macphail 2006:213).

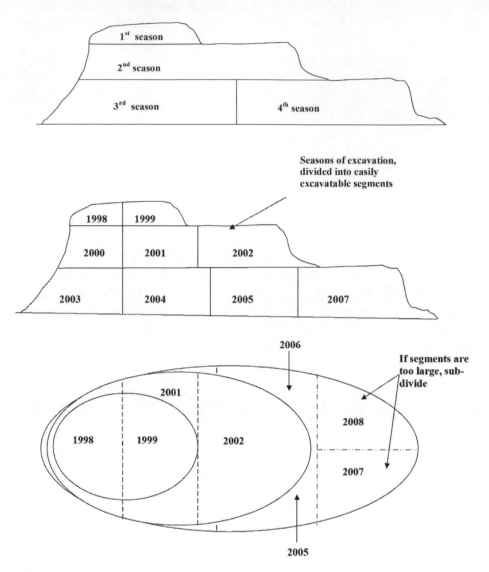

Figure 44: Seasonal excavation of a *kom*, showing the segments of the *kom* that should be excavated each season.

When excavating a *kom* or settlement, the debris layers **must** always be removed first; these are essentially equivalent to the overburden on a flat-land site. Once cleared, you can assess the underlying layers, and begin to understand the various building phases (Dever & Darrel Lance 1978: 152). The friable nature of mud-brick can pose further problems once the overburden has been cleared. For instance, wind, wind-blown dust and salt crystallisation may erode the bases of mud-brick walls, making the walls retreat backwards rather than downwards (Spencer 1994: 315). Therefore, it is sometimes necessary to make a small test pit down to the foundations so as to confirm the walls' original extent. Confusion may occur when attempting to differentiate *in situ* wall remains from fallen fragments; in this instance, observe the orientation and regularity of the bricks and their bonding (Spencer 1994: 317). Discontinuities in brickwork may also indicate other architectural characteristics: doorways can often only be detected from of the lack of proper brickwork articulation, the bricks that have fallen into the doorway, and also the continuous joint lines on each side of the door (Spencer 1994: 317). Once the architectural remains in a specific stratum have been fully excavated and recorded, they must be dismantled to commence excavation of the next stratum Always avoid excavating segments out of the *tell* down to the natural stratum in the form of cake-slices, as this makes it impossible to understand the full extent of the various contexts, and as a result lacunae are likely to be embodied in the spatial record.

Settlement deposits exhibit certain traits that can elucidate their depositional history and socio-cultural activities that helped produce them. Well-sorted water-laid crusts may indicate unroofed areas of a settlement such as streets and abandoned buildings or areas. Dumping episodes can be observed through thick layers with unorientated, randomly sorted sediment particles. These episodes can be observed in middens dumped into abandoned houses, back-filing of graves, defensive earthworks, or landscaping of gardens (Goldberg & Macphail 2006: 221).

It is very easy to become somewhat insular in one's approach to a *tell* site: but it should be remembered that it is only part of the archaeological landscape, and that social activities were also carried out beyond the topographic limits of the actual mound. On-mound excavations must therefore be accompanied by a strategy of off-mound survey by magnetometry, resistivity and drill coring. Excavation may also be appropriate, based on the results derived from these survey techniques.

9. Burials, Graves, Tombs and Cemeteries: Mortuary archaeology deals not only with the detailed analysis of human remains (a domain usually referred to as bioarchaeology, osteoarchaeology physical anthropology) but also with the study of grave or tomb architecture, decoration, grave good placement and assemblage, body orientation, burial type and the spatial and temporal placement of graves within the cemetery. All of these factors provide valuable information about ritual practice, continuation of traditions and customs, sequence dating, ideology, technology, economy, attitudes to death (i.e. separation from the living, or buried under/near residential areas) and much else. This is an ultra-specialised area of research, and cannot be fully summarised here. However, the interested reader is advised to more fully investigate this field (see Aufderheide 2003; Bass 2005; Brothwell 1981; Buikstra *et al.* 1994; Hillson 1986; 1996; Larsen 1997; Mays 1998; Parker-Pearson 1999; Waldron 2001; White 1991; White & Folkens 2005, etc).

There are numerous types of graves and tombs, as well as burial practices, and excavation methods must be highly flexible in order to adapt to all circumstances. That said, graves and tombs should be treated in much the same way as any other context in that they involve the process of preparation (be it digging a grave or building a pyramid) and deposition (of the body, associated artefacts and fills). As with any other feature, this sequence of actions may take place over a period of one day or many years, while secondary use (i.e. later re-use of the tomb) may also occur to confuse the archaeological sequence. All graves and tombs consist of movable (grave goods; the interment itself) and immovable (tomb structure and decoration) elements. Once excavated, the recording of these different elements involves various specialist measuring, drawing and photographic techniques.

Grave Type Definitions: A grave is a pit dug in the ground, sometimes with a simple lining, whereas a tomb is an (large) artificial monument, often with an elaborate superstructure. Both will contain the body, wrappings, receptacles and grave goods; all of these elements should be regarded as equally important, and should be given due regard in terms of recording and publishing. Tombs and graves usually consist of two major elements: the superstructure (the often ornate above-ground section) and the substructure (the plainer, sub-surface section). This architectural division is functional as well as aesthetic. As well as territorially marking the landscape, the accessible superstructure may be repeatedly used for offerings and other mortuary practices, whereas the substructure is generally inaccessible except for instances where the tomb is to be repeatedly used (such as a family vault).

Burial Position: Burials are either primary – where the articulated skeleton reflects the bodies' original position – or secondary, where the bones are reburied after the decomposition of the flesh (this includes cremations). Primary burials come in a vast number of combinations, burial positions and interment styles, some of which are summarised below. Secondary burials are also variable, and may be reburied in a jar, a coffin, or some other container either individually or collectively.

Extended	Legs and spine are in a straight line. Legs together.
Flexed	Usually lying on either the left or right side. Legs are bent up towards the chin; tightly flexed more than 90°, semi-flexed less than 90°
Crouched	Sitting upright with legs bent up to the chin. Hands position variable.
Supine	Lying face-up, resting on the back
Prone	Face down or resting on the side
Kneeling	Sitting upright with legs bent under body. Hands position variable.
Standing	Standing upright with legs straight. Hands position variable.

Table 17A: Burial Positions.

Simple pit graves	Reed-lined pit graves
Graves covered by a tumulus or barrow (mound)	Mud-lined graves, rectangular
Mud-brick lined graves	Chambered graves
Mastabas (tombs)	Rock-cut tombs
Stone & brick built tombs (& mortuary temples)	Shaft-tombs
Pyramid complexes	Boulder tombs e.g. cist graves
Ossuary	Tholos
Mausoleum	Rock-shelter or cave tomb

Table 17B. The Major Grave and Tomb Types Include.

Mummy wrappings	Hide	Own clothes
Shroud (linen)	Reeds	Funerary suite (e.g. jade)

Table 17C: Coverings.

Sarcophagus (stone)	Coffin – oval or round (pottery)
Coffin - rectangular (wooden)	Reed basket
Coffin – anthropoid (wooden, ceramic or metal)	Jar (pithos), urn (cremation)
Coffin – slipper (anthropoid or plain ceramic)	Cartonnage (linen or papyrus with plaster)

Table 17D. Major Receptacles.

Once a tomb or grave has been discovered, it is important to determine its full extent and the layer from which it was dug (or relates to) before excavating it, carefully noting the stratigraphic sequence. Tombs/graves and their contents must **never** be pedestalled, as this will accelerate their deterioration and obliterate the shape of the grave. Neither must any of the bones or grave goods be prised out, as this may damage the objects and obscure their true relationships and provenience. In essence, graves should be treated much as any other pit, ensuring that you have established the layer from which it was dug. If felt to be necessary, the grave can be half-sectioned to assess its profile. However, it is preferable not to do this, and instead to carefully excavate the whole outline of grave. The shape and profile of the grave will help in working out its volume.

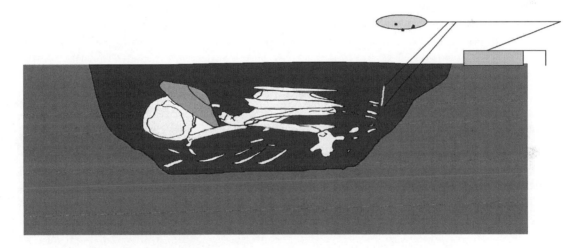

Figure 45: Excavating a simple pit burial.

For larger graves (and tombs), an individual excavation grid must be established over the feature, and be tied into the main site grid to guarantee greater horizontal and vertical control (see **Fig. 57** and **Fig. 58**). A simple twin axis grid (see **Fig. 55**) should be sufficient for a simple pit burial, whereas a local grid (**Fig. 56**) will need to be used for larger tombs, and a much larger excavation grid (such as the cardinal grid shown in **Fig. 6**) for monumental tombs. As well as recording the grave or tomb structure and the inhumation, it is essential to carry out exact three-dimensional recording of all grave goods. Special attention should be given to the recording of artefacts found on or near the body, as the position of durable artefacts often permits the reconstruction of elements that have deteriorated over time. For example, beads strung as jewellery (around wrists, ankles and neck) or on clothing (decoration), or even more unusual items such as headdresses, waistbands or belts (Hester *et al.* 1997: 266).

The first part of a grave or tomb to be discovered is usually the superstructure, be it a mound, a building or a pyramid. A pit burial requires careful recording of the collapsed mound capping the grave, which should be cleared away from the structure while following the contexts or layers. The superstructure should be examined with remote sensing equipment before excavation, then excavated and recorded much as any other standing structure, with elevation drawings, photographs and a detailed written description. If the superstructure is made of mud-brick over a pit, then it should be dismantled layer-by-layer, recording the position of each brick within the layer, and recording each of the layers with single-context planning. Once the superstructure has been fully removed, the substructure must be located and excavated. It is best to excavate mud- or sand-filled graves in 5 cm arbitrary spits, while mud-brick graves should be excavated by following the outline of the brick structure. In some cases, it may not be necessary to dismantle the superstructure, as there will be a clear route to reach the substructure without this added destructive work.

Tomb Considerations and Use-Life: Most tombs are either intentionally (designed to block the tomb) or inadvertently (sediment slumping and accumulation) filled with rubble and other sedimentary material, and their stratigraphic sequence may be further confused by re-use or illicit usurpation of the tomb (Kondo 1997). These can be described as systemic disturbances, still within the use-life of the tomb. The use-life of a tomb is the time-span in which it was used by a defined cultural group (that created it) for burials and related mortuary practices (Polz 1987: 122). Non-systemic disturbances describe those changes brought about by acts/individuals unrelated to the original group (i.e. a Coptic hermit living in a New Kingdom tomb, or a 20th century robber trench). It is therefore important to distinguish between systemic and non-systemic disturbances in order to help understand the cultural and natural transformation processes that have occurred. To this end, it is essential to meticulously record both the non-movable (architectural and decorative) and movable (artefacts) elements of the tomb. All traces of cultural and natural activity in the tomb **must** be recorded, even if certain aspects of the tomb's use-life postdate the intended period of research. For example, when excavating a New Kingdom tomb it is still important to record evidence of usurpation, reallocation or Ptolemaic or Coptic habitation. Only in this manner will the archaeological signature of the tomb be fully comprehensible.

Excavating Rock-Cut Tombs: A sonar or ground penetrating radar survey of the tomb should be undertaken before excavation begins to not only assess its shape and extent, but also its structural integrity. If a tomb proves to be structurally unstable it must be supported with shoring, usually consisting of strong wooden planks set against the faces and roof with internal braces of steel or wood attached to acroprops. This is not a job for amateurs – consult a civil engineer or have a specialist team erect the shoring to ensure its reliability and that it will not damage any delicate paintings or reliefs on the walls and ceiling. A team of conservators may also be required to stabilise the wall-decoration along with a team of epigraphers to record it.

As with other archaeological features, rock-cut and shaft tombs must be excavated in a systematic manner, keeping close control of the context and provenience of artefacts and contexts rather than just clearing the sediments. The tomb, as far as possible, should be excavated in discrete archaeological contexts. If this is not possible (which is often the case in large vertical shafts), use arbitrary lots of 10 or 20 cm, as stratigraphic layers in rubble fills are hard to distinguish. The tomb itself should divided into operational areas (i.e. courtyard, shaft 1, chamber 1, shaft 2, chamber 2, etc,) and must have a vertical as well as a horizontal grid. To make sure that all the evidence from these lots is recovered, the matrix should be sieved and each object labelled and recorded separately (**Chapter 7**). The recording of movable and immovable objects employs the usual written, drawn and photographic media, using the surveying and mapping procedures outlined in **Chapter 6**. Because the amount of potsherds and other artefacts found will usually be smaller than on a settlement site, it should be possible to 3-D plot every object. During finds processing, the potsherds should be sorted into types; and as many potsherds as possible reconstructed into whole or partial vessels. A distribution map should be created of the various vessels, showing the spatial distribution of the potsherds of each vessel. This, in turn, will provide a history of the in-filling process and an indication of the various activities that took place there, as well as indicating where certain pots emanated from and the pattern of disturbances thereby implied (see **Finds Processing**).

Human Remains: Human remains can provide much valuable information about both single individuals and the population as a whole. Areas of investigation include determination of age at death, sex, nutritional status, diet, injury, disease, physiological health, cause of death, social status, activity patterns and biological origin. In order to maximise the amount of information that can be derived from the remains, therefore, they must be meticulously excavated in the presence of - or preferably by - a physical anthropologist (or bioarchaeologist). The manner in which the remains are excavated depends partly upon their condition, which can vary from perfect preservation (intentional mummification in Egypt and elsewhere) to skeletonisation or even just a stain on the ground, only detectable through chemical analysis. However, even poorly preserved human remains can provide much valuable information on the social, economic and cultural life of the population, as well as the local environment, and must be treated with due care and reverence.

Excavating Human Remains: While bioarchaeology is a very expansive field, it is advisable to learn the basics of human osteology so that you can mentally plot the location of human remains under the surface, and will know what to expect as you excavate them. The toolkit one requires for excavating human bones differs in some respects from the usual archaeological repertoire. While they are very effective, dental tools – the standard archaeological tool for fine work – must be used with caution when excavating human remains, although it may be unavoidable if the matrix is very hard. It is preferable to use tools made from material that are softer than the bone itself, such as bamboo or plastic. Each excavator has their own favourite toolset – it is possible to use spoons, porcupine quills, knitting/crochet needles and hardwood skewers. A small plasterer's leaf trowel is as large a tool as you should use when excavating a burial; you should also have a supply of small make-up brushes and paintbrushes. Never dig 'blind' – if you poke where you can't see, you may do untold damage to the remains. Always locate then expose one bone at a time, leaving all in articulation until the entire body is exposed. Be patient: never pull or prise anything out of the matrix as you may break or damage it. Be mindful of associations between bones and also with cultural remains, as everything must be recorded and mapped. Be methodical, but also consider that bones start to deteriorate as soon as they are exposed: twelve hours out of the burial matrix can have as much of a deteriorating effect on human remains as a thousand years under burial conditions. Some matrices are more forgiving than others – those buried in dry sand are comparatively stable, for instance – but changes in temperature, humidity and pressure may do serious damage to human remains unless measures are taken. Place protective covers such as a canopy (usually plastic, or perhaps cloth) or at least an umbrella in a position that will keep direct sunlight off the burial. At night, or when the burial is not being worked on, covers should be laid directly and carefully over the remains. At every stage, original burial conditions should be emulated as closely as possible, so if the conditions are damp, water sprays should be used to **dampen** (not soak) the cloths laid directly on the burial. If you place water-impermeable materials over a dry burial, this may produce condensation that will damage the bones. If working in a dry environment, cover the remains with cotton, layered cheesecloth, jute sacks or linen cloths.

When excavating a grave it is important to make yourself comfortable and to find a working position that enables you to easily reach the bones. If the excavator kneels within the grave, they run the risk of disturbing or crushing bones and associated grave goods. The excavator should therefore kneel or lie on a mat placed on the layer from which the grave was cut (see **Fig. 45**), and lean into the grave. Alternatively, planks can be laid across the grave and rest upon scaffolding poles, and the excavator can rest on these. This may not be possible with larger graves, in which case the excavator should remove their shoes and carefully position themselves within the grave on a mat or other padding.

Recovery Systems: Articulated burials are easier to excavate than disarticulated burials, as the position of the bones can be roughly predicted once the burial position has been ascertained. Likely burial position (E-W extended in Christian cemeteries; flexed on most prehistoric sites, crouched in many Precolombian sites) should be considered. Proceed with caution until you have a general sense of how the body lies. Then continue as indicated above, exposing one bone at a time and leaving everything articulated. Move from the longbones distally, excavating the hands and the feet last as these bones are small and are easily broken, lost or disturbed. Expose the remains on as level a plane as possible; you are aiming to have the completely exposed skeleton lying on its original burial ground surface. The area immediately surrounding the bone must be cleared with great care, in order to assess the condition of the skeletal material and to identify the elements encountered. If the skull is intact and full of damp sediment, it must be emptied or else the sediment inside will contract as it dries and pull the skull into fragments; this sediment should be bagged and tagged. Avoid scratching or zealously over-cleaning the bones – a light brushing (if dry) is all they require; specialist cleaning can wait until the laboratory. Be particularly careful with the teeth, never clean between them in the field, as they are both informative and easily lost. If there are any aberrations – pathological bone, fractures, discolourations etc – take photographs, make accurate descriptive notes, and be particularly careful when excavating that area as pathological tissues are both fragile and bioarchaeologically valuable. Be especially cautious when excavating the abdominal area, as this may contain foetal bones, food remains or pathological by-products (such as gallstones); take a large sample from this area. In dry conditions, it may be possible to see a distinct colour and texture change indicating food remains. This must be sampled as it can provide information about diet and parasitical infestation, as well as other impossible-to-

124

spot conditions such as Chagas disease. Soil samples should also be taken from the skull (see below) and beside the femur. For further sampling information, see below. Always check with the bioarchaeologist before proceeding, as they may wish to take samples of bone or tooth for DNA or stable isotope testing. The entire excavated grave fill must be screened or sieved for small bones, pathological by-products or artefacts such as beads (Roskams 2001: 207). The position of disarticulated bones cannot be predicted, and great care is therefore required both in excavating and recording the remains. Make sure that you can establish whether the disarticulation of the human remains was the result of post-depositional disturbance (i.e. bioturbation) or if the bones were disarticulated before they were interred. As above, clear **all** sediment away before removing any of the human remains.

Recording Processes: The planning of human remains should begin as soon as a grave is discovered. The importance of accurately recording the remains as they are exposed cannot be overstressed. Document all sedimentary changes, as well as the position and condition of the bones, as this information is crucial in the reconstruction of burial patterns and taphonomic processes. A full photographic record of the grave's excavation must be kept. Each skeleton, grave fill and grave cut is given its own context number. However, in multiple disarticulated secondary inhumations, the individual skeletons cannot be given separate context numbers, as they were probably interred in a single action, meaning they would be one context, so it would be better to excavate the feature in spits whilst attempting to define separate contexts. Accurate recording of scattered remains will be of immense help to the bioarchaeologist, and will enable the nature of the bone accumulation to be accurately identified.

Consolidation: If a consolidant must be used, Paraloid B72 and Primal WS24 (acrylic colloidal dispersion) are the best solutions to stabilise degraded human remains in the field. Primal WS24 is best used on damp skeletal material, as Paraloid B72 is usually mixed with acetone and is therefore inappropriate. Paraloid B72 is diluted to a 5% or 10% v/v solution in acetone, and should only be used on dry skeletal material. Primal WS24 is diluted to a 15% v/v solution in water; for highly fragmentary areas of bone a 20% v/v solution can be used to impart greater strength, although this is the maximum concentration which should be used. Only one application can be undertaken using this consolidant solution since, being a colloidal dispersion, it is insoluble in its application medium (water) once it has dried. Both consolidants should be applied by pipette, syringe or sable brush, whichever is the most appropriate. In general, however, consolidant use should be avoided if at all possible, as consolidants may actually accelerate deterioration of osteological material, especially if used by a non-specialist. In addition, small grains of sand can be glued to the surface of the bone. The substrate should be cleaned as far as possible prior to application, using wooden sticks, hog's hair and sable brushes.

Sampling Processes: Sediment samples must be taken from within the area of the body, as these can provide information on the level of certain chemical elements present, such as calcium, lead and strontium. They can also provide evidence of diet in the form of food residues and pollen. Sediment samples should be taken from:

1)   The lower abdominal region

2)   The interior of the skull

3)   Above and below one of the femora

4)   A standard position within the grave fill

5)   A standard position at the edge of the grave

These must be placed in clearly marked plastic bags and recorded on the **Sediment Sampling Form: Sheet 6**. If anything unusual has been buried with the body – such as red and yellow ochre, which has often been used in burial rituals – it must be recorded and samples collected.

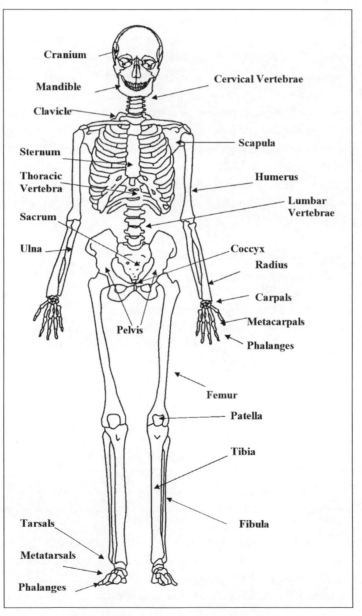

Figure 46: The major bones of the skeleton (adult).

DNA and Stable Isotope Sampling: DNA and stable isotope studies are relatively new approaches that have been used to explore regional and global patterns of animal and human population movement, to explore patterns of kinship, exogamy and residence, create gene maps of ancient pathogens and to provide valuable data on the domestication of animals and plants as well as the spread of agriculture and pastoralism (Jones 2004: 44-8). Stable isotope analysis involves examining various elements within human or other organic remains, enhancing environmental archaeology studies into food-chains and subsistence (Balasse 2002; Fogel & Tuross 2002; O'Connel & Hedges 2004; Peterson 1987; Privat & Schreeweis 2003; Wright & Schwarcz 1998). Human bone, teeth and hair can also be used to this end. Stable isotope analysis on dental enamel will indicate the region in which they were when the teeth developed, whereas bone analysis will indicate where they lived in the last ten years of life. Hair, which grows about 6" (15cm) per year, can inform as to health and diet of the individual in the months or weeks directly prior to death (O'Connell & Hedges 2004). The results can identify population stability, entire population mobility, or whether only males or females moved into a region (Bentley *et al*. 2002; 2003a; 2003b; 2004; n.d.; Price *et al*. 2001; 2002).

Type of Material	Approximate Maximum Age (years)
Human bones	11,000
Human bog remains	7,500
Human mummies	5,000
Neanderthals	29,000
Animal bones	3,500
Plant remains	4,500
Fossilised plant remains	5-24,600,000

Table 18: Various maximum ages of DNA obtained from various types of material, although these limits are likely to be pushed further back in time (after Brown & Brown 1992: 17).

Two of the major problems to consider when collecting ancient DNA are the contamination of ancient samples with modern DNA, and the degradation of DNA over time (Yang & Watt 2005: 332). At certain sites, such as Kafr Hassan Dawood in the Nile Delta, diagenetic processes may have completely destroyed the organic material in the bones, therefore preventing DNA studies (Lovell 2000: 40). Degradation can usually only be detected when the material is examined by the DNA laboratory. However, the invention of PCR (polymerase chain reaction) has made it realistic to analyse ancient DNA, making it possible to amplify the fragments of ancient DNA in human specimens up to 11,000+ years old (frozen remains may contain much older ancient DNA). It has even been possible to extract DNA from Neanderthal remains considerably older than this, thus confirming that Anatomically Modern Humans and Neanderthals are genetically distinct from one another (www.promega.com/profiles/402/ProfilesinDNA_402_09.pdf).

The problem of contamination with modern DNA and infestation with fungi, bacteria and algae can be countered by taking precautions when sampling archaeological materials (Brown & Brown 1992, Brown 1998; Cox & Kneller 2002; Yang & Watt 2005). When taking samples for DNA analysis, the following guidelines should be followed:

1) Wear clean gloves when excavating and handling material destined for DNA analysis. Double thickness disposable medical gloves are best as their outer surfaces are sterile. Change gloves each time you are about to take a new sample. Avoid contaminating the outsides of your gloves by, for instance, scratching your nose.

2) If possible, wear disposable over-suits and shoes. Ideally, head covering and full face masks should be worn, although this is often impractical on an archaeological site. Hairnets, face masks (covering mouth and nose) and synthetic clothing can be worn as alternatives.

3) If not using disposable tools, all tools should be thoroughly cleaned in 10% v/v solution of commercial bleach between taking samples. Nylon, **not** bristle brushes should be used, along with other plastic and metal tools.

4) Do not smoke, eat or drink anywhere near the area where you are taking the samples.

5) The best parts of the skeleton to select for DNA sampling are teeth. Cortical bone is fairly reliable, while the least effective is cancellous (spongy) bone. DNA analysis requires only 1-2 grams of material; fragments of teeth and bones should be sufficient. If possible, set aside another sample of the tooth or bone for reproducibility tests. The remains should be well-preserved and possess good structural integrity. All material used as samples must have undergone *in situ* recording for disease, morphology, measurements and non-metric traits. Bones should generally not be selected if they hold potential for morphological and pathological examinations. However, pathological bone can also be tested in order to identify the disease.

6) Do not add any preservatives or consolidants to 'stabilise' the bones, as these chemicals may inhibit PCR amplifications and may cause contaminant DNA to adhere to the specimens.

7) Do not allow the specimen to come into contact with the ground once it has been excavated. Wrap it in clean aluminium foil and place it in a paper bag for transportation back to the field laboratory. Let it dry naturally before packaging it for transfer to the DNA laboratory.

8) Keep samples of the surrounding matrix and samples of any ancient animal and plant remains: these can be analysed for the possibility of DNA movement between specimens, and also provide useful clues about DNA preservation at the site.

9) Remove excess lumps of sediment, but do **not** attempt to clean the sample in any way as dirt on the sample may prevent contaminants from entering into the bone tissue. Never attempt to wash the sample as the water may cause contaminant DNA to penetrate deeply into the osteological material and also cause hydrolytic damage to the ancient DNA.

10) Keep the material dry; if it is already wet keep it in the aluminium foil and let it dry thoroughly.

11) Once it is completely dry, store the sample in a sterile, dry, airtight container. A screw-cap bottle or canister is ideal; otherwise, use a paper bag. The provenience information must be securely and permanently written on the outside of the container. Do not store in plastic bags as these may encourage the growth of microbes.

12) Store samples in a cool, dry, dark place, ideally in a fridge at 20° C. Keep **out** of direct sunlight.

13) Keep and store all samples separately so as to avoid cross-sample contamination.

14) All personnel who come in contact with the DNA sample should send specimens of their hair (including root) or mouth swab samples to the DNA laboratory as reference samples for comparison with the ancient DNA. This prevents false 'hits' when the DNA is analysed. The number of people who come into contact with the material should therefore be kept to a minimum.

15) The DNA laboratory should be provided with as much contextual information as possible about the provenience of the samples. If a number of different specimens are recovered from the same area (i.e. within a few centimetres of each other), their positions should be recorded and the nature of the surrounding matrix (type of soil, presence of other biological material, dry or wet, etc.) must also be noted.

In the research design and subsequent sampling strategy, provision should be made for the collection of DNA samples. Even if excavating a cemetery it is not viable that all site personnel wear protective clothing for the entire excavation. Therefore, only the bioarchaeologists and conservators who are to handle the DNA samples need to take protective measures, and then only while actually collecting or storing the samples.

The collection of samples for stable isotope analysis does not have to be quite so fastidious in its measures against contamination. However, the use of rubber gloves and the following of points 4 to 12 (above) should be followed when collecting samples. With mummified, frozen or waterlogged remains, special care should be taken to collect hair and finger/toe nails as these can provide a great deal of dietary information.

Lifting, Recording and Storage: It is important to keep the grave goods covered until they are fully exposed. Once the whole burial has been cleared of matrix, it must be fully planned and photographed, with special close-ups as needed. The grave goods must be recorded on the **Special Finds Recording Form: Sheet 9**. If excavating a multiple grave, expose then cover each individual until all have been fully excavated; then carry out a final clean and photograph/plan as outlined above. Once the grave, grave goods, sediment changes and human remains have been completely documented *in situ*, they can be lifted and transported to the on-site osteology laboratory (see lifting in the field). The lifting and bagging of human remains should be done in a set order, so that elements are not missed. It is usually preferable to start with the skull, as this is the source of most information in the analysis stage. The skull is often placed in a box rather than a bag, so as to avoid any damage to the fragile bones. The pelvis should also be treated with particular care, as this provides most reliable data about the age and sex of the individual. Bag by limb; the left and right side shoulder/arm/hand complex should be bagged separately, as should the legs and the thorax. If the vertebrae are very well preserved, it may be appropriate to pass a string through the vertebral canals in the general manner of stringing beads (do **not** lift them by the string – this is only to keep them in the correct order). The string must always be much longer than the line of vertebrae; the process must not be used on pathological specimens, as these are too fragile. The mouths of all bags must be folded over twice, carefully sealed (stapled) and labelled clearly on both the inside **and** the outside. They must then be placed within a larger bag, or a box if available. The heavier bones, especially the limb-bones, should be placed at the bottom, and the fragile elements (skull and pelvis) on top (Roskams 2001: 206).

Infant and Child Bones: Children actually have more bones than adults, as every bone is divided into several pieces that come together and fuse during later childhood or adolescence. Individual bones may be only a tenth of the size of – and much more fragile than – their adult counterparts. This presents problems for the excavator. It may be almost impossible to spot and lift individual bones (especially of the spine, hands and feet), so it may be necessary to collect the sediment around these areas for manual sifting and sorting. If the individual is extremely tiny (pre-term, or neonatal) it may be appropriate to remove the visible bones and then lift/bag the entire sediment block in which the body was found. Even adult hand and foot bones may present recovery issues, especially in unforgiving sediments (i.e. mud); in such circumstances, inexperienced excavators may wish to lift all the sediment around the hands and the feet to ensure that nothing is missed. This might also be appropriate for the skull, to make sure that all the teeth are recovered.

Additional Points to Remember: Some cultures utilised group/multiple burials, which present problems for the excavator. It is important to record the stratigraphic relationship of the skeletal remains and positions of articulated skeletons if present, elements that are attached (i.e. wrist/hand bones) can provide information about the preservation of the remains when they were deposited. It is vital that 3-D recording is implemented and distribution plans are made. This can be done using various techniques described in **Chapter Six**. The minor overlapping of one or two bones from one skeleton of another, or the disturbance of one skeleton by another can indicate whether the skeletons were interred at the same time or if there was a lapse of time between them (Brickley & McKinley 2004: 9-13; Roskams 2001: 205-6). Disturbances of the grave cut and fill can also indicated when the additional inhumations were interred; precise measuring and recording is therefore essential.

Taphonomy of Human Remains: Bones undergo various degrees and stages of decomposition, decay or diagenesis when buried. These changes and alterations are the result of 'taphonomy'. The bones in secondary burials are often disarticulated and some bones may be missing. The bones may also be arranged in unusual configurations. In some cases, the removal of the flesh may be deliberate. The bones may be thrown haphazardly together or carefully arranged in specific positions that may reflect some social or ritual function. Purposeful defleshing may be detected by the presence of cut marks; other traditions, such as scalping, may also be visible in this manner. The period required for the decay of the flesh depends on the environment of the burial site.

The major natural changes that can occur to archaeological bone are:
- Unless the body is desiccated (dried) or frozen (which preserves the body indefinitely) the soft tissues start to decay almost immediately, and depending on the environmental conditions take from one to three years to decompose completely.
- The collagen in the bone is usually lost within a few years, but may take up to

40,000+ years.

- Micro-organisms can invade the bones, making canals, and in some cases can completely riddle the bones making them hard to identify.

- Spaces in the bones get filled with secondary minerals such as calcite (white), pyrite (a brown, black or yellow iron sulphide mineral) or vivianite.

- The primary bone minerals can dissolve totally or partially. This usually happens when the ground pH is between 5.5 and 4.0 pH. In temperate zones the ground pH is usually between 7.0 and 5.0 pH. In arid zones it is usually between 7.0 and 9.0 pH, but in an acid bog it can be as low as 3.0 pH.

- Mechanical damage through ground water, pressure and fire can also affect bones.

- Other site formation processes that may affect skeletal material include abrasion/erosion (including root/fungal activity), trampling, gnawing, 'human modification' (deliberate breakage, burning, skeletal element selection) and any number of other cultural behaviours (Brickley & McKinley 2004).

Samples are rarely representative of all bones, nor of the people originally interred. Very young and very old individuals may be more prone to post-depositional destruction than more robust individuals, while the fragile bones of the skull or the thorax (vertebrae and ribs) have a lower survivorship than larger and more robust bones. Teeth are the most durable part of the body, often surviving after the bones have disintegrated. Partly as a result of this, numerous methodologies have sprung up to assess health, age and diet from the teeth alone (Hillson 1986; 1996). Two of the most important sub-molecular analyses that can be carried out are DNA testing and stable isotope analysis. Note that if a bone is destined for these or other testing, including scientific dating (such as AMS [14]Carbon dating) then consolidants must not be used.

Cremations: Some cultures and periods disposed of their dead using cremation rather than inhumation. Analysing the remains of this process is a specialist sub-discipline that requires the excavator to exercise particular care during recovery. It is the responsibility of the archaeologist and the bioarchaeologist to collaborate in collecting the evidence for pyre technology and ritual reflected in the form and condition of the cremated bone (Brickley & McKinley 2004: 9). Deposits comprising or containing cremated remains must have total deposit recovery, rather than being sampled. It is important to note whether the burnt bones are in their primary place of cremation, or were redeposited after being cremated elsewhere. The condition and type of burnt bones and bone fragments as well as their relative position is important in interpreting the mortuary process. Features to be observed include associated deposits, pyre goods, fragments of pyre debris (fuel ash, fuel ash slag, burnt flint or burnt clay present within the deposit), burial context, position of bone and bone fragments, colour, and fracture patterns. Cremated material may come from various types of contexts, which are summarised below (Brickley & McKinley 2004: 10):

- Pyre sites – with either *in situ* or manipulated pyre debris (including cremated bone).

- Burials – either in a vessel or urn (ceramic, glass or stone vessels) or without a vessel: generally the presence of some form of organic container is apparent, or bone

131

may be spread across the base of a cist grave.

- Redeposited pyre debris – this may be deposited in the grave fill, over the grave, in a pre-existing feature (e.g. ditch), or be a formal deposit in a deliberately excavated feature.

- Cenotaph – may contain a small amount of bone (<25g).

- Cremation-related deposit (i.e. if unsure of the type) – redeposited bone.

- Complete burial *in situ*, with a fragmentary vessel (further affecting fragment size).

- Disturbed (potentially some bone loss, further affecting fragment size).

- Severely disturbed (i.e. noticeable bone loss and increased pressure fragmentation probable).

Burning a corpse creates curved transverse fracture lines, irregular splitting, and marked warping on the bones. By contrast, the burning of dry bones results in cracking or 'checking' of the surface, as well as longitudinal splitting and marked warping. Differentiating between these processes is very important if you aim to understand ancient funerary practices. If the cremated remains are in a whole vessel, the vessel should be block-lifted and taken straight to the osteology laboratory. If the cremated human remains are in a broken vessel (urn) it is essential that the whole context is gathered and bagged, along with any adjacent sediment that may contain fragments of the burial. Once in the laboratory, the vessel should be excavated in a series of 20 mm spits, and gridded into quadrants to allow the horizontal and vertical distribution of individual bone fragments to be accurately recorded. All further analysis of the material should maintain these subdivisions (Brickley & McKinley 2004: 13). This excavation method is also advisable for tightly flexed burials in small round, oval or rectangular coffins. If the cremation is placed straight in a pit, careful cleaning should help define the horizontal limits of the burial. Cremations in pits can also be half-sectioned so that the cremation process may be understood; for example it may be possible to determine whether the bones and ash are from an *in situ* cremation, or were transported to the grave from another location. Cremated remains usually take longer to excavate than inhumations so take account of this in your project design (see Brickley & McKinley 2004: 9-13).

Forms: In archaeological terms, there are no firm rules about what a 'burial' is. For example, a grave or tomb may contain a single interment, in other instances two or more. Alternatively, a grave may contain no detectable human remains at all, but all the other trappings of a burial (i.e. mortuary architecture and grave goods). Therefore, as the number of burials may not always agree with the amount of graves or tombs, there is a separate **Burials Register: Sheet 18** (actual human bodies) and another of **Graves or Tombs Register: Sheet 19**. The two must be cross-referenced. The **Grave Recording Form: Sheet 8** is designed to record the various attributes of the actual grave, whereas the **Burial Recording Form: Sheet 7** is designed to record the human remains.

Pen Mapping: When excavating an extensive cemetery with hundreds or possibly thousands of burials, it may be too time-consuming to draw the precise position of all the individual bones. It may therefore be easier to plot the position of the burials using pen map. Pen mapping can be done manually or digitally, although the basic principle is the same with both media. The general outline and position of the body is drawn, the details being recorded with photographs. Hand-held computers are used with digital media, with a software package such as *Strata Penmap* (www.penmap.com). If using a pencil and draughting film, the same points are recorded on each individual: the shape and position of the head, the position of the shoulders, sternum, sacrum, pelvis, arms and legs. Spot heights are taken at these parts of the body, as well as the top and bottom of the grave cut, and are recorded on the drawing.

After the skeleton has been fully cleaned, two nails with coloured flagging are placed at the head and the feet, with their coordinates recorded on the plan in relation to the site grid. A scale and photographic board are then placed by the remains, with a north arrow, and a vertical photograph is taken (Roskams 2001: 130 & 201). The skeletal remains may then be lifted.

When filling in the details of the skeleton during processing and analysis, the photograph can be blown-up and the missing details filled in, using the nails and the skeleton outline as landmarks (Roskams 2001: 201). Pen mapping puts a higher premium on the photograph being correctly taken and developed, and demands excellent cleaning of the skeletal remains (Roskams 2001: 201) as well as a good level of anatomical awareness. This method should not be used with multiple burials, as it can be difficult to discern different individuals' elements from photographs. Traditional planning should therefore be used for multiple and also disarticulated burials. Pen mapping can also be used to draw other features including building plans and elevations (Anderson 1994).

10. De-watering: Humans tend to settle near water sources, presenting obvious problems for archaeologists who have to contend with sites below, at, or just above groundwater level. Unless groundwater is removed from the excavation area, it is almost impossible to excavate and record the site properly. It also presents serious safety issues for workers in the trenches, as waterlogged deposits are notoriously unstable. The choice of de-watering process will depend on budget, the amount of water present and the types of sediment encountered. Two processes can be used: diaphragms to exclude water from the area of excavation, and lowering the water level in the area of operation by pumping. In very wet areas or if the sedimentary matrix is very unstable, the two processes may be used in conjunction. There are two main pumping methods: sump pumping and wellpoint pumping. These pumps are usually operated continuously or are cycled on and off as necessary to maintain the level of the water in the protected area. Cyclical pumping is generally only sufficient for shallow sites with limited groundwater, and if such sites also have clean gravel and coarse sand, sump pumping with small electric pumps with a motor in a submersible head may be sufficient (Roskams 2001: 107). The pumps must be situated in a sump; this can be specifically dug for the purpose, or adapted from an old excavation feature such as a deep well or pit. It will usually be necessary to shutter the sides of the sump to prevent its collapse and clogging of the mechanism (Roskams 2001: 107). This type of pumping should not be used if small particles of silts and sands are being removed from the sedimentary matrix, as the flow of groundwater and fines towards the pump can cause ground instability; even if using shoring, pumping could therefore lead to collapse of the trench (Fasham 1984).

For more efficient pumping (especially on deeper sites) it is preferable to use well point de-watering, with high-capacity, wheeled engine diesel pumps set outside the trench and

2-3 inch (50-80 mm) pipes (Roskams 2001: 107). Vertical individual wells are secured to rise pipes and sunk into the permeable material under high water pressure 'jetting-in' (Fasham 1984). The well points usually measure 40 mm in diameter by 0.5 or 1 m long, and consist of a perforated steel tube with a ball valve at the base, and surrounded by mesh to prevent fine material from entering the pump (Fasham 1984). These can be sunk 3 to 5 m into the ground and spaced at 1 m intervals around the trenches. The wellpoints are connected to the riser pipes with a swing connection, incorporating a valve to a header pipe which is then connected to the vacuum pump (Fasham 1984). Shoring will usually be required. This type of de-watering can reduce the level of the water table by as much as 3 m; if used in combination with sump pumping, a further 1m can usually be achieved. However, this system has a disadvantage in that it creates a lot of fumes, is expensive, noisy and needs regular maintenance checks and refuelling (Roskams 2001: 107).

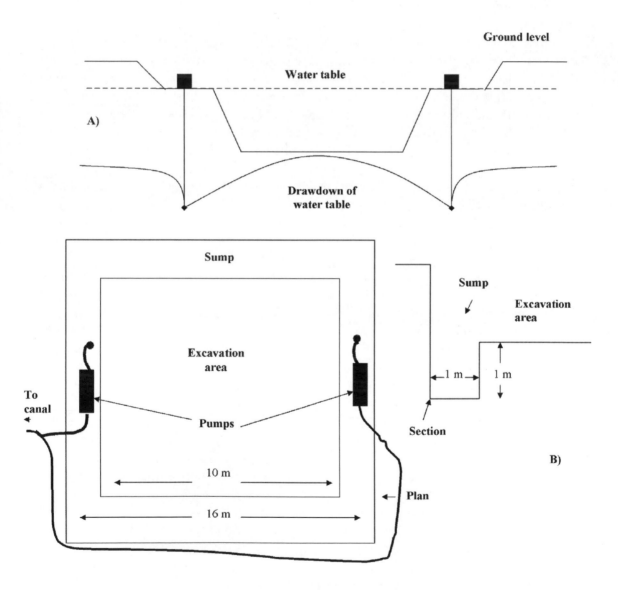

C)

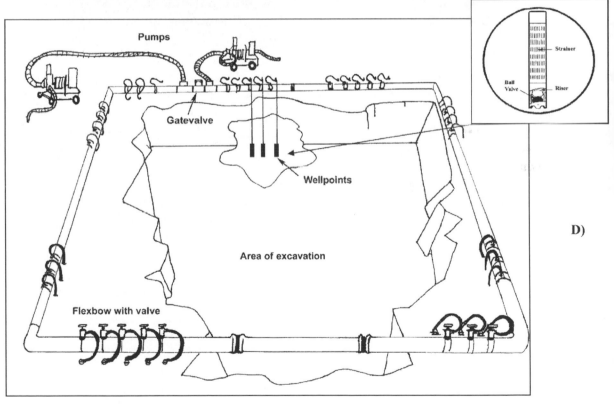

D)

Figure 47: The pumping system for site de-watering A) effect of de-watering, B) sump pumping, C) de-watering at Sais, D) wellpoint de-watering (after Fasham 1984; photograph of Sais Penny Wilson).

The water extracted should be pumped into a nearby canal, river branch, lake or even the sea. However, permission to do so may need to be sought from the local villagers or authorities. It is also best to consult a civil engineer and/or safety expert for advice on installing your system, and to establish whether shoring is needed.

FINISHING EXCAVATION

It is important to protect excavated features both during and after the excavation season, as everything from human remains to mud-brick (and even masonry) walls are liable to deteriorate if left *in situ*. Therefore, before the site is abandoned for the season or at the end of the excavation, it is important to backfill with sand and/or gravel, preferably one with a neutral pH value. Backfilling will not only provide a protective cover to the features, but will also emulate a similar burial environment, thus slowing or preventing deterioration. The depth of backfilling must therefore emulate a similar burial environment, and not just be a thin layer over the top of the features. A layer of sand placed directly on the structures then a layer of geotex material followed by more sand is one of the most effective methods. The most efficient technique may be the rolling method of backfilling, where the spoil out of one trench or grid unit is placed in the previous trench or grid unit.

More elaborate forms of protection, such as specialised housing, can be erected over important features. However, these methods involve many secondary considerations, such as security, interior environment control, temperature, humidity, salinity and groundwater level. These structures, including open-air museums over *in-situ* archaeological remains, should never be erected without first consulting a conservator specialised in their construction. If these structures are erected without due attention to the potential damaging effects, they can cause more damage to the features and artefacts than if they had been left in the open. Any areas that are potentially dangerous - such as deep trenches or high spoil heaps - must be fenced off or made safe.

At the end of each season the tools and other equipment should be packed away and checked off on the inventory made at the beginning of the season. All the tools must be cleaned and oiled if necessary. If it is the end of the excavation, and not just a season, all remaining trenches should be filled-in and spoil heaps flattened. All rubbish that has been accumulated as a result of living on site must be disposed of in a refuse pit, and not be left to blow about the landscape. The health and safety of the local population and the integrity of the environment must be respected when on site, and when leaving it.

CHAPTER SIX

Measuring, Recording and Surveying Techniques

Knowing what to record on an archaeological site, and how to record it, is just as important as using appropriate excavation methodologies. Precise recording of the site is vital, for if the records are not clear, no further questions can be asked of the archaeology in the future (Drewett 1999: 59). Accurate measuring is essential: measuring, in this context, is defined as the calculation of the three-dimensional sizes and spatial relationships of features, contexts, artefacts and ecofacts. The materials used vary from a simple tape measure to a sophisticated total station or state-of-the-art 3D laser scanner that can download directly into a computer. There are drawbacks to digital methods, however: it requires robust equipment that can withstand the often harsh archaeological conditions as data may otherwise be lost. There must also be an infallible system of backing up the data generated by electronic survey and geophysical equipment, geographic information systems (GIS), global positioning systems (GPS) and digital cameras (Green 2002: 106). Therefore, it is essential to have a knowledge of the basic measuring and recording techniques.

MEASURING IN THE FIELD

Large-scale measuring is referred to as 'surveying', while smaller-scale measuring is generally known as 'plotting'. Methods can be technically sophisticated or basic, depending on the money and equipment available. Top-end surveying is carried out using a total station or level; if money is of the essence, then manual measuring with tape measures, Brunton compass, plane table, line-level, steel tape and plumb bob can be substituted. It is advisable to have these basic materials onsite even if you are using a total station or similar, for the sophisticated measuring equipment are sensitive electronic devices and are reliant on batteries and computerised memories (such as the total station), which are prone to damage (Howard 2007: 23-4). Measurements should therefore always be checked with the more traditional methods occasionally, or if you think the reading is wrong. In the plotting of artefacts and contexts, the use of tapes is often a more efficient method for obtaining accurate measurements in the drawing process. Once the measurements have been taken, they are written directly on the recording sheets, plans or section drawings.

Although surveying in the field is sometimes done by a surveyor, the archaeologist should know some of the basic principles of measuring and surveying in the field. The horizontal and vertical control of the site is reliant upon accurate measuring, which should be cross-checked and re-measured where necessary. As outlined in **Chapter 2**, the measuring of the site is done via a grid and a datum. The basic principles of surveying and plotting are based upon triangulation, off-setting, and the use of trigonometry to take linear or angular measurements (for basic methods see Anderson & Mikhail 1998; Bettess 1998; Ghilani & Wolf 2008; Hogg 1980; Moffitt & Bouchard 1992). Teams of three people are ideal for many of the surveying and measuring techniques, one for drawing and two for measuring. The following guidelines are to aid in the measuring of objects, contexts and features in the field. The five essential points are:

1. Establish the full extent of the artefact, context, feature or site *before* measuring begins. Walk around the entity and prepare a sketch plan if it is a large feature or site.

2. Transfer all measurements onto paper as soon as possible; do not trust to memory, and always read back the measurements. Work from the whole to the part, drawing the outline first and filling in the details afterwards.

3. Keep comparing your drawing to the actual entity; work precisely and methodically, but do not become distracted by technology or detail.

4. Always hold measuring tapes taut and horizontal.

5. Ensure that all equipment is in working order, and kept clean, dry and tidy. Keep the measuring and surveying supplies all in one box (ideally a toolbox) or place so they are always to hand.

Basic Equipment and Supplies

The basic equipment required for measuring objects, contexts and features in the field includes:

A 3 or 5 metre steel tape measure, two 30- or 50-metre fibron tape measures; a 1 or 2 metre wooden folding stick measure.
Ranging poles (sharpened red and white poles, 2 m in height), surveyor's arrows or other forms of metal stakes, and a large ball of string.

An A1 size drawing board mounted on a tripod, an alidade, a Brunton or sighting compass, a line level, a plumb bob, builder's line, 6-inch nails and clothes pegs

Scale or graph paper, tracing or draughting film, 2H or 4H pencils, emery board or pencil sharpener, eraser, scalpel, masking tape, beam compass (or a set of spreading compasses with extension bar), ruler, triangular scale ruler graduated at 1:5, 1:10, 1:20, 1:50, 1: 100, etc.

For more technically-advanced survey work, a level and a surveyor's staff, total station and a reflector staff or DGPS will be required.

The Various Methods of Measuring Archaeological Objects and Features in the Field

1. Pythagoras' Theorem: The theory of Pythagoras holds that the lengths of the two shorter sides of a right-angled triangle squared and added together are equal to the sum of the square of the hypotenuse (the long side). Although the 3 - 4 - 5 is probably the most common proportions used to make a right-angled triangle, other proportions such as 20 - 21 - 29, 8 - 15 - 17 and 5 - 12 – 13 can also be used (see **Fig. 48**).

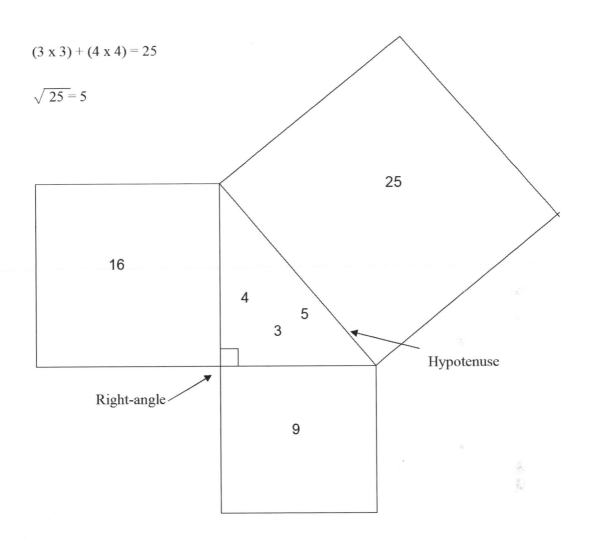

$(3 \times 3) + (4 \times 4) = 25$

$\sqrt{25} = 5$

Figure 48: A 3 - 4 - 5 right-angled triangle.

Using right-angled triangles can help in laying out a grid, surveying a feature or plotting an artefact. It is also useful to know the hypotenuse of a 5.0 x 5.0 m and a 10.0 x 10.0 m triangle, especially when checking that the pegs of the site grid have not moved (see **Fig. 50**). The hypotenuse of a 1.0 x 1.0 m triangle is 1·414 m, that of a 5.0 x 5.0 m triangle is 7·071 m, and the hypotenuse of a 10.0 x 10.0 m triangle is 14·142 m. By using a 50-metre tape measure and three ranging poles or people, these simple mathematical equations can be carried out in the field. A right-angle can also be made using a single tape measure and a baseline. If the tape measure is held at the point you want to locate, the tape measure should be swung in an arc until the shortest point is determined; this will create the right-angle.

139

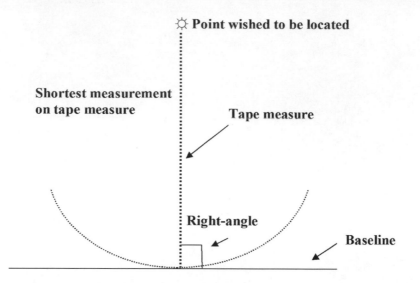

Figure 49: Establishing a right-angle with a tape measure.

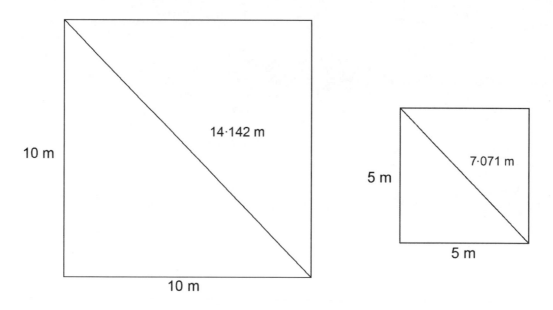

Figure 50: The hypotenuse of a 10.0 m by 10.0 m triangle and a 5.0 m by 5.0 m triangle.

Another simple method of finding a right-angle is by using the ancient Roman *Groma* (**Fig. 51**). This is a square board with two sets of sights aligned at right-angles to one another; the sights can either be sets of nails or cylinders with wire in the centre. One set of sights is lined up with the baseline, then use the second set of sights to form a right-angle. If using nails as sights, then the two nails on the board should be aligned with a ranging pole held by an assistant.

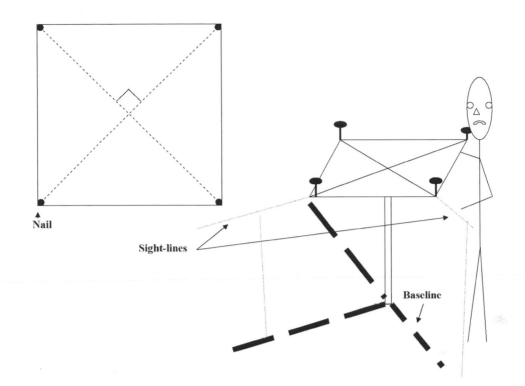

Figure 51: Finding a right-angle with a *groma*.

A more modern variation of the *groma* for finding right-angles is the optical square. This small hand-held device consists of two prisms mounted one above the other. One ranging rod is sighted along the baseline, while an assistant holds another 10 metres away at an approximate right-angle. Looking through the device, the surveyor can see the bottom half of one rod and the top half of the other; directing the assistant to move the rod until the two halves are co-incident, and thus at 90° to one another (Howard 2007: 20).

2. Triangulation: Triangulation involves constructing a series of triangles with tape measures from a known baseline. To make the triangles, first lay-out a baseline (using one of the gridlines is useful for this) then peg one end of a tape measure with a surveyor's arrow or skewer. Then secure the end of a second tape measure at a suitable distance along the same baseline, avoiding the necessity to create an acute or obtuse triangle, and then cross the loose ends of the tapes over the point that you want to locate, creating a triangle. The measurements of the sides of the triangle will be known to you and you will have created a fixed point at the apex of the triangle. The measurements of the baseline and tapes can be scaled down and plotted on the plan using a beam compass or a set of compasses. The process is repeated at several points along the feature (see **Fig. 52**), and the resulting marks where the compasses cross over can then be joined up producing in an accurate plan of your feature or object. The measurements can be checked by positioning another triangle along the same baseline and measuring to the same point. If a large site is being covered with triangulation, then it will be better to move around the site using triangulation and ranging poles as shown in **Figure 53**.

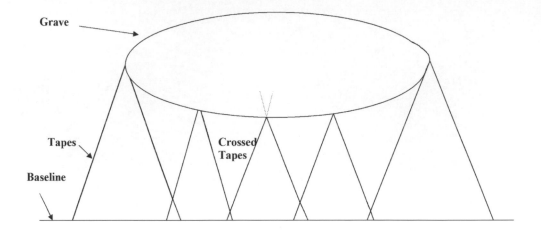

Figure 52: Surveying using triangulation.

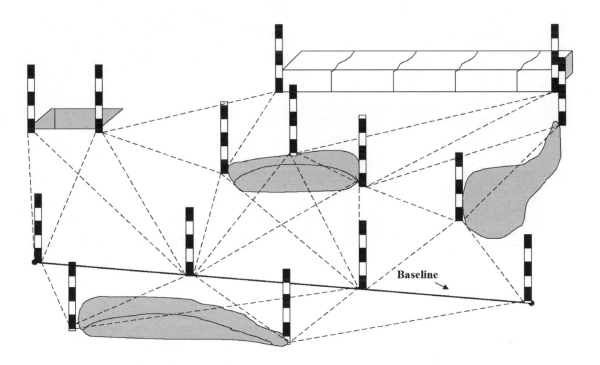

Figure 53: Traversing with triangulation.

3. Off-Sets: As with triangulation, off-setting is done using a baseline; the baseline can be put either inside or outside the feature that you want to locate (**Figs. 54-55**). A perpendicular line is then measured from this baseline to the point wished to be located. The distance from the baseline to the feature is then scaled down and recorded on the plan. It may not always be possible to place your baseline on the ground, in this case it should be placed between the next lowest convenient points and measurements taken from it using a hand tape and a plumb bob to ensure you are over the correct place.

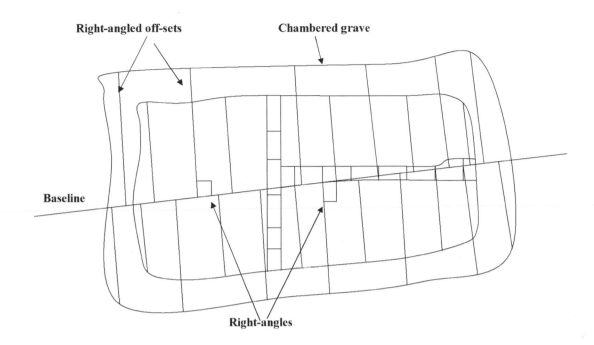

Figure 54: Surveying the outline of a chambered grave by off-sets.

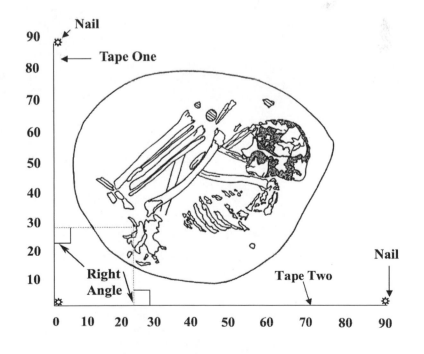

Figure 55: Off-sets from a baseline and meridian line.

Three nails should be set around the feature to be planned with string running between them. Two tape measures must then be securely fixed along these perpendicular baselines. This method of measuring is to make the process easier when planning a burial or other feature that needs lots of very accurate measurements.

A similar method to the local baseline method is the local grid method. This method encloses the feature in four gridlines running parallel to its sides; off-sets are then taken from these gridlines.

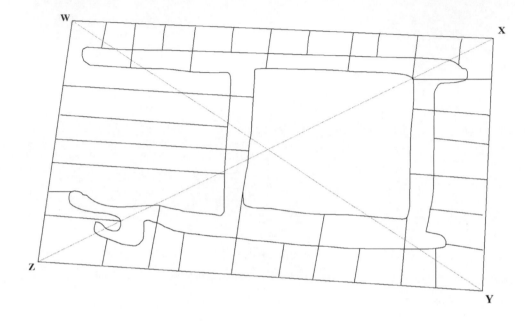

Figure 56: Off-setting from a local grid.

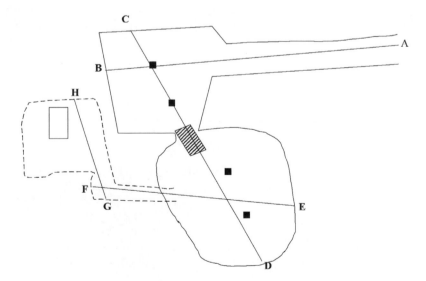

Fig 57: Grid system for drawing/measuring a rock-cut tomb (Dever & Darrel Lance 1978: 163).

When measuring certain monuments, it is necessary to establish a series of baselines from which to take off-sets or triangulation. In the example shown in **Fig. 57**, there are four main axis lines in the tomb. To make an accurate drawing it is essential to record the exact angles and distances that describe the points where these baselines intersect. As long as the pegs laid out on the ground of the tomb or other monument accurately match those on the paper, an accurate drawing should result. If planning tombs, caves and cisterns or other subterranean or multi-level features, it will be necessary to lower the datum or temporary bench mark to below ground level. This is relatively simple, even without sophisticated surveying equipment. All that is required is a line-level and a plumb-bob. First establish a datum point at the entrance to the cave or tomb, run a datum line from A-B, then drop the datum line to C-D while ensuring that it is exactly level by means of a plum-bob and line-level. This procedure can be repeated as many times as necessary, as shown in E-F. The baseline and datum line configurations shown in **Figs. 57** and **58** are applicable to the horizontal and vertical measurements of any tomb or cave.

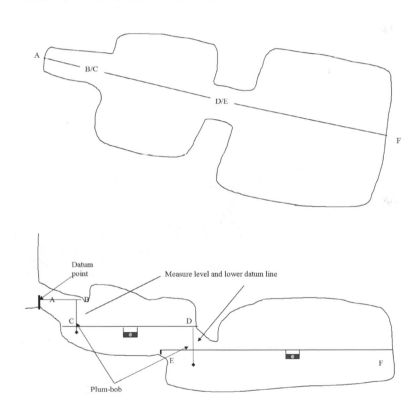

Figure 58: Lowering the datum line (after Dever & Darrel Lance 1978: 161).

4. Traverse Twin Tapes: This method involves laying out a baseline below the object or feature to be measured, with two tapes placed perpendicular to the base line and parallel to one another (see **Fig. 59**). The measurements on the tapes must be exactly in line with one another. A 3-metre metal tape is then placed across these tapes and the readings can

145

be read off. These can then be scaled down and transferred to the plan of the object or feature.

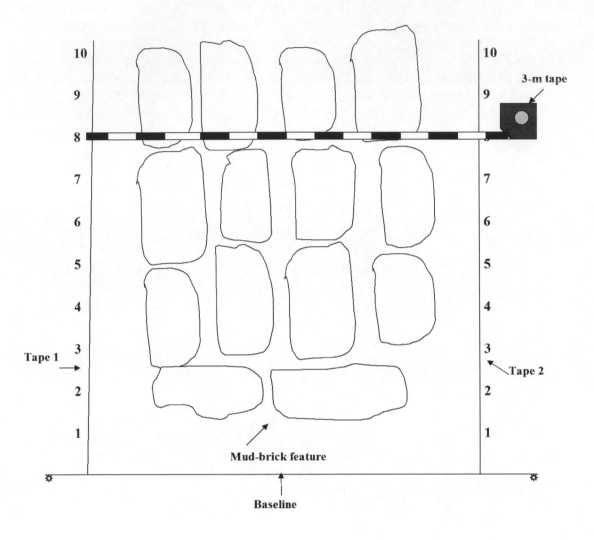

Figure 59: Plotting a mud-brick feature using the traverse twin tape method.

5. Grid Coordinates: The above-mentioned measuring techniques (**Figs. 52-59**) should all be measured into the site grid, and if possible the baseline should be along a gridline. However, if this is not possible, off-sets should be taken from the nearest gridline to establish the local baselines. However, if there is no site grid, then the local grid can become the *de facto* site grid (Hawker 1999: 41). The baseline should then be located on the landscape, either to known landmarks (such as buildings or trees) or to map coordinates. Plotting-in of objects and features may also be taken straight from the grid coordinates, without first establishing a local baseline.

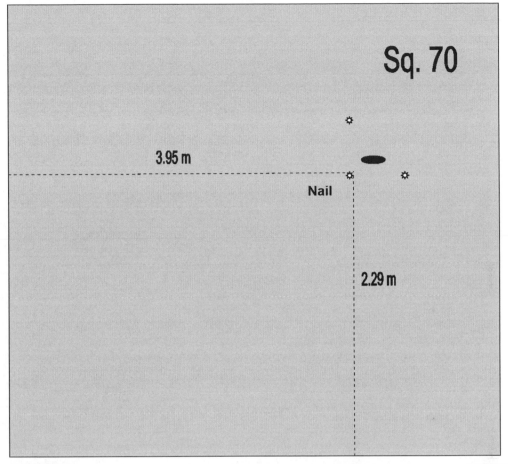

Sq. 70

3.95 m

Nail

2.29 m

110E/250N   115E/250N

Figure 60: Measuring using grid coordinates.

The coordinates of the baseline are recorded as X centimetres east by Y centimetres north from the main axis of the site grid. The east coordinates are always recorded first (Eastings) and the north coordinates are recorded second (Northings). In **Fig. 60**, the position of the first nail of the local grid to measure the artefact (red oval) would thus be recorded as 113.95E/252.29N. Easting 110 m + 3·95 m = 113·95 m, Northing 250 m + 2·29 m = 252·29. The other two nails are likewise measured-in and recorded. The bigger the object, the more baselines are needed from which to take the perpendicular off-sets (Hawker 1999: 41).

6. Horizontal Measuring from a Central Datum: If using grid coordinates, measuring from a central datum is exactly the same as the above-mentioned method. However, if grid points have not been labelled with coordinates, all measurements should be related to the central datum.

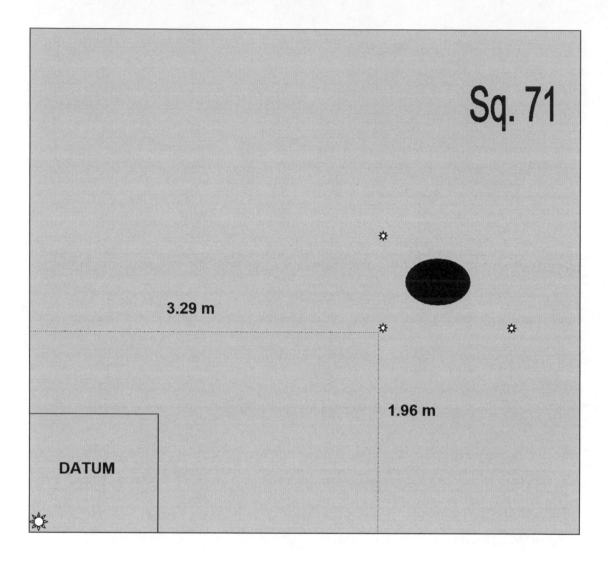

Figure 61: Measuring from a central datum.

The position of the first nail of the local grid set-up to measure the artefact (red oval) would thus be recorded as Sq. 71 329E/196N. In longhand, this translates to 3·29 m east by 1·96 m north of the datum of square 71. The remaining two nails in the local grid should be plotted in the same fashion, and recorded on the plans.

7. The Plane Table: The plane table has been used for surveying since the middle ages, and is still very efficient (Drewett 1999: 62). The plane table itself is an A1 drawing board set on a tripod made precisely level by use of a plumb bob and a level. The drawing board supports graph paper and draughting film, on top of this rests the alidade. The alidade is a straight edged measure with sights at either end (Howard 2007: 25). If a manufactured alidade is not available, a wooden ruler with a nail aligned at either end will suffice. There are two main uses of the plane table on site: the radiation and the intersection (Wass 1992:

69). If planning a feature, the plane table is placed in the middle of the feature and the position of the plane table is likewise marked on the plan. The back of the alidade is placed in the middle of the paper on the place marked for the plane table. The point to be located is sighted through the alidade; the distance between the alidade and the point is then scaled down to 1:20 or greater (depending on the size of the feature) and a mark made at this position along the sight line of the alidade. Radiating sight lines can then be made to the other points you want to locate, and a series of dots made. These dots are then joined up to create the shape of the feature. It is also possible to draw radiating line from the alidade and mark the scaled down position of the feature along these lines. However, this may create a rather messy plan.

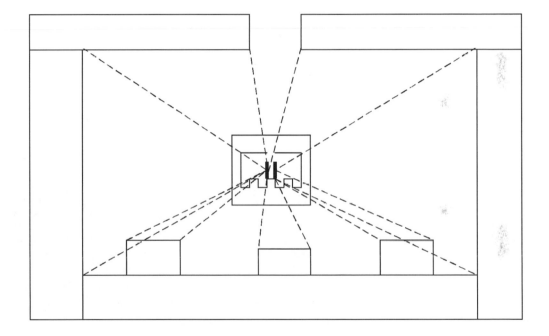

Figure 62: Radiating survey using a plane table.

The second form of plane tabling uses a baseline and a variant of triangulation (Wass 1992: 69). The intersection method allows greater distances to be surveyed than the radiating technique, and is more accurate because each point is sighted and measured twice. A 50.0 m baseline is established and the plane table is set up at one end. The alidade is used to sight the points to be planned as in the radiation method and a set of lines made. The plane table is then moved to the other end of the baseline and the same points re-plotted from this new position. The place which the lines intersect indicates the position of the points measured on the feature.

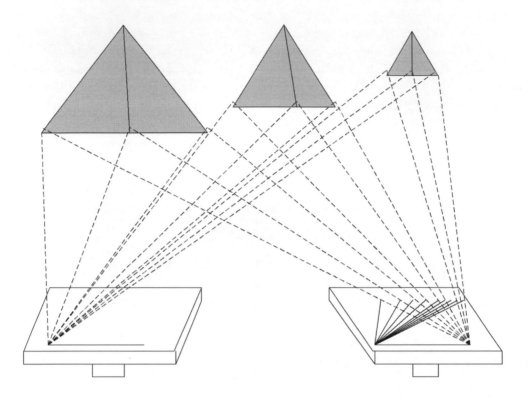

Figure 63: Intersection survey using a plane table.

8. The Level: To complete the three-dimensional plotting of features and artefacts, measurements must also be made in the vertical plane, using levels. There are various types of level, including the dumpy, quick-set, and automatic levels, all of which consist of a sighting line in a telescopic viewer, which can be rotated through 360° and is mounted on a tripod. This is used with a surveyor's staff, a telescopic or folding black and white measure, divided into metres, decimetres and centimetres. A four-metre staff is the shortest practical length to use on site, with a 6-8 m staff being preferable, and vital on deep, highly stratified sites.

When sighting through the telescope, four lines are visible: one pair of cross lines (hairs) and a pair of stadia lines (**Fig. 64B**). The cross hairs consist of a vertical line and a horizontal line – the plane of collimation - which projects an imaginary horizon across the landscape (Drewett 1999: 67). The intersection of this horizontal plane by a vertically-placed surveyor's staff allows the relative heights of different points to be determined (Hogg 1980: 87).

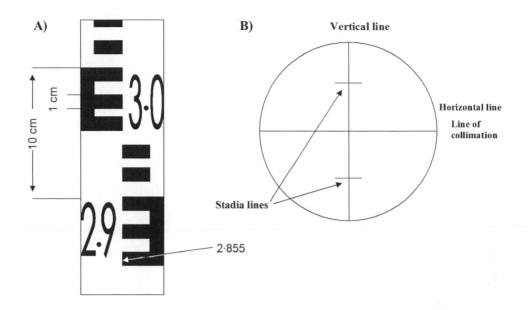

Figure 64: A) The measure on a surveyor's staff; B) The cross hair and the stadia lines on a level.

The vertical line of the cross hairs is to ensure that the surveying staff is held vertically as it is moved around the site. The stadia lines are for tacheometry (calculating distance) and are not used during the levelling process. The distance between the level and the surveying staff is calculated by subtracting the reading of the lower stadia line from that of the higher stadia line and multiplying the result by 100.

Figure 65: Levelling: the line of collimation.

Whatever model you decide to use, it must be set-up properly before taking readings. The tripod must first be set firmly on the ground, with its feet pressed into the sediment or placed on pieces of rubber tyre to stop it slipping, and with the head roughly level. Make sure that any fixing screws between the head and legs are tightened and that the clamps on sliding legs are secure. When taking the level from its protective box, note how it was stored so that you can replace it appropriately. Once the level is screwed firmly on the tripod, the level's eyepiece is adjusted by bring the cross hairs into focus. This can be done by pointing the level's telescope towards a blank surface (i.e. a sand dune or the sky). The image of the staff then needs to be brought into the cross hairs' plane of view by turning the main focusing screw. The instrument then needs to be made level by adjusting the levelling screws in different directions until the instrument's spirit-level(s) are even. The spirit level's bubble will follow the direction of the left thumb in either a clockwise or anti-clockwise direction. The level must then be turned through 90° and the process repeated on the one or two, untouched levelling screw(s). Re-check the level in the first position, and if minor adjustments are needed continue the operation until the spirit-levels bubble remains central regardless of the orientation of the level (Dugdale 1980: 4). The level is now ready for use.

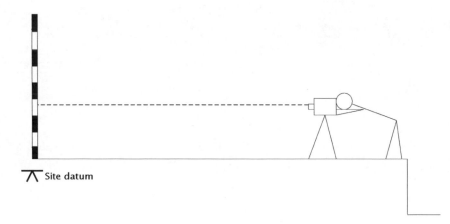

Figure 66: Levelling: the backsight.

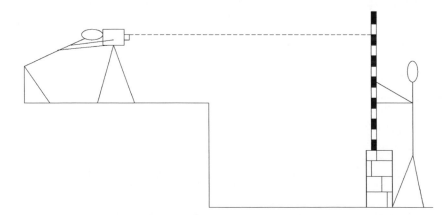

Figure 67: Levelling: the foresight.

The observation and booking of levels is done in relation to the site datum; with all levels recorded as X metres above site datum. The booking of levels should be to the third

152

decimal place (if unclear, estimate to the nearest millimetre, as shown in **figure 64A**). Each staff position is a 'point' and the levels observed on the staff must be booked in the **Level Log: Sheet 3a**. Each operational area should have its own ring binder folder to store these sheets. The levelling process should always start from the site datum (SD) or the nearest control point/temporary bench mark (TBM). This is done by holding a staff on the point (SD) then setting up the instrument at least 10 metres away and looking back at the surveyor's staff. A reading is taken and booked in the log; this is known as the backsight. If the site datum has been given an arbitrary denomination of +100 m and the backsight is known to be +2·960, then the height of collimation is 102·690 m metres above datum. The line of collimation or instrument height (I.H.) is calculated by adding the reading of the backsight to the value of the datum.

No.	Site Datum/ TBM	Backsight	Collimation or I.H.	Foresight	Reduced Level	Comments
1	100·000	2·690	102·690			SD, distance 0 metres
2		0·961	99·898	3·753	98·937	CP 1, distance 50 metres
3		1·762	97·698	3·962	95·936	CP 2, distance 100 metres
4		2·357	98·159	1·896	95·802	CP/TBM, distance 150 metres
5	95·802			4·963	93·196	Head, context 1055
6				4·675	93·484	Sacrum, context 1055
7				4·123	94·036	S. Grave, context 1053
8				4·327	93·832	N. Grave, context 1053
		7·770 –				
		13·938			-100·000	
		– 6·168	✔	13·938	– 6·168	✔

Figure 68: Booking and reducing levels with the height of instrument method: Traversing from the site datum to establish a temporary bench mark.

In the example shown in **Figs. 68** and **69**, 150 metres has to first be traversed to establish a temporary bench mark in a new area of operation. Therefore, a run of levels has to be made, the first being a backsight to the staff held on the site datum. The staff is then moved 25 m in front of the level and a foresight booked. As this was the last foresight taken from the level's original position, the point at which the staff is held is termed a change point (CP). The level is then moved 50 m and set up in the usual fashion, making certain that the staff can be seen from this new position. A backsight is then observed to the staff that is still held at point 2. The staff is then moved 50 m to point 3, and a foresight taken. This process is repeated until a suitable position is located for the temporary bench mark at point 4, convenient for taking levels in the new operational area. The return to the site datum in a closed traverse, and the value at the end of this chain of levels should be the same value as that at the beginning: +100 m. Once the temporary bench mark has been established, levels can then be taken. This is done by taking a backsight to a staff held on the temporary bench mark, and taking a series of spot heights; these are booked as foresights. Each line in the level log corresponds to a single point, so both the foresight and back sight of that point are entered on the same line (Hogg 1980: 100). However, when checking the calculations the spot heights (5-7 in **Fig. 68**) are omitted, except for the last observation made which must always be included.

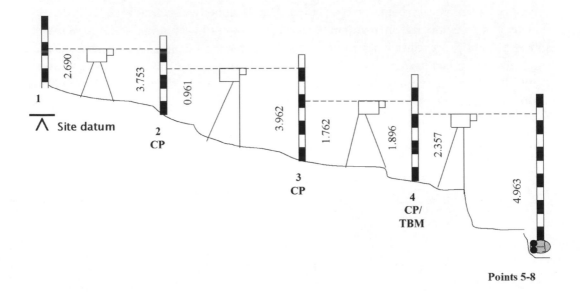

Points 5-8

Figure 69: A run of levels from the site datum to establish a temporary bench mark.

When reading the surveyor's staff it is important that the staff be held vertical. The best way of achieving this is to gently and slowly sway the staff backwards and forwards through the vertical. The lowest reading is the level that indicates the correct level and thus should be booked in the levels log (Hogg 1980: 99).

The method used to calculate the reduced level is the height of collimation or height of instrument method (I.H.). In the I.H. method, the reduced level is calculated by subtracting the foresight from the line of collimation. However, when a run of levels is made traversing the landscape, the line of collimation will dip and rise. To calculate the extent of these dips and rises the backsight must be added to the reduced level of that point:

Point 1 R.L 100·000 + B.S. 2·690 = I.H. 102·690

Point 2 I.H. 102·690 – F.S. 3·753 = R.L. 98·937 + B.S. 0·961 = CP 1 I.H. 99·898

Point 3 I.H. 99·898 – F.S. 3·962 = R.L. 95·936 + B.S. 1·762 = CP 2 I.H. 97·698

Point 4 I.H. 97·698 – F.S. 1·896 = R.L. 95·802 + B.S. 2·357 = CP 3/TBM I.H. 98·159

Point 5 I.H. 98·159 – F.S. 4·963 = R.L 93·196

Point 6 I.H. 98·159 – F.S. 4·675 = R.L 93·484

Point 7 I.H. 98·159 – F.S. 4·123 = R.L 94·036

Point 8 I.H. 98·159 – F.S. 4·327 = R.L 93·832

To reduce mistakes in booking the levels in the log, the staff should always be read twice. If you have an assistant helping with the levelling, the numbers should be shouted back before booking them in the levels log; if not, reading the levels out loud to yourself will also help reduce error (Hogg 1980: 99). To check that the arithmetic has been calculated correctly the backsights must be added together (7·770) and the total of the foresights (13·938) must be subtracted. The resulting figure (-6·168) must match the figure arrived at through the subtraction of the Site Datum (100·000) from the last reduced level (93·832). For the check on the arithmetic to work, the first staff reading **must** be booked as a backsight, and the last staff reading booked as a foresight (Dugdale 1980: 39). If the bookings are being carried onto another page, if the last reading on one page is a foresight, it must be booked as a backsight as the first reading of the new page (Hogg 1980: 100). The allowable closure error must be within a certain margin and in relation to the amount of change points in the course of a run of levels.

$$C = \pm 5\sqrt{n \text{ mm}}$$

Figure 70: The formula for working out the allowable closure error. C = closure error and n = the number of change of points. If the error is within the allowable limits, then it should be distributed equally amongst the reduced levels (Westman 1995: 120).

When establishing vertical height during three-dimensional plotting, the level will not normally be moved that often and should be placed in a position where the instrument can easily sight the operational area's control point (temporary bench mark). It is therefore important that the levelling process should start with a backsight onto the surveyor's staff held on the TBM. All the spot heights will then be recorded as foresight levels. The operational area's level log will usually look more like **Figure 71** than **Figure 68**. This is because most of the levelling done on site (other than contour and profile surveying and establishing a temporary bench mark) will comprise of taking spot levels to transfer onto plans and taking levels to be transferred onto section, elevation and profile drawings. These levels should also be recorded in the relevant recording forms.

The first booking made is the known height of the temporary bench mark, 95·802 metres above site datum. The surveyor's staff is then held on the temporary bench mark and an observation made, the reading is 2·357 m. The height of the instrument or plane of collimation is calculated by adding the backsight to the TBM. The spot heights of the contexts or artefacts are the reduced levels; these should be written on the plans, sections and on the recording forms. To work out the reduced levels, subtract the forward intermediate sight from the instrument height:

Point 1 TBM 95·802 + B.S. 2 ·357 = I.H. 98·159

Point 2 I.H. 98·159 – FS. 3.456 = R.L 94·703

Points 3 to 10 are completed in exactly the same way.

To check that the arithmetic has been calculated correctly the sum of B.S. (2·357) must be subtracted from the last F.S. 2·213 = 0·144. This figure should match the subtraction of the first R.L. 95·802 from the last R.L., 95·946 = 0·144.

No.	Site Datum or TBM	Backsight	Collimation or I.H.	Foresight	Reduced Level	Comments
1	95·802	2·357	98·159			TBM
2				3·456	94·703	E. Profile, context 1293
3				3·792	94·367	E. Profile, context 1293
4				3·814	94·345	E. Profile, context 1293
5				3·793	94·366	E. Profile, context 1293
6				3·679	94·480	E. Profile, context 1293
7				2·859	95·700	Jar, context 1315
8				2·987	95·172	Potsherd, context 1314
9				2·156	96·003	E. Wall, context 1290
10				2·213	95·946	W. Wall, context 1290
		2·357		2·213	-95·802	
		- 2·213		2·213	0·144	✔
		0·144	✔			

Figure 71: The booking of spot heights for three-dimensional plotting.

The theodolite and the transit can also be used for levelling, as can the total station (which is dealt with in section 11). A cheaper option is the Brunton pocket transit, which can perform most of the tasks a full-scale theodolite - take levels, angles, measure degrees for orientation (Farrar 1987). These instruments have an advantage over the level in that they can measure the vertical angle and can be tilted to take readings above and below the line of collimation. Where the site has steep slopes, undulating surfaces or when doing building recording, the theodolite and transit have great advantages over the level. However, transits and theodolites are not as robust as levels. If you are primarily interested in taking spot levels, the dumpy level is the better instrument as it is more liable to resist the rigours faced on an archaeological site (Hogg 1980: 87-95).

9. Central Datum: This method involves leaving a one-metre-square block of sediment in the centre of the excavation area. This is referred to as the 'datum block'. A wooden post is placed in the middle of this block, with a 5.0 m piece of cord attached (usually 0.10 m above the ground level, so that the cord can move easily). A groove should be cut in the post so that the string does not slip down. Measurements can then be taken using a metre stick, a line-level (to check the string is level) and plumb bob (to ensure the metre stick is straight). The line-level is to check that the string is level, and the plumb line is used to make sure that the metre stick is straight. All the level measurements are taken from this central datum post, the actual datum being ground level. The fact that the cord is 0.10 m above the actual level of the datum **must always** be noted on the **Manual Level Recording Form: Sheet 3b** and also in the notebook. The 0.10 m **must** be subtracted when recording all measurements from the local datum. At the end of the excavation, the local data must be levelled with the site datum using an automatic level or Brunton pocket transit. This should be done at the earliest convenient date.

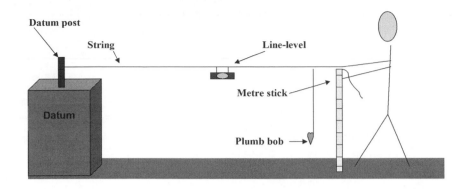

Figure 72: Taking a level from a central datum.

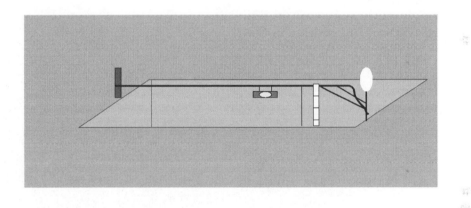

Figure 73: Taking a level from a local datum in a trench.

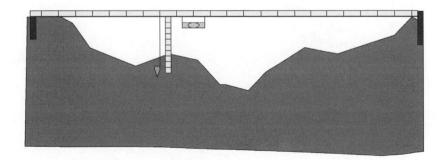

Figure 74: Profiling using a line level and a builder's line.

Profile plotting of ditches and pits by setting up a taut builder's line and placing a 30-metre tape along it. A folding metre rule can then be used to take measurements at various intervals along the tape. These are then scaled down and plotted on graph paper and then transferred onto draughting film.

10. Taking Height Elevations: Elevations of tall buildings and similar features will be recorded with either a theodolite or total station, and will involve the erecting of scaffolding if a stone-by-stone elevation is to be drawn. Façades or solid structures can be measured using tape measures and off-sets, as can their internal layout. However, if a stone-by-stone elevation is not required, some basic measuring methods can be applied to record scaled schematic diagrams of fairly plain buildings.

Depending on the height of the structure, a scale of 1:10 or 1:20 should be used. If the structure is solid, a step ladder may be used (rather than erecting scaffolding) to take the measurements of various features on the façade. If upper floor windows are still present, it is possible to lean out of these to take measurements. An alternative to this is a set of extendable metal rods marked at 0.10 m intervals that can be lengthened to reach up to the features on the structure. A surveyor's staff can be used if the remains are low enough.

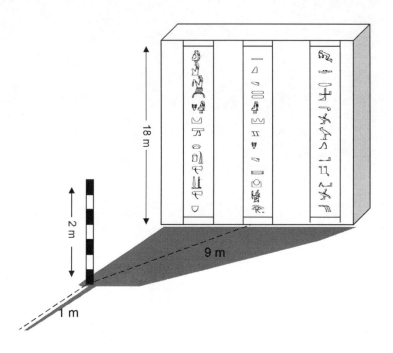

Figure 75: Assessing a structure's height by measuring the length of its shadow.

One of the simplest methods of measuring the height of a structure is by measuring its shadow when the sun is behind it. The height can be worked out with the use of a ranging rod or another object of known length: the length of the structure's shadow divided by the length of the ranging rod's shadow, multiplied by the actual height of the ranging rod equals the structure's height (Wass 1992: 59). Alternatively, the actual height of the ranging pole (usually 2.0 m) can be marked out on the ground. The rod is then placed at the beginning of the ground marking. When the shadow cast by the rod reaches the line marked out as its actual height, the structure's shadow should immediately be measured, as the length of the structure's shadow will be equal to the height of the structure.

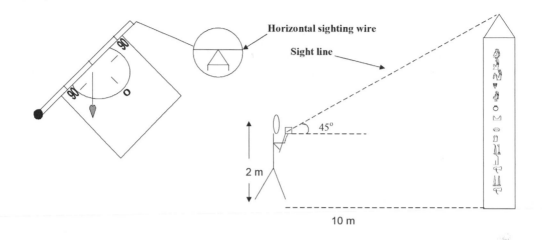

Figure 76: A clinometer.

Clinometers can either be made at home or bought commercially (e.g. Brunton CM ClinoMaster™). They can also be an in-built part of a surveying compass. It consists of a flat board with the markings of a protractor drawn out on one side to measure the angle, and a plumb bob attached to the centre of the top edge to indicate the angle. As the clinometer is raised to sight the target, the plumb bob will swing to indicate the angle of the sight line. This angle of the incline must be noted as must the distance from the structure and the ground-eyes height of the device. By converting these measurements to a scale drawing, the height of the structure can then be calculated (Wass 1992: 59).

11. The Total Station and EDM: The total station (TS) is now a standard piece of equipment on archaeological sites. Often erroneously referred to as an EDM (Electromagnetic Distance Measurer), the TS combines electromagnetic measurements of distances, vertical angles, horizontal angles, and therefore heights by using either infra-red or red lasers, the latter being particularly useful for building surveys as they do not require a prismatic reflector (Howard 2007: 23). Some of the laser models such as the Leica TPS700 can take reflectorless distance measurements on any surface up to 30 or 40 metres away. EDMs were originally attached to theodolites; the two components were later placed in the same housing with the option of a digital datalogger and on-board computer with the whole termed a total station (Bettess 1998: 119; Drewett 1999: 70). The TS resembles a theodolite but is larger, mounted on a small tribrach on a lightweight but sturdy tripod, and has a keypad to enter data and instructions. Three pieces of equipment are normally required for taking measurements: the instrument itself, a tripod and a dedicated staff with a reflective prism on top. Rechargeable batteries, cables, and software will also be necessary to support the TS. There are many different types of TS on the market, each with its own set of specifications; it is therefore necessary to refer to the manual for that type of instrument. Some total stations are 'robotic' allowing the surveyor to control the instrument from a distance via remote control. The surveyor holds the reflector and controls the total station instrument from the observed point, thus making it more efficient in terms of personnel requirements. Recent models such as the Leica SmartStation, Topcon GPT-2005, and Trimble 5600 L1 possess fully integrated GPS capabilities, allowing the instrument to establish its exact longitude, latitude and height above sea level as long as it is within 50 km of a reference or base station. After pinpointing its precise location on the globe, surveying can commence with the TS functions or continue with the real-time kinematic (RTK) GPS surveying capabilities.

The TS can be used for all the same purposes as non-electronic survey equipment, namely establishing grids, taking spot heights and contour and area surveys, and locating plans and sections. The basic principles of TS surveying are the same as traditional surveying; the TS will just make the work easier, quicker and more accurate for most total stations are capable of simultaneous trigonometric conversion of spherical survey coordinates into Cartesian orthogonal measures - usually east, north, and elevation. However, when doing an area survey the approaches are somewhat different. Rather than continually moving the instrument as in manual survey, the TS stays in one position and measurements are taken around the instrument (Drewett 1999: 71). If the TS is set up in viewpoint in the landscape, measurements can be taken up to two kilometres or more away. This eliminates the need for continually moving the instrument, although it does introduce the need for communication via walkie talkies or mobile phones. The TS is accurate to 15 mm over a 1000 m stretch, which exceeds the accuracy required for archaeological work (Bettess 1998: 123). However, this section is not designed for detailing surveying methods and techniques (for surveying practice see Uren and Price 2005), rather for taking measurements on an excavation. The recording of data by the TS makes the manual recording of data redundant, although the levels and distances should be transferred onto recording sheets as a back-up in case of accidents. This must also be done if your TS does not have a datalogger. The major difference between taking levels with a traditional level and the TS is that the figures are read from the TS screen rather than from the surveyor's staff. The TS also makes the acquisition of spatially referenced data easier for transforming into common information systems.

The Baseline, Grid and Control Points: As discussed in **Chapter Two**, a baseline must be established, the starting point of which is termed the site datum. This baseline must always be longer than the diameter or longest dimension of the site. It is desirable for ease of planning (i.e. with north at the top of your plans) to have a grid orientated to the cardinal points of the compass, although at a slight angle to the lines (walls or other features) of the archaeology, as such it is essential to discern north, so that an east-west baseline can be laid out. To establish a baseline with a TS a traverse kit, consisting of two fixed prisms on tripods is useful and means that the surveyor can do it by themselves if necessary. If not using a traverse kit to lay out a baseline, have one person walk out at least 20 to 50 metres due north. Using a properly declinated compass, shoot a bearing from the prism rod to the total station. Adjust the prism rod position until the bearing is due south. Rotate the TS and sight the prism. The TS should now be facing due north. It is critical during this step that the prism rod is exactly vertical and that the cross-hair in the TS optical sight is exactly in the centre of the prism. Set the horizontal angle to zero and enter. Finally, press enter once again to return to the measurement screen (Rick 1996). Once north is located a backsight point can be established there and a series of east-west

90° to 270° control points can then be marked on the ground between which the baseline can be set out (Howard 2007: 27). It may not always be practical to have an east-west baseline, and although it makes no difference for surveying purposes, the closer it is to east-west the better for excavation and planning purposes. The meridian line and other points of the site grid should then be established as discussed in **Chapter Two**. Most total stations have a useful function called 'setting-out'. The coordinates of desired points can be input manually or from data registers, and then the instrument will direct the user to the points, thus allowing a grid to be laid out. The screen will indicate the horizontal and vertical alignments of the point to be found, and then will indicate how far the prism target must be displaced out or in along the radial line of alignment. In this way the instrument can be used to lay out uniform grid systems on uneven ground, quickly locate the widely dispersed units of a random sample, or stake out the corners of perfectly square or rectangular excavation units (Rick 1996).

As the baseline of the grid can be several hundreds of metres from trenches, localised baselines can also be established for measuring various features, or for taking measurements within individual trenches. These baselines are established in the same manner as described above and must be longer than the trench or feature being recorded. The local baseline can be established along a gridline with two control points or stations at either end to enable the TS to locate itself within the site grid and enable a baseline traverse. These control stations must be situated outside of the area of excavation (trenches) so that they are not disturbed during the excavation process. These control stations should incorporate both the vertical and horizontal measurements, the X, Y, and Z coordinates. The coordinates of each control point should be marked on them and they must be given names, e.g. CP 1, CP 2, etc.

Setting up the Total Station: The TS requires line of sight observations and must be set up over a known point (control point) or within line of sight of two or more known points. Before measurements can be made with the TS, check that no previous default settings have been registered by the last person to use the instrument.

- Before the instrument is placed on the tribrach the tripod legs should be spread (not too wide) and their points placed so that the tripod is approximately level over the control point by eye first and if needed with the aide of a plumb bob. Consider the most common sighting direction and try to have one leg pointing that way so that there will be a gap between the two legs behind, avoiding the surveyor having to straddle a tripod leg for the entire session. Tread the tripod shoes firmly into the ground, making sure to press along the leg and not vertically down.

- When the TS is fastened to the tribrach the telescope must be at a convenient height for sighting. If more than one person is using the TS then it should be set to the height of the shortest person, for it is more dangerous for someone to stand on tiptoes to sight as they are more likely to knock the instrument out of position than someone bending slightly to look through the telescope.

- Once the TS is fastened on the tripod it must be exactly positioned over the control point using a laser plummet, which is a spot of red light projected from the base of the instrument, or an optical plummet where you eye in a cross-hair. Once switched on the laser plummet should be centred by rotating the three levelling

161

screws mounted horizontally at the base of the instrument, either together or individually. The cross hairs or laser beam should eventually overlie the control point.

- To check if the instrument is evenly balanced levels called a pond or bull's-eye are also mounted on the TS. By adjusting the length of the three adjustable legs on the tripod the bubble can be centred, thus making the instrument approximately level, with the laser plummet still centred.

- As well as this circular level there will also be a long tubular spirit level (this may be an electronic spirit level on the screen), the bubble of which should be centred by rotating two of the tribrach screws in the opposite direction; the bubble follows the direction of the left thumb. The instrument should be rotated through 90° and the process repeated using the third tribrach screw. This process should be repeated until the bubble remains centred.

- If the laser plummet has moved, then loosen the centre screw and slide it (the TS) until it is over the point again. Tighten the screw. Check that the instrument is still level, if not complete the final levelling process again (Howard 2007: 59-60).

Assembling and Holding the Prism: Although this may seem straight forward there are various points to remember:

- Attach the prism onto the top of the staff. The prism is mounted so that its reflection point is aligned with the centre of the staff on which it has been mounted.

- Place the tip of the staff on the centre of the point to be surveyed.

- A good height for the staff is 1.5 m. This is the distance from the tip of the staff to the centre of the prism. The lower the staff is, the more accurate the measurement. If the surveyor cannot see the prism, then the height of the staff should be raised. The surveyor must be made aware of the new staff height so that they can enter this new height of target (HT) into the total station memory.

- Position the prism so that it is facing the TS. The prism must be held upright directly above the tip; a bull's-eye level is attached to give the person holding the staff a check that it is being held steady with the bubble centred.

- The TS must be aimed at the prism; the TS calculates the position of the prism, not the point to be surveyed. Keep the prism in position until the surveyor says 'Okay'.

Care of the Total Station: Total stations are expensive items of equipment and the electrical and moving parts are sensitive to rain, blowing sand, heat, and being knocked over. Therefore, it is best to avoid using it in heavy winds and/or rain. The plastic hoods provided should be placed over the TS if there is a light mist or moderately blowing sand. The temperature operation range for most total stations is between -20° C and +50° C, although a parasol can provide some protection in high temperatures. When transporting the TS, use the shockproof carrying case; do not carry the instrument on its tripod

The lenses, eyepieces and prisms must be treated with special care. Before packing the TS away, blow dust off lenses and prisms and dust with a soft, clean cloth. If necessary moisten the cloth slightly. The plugs and cables must also be cleaned periodically if they become dirty, use pure alcohol for this. If they TS had to be packed away wet in the field, once back at the research centre it must be wiped dry, cleaned and re-packed.

Total Station Functions: The TS can record data digitally in the vector format, which can be directly downloaded into a compatible computer. If a suitable mapping programme is employed, preliminary and even more advanced data processing can be carried out. The datalogger, which 'remembers' the measurements of each point taken, is the piece of computerised hardware that makes this possible. The parameters are elevation (level), coordinates and the distance from the TS (Hawker 1999: 23). Pre-programmed locations can be entered into the total station's memory (such as the position of a National Grid point or a pre-programmed site grid), which can then be accurately established on the ground. With the free station function, a total station set up at an unknown point can calculate its current position after measurements are made to a couple of known (control) points.

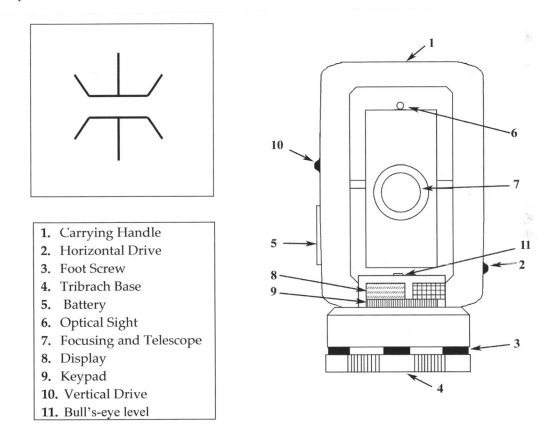

1. Carrying Handle
2. Horizontal Drive
3. Foot Screw
4. Tribrach Base
5. Battery
6. Optical Sight
7. Focusing and Telescope
8. Display
9. Keypad
10. Vertical Drive
11. Bull's-eye level

Figure 77: The total station or EDM symbol (left), and parts of the total station (right).

Total stations have one or two LCD (liquid crystal displays), which usually range from one to eight lines of 16-40 characters, with some capable of simple graphical display showing the map of points to be laid out. There are a number of different keypads, although they all function in a similar manner in that most keys have a dual function.

Some instruments use a single key to act as a switch to change the function of the key, whereas on other instruments a single strike of the key once opens its' first function while a rapid double-strike opens its second function. In all cases, a consultation of the manual should make their function clear. The keypad shown in **Fig. 78** is just one example, but most total stations have similar functions. There will be an on/off switch and a key that allows correction on an entry, abort an operation or get out of a screen. There will be alphanumeric keys and key to allow for transfer between alphabetic and numeric mode. Letters may be shown above the numeric keys on the keypad. These keys should be used in conjunction with other designated keys to input the data to be identified by an alphanumeric code; the coordinates of the instrument station, the coordinates of other known points, the elevation plus the height of instrument and height of the target (staff) (Bettess 1998: 122-3). Other keys will allow the measurement of each individual reading rather than the average of a series to be displayed (Bettess 1998: 121).

The three keys marked with triangles represent the horizontal, vertical and sight distance to the target (Bettess 1998: 122). They are used to display the reading of whichever side of the triangle is emphasised (see the triangles marked 1, 2, and 3 in **Fig. 78**). The V and AZ (azimuth) keys are used to display the values of the vertical and horizontal angles, respectively (Bettess 1998: 122). Most total stations also have keys that will give the values of distance and bearing from the station to the point being measured; with this information the horizontal zero may be set to grid zero and the angles recorded will then be grid bearings (Bettess 1998: 123). There will also be a key that allows the information to be transferred to a datalogger and from there to a computer. The values of the air pressure and temperature may also be entered via the keypad, so that the instrument can make atmospheric corrections, although this is rarely required on an archaeological site (Bettess 1998: 123).

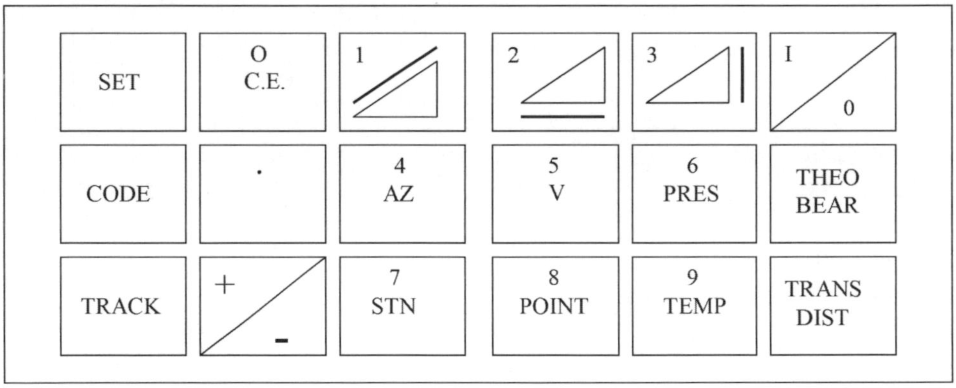

Figure 78: A typical total station keypad (after Bettess 1998: 122).

There are various screens, although the basic measurement screen (BMS) is where all the measurement data is displayed. This screen is usually the default screen when the total station is not performing any functions.

Taking Measurements: The major advantage that the TS has over the level is that it can acquire the X, Y, Z position of contexts and artefacts. The TS cannot record the fine details that planning can, but can quickly acquire multiple X, Y, and X coordinates of contexts. The three or two-dimensional point plotting of artefacts can also be acquired by the TS.

Once the TS has been set-up and turned on it emits an infra-red beam; a wave form is superimposed on this beam, which is returned to the TS from the prism on the staff held on the point to be located. The computerised electronics calculate the distance by the length of time the beam takes to travel back to the instrument (Bettess 1998: 118); the displayed figure is the mean of about eight readings of the distance (Bettess 1998: 119). When the instrument is set up and turned on, it sets itself to be pointing to zero degrees (north) when power is first supplied. The user must then re-set the instrument to zero degrees when it is actually pointing north (as described above). To start taking measurements bring up the menu screen.

- Either open an already created job, or create a new job by inputting the job name (i.e. 161209), such as the date or (GT161209) for your initials and the date. The total station usually has one job every day or for each task. A job organises all recorded data into a database.

- Look to see if co-ordinates of the control point that the TS is located over are already logged in to the memory? Type in the control point name (usually a number or combination of alphanumeric symbols, e.g. CP01, CP02, etc), if the point number/name has already been recorded its coordinates are displayed.

- If the control point is not logged in the memory, the screen will wait for the input of coordinates of the point that the instrument station is set over. Input the station name and the X. Y, Z coordinates of the point. As control points are also usually grid points or can be measured from a nearby one, the X and Y coordinates will be known, the Z, the elevation will have to be ascertained. To find the height of the new control point this must be measured in from a station of a known elevation.

- Input the height of the instrument (I.H.) by measuring and recording in metres the instrument height using the small indentation or TS symbol on the right side of the total station (**Fig. 77**) to the top of the nail/peg.

- Focus the reticle cross hairs in the telescope by pointing the telescope at some other uniformly light surface (i.e. the sky), and rotate the inner black portion of the eyepiece until the cross hairs are sharp and black. Sight the reflector so that the crosshairs on the telescope are in the centre of the prism. Use the optical sight (finder) and align the optical sight arrow with the prism staff or prism and lock the upper clamp. Look through the telescope and find the prism and lock the vertical clamp. Use the fine-tuning knobs on the ends of the clamps to centre the crosshairs on the centre of the prism.

- In the menu display there are methods of setting the backsight point, select coordinates. Input the backsight point name or number. The TBM is a good point to use as a backsight, although the next control point after the station point the TS is set over can also be selected. Input the code which is usually 'BS' for backsight. Enter the coordinates of the backsight point.

- Check that the height of target (HT) is correct. The height of target is the height from the tip of the staff to the centre of the prism. If the height of target is incorrect, input the height of the target that the rod person reads to you from the prism staff.

- Set the prism on the backsight point and sight in the prism. Enter this information and the station is recorded and the HAZ (horizontal azimuth) is calculated between the two points from the input coordinates. Now all of the points measured will be spatially referenced.

- To make sure that the TS is on the grid system, take a measurement of a known point. If the measurement is correct then record the shot as the next consecutive point number after the backsight and the code. If the measurement is incorrect then the TS must be re-set up, although it may be various other problems.

- When taking measurements make sure that the X, Y, Z coordinates are displayed on the basic measurements screen menu. If they are not displayed press the relevant display key until they are displayed. Have the staff person position the prism on the point wished to be measured. Sight the centre of the prism with the crosshairs. Record the measurement into the specified job's database. Raw and coordinate (XYZ) data are recorded. The point name input screen is displayed. Enter the point information for the point name, e.g. 9. Enter the height of the target (i.e. height of the staff). Enter the code followed by a / (slash) followed by the initials of the surveyor who is taking the shot (to know whose point the shot is) (e.g. GJT). If wished the X, Y, Z coordinates can be recorded on one of the various level forms (**sheets 3 to 4**) along with any comments about the shot that might help when planning.

The information in the TS can be printed out in database form once it has been downloaded into a computer, which must occur regularly to avoid it being wiped by mistake. A time should be set for all the downloading of information into a computer. Anyone who has data stored in the datalogger should be present at this downloading or make the operator aware that they have data stored in the TS. The information stored in the TS will usually be downloaded into survey processing software, such as *Surfer, Geoplot* or *Geo Office* by Leica (for use with their range of high precision total stations) to locate your trenches on the base plan. Some of the new total stations have in-built software, such as the Trimble 5600 One Man Direct Reflex Total Station plus *FastMAP* on-board software. However, programmes such as ESRI's *ArcGIS,* Cadcorp's *SIS* or *Terraform* will allow more sophisticated manipulation of the data, including 3-D imaging, digital elevation models (DEM), and even virtual sectioning of any part of the site (Hawker 1999: 23; Hughes 1999; Lock & Stančič 1995). By using a light pen and/or digitising tablet to digitise plans and sections drawn in the field, this information can be imported to your mapping programme and added to the point information made by the TS in order to create a detailed picture of the site. These data sets form an integral element of Geographic Information Systems (GIS), with the GIS programme acting as the central data centre for digital storage, retrieval, analysis, and publication. Spatial data are recorded in two formats to facilitate using the data in GIS: points and polygons. A point is a single X, Y, Z coordinate that is recorded for a special find or elevation recording. A polygon is a closed plane figure with at least three vertices or more (e.g. triangle, rectangle, or octagon). Polygons are used to draw, digitally, archaeological contexts in the field. A polygon is recorded using a total station by collecting multiple coordinates of the different vertices of the desired context (Conolly & Lake 2006). Plans and architectural drawings from past archaeological missions are also being digitised to modern standards (Johnson In Press).

Figure 79: The total station in use. In the foreground is a traverse unit prism mounted on a tripod located over the backsight, the surveyor has her TS located over a control point and the first staff person (behind the water tank) holds a roving prism and staff on the foresight point and the second staff person (to the left of the photograph) holds one over a second point to enable the laying out of a new trench.

Alternatively, directly transfer in the field by linking the total station to a ruggidised laptop computer. Each shot is recorded directly to hard or removable disc, circumventing any on-board TS storage. However, storage is only one aspect this direct link. When attached to the total station, the computer's greater memory and computational capabilities become available. Control of the total station usually passes to the computer, and complex annotation of points (types of shots, context numbers, artefact numbers, and contextual information, etc.) can be input through menus, pointing devices, or the keyboard. This alphanumeric information is not easily added from the cramped and limited keypads of the TS. Immediate data reduction and display are another obvious outcome - the larger screens of laptop computers are much more effective than TS displays in showing data point positions as they are shot (Conolly & Lake 2006: 61-77; Rick 1996). Data relationships can therefore be identified during fieldwork, and anomalous point positions can alert the survey team to errors in instrument setup or alignment before significant amounts of inaccurate data are collected. A more portable means of adding greater memory and computational capabilities is by attaching a PDA, such as the ruggidised TDS Recon, which uses *SoloField TDS* software, although Palmpilot or iPAQ can also be used. The surveyor can enter data on a specific point (special find) or set of points (a polygon shape representing a context) and triggers the TS to record the coordinates for the point or polygon data. After finishing the day's excavation, these data are exported to a designated laptop as an ArcGIS shapefile, which contains both the spatial information for every point and polygon as well as a database with the data entered for each recorded artefact or context (Conolly & Lake 2006: 61-77).

*12. **High-Definition Three-Dimensional Laser Surveying**:* Range or distance measurement using lasers has been used by surveyors for more than three decades (Fangi *et al.* 2001), while advances in technology have enabled the automatic collection and processing of large volumes of range data using 3D laser scanning systems. Historic Scotland, the Glasgow School of Art and CyArk have been using this technique to create three-dimensional computerised models of World Heritage Sites, to enable better preservation of these important sites. The scanner is set up on a tripod in the same manner as a total station and can be set to remotely capture the complete geometry of the exposed surface of an object in the form of a dense, accurate three-dimensional point cloud related to the sensors local coordinate system. Conversion software can then be used to turn the point cloud data into a more advanced three dimensional model or a two dimensional drawing that can be exported to Computer Animated Drawing (CAD) packages such as *AutoCAD* and *Microstation*. The information provided by laser scanners has a high level of true geomatic completeness and detail, and virtually eliminates costly site re-visits to gather more detail (Coiner *et al.* 2001). In addition, the operation of laser scanners is independent of daylight, so they can measure in complete darkness. Laser scanning can be used to record architecture, measured building surveying, rock art, civil engineering, heritage preservation and virtual reality scene acquisition.

In principle laser scanners measure the distance to a target point and also the respective vertical and horizontal angles. The instrument can be sited tens or even hundreds of metres from the target object, and even a complex building façade can be recorded in just over an hour (Howard 2007: 24). Two different types of scanner are available – ranging lasers and triangulation based systems, which are outlined below.

Ranging Laser Systems

Pulsed Laser
A series of laser pulses are sent to the target and reflected back to the scanner by natural and artificial surfaces. By calculating the time of flight of the pulse along with the speed of light, the scanner can deduce object distance with an accuracy of a few millimetres. The laser pulse is scanned horizontally and vertically by rotating mirrors over the scene.

Scanning proceeds as consecutive columns of sequenced points that rapidly paint a detailed, raster style 3D image of the target area. The intensity of the reflected laser pulse is also often recorded, which provides an indication of the reflective characteristics of the surface, enabling the creation of quasi images (Lemmens & van den Heuval 2001 GIM Int). In some systems the true colour of the target point is supplied via an additional passive

168

channel, allowing an instantaneous automatic texturing of the three dimensional model. The scanner must be stationary (usually tripod-mounted) while it is scanning. Two of the most popular makes of laser scanner are Leica's Cyrax, HDS3000 and HDS4500 and Riegl's HS2.

Modulated Laser

A continuously varying laser beam is swept over a surface via rapidly rotating mirrors. The returned beam is captured by a receiver that detects the reflected energy. The receiver matches the return waveform to the output modulation and calculates the distance to the object (Goldberg 2001).

Triangulation-based Systems

These scanning systems use optical triangulation over a projected laser line. A low-powered laser beam is deflected by a mirror, and a linear CCD camera observes each point of the laser spot on the object. Laser scanning using triangulation is effectively independent of reflectivity, texture or colour of the object surface. Laser triangulation systems are advantageous over camera-based ones, although triangulation is only applicable to small objects because as the distance to the object increases the angle becomes more acute and therefore less accurate.

There are a number of problems with all laser scanning systems. They are line-of-sight dependent, so may be areas of an object cannot be recorded in a single scan. Furthermore, divergence of the laser beam increases with range, i.e. the laser beam spreads out over a distance. Unfocused, the beam can spread to as much as 120 millimetres at 100 metres (Goldberg 2001). This makes the accurate capture of fine detail impractical at longer distances. Another problem is dark and transparent objects (i.e. marble and shiny black objects), because laser light is absorbed more than reflected. For example, marble will cause subsurface scattering, resulting in a degradation of the quality of range data. A small amount of noise is also inherent internally in all laser scanners. However, technological improvements are continually improving the range and definition of these promising systems.

Structured Light Scanner

Structured light scanners, such as the Breuckmann triTOS-HE, are able to acquire both chromatic and geometric data about an object through a single camera lens, allowing accurate mapping of the object's colour in relation to the 3-D data. The scanner consists of a small projector, which displays a structured light pattern on the object, and a separate 1384 x 1036 pixel resolution colour, digital camera. These two instruments are mounted at opposite ends of a tubular frame with an interchangeable middle segment so that the distance between the camera and the projector can be modified. By changing the length of the middle segment and the focal length of the lenses on both the projector and the camera, the size of the area to be scanned can be changed. Thus depending on the configuration of the scanner, it can capture 3D information at scales ranging from a single tooth to an area approximately 0.75 x 0.55 m (McPherron *et al.* 2009). The scanner projector uses a 100W halogen lamp to project a series of patterns, consisting primarily of alternating black and white vertical stripes onto the object. Measuring the deformation of these patterns the scanner is able to calculate the X, Y, and Z coordinates for each pixel captured by the camera. The scanner then floods the scene with the projector lamp or optionally with external lamps to capture a colour image. These data are passed to a computer via a controller box, pre-processed, and saved (McPherron *et al.* 2009). Surfaces of deposits with *in situ* artefacts are able to be scanned via this method and 3-D images produced.

Distance and Ultrasonic Measurers

Sonin 45 Ultrasonic Tape

Electronic distance measuring tools send out narrow beams of sound waves that bounce off solid objects back to a hand-held receiver. They contain custom electronics and a microprocessor that convert elapsed time into a distance measurement and display it on a LCD screen. This is not a three-dimensional measuring tool, but an electronic tape measure that gives millimetre accuracy. These are very suitable for measuring buildings, both inside and out, but their short-range makes them less useful for field surveys (Howard 2007: 17).

Disto Plus Laser Measure

Laser measures such as the Disto Plus give high-precision single distance measurements, and enable further electronic processing of measurement data. A series of laser pulses are sent to the target and reflected back to the scanner from natural and artificial surfaces. The measurement data is stored in the hand-held device, which can then be downloaded to a PDA (Pocket PC) or directly to a laptop, and easily used for other purposes. Software programs such as *PlusDraw* allow the creation of simple sketches with values; the sketches can be transferred as a graphic file (bmp) to the PC, while the recorded data is stored in a dedicated Excel file. Advances in this technology are enabling long-range (1000 m) to be measured and certain models incorporate electronic compasses and clinometers for measuring slope, and the ability to directly connect to a GPS device (Howard 2007: 18).

13. Global Positioning Systems (GPS): A GPS calculates the grid reference for your position from orbiting satellites, and operates on the same map projection system as officially published maps (for most modern ones this is WGS84). There are various types of GPS systems, giving varying degrees of accuracy. It you are conducting a landscape survey to locate sites then a navigation grade GPS will normally be sufficient. Many topographical surveys nowadays are being conducted with survey-grade GPS or Differential GPS (DGPS) to give 0.10 m accuracy (English Heritage 2003). These GPS surveys use either static or real-time kinetic data collection and allow rapid and accurate gathering of three-dimensional points on the landscape to allow ground modelling in CAD and GIS software packages. Pay close attention to the manufacturer's directions to heighten accuracy, and always wait a few minutes for the receiver to lock on to the available satellites after switching on.

Navigation Grade (Hand-Held) GPS: These allow map and absolute accuracy of approximately 10 m. These are good for finding locations in relation to maps and relocating sites. These are not suitable for site survey, and are notoriously inaccurate for elevations. Brunton have produced a digital altimeter and compass called the Nomad™ V2 Pro, which records the altitude to within 30 cm, which is an affordable means of recording height a.s.l. Some models by Garman and Magellan now include DGPS options and have real-time Satellite Based Augmentation System (SBAS) solutions such as WAAS and EGNOS capabilities, which increase the accuracy to within 3 metres.

Mapping-Grade (GIS Data Collection) GPS: These allow map and absolute accuracy of 1 m to be achieved in real-time or in post-processing. These are suitable for mapping at up to 1:2,500 scale, but are not suitable for site surveys.

Survey-Grade (Differential) GPS: These allow map and absolute accuracy of approximately 0.10 m to be achieved in real-time or in post-processing. These use a static base station and a roving receiver. They can create accurate, measured survey plans at 1:1,000 and larger scales as well as three-dimensional data.

Relative accuracy can easily be achieved in laying-out and measuring within a grid using total stations, dumpy levels and tape measures (Bowden 1999, 2002). For these functions survey-grade GPS offers no advantages over traditional technologies. Survey-grade GPS is particularly good at locating site surveys, objects, monuments and landscapes relative to maps (English Heritage 2003: 8). For speed of data collection - particularly where accurate three-dimensional modelling is a requirement - then survey-grade GPS is the most cost efficient method to gather large volumes of data to a high degree of accuracy (English Heritage 2003: 7-8). A real-time kinematic (RKT) GPS gridless survey requires survey-grade GPS equipment, such as a Trimble R8 or Leica GPS900. The receiver, or base station (one is located on top of the Centre d'Études Alexandrines [CEA] in Egypt) is located at a fixed point and transmits GPS correction data to one or more roving units in real-time via a telemetry link, VHF/UHF radio or mobile telephone (English Heritage 2003: 11). The roving unit is then set to record continuously or by short stops at the points of interest to be surveyed. The amount of time that a point of interest is occupied depends on the amount of accuracy required, from a few seconds to a couple of minutes. To survey a large linear feature, the surveyor walks along the feature and records it as they walk, with two other members of the team scanning the area either side of the feature. Any additional features observed during the scanning are flagged and the surveyor records these with the roving unit after surveying of the linear feature. Attribute data can be recorded in Trimble's *TerraSync* software. The data collected is then downloaded to a laptop running software such as Trimble's *Pathfinder Office* where it can be further differentially corrected and exported as shape files for use in GIS programmes.

14. *Measuring and Recording in the Digital Age*: Any combination of the above methods may be used on site, but ultimately the type of methods used will depend on the type of site and the tools and instruments available. Consideration of the storage of the vast amounts of digital data produced during an archaeological project must form part of the research design. Mass storage devices, such as mini disc drives and other forms of external disc drives can now store from 160 gigabytes to a terabyte of data. However, these devices can malfunction, so **always** backup your data in at least three different places, also utilising DVDs that can store 4.7 GB or CDs that can hold 700 MB of data.

Advances in technology, accuracy and multi-functionality are being made all the time and it is worthwhile keeping a-breast of these changes. It is possible to record to millimetre accuracy, but this takes longer and is usually more expensive than recording to centimetre accuracy (Howard 2007: 8). Remember that the degree of accuracy required should be decided upon before choosing your measuring technique. This will largely be dependent on why you are recording the site and what you want to know. If you are recording the site with a view to either physically or digitally reconstructing it, a higher degree of accuracy will be required than if it is to produce scaled plans for a monograph. Although a record should always aim to be accurate, as Howard (2007: 8) states: you must always bear in mind 1. How much detail needs to be recorded to conform to the research design; and 2. What is the maximum intended scale of use of the survey product? As the reduced scale becomes larger, so the required level of accuracy also increases (Burke & Smith 2004: 112-3). The maximum ranging errors are provided below.

Scale of Final Plan	Acceptable Error
1:5	2 mm
1:10	5 mm
1:20	10 mm
1:50	20 mm
1:100	50 mm
1:250	100 mm
1:500	200 mm
1:1000	500 mm

Table 19: Acceptable levels of accuracy for features, site plans and sections (after Burke & Smith 2004: 113).

15. *Computing and Archaeological Recording Systems*: The use of computing in archaeology is a fast-growing area, and on-site digital data capture is becoming increasingly important to reduce time and errors in transferring manual data to digital formats (Ziebart, Holder & Dare 2003: 58). The instruments used for digital capture include those listed above; rather than downloading the digital data direct into a laptop computer, Penmap, Palmpilot and iPAQ handheld computers in conjunction with data acquisition software are increasing the mobility of digital technology. Handheld computers can run various mapping software for recording spatial and attribute data, such as ESRI's *ArcPad*, which runs on Windows. GPS units can be attached directly to handheld computers to increase their efficiency. The digital data is then first transferred to a CAD programme, then into a GIS programme such as *ArcGIS* on a laptop computer back in the research centre or base-camp. However, the use of handheld computers for running recording systems is still in its infancy. Moreover, as archaeological sites often have difficult working conditions and a hard copy is required for the archives, most field units still prefer to fill out the paper recording forms at present. These forms can then be manually entered into a database and plans can be digitised by means of a digitising tablet.

The *Abydos Survey for Prehistoric Sites* (ASPS) project is documenting and explaining the distribution of lithic artefacts across a desert pavement landscape. Artefact visibility on this surface is quite high and artefact densities are such that tens of thousands of stone tools are dealt with. To accommodate the recording of these an integrated data collection system was developed to and the multiple survey teams were equipped with GPS units, digital cameras, handheld computers, and digital callipers to document localities and to analyse but leave behind the stone tools in a field scanning programme (McPherron *et al.* In Press). The team used PocketPC based handheld computers running ESRI's *ArcPad* software with customised data entry forms and directly connected to GPS units through a serial connection for collecting spatial data. For the on-site lithic analysis, these same handhelds ran a self-authored data collection programme that communicated with digital callipers through a CF card to a serial communications adaptor. At the end of each day the data from the teams were transferred to a laptop in the field camp and organised using ESRI *ArcMap* and Microsoft *Access* software (McPherron *et al.* In Press).

Eiteljorg & Limp (2007) discussed the problems of integrating the three critical technologies: database management systems, CAD and GIS, and how to gather, store, analyse, and preserve all relevant data. The questions of specific programmes – entry systems, software choices, etc. – must then be approached as must be linkage of the programmes. An integrated, holistic approach demands consideration from the very beginning of the project, regarding such things as interconnectivity of digital data, systems of labelling that permit the same item to be labelled in the database, CAD model, and GIS dataset so that information can be retrieved (Eiteljorg & Limp 2007: 229). Single-context recording gives each item an unambiguous number, with the context as the base identification number for all associated objects. Every item can thus be traced in any computer technology.

Digital documentation methods enable excavations to be conducted more rapidly and with huge improvements in the quality and objectivity of field data. The integrated archaeological information system developed by ArcTron 3D, incorporates digital surveying data with CAD manipulation and database technology to record the data generated during fieldwork (Ring In Press). ArcTron's central application, ArchaeoCAD, is based on AutoCAD and can be used to automatically generate and edit archaeological plans. Using the integrated total station interface, appropriately coded data can be downloaded and directly converted into publication-standard, scientifically pre-structured plans. ArchaeoDATA is a database solution which can be used to record, manage and automatically cross-reference archaeological field data. ArchaeoMAP is a mapping module which acts as a connector between ArchaeoCAD and ArchaeoDATA allowing database queries to be automatically mapped (Ring In Press). This information system allows data of many different kinds to be combined and compared, a solution to the common problem of data format incompatibility. This, and the high-precision of plans generated from total station data, makes the system a powerful tool for the comprehensive documentation and management of archaeological excavations (Ring In Press).

The Museum of London Archaeological Service (MoLAS) uses a pencomputer with data acquisition software attached to a total station. The x, y and z co-ordinates of the TS are recorded along with those of a reference object and a backsight, before recording points of interest. When the staff-mounted prism retro-reflector is placed over a point of interest (e.g. an edge of a pit) an observation of the horizontal and vertical angle and slope of distance to the reflector from the TS is converted to a three-dimensional position of the point of detail, which is stored in the pencomputer's database (Ziebart, Holder & Dare 2003: 59). Further spatial elements can then be built up, and text-based and numeric data can be attributed to the surveyed spatial data, either as simple identifiers or as descriptive data (Ziebart, Holder & Dare 2003: 59). This data is then downloaded to CAD, terrain modelling or GIS packages for further manipulation, allowing a three-dimensional plan of the site or monument to be produced.

The Archaeological Recording Kit (ARK) is a web-based system that is capable of holding the spatial, graphic, identification and descriptive data required on an excavation (Eve & Hunt In Press). ARK uses open-source software that is designed to work with a digital or paper recording system, such as that presented in **Chapter 7**. The software is basically a database linked to GIS and includes data-editing, data-creation, data-viewing and data-sharing tools stored on a server, which are delivered using a web-based frontend. These make it possible for a reflexive approach in the recording, and for the various people working on the project to interact with each others' production almost instantaneously. It is also possible for people or groups working on the project to offer various interpretations of the data (Eve & Hunt In Press).

A similar web-based system using open-source software is the Integrated Archaeological Database (IADB), which is designed to address the data management from initial excavation recording, through post-excavation analysis and research to eventual dissemination and archiving (Rains 2007). The major difference between IADB and ARK is that the former does not contain a GIS component. The IADB allows the recording of finds, contexts, sets of contexts (i.e. cut with its fills), groups (associated sets of contexts – features), phases (chronological groups), objects (an assemblage of finds, contexts, sets groups and phases), images (digital raster images), illustrations (digital vector illustrations), diagrams, documents and bibliographic references. These documents can all be edited on-line (Rains 2007).

Whether millimetre- or centimetre-accurate, three-dimensional measuring of the site is essential to its recording and placing it within time and space. Without accurate measurements of the artefacts, ecofacts, contexts, features and structures the archaeological data cannot be quantified against other intra- and inter-site data. It is always best to learn to take measurements with a tape measure and dumpy level, in order to not only compliment the electronic instruments and methodologies, but better understand how they work. Knowledge of basic measuring techniques can therefore save time and money.

CHAPTER SEVEN

The Written Record

"The object of all excavation recording is data retrieval. At the end of the excavation all that remains are the site records, the drawings and photographs, and the finds. Any information which is not contained in one of these is lost for good."

(Barker 1982: 146)

THE RECORDING SYSTEM

	Sheet	What to Record
Excavation	1 Context Recording Form	For recording the characteristics of each separate context.
	2 Arbitrary Lot Recording Form	For recording the characteristics of each spit or lot.
	3a Levels Log Sheet	For logging the levels taken using a level (dumpy, etc)
	3b Manual Level Recording Form	For recording the levels taken with line-level
	4 Total Station Form	For keeping a record of the total station points and data
	5 Finds Register	For logging individual special (primary) and specific (secondary) finds
	6 Sediment Sampling Form	For recording special sediment samples for environmental or chemical analysis
	7 Burial Recording Form	For the bioarchaeologist to record the human remains
	8 Grave Recording Form	For recording the vital statistics of the grave or tomb
	9 Special Finds Recording Form	For recording the details and characteristics of special finds either *in situ* or in processing
Indices	10a Building Recording Form	To record standing or partially-standing structures.
	10b Room Recording Form	To record individual rooms in standing structures.
	11 Mud-brick Recording Form	To record details of any mud-brick found
	12 Masonry Recording Form	To record details of masonry
	13 Photographic Index	To keep a record of photographs taken
	14 Drawing Index	For logging drawings done on site
	15 Context Register	For logging contexts identified on site
	16 Pottery Register	For the small finds analyst to log the pottery found within a given context
	17 Stone Vessel Register	For the small finds analyst to log the stone vessels
	18 Burial Register	To keep a log of all the burials on site *
	19 Grave Register	To keep a log of all the graves on site **
	20 Structure Register	To keep a log of all the structures on site
	21 Worked Stone Index	To keep a log of all the worked stone on site
	22 Environmental Sample Register	To log all the sediment and environmental samples taken
	23 Environmental Processing Form	To record the results of the sieving or flotation process
	24 Archaeobotanical Analysis Form	To record the results of the analysis of plant remains
	25 Chronometric Recording Form	To be filled out by the director or geoarchaeologist to record the details of radiocarbon or OSL samples
Environmental	26 Macro-Faunal Recording Form	For recording large animal remains
	27 Micro-Faunal recording Form	For recording small animal remains
	28 Environmental Sampling Form	For recording single environmental samples for analysis
	29 Wood & Timber Recording Form	For recording wooden objects or timber used in construction

30 Pottery Recording Form	For the ceramicist to record the characteristics of pottery
31 Stone Vessel Recording Form	For the small-finds analyst to record the stone vessels
32 Lithic Tools Recording Form	For recording all the details and characteristics of lithic tools
33 Coffin Recording Form	For recording all the details and characteristics of coffins
34 Hair Recording Form	To be filled out by the palaeoethnotrichologist or bioarchaeologist to record the details of any hair samples
35 Textile Recording Form	For the small-finds analyst to record the characteristics of textile samples
36 Basketry Recording Form	For the small-finds analyst to record the characteristics of basketry
37 Rope & Cordage Recording Form	For the small finds analyst to record details of rope or cordage
38 Worked Stone Recording Form	For recording all the details and characteristics of worked stone
39 Building Material Recording Form	For recording all the details and characteristics of building materials
40 Conservation Recording Form	To be filled out by the conservator to record the condition and treatment of objects
41 Object Invigilator Form	For keeping track of objects handed over to specialists
42 Object Distribution Map	To create a distribution map of artefacts
43 Unit Inventory Form	For cataloguing all the finds found in a single-context or feature
44 Site Inventory Form	For cataloguing all the finds found on site
45 Age, Sex and Wealth Analysis	For spatial analysis of the artefacts
46 Expenses Log	For the director to keep a detailed record of all expenses incurred
47 Additional Pages	For any additional information not included in the above forms

48 Drill Core Recording Form	For recording the cores obtained through drill coring
49 Survey Recording Form	For recording sites located through survey

* While graves may contain two or more bodies, each body gets its own burial number.
** Each grave - whether it contains only grave goods and no body, or more than one body - gets a single grave number.

Excavation is a destructive process. Once a site has been excavated, all that is left are the buildings, artefacts and biological remains and - most importantly - the site records. Anything that is not either recorded or preserved is lost forever; as such 'recording is the absolute divide between plundering and scientific work' (Petrie 1904: 48). Therefore, the recording system should be designed to optimise data collection and retrieval, and facilitate the interpretation of the site. Recording of an archaeological site is done with three different media: the written record (recording sheets, note books and index cards), the drawn record (plans, sections, contour maps and artefact drawings) and the photographic record (print, slide and digital photographs and video film). Because there are many different types of site, it is important to have a simple, logical and flexible recording system. Using pre-printed recording sheets helps to make the recording of a site as standardised and objective as possible.

It is important to fully describe a context in order to clarify the formation processes that created it, and any transformation processes that it may have undergone (Roskams 2001:

169). The standardised and uniform recording of contexts in a systematic manner enables a consistent comparison to be made between all the contexts being recorded, thus allowing more efficient intra-site and inter-site analysis. The written description of contexts must begin when they have first been fully exposed; it can then be modified as they are excavated. The use of *pro forma* recording sheets ensures consistency in the recording of data throughout the site, keeping the information recorded as objective as possible. Recording the written evidence in this manner cuts down on human error, which can occur when filling out free-hand records such as notebooks, as interpretation can often colour observation, leading to important data being omitted (see **Chapter 4** on levels of interpretation). However, the recording system aims to incorporate individual field notebooks, which should complement the recording system and add additional – non-standard – information where necessary. The standardised format of the prompt questions on the forms is designed to force the recorder to address important aspects of the context, artefact or ecofact in question. Actions are instigated by the recording sheets, indeed they are an integral part of the document's design, however this does not negate the agency of the individual in filling out the forms and encourages free interpretation (Yarrow 2008). The use of pre-printed forms also makes the presentation more computer compatible, and is more flexible since the forms can be sorted into any order and later additions can be inserted quickly and easily. When the forms are checked by the field supervisor or director, they can see at a glance all the information contained, and whether additional data is required.

The recording system consists of 49 *pro forma* recording sheets on which to record the various categories of information (**Appendix 2**). The above table shows the complete list of recording forms; however, not all the sheets will usually be used on any one site. The system has been subdivided into four sections: Excavation, Indices, Environmental, and Processing & Analysis (the Survey forms are additional). The excavator will usually be concerned with between four and eight forms – the context recording form, lot recording form, levels log, finds register, special finds recording form, environmental sampling form and sediment sampling form (and related registers). The other forms are more specific and will be less frequently employed; many to be used by specialists. The assigning of context and find numbers can only be done by the site supervisor and as such they hold most of the indices, unless blocks of numbers are assigned to area supervisors. All indices should be sequentially numbered. The various categories of forms should be printed on different coloured paper (i.e. light yellow, light green, pink, white, light blue) to make recognition easier. The Processing & Analysis forms are only used during processing, unless an object cannot be lifted without causing severe damage to it. The Analysis forms – 41, 42 and 45 are either for use when a computer is not available or as a template for a database, making the analysis of the data easier. While the system may look a little daunting, it has been designed so as to divide the labour as efficiently as possible. The format of the forms can be adapted for other specific areas of recording that are not included in the forms.

FILLING OUT THE RECORDING SHEETS

The recording sheets have been designed to make recording, analysis, archiving and eventual publication as easy and efficient as possible. The sheets are also designed to be computer friendly, so that all data can be easily logged into a database or form the digital design template. Examples of filled-out recording forms can be seen in **Appendix 3**.

The Numbering System

To avoid confusion and replication, each context, feature, artefact, drawing, photograph and recording sheet has its own individual number. Many archaeological units number their single-context plans by the same number as the context they represent, and this is the system advocated here. A logical, cohesive, all-encompassing numbering system has been developed to accommodate all the different aspects of site recording (including contexts, artefacts, drawings, recording sheets and photographs). The maintenance of indices and registers is essential if the numbering system is to work efficiently, and on large sites certain indices must be maintained by only one person in order to avoid confusion. The comprehensive numbering system is presented below.

Recording Sheet Number: Each form is numbered in the top left-hand corner, so they can be quickly identified and easily filed.

Drawings: The single-context plan is the primary unit in the single-context recording (SCR) system; these plans simply take the number of the context they represent. These drawings should be kept in numerical order in an individual operational area folder before being transferred for processing and evaluation. The **Context Register** thus doubles as the single-context plan register. All other on-site drawings, such as multi-context plans and sections, should have a drawing number that consists of the site code and the sequential drawing number (i.e. TAD09-1, TAD09-2, TAD09-3, etc). Each area supervisor (or finds processor) should be allocated blocks of drawing numbers to avoid replication, as the drawing number sequence relates to the whole site rather than individual excavation units. These drawings are logged on the drawing index kept for that operational area. All drawings done during finds processing should be kept on a separate index and have the prefix FP. If more than one drawing is done per sheet, then it should be suffixed with a letter. Therefore, the 2nd potmark drawn on the 79th drawing sheet would be recorded thus: FPTAD09-79b. The **Drawing Index** should be kept and maintained by the area supervisors or finds manager.

Photographs: The site photographer is responsible the **Field Photography Index**. The photographs are recorded by roll and frame number; therefore, roll 9, frame 36 is recorded as 9/36. You may wish to keep different registers for black and white, slide or digital media.

Site Code: The site code comprises the abbreviation of the site's name and the year of work. If there is more than one season per year, a suffix must be added. The second season of excavation at Tell Abu Dawood in the year 2009, would thus be recorded as TAD09.2, if only one season of excavation was conducted in that year it would be recorded as TAD09.

Contexts: The **Context Register** must be kept and maintained by only one person, usually the site supervisor. Each context is allocated a sequential number. The allocation of context numbers relates to the whole site rather than individual excavation units. Area supervisors may be allocated 10 to 50 context numbers, which the area supervisors then allocate to contexts as they appear and log the information in their own register. The site supervisor should transfer these data to the main context register at the earliest convenient moment.

Graves: Graves are allocated a sequential number (1-n) for the whole site; the number must be prefixed with a 'G' (G1, G2…). The **Graves Register** must be kept and maintained by only one person - usually by the bioarchaeologist.

Burials: Burials are numbered sequentially for the whole site, and are prefixed with a 'B' (B1, B2…). The **Burials Register** must be kept and maintained by the bioarchaeologist.

Structures: Structures are numbered sequentially from 1 upwards for the whole site. These are prefixed with an 'S' (S1, S2…). The **Structures Register** must be kept and maintained by only one person, usually by the site supervisor.

Finds: There are two different categories of finds: bulk finds and special finds. Bulk finds are deposited in plastic bags with a label placed inside with their provenience information and sequential bag number (the find number is thus the context number and sequential number, i.e. 395-1). However, if there are lots of finds of a particular category, such as pottery, they should be put in a pottery 'basket' (usually a bucket) and labelled the same way as the finds bags, but the finds number is the context and sequential basket number. The amount (and sequential number if wished) of bags for each category of finds are then entered on the back of the context form before being sent for finds processing and cataloguing on the **Single Unit Inventory Form: Sheet 43** and subsequently **Site Inventory: Sheet 44**. Special finds are numbered sequentially for the whole site and placed in their own bag or other container with a label detailing their provenience information and SF number written in a triangle. The SF should then be registered on the **Finds Register: Sheet 5** and then recorded on the **Special Finds Recording Form: Sheet 9**. The finds register must be kept and maintained by only one person, usually by the site supervisor, although batches of numbers can be given to an area supervisor if they are excavating a feature producing lots of special finds, such as a large grave. Coffins are also treated as special finds, receiving a sequential number. Specific finds that are of intrinsic value (those found *ex situ*), such as figurines or coins, are treated in the same manner as special finds, but their find number is not placed within a triangle. Special mud-bricks and masonry should also be treated as special finds, receiving a sequential find number.

Samples: Samples are numbered sequentially for the whole site and placed in their own bag or other container with a label containing their provenience information and sample number written in a diamond. The sample number must be entered on the back of the context form and recorded on the **Sediment Sampling Form: Sheet 6** or the **Environmental Sampling Form: Sheet 28** and registered on the **Environmental Sample Register: Sheet 22**.

Levels: Levels should be labelled specific to each drawing (see **Fig. 133**).

Universally Applicable Codes: Without proper contexts, archaeological evaluations and research are valueless as they cannot otherwise ascertain the physical origin – and therefore the social relevance - of artefacts, ecofacts and other features. The grid reference and site sub-division are the most important reference markers to ensure that data are not threatened in this way; as they are used in almost all recording sheets, they have been summarised here for the purposes of clarity.

Site Code: Each site is to be allocated a unique code that reflects its name and numerical registration. For example, the site code such as **TAD09** reflects the name of the site (Tell Abu Dawood) and also the season in question (2009).

Operational Area: This may either be identified by a number or a letter or a combination of the two, or a name, such as temple, shaft 1, industrial area, cemetery, settlement, etc. This field is only applicable on large sites where two or more distinct regions are being concurrently investigated.

Site Sub-Division: This is the number of the trench or square you are working in. Trench 3 thus becomes T3, whereas, Square 97, Quad A, becomes 97A.

Grid Reference: The excavation grid is identified by the coordinates of the south-west corner grid peg. The coordinates of the grid squares in which the context is located must be recorded in this box. If the context is located in just one grid square, the coordinates of the south-west grid of that square is required (i.e. 115E/205N). If the context runs into two adjacent grid squares, each of the squares' south-west peg coordinates should be recorded. If a context runs E-W, it might be recorded 115-120E/205N; however, if running in a north-south direction, it would be recorded as 115E/205-210N.

The Recording Sheets

1.00 Sheet One: Context Recording Form: Each context (deposit or cut) must be allocated a context number (see Introduction for further definition of a context). Sheet One (with two layouts) should be used to record these individual contexts. Completion of the sheet must begin immediately, even if stratigraphic relationships are still unclear. If there are uncertainties, then the relevant spaces on the context sheet may be left blank but the excavator **must** complete the sheet when the necessary information has been uncovered. This may occur after the context has been fully planned, sectioned (if necessary) and excavated. The sheets must be completed by the end of each day's excavation, or by the end of the excavation of the context in question. The information listed below is necessary to fill-out the context recording form accurately.

1.01 Site code: The site code is an abbreviation of the site name and year, so the 2009 season at Tell Abu Dawood becomes **TAD09**.

1.02 Operational area: The area of the site you are excavating in.

1.03 Site sub-division: The number of the square or trench being worked in, i.e. Trench 3 becomes T3.

1.04 Context number: Each new context will have a new number that must be entered here.

1.05 Grid reference: Squares within the excavation grid are identified by the coordinates of the south-west corner grid peg. If the context is located in just one grid square, then only enter the SW peg coordinates for that square (i.e. 115E/205N). If the context runs into two adjacent grid squares, it would be recorded as 115-120E/205N (or, if the context runs in a north-south direction, 115E/205-210N).

180

1.06 Feature or context group number: If the context is part of a feature, the feature number must be put here.

1.07 Type: This is used to describe the entity, be it a deposit or layer of sediment, cut of a pit or ditch or feature such as a pottery cache, structure, hearth, etc. Mud-brick and masonry should be recorded on the special forms provided. This is also the case with skeletons, graves and coffins.

1.08 The reduced level for layers, spreads and fills means the highest (minimum) and lowest (maximum) level **on top** of the deposit (only one level is necessary if it is flat). For cuts this means the highest level on the top of the feature and the lowest level on the base of the feature.

1.09 Length of context: The full length of the context should be given in millimetres (0-99 mm), and thereafter in metres (0.1-0.9 m, 1.0-n.0 m) in accordance with architectural conventions. Indicate orientation (i.e. 0.40 m N-S or 0.26 m E-W), range of dimensions, (i.e. maximum 1.80 m E-W, minimum 1.40 m E-W) and note if one or more dimension is limited by the edge of excavation or truncation.

1.10 Width/diameter of context: The width (or diameter, if circular) of a context must be given in millimetres (0-99 mm), and thereafter in metres (0.1-0.9 m, 1.0-n.0 m) in accordance with architectural conventions and indicate the orientation of the measurements.

1.11 Thickness/depth: The thickness of the deposit should be given in this format: "thickest part in the east 90 mm; thinnest part in the west 62 mm". A maximum thickness is not sufficient. If the context lenses out, this must be noted in the comments, as should any lenses of organic material. If the context is a cut, then the depth of the pit should be noted. The depth of a cut should be recorded longest side first, followed by the shortest side. It the cut is large and complex, depth can be calculated from the difference between surface and base elevations taken with a level. If it is a small, angled stake-hole or post-hole, then the axis should be measured. This can be done by placing a rod into the cut and marking the depth that the rod goes into the cut (see **Fig. 80**).

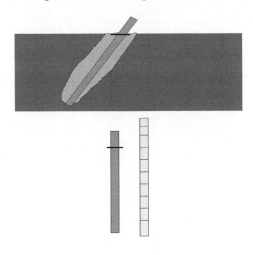

Figure 80: Measuring the depth of a cut. Measure the rod once out of the cut.

1.12-17 Sedimentary deposits are the overwhelming majority of stratigraphic units encountered on an archaeological site. The understanding of the environmental and anthropogenic formation processes is vital for understanding archaeological sites. Many of the descriptive parameters used in archaeology are borrowed from sedimentology and reflect either individually or collectively – the history of the deposit, including its 1. origin, 2. transport, and 3. the nature of the locale where it was deposited – the environment of deposition (Goldberg & Macphail 2006: 11). Sediments can be divided into three main types: clastic, chemical, and organic, the first two being the most pertinent to archaeology. Clastic sediments are the most abundant sediment type. These are composed of fragments of rocks, other sediments, or soil material that reflects the history or erosion, transportation and deposition (Goldberg & Macphail 2006: 11). The majority of clastic sediments are terrigenous, being deposited by agents such as wind, running water, or gravity (see **Tab. 20** for typical clastic sediments). The other type of clastic sediment is volcaniclastic debris (tephra), which consists of bombs, blocks, lapilli (2-64 mm), and volcanic ash (<2 mm). Bioclastic sediments such as coquina and chalk consist of fine fragments of marine organisms, such as molluscs and corals mixed with other sediments. Non-clastic sediments are less common, and can be divided into chemical such as carbonates (limestones), evaporates (chlorides, sulphates, silicates and phosphates), and travertines and flowstones (cave and karst settings). These types of sediments are produced by direct precipitation from solution (Goldberg & Macphail 2006: 13). The second non-clastic sediment types are biological sediments, such as peats (coal, lignite), algae, bacteria, diatoms, ostracods and foraminifera. These types of sediments are composed mainly of biological, mainly plant matter (Goldberg & Macphail 2006: 13). There are six data fields for description of sediments.

12 – Colour: Sediment colour should be described using a *Munsell Soil Colour Chart*. A typical entry might be: "10YR 6/4 - dull yellowish brown". The colour should be registered in daylight, preferably in a moist, but not wet condition. However this may not always be possible, so always denote the dampness of the sample by the suffix D = dry, M = moist and W = wet. If a *Munsell Soil Colour Chart* is not available, colours should be described by their value (darkness), hue (e.g. greyish), and chroma (e.g. brown). Accurate colour determinations are valuable in recognising subtle microstratigraphic details and can contribute to the interpretation of the mode of formation. Oxidation can produce reddish or yellowish colours, whereas reducing conditions produce dark bluish or grey colours. High organic matter content often produces dark brown, black or grey sediment. Good drainage and aeration are often conducive to the development of reddish and yellowish colours, whereas poor drainage usually produces mottled greyish, brownish, and yellowish colours (Hassan 1978: 201).

13 – Composition/texture/particle size: Description of the size of the sedimentary particles (see **Tab. 20**) and relative proportions of sand, silt or clay contained in the sedimentary matrix; and percentages of sand, silt and clay should be provided (see **Figs. 84, 85**). The particles can also be grits, pebbles, pottery, mortar, molluscs, tile, bone or organic matter. If there is more sand than silt in the deposit it should be described as silty sand. The size of the grains is a good indicator of the velocity regime that deposited the grains. Fine grains usually settle down at lower velocity than large grains. Flood basins and lakes are characterised by a lower energy regime than rivers (Hassan 1978: 202). Recording how well the sediments are sorted is useful in determining the winnowing effect of the depositional environment, the mixing of materials from different sources, and the rate of sediment accumulation (Hassan 1978: 202). If the sediments are roughly all the same size, then it is well sorted; if the sediments vary greatly in size it is poorly sorted, **Fig. 81**. The sediment formed from the sudden dumping of particles will be poorly sorted, e.g. slope deposits where a mass of material has been moved downhill (colluviation) and till from glacial meltwater. Wind blown deposits, such as dune sand are usually well sorted, as are beach deposits (Goldberg & Macphail 2006: 16; Hassan 1978:202-3). Measures of 'roundness' - indicating the degree of abrasion, wear or corrosion - should be recorded (see **Fig. 82**) to determine if the grains are fresh, transported for short or long distances, or subjected to solutions after deposition. Increased roundness in sand sized clasts is commonly associated with being wind blown, which is more effective than water for rounding grains. Limestone pebbles round much easier in a fluvial environment then chert pebbles, which tend to fracture before rounding. The presence of small round chert pebbles indicates many reworking cycles and relatively greater age than chunks. Well rounded pebbles generally indicate fluvial transport (Goldberg & Macphail 2006: 17-8). The shape of the grains should also be noted (**Fig. 83**). High energy riverine environments tend to create accumulations of spherical and rod-shaped particles, whereas low energy environments like lakes favour bladed and discoidal particles (Hassan 1978: 203). If possible also note the lithology of individual stones, e.g. chert. The full description of the sediment in this field should for example be: sandy silt (40%/60%), well sorted, rounded, discoidal. In the field the use of a magnifying glass or graduated lens and a sediment size comparator chart are useful until further laboratory analysis can be undertaken.

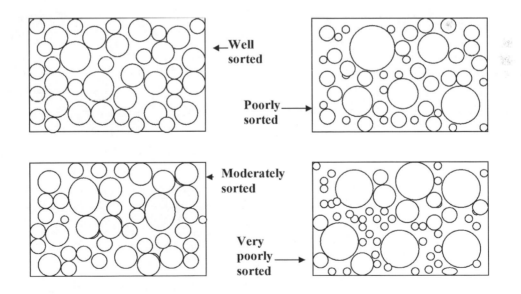

Figure 81: Chart for the estimation of degree of sorting (after Westman 1994: 33).

Mineral Size Class		Metric size	Phi (Φ)	Sieve µm	Comment
Boulders	Large	Above 409.6 cm	-9 to <-10		Rounded or angular and visible to the naked eye
	Medium	102.4 - 409.5 cm			
	Small	60.0 - 192.3 cm			
Cobbles	Large	25.6 - 59.9 cm	-8 to -9		Rounded or angular and visible to the naked eye
	Medium	15.0 - 25.5 cm	-7 t0 -8		
	Small	7. 0 - 14.9 cm	-6 to -7		
Pebbles	Large	6.4 - 6.9 cm	-5 to -6		Rounded or angular and visible to the naked eye
	Medium	3. 4 -6.3 cm			
	Small	1. 6 -3.3 cm			
Stones	Large	1.4 -1.5 cm	-4 to -5		Rounded or angular and visible to the naked eye
	Medium	1.0 -1.3 cm			
	Small	8.3 - 9.9 mm			
Gravel	Large	7.0 - 8.2 mm	-3 to -4		Particles gritty and visible to the naked eye
	Medium	6.0 - 6.9 mm			
	Small	5.0 - 5.9 mm			
Grits	Large	4.0 - 4.99 mm	-1 to -2		Particles gritty and visible to the naked eye
	Medium	3.36 - 3.99 mm			
	Small	2.83 - 3.35 mm			
Very Coarse Sand		1.01 – 2.00 mm	0-1		Particles gritty and visible to the naked eye
Coarse Sand		0.50 mm – 1 mm	1-0		Particles gritty and visible to the naked eye
Medium Sand		250 - 499 µm	2-1	500-300	Mineral particles gritty and visible to the naked eye
Fine Sand		125 - 249 µm	3-2	250-149	Particles, gritty and visible to the naked eye
.Very Fine Sand		63 – 124 µm	4-3	125-74	Particles, gritty and visible to the naked eye
Coarse Silt		31 – 62 µm	5-4	62.5-37	Particles, gritty and visible to the naked eye
Silt	Medium	16 - 30 µm	6-5	31-3.9	Particles have a silky feel, not visible to the naked eye
	Fine	8 - 15 µm	7-6		
	Very Fine	4 - 7 µm	8-7		
Clay		0.06 - 2 µm	9-8	2.0-0.06	Mineral matter sticky, plastic feel when wet
Loam		_____	>10		Mixture of sand, silt, clay and humus (organic matter)

Table 20: Size of sediment grains.

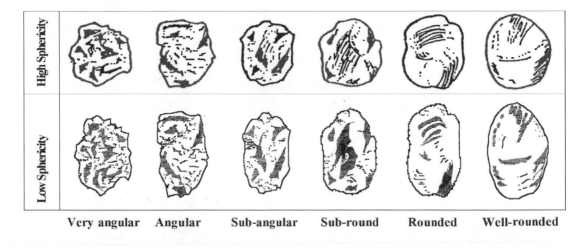

| | Very angular | Angular | Sub-angular | Sub-round | Rounded | Well-rounded |

Figure 82: Table to show degrees of roundness (after Powers 1953: 117-9).

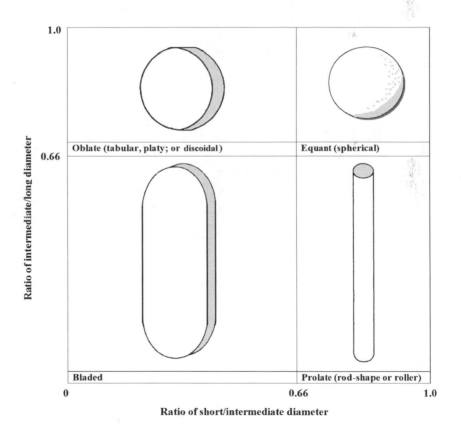

Figure 83: Shape of the sedimentary particles (after Goldberg & Macphail 2006: 18).

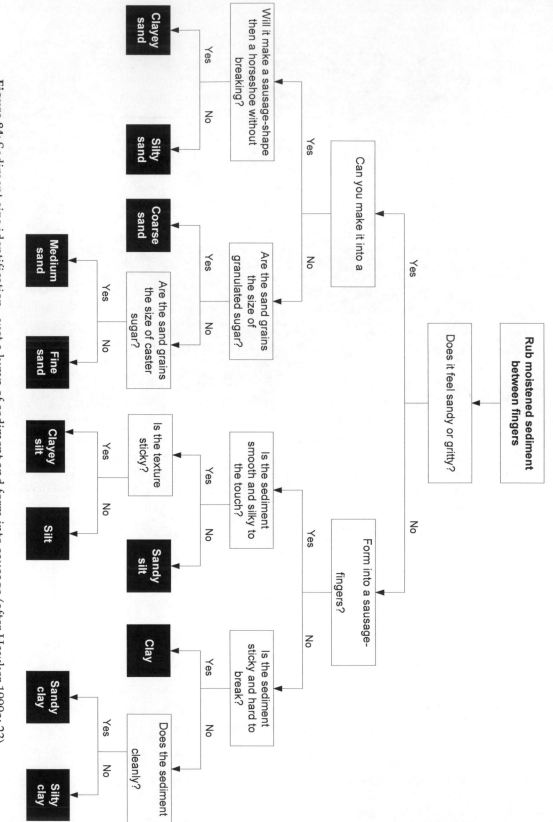

Figure 84: Sediment size identification - wet a lump of sediment and form into sausage (after Hawker 1999a: 23).

14 – Compaction/consolidation: The description of sediment cohesion, adhesion, strength and cementation (see **Tab. 21**) is important to note, and if this varies throughout the context. Take a dry or slightly moist cube of sediment and crush between thumb and forefinger. If it offers no resistance it is loose; if low pressure is necessary to break it, it is weak or friable. If greater pressure is required, the sediment would be described as firm. If it cannot be broken, it is compact, or hard. If it is bound together, it is cemented. Cementation refers to the precipitation of minerals between sedimentary grains. The common cements are: carbonates (e.g. calcite) whitish colours, iron oxides (e.g. hematite) yellowish to red colours, and silica (e.g. quartz) colourless to white. The compaction of a deposit at a particular point may indicate the insertion of a load bearing wall, at say 0.50 m above it (Roskams 2001: 180). The absence of compaction of layers in between would suggest more local compact, possibly from increased traffic on the context in question. In a series of dumping episodes the uppermost event may be more compact at its surface than its base, with the underlying dumps loose throughout. This compaction may be the only indication that it was once a surface of a road or street, with the other contexts being preparatory road make-up (Roskams 2001: 180).

Sediment type	Term	Definition
Coarse-grained Sediments	Indurated	Can only be broken with a sharp blow from a pickaxe.
	Strongly cemented	Cannot be broken with the hands.
	Weakly cemented	Large lumps thrown up by pickaxe, but these can be broken with the hands.
	Compact	Requires the use of pickaxe to excavate it.
	Loose	Loose enough to be excavated with a trowel
Fine-grained sediments	Hard	Brittle to very tough.
	Stiff	Cannot be moulded with fingers.
	Firm	Moulded only with firm strong finger pressure.
	Soft	Easily moulded with fingers.
	Very soft	Exudes between fingers when squeezed.
	Friable	Non-plastic, crumbles in fingers.
Very-fine organic rich soils	Firm	Fibres compressed together.
	Spongy	Very compressible and open structure.
	Plastic	Can be moulded in hands and smeared between fingers.

Table 21: Sediment typology (after Westman 1994: 31).

15 – Structure: This refers to the geometric relations of the grains within a bed, patterns of bedding deformation, and surface features of bed surfaces. Sediments may show primary structures, such as cross bedding, lamination, rill marks, scour and fill structures or post depositional secondary structures such as mud-balls, desiccation cracks, water level marks, bioturbation or fissures. Surface ripples and cross-stratification indicate wind or water flow directions (Hassan 1978). The help of a geoarchaeologist may be needed to fill out this section. Anthropomorphic structures, such as tip-lines, are usually only relevant for features that have been deliberately infilled, and denote the direction from which the fill was deposited. This is characterised by a sloping layer, often with stones gathering at the bottom. The side from which it was thrown into the pit should be noted as a compass coordinate. Discontinuous lines of greyish brown silt on a deposit's surface may indicate that the area was once covered by wooden flooring, the silt having fallen through the cracks (Roskams 2001: 182). Greenish staining on the deposit surface may indicate that there was once a copper object there and has either disintegrated or been removed. Undulations in a deposit's surface due to differential wear may indicate access points, whereas unworn surface may indicate that there was once furniture in that location protecting it from being walked on (Roskams 2001: 182).

16 – Coarse archaeological components: Estimate of relative proportions of pottery, bone, worked stone, shell (etc) not exceeding 10% that are contained in the sedimentary matrix. The size of the larger inclusions should be recorded as an average size with a maxima and minima. The proportion of each material should be described as frequent, moderate or occasional (see **Fig. 85**). Any mottles and patches should also be recorded, noting their size, location (on the plan), proportion of the deposit and material. Any concentrations of inclusions should be recorded, also noting their shape, size and location (on the plan).

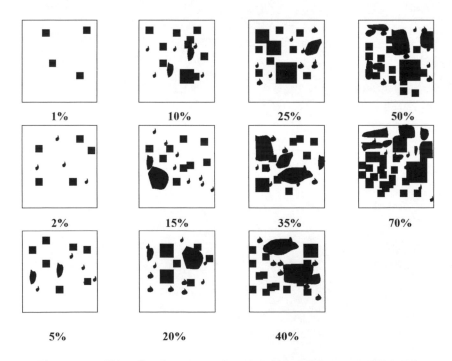

Figure 85: Chart for density estimation (after Westman 1994: 32).

17 - Coarse natural components: Description of coarse natural inclusions present in the sediment, which comprise between 1-10% of the deposit. The packing of these are termed as either open or close packed. Where the grits, gravel, shells, stones, pebbles, cobbles or boulders are separated from one another and interspersed with a finer sedimentary matrix, this is indicative of sediments formed by sudden deposition, such as dumping. Close packing - where the sediment particles are close to one another - is characteristic of slow deposition. The nature of the components should always be noted. Alongside inclusions flecks and fragments must be recorded – flecks <60 mm, fragments 60 mm – 120 mm - such as carbonates (calcite, aragonite), silicates (opal, microcrystalline quartz/chert), sulphates (gypsum, barite), oxides (iron, manganese, copper). The frequency of these components should be described as frequent, moderate or occasional with a description of their shape. The patterning or abrasion of surface inclusions can suggest a deposit was subject to wear, whereas the reverse is true if inclusions protrude from the surface, indicating that it was not an occupation surface (Roskams 2001: 182). The types of inclusion are one means of correlating deposits in post-excavation analysis (Roskams 2001: 181).

1.18 Fill of: If the deposit is a fill of a pit or hearth, the context number of the cut should be put in this field.

1.19 Context boundary interface: The interface boundary is the meeting point between contexts, and may be very abrupt, abrupt, gradational, diffuse, very diffuse, smooth, wavy, irregular or very irregular. The definitions are presented below. It is important to establish whether artefacts found within the critical transition layer pertain to the superior or inferior horizon, particularly if they are on a potential living surface. The physical stratigraphic relationship should also be recorded here, such as cuts/is cut by, overlies/underlies, abuts/is abutted by so the finds personnel can retrieve information about the physical contact between deposits, vital to understanding patterns of discard on site and for understanding the structural development of the site (Roskams 2001: 154). The numbers of all the contexts that physically interface must be recorded. This section can also be used to record cuts if they cut several other deposits.

Very Abrupt	Change occurs over a distance of 1 mm (or less)
Abrupt	Change occurs over a distance of 5-25 mm
Gradational	Change occurs over 25–30 mm
Diffuse	Change occurs over 30- 60 mm
Very diffuse	Change occurs over 60–130 mm
Smooth	The boundary surface is plane with a few irregularities
Wavy	The boundary has surface with broad shallow relatively regular pockets that are wider than they are deep
Irregular	The boundary surface has pockets that are deeper than they are wide
Very irregular	Broken boundary, very interrupted

Table 22: Boundary interfaces (after Hassan 1987 & Westman 1994:34).

1.20 The shape of the top of the cut in plan should be noted here. The categories are circular, sub/semi-circular, oval, square, rectangular or linear. If the cut is linear, note whether the sides are parallel, curving or irregular. If the cut cannot be described by one of the above terms, state 'irregular' and try to describe it in your own words.

1.21 Corners: The corners of the cut as present in plan view should be described as square, rounded, or irregular.

1.22 The top break of slope: The meeting of the surface and the top of the cut should be described as sharp, gradual or not perceptible.

1.23 Sides: These can be very shallow, shallow, moderately shallow, moderately steep, steep, very steep or vertical. The shape of the sides should be described as straight, concave, convex, tapering or stepped. If possible, state the gradient and angle of the slope. This should be worked out by measuring the height of the cut from the break of slope at the base vertically upwards, the 'D' or down axis and then forming a right-angle to the top of the cut, the 'A' or across axis. The gradient is then recorded as 'D' in 'A' – which means that the slope rises 'D' millimetres over 'A' millimetres. These measurements should be rounded (i.e. 10 mm in 5 mm becomes 2:1) and this should be put alongside the actual measurements of 'D' and 'A' along with the angle in degrees ('X'). Angle 'X' is worked out using simple trigonometry on a scientific calculator. If the tangent (tan) of 'X' = 2:1, then the angle is 63°43'50'. On the calculator you need to use the inverse of tan, which may be shown as tan⁻¹, invtan or arctan and is usually marked above the tan button. To access invtan, you usually press the top left button, marked inv or 2ⁿᵈ fn or shift then tan and the measurements. See **Figs. 86** and **87** for further details.

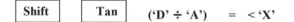

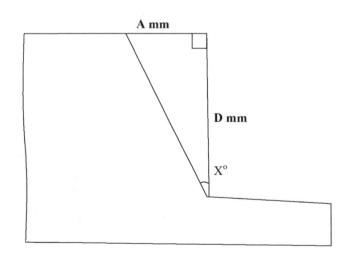

Figure 86: Measuring the gradient of a slope. If 'A' is 5 mm and 'D' is 10 mm, the gradient is 2:1.

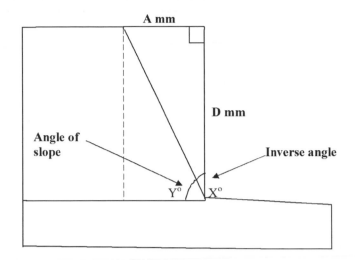

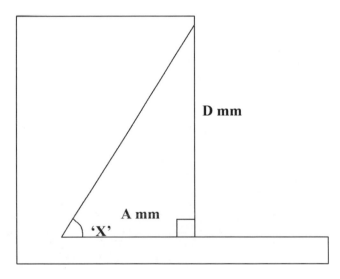

Figure 87: Measuring the gradient of the sides of an undercut. To be recorded as – 'A' in 'D'.

A simple check to see that you have got the measurements right is to draw a triangle matching your measurements on a piece of graph paper, the hypotenuse being the side of the cut, and then measure the angle with a protractor. However, **Tab. 23** is also designed to show what sort of an angle you should expect from certain gradients. The calculations given on the previous page are to work out the inverse angle of a slope. The inverse angle, plus the angle of slope, should equal 90 degrees. These measurements are important for drawing profiles and sections of cuts. To work out the angle of slope use the following formula:

| Shift | | Tan | | ('A' ÷ 'D') | = < 'Y' |

Gradient	Angle of Slope in Degrees (hours) minutes and seconds	Inverse Angle in Degrees (hours) minutes and seconds
1:5	78°69'01'	11°30'99'
1:4	75°96'38'	14°03'62'
1:3	71°56'51'	18°43'49'
1:2	63°43'50'	26°56'50'
1:1	45°	45°
2:1	26°56'50'	63°43'50'
3:1	18°43'49'	71°56'51'
4:1	14°03'62'	75°96'38'
5:1	11°30'99'	78°69'01'

Table 23: Chart of gradients showing their equivalents in degrees and minutes.

1.24 Break of slope at base: How the sides of the cut break into the base of the cut. This should be described as sharp, gradual or not perceptible.

1.25 Base: The shape of the base of the cut should be described as flat, concave, convex, sloping (direction of slope to be stated), pointed, or tapered (sharply or bluntly tapered).

1.26 Orientation: The direction should be noted, the head of the cut being given first (i.e. NE by SW).

1.27 Inclination of axis: This is only relevant to post-holes, and should be measured as shown in **Fig. 88**. The measurements of the triangle are noted as 'D' in 'A' and the inverse angle given.

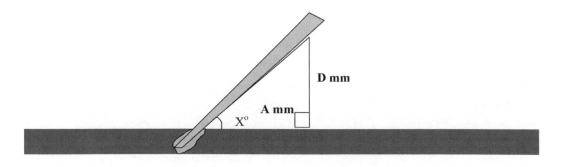

Figure 88: Measuring the angle of a post-hole.

1.28 Truncation: If the cut is truncated, state where this has occurred and, if possible, the context number of what has truncated it or, e.g. horizontal truncation by ploughing, modem construction, etc.

1.29 Fills: A list of the deposits filling the cut, stating their context numbers.

1.30 Any other relevant comments such as presence of erosion, if it is a natural context, etc.

1.31 Comments and further description of context: The first line requests basic information: is this context part of an internal (roofed) space, an external (open-air) space, a structural activity (e.g., a wall, a posthole, a ditch, a foundation cutting), or something else? Circle the relevant word; if in doubt, explain the situation under 'other'. This section is provided for any aspects that you feel need further explanation or comment beyond the abovementioned characteristics, especially the surface detail of the context. It is usual to start with a **brief** description of the context, i.e. a hearth fill, a pit cut, building debris, or "primary fill of grave \1157/". Then give a brief stratigraphic description such as "stratum of Upper Nile Mud Unit, which overlays whole site", or "appears to be a singular and isolated pit". The positions of notable artefacts, rocks or ecofacts within or on the context should be noted. Sometimes the description of the context will suffice and no further interpretation will be needed. Details of any drawings or photographs that cannot be fitted into the space provided should be put here.

1.32 Interpretation: Attempt a basic interpretation of the function of the context, differentiating between categories such as floor, midden, a tree trench (bowl), sterile layer, pit lining, rubbish fill, wall foundation trench and post-hole (and, if so, is it part of a feature or structure?). The interpretation should be made whilst you are front of the context. If assignation is tentative, provide an alternative. The reasons for your interpretation(s) must be given. The formation processes should also be noted. Cross-reference your context to other contexts or geological/archaeological features in support of your interpretation.

1.33 The method of excavation will be JCB, pickaxe, shovels, trowels, brushes, etc. Note whether the sediments were sieved or un-sieved.

1.34 The weather conditions, if it was sunny, rainy, hot cold, etc. should be recorded along with the time of day.

1.35 The numbers of the contexts above and below should be placed in the *Running Matrix*. The context being described should be placed in the central box. This is for stratigraphic relationships **not** physical relationships. Always keep a running matrix when you are excavating an area, and cross-reference with other excavators if their features or deposits have stratigraphic relationships with yours. Check with the site supervisor if at all uncertain about stratigraphic relationships - they must be accurately determined on site. The rules of contextual procession are self-evident but are nonetheless re-stated here for the purposes of clarity. Contexts that are above or within others will be later than that context, whereas contexts that are below or are filled with another context will be earlier than the overlying/infilling context. It is difficult to establish specific contemporaneity, although the placing of a post within its post pit, and the digging of a series of post-holes that form a house, are likely to be roughly contemporaneous. The lower boxes can only be filled out once the earlier context has been excavated, so remember to constantly reassess previous forms to tighten up on the stratigraphic relationships.

1.36 Note the numbers of any finds (bags or baskets) associated with the context.

1.37 Note the number(s) of any special finds found in the context.

1.38 Note the number(s) of the samples collected from the context.

1.39 Record the numbers of any plans, sections or other drawings made of the context.

1.40 List the numbers of any photographs taken of the context.

1.41 The value of the temporary bench mark or datum should be entered here, as well as the measurement from the backsight to the TBM, and the instrument height.

1.42 A brief sketch of the context should be put in the grid provided, showing any notable aspects and relationships; include a grid peg square reference, the scale, and annotate with dimensions and other relevant information. Do **not** simply copy the formal plan.

1.43 A list of all the foresights taken on the context should be placed here. A brief sketch of the section or elevation can be included if necessary.

1.44 It is very important that the supervisor who completed the recording form signs and dates it.

1.45 The form and interpretation must be approved and counter-signed by the director or site supervisor, and any conflicting and differing interpretations of the same data entered.

1.46 The database manager must sign and date this field once the process has been completed.

2.00 Sheet Two: Lot Recording Form: This form is for recording lots (10 or 20 cm spits or levels), which are sequentially numbered from the surface down, with the uppermost level being given the number **Lot 1**. A lot may contain several contexts or be spits of a large context. State the context number and lot number, as well as the context numbers and features that the lot may contain. If, for example, the context number is 1025, and the lot was number 6, it would be recorded as 1025/6. If a new context begins in the middle of a lot (i.e. 5 cm into a 10 cm lot) then the lot is stopped and recorded as a 5 cm lot. Any contexts discovered within a lot must be excavated separately. If these also need to be excavated in arbitrary lots, then a new context-specific lot system must be started (beginning with 1).

Information about the sedimentary matrix and any stratigraphic relationships **must** be recorded on the context recording forms. The lot forms must show the size and location of the lots and any contexts they are part of or may contain. The lot system can be used with either the box-grid or open-area method of excavation.

2.01 Site code: An abbreviation of the site name and year, so the 2009 season at Tell Abu Dawood becomes **TAD09**.

2.02 Operational area: This is the area of the site in which you are excavating.

2.03 Site sub-division: The number of the square being worked in, i.e. Trench 3 becomes T3.

2.04 Context number: The context number that the lot is a component of must be noted here

2.05 Grid reference: Squares within the excavation grid are identified by the coordinates of the south-west corner grid peg. If the context is located in just one grid square, then only enter the SW peg coordinates for that square (i.e. 115E/205N). If the context runs into two adjacent grid squares, it would be recorded as 115-120E/205N (or, if the context runs in a north-south direction, 115E/205-210N).

2.06 The lot number, which consists of the context number, and sequential lot number, e.g. **123/1** (the next would be **123/2**).

2.07 The thickness of the lot being excavated should be stated here (e.g. 0.1 m or 0.2 m).

2.08 Type: Is the context a deposit, layer of sediment or a spit within a feature. If it is part of a feature, then the feature number must also be entered in this space.

2.09 The value of the temporary bench mark or datum should be entered here, as well as the measurement from the backsight to the TBM, and the instrument height.

2.10 The reduced level of the top of the lot and bottom of the lot must be placed here.

2.11 Width and Length of Lot: The width (or diameter, if circular) must be given in millimetres (0-99 mm), and thereafter in metres (0.1-0.9 m, 1.0-n.0 m). The full length of the lot should be given in millimetres (0-99 mm), and thereafter in metres (0.1-0.9 m, 1.0-n.0 m).

2.12 The general appearance of the lot's matrix should be described here, referring to the context recording sheets used to describe the matrix in greater depth.

2.13 Contains: The codes for any features and contexts contained within the lot.

2.14 The method of excavation and any additional remarks should be noted here.

2.15 The numbers of any finds (bags or baskets) associated with the lot.

2.16 The number(s) of any special finds found.

2.17 The number(s) of the samples collected.

2.18 List any plans, sections or other drawings made of the lot.

2.19 The numbers of any photographs taken of the lot.

2.20 Any other relevant information must be put in this field.

2.21 A general sketch of the lot, showing the position of (and labelling) any features or contexts.

2.22 It is very important that the supervisor who completed the recording form signs and dates it, and that it is then checked and counter-signed by the director or site supervisor.

3a.00 Sheet Three a: Levels Log Sheet: At the top of the document are spaces for the following fields: Site code: (i.e. TAD09), Datum: the height of the site datum and the TBM: the height of the temporary bench mark.

3a.01 If taking levels with a dumpy level, consult **Chapter 6**.

3b.00 Sheet Three b: Manual Levels Log Recording Form: At the top of the document enter the Site Code, Grid Reference (i.e. 115E/220N), Site Sub-division (i.e. Trench 3), Context Numbers (that the levels relate to), Operational Area, Datum, TBM and Date. Follow the guidelines above, and in section 3a.0. At the bottom of the document there are spaces for the supervisor to sign and the site supervisor to counter-sign.

3b.01 Column one contains prewritten numbers referring to the eight points to be recorded if excavating in arbitrary lots.

3b.02 Before each set of eight levels are taken, the height of the datum (pole) must be taken and entered here.

3b.03 The starting and reduced levels (in millimetres or metres) must be entered in this field.

3b.04 The lot number must be entered in this field, i.e. **123-1**.

3b.05 The new lot number must be entered in this field, i.e. **123-2**.

<u>**N.B.**</u> The starting context must also be recorded, as must any new contexts. These are put in columns 4 & 5 respectively, and are recorded so that context 107 is detailed as C.107.

4.00 Sheet Four: Total Station Datum Table: This form is for the site surveyor to complete when using a total station and should by now be self-explanatory. It should be filled out in accordance with previously-explained conventions, consult **Chapter 6** for further details.

5.00 Sheet Five: Finds Register: This form is for special finds or specific finds found *ex situ* and should be filled out as stated above, consult **Appendix Two** for further details.

6.00 Sheet Six: Sediment Sampling Index: Sedimentary samples are primarily taken for environmental analysis or as a control sediment sample. Environmental samples can provide information on the economic, climatic, ecological and, human behavioural patterns. Control sediment samples are required so that the archaeologists can recognise the various types of sedimentary strata or contexts on site through morphological and chemical analysis. Each type of new sedimentary context must be sampled, especially those where organic material has preserved well (i.e. waterlogging or desiccation). Samples should only be taken from well provenienced and datable contexts, and must be sufficiently large to allow a series of tests to be carried out. The sample must not be contaminated with modern material, or include material from other contexts. If in doubt, take a sample. The sediments inside pits, wells or in houses or hearths are prime sediments for field sampling; the sediments contained inside pottery or stone vessels must be taken straight to the laboratory for specialist sampling along with the vessel that contains them. The size and sampling techniques are given in **Tabs. 3, 8** and **Fig. 25**. All samples must be double-bagged in strong finds bags; the context information must be written on the outside of the bag and on an additional spun-bonded polythene label placed inside the bag.

6.01 Site code: To be recorded as outlined above.

6.02 Operational area: To be recorded as outlined above.

6.03 Site sub-division: To be recorded as outlined above.

6.04 The number of the context from which the sample was obtained should be noted.

6.05 Grid reference: To be recorded as outlined above.

6.06 If the sample comes from a feature or group of contexts, the feature's code number should be entered here.

6.07 Samples are numbered sequentially for the whole site and placed in their own bag or other container with a label containing their provenience information and sample number written in a diamond (see **Fig. 26**). The sample number must be entered on the back of the context form and recorded in the **Environmental Sample Register: Sheet 22**.

6.08 The category has already been entered, for it will be a deposit.

6.09 Type: Variants include ash from a hearth, sand, silt, soil, rock or other type of sample.

6.10 The exact 3-D provenience of the samples must be recorded.

6.11 The sample must be described as dry (desiccated), moist (damp) or wet (waterlogged).

6.12 The nature and amount (none, some, heavy) of contamination should be recorded.

6.13 Describe the sedimentary matrix, including compaction, colour, composition and inclusions. Provide other comments if necessary.

6.14 The volume or dimensions of the sample must be entered in this field in either litres, or number and size of bags. One bucket holds approximately 10 litres. Alternatively, bag size should be recorded.

6.15 Give the size of the sample as a proportion of the entire context from which it came. This will give an indication of the entire environmental material.

6.16 State your opinion on the quality and reasons for taking the sample. Variables include visible botanical/faunal remains or good sediment consistency.

6.17 Further points about the sample or the proscribed tests that have not yet been addressed, i.e. the nature of any visible biological remains, the characteristics of the assemblage, the hypothesised use of the context or the nature of the local environmental conditions, etc.

6.18 Provide a sketch of the section and plan of the context, marking the sample's provenience.

6.19 The current context number (central box) and those of the contexts stratigraphically above and below should be placed in the *Running Matrix*.

6.20 The value of the temporary bench mark or datum and the measurement from the backsight to the TBM, and the instrument height.

6.21 The method of sampling (i.e. trowel, column, sieving or flotation).

6.22 Note the find numbers of any special finds associated with the sampled context.

6.23 List the numbers of any plans, sections and other drawings.

6.24 List the numbers of any relevant photographs.

6.25 Note the reference numbers for related samples (and the type of samples collected).

6.26 Note whether it is necessary to take any sub-samples from the main sample (for radiocarbon dating, etc).

6.27 Enter the date here, along with the supervisor's name and that of the data cross-checker.

7.00 Sheet Seven: Burial Recording Form: This form is for recording human remains. At the top of the document are spaces for the **Site Code (7.01)**, **Operational Area (7.01)**, **Site Sub Division (7.03)** and **Grid Reference (7.05)**. These should be filled-in as outlined above.

7.04 Context number: The context number pertains to the skeleton.

7.06 Each burial receives its own new number, which runs in a continuous sequence from 1 upwards. Consult with the bioarchaeologist or site supervisor to establish the last burial number recorded.

7.07 The grave number: Allocated by the bioarchaeologist or site supervisor.

7.08 Coordinates **A**: The coordinates must be taken from the site grid.

7.09 Coordinates **B**: The coordinates must be taken from the site grid.

7.10 The skeleton diagram: Provide a general record of the skeleton and a record of which bones are present. If a bone is present it should be shaded; if it is partially present only that part present should be shaded. Also indicate how the bones were bagged, the percentage of whole skeleton present, and any truncation with a line drawn in the following manner: ━ ·· ━.

7.11 Burial measurement statistics (you are measuring the burial, not the deceased's height):

    a. **Length** - Maximum length of the body, from the top of the skull to the furthest point of the body.

    b. **Width** - Maximum width of the skeleton.

    c. **Thickness** - Maximum thickness of the skeleton.

  Levels: The three most important levels to take are

    1. the highest point on the skull

    2. the base of the sacrum (if possible)

    3. the highest point of the feet

Any additional levels taken should be recorded on the skeleton diagram.

7.12 Type of burial: This space is for describing if the burial is a 'cremation', 'chalk burial', 'bog body', 'single interment', 'multiple interment', 'disarticulated', or 'mummified'? If the human remains are mummified state if: **a. Type** – is the body fully or partially wrapped? **b. Material** – mummification materials (i.e. linen, matting, resin or plaster)? and **c. Evisceration** – have any of the internal organs been removed? It should also be recorded if soft tissue is present but not mummified.

7.13 Orientation:

The Head: the position the top of the head is facing should be put down as either

N = North	**S = South**
E = East	**W = West**

The Face: the position the face is facing should be recorded as either

N = North   E = East   S = South

W = West   U = Upwards (facing the sky)   D = Downwards (facing the earth)

The Side: that the skeleton is lying on should be recorded as either

L = Left   R = Right

B = Back   F = Front

7.14 The layout of the body should be recorded by ticking the appropriate box (see **Burials, Grave, Tombs and Cemeteries**).

7.15 Position of the Limbs: Two charts are here provided so that the position of the limbs may be given a number, this should then be put in the space provided.

Chart One Arms

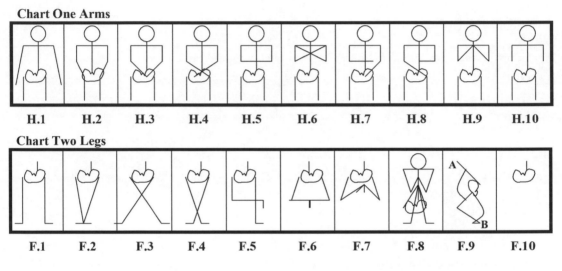

H.1   H.2   H.3   H.4   H.5   H.6   H.7   H.8   H.9   H.10

Chart Two Legs

F.1   F.2   F.3   F.4   F.5   F.6   F.7   F.8   F.9   F.10

Figure 89: Charts of burial positions.

H.10 and F.10 are for the excavator to put in their own position of the arms and legs; this should be drawn and put in the top right hand corner of the sketch, **7. 43**.

If the hands are crossed, the difference between left over right and right over left should be indicated using L.O.R or R.O.L. after the position number. For example H.10/L.O.R. or F.5/R.O.L. When the position of the hands is in H.9, then the angle of the elbow to the wrist can also be recorded, along with that of the shoulder to the rib cage, as can the knee angle from the ankle to the bottom of the pelvis, and the groin angle between knee and sternum when they are in F.8.

The full writing of this (contracted) position would be:

HANDS - H.9/L.O.R. (A. r 30, l 32); (B. r 45, l 40).
FEET   - F.8/L.O.R. (A. r 80, l 90); (B. r 60, l 65).

If the hands are not crossed, the LOR/ROL is redundant. Do not write anything in this position.

7.16 It should be noted whether the body is articulated, disturbed, completely disarticulated or grouped together with other skeletal material.

7.17-29 Must be entered by the specialist.

7.30 Any other comments.

7.31 The bioarchaeologist will usually score all the anatomical features of the skeleton recovered. However, it is advisable to have some basic training in scoring these features if a bioarchaeologist is not present at the site, or if the number of skeletons recovered exceeds expectations. Familiarity with the human skeleton will mean that you will be able to predict roughly what is coming next when exposing a skeleton, and will be able to identify unpromising-looking bones such as the carpals and tarsals (which look rather like stones to the untutored eye). You will also be able to recognise valuable pathologies, etc and treat them with the appropriate care. The charts on the right of this field are to show the presence or absence of teeth, and the development of deciduous and permanent dentition: erupted, partially erupted or unerupted. Caries, abscesses, calculus, dental wear, hypoplasias and opacities can all be recorded, although this analysis should only be undertaken by a bioarchaeologist. The space on the left is for making any further comments on the dentition. Brothwell's (1992: 52-4) dentition formula is shown below:

A) Formula for permanent dentition.

Right 8 7 6 5 4 3 2 1	1 2 3 4 5 6 7 8 Left	Palate
8 7 6 5 4 3 2 1	1 2 3 4 5 6 7 8	Mandible

Always orient skeletal remains as they would have been in the live individual. Therefore, the sides are as they would be recorded in the live individual, so if you are scoring teeth in a maxilla (palate) and the skull's face is pointing away from you, your left and the individuals' left are polarised.

B) Formula for deciduous (milk/baby) dentition.

If the individual is maturing, the dentition may be a mixture of deciduous and permanent teeth.

Right e d c b a	a b c d e Left	Palate
e d c b a	a b c d e	Mandible

1 = Medial incisor   5 = Second premolar   a = Medial deciduous incisor
2 = Lateral incisor   6 = First molar   b = Lateral deciduous incisor
3 = Canine   7 = Second molar   c = Deciduous canine
4= First premolar   8 = Third molar (wisdom tooth).   d = First deciduous molar
                                                  e = Second deciduous molar

C) The basic symbols.

A

\8̷7 6 5 4 3 2̶1 | 1 2X̶4 5 6 7̶8̲

8̲7 6 5 4 3 2 1 | 1̶2 3 4 [Area missing]
C

Area
missing

Key

X̶ = Tooth missing but socket present

2̶ = Tooth present but socket missing

X̶ = Tooth lost ante-mortem

\8̷ = Tooth not yet erupted

8̲ = Tooth probably erupting

5 = Tooth has a caries (cavity)
C

3 = Tooth displays an abscess at the root
A

D) A child's dentition with permanent teeth erupting.

\7̷6 e d 3 b 1 | 1 b 3 d e 6 7̷/

\7̷6 e d 3 2 1 | 1 b 3 d e 6 7̷/

7.32 This field is for recording any conservation treatment carried out, and must be filled out by the conservator.

7.33 The method of lifting should be noted, such as bloc-lifting or elements being collected in plastic bags. The bag numbers should be recorded in this field.

7.34 Record the weather conditions, along with the time of day the remains were excavated.

7.35 A description of the burial and your interpretation of the burial should be entered in this field. Special attention must be given to multiple burials, noting any apparent sequence of interments (i.e. overlapping bones), and if/how the burial was disturbed by another. The nature and position of any truncations must also be recorded.

7.36 Any plans, sections or other drawings made of the burial must be listed here.

7.37 The numbers of any photographs taken of the burial must be entered here. Take many varied photographs of the *in situ* skeleton, including all details, juxtapositions, truncations, a vertical shot, and associations.

7.38 The amount of any finds (bags or baskets) found on/by the burial must be placed in this field. There will probably not be any secondary finds, as the majority will be grave goods.

7.39 The special find number(s) of the grave good(s) are required here; only those that are actually on/by the body need be indicated. If the burial was contained within a coffin, provide its excavation number.

7.40 Record the number of samples taken from the burial for stable isotope, DNA, ^{14}C, etc., and chemical elements such as calcium, lead and strontium. Soil samples can also provide dietary evidence in the form of food residues, and palaeopathological evidence in the form of parasite eggs, organic concentrations (e.g. renal and biliary stones) and hydatid cysts. Sediment samples should be taken from:

a) the interior of the skull.

b) the lower abdominal region (and inside pelvis – sample blocks of fibrous matter if body is   preserved in desiccated condition).

c) above and below one of the femora.

d) a standard location in the grave fill (such as the centre of the fill).

e) a standard location at the grave edge (such as the top northern edge).

The samples should be placed in clearly-labelled, sealed plastic bags with an approximate size of 25 cm x 15 cm, and the number sequence logged in the space provided on the sheet.

7.41 Any other relevant information must be put in this field.

7.42 The value of the temporary bench mark or datum should be entered here, as well as the measurement from the backsight to the TBM, and the instrument height.

7.43 A brief sketch of the burial should be drawn in the space provided, paying particular attention to the position of the body. As always, North should be marked, as should the position of any grave goods.

7.44 It is very important that the supervisor who completed the recording form signs and dates it.

7.45 The form and interpretation must be approved and counter-signed by the director or bioarchaeologist, and any conflicting and differing interpretations of the same data entered.

7.45 The person that enters the data into a database must sign and date this field once the process has been completed.

8.00 Sheet Eight: Grave Recording Form: This form is for recording graves, and can be adapted to record tombs. The individual fills must still be recorded on the single-context form (**Sheet One**), mud-brick, masonry and timber elements on (**Sheets Eleven, Twelve** and **Twenty-Nine**) and the grave goods must be recorded on the special find forms (**Sheet Nine**). The overall statistics of the grave (other than the skeletal remains) should be recorded on this form.

At the head of the form there are boxes for the **Site Code (8.01)**, **Operational Area (8.02)**, **Site Sub-Division (8.03)** and **Grid References (8.04)**, which should be recorded as outlined above.

8.05 Context numbers: The context number of the grave cut must be placed within the box, and all other related context numbers for the grave (fills, etc) entered in the greater field area.

8.06 Each new grave found is allocated its own number. The numbers run in a continuous sequence from 1 upwards. Consult with the bioarchaeologist or site supervisor to establish the last grave number recorded.

8.07 The burial numbers of all skeletons or mummies contained within the grave must be entered here.

8.08 If the grave contains a coffin(s), the coffin number(s) must be entered here.

8.09 A general description of the grave fill matrix must be entered here, along with its context number.

8.10 The value of the temporary bench mark or datum should be entered here, as well as the measurement from the backsight to the TBM, and the instrument height.

8.11 The reduced level of the top of the grave cut must be entered here. If the cut is large, take the (N-E-S-W) readings.

8.12 The reduced level of the bottom of the grave cut must be entered here. If the cut is large, take the (N-E-S-W) readings.

8.13 The full length of the top and bottom of the grave cut should be given in millimetres (< 99 mm) and thereafter in metres (0.1m>) in accordance with architectural convention.

8.14 The full width (or diameter) of the top and bottom of the cut must be given in millimetres (< 99 mm) and thereafter in metres (0.1m>).

8.15 The depth of the grave cut should be put here.

8.16 The volume of the substructure or grave pit should be entered here, and, if possible, that of the grave superstructure. To work out the volume of a rectangular or square grave, multiply the length by the width by the depth. To find the volume of a circular grave, use Π (Pi – 3.142) and R (radius) in the following formula: ΠR^2 x the depth. The volume of an oval grave can be calculated as Π divided by 12 x depth x $(L_1 \times W_1 + \sqrt{(L_1 \times W_1 \times L_2 \times W_2)} + L_2 \times W_2)$ = volume of oval grave: Π divided by 12 x 0.5 x (1.1 x 0.8 + $\sqrt{(1.1 \times 0.8 \times 1.0 \times 0.7)}$ + 1.0 x 0.7) = 0.3095590149 or 0.3095 m^3 (see **Fig. 90**). Calculations **must** be done on a scientific calculator. If you do not have time to do it in the field, it can be done back at the research centre.

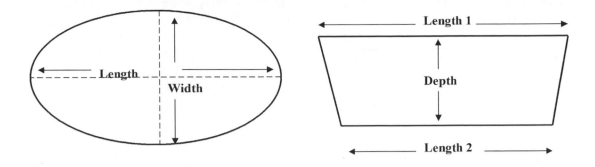

Figure 90: Diagram showing the measurements to calculate the volume of an oval grave:
Length 1 = 1.1 m, Length 2 = 1.0 m, Width 1 = 0.8 m, Width 2 = 0.7 m, Depth = 0.5 m.

To find out the area of a feature, omit the depth of the object from the calculation. However, to calculate the area of an oval: π x ½ length x ½ width.

8.17 Describe the type of any superstructure (e.g. tumulus, cairn, mastaba, pyramid, etc).

8.18 The material from which the superstructure is constructed (e.g. mud-brick, stone, etc).

8.19 The full length of the grave superstructure should be given in millimetres (< 99 mm), and thereafter in metres (0.1m >).

8.20 The full width (or diameter) of the superstructure must be provided here.

8.21 The height of the superstructure should be entered here.

8.22 The number of rooms in the superstructure must be provided here.

8.23 Any special features noted in the superstructure must be entered here.

8.24 Truncation: Note whether the grave cut has been truncated, and what part of the cut has been truncated. Also specify if there is a robber trench, stating its size and location.

8.25 State the shape of the top of the grave cut in plan view. The main categories are circular, sub/semi-circular, oval, square, rectangular and linear. If the cut is linear, state whether the sides are parallel, curving or irregular. If the cut cannot be described by one of the above terms, state 'irregular' and describe it in your own words.

8.26 Corners: The shape of the corners of the grave cut as seen in plan view. Categories include square, rounded and irregular.

8.27 The top break of slope: The extent or degree with which the surface breaks into the top of the grave cut. This should be described as sharp, gradual, or not perceptible.

8.28 Sides: These can be very shallow, shallow, moderately shallow, moderately steep, steep, very steep or vertical. The shape of the sides should be described as straight, concave, convex, tapering or stepped. If possible, state the gradient and angle of the slope (see **Figs. 86-88** and **Tab. 23**).

8.29 Break of slope at base: The extent or degree with which the sides of the grave cut break into the base of the cut. This should be described as: sharp, gradual, or not perceptible.

8.30 Base: The shape of the base of the grave cut should be described as flat, concave, convex, sloping (state direction) or tapered (differentiate between sharply or bluntly tapered).

8.31 The cut's orientation should be noted, with the head of the cut being given first (i.e. NE/SW).

8.32 State if there is a special entrance to the grave, describing any notable features such as steps, portcullis, doors, etc.

8.33 The type, thickness and context number of grave lining (if any) such as mud lining, mud-brick, matting, etc.

8.34 This field is for describing the material and structure of the grave roofing and note context number.

8.35 The number and sizes of any chambers in the substructure must be noted here.

8.36 Fills: Provide a full list of the deposits filling the grave cut, stating context numbers.

8.37 Comments and descriptive text of grave: This section is provided for any aspects that you feel need further explanation or comment. Special attention must be paid to intercutting or adjacent burial pits, considering the nature of their interaction. For example, the grave may have been re-opened to insert another inhumation. There is also a field for grave type; the main Egyptian categories include:

G.1 = Simple Pit Burial = The body was placed in a round, oval or rectangular grave dug into the surrounding sedimentary matrix.

G.2 = Jar Burial = The deceased – usually a child - was buried in a large amphora-like pot. Although the jar is technically a receptacle and should be recorded under the coffin burial form, the grave measurements and type should be recorded on this form.

G.3 = Grave with Reed or Skin Matting = As G.1, but with additional wrapping of the body in reed matting or animal skin. Reed mats can also be placed as lining for the bottom of the grave and also to cover the deceased. Plaster can also be used to line the pit.

G.4 = Mud-Filled Pit = The walls of the pit are sometimes lined with mud to provide more stability, or the grave is dug into the sand and mud is poured over the interment with no separate mud-lining. The grave can be either rectangular or oval with sloping walls. Traces of wooden sticks may indicate a roof. A wooden or ceramic coffin may also be present.

G.5 = Simple Chamber Graves = A large, deep rectangular pit, with one or more chambers. The walls are straight and usually mud-lined. The body is sometimes placed in a coffin, or just placed on the floor and covered with plaster, twigs or wood and matting. A roof of wooden beams and mats, supported by upstanding wooden beams, may also be present.

G.6 = Mud-Brick Chambered Graves = The walls of a large rectangular pit are built up using mud-bricks, and the pit is divided into multiple chambers by cross walls. A main chamber holds the burial, flanked by one or more annexes. A roof of wooden beams and mats was placed over the grave. The floor can be of mud-brick or of plaster, twigs or wooden planks and matting. The walls may be plastered with clay. The body is sometimes placed in a wood or ceramic coffin.

G.7 = Complex Mud-Brick Chambered ('Mastaba-Like') Graves = The walls of a large deep pit are built up using mud-bricks, and the pit is divided into multiple chambers by cross walls, often several bricks thick. A main chamber holds the burial, flanked by several annexes. A roof of mud-brick vaulting may used to cover the various chambers, with a mud-brick superstructure over the whole substructure. The floor can be of mud-brick or of plaster, twigs or wooden planks and matting. The walls are sometimes plastered with clay. The body is sometimes placed in a wood or ceramic coffin.

G.8 = Cobble Tombs = These tombs have a superstructure constructed from a heap of cobbles and boulders arranged like a tumulus over the burial. These tombs can take various forms, including: cairn (cobble pile), long rectangular, 'empty' tomb (a cairn with a built entrance and a separate wall around it), 'full' tomb (a cairn with a built entrance and retaining wall), nawamis (circular tomb with carefully laid stones and corbelled entrance), and a circular tomb (a cairn with a built entrance and large slabs for a retaining wall) [see Rothenberg 1979: 125 for typology].

G.9 = Mastaba = Mastaba tombs get their name from their likeness to benches, and are essentially a subterranean pit covered by a roof and with a rectangular superstructure. The earliest mastaba tombs were mud-brick buildings; by Dynasty IV most were built entirely of stone.

G.10 Monumental = There are two major types of Egyptian monumental tomb: the rock-cut tomb and the pyramid. Both of these types of tombs will require the use of building forms, masonry forms and/or mud-brick recording forms. The pyramids can be divided into two major types, the step and true pyramid. Rock-cut tombs again can be divided into numerous categories, including the gallery tombs (Serapeum), shaft and *saff* tombs.

The burial type number should be recorded in this field. If it does not resemble any of the types outlined above, a new description should be logged under **G.11** so that a new site (or country) specific tomb typology can be made.

8.38 Interpretation: Attempt a basic interpretation of the grave. The main categories of information include whether it is intact or robbed, rich or poor, a single grave or part of a cemetery? The interpretation should be made whilst in you are in front of the feature; provide an alternative interpretation if you think it necessary. Cross-reference to other contexts in support of your interpretation.

8.39 Detail any conservation or chemicals used to consolidate the grave.

8.40 Note the method of excavation (trowelling, etc). Note if the spoil was sieved.

8.41 Record whether the weather was sunny, rainy, hot or cold along with the time of day.

8.42 Provide a sketch of the grave, showing the burial position and matrix with a blow-up of any special features. There should be two views - a plan and section (if relevant). These sketches must have the context numbers written on them, along with the reduced levels and the north arrow.

8.43 The amount of any finds (bags or baskets) found in the grave must be placed in this field. There will probably not be any secondary finds, as the majority will be grave goods.

8.44 The number(s) of the sample(s) collected should be written in this space.

8.45 The number(s) of any special find(s) found in the grave should be put in this space, continuing on **Sheet 47** if there is a large amount of grave goods.

8.46 Any plans, sections or elevations made of the grave must be listed here.

8.47 Any special drawings made of the grave and burial must be entered here.

8.48 The numbers of any photographs taken of the grave must be entered here.

8.49 The excavator or area supervisor must sign the form and have it countersigned by a bioarchaeologist or site supervisor. The date that the grave was found (and the date its excavation was finished) must be entered here.

8.50 The person that enters the data into a database must sign and date this field once the process has been completed.

8.51 The form and interpretation must be approved and counter-signed by the director or bioarchaeologist, and any conflicting and differing interpretations of the same data entered.

9.00 Sheet Nine: Special Find Recording Form: These forms are to be used both in finds processing and in the field. In finds processing they are for small finds (both *ex* and *in situ*) and in the field for objects found in their primary context (*in situ*), such as grave goods, so that no information on the object is lost and an exact reconstruction of the feature can be carried out at a later date. If the special find cannot be moved without it disintegrating then the majority of the form must be filled out in the field. However, if the object is robust, fill out the provenience information, make a sketch and pass the form with the artefact to finds processing to fill out the remainder of the information. Special finds should be logged in the **Finds Register - Sheet 5**.

9.01A The catalogue or registration number given by the finds manager, e.g. TAD1002 (see **Fig. 193**) must be entered here after finds processing.

9.01B The sequential special find number (the excavation number given in the field) must be entered here.

9.02 Site code, e.g. **TAD09**.

9.03 Operational area: The area of the site in which you are excavating.

9.04 Site sub-division: The number of the square being worked in, i.e. Trench 3 becomes T3.

9.05 Context number: the number of the context containing the special find should be placed here

9.06 Grid reference: Enter the grid reference here. If the context is located in just one grid square, enter the coordinates of the south-west peg of that square (i.e. 115E/205N). However, if the context runs into two adjacent grid squares, it should be recorded as 115-120E/205N, or if the context runs in a north-south direction 115E/205-210N.

9.07 The category has already been filled out, as it will be a deposit.

9.08 The type of deposit: If found in a grave or structure, the feature number must be noted here.

9.09. The 3-D provenience: The X, Y and Z coordinates of the object should be entered in this space.

9.10 Associated finds numbers: Enter the excavation numbers of any special finds associated with the special find here.

9.11 Enter the drawing number(s) of the special find here.

9.12 The numbers of any photographs taken of the find must be put here.

9.13 Description and interpretation: An overall description of the special find. The location, how it was lying, other objects associated with it, etc. The excavator should attempt a basic interpretation (are there any biological remains associated with it, therefore possibly a food offering, is it a possible indicator of gender, etc). Fields **a, b** & **c** are to list the material, industry and object names (see **Tabs. 28** and **50**).

9.14 A spot date (estimate) of the period of manufacture should be put in this field.

9.15 Length of artefact.

9.16 Width of artefact.

9.17 Diameter (if necessary).

9.18 Thickness (if necessary).

9.19 Height or depth of artefact (if necessary).

9.20-22 Three data fields for description of the special find are provided.

> **20 – Material of Construction:** Type of material (ceramic, stone, ivory, metal, etc), texture of artefact (feel of the object - rough, coarse, smooth), colour of artefact (use the Munsell colour chart if available). Are there any inclusions, such as temper? Is it an imported material?

> **21 – Forming Technique:** How was the object made, what technologies were used?

> **22 - Decoration:** To describe decorative patterns or potmarks.

9.23 Record if any residues are present. Those to be sampled for phytoliths should be put in a sterile zip-seal bag immediately. Any other samples taken must have their numbers written here.

9.24 State the nature of the fill of the special find along with its context number.

9.25 Any signs of ancient repairs must be put in this field.

9.26 The presence of any drill holes, the number and purpose should be entered in this space.

9.27 Any other relevant information about the fabric of the object should be entered here.

9.28-32 This section contains five data fields for interpretative stratigraphic relationships, and relationships with other grave goods. In most cases it is a special find number required under the following headings:

> **Above** special find?
> **Below** special find?
> **Filled with** sediments?
> **Contains** special find?
> **Within** special find?

The excavator should use one or more of these fields to attempt to identify the relationship of the special find with surrounding or associated artefacts.

9.33 Is the object intact, yes or no?

9.34 If it is a whole object but in pieces, or just a few fragments, the number of fragments should be entered here.

9.35 Is there any soluble salt efflorescence visible?

9.36 Are there signs of any other encrustations?

9.37 Are there any stress cracks visible?

9.38 Is the outside or inside of the object flaking or powdering?

9.39 Condition/Friability: Solid, stable or friable – high, medium or low?

9.40 The method of lifting should be recorded here. Note whether the sediments surrounding the special find were sieved (the contents of the pots, etc. go straight to the lab with the pot; make-up palettes and querns should **never** be cleaned in the field, and must be sent to the lab with the surrounding material still intact for sampling).

9.41 State if and why samples of the objects fabric or material were taken (thin section analysis, thermoluminescence dating, isotope analysis, etc).

9.42 Note if conservation was carried out in the field, and what type of specialist treatment was conducted.

9.43 A brief sketch of the special find with its associated artefacts should be provided.

9.44 A sketch of the special find is required in this space.

9.45 It is very important that the supervisor who completed the recording form signs and dates it.

9.46 The form and interpretation must be approved and counter-signed by the director or finds manager and any conflicting and differing interpretations of the same data entered.

9.47 The person that enters the data into a database must sign and date this field once the process has been completed.

10a.00 Sheet Ten a: Building Recording Form: This form permits the recording and description of a standing or semi-standing building.

At the head of the form there are boxes for the **Site Code (10a.01)**, **Operational Area (10a.02)**, **Site Sub-Division (10a.03)** and **Grid References (10a.05)**, which should be recorded as outlined above.

10a.04 The structure number (acquired from the site supervisor or director) is required here.

10a.06 The type of building is required here (i.e. temple, rock-cut tomb, wattle and daub house).

10a.07 The numbers (and reference numbers) of the rooms inside the building are required here.

10a.08 State the reduced level of the ancient ground level, if known.

10a.09 Note the general location of the building within the site or complex of structures.

10a.10 The number of storeys. Estimate if uncertain, and justify your answer.

10a.11 The period to which the building pertains.

10a.12 The entire length of the building.

10a.13 The entire width of the building.

10a.14 The greatest height or depth of the extant building

10a.15 If the building is part of a complex or village, the name/number of the complex is required here.

10a.16 Note the overall ground area of the building.

10a.17 Note the overall shape of the building (round, rectilinear, pyramidal, etc).

10a.18 Your interpretation of the function of the building and any additional comments. Give your reasons for the interpretation, and note any other relevant evidence.

10a.19 The total number of walls in the building, state whether internal or external; the structural material of the walls; the finish of the walls (plaster or decoration); the percentage of walls left standing; and the minimum and maximum height of the walls.

10a.20 The total number of floors and pavements in the building, state whether internal or external; the structural material of the floors and pavements; the finish of the floors (plaster or decoration); the percentage of floors and pavements left *in situ*; the minimum and maximum thickness of the floors and pavements.

10a.21 The total number of roofs in the building; the structural material of the roofs, the finish of the roofs, such as any plaster or decoration; the percentage of roofs left *in situ*, the minimum and maximum thickness of the roofs.

10a.22 The number of windows in the building; the locations of the windows; the type of windows; the largest and smallest dimensions of the windows; materials the windows are made from, window furniture such as catches or hinges; any other details.

10a.23 The number of doors and doorways in the building; the locations and types of doorways (provide the same information for the door, if present); the largest and smallest dimensions of the doors and doorways; the materials the doors and doorways are made from, and furniture such as catches or hinges; any other details.

10a.24 Note the presence, number, location, type and vital statistics of any obelisks around the building.

10a.25 Note the presence, number, location, type and vital statistics of any courtyards and/or gardens around the building.

10a.26 Note the presence, number, location, type and vital statistics of any columns in the building.

10a.27 Note the presence, number, location, type and vital statistics of any stairs in the building.

10a.28 Note the presence, number, location, type and vital statistics of any pylons (if any) in the building.

10a.29 Note the presence, number, location, type and vital statistics of any arches, vaults or corbels in the building.

10a.30 Enter details of any foundations here, providing a sketch if you feel it to be necessary.

10a.31 Record details of any facing, sculpting or painting in the building here.

10a.32 Describe any fixtures and fittings, such as any provisions against rain, any drainage systems, cupboards, cornices, etc.

10a.33 The numbers of any finds associated with the building must be entered here.

10a.34 The number(s) of any plans, elevations or other drawings must be put in this field.

10a.35 The number(s) of any photographs must be put in this field.

10a.36 The value of the temporary bench mark or datum should be entered here, as well as the measurement from the backsight to the TBM, and the instrument height.

10a.37 A brief sketch of the building showing its rooms should be provided here.

10a.38 A brief sketch of the section or elevation should be put here; illustrate the bonding of the wall.

10a.39 The supervisor who completed the recording form must sign it, and have it counter-signed by the director or site supervisor.

10b.00 *Sheet Ten b: Room Recording Form*: This form is to record the general description and dimensions of a single room in any standing or semi-standing building.

At the head of the form there are boxes for the **Site Code (10b.01)**, **Operational Area (10b.02)**, **Site Sub-Division (10b.03)** and **Grid References (10b.05)**, which should be recorded as outlined above.

10b.04 The room number, acquired from the site supervisor or director is required here.

10b.06 The type of room is required here (bedroom, kitchen, etc).

10b.07 The building number is required here.

10b.08 The reduced level of the ancient ground level, if known, is required here.

10b.09 State the building materials that the room is constructed from here.

10b.10 Note the general location of the room within the building (e.g. north-east corner of building) here.

10b.11 Note the overall ground area of the room here.

10b.12 The overall shape of the room is required here (round, rectilinear, etc).

10b.13 Record the overall length, width and height of the room here.

10b.14 Record the structural materials that the walls are constructed from; their finish (i.e. plaster or decoration); the percentage of walls left standing; their minimum and maximum height; the number of courses of brickwork in the walls; and the length and thickness of each of the walls.

10b.15 The materials that the floors of the room are constructed from; their finish (paving stones, mosaics or other decoration); the percentage of floors left *in situ*; the amount of floors that have been relaid; the length and width of the floors and their minimum and maximum thickness.

10b.16 The structural material that the ceilings are constructed from; their finish (such as any plaster, paint or other decoration); the percentage of ceilings left *in situ*; their length and width and their minimum and maximum thickness.

10b.17 The number of windows in the room; their locations; type; largest and smallest dimensions; the materials the windows are made from, and any window furniture such as catches or hinges, any other details.

10b.18 The number of doors and doorways in the room; their locations; types; largest and smallest dimensions; the materials the doors and doorways are made from, and furniture such as catches or hinges; any other details.

10b.19 Note the presence, number, location, type and vital statistics of columns in the room.

214

10b.20 Note the details of any facing, sculpting, or painting in the room.

10b.21 Note the presence any fixtures and fittings (cupboards, cornices, light fittings, etc).

10b.22 Your interpretation of the room's function and any additional comments should be entered here. Justify and cross-reference your interpretation.

10b.23 The numbers of any finds associated with the room must be entered here.

10b.24 Note the numbers of any plans, elevations and other drawings of the room in this field.

10b.25 Note the numbers of any photographs of the room here.

10b.26 Record the type(s) and number(s) of any samples collected. Collect samples of the mortar, bricks and any matting, plaster or additional material.

10b.27 The value of the temporary bench mark or datum should be entered here, as well as the measurement from the backsight to the TBM, and the instrument height.

10b.28 Provide a brief sketch of the room, indicating its location in the building.

10b.29 Provide a brief sketch of the section or elevation. Illustrate the bonding of the wall, if visible.

10b.30 The supervisor who completed the recording form must sign it, and have it counter-signed by the site supervisor.

11.00 Sheet Eleven: Mud-brick Recording Form: Mud-brick was one of the most common building materials in the ancient world, particularly in ancient Western Asia and Egypt, where it was used from the Neolithic to the Roman Period and beyond. The use of mud-brick favoured rectangular buildings, which are more conducive to the extended family unit, and encouraged intensification of production and differentiation in wealth. The rectangular village community rewarded occupational specialisation, wealth differentials, and other aspects of complex societies; therefore architecture is a reflection of the socio-economic organisation (Wenke 2009: 216-7). In Egypt it was used for building private, public and some elements of monumental structures (such as the magazines of many of the temples). The types of buildings that mud-brick was used for can be divided up into five categories: funerary, religious, administrative and official, domestic, and fortresses/defensive town walls. Although the ancient Egyptians were aware of the practice of baking bricks, it was not extensively used before the Late Period, where bricks measuring up to 0.71 m in length have been discovered.

Mud-bricks are made by mixing various quantities of clay, fine sand, silt, coarse sand and chopped straw. The sand and the straw prevent the formation of cracks as the mud shrinks (up to 30%) during drying. Other varieties regularly occur, such as sand combined with gravely desert sediments, but the most common consists of mud and straw combined with a little sand. The strongest combination is 1 m³ of mud, combined with ⅓ of a cubic metre of sand and with 20 kg of straw. This combination can withstand the compressive stress of 52 kg /cm^2 (Spencer 1979: 3, also see Kemp 2000: 79-83). Although the bricks can be made entirely by moulding with the hands, the vast majority of ancient bricks were made in wooden moulds. This process involves mixing the ingredients together, then pushing the mixture into a rectangular wooden mould, smoothing the top by hand. The mould is then loosened from the brick and the wet brick is laid on the ground. This process is repeated until the whole area of brick making is covered, leaving a grid-pattern between the bricks the width of the mould's frame. After three days of drying the bricks are turned over. After a week the bricks are strong enough to be stacked into a pile.

Brick shape, size, bonding, and coursing can assist in the dating of various structures. Impressions of plants and pollen grains can also be caught in the mud-bricks, and can provide environmental and economic data on past agricultural practices and vegetation history (Ayyad 1991). The recording of ancient mud-bricks is therefore an essential archaeological practice. This form is to record single mud-brick contexts, so repairs, rebuilds or unusually constructed areas receive a new context number and a new sheet.

11.01 Site code, e.g. **TAD09**.

11.02 Operational area: The area of the site in which you are excavating.

11.03 Site sub-division: To be recorded as outlined above.

11.04. The number of the mud-brick context.

11.05 Grid reference: To be recorded as outlined above.

11.06 The mud-brick context will usually be part of a wall of a building or the lining of a grave. Note the number of the feature that the mud-brick context is a part of.

11.07 There may be elements of the context that are constructed or clad in worked stone, such as doorways, windows, columns, pilasters, arches, or decorative elements. The numbers of any worked stones are required here. Each individual worked stone receives an accession number, as well as being recorded as part of the context. The worked stone number is a sequential finds number, obtained from the site supervisor or site director and recorded on the **Worked Stone Index: Sheet 21**; this number must be written on an indestructible label and securely attached to the stone. The individual stone is then recorded on the **Worked Stone Recording Form: Sheet 38**. The placement and dimensions of the worked stone element must be clearly shown in the sketch (**11.41**).

11.08 Type: Variables include a course of mud-bricks in a building, a retaining wall or great wall, undulating wall, palace-niche-façade, a grave, floor, foundation, arch, vault, dome, corbel or just a single mud-brick.

11.09 The reduced level **<u>on top</u>** of the highest and lowest point of the feature (only one level is necessary if it is flat). The level of the contemporary ground level should also be given, if known.

11.10 The overall length of the context.

11.11 The overall width of the context.

11.12 The overall height or depth of the context.

11.13 The colour of the mud-bricks and mortar should be recorded using a *Munsell Colour Chart*.

11.14 The composition refers to the varying amounts of mud, sand, straw, gravel, *tafl*, etc. in the brick. The tables for sediment analysis for **Sheet One** will be of use in this task. It must also be noted whether the brick is sun-dried or oven baked.

11.15 Any coarse natural or archaeological components (other than straw) that are observed in the brick should be noted here. The tables for **Sheet One** should be of help.

11.16 The average dimensions of the individual bricks must be recorded, giving the paired measurements of the length, width and depth of the brick. Bricks will usually have a length/width ratio of 2:1. Up to a hundred bricks should be recorded in a single mud-brick context to get the average size (Kemp 2000: 85); **Sheet Forty-Seven** will be in useful in this respect. If there are any odd-sized bricks these should also be recorded. The range of brick sizes can then be expressed both diagrammatically and as a statistical mean (Kemp 2000: 85). This may help establish the function of a fragmentary building, as large bricks were usually used for major public buildings, whereas small bricks were used in houses and private tombs.

11.17 Record the shape of the bricks, whether they are rectangular, square, round, or special vault-bricks, circular column-bricks or cornice-bricks. Bricks can also be flat or hog-backed.

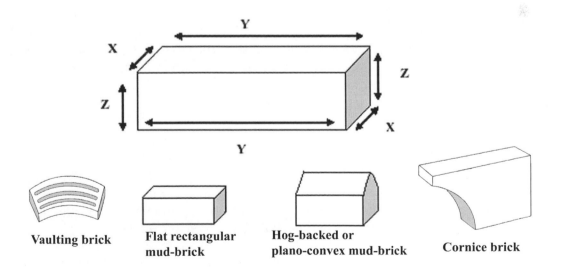

Vaulting brick   Flat rectangular mud-brick   Hog-backed or plano-convex mud-brick   Cornice brick

Figure 91: Basic brick shapes and how to take the brick's measurements.

11.18 The coursing or bond is the pattern in which the mud-bricks are laid. Two common terms used in brick bonding are headers and stretchers. A header is the end of the brick facing out, and a stretcher is the side of the brick facing out. The maximum (and minimum) number of vertical courses must be entered.

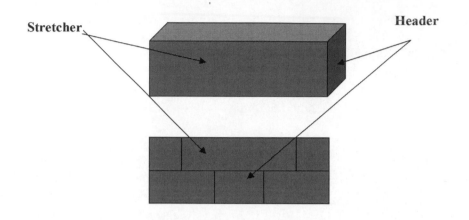

Figure 92: Headers and stretchers.

The best way to record bonding is by the use of a standardised bonding corpus, such as that created by Spencer (1979). The use of letters and numerals in this corpus makes the recording of the brick bonding easier and less time-consuming than describing it in words. After the corpus code (e.g. A1) numbers can be added (A1/ 2·5 [to indicate that the wall is 2·5 brick lengths thick]). Although the thickness of walls may vary from two to twenty bricks, the bonding pattern will not alter. For this reason, only the basic bond is shown in **Fig. 93**. One of the deciding factors in the choice of bonding is the thickness and height of the wall. Complex bonds should be classified by giving the relevant code letter for each face of the wall (if different), and writing them together. Therefore, code AC describes an arrangement where one face of the wall has the characteristic appearance of a class A bond, whilst the other face conforms to type C. The basic brick corpus is denoted by capital letters: A, B, C, whereas arches, vaults and corbels are denoted with small letters: a, b, c. If unusual bonds have been used, as in the Predynastic Period, then the corpus should be expanded to accommodate these bonds (Zdziebłowski 2008a; 2008b).

Some forms of mud architecture do not consist of bricks, such as mud-lining of tombs or *pisé* constructions, which comprises of stiff mud rammed between boards or reed and log walls plastered with mud. These types of constructions have been found in Predynastic sites such as Hierakonpolis. Indeed, reeds and papyrus supplied many of the supportive elements in Predynastic and Early Dynastic buildings, such as bundles of papyrus tied together to form columns. Reeds could be bent to form archways. Many of these elements were later replicated in stone in the form of cornices, screen walls, false-doors, and columns (Arnold 1991: 3). As some of these elements seem to fall between the **Mud-Brick** and **Timber Recording Forms** elements of both forms should be taken to create a new form.

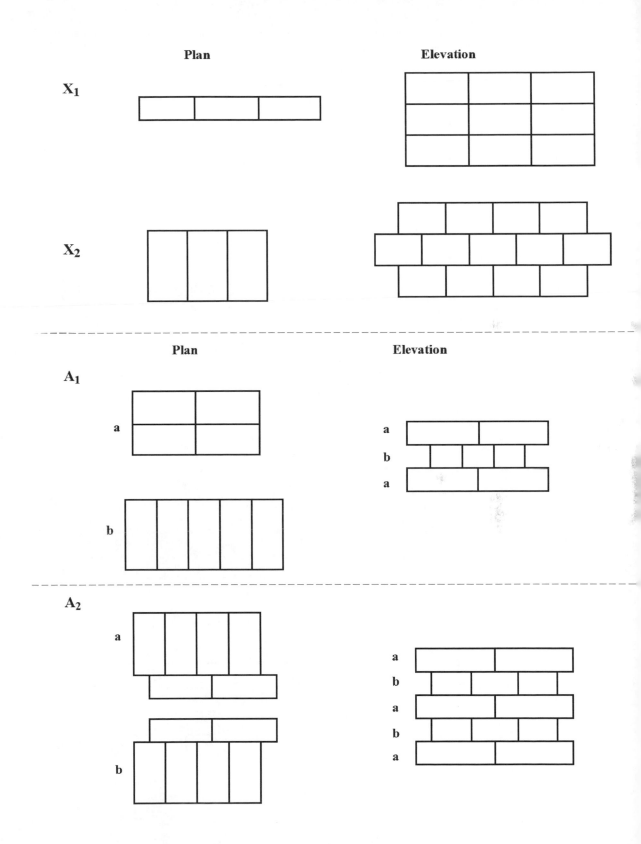

Plan	Elevation

X₁

X₂

Plan	Elevation

A₁

a

b

a
b
a

A₂

a

b

a
b
a
b
a

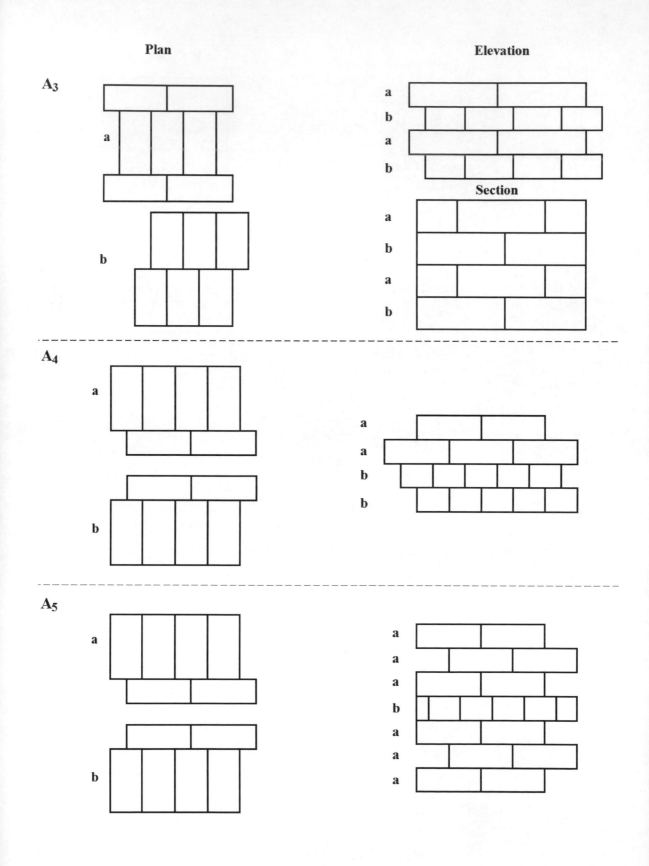

Plan   Elevation

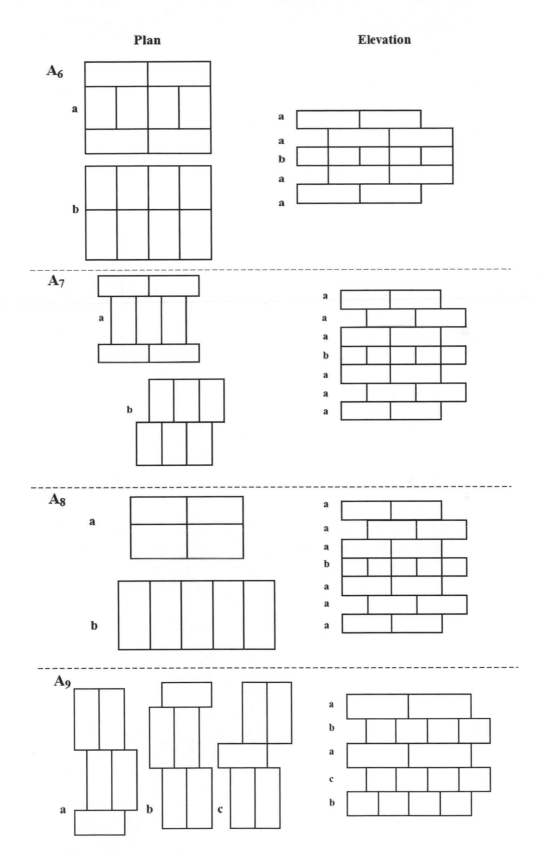

221

Plan

A_{10}

a   b   c

Elevation

The Corner
bond usually
accompanying
A_{10} bonding

a
b
c
b
a
b

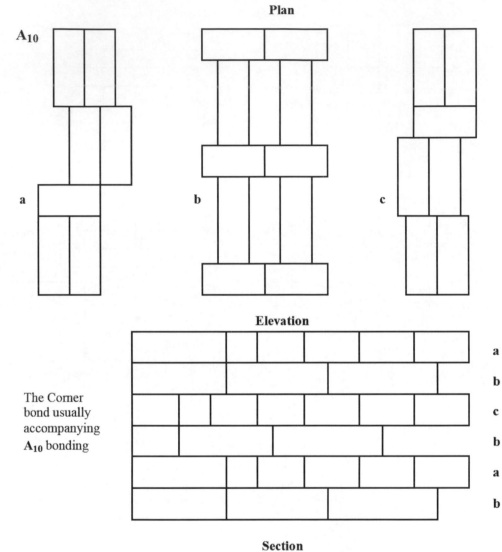

Section

The hatching
indicates the
changes of
arrangement
of the internal
stretchers

a
b
c
b
a
b

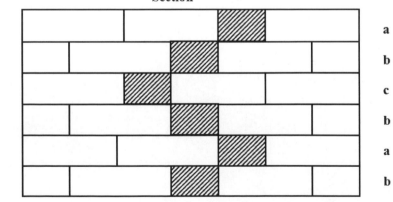

Plan

A_{11}

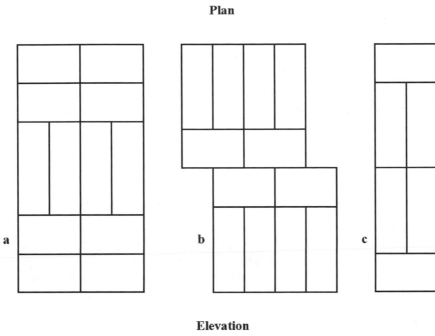

a   b   c

Elevation

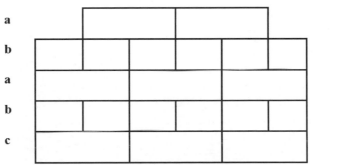

a

b

a

b

c

Plan

A_{12}

Elevation

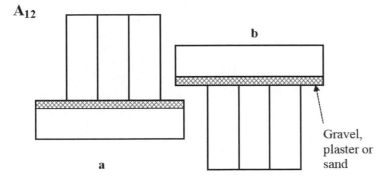

b

Gravel, plaster or sand

a

a

b

a

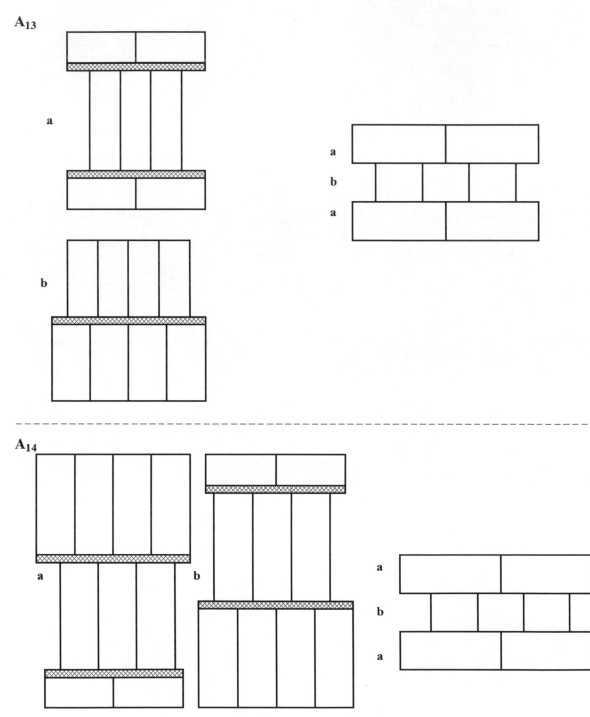

Plan   Elevation

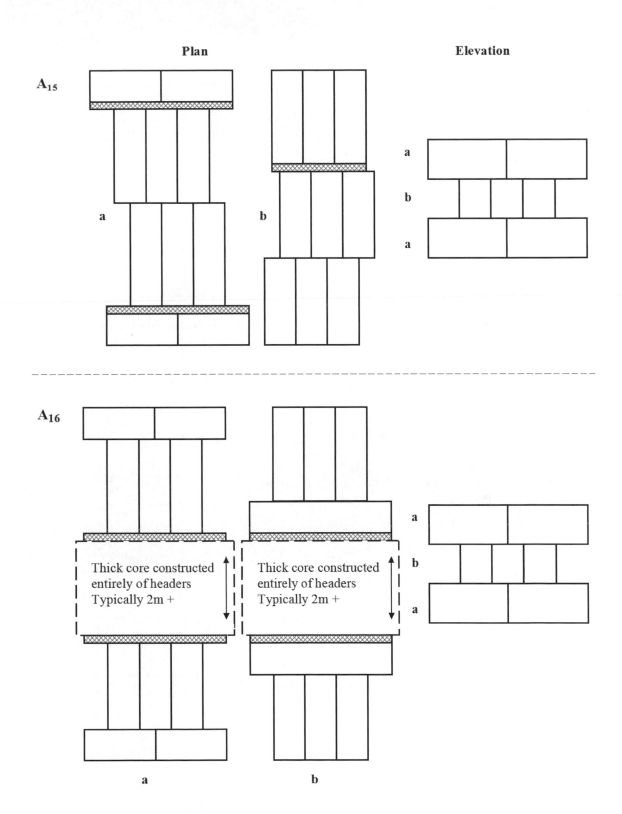

225

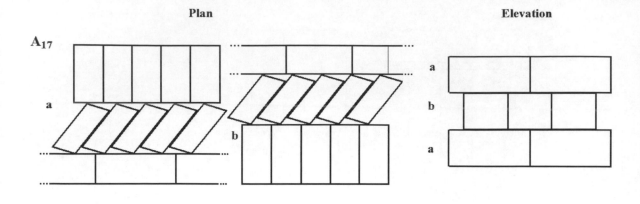

Plan   **Elevation**

A_{17}

Plan

A_{18}

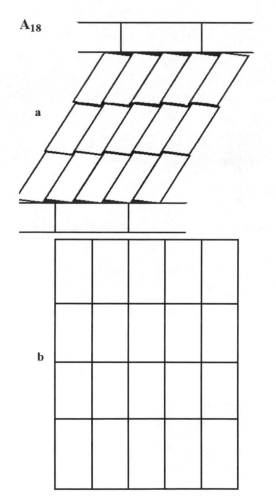

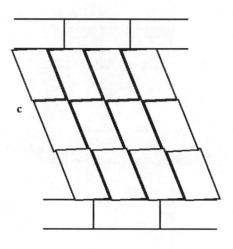

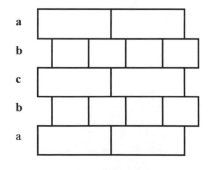

Elevation

226

Plan	Elevation

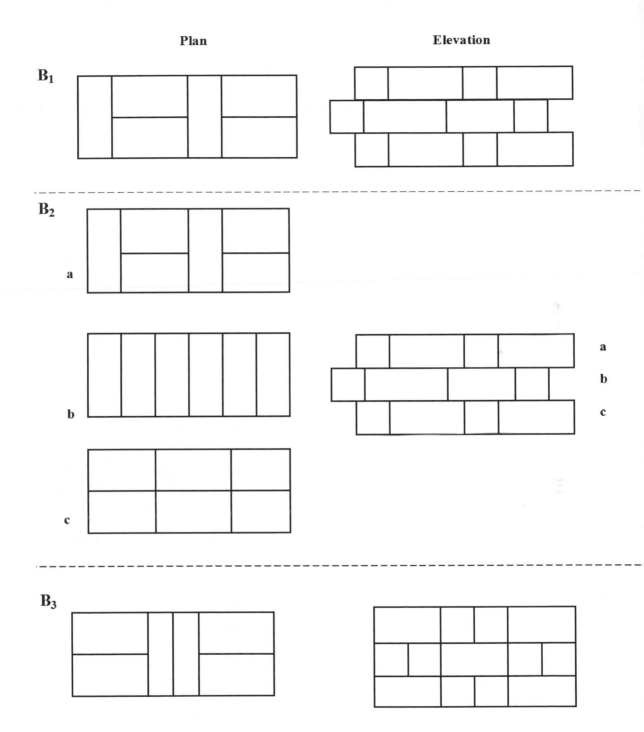

B₁

B₂

a

b

c

a

b

c

B₃

Plan	Elevation

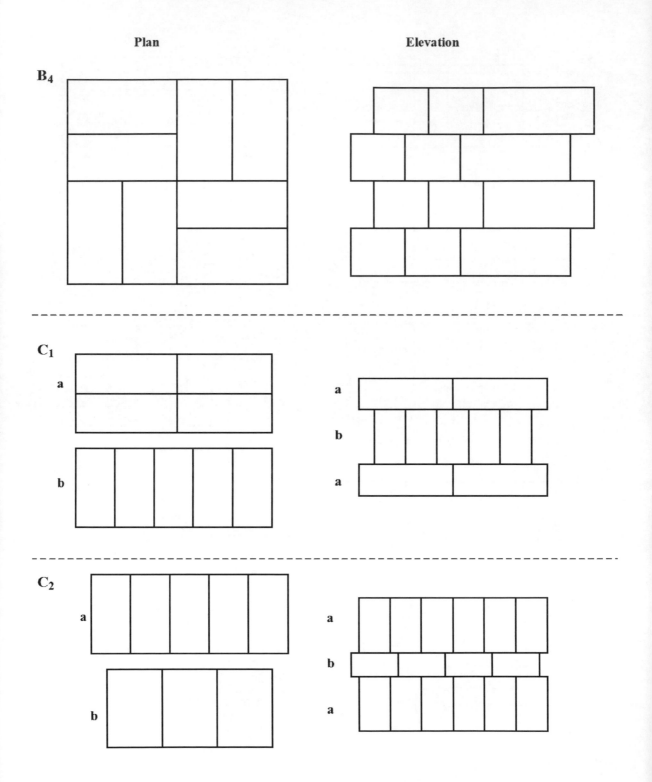

B₄

C₁

   a

   b

   a

   b

   a

C₂

   a

   b

   a

   b

   a

228

Plan   Elevation

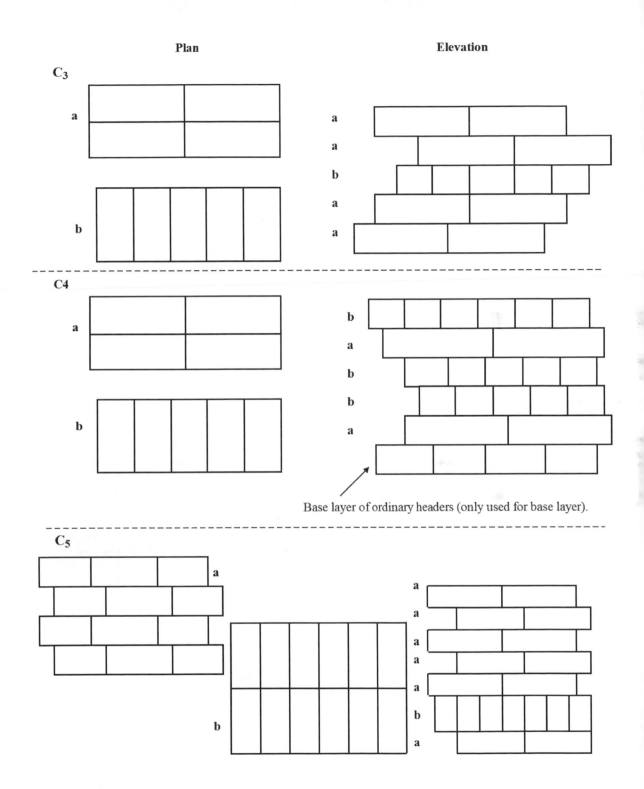

Base layer of ordinary headers (only used for base layer).

229

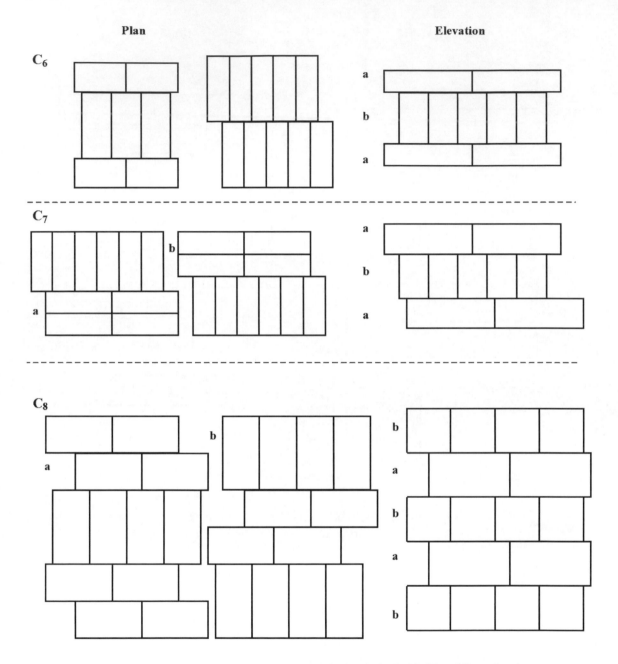

Plan   Elevation

C₆

C₇

C₈

Note: The bond requires bricks with a ratio of
6:4:3 between the length x width x thickness
[normal bricks are 6:3:2].

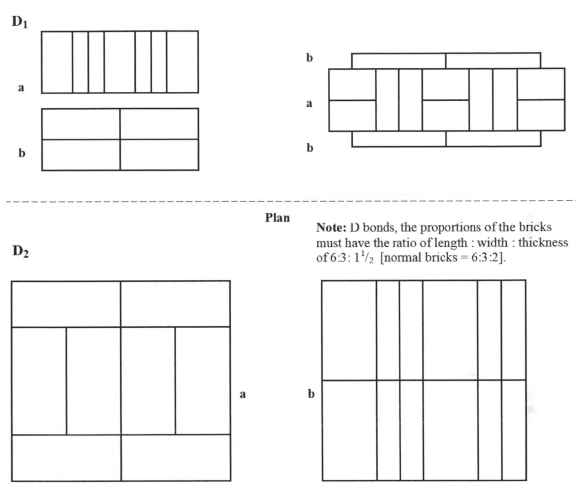

Plan   **Elevation**

D₁

Plan

D₂

Note: D bonds, the proportions of the bricks must have the ratio of length : width : thickness of 6:3: 1¹/₂ [normal bricks = 6:3:2].

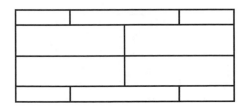

Section (x -----x)   **Elevation**

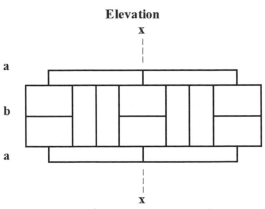

Plan

Section

AC₁

a

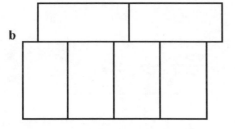

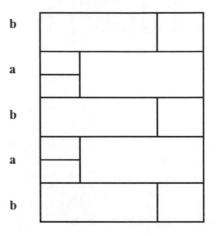

b
a
b
a
b

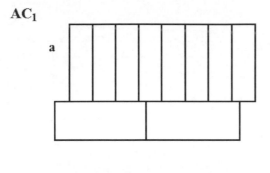

b

Elevation

Reverse

Obverse

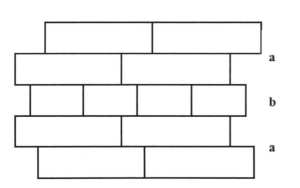

a
b
a

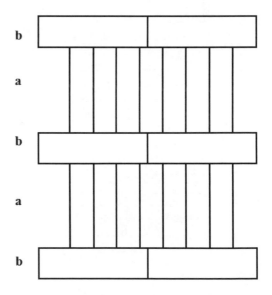

b
a
b
a
b

232

Plan

AD₁

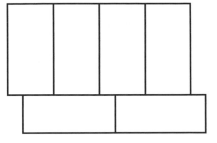

a

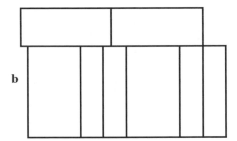

b

Elevation

(Obverse)

x   y

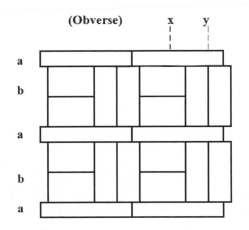

a

b

a

b

a

(Reverse)

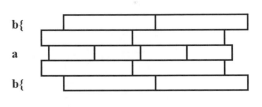

b{

a

b{

Section

y…y

a

b

a

b

a

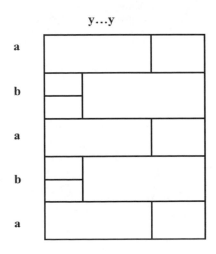

x…x

a

b

a

b

a

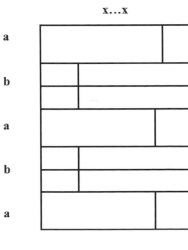

Plan

CE$_1$

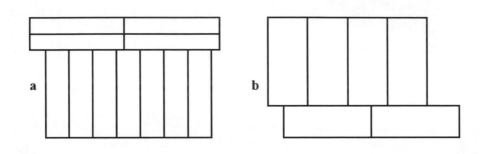

a   b

Section

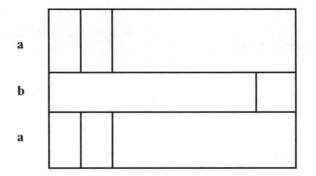

a

b

a

Elevation

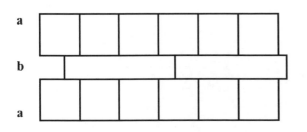   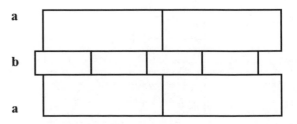

a   b   a   a   b   a

234

Arches and Vaults

Cross-Section   **Side Elevation**

x_1

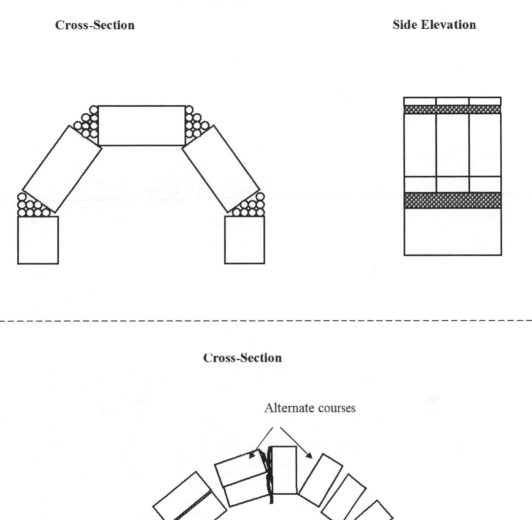

Cross-Section

a_1

Alternate courses

235

a₂

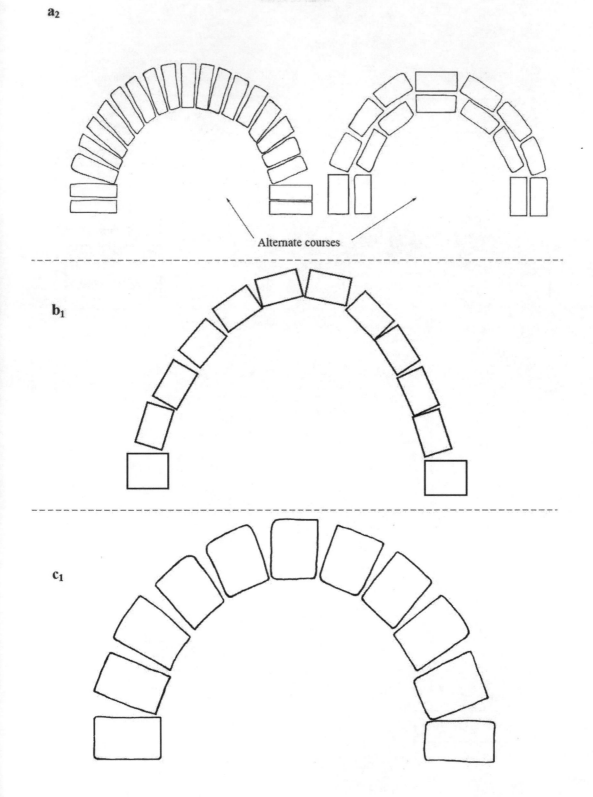

Alternate courses

b₁

c₁

Cross-Section

c₂

Cross-Section

Longitudinal Section

d₁

d₂

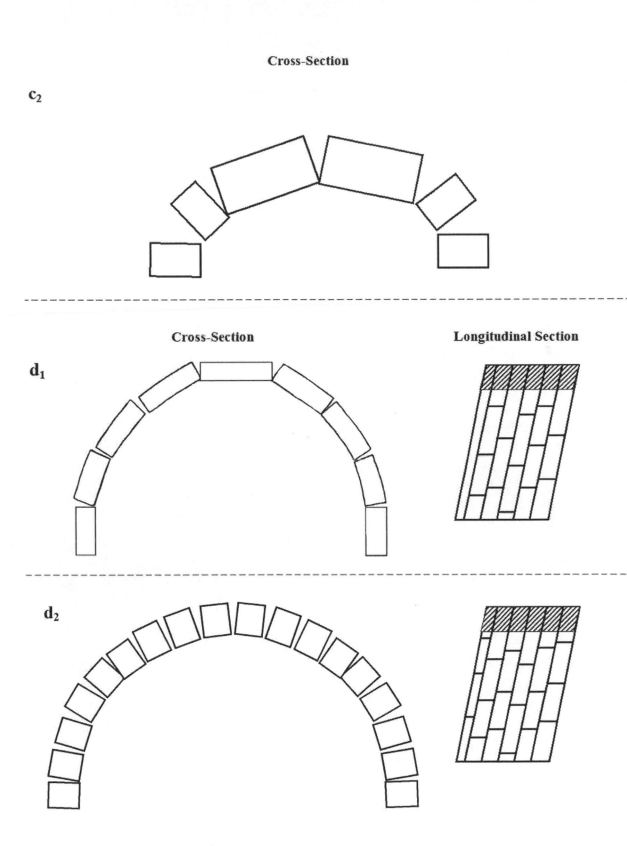

Cross-Section

Longitudinal Section

e₁

Cross-Section

f₁

Interstices filled with
stones or potsherds

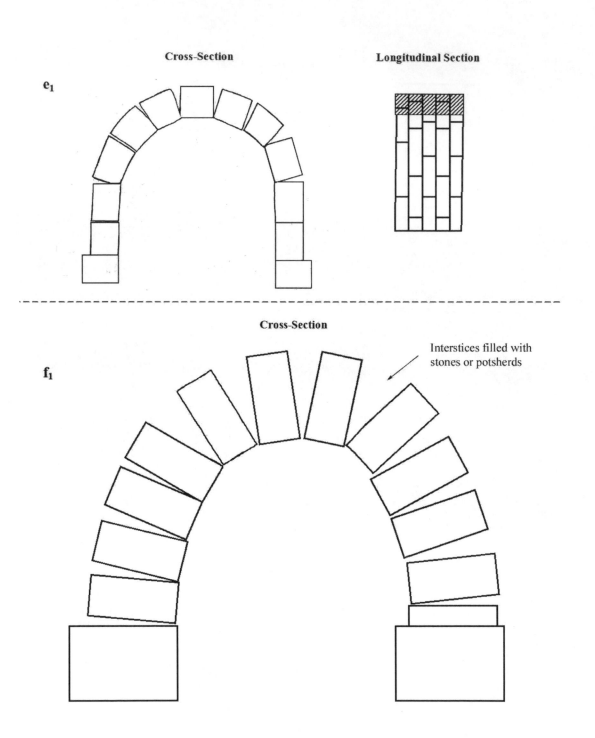

238

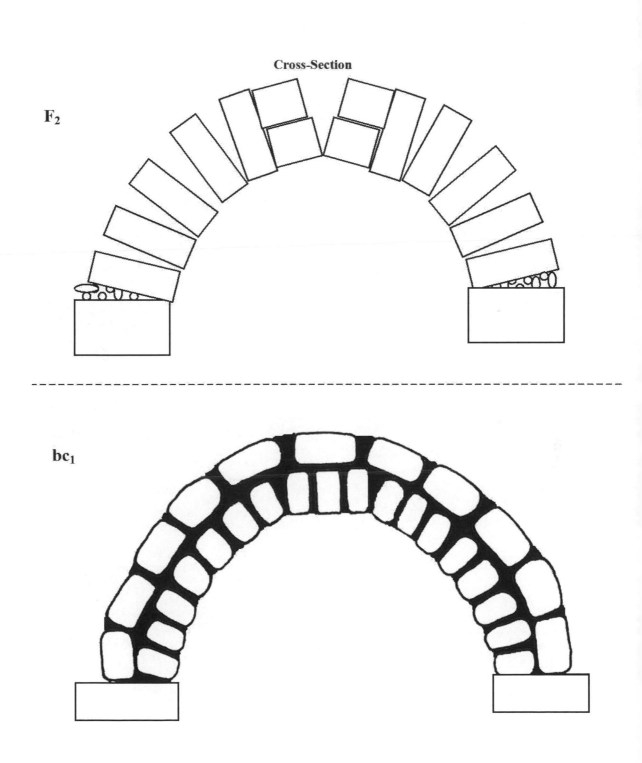

Cross-Section

F_2

bc_1

239

Cross-Section   Longitudinal Section

bd₁

bx₁

cd₁

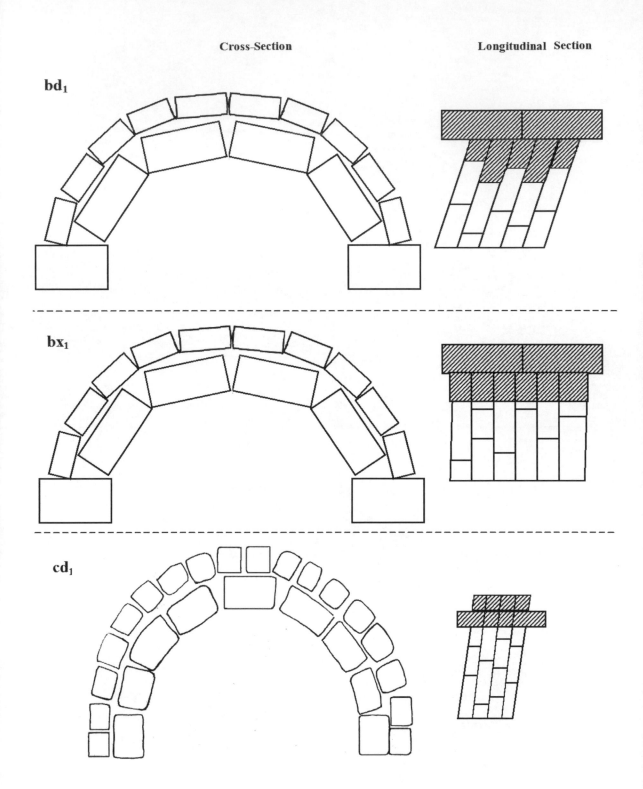

240

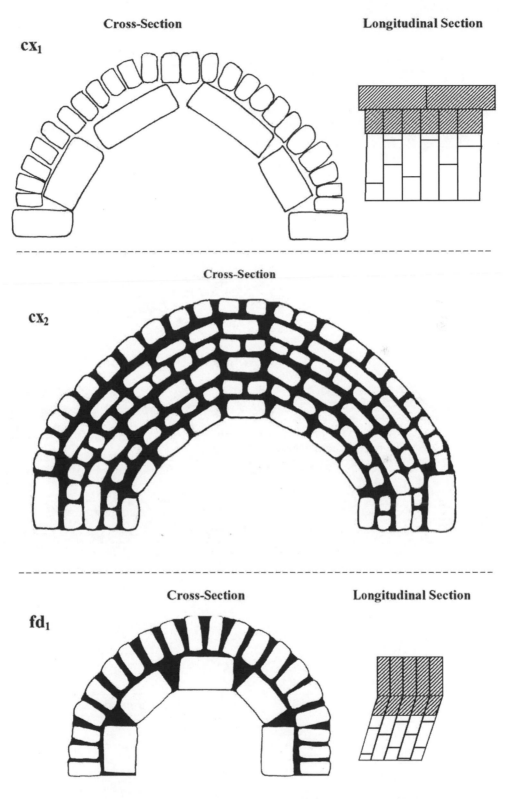

Figure 93: The mud-brick bonding corpus (after Spencer 1979: Pl. 1-20).

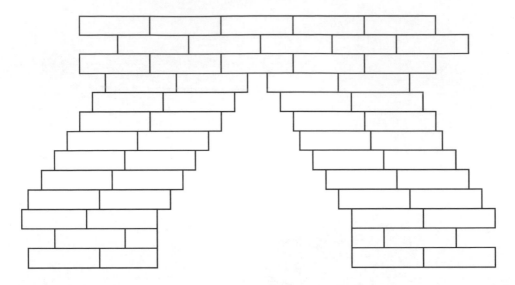

Figure 94: The construction of a corbel.

Bond	Chronological Range
X1	Common in all periods as it is the only one that can be used in walls of 0.5 m thickness and less.
X2	Although this is an uncommon bond, it occurs throughout time and is mainly used in door-blocking.
A1 A2 A3	Universally common in all periods, and interchangeable with **C type** bonds in the Roman and Coptic periods.
A4	An uncommon bond sometimes found in the Late Period.
A5 A7 A8	Popular in the in the Protodynastic and Early Dynastic Period; some **A8** bonds continue into the Old Kingdom.
A6	Common in Early Dynastic Period mastabas, especially in Dynasty II and III.
A9	Rare in the Old and Middle Kingdoms; more frequent use in the Ptolemaic and Roman periods.
A10	An uncommon bond, with a few examples from the Old Kingdom and Late Period.
A11	One recorded example in the Dynasty I Tomb 3357 from Saqqara.
A12	Found at Armant and in Dynasty XIII.
A13 A14 A15	Only found at Armant.

A16	Very uncommon; New Kingdom only.
A17 A18	A not infrequent bond of the Late Period to Roman Period.
B1	Common in the Roman Period; only used as door-blocking in early periods.
B2 B3 B4	Roman, with B3 continuing into the Coptic Era.
C1	A common bond in Roman and Coptic periods, with one example from the Early Dynastic Period and another from Dynasty XXX.
C2 C3 C4	Fairly common in the Roman and Coptic periods.
C5	A weakly-defined bond, possibly found in some of the Dynasty I Saqqara mastabas.
C6 C7 C8	Fairly common – especially **C6** – in the Roman and Coptic periods.
D1 D2	An uncommon bond, only found in the Late Roman Period.
AC1 AD1	An uncommon bond, only found in the Late Roman Period.
CE1	Found only in the Early Dynastic Period.
a1 d2 e1 f2	Ptolemaic and Roman periods, with **e1** continuing into the Byzantine Period.
cd1 cx1 cx2	Frequently used in thick arches from the Old Kingdom to the Late Period, and in small arches of all periods. **cd1** is common in Roman houses.
bc1 cd1	Used in thick arches of the New Kingdom and tomb structures of the Middle Kingdom; common in Roman and Coptic houses.
bx1	Commonly used in arches of Roman and Coptic Period date; rare in dynastic buildings.
x1	This bond is common in all periods, and was used over wide spans in the Roman era
b1	Uncommon in all periods.
c1	Commonly used from the Early Dynastic Period onwards in both small and large arches.
c2	Only one example survives - an Old Kingdom tomb at Dahshur.
d1	Commonly used from the Early Dynastic Period onwards for both small and large vaults.
f1	Only two examples survive, in the Middle Kingdom tomb of King Hor at Dahshur.
fd1	Only one example survives, in an Old Kingdom tomb at Matmar.

Table 24: Chronological table of Egyptian mud-brick bonds (after Spencer 1979: 138-9).

11.19 The position and type of any reed matting, stone or timber in the brick bonds must be described, stating its dimensions and purpose (if known). Note context number and the number of any special forms used to record the context.

Reed matting was commonly used in mud-brick constructions from the Early Dynastic Period onward. Reed matting was set transversely at various levels between the brick courses, or along and across the axis of the wall, to bond the brick courses. Reed matting was also used as a roofing material (with beams) or for floors (with plaster). Structural wood is usually found in the remains of roofing, usually planks supported on beams or on posts, and wooden door- and window-frames. Wood was also used for flooring and to reinforce mud-brick walls. Stone found widespread use – both as an independent medium and also to reinforce mud-brick structures. It was sometimes used to encase brickwork, and many mud-brick mastabas and pyramids were covered by stone casing. Stones were also used for flooring, door-jambs, lintels, sills and grills. Similar patterns of use are found elsewhere in the world, such as Western Asia and adobe structures in the Americas.

11.20 Most mud-brick structures were covered with an initial layer of mud plaster, then a layer of gypsum plaster. You are likely to encounter four main types of plaster in ancient Egypt: **1)** mud plaster, made from alluvium mixed with sand and chopped straw. The colour of the plaster varies from dark grey-brown to yellow, depending on the amount of sand and composition of the mud. It was sometimes used in the manufacture of precast slabs; **2)** *tafl* plaster, made from gravel, sand and chopped straw, with a little clay. This plaster is usually confined to buildings on the desert edge, especially the superstructures of small tombs; **3)** gypsum plaster, usually the finishing coat laid over the mud plaster to make the walls white; these were often painted; **4)** lime plaster, used from the Ptolemaic Period onwards, usually with burnt brick constructions. The presence and percentage of plaster must be recorded, and a brief description of the type with its context number is needed here. As plaster was usually applied annually, the plaster must have its own context number and recorded on its own **Single-context Recording Form**: **Sheet One**.

11.21 The bonding material or mortar used in ancient Egypt can be divided into three main types: **a)** mud mortar, made from Nile alluvium (the most common variety); **b)** *tafl* mortar, made from desert gravel and sand (usually found in small buildings on the desert edge); and **c)** lime mortar, a hard, lime-rich white mortar (used in Ptolemaic and Roman times, which is impermeable to water and therefore used mainly for baths and conduits) (Spencer 1979: 133). The mortar was usually applied roughly, and restricted to the horizontal joints. However there are exceptions to this on the outer faces, where both the vertical and horizontal joints were sometimes well pointed. Where there is a thick core of mud-brick, the internal brickwork often had no bonding material at all or just a layer of sand between the courses. In joints of A12 and A16, a special wide joint is filled with gravel or plaster. The first line of this prompt asks you for as description of the form of mortar pointing (see **Fig. 103**), a description of the mortar and its texture is then required followed by prompts for the thickness of the mortar in the horizontal and vertical beds.

The type of mortar must be recorded, along with its thickness. To record the thickness, it is best to record the height of four courses and four bed joints, this will allow an accurate recording (average) of the bed joints to be made. The interstices in arches and vaults are often filled with pebbles, potsherds or chips of stone, these must also be recorded.

11.22 Stamped bricks are very useful to the archaeologist as they can be easily dated and contextualised. In Egypt from Dynasty XVIII to XXVI they occur stamped with the king's name in a cartouche (or simple oval) and (more rarely) the queen's name, or the name of the building in which the brick was laid. The vast majority of bricks with royal stamps come from mortuary temples. Bricks bearing the name of private individuals are sometimes found, with the person's name and titles in a rectangle or oval frame. A major catalogue and study of brick types has been published by Spencer (1979: Pl. 21-38).

Describe the stamp on the brick, along with its dimensions. Make a sketch of the stamp on the reverse of the recording form, a scale drawing, and take several photographs. The reference numbers of these images must be recorded in the spaces provided.

11.23 This space is for recording unusual construction and materials such as burnt bricks, *tafl* bricks, specially-shaped bricks (including burnt frieze bricks, fire-dog bricks, thin bricks, semi-circular bricks, quadrant form bricks, interlocking bricks, circular bricks, cornice-bricks, square bricks and segmental bricks) and bricks that are exceptionally large or small.

11.24 Record any impressions of plants in the mud-brick, and whether it has been sampled for pollen.

11.25 Comments and descriptive text: The first line asks you for basic information: is this structural context part of an internal (roofed) space, an external (open-air) space, or something else? Circle the relevant word; if in doubt, explain the situation under 'other'. The descriptive text usually starts with a statement such as "Four courses of brickwork inside grave <\1157/>". You must also record in which direction the feature is facing. Then give a brief stratigraphic description. Relationships with artefacts, rocks or ecofacts within or on the context should be noted. Sometimes the description of the context will suffice and no interpretation will be needed. Details of any drawings or photographs that cannot be fitted into the space provided should be put here.

11.26 Interpretation: The excavator should attempt a basic interpretation of the context. It is most important to differentiate between, for example, a superstructure or substructure, and also to provide some idea of how it was formed and used. The interpretation should be made whilst in you are front of the context. It is advisable to provide an alternative interpretation, along with your reasons for giving both the main interpretation and the alternative. Cross-reference your context in support of your interpretation. Associated mud-brick contexts should be listed in this section, along with their context numbers.

11.27 The method of excavation will be *fas,* shovels and buckets, trowels or brushes. Note whether the spoil was sieved.

11.28 The weather conditions: State whether it was sunny, rainy, hot cold, etc., along with the time of day.

11.29-32 This section is for the *Physical Stratigraphic Relationships* and contains three data fields for interpretative stratigraphic relationships: earlier than, later than and contemporary with, if same as another context this should be indicated here. The excavator should use one or more of these fields to establish the relationship of the context with surrounding or associated contexts. Provide the context number(s) (if different) and a description of the foundation upon which the mud-brick context rests (bedrock, riprap, undisturbed natural), and the base course or footing of the wall, which is usually wider than the wall itself.

11.33 The context numbers of the contexts above and below should be placed in the *Running Matrix*. The context being described should be placed in the central box. This is for stratigraphic relationships **not** physical relationships. Always keep a running matrix when you are excavating an area, and cross-reference with other excavators if their features or deposits have stratigraphic relationships with yours. Check with the site supervisor if at all uncertain about stratigraphic relationships - they must be accurately determined on site.

11.34 The amount of any finds (bags or baskets) associated with the context must be placed in this field.

11.35 Record the number(s) of any special finds found in this space.

11.36 The number(s) of the samples collected, such as mortar, bricks, matting and any other material must be entered in this space.

11.37 Any plans, sections or other drawings made of the context must be listed here.

11.38 List the numbers of any photographs taken of the context here.

11.39 Any other relevant information must be entered here.

11.40 The value of the temporary bench mark or datum should be entered here, as well as the measurement from the backsight to the TBM, and the instrument height.

11.41 A brief sketch of the context should be put in the grid provided, showing any notable aspects and relationships; include a grid peg square reference, and put in the scale, annotate with dimensions and other useful information. Do **not** simply copy the formal plan.

11.42 List all the foresights taken on the context here. A brief sketch of the section or elevation may be put here if necessary.

11.43 It is very important that the supervisor who completed the recording form signs and dates it.

11.44 The form and interpretation must be approved and counter-signed by the director or site supervisor and any conflicting and differing interpretations of the same data entered.

11.45 The person that enters the data into a database must sign and date this field once the process has been completed.

12.00 Sheet Twelve: Masonry Recording Form: While the following section is formulated with Egypt specifically in mind, the large array of building styles and masonry traditions in Egypt covers many international eventualities. As in all previous and subsequent sections, therefore, use these definitions so far as they are applicable, and add to them if necessary. The country or regionally specific books relating to African (Garlake 2002), Western Asian (Bretschneider *et al.* 2007; Crawford 1977; Lloyd *et al.* 1974), Indian (Gupta 1980), and Chinese (Sickman 1956) architecture should be consulted for culturally specific nuances.

Stone has been used for building structures in Egypt since the Early Dynastic Period (Dynasty II) though some masonry techniques go back as far as the early Predynastic. The principal building stones of ancient Egypt can be divided into soft stones and hard stones. The most popular soft stone was limestone (found from the Memphite Region down to Esna), with sandstone (found from Esna to deep into Nubia) being used to a lesser extent as well as a small amount of Egyptian alabaster (Aston *et al* 2000; Klemm & Klemm 2008). The main hard stone used was granite, with lesser amounts of basalt, diorite and quartzite. However, due to the difficulty of quarrying and dressing, the hard stones were used sparingly. The quarrying and working of stone was governed by the state, leading to the development of standardised methods of working.

Stone is intimately associated with permanence, and was generally used for monumental buildings that were designed to last, such as temples and tombs. It was more rarely used for residential buildings. Despite the fineness of the jointing and the expert manoeuvring of the vast blocks in the Old Kingdom, there seems to be little use and understanding of the 'breaking joint' or the value of sturdy foundations before the Roman Period (Somers Clarke & Englebach 1939: 3). The foundations of Pharaonic buildings were generally made separately for each part of the building, e.g. separate foundations for the walls, obelisks, columns, etc. However, occasionally great platforms were built, such as the one under Luxor Temple (Arnold 1991: 113). The idea behind the foundations was to lay the upper courses on a flat, stable surface. To this end foundation trenches often contained clean freshly sieved sand (Arnold 1991: 113). This sand provided protection against rising groundwater and earthquakes, and may be symbolic of the primeval mound on which the first temple was built (Arnold 1991: 113). The foundations themselves were usually between one and five courses of masonry deep and packed with gravel; Early Dynastic Period foundations were usually very shallow, and mud-brick was often used for the foundations of masonry buildings. During the Roman Period stone became a more common material for secular buildings, while the use of previously marginal ceramic bricks (especially tiles) really exploded during the Late Antique era. More solid foundations were constructed from the Ptolemaic Period onwards, often consisting of very deep, solid platforms.

The written recording of ancient masonry is an essential archaeological practice, and must be compiled together with any epigraphic work in as accurate a manner as possible. This form is designed to record intact structural masses of worked, unworked (roughly hewn) masonry blocks (contexts), or ceramic bricks, or combinations of masonry, and how constituent masonry blocks fit together to form a structure. Every element of the masonry context must be detailed in the masonry recording form. However, areas with evidence of repair, rebuilding or unexpected construction receive a new context number and a new sheet. If applicable, a general building number and overall description on the building form should be given.

12.01 Site code, e.g. **TAD09**.

12.02 Operational area: The area of the site in which you are excavating.

12.03 Site sub-division: The number of the trench/square you are working in.

12.04. The number of the masonry context.

12.05 Grid reference: To be recorded as outlined above, using the south-west corner grid peg. If the context runs into two adjacent grid squares, it should be recorded as 115-120E/205N, or if the context runs in a north-south direction 115E/205-210N.

12.06. The masonry context will usually be part of a building. State the feature of which the masonry context is a part of.

12.07 The numbers of any worked stones are required here. Each individual worked stone receives an accession number, as well as being recorded as part of the context. The worked stone number is a sequential finds number, obtained from the site supervisor or site director and recorded on the **Worked Stone Index: Sheet 21**; this number must be written on an indestructible label and securely attached to the stone. The individual stone is then recorded on the **Worked Stone Recording Form: Sheet 38**.

12.08 Type: Describe whether the context is a course of masonry in a building, a retaining wall or great wall, architrave, roof, a tomb wall, floor, pavement, foundation, arch, vault, dome, corbel, ventilation system, doorway, stairs, column or pillar, facing or just a single masonry block.

12.09 The overall length, width and thickness/height of the masonry context must be recorded. The average dimensions of individual masonry bricks or blocks must also be recorded, giving the paired measurements of the length, width and depth of the stone or brick. Up to a hundred blocks can be recorded in a single masonry context to get the average size; **Sheet Forty-Seven** may be useful in this respect. The range of masonry brick or block sizes can then be expressed both graphically and as a statistical mean. If there are any odd-sized bricks or inclusions, these should also be recorded.

12.10 The colour of the masonry and mortar should be recorded using a *Munsell Colour Chart*.

12.11 Provide the reduced levels of the highest and lowest points of the contexts. The level of the contemporary ground level should also be given, if known.

12.12 The condition of the masonry context; has it been weathered, demolished, painted, burnt. Does it need conservation treatment? Also state whether the original surfaces are absent or present.

12.13. Tick the type of material(s) that the masonry context is built with. Four fields are provided: ceramic bricks, stone, mortar and other (i.e. plaster or rendering).

12.14 Materials description: All the materials must be further described in this field. Any inclusions should be noted, such as reuse of older building material. The use of unusual bricks or stones is also worthy of note. The bricks and/or stones must be recorded by plan and elevation *in situ*. If there is any doubt as to the identification of a stone, consult the site geoarchaeologist.

12.15. This field is for recording the finish of the blocks or bricks. Categories include roughly hewn, squared, and ashlar (see **Fig. 101**). It **must** also be recorded if the stone has been pecked, ground, flaked or is unshaped. If the whole context is of worked stones, state how many faces of worked stone are cut and dressed, in addition to indicating which faces they are, the number (if any) that are partially dressed or left roughly hewn. The presence/absence of bevelled edges must also be noted.

Terminology	Definition
Abacus	The flat, square member connecting the column capital to the architrave.
Abutment	The supporting wall or pier that receives the thrust of an arch; a solid stone springer at the lowest point of an arch, vault or beam.
Aggregate	Materials that are added to mortar or grout at time of mixing to impart special properties to the mortar or grout; quantities of loose fragments of rock or mineral.
Anathyrosis	A method of creating a precise joint by smoothing the contact surfaces of two blocks along a narrow border just around the edges of the stones.
Arcade	A range of arches with their supports; also, a passageway, one side of which is a range of arches supporting a roof.
Architrave	A horizontal member that connects different components of the building (i.e. lintels, columns and walls) and which also carries the roofing slabs.
Ashlar	A block without a moulding, but with one or more faces dressed and at right angles (or parallel) to each other.
Atrium	The open-roofed entrance court of a building.
Back filling	Rough masonry built behind a facing or between two faces. Or, filling over the extrados of an arch; brickwork in spaces between structural timbers, sometimes called brick nogging.
Backing stones	Stones that connect the facing blocks to the core masonry.
Banker	A bench of timber or stone (can be a single block) on which stone is worked.
Base	Shaped block upon which columns sit.

Basketweave	A checkerboard pattern in paving.
Batter	Recessing or sloping masonry back in successive courses; the opposite of corbel.
Bench	Steps formed in a quarry by the removal of stone following bed joints. Alternatively, a long seat of cubic stone.
Boss	An extra stock or rough, undressed block face that protrudes from the wall surface.
Cantilever	A structural member, supported at only one end, which projects from a wall: a long bracket or beam supporting a balcony or truss in a bridge.
Capital	The decorated top of the column.
Capstone	The crowning stone of a structure, differing from capital in that it is not a supporting member.
Cavetto	A hollowed moulding used in the cornices that crown buildings.
Chamfer	A bevelled corner, or the method of cutting a right-angle slope.
Collar	The part of a column shaft that lies immediately below the capital.
Cornice	A moulded projecting stone at the top of an entablature or façade.
Cramp	A dovetail-shaped dowel joining two blocks of stone.
Cubit	An ancient Egyptian unit of length equal to 52.5 cm. It was sub-divided into 7 'palms' of 7.5 cm, which was again sub-divided into 4 digits of 1.875 cm in length.
Diaper	Any continuous pattern in brickwork, usually applied in a diamond or other diagonal patterns.
Dressed face	A stone face that has been worked further with hammer, chisel and an abrasive to give a relatively smooth surface.
Entablature	A horizontal, projecting group of stones immediately above a column capital. Consists of three major parts: architrave, cornice, and frieze.
Entasis	A bulge in the profile of a column shaft.
Extrados	A rounded upper surface of an arch or vault.
Impost	The upper surface of a structure that carries the vault.
Isodomic	Wall bonding with courses of equal height.
Jamb	The side posts or surfaces of a door, window or fireplace.
Keystone	The topmost stone (or voussoir) of an arch or vault, regarded as binding the whole.
Ledger	A slab of stone used horizontally to cover a tomb.
Lintel	The weight-bearing uppermost horizontal support of a door or a window.
Lug	A small projecting member of a larger stone piece, to engage an adjoining unit or to serve as an aid in handling.

Moulding	The tradition of cutting/dressing the outer faces of the block so that when several such blocks are fitted together the design forms a distinct continuous architectural feature or ornamentation (such as a cornice or capital of a column).
Mullion	Vertical division member between windows or doors.
Ogee	A stone moulding with a reverse curved edge, concave above, convex below.
Orthostats	Tall, upright slabs of stone that form the lowest courses of a wall, often used to case poor quality masonry.
Packing stones	Smaller stones placed to fill the gaps between the backing stones and core masonry.
Parapet	A low wall around the perimeter of a building at roof level, or around balconies.
Pilaster	Engaged pier of shallow depth; in classical architecture, it follows the height and width of related columns, with similar base and cap.
Plinth	The lower square part of the base of a column, a square base or pedestal. The base-block at the juncture of base-board and trim around an opening.
Portcullis	A stone slab lowered vertically from a recess in the ceiling to block a passageway.
Predella	Platform surrounding an altar.
Putlog hole	A hole in the face of a wall, used to receive horizontal beams. Often used to stabilise scaffolding.
Pylon	A truncated pyramidal structure that serves as a gateway to a building, usually forming a temple façade.
Pyramidion	The apical block of a pyramid, formed in the shape of a small pyramid.
Quoins	The external interlocking stones that form the corners of two walls meeting at a right-angle, so that the header block of one wall becomes the stretcher of the other.
Rake	An angular cut on the face of stone.
Riprap	Irregular shaped stones used for facing bridge abutments and fills; stones thrown together in a disorderly manner to form a foundation, sustain walls, or minimise soil erosion. Also used for rustic stepping stones and patios.
Riven	To split along natural cleavage planes.
Rubble	Irregularly shaped pieces of stone, partly trimmed or squared, used chiefly in walls and foundations.
Scamilus	A block supporting the pedestal of a statue or the plinth of a column; a surplus bevel of stone adjoining a sharp edge, to prevent chipping when the cubic piece is being set.

Scoinson	A block without moulding but with two or more faces dressed. Unlike an ashlar, these faces are at neither at right angles nor parallel to each other. Trapezoidal masonry walls, inner parts of window frames and door jambs are often constructed with scoinsons.
Shaft	The major part of a column extending from the base to the capital. They can be square, rectangular, round, polygonal, octagonal, Doric, fluted, ribbed or reeded.
Sill	The lowermost horizontal slab that supports a window or door. Doorsills usually have an elevated ledge with the stop face for the door wing.
Tafl	Arabic term for layers of marl clay and gravel that often underlie desert conglomerate.
Talatat	A block without a moulding, similar to, but smaller than an ashlar block with one or more faces dressed and at right angles (or parallel) to each other.
Torus	A semicircular or three-quarter-circular moulding along the edges of a building placed either vertically along the corners or horizontally along the upper edges.
Toothing	Gaps or projections in alternate courses, usually indicative of a return wall or buttress at this point (subsequently removed).
Tumbling in	Blocks or bricks set at a diagonal angle to the wall, usually to create a buttress.
Typestone	The best surviving example of a particular type of ashlar, scoinson, moulding, etc. A typestone must always be fully recorded in every detail. Recording stones of the same type is facilitated by reference to this typestone.
Voussoir	One of the stones in an arch between the impost and keystone.
Worked Stone	A stone is deemed to be worked if any part of its surface has been cut and finished to form a dressed face or moulding. Whereas most building stone will have been quarried, hewn and cut to size, worked stone has a distinctly finished appearance. Unworked or roughly hewn blocks and rubble need not be recorded individually.

Table 25: Terms used to describe the finish of stones (after Arnold 1991: 295-7 and Westman 1994: 65-6).

12.16 Record the shape of the bricks or stones here. Some typical ceramic brick types are shown in **Fig. 95**, others include dog-leg, bull-nose bricks, plinth bricks, or special vault-bricks, circular column-bricks or cornice-bricks. The stones can be blocks, tabular, irregular, ashlars, or scoinsons.

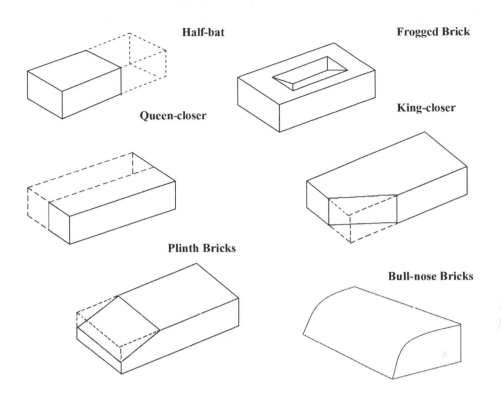

Figure 95: Types of ceramic bricks.

12.17 The coursing or bond is the pattern in which the bricks or masonry blocks are laid. The most common terms used in describing brick bonding are:

- **Stretcher -** When a brick is laid so that a long, narrow side is the one that is exposed, that brick is said to be a stretcher. The long edge is horizontal.

- **Header -** A header brick is laid so that a small end is exposed and the wide edge is horizontal.

- **Rowlock Stretcher -** A stretcher laid so that the long, wide face is exposed.

- **Rowlock Header -** A header laid so that the narrow edge of the face is horizontal.

- **Soldier -** A brick is called a soldier when it stands vertically with the narrow, long face exposed.

- **Sailor -** A sailor also stands on end. However, the long, broad face is exposed.

- **Wythe -** Wythe is the term for all the vertical courses together. A brick wall may be one, two, or three wythes thick for most purposes.

- **Closure Brick -** In any course, bricks are laid from the outer edges in toward the centre. The final brick, the one that fills the opening to complete the course, is called a closure brick. This brick almost always has to be cut to fit properly in its niche.

Bricks are usually laid on their bed, on end or on edge (see **Fig. 96**). If the brick bonding is unusual, these are the terms that should be used to describe how the bricks are laid.

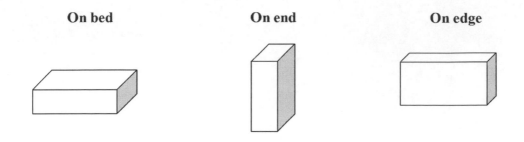

On bed   **On end**   **On edge**

Figure 96: Basic brick positions.

Ancient Egyptian masonry can be divided into two main categories: small-block masonry (such as that found in Djoser's Pyramid Complex at Saqqara) and megalithic masonry (such as that found in Khufu's Pyramid Complex at Giza). In both types of masonry, only the casing blocks were dressed, surrounding packing blocks and core made of roughly hewn stones. The faces of both types' bedding and rising joints were usually dressed before the blocks were laid. The top surface of the block was cut to receive the blocks of the next course, while the front (external) face was only cut and dressed after all the courses had been laid. Sometimes when cutting the bedding for the next course, the packing or and core blocks were also cut to receive the next course of blocks.

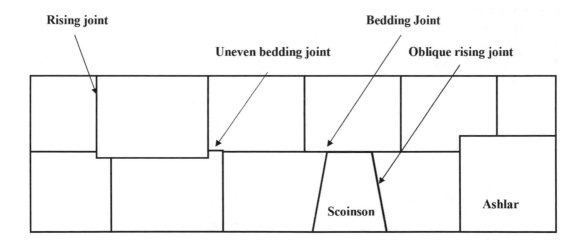

Figure 97: Monumental courses, showing the variations in bedding and rising joints.

A)

B)

Figure 98: A) Showing a stepped core resulting in increase casing block height, and B) Section of the Bent Pyramid of Sneferu, Dahshur, showing how the dressed casing blocks interlock with the core blocks (photograph G. J. Tassie).

Ancient Egyptian builders often used both ashlars and scoinsons when laying courses (see **Fig. 99**). Two main types of bonding were used in monumental buildings: Type A bonding contains oblique joints, with the rising joints at a right-angle to the bedding joints. In Type B, the rising joints are at a right-angle to the front face of the block, although a secondary Type B also occurs where all the joints are at oblique angles to each other. Both types were used interchangeably until the end of the Old Kingdom. At the end of this period, however, Type A vanishes, while Type B was used until the end of the Pharaonic Era.

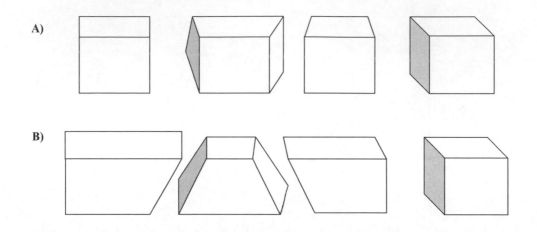

Figure 99: Showing Type A with the planes of all the rising joints vertical and Type B bonding, showing the planes of the rising joints at a right-angle to the front faces of there block (after Somers Clarke & Engelbach 1990: 101).

The best way to describe and record bonding is by use of a standardised bonding corpus. The mud-brick bonding corpus shown in **Fig. 93** may also be used to describe masonry bonds. The diagrams of coursing and brick bonding types shown in **Figs. 100** to **101** may be of some help. The maximum (and minimum) number of vertical courses must be entered. It may be best to make a site-specific corpus using the terms outlined in this section (see Aston *et al* 2000). Another problem encountered in classifying ancient (Egyptian) masonry bonds is that several types were often used in the same building. In monumental buildings the core of the structure was often built of poorer quality stone and then faced with higher quality stone, this core was often made of irregular shaped blocks or even rubble. To fully understand the construction of masonry buildings it may be necessary to dismantle the building. However, this can only be done with special permission from the Supreme Council of Antiquities (SCA) or local equivalent.

12.18. The direction in which the outside faces of the context face must be recorded in this field.

12.19 The bonding material or mortar used in ancient Egypt can be divided into three main types, which are also commonly found elsewhere: **a)** gypsum mortar, which is made from burned gypsum, sand and a little carbonate of lime or limestone chips (all periods); **b)** a hard, white and impermeable lime mortar (Ptolemaic and Roman); and **c)** cement mortar, which was associated with hollowed joints (Roman onwards). As in all sections of this book, you may wish to adapt this catalogue to take in regional variations of mortar manufacture.

256

Mortar was usually applied roughly, and restricted to the horizontal or bedding joints. It was sometimes poured into the rising joints in core/facing walls before the packing stones and outer casing stones were laid. Very rough mortar – including many large inclusions – was sometimes poured into the core of monuments where the internal joints were uneven and spaced comparatively far apart, in order to give the core a greater solidity.

A₁

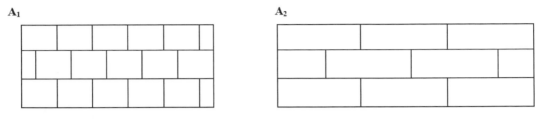

Headers

Stretchers

Elevations of Freestanding Walls

A₃

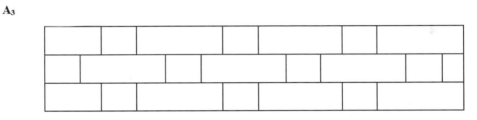

English

A₄

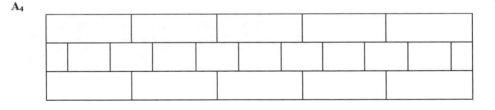

Flemish

A₅

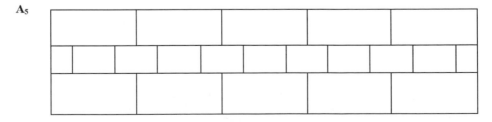

Dearne's or Rat Trap

A₆

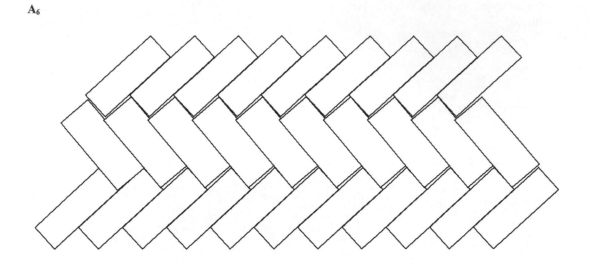

Herringbone

B₁

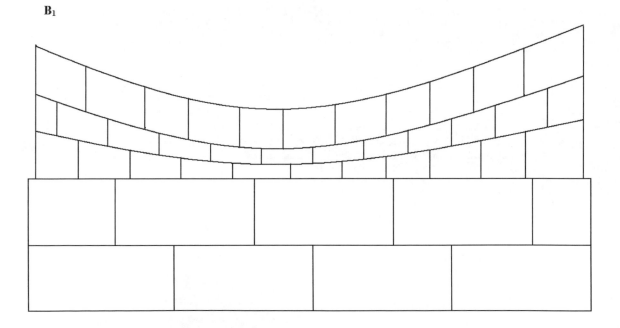

Concave bed

B₂   Stepped (broken courses)

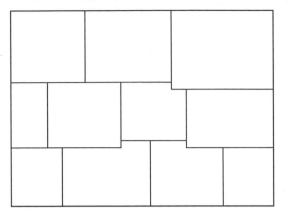

B₃ Trapezoidal masonry

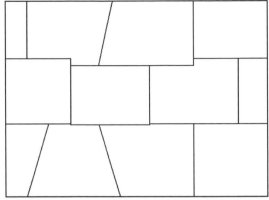

B₄   Ashlar (regular)

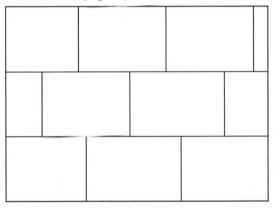

B₅ Monumental Rat Trap

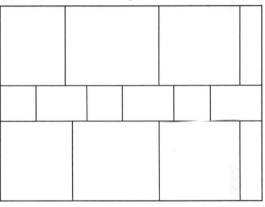

B₆   Irregular

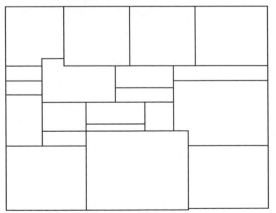

B₇   Mixed masonry courses

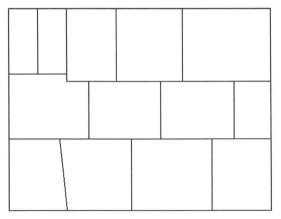

Sections of Freestanding Walls

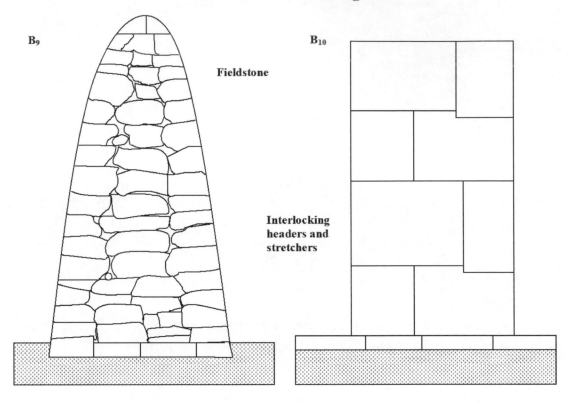

B₉

Fieldstone

B₁₀

Interlocking
headers and
stretchers

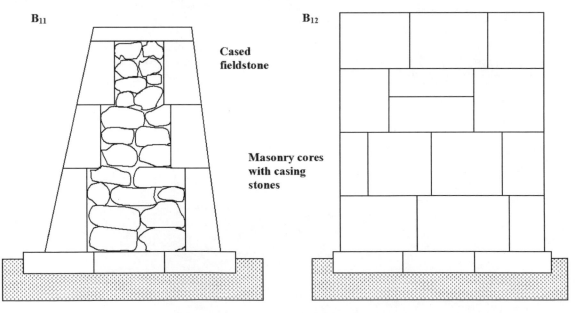

B₁₁

Cased
fieldstone

B₁₂

Masonry cores
with casing
stones

Sections of Retaining Walls

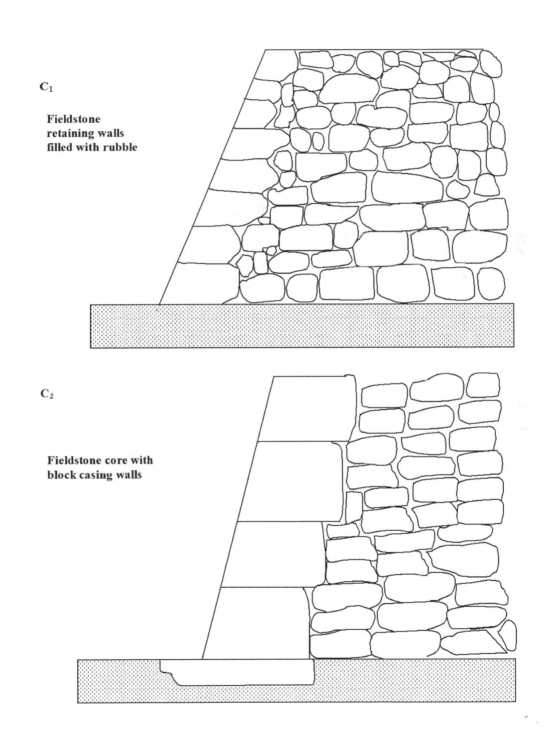

C₁

Fieldstone retaining walls filled with rubble

C₂

Fieldstone core with block casing walls

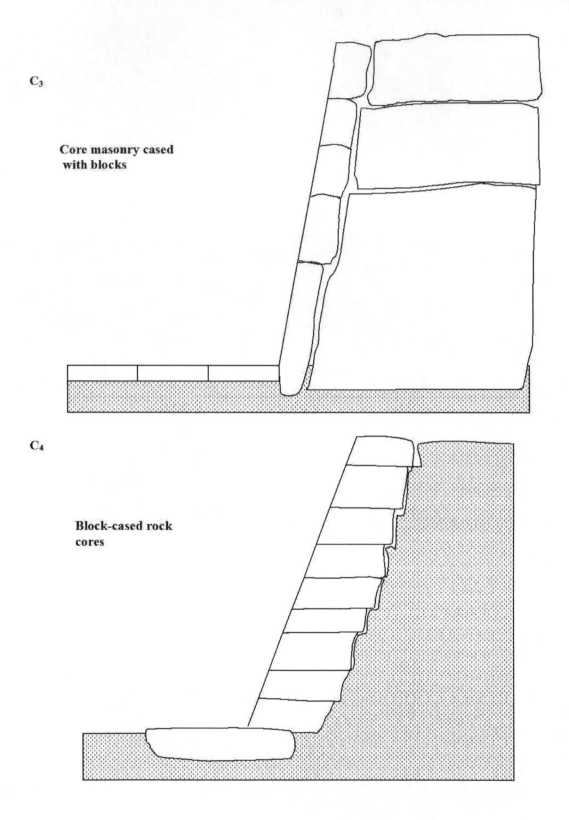

C₃

**Core masonry cased
with blocks**

C₄

**Block-cased rock
cores**

d₁

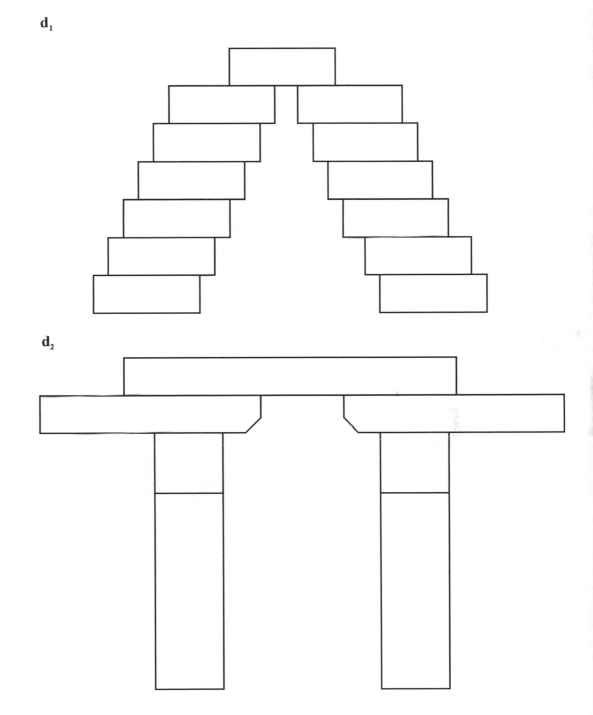

d₂

d₃

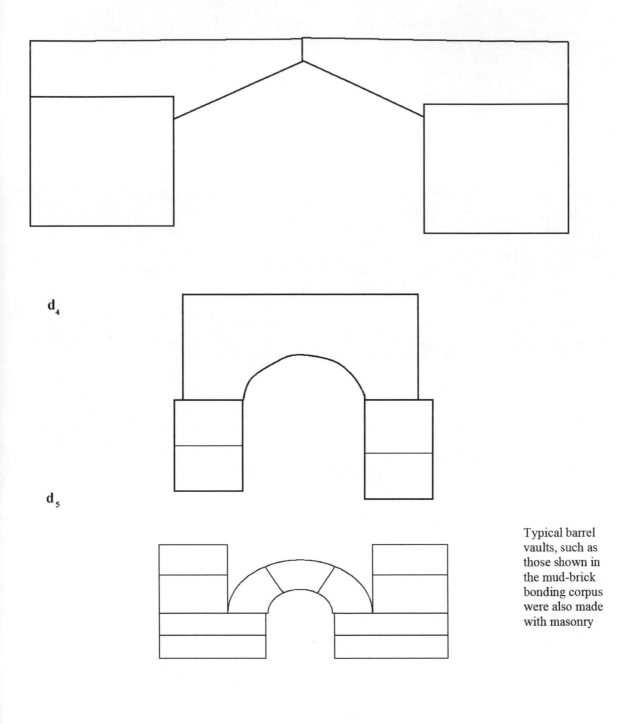

d₄

d₅

Typical barrel
vaults, such as
those shown in
the mud-brick
bonding corpus
were also made
with masonry

264

d$_6$

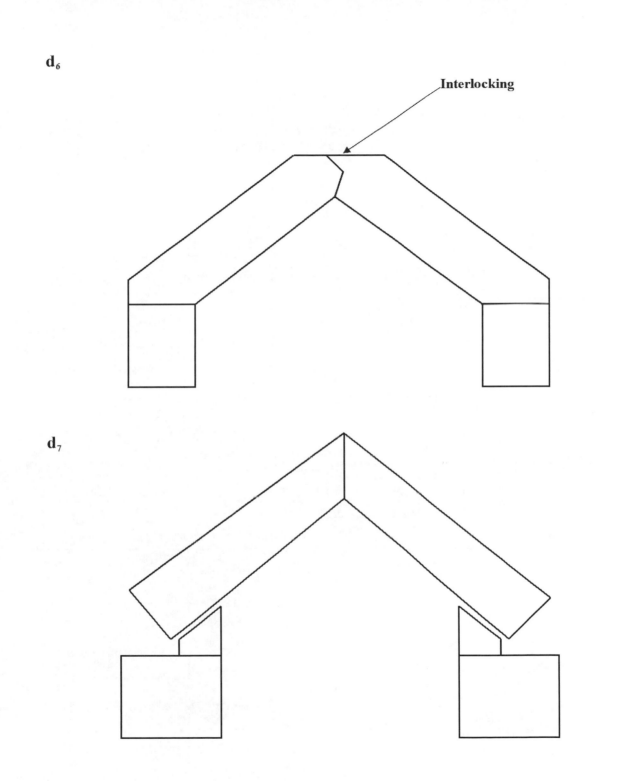

Interlocking

d$_7$

Figure 100: Typical brick bonds (after Arnold 1991: 183-201).

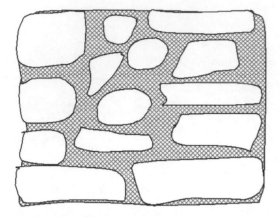

1. Random uncoursed

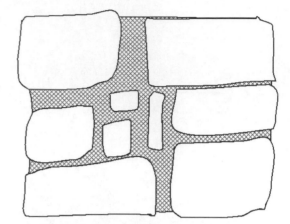

2. Squared random

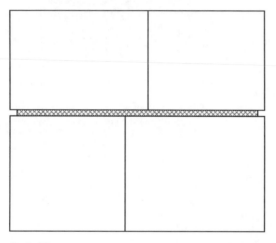

3. Ashlar

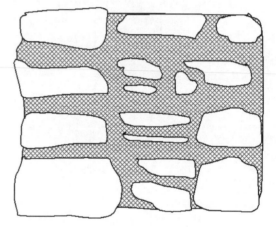

4. Random coursed

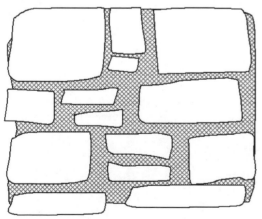

5. Squared, built to courses

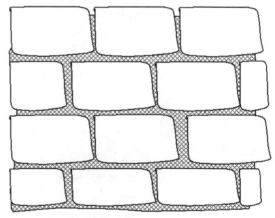

6. Regular courses

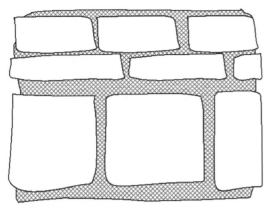

7. Uneven courses

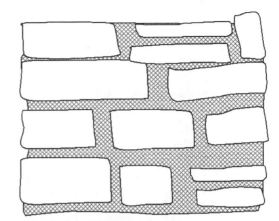

8. Quoins (corners) stressed

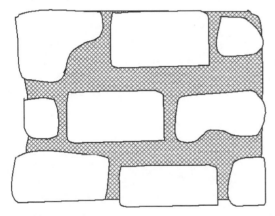

9. Quoins unstressed

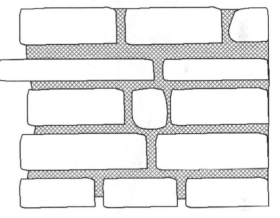

10. A string

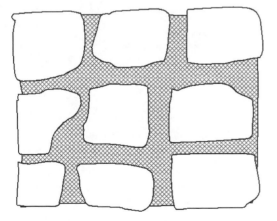

11. Fair face

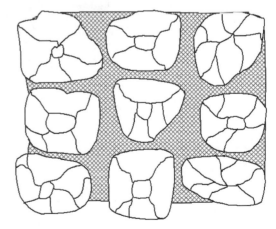

12. Rough face

Figure 101: Typical styles of stone coursing and finishing (after Westman 1994: 56).

In megalithic monuments, the component parts of the structure are held in place by the friction exerted by the dead weight (Somers Clarke & Engelbach 1990: 78). Mortar was therefore most important in the bedding-joints so that the lower courses could support the weight of the upper courses evenly without producing weak spots. A coat of hard-setting mortar provided an even surface and distributed the weight evenly, acting like a lubricant, preventing cracking and also acting as a binding material (Somers Clarke & Engelbach 1990: 78-9).

The first line asks you for the form of mortar pointing (see **Fig. 103**) and a description of the type of mortar and its texture. To record the average thickness of the mortar in the horizontal and vertical beds, it is best to record the height of four representative courses and bed joints, thus allowing accurate recording.

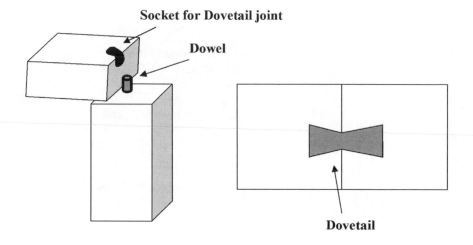

Figure 102: Examples of dovetail and a dowel (after Somers Clarke & Engelbach 1990: 112).

Dovetails of wood, lead, copper and stone were sometimes used to keep the blocks together, and can measure up to 1.5 m long (Somers Clarke & Engelbach 1990: 113). A dowel peg was also sometimes used to unite an architrave with the top of a column (Somers Clarke & Engelbach 1990: 112).

12.20 Describe the shaping or decoration on the bricks or blocks. A sketch of the decoration must be given on the reverse of the recording form, a scale drawing made and photographs taken. The reference numbers of these records must be written into the spaces provided. The decoration on the blocks may be a painted or carved scene, or a frieze or architrave. In such a case, the individual blocks of worked stone must be recorded on the **Worked Stone Recording Form: Sheet 38** and epigraphic drawings made. Describe any plastering or rendering, and the percentage of the context face that is covered. Record where and how it terminates at the base and sides, as this may indicate floor levels or wooden partitions.

It is also important to record any visible tool marks; it is possible to differentiate between marks left by axe, chisel or saw. There may also be mason's marks (which

268

indicate the 'true' face), construction grooves, sockets or graffiti on the stone or bricks. All these must be recorded.

12.21 Describe if the stones have been re-cut, or have been reused from an earlier building.

12.22 Comments and descriptions of the context: The first line asks you to distinguish: is this structural context part of an internal (roofed) space, an external (open-air) space, or something else? Circle the relevant word; if in doubt, explain the situation under 'other'. It is usual to start with a statement such as "Five courses of un-worked limestone blocks surrounding a rubble core forming the southwest corner of building <9>", and then to give a brief stratigraphic description. The nature of the context will dictate what needs to be recorded – sometimes the description of the context will suffice and no interpretation will be needed. Is there any difference between the context's face and core? Positions of artefacts, rocks or ecofacts within the context should be noted. Describe how the foundation or brickwork walls were constructed. Each column should receive an individual context number, and particular attention should be paid to the type of capital (in Egypt categories include lotus, open/closed papyrus, palm, Hathoric, etc). The shape of the pillar shaft (square, circular, octagonal, 16-sided, Doric, papyrus stem, papyrus bundle, lotus bundle, polygonal etc) should also be noted, as should the shape of the base and the foundations.

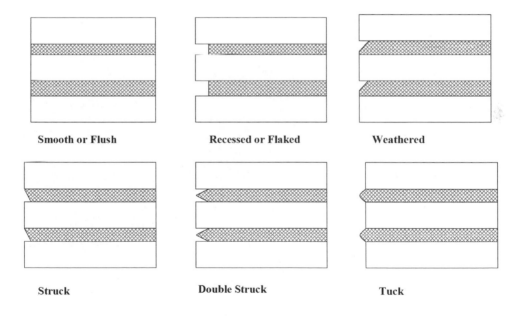

| Smooth or Flush | Recessed or Flaked | Weathered |
| Struck | Double Struck | Tuck |

Figure 103: Pointing types (after Westman 1994: 64).

12.23 Interpretation: The excavator should attempt a basic interpretation of the function of the masonry context, differentiating between floors, walls, supporting columns, superstructures, substructures, foundations, etc. The interpretation should be made whilst in you are front of the context; provide an alternative interpretation if you feel it is necessary. Try to cross-reference the context in support of your interpretation.

12.24 The method of excavation should be stated. It should also be noted whether the spoil was sieved, and whether the weather was sunny, rainy, overcast, etc. during excavation, and time of day.

12.25-28 This section is for the *Physical Stratigraphic Relationships* and contains three data fields for interpretative stratigraphic relationships: earlier than, later than and contemporary with, if same as another context this should be indicated here. The basic principles of stratigraphic interpretation have already been outlined above and do not need to be reiterated here. Other masonry or mud-brick contexts clearly associated should be listed. The excavator should use one or more of these fields to establish the relationship of the context with surrounding or associated contexts.

12.29 Provide a list of the context number(s) and a description of the foundation upon which the masonry context rests (bedrock, riprap, undisturbed natural), and the base course or footing of the wall, which is usually wider than the wall itself or consists of wooden piles or horizontally-laid timbers. How deep are these foundations of the masonry context? Foundations and foundation trenches, footings and any fills should all be allocated their own context numbers, as should any robber-trenches.

12.30 The numbers of the contexts above and below should be placed in the *Running Matrix*. The context being described should be placed in the central box. This is for stratigraphic relationships, **not** physical relationships. Cross-reference with other excavators if their features or deposits have stratigraphic relationships with yours and check with the site supervisor if at all uncertain about stratigraphic relationships - they must be accurately determined on site.

12.31 The amount of any finds (bags or baskets) associated with the context must be noted here.

12.32 The number(s) of any special finds found should be put in this space.

12.33 The number(s) of the samples collected should be written in this space. A petrological sample from a non-exposed face should be taken of each type of stone in the context/feature. The mortar, stone / brick and any paint must also be sampled.

12.34 Any plans, sections or other drawings made of the context must be listed here.

12.35 The numbers of any photographs taken of the context must be entered here.

12.36 Any other relevant information must be entered here.

12.37 The value of the temporary bench mark or datum should be entered here, as well as the measurement from the backsight to the TBM, and the instrument height.

12.38 A brief sketch of the context should be put in the grid provided, showing any notable aspects and relationships; include a grid peg square reference, the scale, and annotate with dimensions and other relevant information. Do **not** simply copy the formal plan.

12.39 A list of all the foresights taken on the context should be placed here. Provide a brief sketch of the section or elevation if necessary.

12.40 It is very important that the supervisor who completed the recording form signs and dates it.

12.41 The form and interpretation must be approved and counter-signed by the director or site supervisor and any conflicting and differing interpretations of the same data entered.

12.42 The person that enters the data into a database must sign and date this field once the process has been completed.

13.0 Sheet Thirteen: Field Photography Index: If photo accession numbers are not rigorously controlled, the number of photographs taken on the average excavation makes it very easy to become confused. A separate recording sheet should be kept for the different rolls, e.g. black and white print, colour transparencies and digital. With digital, there will be no roll number, instead enter the download number, e.g. first download, second download, etc.

13.01 Site code.

13.02 Note the date the film was started.

13.03 Note the date the film was finished (or downloaded).

13.04 The make and camera number should be entered in this field.

13.05 Enter the make of film (or memory card) here.

13.06 Enter the type of film (prints, slides or digital in either black and white or colour) in this space.

13.07 Enter the roll number (or download) in this space. Each roll must be marked with its roll number on its metal casing with an indelible marker. A small piece of drafting tape must be fixed to the back of the camera body detailing information on the roll of film currently held in the camera (roll number, film type, number of exposures, ASA). The folder number or name that the digital images are downloaded into must be substituted for the roll number when taking digital photographs.

13.08 The DIN/ASA (film speed) should be entered here.

13.09 If known, the date the film was processed should be entered here.

13.10 The frame or image number is required here.

13.11 A brief description of the frame's subject should be entered here.

13.12 Enter the subject information, i.e. context number, feature number, site sub-division and operational area.

13.13 Enter the direction in which the camera was pointing when the photo was taken.

13.14 Enter the size of the scale used in the photograph.

13.15 Date frame was taken.

13.16 The initials of the photographer must be entered here.

When entering the photographic record onto other sheets abbreviate photographic information as follows: roll number; exposure number (1/1 for roll 1, exposure 1).

14.0 *Sheet Fourteen: Drawing Index*: This form is for registering all drawings other than single-context plans.

14.01 The drawing number, of multi-context plans and sections, etc, should have a drawing number that consists of the site code and the sequential drawing number, i.e. TAD09-1, TAD09-2, TAD09-3, etc.

14.02 The numbers of the context(s), feature(s) (i.e. grave or building) or artefact must be recorded here.

14.03 The site grid reference in the form of grid coordinates or/and trench/operational area. If an object, its provenience must be written here.

14.04 The date that the plan or section was drawn.

14.05 Initials of the person that drew the plan or section.

14.06 A fuller description of the drawing must be written here, stating if it is a multi or composite context plan, and what it represents. If it is a section, state orientation (i.e. West profile, which is East facing) and any special features that are visible. Any further information about the drawing should be written in the space provided.

15.0 *Sheet Fifteen: Context Register*: This sheet is to keep control of the various contexts excavated on the site.

15.1 The context number **<u>must</u>** placed within the appropriate symbols, i.e. (22) deposit, [323] cut (see **Tab. 37**).

15.2. Note the context category and type (i.e. deposit-fill, deposit-masonry, deposit—layer, cut-grave, cut-pit, cut-hearth).

15.3 A description of the context, i.e. "the uppermost fill of hearth [769]", or "limestone wall abutting basalt wall (329)".

15.4 The site sub-division, operational area or grid coordinates.

15.5 The date and the supervisor's name or initials.

16.0 *Sheet Sixteen: Pottery Register*: This form is to be filled out by the ceramicist to keep a log of all the pottery vessels that they have registered, and should be filled out in accordance with the conventions explained above.

17.0 *Sheet Seventeen: Stone Vessel Register*: This form is to be filled out by the small finds processor to keep a log of all the stone vessels that they have registered, and should be filled out in accordance with the conventions explained above.

18.0 *Sheet Eighteen: Burial Register*: This form is to be filled out by the bioarchaeologist, director, or field supervisor.

19.0 *Sheet Nineteen: Grave Register*: This form is to be filled out by the bioarchaeologist, director, or field supervisor.

20.0 *Sheet Twenty: Structure Register*: This form is to be filled out by either the director or the field supervisor.

21.0 *Sheet Twenty-One: Worked Stone Index*: This form is to be filled out by either the director or the field supervisor.

22.00 *Sheet Twenty-Two: Sediment Sampling Register*: At the top of the document is a space for filling out the Site Code.

22.01 Enter the number of the sample taken here.

22.02 Record the context number in this field.

22.03 Enter the operational area and site sub-division here.

22.04 Enter a brief description of the sample and where it came from in this field.

22.05 Record the date the sample was taken and initials of the person who collected the sample.

23.0 *Sheet Twenty-Three: Environmental Processing Form*: This form is for the processing archaeobotanical or zooarchaeological samples. Side one is for the sieving record, and side two is for the sorting of the material.

At the head of the form there are boxes for the **Site Code (23.01)**, **Operational Area (23.02)**, **Site Sub-Division (23.03)**, **Context (23.04)** and **Grid References (23.05)**, which should be recorded as outlined above.

23.06 The category has already been filled out, as it will be a deposit.

23.07 The type of deposit: hearth, threshing floor, etc.

23.08 Enter the reduced levels (top and bottom) of the context from which the sample was taken.

23.09 Enter the number of the feature from which the sample was taken.

23.10 The number of the sample is required here.

23.11 Enter the flot number (if flotated) here.

23.12 Record the date that the sample was collected.

23.13 Record the date that the sample was sieved here.

23.14 The context type must be indicated in this space, showing the sample's exact position in the hearth, pit, etc. The length and width of the context can also be indicated here.

23.15 Describe the sedimentary matrix's compaction, colour, composition and inclusions, and give other comments if necessary. A fuller description of the feature's probable function must also be entered here.

23.16 The exact 3-D position of the feature from which the sample was taken. Draw the position of the feature in the diagram of the grid square provided.

23.17 Enter the numbers of any artefacts recovered from the sample, either before or after sieving.

23.18 Give the archaeological date of the sample, if available.

23.19 Record whether any sub-samples have been taken from the main sample.

23.20 The name of the person undertaking the sample processing.

23.21 Estimated sample volume processed, both the number of buckets and litres. One bucket holds approximately 10 litres.

23.22 Note how the biological remains were extracted from the sample matrix, i.e. coarse bulk sieving, fine dry sieving, in a flotation tank or floated in a bucket. Tick one field.

23.23 The size of the meshes used in sieving or flotation.

23.24 Describe the residue composition after flotation but before sorting, and any further comments.

23.25 Note whether the 5 mm heavy residue was sorted, and give the percentage of heavy residue.

23.26 Weight of dry sample after flotation or sieving.

23.27 Field comments and description.

23.28 Note the presence of any modern intrusions in the sample.

23.29 After sorting tick the constituents of the flot of sieved remains, giving their abundance, diversity and any further comments.

24.0 Sheet Twenty-Four: Archaeobotanical Analysis Form: This sheet is to be filled out by the site archaeobotanist.

25.0 Sheet Twenty-Five: Chronometric Sampling Recording Form: This form is for ^{14}C, OSL and TL dating samples, and should be filled out by the site director.

26.0 Sheet Twenty-Six: Macro Faunal Recording Form: This form is to be used for larger animals such as goats, crocodiles, sheep, falcons, donkeys, gazelle, cats, dogs, and cattle, etc. This form can be used for recording various bones from a single context, or for recording a single animal. Separate forms must be used if a group of animals has been found together in a grave, one for each animal; it should be filled out by the site zooarchaeologist who may wish to consult von den Driesch (1976) for taking the standard measurements of the animal bones.

At the head of the form there are boxes for the **Site Code (26.01), Operational Area (26.02), Site Sub-Division (26.03), Context (26.04), Grid References (26.05),** and **Feature (Grave) Number (26.06),** all of which should be recorded as outlined above.

26.07 The find (or sample) number is required here.

26.08 Coordinates **A**: The coordinates must be taken from the site grid.

26.09 Coordinates **B**: The coordinates must be taken from the site grid.

26.10 The skeleton diagram: Provide a general record of the skeleton and a record of which bones are present. If a bone is present it should be shaded; if it is partially present only that part present should be shaded. Also indicate how the bones were bagged, the percentage of whole skeleton present, and any truncation with a line drawn in the following manner: ▬ · · ▬.

Shown on the form is a skeleton of a *Bos* (cattle), but skeletons of any other animal can be treated in a similar manner.

26.11 Give a short description of the context where the macro faunal remains were found, giving an interpretation of the context (or feature); is it a floor, midden, fill of a pit, or a grave? Give any relevant numbers, and the basic shape and dimensions of any cut or fill.

26.12. Describe the sedimentary matrix - basic type, colour and consistency of any sediments encountered, main stratigraphic relationships and level of modern contamination, if any.

26.13 Describe the faunal assemblage, containing large and small mammals, birds, reptiles or amphibians. The minimum number of individuals (MNI) must be given, the elements of the animals present, the weight of each taxa present, and an identification of the genus and species.

26.14 The minimum number of individuals (MNI) in the context.

26.15 The number of individual species (NISP) in the context.

26.16 Total weight of mixed sample.

Description of macro faunal remains from an individual animal or burial

This section should be filled out by a zooarchaeologist if present.

26.17 Burial measurement statistics:

   a. Length - the maximum length of the body must be recorded from top of the skull to the furthest point of the body.

   b. Width - Maximum width of the skeleton.

   c. Thickness - Maximum thickness of the skeleton.

   Levels: The three most important levels to take are

   1. the highest point on the skull.

   2. the base of the sacrum (if possible).

   3. the highest point of the feet.

Any additional levels taken should be recorded on the skeleton diagram.

26.18 Type of burial: This space is for describing if the burial is a 'cremation', 'interment', or 'mummified'. If the animal remains are mummified state if: **a. Type** – is the body fully or partially wrapped? **b. Material** – mummification materials (linen, matting, resin and plaster)? and **c. Evisceration** – have any of the internal organs been removed? It should also be recorded if soft tissue is present but not mummified. Is it an intentional burial in an animal grave, cemetery or catacombs?

26.19 The value of the temporary bench mark or datum should be entered here, as well as the measurement from the backsight to the TBM, and the instrument height.

26.20-30 These fields are asking specific questions about the macro faunal remains, and require the identification of species and body parts.

26.31 Note any specialist treatment that the find has had (i.e. from a conservator).

26.32 The method of analysing the find must be entered here, along with storage particulars, i.e. materials, references numbers, location, etc.

26.33 The method of excavation; and state whether or not the matrix was sieved.

26.34 What were the weather conditions while the remains were being excavated, and what was the time of day?

26.35 Your interpretation of the remains: were they an offering or natural deposit? Are they part of a rubbish dump, butchering site or kill site? Give any numbers of associated macro faunal remains.

26.36 A sketch of the context and related features where the macro faunal remains were found.

26.37 Record the amount and numbers of any finds (bags or baskets) associated with the remains in this field.

26.38 Record the number(s) of any special finds found in association with the remains in this space.

26.39 List the numbers of any plans, sections or any special drawings made of the remains.

26.40 Insert the numbers of any photographs taken of the remains here.

26.41 Any other relevant information must be entered here, such as the number(s) of any samples collected.

26.42 The supervisor or zooarchaeologist who excavated and examined the macro faunal remains must sign and date the form.

26.43 The form should be countersigned by the director or site supervisor.

27.00 *Sheet Twenty-Seven: Micro Faunal Recording Form:* This form is to be used for smaller animals such as fishes, insects, crabs, and snails, etc. many of which may have been intentionally placed in a midden. It should be filled out by the site zooarchaeologist.

At the head of the form there are boxes for the **Site Code (27.01)**, **Operational Area (27.02)**, **Site Sub-Division (27.03)**, **Context (27.04)**, **Grid References (27.05)**, and **Feature Number (27.06)**, all of which should be recorded as outlined above.

27.07 Note the type of sample (shells, fish bones, insects, etc).

27.08 Enter the reduced levels (top and bottom) of the context from which the sample was taken.

27.09 The sample or find number is required here.

27.10 Note the size in litres of the sample before and after sieving.

27.11 The total weight of the sample.

27.12 Make a sketch of the various animals in the faunal assemblage. This space can also be used to show the exact X, Y, & Z location of the sample in the feature.

27.13 Describe the context, giving an interpretation of the context (or feature). Is it a floor, midden, pit fill, or a grave? Give any relevant numbers, the basic shape and dimensions of any cut or fill.

27.14 Record the sedimentary matrix, giving a description of the basic type, colour and consistency and main stratigraphic relationships, and the degree of contamination, if any.

27.15 Describe the faunal assemblage, i.e. fish, eggshells, insects, crustacea or mollusca. The minimum number of individuals (MNI) must be given, the elements of the animals present, the weight of each taxa present, and an identification of the genus and species.

27.16 Record the measurements of typical or control samples of the different taxa of micro faunal remains. The name of the species must be written along with its measurements and shape.

27.17 Number of individual species (NISP).

27.18 Are the micro faunal remains made into an artefact or part of an artefact, or modified in any way?

27.19 State how the remains were excavated, and whether it was by trowel, sieve, flotation, and also any treatment the remains may have received.

27.20 The method of analysing the find must be entered here, along with storage particulars, i.e. materials, references numbers, location, etc.

27.21 Your interpretation of the assemblage. Was it an offering, a working area, a natural deposit or part of a midden site?

27.22 Record the amount and numbers of any finds (bags or baskets) associated with the remains in this field.

27.23 Record the number(s) of any special finds found in association with the remains in this space.

27.24 List the numbers of any plans, sections or any special drawings made of the remains.

27.25 Insert the numbers of any photographs taken of the remains here.

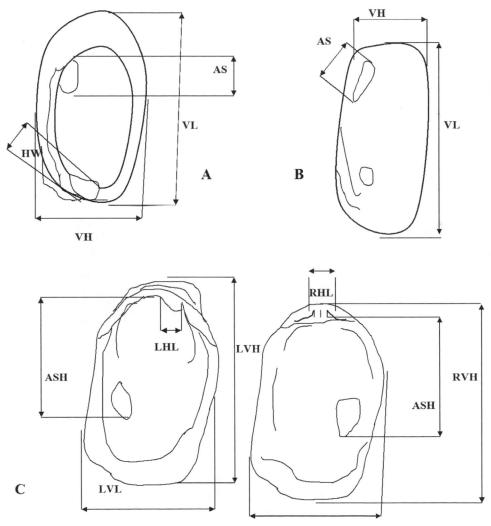

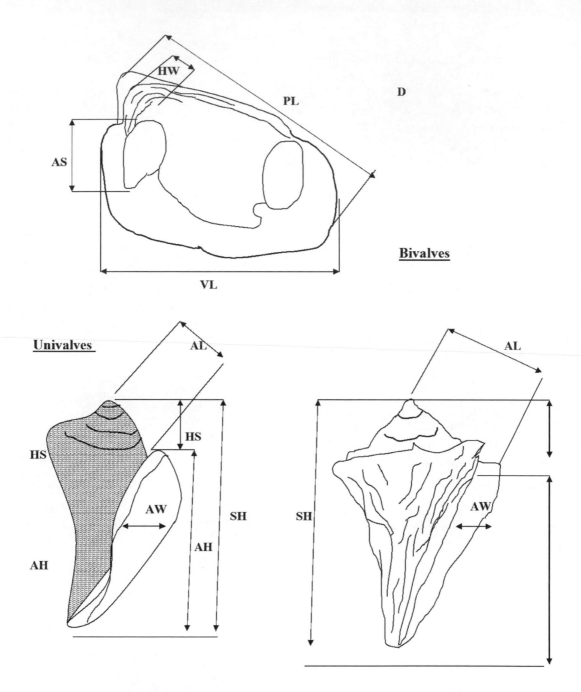

Figure 104: Measurements of shells, to be taken by specialist. Key: Bivalves: HW = hinge width, VL = valve length, VH = valve height, HL = hinge length, ASH = anterior scar height, PL = posterior slope length. Univalves: AW = aperture width, AH = aperture height, HS = shell height, AL = apex length, HS = height of spine, (after Claassen 1998: 109-10).

27.26 Record the numbers of any sub-samples taken here.

27.27 Any other relevant information must be put in this field.

27.28 The supervisor or zooarchaeologist who excavated and examined the micro faunal remains must sign and date the form.

27.29 The form should be countersigned by the director or site supervisor.

28.00 Sheet Twenty-Eight: Environmental Sample Recording Form: This form is for recording any individual object or specific sample that requires identification or sending to a laboratory for analysis, e.g. radiometric dating. The category of the sample should be ticked, whether it is wood, shell, charcoal or miscellaneous.

At the head of the form there are boxes for the **Site Code (28.01)**, **Operational Area (28.02)**, **Site Sub-Division (28.03)**, **Context (28.04)**, **Grid References (28.05)**, **Reduced Level (28.06)**, and **Feature Number (28.07)**, all of which should be recorded as outlined above.

28.08. Note the type of feature from which the sample came, i.e. hearth, cess pit, etc.

28.09 Record the size of the environmental sample.

28.10 Record the weight of the sample, in grams.

28.11 Note the number assigned to the sample and recorded in the environmental sample register.

28.12 Note if any sub-samples were taken, and their assigned number(s).

28.13 These fields are used to describe single wood samples.

Sampled for: tick appropriate box(es).

Sample is: tick the appropriate box.

Original use: If the wood has been reused, it may still be possible to ascertain its original use.

Evidence for reuse: If the sample or item has evidence of reuse, what is it? Tick the appropriate box, and give a brief explanation of your reasoning.

Is the item or sample in its original position as part of a structure, or is it a stray piece of wood with no other associated finds?

If the sample is from a structural element, describe the structure or item it is from and give the context, special find or structure number.

28.14 These fields are used to describe single shell samples.

Sampled for: Tick appropriate box(es).

Sample is: tick the appropriate box.

Recovered from: tick the box where the shell was recovered from and describe its provenience and relationship to other finds.

28.15 These fields are used to describe any single charcoal samples.

Sampled for: Tick appropriate box(es).

Sample is: tick the appropriate box.

Taken from: tick the box where the charcoal was recovered from and describe its provenience and relationship to other finds.

28.16 These fields are used to describe any environmental samples that are not wood nor shell nor charcoal, such as coprolites or modified sediments.

Material Type: The class of sample.

Description: Describe both the context from which the environmental sample came and the sample itself, along with any other information that may assist in identification and interpretation.

Sampled for: Tick appropriate box.

28.17 Make a note of any specialist treatment the sample received in the field.

28.18 State how the sample was lifted (e.g. manually by trowel, undercutting or sieving).

28.19 Give a description of the weather conditions when the sample was taken, and the time of day.

28.20 Sketch in plan and section showing where the sample came from.

28.21 Sketch of the sample; state the scale at which it is drawn.

28.22 Record the amount and numbers of any finds (bags or baskets) associated with the remains in this field.

28.23 Record the number(s) of any special finds found in association with the remains in this space.

28.24 List the numbers of any plans, sections or any special drawings made of the remains.

28.25 Insert the numbers of any photographs taken of the remains here.

28.26 Any other relevant information must be put in this field.

28.27 The estimated period or date of the sample.

28.28 The document must be signed and dated by the area supervisor.

28.29 The document must be signed and dated by the director or site supervisor.

28.30 The method of packaging the sample.

28.31 Date that the sample was sent to the lab.

28.32 State who authorised the sample's transfer to the lab (especially if it has to leave the country). Has the relevant permission been granted?

28.33 Is the sample in storage awaiting analysis? If so, where and does it have a storage number?

28.34 Date received back from the lab.

28.35 A summary of the lab results.

28.36 The identification of the sample.

29.00 Sheet Twenty-Nine: Wood and Timber Recording Form: Dry climates are excellent for preserving desiccated wood, however, if there have been fluctuations in the microenvironment the wood has been laying in, it is unlikely to survive. Waterlogging is another good means of preserving timbers, and is particularly common in Northern European bogs, swamps and marshes, as well as marine/riverine sediments. It should be noted that waterlogged wood tends to shrink as it dries, therefore all measurements must be taken as soon as the timbers are exposed (as they shrink by up to 25% radially (in width), regardless of how much and often they are sprayed). The thinner the timbers, the greater the likelihood of shrinkage and distortion (Westman 1994: 73).

In the Egyptian case, numerous types of indigenous wood were used, including acacia, tamarisk, willow, sycamore and fig (see Gale *et al* 2000). However, large scale timber production from native trees was rare, even in the Predynastic Period, and as the demand for better quality timber increased in the Early Dynastic Period, wood started to be imported from the Levant. Large quantities of cedar were imported into Egypt from the Early Dynastic Period onwards, especially from the Lebanon. Ash and elm were imported from Libya and the Levant, and oak was imported from Anatolia, and ebony was shipped from Punt and elsewhere south of Egypt. Wood and timber were used for making a variety of objects and structures in ancient Egypt. While whole buildings were generally not constructed wholly from timber, it was usually used as a framework or for certain features of both masonry and mud-brick buildings. Construction timber in the early periods usually takes the form of rough-hewn logs, whereas in the later periods (such as the Roman houses in the Faiyum) the timbers are neatly cut and planed. In later buildings timber was decorative and was not covered-up by plaster as it was in the Dynastic period. It was also widely used for domestic items, as elsewhere in the world.

This form is to record single pieces of wooden furniture, including boxes or single timber contexts within a wooden structure (this is in addition to the structure number and description on the building form). This form can also be adapted to record wooden boat-building techniques (see Ward 2006). The recording must provide sufficient information regarding stratigraphic position in relation to other features on site, establish its form, enable it to be dated and enable an isometric projection to be drawn (Westman 1994: 64). Wood can provide two distinct types of information: **a)** structural and constructional aspects of an object or structure, gained from studying the wood as *timber*, and **b)** environmental and dendrochronological data, gained from studying the timber as *wood* (Westman 1994: 70).

At the head of the form there are boxes for the **Site Code (29.01)**, **Operational Area (29.02)**, **Site Sub-Division (29.03)**, **Context (29.04)**, **Grid References (29.05)**, **Reduced Level (29.06)**, and **Structure Number (29.07)**, all of which should be recorded as outlined above.

29.08 Type: State whether it is a feature of a building (baseplate, post, brace, stake, top-plate, plank), artefact, piece of furniture, or just a single piece of timber.

29.09 Record the overall length, width, height or depth of the wooden context or artefact.

29.10 The dimensions of the individual logs or planks must be recorded, giving the paired measurements of the length, width (diameter), and depth of the planks. The measurements of all the various pieces of wood used in one context or artefact must be recorded. Sheet **Forty-seven** may come in useful in this respect.

29.11 The colour of the timber should be recorded, using a *Munsell Colour Chart*.

29.12 If known, state all the species of wood, giving both the English and Latin names.

29.13 This field is to describe the type of timber: post, brace, plank, baseplate, top-plate, stake, etc.

29.14 This field is to describe the position of the timber, variants include vertical, horizontal, diagonal (if leaning, note the angle: also distinguish between original and post-depositional lean).

29.15 Which compass direction is the timber facing?

29.16 The presence of any accessory items must be recorded here. Note the type of fitting (i.e. hinges, handles or bolts) and the material from which they are made (wood, gold, copper; bindings made from leather or reeds) and the presence of any appendages or decoration.

29.17 Note how the timber was cut from the tree trunk. In ancient Egyptian contexts, the trunk was cut into lengths of approximately 1.70 m (Killen 1994: 12). Sometimes

284

unconverted tree trunks were used as supports in buildings, although the through-and-through process was also used, cutting the tree-trunk into planks with a pull-saw to produce tangentially faced timbers. Boards produced in this manner are liable to cup, due to tangential shrinkage (Killen 1994: 13). Another method was to box the heartwood, where the bark and sapwood were removed by axe and the surfaces trimmed and smoothed with an adze (Killen 1994: 16). This method produces long solid pieces of timber, such as used in major constructions or for large wooden statues. Other methods (such as halved, quartered, radially cleft, box halved and box quartered) only start to appear in Egypt from the Graeco-Roman Period. The space provided is to describe the method of conversion.

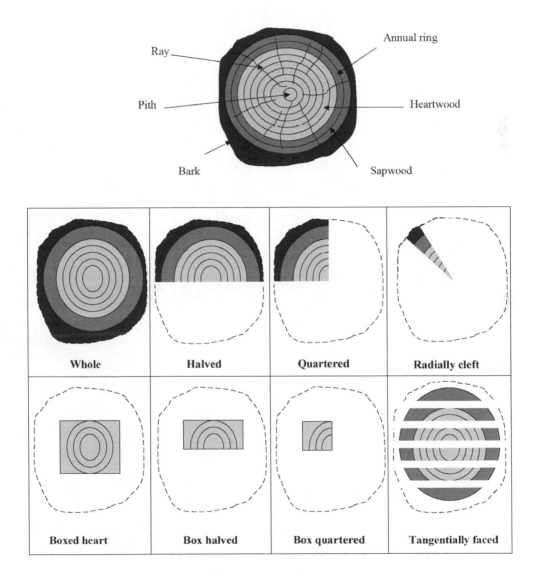

Figure 105: Timber conversion (after Killen 1994 & Westman 1994).

29.18 Describe the shape of the cross-section, and state if it changes along the length of the timber. The shape must also be indicated on the diagram in **29.41**.

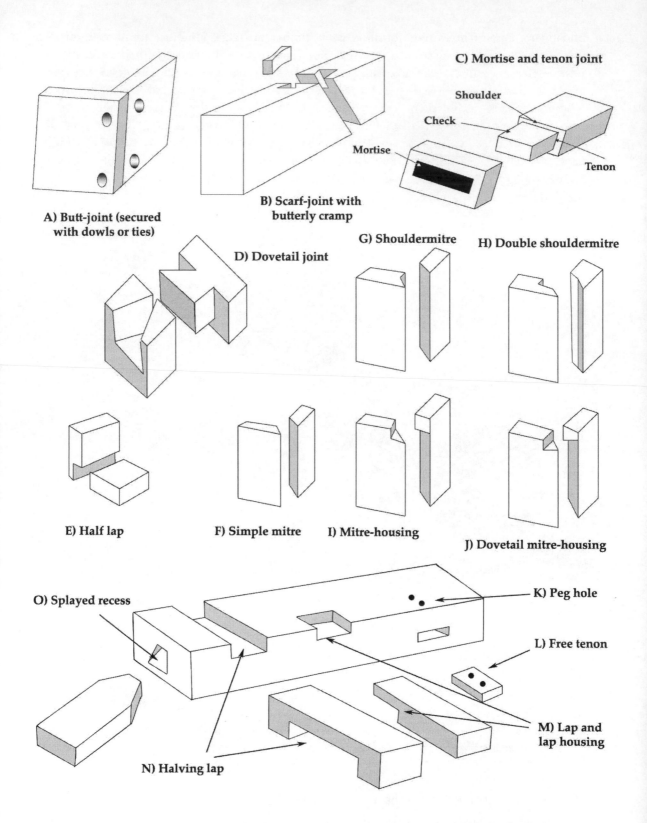

Figure 106: Joining techniques (after Killen 1994: 14-16).

29.19 Tool marks are often found on the timber surfaces. The through-and-through process creates a slash-grain effect, while there may also be evidence for marks made by a flint saw or knife, or from copper drills, pullsaw, adze, axe, awls, mortise/firmer chisels and sandstone smoothing blocks. These marks should be described and a 1:1 drawing made as soon as possible.

29.20 If there are any guidelines marking out the joints or where to cut the timber, assembly marks, tally marks or any graffiti, these must be described and included in the main drawing of the timber.

29.21 Note any applied techniques that have been used on the timbers. Treatments include coating with gypsum or gesso, painting, gilding (gold-leaf) and veneering with wood, ivory or ebony. Inlaying with semi-precious stones, marquetry and parquetry and coating with clear and black varnishes, beeswax and glue may also be found. If there is any moulding or carving on the timber, this must also be described and drawn at 1:1.

29.22 The type and number of joints must be recorded, along with their dimensions, and drawn at a scale of 1:1. The major types of joints used in ancient Egypt are shown in **Fig. 106** (also see Gale *et al* 2000)**.**

29.23 Any other comments, i.e. colour stains from a fitting.

29.24 The preservation of the timber must be recorded. In all cases, differentiate between ancient or recent/post-depositional damage. State if it is whole or partial, and note any burning or charring, wearing, insect or fungal damage.

29.25 Describe the timber's original context i.e. the identity of the artefact/feature of which it originally comprised a part.

Term	Definition
Brace or shore	Any supporting structural timber that is diagonally-set.
Cheeks	The exposed cut faces of a joint.
Edge & Face	Dressed timber usually has two faces wider than its two edges, except when it has been literally squared. The upper face is the surface most radial to the circle of the log.
Plate	A horizontal timber placed either at the top (top-plate) or bottom (base-plate) of a framing. Principal posts are often tenoned into the base-plate.
Shakes	Defects due to incorrect seasoning, usually splits that open into holes occurring across or along the grain.
Soffit	The underside of a timber.

Table 26: Glossary of woodworking terms (Coutts 1977; Killen 1994 & Westman 1994).

29.26 Provide an interpretation of the timber's use, substantiating your interpretation with reference to other timbers, contexts and documentary evidence. State whether there are any signs of recutting of the timbers, or if they were reused from an earlier building or structure.

29.27 Note how the wood was excavated, and also whether or not the matrix was sieved. It should also be recorded whether the description was made before or after the timber was removed from the matrix.

29.28 Note the weather conditions at the time of excavation, along with the time of day.

29.29-32 This section is for the *Physical Stratigraphic Relationships* and contains three data fields for interpretative stratigraphic relationships: earlier than, later than and contemporary with. The basic principles of stratigraphic interpretation have already been outlined above and do not need to be reiterated here. The excavator should use one or more of these fields to establish the relationship of the context with surrounding or associated contexts.

29.33 The context numbers of the contexts above and below should be placed in the *Running Matrix*. The context being described should be placed in the central box. This is for stratigraphic relationships **not** physical relationships. Always keep a running matrix when you are excavating an area and cross-reference with other excavators if their features or deposits have stratigraphic relationships with yours. Check with the site supervisor if at all uncertain about stratigraphic relationships - they must be accurately determined on site.

29.34 Record the amount and numbers of any finds (bags or baskets) associated with the timber(s) in this field.

29.35 Record the number(s) of any special finds found in association with the timber(s) in this space.

29.36 The numbers of the samples collected should be put here. You should take a carbon 14 sample from a non-exposed face. It is also important to take dendrochronology sample cores, and any paint, should also be sampled. Samples should be able to supply data on how many species were involved, the age of the timber when cut, how the timbers were converted/dressed, the MNI trees, calendar dates for the felling of the timber, any climatic changes, and woodland management practices.

29.37 List any plans, sections or other drawings made of the context. All structures are drawn at 1:20 in plan and elevations and sections at 1:10. Each individual structural timber (unless identical to others already drawn) must be drawn, showing the faces and edges at 1:10.

29.38 List the numbers of any photographs taken of the context. Timber structures should be photographed so that their three-dimensional nature can be observed. Record details, i.e. joinery, joint assembly marks and individual timbers.

29.39 The value of the temporary bench mark or datum should be entered here, as well as the measurement from the backsight to the TBM, and the instrument height.

29.40 A brief sketch of the context should be provided, showing any notable aspects and relationships; include a grid peg square reference and the scale, and annotate with dimensions and other useful information. A list of all the foresights taken on the context should be placed here. A brief sketch of the section or elevation can also be put in this space if deemed to be necessary. Do **not** simply copy the formal plan.

29.41 Sketch the type of wood conversion on the cross-section of tree trunk provided, and tick the boxes to indicate whether the wood has bark and/or sapwood, and is knotty or straight-grained.

29.42 It is very important that the supervisor who completed the recording form signs and dates it.

29.43 The form and interpretation must be approved and counter-signed by the director or site supervisor and any conflicting and differing interpretations of the same data entered.

29.44 The person that enters the data into a database must sign and date this field once the process has been completed.

30.00 Sheet Thirty: Pottery Recording Form: Although ceramics are usually associated with pottery vessels, 'ceramic' applies to all artefacts made from clay or silicates, such as baked clay figurines, musical instruments, tiles, bricks, faience, and glass objects. Pottery is the most important category of ceramics for investigating aspects of socio-cultural change, and as such this form is for recording pottery vessels rather than other categories of ceramics. The variables that can be recorded in this form allow a chronology (relative dating) to be established for the site, as well as an opportunity to investigate the manufacturing technology, deposition patterns, production distribution, function and use, settlement organisation and socio-cultural expression. The nature of the variables scored depends upon the period and geographical area under assessment. Non-specialists are advised to acquaint themselves with the corpus of pottery types likely to be recovered at the site, although this form should ideally be filled out by the site ceramicist. This form is for the recording of individual pottery vessels or important diagnostic components thereof, whereas **Sheet 30a** is for the recording of all the bulk pottery; all registered vessels or sherds should also be placed on the **Pottery Register: Sheet 16**.

Raw material sourcing can help establish the trade routes and site catchment areas, while the residues inside the vessels are a source of information about diet and other social activities. Scientific methods such as thin section analysis can be used to identify the type of clay used, locating the distinctive clay of a region by its grain size and inclusions under a microscope. The social aspects of pottery manufacture and the gendered roles within are also important aspects that can be investigated. It is thus very important to adequately record the ceramic corpus.

At the head of the form there are boxes for the **Site Code (30.01)**, **Operational Area (30.02)**, **Site Sub-Division (30.03)**, **Context (30.04)**, and **Grid References (30.05)**, which should be recorded as outlined above.

30.06 The category has already been filled out, as it will be a deposit.

30.07 Describe the type of deposit that the pottery vessel was extracted from, i.e. fill, layer, floor, etc.

30.08 Note the number of the feature in which the pottery vessel was found.

30.09 Record the exact 3-D provenience of the artefact.

30.10 Note the artefact's find number.

30.11 Note the artefact's catalogue number.

30.12 Completeness: The prompt asks if the vessel is complete, if yes, how many potsherds is the whole vessel comprised of and what is the weight of the vessel? If the potsherds do not constitute a whole vessel, how many are there, and what extent are the potsherds? Potsherds from the same vessel may fit together, certain groups of potsherds from the same vessel may fit together but the groups may be unconnected. The extent of the sherds may be described as:

1. Rim	10. Shoulder
2. Decorated body	11. Neck and shoulder
3. Base	12. Rim, neck and shoulder
4. Handle	13. Rim and shoulder
5. Spout	14. Base and body
6. Rim and handle	15. Rim, neck and body
7. Rim and shoulder	16. Rim and neck
8. Rim, body and base	17. Neck and body
9. Rim and body	18. Rim, neck, shoulder and body

The total weight of the sherds must then be entered.

30.13 Dimensions: The maximum/minimum diameter of the rim and base, and the maximum girth of the shoulder and vessel. The radius chart (**Appendix 6**) should be used to assess the diameter of the potsherds. The potsherd(s) or vessel should be placed on the chart and the stance ascertained by rocking the rim or base on the chart until no light (or the minimum light) can be seen between the potsherd and the chart. The thickness of the wall of the vessel must be recorded in millimetres, measuring the rim, body and base.

The radius chart should also be used to assess the percentage of the rim or base preserved. The reason for ascertaining the percentage of the diameter present is to more easily quantify the material present at the site and facilitate intra-site and inter-site comparisons. The creation of what Orton (1993) terms estimated vessel equivalents (EVE) is one of the most accurate methods to statistically represent pottery for comparative purposes. This may be complimented by the counting and weighing of sherds. To

290

determine the EVE of-say-five Nile A fabric wine jars with the following measures (as calculated from the radius chart), 22%, 5%, 10%, 12% and less than 5%, then 50% of the wine jars made from Nile A fabric are present, which is equal to 0.5 of an EVE. If the percentages had added up to 600%, then 6 EVES are present. If only 0.5 of an EVE of his type of wine jar is present in context 10 where all EVES in all fabrics and forms came to a total of 25, then there is only 2% of wine jars of fabric Nile A present in this context (after Orton 1980). This method therefore allows for the various percentages of each type of pottery present in the various contexts to be assessed and should be recorded in a database. This process is not without its problems, as rims of storage jars in comparison with their bases seem to be under represented in the archaeological record. Also rims and bases should generally not be lumped together but analysed in separate sets (see Orton 1993 for a discussion of the problems).

The height is only recorded when a whole profile of a vessel is present, and the maximum height (height from base to shoulder, and the height of the neck) should be recorded.

30.14 Fabric type: Note the name of the fabric, if known. To ascertain the fabric type both macro and microscopic analysis should be used. There are various types of *primary* clay, which contain only impurities from their mother rock, such as kaolin (China clay), fire clay, infusible clay, refractory clay and *secondary* clay, which has been transported from site of formation and contain impurities from the process, such as marl or calcareous clay, ball clay, fusible clay, red clay, earthenware clay, sandy clay, siliceous clay and stoneware clay. The Vienna system (see **Tab. 27**) was devised for the classification of fabric types found in Egypt (Arnold & Bourriau 1993).

Nile Silts	Marl Clay	Foreign
Nile A	Marl A1	Nubian Kerma ware
Nile B1	Marl A2	Mycenaean fine ware
Nile B2	Marl A3	Cypriot I/II ware
Nile C	Marl A4	Cypriot red lustrous ware
Nile D	Marl B	Syrian red lustrous ware
Nile E	Marl C1	Palestinian - Canaanite fabric with combed
	Marl C2	surface
	Marl C compact	Palestinian - Canaanite fabric with fine mineral
	Marl D	inclusions
	Marl E	Palestinian - Canaanite fabric with shell inclusions

Table 27: The Vienna system fabric classifications.

However, for Naqada III fabrics from Lower Egypt, based on analysis from the pottery corpus at Helwan Köhler & Smythe (2004: 126-128) have re-classified the fabrics due to the limited types of Predynastic pottery originally used for the compilation of the Vienna system. The fabric types are now classified as: Alluvial Silt Fabric Type A (none to very finely tempered) (nearest Vienna-system comparison is - Nile A), Alluvial Silt Fabric Type B (tempered with chaff and limestone) (comparison is – D variant of Nile B & C), Alluvial Silt Fabric Type C (tempered with chaff) (comparison is - Nile B1 or B2), Marl Clay Fabric Type A (tempered with limestone) (Comparison is - Marl A1), Marl Clay Fabric Type B (tempered with limestone and chaff) (comparison is – Marl A).

The next field asks for the overall firing conditions (see **Fig. 107**); terms used should be oxidised, unoxidised (incompletely oxidised or reduced), irregularly fired, overfired, spalled and adjusted firing (unoxidised surface over oxidised band or core).

The next set of prompts relate to specific questions about the fabric: firing, colour, hardness, texture and fracture (see Orton, Tyres & Vince 1993: 134, 231-42)

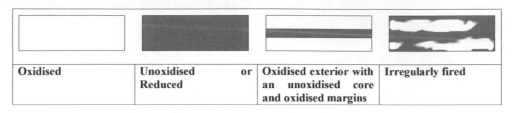

| Oxidised | Unoxidised or Reduced | Oxidised exterior with an unoxidised core and oxidised margins | Irregularly fired |

Figure 107: General firing conditions (after Rye 1981: Fig. 104).

Firing – Five columns (the external surface, external margin, core, internal margin and internal surface) are provided to record how well the pottery vessel was fired. The terms that should be used are oxidised, unoxidised or incompletely oxidised and irregularly fired (Rye 1981: 146)

Colour – Record the colour of the various parts of the section or break as well as the interior and exterior of the vessel, using a *Munsell Colour Chart* or a *Panetone Colour Chart*. If neither are available the choices are usually orange-brown red spectrum, the pale pink-buff-off-white spectrum, white, and the black-grey-uncertain spectrum (Prehistoric Ceramics Research Group 1992: 12).

Hardness – The hardness of the fabric should be determined by scratching it with a fingernail. If it can be scratched then it is soft. If it cannot be scratched with a fingernail, but a blade makes a scratch then it is hard. Very hard is stoneware or overfired and cannot be scratched with a blade. The Mohs scale can also be used if wished:

Mohs Scale	Mineral	Can Be
1	Talc	Crushed with fingernail
2	Gypsum	Scratched by a fingernail
3	Calcite	Scratched by iron nail
4	Fluorite	Scratched by knife or glass
5	Apatite	Scratched with knife with difficulty
6	Orthoclase feldspar	Scratched quartz, and scratches glass with difficulty
7	Quartz	Scratched by steel nail, scratches glass with ease
8	Topaz	Scratched by emerald, scratches glass easily
9	Corundum	Scratched only by a diamond, cuts glass
10	Diamond	Used to cut glass

Table 28: The Mohs scale of hardness.

Texture – This refers to the 'feel' of the surface of the vessel or sherd. Fineware will usually have a smooth texture, while a soapy feel is common to shell-gritted limestone or grog-gritted wares. Sandy and very sandy vessels feel like sand paper and can be sand or straw tempered. Granular ceramic feels like grit (Prehistoric Ceramics Research Group 1992: 12).

Fracture – This refers to the broken section, which should be a fresh break done with a pair of pliers. There are various terms to describe how the fabric fractures:

Conchoidal – curved, shell-like striations (like flint surfaces).

Fine – unequal small closely-spaced irregularities or porous structure.

Hackly – uneven, rough break, which is typical of sandy fabrics with spaces between the matrix and inclusions.

Smooth – flat or slightly curved.

Irregular – large or more widely-spaced gaps or porosity.

Laminated – layers like slate or shale.

Inclusions – Most pottery fabrics have inclusions; some can be identified with the naked eye, whereas others require a magnifying glass or binocular microscope. A 10% vv solution of hydrochloric acid (HCl), a magnet and dental pick will be required to investigate the inclusions (Prehistoric Ceramics Research Group 1992: 13). Some inclusions may be natural, such as clay pellets and mudstone, whereas others were used as temper, such as grog or chaff. The calcareous matter is best tested with the HCl solution; shell, oolitic limestone and chalk will fizz on contact. Voids in the fabric usually indicate where inclusions have been burnt or leached out.

Once the material of the inclusion has been identified (see **Fig. 108**), the frequency of the inclusions must be recorded. This is best done as a percentage with reference to the density chart (**Fig. 85**). The sorting of the inclusions can be ascertained by reference to **Fig. 81**, whereas the degrees of roundness and sphericity can be judged with reference to **Fig. 82**. Inclusion size should be measured with a microscope and ruler, and then referenced to the sediment size chart (**Tab. 20**). Inclusions are either natural (e.g. clay pellets, mica, iron oxides), temper (e.g. chaff, grog, flint) or uncertain (both sand and shell can be natural and used as temper).

30.15 The likely source of the inclusions. Are they:

1. Local = within 10 km radius of the site.

2. Non-local/Regional = a source exists in the region but over 10 km from the site.

3. Regional = from the region, but is to too general to determine if local or regional.

4. National = sources available somewhere within the country.

5. Foreign = sources unavailable within the country but possibly from neighbouring polities.

6. Uncertain = not able to distinguish the origin.

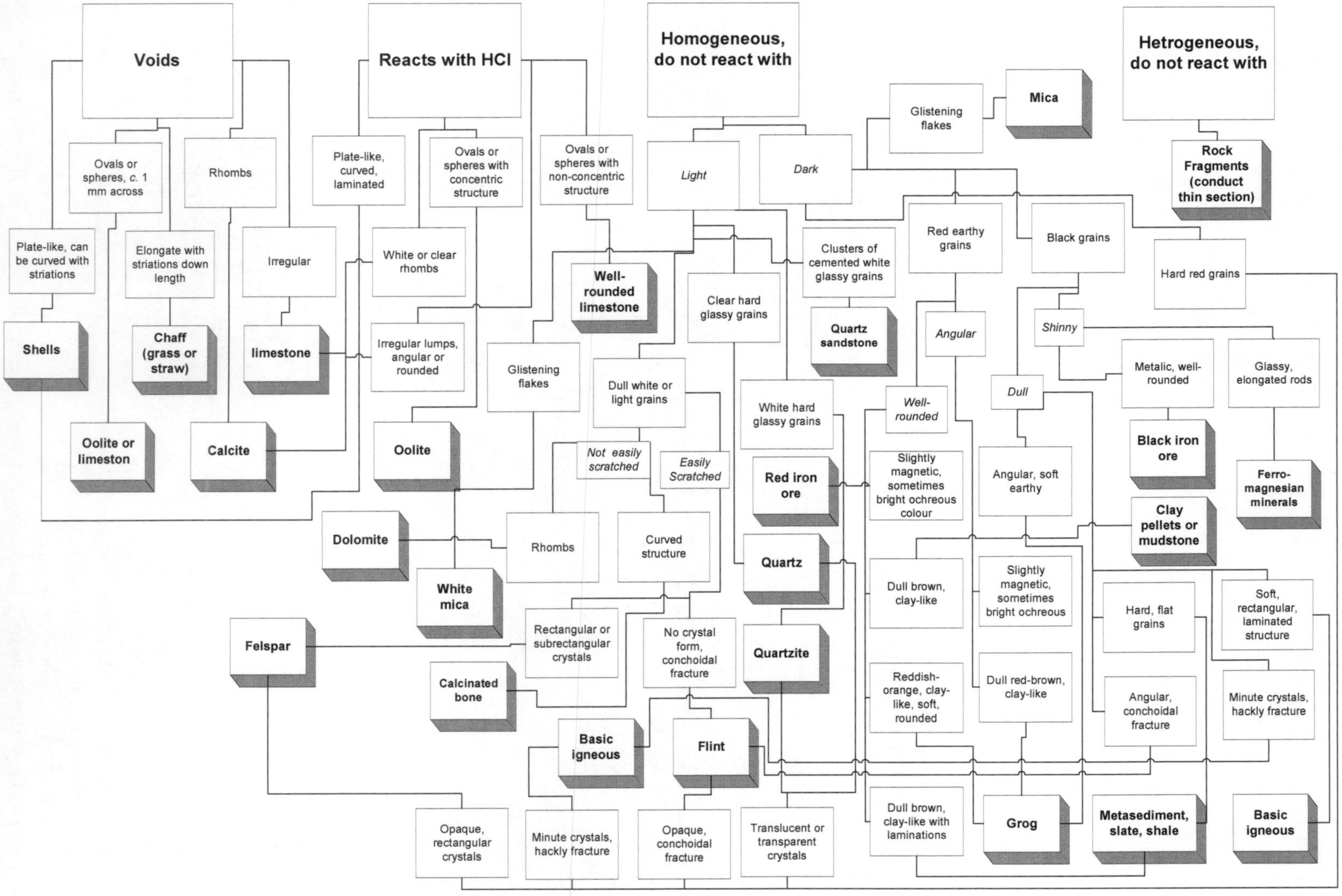

Figure 108: Pottery inclusions identification chart (after Orton, Tyres & Vince 1993; Peacock 1977).

State if the exact source of the inclusions is known (Arnold 1981; Prehistoric Ceramics Research Group 1992).

30.16 Note the likely source of the clay using the same options as above.

30.17 Record the porosity of the fabric as: open porous texture, moderately porous, elongated pores, decomposed limestone, dense or incipient vitrification.

30.18 A brief account of the petrology of the fabric of the vessel and state if a specialist report is available, usually written by the site geoarchaeologist.

30.19 Brief comments on the fabric, which are useful to its identification. Note anything unusual or what types of vessels the fabric is used for. After all the fabric/pottery analysis has been completed it is useful to have a record of the operational areas, features and contexts where the fabric was recovered. Finally the fabric should be cross-referenced to other sites.

30.20 The construction or manufacturing techniques must be recorded. Various methods may have been used in the construction of one vessel, it must be noted how each part of the vessel was made. The various methods of construction are detailed in Arnold & Bourriau (1993) and also Rye (1981). Some of the techniques used are shown in **Tab. 29**.

Non-Radial	Free-Radial	Central-Radial
Pinching and hollowing	Slab and coiling	Simple low wheel
Pounding using paddle and anvil	Turning device	Tall-stemmed single wheel
Shaping over a core or lump	Turning mat	Extra low simple wheel
Moulding and slip-casting		Kick-wheel
Mortised or riveted		Wheel-thrown
Applied or attached		Wheel-finished

Table 29: Techniques of pottery vessel construction.

30.21 The form of the vessel is closely related to its function, such as a breadmould or pot stand. Closed forms include bottles, flasks, jars and jugs, contrasting with open forms such as bowls, cups, dishes, plates and vases. These basic forms of vessels can then be prefixed by their type, such as storage jar or carinated bowl. What is required in this field is the form of the vessel. The basic forms are given in **Tab. 30**.

30.22 The form type is required in this field, is it a beer jar, *hes*-vase, Bes jar, flanged bowl, etc. The type is often dictated by certain features, such as the rim, foot or handles or shape such as cylindrical vase or ovoid jar. The form type is required in this space. If using a computerised system, various alphanumeric codes can be allocated to the various elements of the vessel (i.e. rim, base, handles, spout, etc) as well as to its form type (see Wodzińska 2009a; 2009b).

Form	Description
Beaker	A drinking vessel without handles, height exceeds diameter, can be either open or closed
Bottle	A vessel with a constricted, often narrow neck, no handles designed to stand with the neck upright
Bowl	An open vessel form, rim diameter generally exceeds that of base, sides deeper than a dish, with the deep form having a 1:1 ratio of height to rim diameter
Cup	A small drinking vessel; rim diameter always greater than both the base diameter and the height, sometimes has loop handle(s)
Dish	An open vessel with a height between one third and one seventh its rim diameter
Flask	Round base with a narrow neck and no handles, not designed to stand upright
Jar	A closed vessel with a wide neck opening, a short neck/rim with a shoulder and a base smaller than the maximum diameter
Jug	A closed form with handles, designed to stand with the rim upright. There may be a lip or a spout for pouring liquids
Lid	Similar to inverted dishes, sometimes with a central knob for lifting
Mug	Tall drinking vessel with loop handle(s) that has a height greater than the rim, base and maximum diameters
Plate	An open vessel with a height less than one fifth its rim diameter, with the upper part of the wall everted
Vase	An open vessel, where height exceeds maximum diameter, often flared

Table 30: Vessel forms (after Medieval Pottery Research Group 1998).

30.23 The various functions for which pottery vessels were produced influenced the forms, types, sizes and fabrics used. Many of the other variables recorded on this form can also be used to determine its original function, such as decoration and other surface treatments such as burnishing, use of perforations and attachments like handles can indicate its intended usage (Hendrickx *et al.* 2002; Mountjoy 1993: 122-8). In addition to style, the use of residue analysis (Heron & Pollard 1988; Needham & Evans 1987; Renfrew & Bahn 1991) and usewear patterns (Hally 1986) are invaluable in deducing vessel function. Some vessels were produced purely as funerary objects; never having a utilitarian use. Some of the various ceramic type-function classifications are:

Alembic	Breadmould	Cupel
Aludel	Candlestick	Curfew
Amphora	Churn	Dutch oven
Baking tray	Cooking pot	Fish trap
Base	Cooking pot stand	Flower pot
Basin	Crucible	Fuming pot
Beer jar	Cruet	Grenade
Bottle	Cucurbit	Horn
Brazier	Cup and saucer	Incense burner

Inkwell	Mousetrap	Spindle whorl
Krater	Oil lamp	Spittoon
Lantern	Olive jar	Stamp seal
Lavabo	Pan	Stand
Lid	Pitcher	Storage jar
Mantel	Plaque	Unguentarium
Milk churn	Platter	Urn
Milk jar	Sieve	Whistle
Mortar	Strainer	Wine jar

30.24 The rim shape is the form of the rim and along with the stance, profile and embellishments is one of the most diagnostic elements of pottery vessels, the most common are depicted in **Fig. 109**. The shape is usually described as plain or simple (vertical/upright or sloping), articulated (inverted or everted), thickened (internally, externally, symmetrically), thinned, collared, rolled, flanged, hammerhead or clubbed.

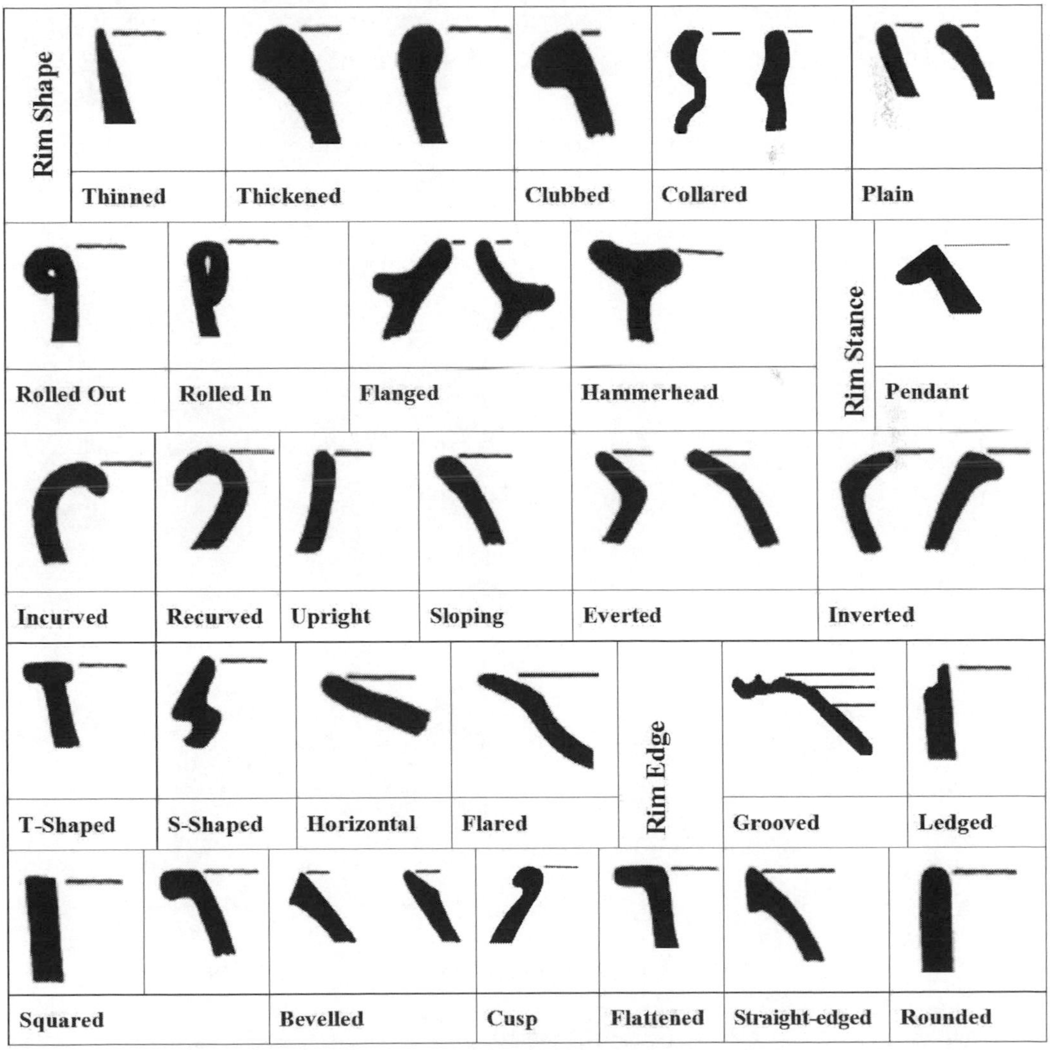

Figure 109: Various categories of rims (after Medieval Pottery Research group 1998).

30.25 The rim stance is the angle of the rim in relation to the vessel. The stance is usually described as vertical or upright, sloping, flared, everted, inverted, hooked – recurved or incurved, T-shaped, S-shaped, pendant, or horizontal (flat).

30.26 The rim edge is the lip or profile of the rim and is usually described as rounded, squared, ledged, bevelled or wedge, flattened, crenellated, straight-edged, cusp, or grooved (in-out-up).

30.27 Rim embellishments describe how the rim is decorated; variants include ribbed, thumbed, crenellated, cordoning and castellations.

30.28 The shape of the base is an important diagnostic element and is normally described as round, pointed, knob, flat, disk, concave, convex, plain ring, ring with flattened base, hollowed trumpet, unhollowed trumpet, footed, pod or loop.

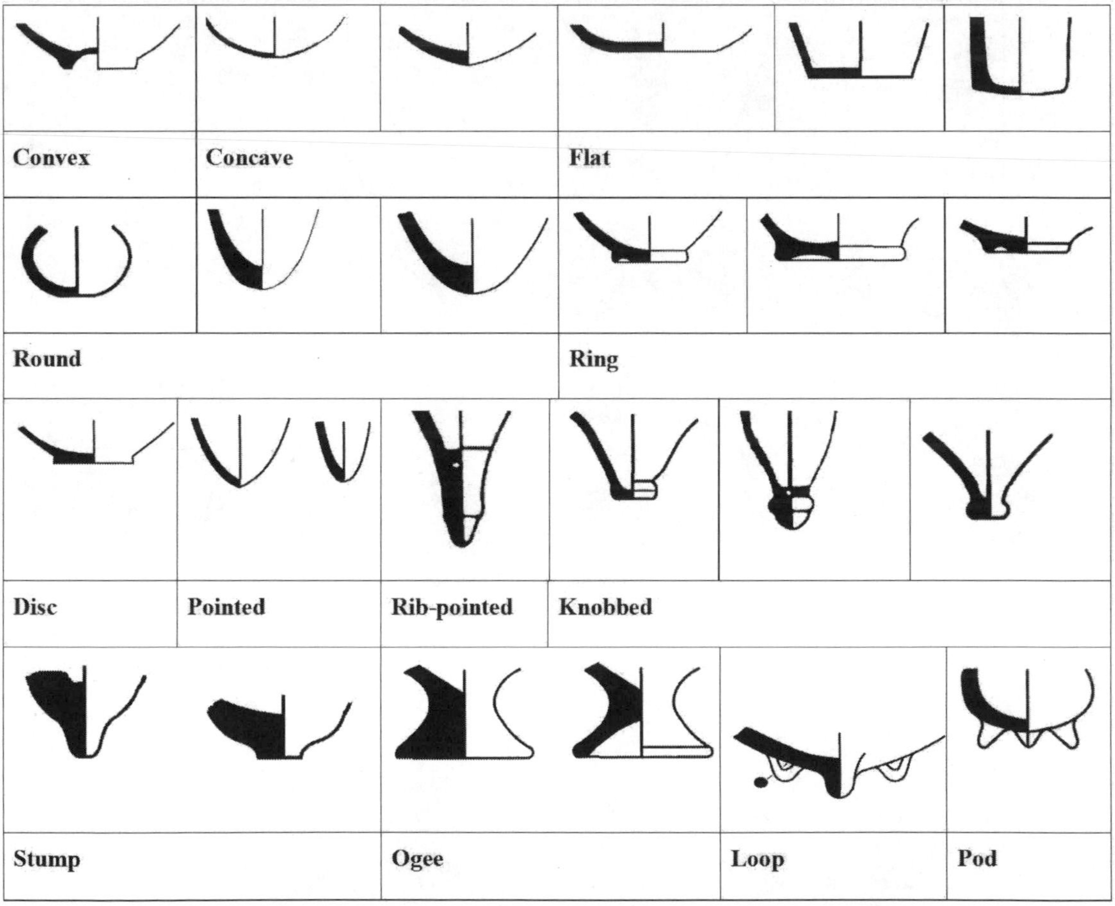

Figure 110: Various types of bases (after Joukowsky 1980).

30.29 Base embellishment describes how the base is decorated; variants include: faceted, foot ring, frilled, splayed, cordage, thumbed, pedestalled and recessed.

30.30 The shape of the body of the vessel is described as spherical, ovoid – vertical, ovoid – horizontal, ovoid – inverted, date-shaped, pyriform/pear-shaped – vertical, pyriform – inverted, cylindrical – horizontal, cylindrical – vertical, conical – vertical, conical – inverted, biconical –equal, biconical – unequal, tricornate or spherical.

30.31 The neck can be: not present / indefinable, convex, concave (or carinated) or vertical.

30.32 The height of the neck should be described as short or tall.

30.33 The girth of the neck should be described as narrow or wide.

30.34 How many handles or handle emplacements are present? However, if it is only the scar present where the handle was once attached, this should be recorded but clearly indicated.

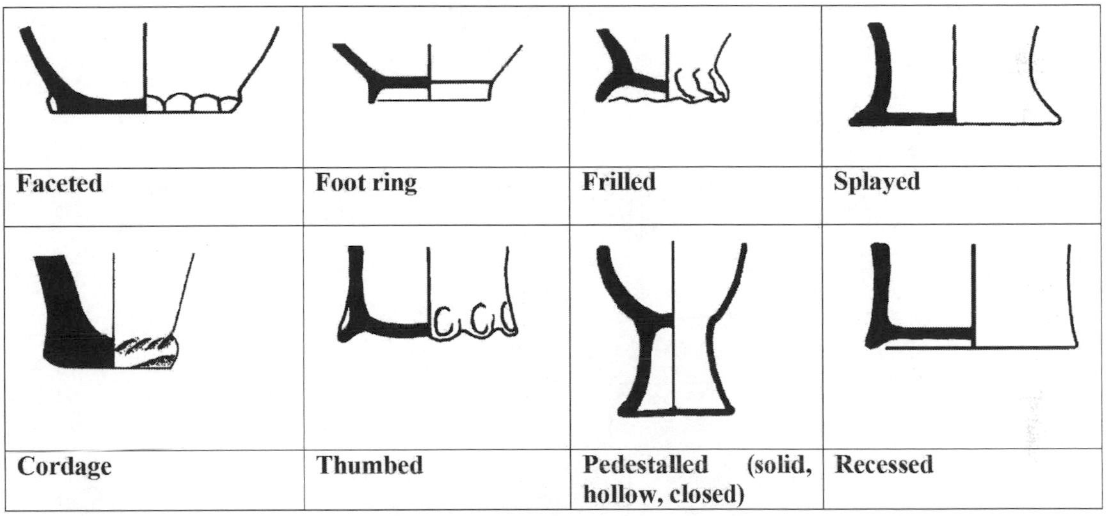

Faceted	**Foot ring**	**Frilled**	**Splayed**
Cordage	**Thumbed**	**Pedestalled (solid, hollow, closed)**	**Recessed**

Figure 111: Base embellishments (after Medieval Pottery Research Group 1998).

30.35 The type of handle is usually described as loop (D-shaped, right-angled or ring handle), ear, basket, strap, lug – plain, lug – envelope, ledge – plain, ledge – envelope, ledge - thumb-indented (wavy), ledge - pushed up, ledge – vestigial or wishbone. The section of the handle should also be noted: is it round, oval, flat, irregular, double strand, triple strand, composite, hollow, rod, strap, socketed, tubular, grooved or twisted?

30.36 The placement of the handles should be described in terms of their angle: vertical, horizontal, or oblique, and their attachments to/from: rim, neck, shoulder, upper body, lower body or base.

30.37 The presence/absence or number of spouts must be recorded here.

30.38 The type of spout should be recorded as: plain trough, trough with strainer, cylindrical tubular, tapered tubular, S-shaped tubular, cup, bridge or parrot beak, cut-out or open, gutter, pinched, trefoil, or animal. Also note if it is a long or short spout.

30.39 The placement of the spout(s) is recorded in terms of angle, is it located horizontally, vertically or obliquely in the rim, neck, shoulder, upper body, lower body or base.

30.40 The presence, number and type of feet should be recorded in this field. Feet in profile can be circular, oval and triangular with the modification of clubbed or trefoil. The feet may be applied, pulled or thumbed.

30.41 If the vessel has a lid it should be recorded on a separate pottery recording form; the catalogued number of the lid should be put in this space. The lid must always be made referred to the vessel it relates to. On the sketch of the vessel the lid and any other directly associated pottery objects must be shown together. Lids are normally described as collared, conical, dish, domed, flat, flat-topped, saucer-shaped or flanged.

30.42 The presence, number and type of knobs should be recorded in this field. Knobs can be clubbed, rounded, squared, triangular, wedge-shaped, floral, anthropomorphic or zoomorphic.

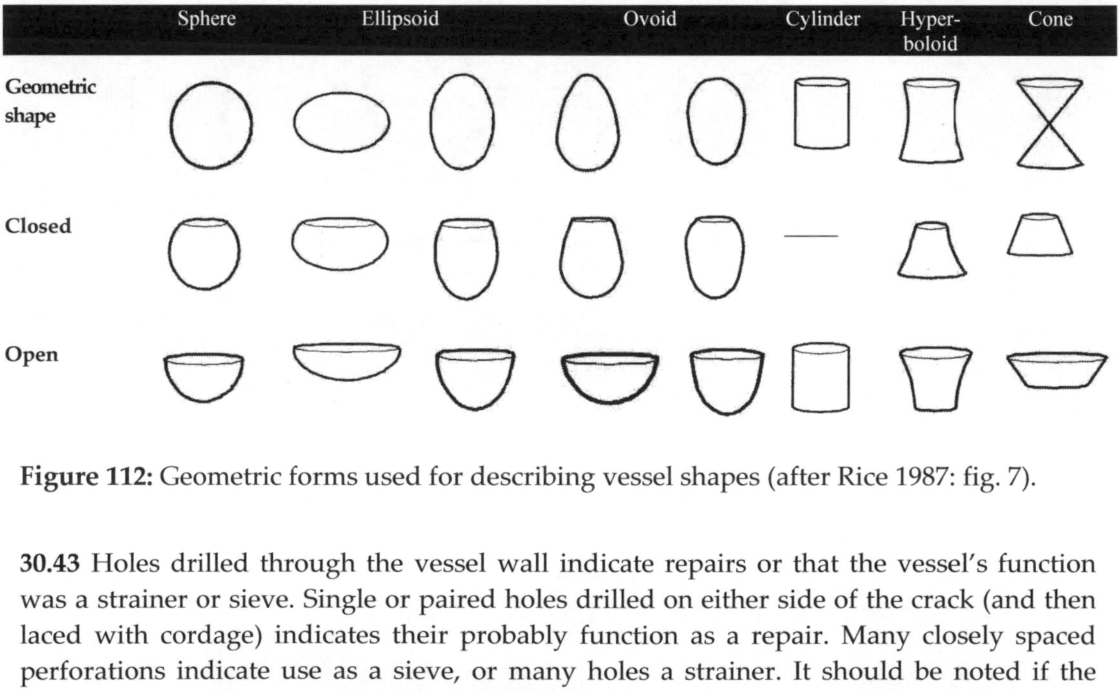

Figure 112: Geometric forms used for describing vessel shapes (after Rice 1987: fig. 7).

30.43 Holes drilled through the vessel wall indicate repairs or that the vessel's function was a strainer or sieve. Single or paired holes drilled on either side of the crack (and then laced with cordage) indicates their probably function as a repair. Many closely spaced perforations indicate use as a sieve, or many holes a strainer. It should be noted if the holes were made pre- or post-firing, as this will help indicate their function.

30.44 Perforation placement: Where are the holes placed on the vessel?

30.45 Any other plastic or non-plastic elements should be recorded in this field, such as the presence of string or wrapping in cloth.

300

30.46 Surface treatment refers to the manipulation of the vessel surfaces prior to the firing process, and is typologically significant. Many of the methods used were to achieve smooth surfaces on the vessel, such as wiping, burnishing, scraping or the application of slip. Plain surfaces are those that were wiped, finger-smeared, scraped, with no other surface manipulation. Corrugated surfaces were produced by indenting the exterior surface as clay coils were applied. Polished surfaces were produced by burnishing or rubbing with a polishing stone or similar, producing a sheen with polishing striations. This method also strengthens the surface bond of clay particles. Slip consists of extremely fine-grained clay particles which are separated from the clay matrix by soaking in water. Slip is often applied to exterior and interior vessel surfaces as a method for strengthening the bonds between coils, and also to create a smooth surface. When viewed in profile, slips appear as thin lines of contrasting colour and texture to the fabric matrix. Slips can be divided into self-slip (smoothing) and slip (coated). A vessel may also be washed in slip or other substance. Glazes consist of glassy or metallic chemicals painted onto a vessel surface, which vitrify and create a glassy surface when fired, strengthening the vessel body. The brushing technique is decorative and also creates a surface bond between the coils. Combs were also used for the same reason, as was scratching with a sharp tool such as a stylus. Painted designs were also sometimes applied prior to firing on the slipped, polished or plain ceramic surfaces.

The surfaces treated must be recorded as must the tool that was used to execute the surface treatment, such as a finger, knife, reed brush, comb, hard pebble, or pointed instrument/stylus. The colour of the surface treatment must be recorded using a *Panetone* or *Munsell Colour Chart*.

30.47 Decoration: This is also highly diagnostic, both temporally and spatially. As such, pottery decoration effectively serves as social or ethnic markers. While internal variability can denote social and political organisation.

The first field is for entering the location of the decoration. The second space is for detailing the technique of applying or creating the decoration. Many different techniques have been employed, fluid or liquid decoration techniques include glaze, blusterous slip, hand painted (e.g. the D-Ware pottery of Predynastic Egypt [see **Fig. 155**] or the black or red figured pottery of Classical Greece), spatter or sponge decoration, transfer printing, secondary slip, or a thin creamy wash applied after firing. Plastic decoration or appliqué (applied) is the additions of various elements to the basic vessel. The vessel itself can be made into a fancy shape, such as an animal or human. Other methods include cut out, incised, impressed/stamped, roughcast, rusticated, knife trimmed, stamp and drag, squeezed, pinched, embossed, barbotine, tooled, shell-stamping, finger impressed, fingernail impressed, scored, notched, slashed, scratched, excised (carved out), moulded relief, fretwork, incisions filled with paste, linear dentate stamping (marks made by a tool resembling a comb) and rocker dentate (the tool is impressed and then pivoted at one end creating a 'saw-toothed' design).

The decorative elements or type include: sculptural, wavy walls, angular indentations, ribbing, triangular voids, other void shapes, knobs, round flat pads, bands – ropes, bands - ring hatching, bands – smooth round, scalloping, animal body parts, human body parts, Bes face, Hathor head, incised straight line, incised wavy line, dotted wavy line, small waves, long waves, running spiral, zigzag, dots, dashes, herringbone, buttons, geometric shapes, pictorial, floral designs, faunal designs, rope impressed, leaf impressed, basket impressed, textile (fabric impressed), ridging, cordage, stamps, furrowed, roulette, 'saw-toothed' design, single point dentate decorations (marks of a tool which is repeatedly pressed into the clay surface), pellets, scales, foil, and rim notching,

The last two fields ask for the colour of the decoration and the dryness of the pottery vessel when the decoration was applied. The terms used should be plastic/moist, leather-hard, very dry, and after firing.

30.48 Marks may be made on the vessel, some are termed potmarks (see Tassie *et al.* 2008), others may be potters marks made to identify the person who made the vessel. A description of the mark must be given here along with the location of the mark.

30.49 Is there any evidence of residues on the surface of the vessel, such as limescale (possible evidence of boiling or storing water), food residues, slags or pigments?

30.50 Is there any evidence of usewear on the interior or exterior surfaces? Use wear categories include exterior sooting, interior sooting or carbon deposits, interior mineral deposits, rim chipping and basal abrasion among others (Skibo 1992). Because post-depositional wear and residues are common, use wear categories such as sooting and rim chipping may be the result of post-depositional activity as well as pre-depositional use (Beck *et al.* 2002). However, sooting is generally the direct result of a pot being used over an open fire. Sooting can occur as secondary use (e.g. a sherd used as a cooking pot support during a later occupation). Therefore, this attribute has its best interpretive value when complete or nearly complete vessels are being examined.

If interior abrasions are present they can represent direct evidence of mechanical use impact such as mixing, food preparation, parching, boiling and stirring (Hally 1983; 1986; Skibo 1992). Suspension marks may be visible from the suspension of the vessel by a rope or chain. There may also be rubbing scars around the lip of the rim from the presence of a lid.

30.51 Condition of sherds: The condition should be recorded as fresh, slight abrasion, light abrasion, heavy abrasion, flaked, or pitted.

30.52 Reuse: If the pottery object has been reused it should be described here. Some potsherds have been modified into Clayton discs, jar stoppers, counters, spindle whorls, pendants or tools. This normally takes the form of rounding the sherd and/or drilling a hole through it. Whole vessels may also be cut down and reused; jars may be modified into bowls or saucers. Identification of post-firing modifications assists in further characterising the range of activities that took place at a site and the role ceramic artefacts had in these activities.

30.53 Any comments on the vessel or potsherd should be recorded here. If interlocking sherds have been found in different contexts space is provided to record this fact. This will help in investigating post-depositional processes and chronological relationships. It can also be used to alert the excavators of miss-assignation of material if the contexts concerned are not related or of the fact that the two contexts might correlate with one another. Any unusual elements or attributes should also be commented upon, as should the decoration. The presence of this type of vessel in the various operational areas, features and contexts should also be recorded, possibly using a correlation table. At the bottom of the field is space for the preliminary dating of the pottery vessel or potsherd. Typologies and chronological sequences have been created for various countries, cultures and time periods, either this number or the sites' should be put in the corpus field. For Predynastic Egypt, Petrie devised one of the earliest, which he termed sequence dating. This has been modified by Kaiser (1957) and then by Hendrickx (1996; 1999). References should be made to any other publications with similar pottery vessels.

30.54 The numbers of the samples collected from the pottery vessel must be recorded here. Samples of the fabric and any residues, such as food or soot must be taken as well as any paint on the vessel. The residue samples can then be tested to aide in diet reconstruction or soot for radiocarbon dating.

30.55 List any plans or other drawings made of the pottery vessel or sherd here.

30.56 Insert the numbers of any photographs taken of the pottery vessel or sherd here.

30.57 A sketch of the pottery vessel is required here with a blow-up of any special features (such as base, rim, handles or spout).

30.58 A 1:1 scale drawing of any writing, potmarks, *serekhs*, cartouches, potters marks or other signs is required here.

30.59 It is very important that the supervisor who completed the recording form signs and dates it.

30.60 The form and interpretation must be approved and counter-signed by the director or finds manager and any conflicting and differing interpretations of the same data entered.

30.61 The person that enters the data into a database must sign and date this field once the process has been completed.

30a.00 Sheet Thirty a: Bulk Pottery Processing Form: This form is for the quantification of bulk potsherds and relates to the main form in so much as the fabric type, vessel form and corpus number derived from the first should be entered into the various fields. The main form 30 need only be filled out when new types of pottery are discovered.

31.00 Sheet Thirty-One: Stone Vessel Recording Form: This form is filled out by a specialist, and as such has its own criteria depending on the date of the vessels being recorded, although the guidelines for recording pottery vessels may be of assistance. For the non-specialist, Ashton's corpus of stone vessels will be of a great help in identifying your specimen. A geoarchaeologist may be required, to identify the stone from which the vessel is made.

32.00 Sheet Thirty-Two: Lithic Tools Recording Form: These forms are designed for the recording of chipped stone tools only and should be filled out by a lithicist; the other types of stone tools should be recorded on the **Special Finds Recording Form**. The nature of the factors scored depends upon the period and geographical area under assessment. If a specialist is not available, the archaeologist should acquaint themselves with the corpus of lithic types that are likely to be recovered at the site. For Palaeolithic tools a computerised recording programme (e4) is available from www.oldstoneage.com, which gives easy steps for recording stone tools. Two excellent books to aid the analysis of stone tools are Andrefsky (1998) and Odell (2004), which guide the analyst in the various methods that can be used to investigate the lithics. A brief introduction is provided below.

For each tool or collection of tools to be produced the knapper will have had a specific reduction strategy. If the goal was to produce flakes, the remnant lithic core will have probably been discarded once it became too small to use. However, if the goal was to produce a core tool the objective nucleus will have been reduced to a rough unifacial or bifacial preform, reduced further using soft hammer flaking techniques or by pressure flaking the edges. Some tools were hafted, while others used as they were. Therefore, three different forms are provided for recording different types of lithics: **Sheet 32 A**, for recording flakes and blades, **Sheet 32B** for recording cores and **Sheet 32C** for retouched tools. It is essential that the processor makes a key of the abbreviations used in the recording of the various attributes of the lithics. After typology (**32.13**) the forms diverge, and so there are three sets of guidelines for filling out the forms after this point. The layout of these forms can be copied into a computerised database to make the task easier. The forms have been devised for ease of classification of the lithic assemblage. Classification is an aid to the summarisation of data for descriptive purposes, facilitating greater comparison and generating questions about the data. There are two approaches commonly used. 1) It is much easier for people to understand the composition of an archaeological site if numbers of each tool class are given, as opposed to describing each tool individually, e.g. 119 broken bifaces, 56 whole bifaces, and 601 blades is much more concise than describing the morphology of 776 individual artefacts found at the site. Each individual class or type of tool should be fully described and illustrated, and a table of the statistics should be presented. Indeed, it is advisable to illustrate a representative sample of the total assemblage both in the drawn and photographic media for sites that contain even well known industries. 2) Certain sites however, may require the total assemblage to be presented; these are usually type sites of an unknown or little known industry or sites that can answer major questions on the character of an industry. For certain lithic tools more information may wish to be recorded, the **Special Finds Recording** form, or **Additional Pages** should be used in this case.

The use of chipped stone tools dates back over 2.6 million years ago, starting with simple choppers and hand-axes and evolving into beautiful pressure flaked bifacial tools. Even after the advent of copper, bronze and iron, stone tools continued to be used for certain purposes. Chipped stone tools and debitage represent the most abundant form of artefacts found on prehistoric sites. Indeed, stone tools may represent the only material remains to have withstood erosion, decay, and landscape development. As such lithic tools represent one of the most important data sets for understanding prehistoric lifeways and behaviour (Andrefsky 1998: 1). There are, however, other forms of stone artefact which should be mentioned briefly. Industries that included chipped stone tools, are often accompanied by ground and polished tools, such as axes, adzes, hoes and chisels, which were usually made from coarser-grained materials such as basalt, greenstone, rhyolite, granite, and also finer-grained stones such as chert, flint and jade. Other ground stone tools such as grinders, mortars and pestles, manos and metates, querns, palettes, maceheads, and weights, were also usually made from coarser-grained rocks such as granite, quartzite, and limestone, and are all forms of core stone tools. Beads and pendants made from semi-precious stones were common elements of jewellery. Pecked stone tools also occur in many areas of the world; these have a surface similar to the skin of an orange. Some tools were created by a mixture of various techniques, such as chipping or pecking and then grinding.

Manufacture of Lithic Tools

Only a limited amount of rock types can be used for chipped stone tools manufacture. The most desirable ones are relatively hard and brittle, with very small to invisible grains that fracture conchoidally when struck, and have a smooth, homogeneous internal consistency (Andrefsky 1998: 57). The volcanic glass obsidian is the best example of this type of material, being easily susceptible to the designs of the knapper. It was extensively exploited in those limited areas of East Africa, Anatolia, the Cycladic island of Melos and Mexico where it occurs naturally. Among other widespread rock types, the ones that best meet these criteria are very fine-grained cryptocrystalline silicates (also known as quartz), such as chert, flint, chalcedony, agate, jasper, hornstone, and novaculite. Although flint is common throughout Europe, and chert in North America, not all tools were made of chert or flint in these regions. In certain parts of the world, such as some parts of Africa, large nodules of flint and related rocks do not occur, so people were compelled to use other materials, mainly quartzites or volcanic rocks. Some fine-grained quartzites approach chert in quality and some fine looking tools have been produced. Basalts, andesite, quartzites, and rhyolites have also been used to produce chipped stone tools, but have a lesser degree of homogeneity, are less brittle, and as such display progressively less predictable fracture characteristics (Andrefsky 1998: 23). Volcanic rocks, such as basalt, which are more difficult to work, generally result in relatively crude-looking artefacts. Even the very earliest stone-tool makers preferentially selected the most desirable rock types at their disposal. Stones, particularly special stones such as obsidian were traded; these manuports can be identified as stones not found locally in the area.

It is advisable to become acquainted with the geologic deposits in the region you are working. In that way it may be possible to trace the origin of the stones found on the site, or at least know if they were locally procured or imported. The exact type of stone is sometimes difficult to ascertain, even if using geochemical techniques as there may be no observational differences, with the only difference being the genesis (Andrefsky 1998: 57). Holmes (1989: 462) found that the majority of stone used in Egypt was a beige coloured chert, sometimes with pink banding, with a small amount of chocolate brown to dark brown. Most of the chert used in Egypt was matt in texture. The names of rocks are important if particular rock types are linked to specific raw material locations, or linked to particular technologies or chronologies. However, it may be better to describe the rock, i.e. microcrystalline silica with fossil inclusion, than give it a name such as siliceous siltstone with high iron content or fine-grained ferruginous metaquartzite (Andrefsky 1998: 58).

An excellent study of chert and flint has been conducted by Luedtke (1992) examining their genesis, and chemical, visual and mechanical properties. There are two main types of chert or flint: nodular (formed in pebbles) and tabular (formed in sheets). The stones can be obtained directly from its chalk or limestone matrix by quarrying. Stones can also be collected from the surface where they have been redeposited due to weathering and mechanical action on the primary seams, sometimes forming large gravel beds or along river terraces.

Rocks, such as chert and flint, are covered with an outer skin called a cortex, which can very in thickness from a few millimetres to a couple of centimetres. This cortex is generally white to buff in colour, although darker varieties also occur. On pebbles, such as those found on a beach or river terrace, the outer surface is often pitted and battered. Where the cortex has been removed it is often discoloured to grey or buff-brown in colour (Butler 2008: 20). The recording of the percentage of the cortex is useful in the *triple cortex typology*, by which the lithicists classify the debitage as either primary, secondary, or tertiary. These types are based on the relative amount of cortex found on the dorsal surface of the flake: primary flakes have more cortex on them than secondary flakes, which in turn have more cortex than tertiary flakes. Flakes with more cortex on them are representative of an earlier stage of reduction than those with less cortex remaining on them. However, it is important for the researcher to define what they mean by primary, secondary and tertiary detached pieces. As Andrefsky (1998: 113-4) points out, the amount of cortex present on a flake is dependent on the amount of cortex originally present on the objective piece. A more reliable method is the *dorsal cortex count*. This method involves the amount of cortex present being measured on an ordinal scale. If the entire dorsal surface is covered with cortex it receives a value of 3, if there is no cortex present a value of 0 is assigned. A value of 2 is given when there is more than 50% but less than 100% of cortex covering the dorsal surface. A value of 1 is assigned when there is more than 0% and less than 50% of cortex coverage. Trends should then be looked for in the population of the lithic assemblage.

The process of chipping or flaking stone is called *knapping* (see Inizan *et al.* 1999; Whittaker 1994). Three principal techniques exist for the removal of detached pieces from the objective piece and a further method for shaping tools:

(1) *Direct percussion*: Direct percussion can take two basic forms. In the most common variant, the knapper uses a hammerstone to strike a flake from a core. For best results, the hammerstone should be softer than the core, so that the core bites into it and slippage between the two pieces is minimised. If the core is flint, quartzite and certain kinds of volcanic rock generally make good hammerstones. Limestone is usually too soft. The hammerstones are usually ball-shaped and often have usewear (pitting, flaking and crunching) focused in one area. A hammerstone usually produces a wide a platform, whereas a soft hammer normally produces as thin butt (Butler 2008: 37). A wooden or bone rod (billet or soft hammer) may be substituted for the hammerstone if the goal is to detach relatively long, thin flakes with feather termination—for example, in the final shaping of a hand-axe. Wooden or bone rods were almost certainly used to finish some finely made late-Acheulian hand-axes from Europe, dating from between about 400,000 and 200,000 years ago. In some cases the objective piece may have been held between the feet and a long handled soft hammer used to detach the flakes. Striking the core with the billet initiates a fracture but the soft hammer material tends to catch the edge of the flake, allowing the experienced knapper to pull the flake off of

306

the core. This works because the stone is actually shearing or tearing, rather than splintering. Soft hammers also produce a diffuse cone of percussion, less ripples on the ventral surface and a pronounced lip at the interface between the butt and bulb (Butler 2008: 38-9). In the second basic, less common variant of direct percussion, the hammer and anvil technique, the core is mobile and the hammerstone is stationary. The knapper uses the core as a hammer, striking the edge of the objective stone against a large, stationary stone (the anvil) in order to remove a flake. Although the knapper has less control using this method, it is quite effective for making large flakes which can be used either as tools, or as blanks from which retouched tools can be made. A modification of the hammer and anvil technique is the wedging technique. With this method the core is placed on the anvil for support, and then struck with a large heavy hammer. The compression from both ends of the bipolar core causes it to fracture into flakes, some of which are large enough to be further flaked into tools. This technique is often found in areas where the only reliable source of workable stone is cobbles. Like the hammer and anvil technique, there is little control over the flake making process, and it wastes a great deal of raw material.

(2) *Indirect percussion*: In indirect percussion, a third object (punch), such as a wooden or antler rod, is interposed between the core and the hammer-stone. This gives the knapper fine control over the point where the hammer blow enters the core. Indirect percussion was invented later than direct percussion, and indications are that it was rarely practiced before the emergence of Upper Palaeolithic and related cultures about 50,000-40,000 years ago. Indirect percussion was used to produce blades or bladelets. The butt of blades and bladelets formed by this method will usually be quite thin as the punch will normally have been placed close to the edge of the core platform, and the blade will have a prominent, but small cone of percussion (Butler 2008: 38).

(3) *Pressure flaking*: In pressure flaking, the knapper removes a flake by gradually pressing a pointed antler rod, bone or other hard object against the edge of the objective stone. Alternatively, the object to be flaked can be forced against a stationary compressor. With gradual pressure predominately in the direction that the flake is being removed with a slight downward force a longer flake is produced, whereas more downward pressure will create a shorter deeper flake (Butler 2008: 38-9). In the Upper Palaeolithic peoples used it mostly for modifying (retouching) the edges and surface of a flake. During the Neolithic it was used more extensively to produce pressure flaked items, such as concave base arrowheads. During the Bronze Age it is possible that copper punches were used instead of, or as well as, bone or antler punches to produce ripple-flaked knives and other tools.

(4) *Ground Stone*: Two basic forms of ground tool are the chopping tools, which were usually ground and polished, and the grinding tools, which were usually left un-polished. The chopping tools such as axes and adzes could be made from nodules or large stone flakes, which were initially made into what is termed a roughout (flakes removed from the surfaces in the form of the intended tool) using hard hammers. These primary flakes will have broad butts and pronounced cones of percussion, with cortex on the dorsal face and multi-directional negative scars on the ventral face. These roughouts were then turned into what are called preforms by the removal of any remaining cortex, reducing the high ridges and retouching the cutting edge with a

soft hammer. These secondary flakes will have a thin curving profile, narrow butts, and diffuse cones of percussion and an associated lip and multi-directional negative scars on the dorsal face. After the final retouching around the edges the tool was ground repeatedly, either against an abrasive stone or by a hand-held abrasive stone rubber (*polissoir*). Water was often used as a lubricant and coolant, and sand used as a smoothing/polishing medium. This last stage was very labour intensive and could take up to 40 hours, whereas the initial preform stage may have taken 20 minutes. Polishing increased the tensile of the implement, lessening the likelihood of chipping and breakage, making these tools useful for felling trees and splitting wood (axes), stripping off branches and shaping logs and planks (adzes), and also for breaking up soil (hoes). The second form of ground stool production was for the grinding tools, such as querns and mortars and usually utilised coarser-grained materials, such as basalt, granite, limestone, quartzite, and sandstone. As with polished stone production the final shaping of roughouts and preforms followed and was done by pecking and drilling. The object was often only coarsely finished by grinding and this often only on the internal or working surface, with the external surface left rough. This was because the rough internal or work surfaces made excellent surfaces for grinding plant material and pigments, resulting in these work surfaces being further polished by use (Butler 2008: 139-145; Joukowsky 1980: 322; McCarter. 2007: 137)

The place, angle, force and tool with which a core is hit will determine the type of fracture that will occur. There are three main types of fracture mechanism: 1) Hertzian initiation, 2) bending initiation, and 3) wedging initiation, producing respectively conchoidal, bending, and compression or bipolar flakes. When a rock is struck near the edge a Hertzian cone (a series of concentric cracks growing larger as they radiate out, with one usually dominating to form a 136° cone [Andrefsky 1998: 23-6]) is produced. The impact of knapping sends a series of ripples through the stone causing a crack, and a cone begins to form with the widest part of the cone being on the opposite side to the point that was struck (Joukowsky 1980: 326). The formation of this cone increases outward pressure and causes the crack to curve away from the core and forms the cone of percussion on the conchoidal flake. This type of knapping requires a great deal of pressure and tools are normally created by a hammerstone, but can be caused by pressure flaking (Andrefsky 1998: 23-4). Bending flakes are formed when cracks start away from the point of applied force, usually by applying force at an acute edge of the objective piece. As such, no Hertzian cone and cone of percussion are formed. The initial crack travels into the objective piece at a right-angle before turning to the outside. The resultant flake is a smooth looking flake with few undulations on the surface (Andrefsky 1998: 27-8). Bipolar or compression flakes are formed by wedging initiation during core reduction. This type of knapping is usually conducted with a sharp hammer, with the force of application concentrated in the centre of the radii and a crack is formed where the centre of the Hertzian cone would normally have formed. Wedging can also occur when the point of applied force is near the centre of the core, or when detrital particles are placed in an existing flaw on the surface. Bipolar technology typically uses wedging, but in this instance the core is placed on an anvil and struck from above with a hard hammer, often resulting in the fracture being initiated from the anvil end as well as the hammer end.

Bipolar flakes may therefore appear to have two points of applied force (Andrefsky 1998: 26-7).

When a flake or blade is removed from a core, there is often a distinctive mark on the bulbar end where the hammerstone has hit the striking platform causing a ring crack. As the cone of percussion radiates out from the precise spot where the hammerstone hit the core, the point of force application (PFA) should be looked for at its base (Burke & Smith 2004: 209-20). Below the cone of percussion is the bulb of force (the two sometimes collectively called the bulb of percussion), which may have further ripple marks radiating away from it. These marks give an indication of the angle and type of hammer blow. Another characteristic found in association with the cone of force is the bulbar or eraillure flake scar (see **Fig. 113**). This scar is produced during the original impact for the flake or blade removal if more than one location on the striking platform was hit. When a stone is hit waves travel through it, one of these will usually dominate. When one of the inferior waves hits the dominant wave the contact results in the removal of a chip from the cone of percussion, the eraillure flake (Andrefsky 1998: 19-20).

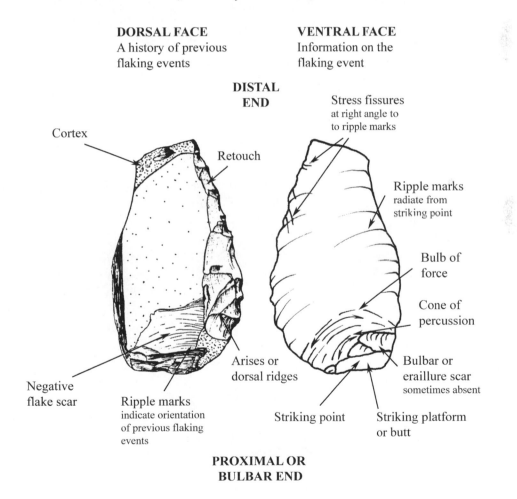

DORSAL FACE
A history of previous flaking events

VENTRAL FACE
Information on the flaking event

DISTAL END

Stress fissures at right angle to to ripple marks

Cortex

Retouch

Ripple marks radiate from striking point

Bulb of force

Cone of percussion

Negative flake scar

Arises or dorsal ridges

Bulbar or eraillure scar sometimes absent

Ripple marks indicate orientation of previous flaking events

Striking point

Striking platform or butt

PROXIMAL OR BULBAR END

Figure 113: The main features of a lithic blade (Griffiths *et al.* 1991: 94; Hurcombe 2007: fig. 8.9).

Flake scars are caused by the removal of previous flakes from the objective piece. Dorsal surfaces either have cortex or flake scars or a combination of both on them. It has been suggested that the more flake scars the blade of flake has the later it is in the sequence of removal. A piece in the earliest stages of removal usually only have a few large flake scars. However, the amount of flake scars is also determined by the size of the flake, with larger flakes having more scars, the type of stone, the type of artefact, and the chipping technique used (Andrefsky 1998: 106). Between the flake scars are ridges or arises, which give chipped tools their distinctive appearance.

Recognition of lithic Tools

The term *chaîne opératoire* is used to describe the end to end production of a tool and its wastage (debitage). The production of a tool involves the procurement, reduction sequence, the conceptual model held by the flint knapper, the use and reuse of the tool and final discard (Courboin 2009). The understanding of this sequence leads to a classification and interpretation of tools and acts to embed lithic technology into other aspects of human behaviour and organisation (Andrefsky 1998: 37). The stone tools and debitage found at archaeological sites are a result of a complex object biography influenced by cultural influences, technological and situational constraints and raw material availability.

1. Core: A piece of raw stone from which flakes, blades, or bladelets have been detached by the knapping process. In some cases these can form the actual tool, such as choppers and handaxes, or be part of the waste material, particularly if blades or flakes were the intended tools.

2. Debitage: Detached pieces that are discarded during the core reduction process, such as flakes and chips (see **32.27a**).

3. Completed tool: Completed tools can be core-based, flake-based or blade-based. Completed tools often have retouch on their edges, and can be either unifacially and bifacially worked into the tool shape.

Archaeologist will rarely find the full range of tools and debitage at any one site. A manufacturing site, for example, may provide a full range of waste material and broken tools, but few completed tools. The finished tools were usually removed to the site in which they were to be used. This indicates that types of tools found at a site can indicate the function of the site. A site with lots of projectile points might indicate a temporary hunting camp (Renfrew & Bahn 2004: 327). A wide range of tools might indicate a base camp or permanent settlement.

Field archaeologists are usually engaged in describing cores, finished tools or debitage. (1) Finished tools, particularly bifacial ones such as concave based arrowheads, hand-axes, ripple flaked knives, and fishtail knives are fairly easy to recognise. Flakes, blades, cores and parts of tools are sometimes less easy to spot immediately. (2) Debitage, chipped stone flakes and blades have many distinctive features (see **Fig. 113**), the most characteristic of these being the striking platform and cone of percussion, although negative dorsal scars (also called facets), ripple marks and retouch are also typical features. (3) Cores will have the opposite, complementary characteristics to those of a blade or flake, such as the negative imprint of the cone of percussion and flake scars. Cores may also have a prepared platform surface with distinctive edge strengthening attributes.

There are two main types of cores, unidirectional and multidirectional. Unidirectional cores usually have a single flat surface or striking platform, and the pieces are detached in one direction away from this platform. Sub-types of this core exist all around the world, such as polyhedral cores and some microblade cores. Multidirectional cores always have more than one striking platform, and have flakes removed in multiple directions. Sub-types of this type of core consist of bipolar cores, radial or discoidal cores, irregular flake cores, and Levallois cores. Core reduction strategies seem to be linked to the size and shape of the raw material. Centripetal reduction is when the core has flakes removed from the perimeter towards the centre, producing a scar pattern which radiates around the centre. These are multidirectional cores. Parallel reduction is when blades or flakes are removed along a single axis of the core. These cores are unidirectional cores. Centripetal cores were used to produce large wide flakes, whereas parallel cores produce lots of long narrow blades or flakes. In the Epi-Palaeolithic and Neolithic cores tended to be fairly well worked out, and be quite small. In the Bronze Age and later less care was taken in selecting good raw material, and less care taken during the knapping process and cores tended to be discarded after only a few flakes had been removed (Butler 2008: 30).

There are many flake debitage typologies, generally dependent on what questions the researcher is aiming to answer (see Andrefsky 1998: 110-88). Some of the common flake types identified are: bifacial thinning flakes, retouched scrapper flakes, bipolar flakes, striking platform preparation flakes, and notching flakes. The typologies based on technological attributes can be very useful in making behavioural inferences (Andrefsky 1998: 121). Typologies for microlithic blade tools have been created by Clark (1934), Jacobi (1978) and Tixier (1963).

Both natural and human activity can produce features that may be mistaken for those of a chipped stone. Frost fracturing, where the stone reacts to repeated hot and cold events, can cause small generally circular flakes being forced off the surface. However, there is no cone of percussion on any of the edges, no platform, and frequently no negative scars (Butler 2008: 43). Starch fractures are a result of impurities in the stone and can resemble a blade core. Bladelet-like scars appear on the surface, but some of the negative scars extend beyond the 'platform'. Natural flaws and impurities in the stone can lead to flake-like scars and breakages when the stone is subjected to stress. Agricultural activity can also produce convincing flakes. A machine-struck flake may have a cone of percussion, but will not have a platform, and will often look quite fresh with no patination (Butler 2008: 43). Retouch can also be caused by mechanical activities. This damage will usually be indiscriminate, lacking the uniformity of humanly retouched edge. This damage will also usually occur much later, and have no patination on it (Butler 2008: 45).Stones rolled in water, such as rivers or the sea where they have smashed into one another can also create cones of percussion, but again there will be no striking platform.

The data fields involved in recording lithic materials are provided below:

32.01 Site code, e.g. **TAD09**.

32.02 Operational area: The area of the site in which you are excavating.

32.03 Site sub-division: To be recorded as outlined above.

32.04 Grid reference: To be recorded as outlined above.

32.05 The number of the context in which the lithic tool or debitage was discovered.

32.06 The lot or spit number (if used) is required in this space.

32.07 Two boxes are provided to indicate whether the artefact was found during excavation or was part of a surface scatter found during survey.

32.08 The numbers of any photographs taken of the lithic or its context must be entered here.

32.09 The numbers of any drawings made of the lithic must be entered here.

32.10 The person that enters the data into the recording form must sign and date this field once the process has been completed.

32.11 Artefact number: To be recorded as outlined above.

32.12 The type of rock used for making the lithic must be entered in this field (see **Tab. 33**).

32.13 Typology: Many typologies exist for different periods and regions of the world to help with identifying the type of lithic Typologies are used: 1. as a means of establishing recurring sets of similar attributes, 2. as a common language for communication, 3. as a way of determining relative dates, 4. as a way of establishing distinct social groupings. The construction of typologies and chronologies using stone tool analysis has been conducted for over a hundred years. Some particularly important texts that will help in the identification of lithics are Allchin & Allchin (1982), Bar-Yosef (1992; 1994), Bordes (1961; 1968), Brennan (1975), Butler (2008), Camps *et al.* (1973), Chen & Zhang (1991) Clark (1951), Holmes (1989), Inizan *et al.* (1999), Jia & Huang (1985), Marks (1990), McBurney (1960; 1967), Midant-Reynes (2000), Tixier (1963), and Wymer (1984). There are some types of lithic tools that occur in all, or almost all periods of prehistory from the Middle Palaeolithic Period onward, with variations in shape, size and sub-types, which include scrapers, burins, piercers and awls, knives, notched pieces, and axes (Butler 2008: 49). Formal variations in stone tool types can be attributed to style and function. However, artefact form does not always equate to function, and an arrowhead can be used for cutting or scraping as well as functioning as a projectile point.

Tool Type	Description
Adze	A bifacial core tool with the blade hafted perpendicular to the wooden, antler or bone handle. The cross-section is often plano-convex and the profile curved.
Aeolith	A stone chipped by natural processes, not human, and not an artefact.
Arrowhead	A small projectile point shaped for maximum aerodynamics. Many types existed to fulfil various functions.
Awl	A pointed flake tool, with abrupt retouch along one or both edges of the point. Usually have a thin cross-section.

Axe	A core tool with the cutting edge hafted parallel to the handle. Two major types existed, thick-butted and thin-butted, and two categories, ground and bifacial.
Backed blade	A blade that has been blunted by continuous abrupt retouch on the opposite side to the cutting edge.
Barbed-and-tanged arrowhead	These are typical arrow-shaped points that have both a tang and barbs with invasive pressure-flake retouch that can entirely cover one or both surfaces, or just be confined to the edges.
Biface	A tool chipped over both surfaces.
Bifacial knife	A knife that has the cutting edge modified by invasive retouch on both faces and opposing lateral edge. The working of these knives can vary from irregularly flaking to extremely fine pressure flaking over both surfaces. The haft end can be rounded or tanged.
Blade	A thin parallel sided tool struck from a core with its length more than twice its width. It will also have parallel ridges.
Blade core	A blade that has been used as an objective piece, from which another tool such as a burin could be produced.
Blade knife	A knife with a slightly curved cutting edge that meets the backed edge at the knife end. The haft end is usually narrower and rounded. These knives vary in length between 80 to 150 mm.
Bladelet	A blade that is less than 12 mm wide.
Blank	A detached flake of blade potentially modifiable into a specific tool form.
Borer	See Piercer
Burin (graver)	A blade of flake that has been modified by the removal of a narrow splinter (spall) from a break, unmodified surface, or platform to create a sharp edge.
Byblos Point	A long thin tanged point with a single ridge and steep retouch on either side.
Celt	An old fashioned name for ground stone axes, adzes and hoes.
Chip	A small waste piece a by-product of chipping, core preparation, or of retouching.
Chisel	Long thin bifacial tools with parallel sides and a lenticular cross-section. The cutting edge is usually narrower than the body. Usually hafted in direct line with the handle.
Chopper	A core tool with either a unifacial or bifacial cutting edge and the main tool left covered with cortex.
Circular-scraper	A flat circular flake tool with flat invasive retouch all around its periphery, with an angle between 60° to 90°.
Cleaver	A bifacial core tool that is generally lingulate in plan, with a transverse cutting edge.

313

Concave-base arrowhead	Also called hollow-based, it has a concave base and two long parallel or incurving barbs with pressure-flaked invasive retouch that can entirely cover one or both surfaces, or be just confined to the edges.
Core	A nucleus of stone from which flakes or blades have been detached. The flakes may then be further modified into tools or the core may be further shaped into a tool.
Crescent drill	A comparatively thick bifacial tool with a concave upper margin and convex lower cutting edge often showing signs of usewear.
Cresting	The use of either bifacial or unifacial flaking to create a ridge on the face of a core running perpendicular from the platform, to act as a guide to remove the first (crested) blade.
Denticulate	A flake or blade that has had a line of successive notches removed from one or more edges, producing a serrated effect.
Discoidal core	A disc-shaped multi-directional core from which flakes have been removed, often with the centripetal or preferential method.
End-scraper	A flake tool that has been retouched on the distal end. The retouch area has an edge angle of between 60° to 90°.
Fabricator	Bifacially worked tools that were made on an elongated thick flake, blade or core. They are generally rod-shaped with one or both ends rounded through use, the lateral edges also usually show some use-wear. The cross-section can be oval, circular, diamond or rectangular.
Fishtail knife	These bifacial tools which have a forked end that resembles a fishtail. The forked end can be a shallow concave end or a steeper v-shape. There is usually fine serration around the cutting edge in the centre of the fishtail. Some of the better examples can be ripple flaked. The haft end is long and sometimes thin.
Flake	A general term for all fragments of stone that have been detached from a core. These flakes can be modified into tools or simply be debitage.
Flake tool	Flake tools have a width more than half their length.
Halfan technique	A microlithic blade technique where the core had two platforms, one to produce six fine, parallel bladelets, and the other to produce a series of convergent flakes.
Hammer-axe	A roughly worked core tool with much of the cortical surface still remaining. The butt end usually shows signs of impact damage and the distal end bifacially worked to form a cutting edge. A utilitarian pounding and cutting tool that was hafted with the cutting edge parallel to the handle.
Hammerstone	A stone, usual globular, that is used to detach flakes from a core. These stones will usually show signs of impact damage in one or more focal points.

Handaxe	A bifacially worked core tool, with the two faces meeting to form a single edge that circumscribes the tool. Generally oval or pear-shaped and hand-held not hafted.
Helwan point	A point similar to the el-Khiam point, consisted of a truncated and symmetrically notched bladelet, sharpened at the tip by marginal retouch.
Hoe	Similar to an adze, but usually larger with a wider cutting edge.
Knives	Made on a long thin blade or flake with a straight unretouched cutting edge, with the opposite thicker lateral edge either abruptly retouched (backed) or with the cortex left intact. In the latter case these are often termed cutting flakes.
Lanciolate point	A point that tapers at both ends with the edges retouched.
Leaf-point	A bipointed arrowhead with invasive retouch that can entirely cover one or both surfaces, or just be confined to the edges.
Levallois technique	A method of shaping the core in advance so that it would provide a flake of predetermined size and shape
Lunate	A half moon-shaped microlith with retouch on the curved edge.
Microburin	A microlith that has been made by breaking down a bladelet into a number of smaller pieces that are then turned into microliths. The microburin is the piece that has the original butt, together with the notch used to split the bladelet and the intersecting break facet.
Microdrill	They are similar to a small awl (15-60 mm) made on a bladelet, with the retouch sometimes continuing along both lateral edges.
Microlith	Small blade tools, often geometric in shape, usually less than 3 mm long.
Notch	A small concave area on the edge of a flake created by retouch.
Ounan point	Ounan points are lens-shaped with limited tip and/or basal inverse or *couvrante* retouch.
Piercer	A flake tool with abrupt retouch on two lateral edges converging to create a point. These tools normally have a thick triangular cross-section.
Pick	Similar to an axe or adze but with a pointed working edge and with an oval or quadrangular cross-section.
Plane	These are axe-like tools, made on thin nodular stones and have an expanding shape with the cutting edge on the broad end. The dorsal surface was flaked all over creating a steep cutting edge, leaving the ventral surface a smooth, flat plane, sometimes with flat retouch.
Projectile point	A chipped tool with a haft area that was used as the point of an object thrown through the air, such as a dart, arrow, or spear.
Rhomboidal knife	A bifacial knife with an elongated form with a bulge in the middle tapering to the rounded or ogival ends.

Ripple-flaked knife	A knife with a straight to slightly convex back and a knife edge that curves to meet this back. The haft end is normally rounded. The knife will either have ripple flaking on one or both surfaces. If only on one surface the other will be ground and polished.
Ripple-flaking	Large, flat, parallel, lamellar retouch so that the scars overlap in a regular pattern.
Scraper	A flake tool with a retouched curved edge, with an angle between 60° to 90°.
Sidescraper	A flake tool with one of its long edges retouched to serve as the scrapping edge.
Sickle	A blade, sometimes with serrated edges used to harvest grasses and hafted in a wooden handle along with other blades. These can have either unifacial edge retouch or bifacial retouch.
Spearhead	A lens-shaped blade often bifacially worked that is similar to an arrowhead but larger.
Tabular scraper	These are made on large thin cortical flakes ranging from 50 to 150 mm in length and width, and can be ovoid, circular or rectangular in shape. They have retouch around their entire periphery.
Tranchet adze	An adze that has had its cutting edge sharpened by the removal of one or more tranchet sharpening flakes.
Tranchet flake	A flake removed by a blow from one lateral edge to remove a transverse flake across the blade of an axe or adze to create a sharp cutting edge.
Transverse arrowhead	An arrowhead made on a section of a blade with one of its lateral margins left unretouched to serve as a sharp projectile edge.
Trapeze	A microlith with a narrow base, straight or curved retouched edges and a broad end.
Triangle	A triangular shaped microlith with retouch down one or both edges.
Truncation	A blade tool with many sub-categories, such as straight, convex, oblique and double. The truncation is usually finished with retouch and the tools will have at least one functional lateral edge.
Truncation knife	A blade tool with the truncation shaped to make a definite corner with the functional edge that is either straight or slightly curved. The end opposite the truncation is normally round or ogival. These knives vary between 45 to 85 mm in length.
Uniface	A tool that has been modified on only one side.
Winged drill	These are bifacially worked Y-shaped tools with the drill bit having a circular cross-section, sometimes referred to as a tribrach. The drill bit will usually show use wear.

Table 31: Types of tools (after Butler 2008; Holmes 1989, Joukowsky 1980; Tixier 1963).

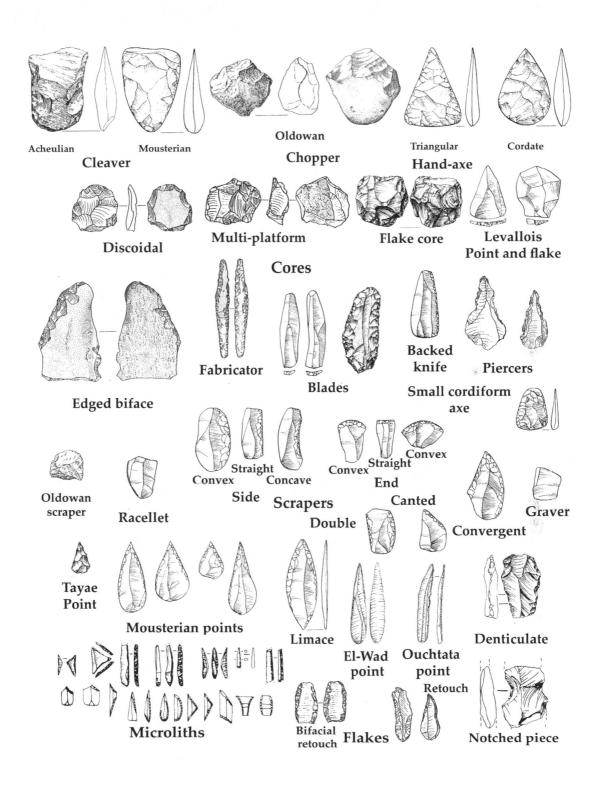

Figure 114: Various types of Palaeolithic to Epi-Palaeolithic tools (from F. A. Hassan's archives and after Holmes 1989; Wymer 1984).

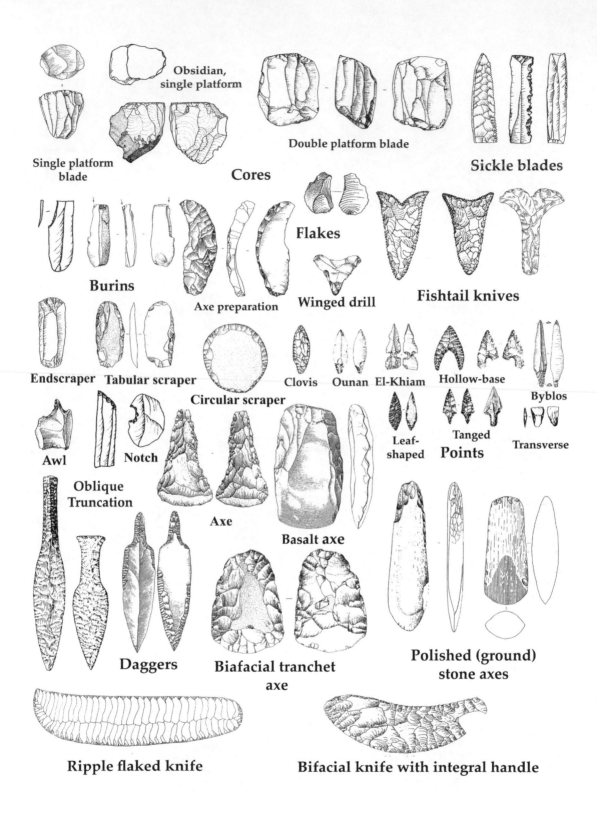

Figure 115: Various types of lithic tool from the Neolithic to Early Bronze Age (from F. A. Hassan's archives and after Holmes 1989; Wymer 1984).

Flakes and Blades

32.14a The length of the lithic should be measured on the ventral surface at the maximum dimension perpendicular to the striking platform and recorded in millimetres (see **Fig. 116**).

32.15a The width of the lithic should be measured on the ventral surface at the mid-point, perpendicular to the length and recorded in millimetres.

32.16a The thickness of the lithic should be measured at the mid-point of the lithic and recorded in millimetres.

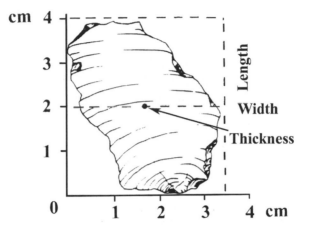

Figure 116: The measurements of a flake for length, width and thickness (after Butler 2008: 197).

32.17a The weight of the lithic should be measured in grams.

32.18a Record the width of the striking platform from one lateral edge to the other.

32.19a Record the thickness of the striking platform perpendicular to the platform width at the widest point of the platform.

32.20a Record the diameter of the point of force application (PFA), from one side of the ring crack to the other.

32.21a Record the PFA to dorsal ridge relationship by examining the dorsal surface and seeing if it is: 1. directly behind a clear ridge, 2. to one side of a clear ridge, 3. between two ridges, 4. behind a previous PFA but no ridges, 5. no relationship, which usually indicates the core has been rotated, or 5. is indeterminate.

32.22a Record the platform focalisation: broad platforms are as wide as the width of the flake, whereas focal platforms are narrower than the width of the flake.

32.23a Record the type of platform. There may be: 1. no platform preserved (the platform and cone of percussion may have been removed by subsequent manufacture), 2. a flat smooth platform that has been impacted to remove a flat a detached piece, 3. a cortical

319

platform (within the cortex), 4. a complex platform (a rounded surface or surface composed of multiple flake scars, 5. an abraded platform (this is a complex platform that has been smoothed by abrasion or rubbing), 6. was it unprepared, or 7. is the lithic broken so that the presence of the striking platform is uncertain.

32.24a Record if the over hang or lip has been removed. This can be observed by examining the lithic for small negative scars on the dorsal ridge below the platform. These have been created to correct the angle of the flake, or to remove previous ridges.

32.25a The percentage of cortex covering the flake must be recorded either as a percentage or on an ordinal scale.

32.26a Record the amount of negative flake scars on the dorsal surface, not counting the small flake removals that resulted from preparation of the striking platform, breaks, modification after detachment, and shattering. To simplify this task Andrefsky (1998: 106-7) suggests that an ordinal scale, with 0 = no flake scars, 1 = one flake scar, 2 = two flake scars and 3 = those with more than two flake scars.

32.27a Record if the artefact is flake shatter or non-flake angular shatter. During the knapping process there are discarded and unused detached pieces, these are called debitage. Debitage can be divided into detached pieces that have flake characteristics, and those that do not. If an artefact has recognisable dorsal and ventral surface attributes it is termed a flake. Those that do not have recognisable surface features are termed as non-flake debitage. Flake debitage is divided into two categories, flakes and flake shatter (Andrefsky 1998: 81). Flake debitage has a discernable PFA or striking platform, whereas flake shatter has no discernable striking platform. The point of this distinction is to discern between actual flakes, and waste products that may in theory be from the same flake, e.g. a distal portion. Flake pieces may break into numerous pieces at any point in the objects biography. This works a bit like a MNI count on bone, and keeps your actual flake sample non-skewed. The flake shatter count becomes an indication of post-use or post-depositional processes rather than skewing the knapping/production data allowing for more accurate comparative material. Non-flake debitage includes general waste chunks and chips, which you might not be able to call core fragments and are termed non-flake angular shatter or angular debris (Andrefsky 1998: 82-3).

32.28a Describe the type of termination of the flake of blade (see **Fig. 117**), which will usually be one of six types: 1. feather termination, 2. hinge fracture, 3. step fracture, 4. plunging fracture or overshot, 5. snap fracture, or 6. spontaneous retouch or pseudoretouch. The type of termination indicates how the objective piece (core) was struck and how the force travelled through the stone. A feather termination increases the usable edge, whereas in a plunging fracture the striking force was too hard and broke off the bottom of the core along with the intended flake. In step terminations the flakes have broken off prematurely, leaving behind a perpendicular ledge. With hinge fractures the force of impact has turned or rolled away from the objective piece leaving behind an inwardly curved ledge. If hinge or step fractures occur once, they are likely to occur again with subsequent flakes and may result in the knapper abandoning the core (Burke & Smith 2004: 215; Andrefsky 1998: 18).

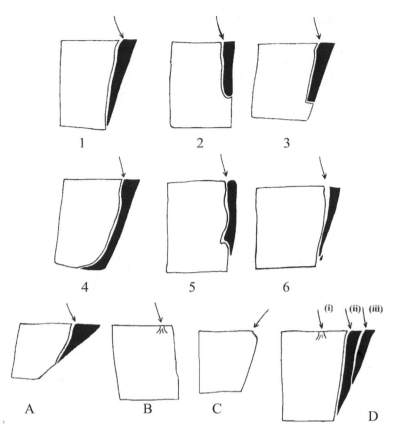

Figure 117: The main types of termination: 1. feather termination, 2. hinge fracture, 3. step fracture, 4. plunging fracture or overshot, 5. snap fracture, or 6. spontaneous retouch or pseudoretouch, A. smaller flake angle (shorter and thicker blade), B. flaking angle over 90°, no flake produced, C. incorrect angle of blow, no flake and crushed edge, D. depth of blow: i. too deep, no flake, ii. Correct position, iii. too close to the edge, short flake (after Butler 2008: 30; Hurcombe 2007: 8.10).

32.29a Record the colour of the lithic using a *Munsell Soil Colour Chart*. This is important, for this may have been selected for various tool types or by certain groups of people. The colour of the rock can also help indicate its source of origin. Stones can also change colour under certain circumstances by absorbing colour from their surrounding matrix.

32.30a Record if the artefact is complete or if there is any breakage after the flake was made and where the breakage occurs. Flakes and blades can be broken longitudinally (along the blade) or transversely (across the flake). The part of the artefact that is missing must be recorded

32.31a The length of the functional edge of the tool should be recorded. This is done by taking the maximum linear distance with a piece of string stretched along the edge following any contours, then measuring the piece of string.

32.32a Record the angle of the functional edge of the tool.

32.33a Record the placement of the functional edge: left margin, right margin, proximal end, and/or distal end.

32.34a Record the presence of any use polish, also termed sickle gloss. The field of usewear or microwear analysis covers many aspects, such as abrasion of lithic tools, tool function, fracture of lithic tools, and use polish (Anderson-Gerfaud 1988; Fullagar 2006; Hayden 1979; Kooyman 2000; Sievert 1992). Although use polish can sometimes be seen by the naked eye, minute striations, pitting and fracturing, and also gloss can better be identified with the use of an eye glass or microscope. It may be possible to determine the type of substance that was being worked by the stone tools, such as cereals, wood, bone, or leather, and how the tool was being used: scrapping, sawing, cutting or boring (Butler 2008: 199).

Cores

32.14b The length of the core should be measured at its maximum dimension and recorded in millimetres.

32.15b The width of the core should be measured perpendicular to and at the mid-point of the length and recorded in millimetres.

32.16b The thickness of the core should be measured perpendicular to and at the mid-point of the width and recorded in millimetres.

32.17b The weight of the core should be measured in grams.

32.18b Record the colour of the lithic using a *Munsell Soil Colour Chart*.

32.19b Record the number of platforms from which detached pieces have been struck. A second or third platform is often found at the opposite end to the first, parallel to it, at a right angle to it, or frequently at irregular angles (Butler 2008: 29). The amount and position of the platforms indicates the type of core and how much use it had. Cores were also rejuvenated, this entailed removing an old platform, and the only clue that this has happened is the remains of a few negative scars. Cores would be rejuvenated if good quality raw material was scarce or cores were being curated (carried around by mobile or semi-sedentary groups).

32.20b Record any platform preparation, such as overhang removal, or strengthening of the edges, the categories of which are: 1. no edge strengthening removals, 2. tiny edge strengthening removals, 3. continuous edge strengthening removals, 4. irregular, large and small chip scars, 5. grinding or abrading, and 6. other. The preparation of the core increases the coefficient of friction and creates micro-flaws in the surface enabling better knapping of the core.

32.21b Calculate how much of the core still remains as cortex. This is another means of calculating how much the core was used. Cores will have been discarded at different stages of the reduction process. On core tools like choppers and cleavers, the amount of cortex remaining is an indicator of the tool type and the knapping process.

32.22b Has the core been bifacially worked? Bifacial cores are preferred by highly mobile societies as they are multifunctional, readily modifiable, and portable tools (Andrefsky 1998: 150). Core tools were used for cutting or scrapping, but were also a more reliable source than pebbles for tool production.

32.23b Count the amount of distinct cortical surfaces.

32.24b What was the core, was it a pebble, a tabular outcrop, a nodular outcrop, flake or indeterminate?

32.25b Record the type of platform surface. The major categories are: 1. large flake scar, 2. scars of previous flake removals, 3. scars of platform surface preparation removals, 4. cortex, 5. ancient patina, 6. unpatinated, natural flint surface, and 7. other/irregular.

32.26b Record the amount of feather terminations observable.

32.27b Record the amount of step and hinge terminations observable.

32.28b Record the core platform type, are they: 1. opposing, 2. irregular, 3. parallel, or 4. right-angled? Bipolar cores have opposing platforms, whereas radial cores, irregular flake cores, and Levallois cores will have irregular platforms.

32.29b Note whether there is any weathering on the core. This usually occurs when it has had prolonged exposure to the elements and can affect all surfaces. Chemical processes in the ground can react gradually and create a white a patina, or a glossy patina. The initial stages of white patination can create an optical effect that appears speckled or bluish, and flint is never blue in colour (Hurcombe 2007: 160). Heat and cold can also damage the rocks. Heat can create a myriad of small cracks, whereas frost can create pitting.

Retouched Tools

32.14c The length of the artefact should be measured at its maximum dimension and recorded in millimetres. If it is a hafted tool with a tang and barbs the blade should be measured from the tip to the tip of the shoulder.

32.15c If it is a hafted tool measure the height of the neck to the base.

32.16c If it is a hafted tool measure the haft length from the top of the haft element to the base.

32.17c The width of the artefact should be measured perpendicular to and at the mid-point of the length and recorded in millimetres. If it is a hafted tool measure the width from shoulder to shoulder.

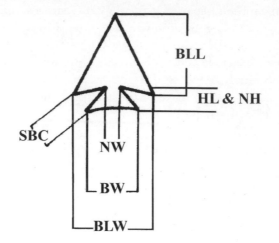

Figure 118: Measurements for hafted tools (after Andrefsky 1998: 179).

32.18c If it is a hafted tool measure the neck width from neck edge to neck edge.

32.19c If it is a hafted tool measure the base width from base edge to base edge.

32.20c If it is a hafted tool measure the shoulder to corner distance, from shoulder edge to basal corner.

32.21c The thickness of the artefact should be measured at the mid-point from face to face and recorded in millimetres.

32.22c The position of the retouch must be recorded. There are two basic forms of retouch: 1. edge retouch, and 2. *couvrante* retouch ('covering' retouch that covers most or all the surface). There are various terms for use in describing the extent of edge retouch 1. direct, 2. inverse, 3. bifacial, 4. alternating, and 5. alternate. The location can be further defined by stating if it is on the left lateral edge/margin, right lateral edge/margin, proximal or distal end, or circumscribing the tool.

32.23c The extent of the retouch must be recorded. When a flake or blade is freshly struck from a core it will usually have sharp edges, so that it could immediately be used as a tool. However, to use tools for some tasks some kind of modification may be necessary. Abrupt retouch is usually done with a soft or hard hammer to create a steep edge angle of just less than 90° (Butler 2008: 44). This type of retouch is restricted to the edges of the tool and is used to blunt them, either so they can be held by that edge, hafted, or so that that edge can be used for scraping or other non-cutting activities. Two alternate edges may be modified with abrupt retouch to form a point, as in a piercer. Tangs for inserting into a haft can also be formed in a similar manner. Semi-abrupt retouch is similar to abrupt, but a less acute angle, normally 45° and beginning to invade the surface of the tool. This can be used for the same purposes as abrupt retouch but is usually applied to a much thinner flake. Invasive retouch is created by either a soft hammer, or more usually pressure-flaking. This is a very flat form of retouch with an angle that is usually 10° or less that extends across much of the face and follows the shape of the tool (Butler 2008: 45). This type of retouch is used for creating or re-sharpening a cutting edge on knives, arrowheads and other cutting implements.

32.24c The size of the retouch must be recorded. The dimensions of the individual retouch scars should be recorded using the following descriptions:

Very small: <1 mm
Small: 1-2 mm
Medium: 2-4 mm
Large: 4-8 mm
Very Large: >8 mm

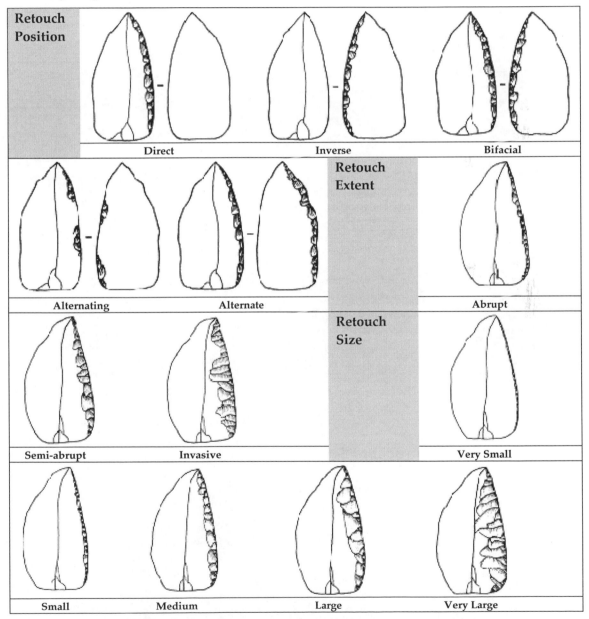

Figure 119: Types of retouching (after Holmes 1989: 450-6).

32.25c There are numerous terms to describe the various types of retouch. Holmes' (1989:450-6) divided the various types into convenient categories for describing the main types of retouch (see **Fig. 120**).

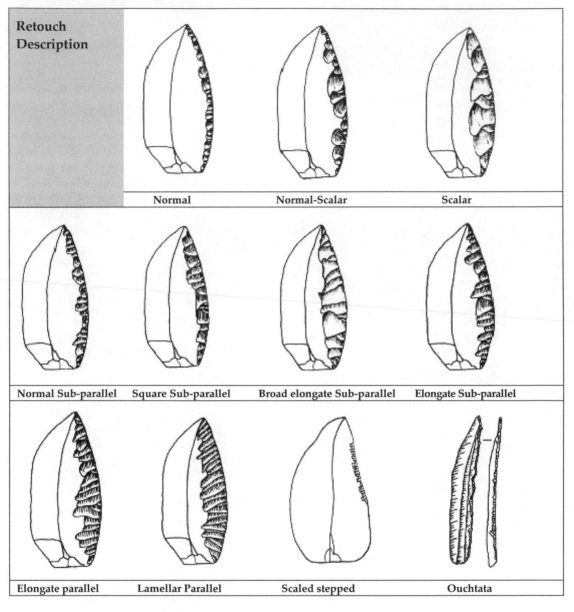

Figure 120: Descriptions of retouch types (after Holmes 1989: 450-6).

Normal: A non-invasive form of retouch consisting of scars of equadimensional proportions with approximately parallel sides and rounded terminations.

Normal-scalar: A retouch consisting of a mixture of scalar and normal scars.

Scalar: Broad scars that expand towards their termination.

Normal sub-parallel: A mixture of normal and sub-parallel scars (longer than they are wide).

Square sub-parallel: A retouch consisting of both sub-parallel and square scars, with the square scars being equadimensional with parallel sides and straight terminations.

Broad elongate sub-parallel: A retouch comprising a series of broad sub-parallel scars.

Elongate sub-parallel: Sub-parallel scars tending to be twice as long as they are wide.

Elongate parallel: Elongate sub-parallel scars that are more regular.

Lamellar parallel: A retouch comprising of regular parallel-sided scars that have a length-width ratio of well over 2:1.

Scaled Stepped: A retouch comprising of wide and short scars, which resemble fish scales. If it is accentuated in a series of overlapping rows, usually on large thick tools such as notches, then the qualificative 'stepped' can be added.

Ouchtata: A fine direct abrupt or semi-abrupt non-invasive simple retouch confined to the edges along one or rarely both sides of a blade tool often giving a roughly serrated edge but never forming true notches.

   Nibbled or *grignotage* describes continuous, short, irregular retouch along one or both edges, whereas smoothed retouch describes retouch scars that have been obliterated or dominated by abrasion or polishing. The retouching can also be described by the way the scars terminate, such as stepped or feathered (Andrefsky 1998: 171). In general the same terminology can be used for describing *couvrante* retouch with a few modifications. Other types that are not covered in these descriptions can be added and a key made.

The size of *couvrante* retouch can be described as:

   Small: <10 mm
   Medium: 10-20 mm
   Large: >20 mm

The flatness of the *couvrante* retouch can be described as:

   Flat,
   Relatively deep
   Deep

The distribution of the *couvrante* retouch can be described as:

Central, which extends over the central part of the tool.

Edge, which is essentially non-invasive retouch applied after the main *couvrante* retouch.

   For describing the type of *couvrante* retouch the same categories for edge retouch can be used (Holmes 1989: 254-6).

32.26c The length of the functional edge of the tool should be recorded. This is done by taking the maximum linear distance with a piece of string stretched along the edge following any contours, then measuring the piece of string.

32.27c Record the angle of the functional edge of the tool.

32.28c Record the placement of the functional edge: left margin, right margin, proximal end, and/or distal end.

32.29c Record the type, if any, of platform preparation. The terms used to describe the preparation are: 1. remaining natural surface (RNS), 2. unfaceted, 3. dihedral, 4. multifaceted, 5. thinned, crushed, or 6. irregular/other. The platform shape can be: 1. rectangular, 2. lenticular, 3. irregularly lenticular, 4, triangular, 5. irregularly triangular, 6. gull-winged, semi-circular, 7. irregularly-shaped wide platform, or 8. irregular/other.

32.30c Has the tool been bifacially worked? Both unifacial and bifacial tools can have retouch, although unifacials can be modified into bifacials. Bifacials are flexible, portable and are ideal tools for groups conducting activities away from the residential camps or settlements (Andrefsky 1998: 185).

32.31c Record the shape of the tool. Although the type of tool will give a good indication of the shape, this category further refines this, e.g. a sickle blade can be rectangular, rectangular with one or both ends broken, one end ogival, one end ogival, the other broken, serrated edged and barbed arrowheads can have various types of barbs: 1. pointed barbs, 2. squared barbs, 3. base of barb obliquely shaped, or 4. rounded barbs.

32.32c Record if the tool has a haft element, and the type of haft element. The various types of haft element are: 1. squared tang, 2. rounded tang, 3. pointed or triangular tang, and 4. curved or hook tang.

32.33c Record the amount of feather, hinge and step terminations observable.

32.34c Note whether there is any weathering on the tool.

32.35c Record the colour of the lithic using a *Munsell Soil Colour Chart*.

32.36c Record the presence of any use polish, also termed sickle gloss.

All Tools

32.37 Record if the stone has been heat treated or not. Stone heated to a high temperature and then allowed to cool can improve its flaking quality, allowing better control over the length of blades being produced and reducing the likelihood of hinge and step terminations (Butler 2008: 46). The heating of stone removes some of the moisture and can change its texture and colour, giving it permanent greasy or soapy lustre and a reddish hue (Holmes 1989: 459-64). However, sometimes only a limited change in colour or texture occurs making it difficult to distinguish from un-heat treated flint.

32.38 Comments and Period of the lithic. There may be other features that you want to comment on or special features that need further explanation. The period of the lithic should also be recorded here. The stone artefacts from contemporary contexts, such as a cultural layer within a site, are usually referred to as an assemblage. Generally similar assemblages from the same region and time interval are lumped into an industry, and groups of related industries are placed in the same industrial complex or tradition. Sometimes, culture and cultural are used instead of industry and industrial, although, even where artefacts are abundant and diverse, they clearly reflect only a small part of culture in its anthropological sense (Wymer 1984: 30-1). As these terms can be used in both a cultural and chronological sense, the only hope of assessing the developments and trends in this complex cultural process lies in placing the evidence into a chronological framework. The evidence must consist not just of pure archaeology (i.e. deductions made from artefacts and their direct associations), but of everything found with them that can help reconstruct the environment as near to its totality as possible (Wymer 1984: 34). As noted above, lithics were used in periods other than the various stone ages, but generally once pottery starts to be used the ceramics are the predominant relative dating tool.

Clark (1968) devised five general technological modes of stone tool production based on how the flake-core relationship occurred, upon which were superimposed the varieties brought about by cultural preference, economic need, and raw material availability:

Mode One: Industries that comprise of simple flake pebble tools and flakes, the Lower Palaeolithic Oldowan tradition and derived industries, such as the Oldowan (sub-Saharan Africa), Moulouyen (North Africa), Vallonet, Buda, Clactonian (Europe), Patjitanian, Choukoutien, and Ordosian (East Asia). The tool kit consisted of: chopper-core, biconical-core, proto-handaxes, un-retouched flakes, and semi-abruptly and abruptly retouched flakes. The system of production is typified by the simple striking platforms and lack of preparation involved. There was relatively little diversity in tool types. The detached flakes tended to be small and there was a lack of invasive retouch. In sub-Saharan Africa Mode 1 industries occur primarily in the Pliocene and into the Lower Pleistocene, whereas in Eastern Asia they continued into the Upper Pleistocene. In Europe they occur in the Middle Pleistocene (Butler 2008: 60-2; Foley & Lahr 2003: 114).

Mode Two: Industries that predominantly comprise of handaxes and retouched flakes, the Lower Palaeolithic Acheulian tradition and derived industries such as the Acheulian, Fauresmith (sun-Saharan Africa), Acheulian, Micoquian (Europe), Tabunian, and Jabrudian (Western Asia). The tool kit consisted of: bifacially flaked hand axes of different styles (crude stone struck, small, ovate, pointed, sub-cordate, and cordate), cleavers, segmental choppers, ficron handaxes, scrapers, retouched flakes, and flaked flakes. This system of production allowed relatively large flakes to be detached from the core, having some of the size properties but with a narrower cross-sectional area, and therefore suitable for a greater amount of invasive retouch. It became possible to detach secondary flakes from the whole surface and edges of these flakes, resulting in bifacial flake tools. Although the Acheulian is known in Africa from 1.5 mya, until 1.0 mya it is difficult to distinguish it from the Developed Oldowan. The bulk of well documented African sites occurred in the Middle Pleistocene. In Europe, the Indian sub-continent and Western Asia the sites fall mainly within the Middle Pleistocene, although some sporadic earlier instances are

329

recorded. In East Asia although there was bifacial technology, it is not as developed as the Acheulian (Butler 2008: 62-6; Foley & Lahr 2003: 114).

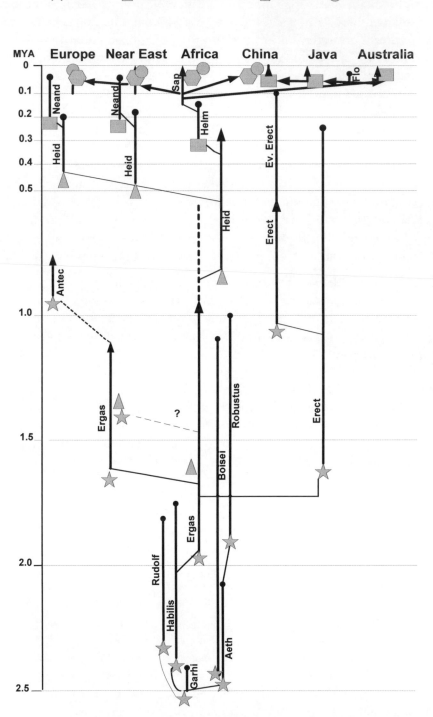

Figure 121: Comparison of chronological and geographical distribution of lithic modes and Hominin taxa (after Foley and Lahr 2003: 118).

Mode Three: Industries that comprise of flaked tools from prepared cores defined by the presence of Levallois flakes, retouched flakes and some handaxes, the Middle Palaeolithic Levalloisian and derived industries, such as the Aterian (North Africa), Khormusan (Egypt), Mousterian (Africa and Europe) and Soanian (East Asia). Although the Levallois technique can be found in both Mode 2 and Mode 3 assemblages, it is more common in Mode 3 assemblages. The tool kit consisted of: Levallois flakes, Levallois points, side-scrapers, transverse scrapers, end-scrapers, backed knives, blades, denticulates, notched pieces, burins, flake cleavers, and *Bout Coupé* (sub-rectangular, thin with a rounded tip and straight/convex base) handaxe. This mode shows a significant advance in the system of lithic production, with the key difference being the preparation of the core before a major flake was struck off; this is known as the Levallois and disc core techniques. These two techniques give greater control over the shape and thickness of the flakes, which resulted in a more diverse tool kit and greater variability. In Europe Mode 3 industries occurred during the Middle Palaeolithic of the Late Pleistocene and the African and India Middle Stone Age (MSA). Although its occurrence in the East Asian Pleistocene is disputed, it seems to have had an extensive distribution during the Upper Pleistocene (Butler 2008: 66-72; Foley & Lahr 2003: 114-5).

Mode Four: Industries that are characterised by long narrow blades, which were used as blanks for a whole range of different tools often punch struck with steep retouch, the Upper Palaeolithic industries, such as the Magosian, Robberg, Kenyan Capsian, Elmenteitan (sub-Saharan Africa) Dabban (North Africa), Halfan, Sebilian, Fakhurian, Menchian, Kubbaniyan (Egypt and Nubia), Amudian, Antelian, Baradostian, Zarzian, Ohalo, Nerve David, Ahmarian (Western Asia), Perigordian, Aurignancian, Gravettian, Solutrean, Magdalenian (Europe), Clovis and Paleoindian (Americas). This mode can be split into three broad categories, the Early Upper Palaeolithic, Late Upper Palaeolithic and the Final Upper Palaeolithic. In the earliest phases remnants of the disc core technique still persisted in some of the traditions, and the general trajectory of Mode 3 continued, in that it was concerned with detaching pieces from a prepared core. The aim in Mode 4 industries was to detach long thin blades from the objective piece, resulting in cylindrical prismatic cores, and long blades with narrow cross-sections, which were reworked into diverse sets of subsidiary tool types. Although long blades had been produced by the Mode 3 industries, these were not flaked from prismatic cores and did not make up as large a percentage of the tool kit. The tool kit witnessed a sharp increase in the diversity and variety of tool types, consisting of various types of projectile points including lens-shaped, shouldered and tanged points, burins, denticulates, curved and straight backed blades, scrapers, bladelets, truncations, and drilling and piercing tools. For the first time bone artefacts and art appear in the fossil record in Africa. Mode 4 is mainly associated with the Eurasian and North African Upper Palaeolithic of the Late Pleistocene (after 50 kya), for the first time humans enter the Americas, with the Clovis industry having similar elements to the Solutrean (Butler 2008: 72-81; Foley & Lahr 2003: 115).

Mode Five: Industries that are characterised by microlithic technologies, the production of very small flakes and blades that are retouched and worked into various shapes, or used unmodified as composite tools, the Leptolithic (light stone) Epi-Palaeolithic, Mesolithic, and Late Stone Age (LSA) industries, such as the Kenyan Capsian (sub-Saharan Africa),

Oranian, Capsian (North Africa), Khartoum Mesolithic, Arkinian, Shamarkian, Qadan, Afian, Silsilian, Qarunian, Elkabian, Khatatbian (Egypt and Nubia), Kebaran, Natufian (Western Asia), and Maglemosian, Tardenoisian, Azilian (Europe), Jomon, Xichuan, and Hoabinhian (East Asia). During this period it is more accurate to define a culture by their economy than a generic term, as there were various modes of living that used of microliths, semi-sedentary pottery users, pastoralists and those manipulating cereals. Microliths were either produced from bladelets or by snapping blades in a controlled manner. The tool kit consisted of microblades, bladelets, microburins, burins, geometric microliths (triangles, lunates, trapezes), points, tranchet adzes, axes, denticulates, fabricators, piercers, drill bits, notches, scrapers and flake tools. A few bone tools and some ground stone tools also occurred during this period. In Eurasia the Mesolithic and Epi-Palaeolithic industries occurred during the latter part of the Upper Pleistocene to Early Holocene (*c.* 15 kya), whereas in sub-Saharan Africa the LSA starts in the Upper Palaeolithic (*c.* 30 kya). However, earlier occurrences of microlithic industries have been found at Howieson's Poort in southern Africa *c.* 80 kya. In Southern Asia Mode 5 industries also occur at 30 kya and by the mid-Holocene in Australia (Butler 2008: 66-72; Foley & Lahr 2003: 114-5).

The **Neolithic Period** although not included in Clark's modes of lithic production, the cultures were characterised by tanged points, pressure flaked, ground and polished stone tools, such as the Merimdian, Faiyumian, Maadian, Badarian, Abkan, Khartoum Neolithic (Egypt and Sudan), PPNA, PPNB, PPNC, Pottery Neolithic, Jarmo, Hassuna, Halafian, Ubaid, Amuq, Hacilar (Western Asia), Sesklo, Dhimini, Karanovo, Linearbandkeramik (LBK), Almerian, Lengyel, Ertebølle, Ellerbek, Roessen (Europe), Tahsi, Peilikang, Pengtoushan, Yangshao, Homudu, Dawenkou (Eastern Asia), and Late Archaic (Americas). Although the microlith and composite microlithic tools continued into the early Neolithic, they was soon replaced as a hunting tool by leaf-shaped, corner-notched and concave base bifacial points and other arrowheads. The tranchet adze prominent in the Mode 5 industries, although continuing throughout the Neolithic was largely replaced by ground stone implements. As bladelets disappeared, they were replaced by blades and flakes for turning into tools. The tool kit consisted of: polished stone adzes, hoes, and axes, ground stone querns and mortars, and chipped stone concave or hollow based arrowheads, leaf-shaped arrowheads, barbed and tanged arrowheads, bifacial axes, scrapers, awls, piercers, knives on both flakes and blades, sickle blades, fabricators, notches, dihedral burins, truncation burins, ovates, fishtail or Y-shaped tools, and rods. As with the Mode 5 industries attention was given to the preparation and maintenance of the core and its platform, although when the platform was exhausted, unlike in Mode 5 industries, a new platform was sought by rotation of the core rather than creating a new platform by detaching a flake. This resulted in cores often having multiple irregular platforms, although if only two platforms were used these were often at right-angle to one another. Although had hammers were used for the initial shaping, soft hammers were used for extensive retouch and pressure flaking was common on many tools. In Western Asia, in the 'Fertile Crescent' Neolithic cultures start *c.* 10 kya, and spread out from there into Egypt by 7.2 kya and Europe by 9 kya. In East Asia Neolithic industries occur by 8 kya and in the Americas by 6.5 kya (Butler 2008: 119-150; McCarter 2007; Midant-Reynes 2000; Scarre 2005).

Although these broad groupings are a useful guide to the age of a lithic tool, it is advisable to familiarise oneself with the specific typologies and chronologies of the region in which one is working (see **32.13** for various regional references). Midant-Reynes (2000) has many good references for the major periods of Egypt's prehistory and the series of publications resulting from the Dymaczewo symposia founded by Lech Kryżaniank and Michal Kobusiewicz contain excellent studies on the prehistory of Northeastern Africa.

33.00 Sheet Thirty-Four: Coffin Recording Form: This form can be used for not only wooden, ceramic and lead coffins, but for stone sarcophagi, tile lined graves and mud-brick lined graves. Although the finds number should be sufficient and can be placed in the running matrix (instead of the context number) the coffin can also be assigned a context number if wished.

At the head of the form there are boxes for the **Site Code (29.01)**, **Operational Area (29.02)**, **Site Sub-Division (29.03)**, and **Context (29.04)**, which should be recorded as outlined above.

33.05 This space is for recording the coffin's special find number, which should be taken from the finds register along with normal special finds.

33.06 The category is already filled out - **deposit**.

33.07 The type of deposit is already partially filled out – **coffin**, the variety of coffin should be added as a prefix.

33.08 The grave number must be given here along with the context numbers of the grave cut and fills.

33.09 Note the skeleton's burial number here.

33.10 Provide a sketch of the coffin base, lid, head and foot and matrix here. Make a note of their dimensions in the relevant places and put in the reduced levels and the coordinates of the head and foot of the coffin. Include any coffin furniture in the sketch.

33.11 Grid reference: Enter the grid reference here. If the context is located in just one grid square, enter the coordinates of the south-west peg of that square (i.e. 115E/205N). However if the context runs into two adjacent grid squares, it should be recorded as 115-120E/205N, or if the context runs in a north-south direction 115E/205-210N.

33.12 A brief description of any specialist treatment given to the coffin must be given here.

33.13 A brief description of excavation/lifting method must be entered here.

33.14 A note on the weather conditions and time of day the coffin was excavated.

33.15 Record the dimensions of the coffin's base here.

33.16 Record the dimensions of the coffin's lid here.

33.17 A description of the fabric from which the coffin is made.

33.18 A few words on the state of preservation - good, medium or poor.

33.19 Note the reduced levels of the head of the coffin base and lid here.

33.20 Note the reduced levels of the foot of the coffin base and lid here.

33.21 Give a description and amount of any coffin furniture or decoration on the coffin.

33.22 The type of coffin and a description of it must be put in this field. The main types of Egyptian coffin are listed below, although Ikram & Dodson (1998: 193-275) give a fuller list of the various sub-types.

> **C.1 = Ceramic Oval Coffin**
> **C.2 = Ceramic Rectangular Coffin**
> **C.3 = Anthropoid Pottery Coffin**
> **C.4 = Rectangular Wooden or Reed Coffin**
> **C.5 = Oval Wooden or Reed Coffin**
> **C.6 = Wooden Painted Anthropoid Coffin**
> **C.7 = Jar Coffin**
> **C.8 = Ceramic Slipper Coffin**
> **C.9 = Ceramic Barrel Coffin**
> **C.10 = Anthropoid Stone Coffin**
> **C.11 = Sarcophagus (a container for coffins)**

Adapt and expand this list according to the country/period in which you are working. The shape of the coffin (oblong, oval, etc.) should also be stated. An estimate of the age or period of the coffin is also required here.

33.23 Your interpretation of the coffin burial must be placed in this space.

33.24 Record the amount and numbers of any finds (bags or baskets) associated with the coffin in this field.

33.25 The numbers of the samples collected from within or around the coffin must be recorded here.

33.26 The number(s) of any special finds found on, within or with the coffin should be put in this space.

33.27 List the numbers of any plans, sections or any special drawings made of the coffin here.

33.28 Insert the numbers of any photographs taken of the coffin here.

33.29 The value of the temporary bench mark or datum should be entered here, as well as the measurement from the backsight to the TBM, and the instrument height.

33.30 It is very important that the supervisor who completed the recording form signs and dates it.

33.31 The form and interpretation must be approved and counter-signed by the director or site supervisor and any conflicting and differing interpretations of the same data entered.

33.32 The person that enters the data into a database must sign and date this field once the process has been completed.

34.00 Sheet Thirty-Five: Hair Recording Form: Despite the wide range of objects it must cover, the recording of hair and wigs, and objects made from hair uses a single system of description. The main categories cover hair still attached to the human body, postiches and full wigs with reticulated bases, hair offerings and hair made into jewellery. A basic knowledge of physical anthropology is helpful when completing this form, and Cox (1977) is essential reading, as is the guidance of a conservator. Most of this work is specialised, but as palaeoethnotrichology is rather an unusual specialty it might be advisable to train a volunteer to carry out this work if any significant amount of hair (or hair-based products) are likely to be recovered from the site at which you are working (see Fletcher 2000; Tassie 2002).

At the head of the form there are boxes for the **Site Code (34.01)**, **Operational Area (34.02)**, and **Site Sub-Division (34.03)**, which should be recorded as outlined above.

34.04 The number of the context in which the hair remains were found.

34.05 Grid reference: Enter the grid reference here. If the context is located in just one grid square, enter the coordinates of the south-west peg of that square (i.e. 115E/205N). However if the context runs into two adjacent grid squares, it should be recorded as 115-120E/205N, or if the context runs in a north-south direction 115E/205-210N.

34.06 The category has already been filled out, as it will be a deposit.

34.07 The type of deposit, wig, postiche, natural hair (i.e. still attached to the scalp).

34.08 Record the number of the feature in which the hair was found here.

34.09 Record the exact 3-D provenience of the remains in this field.

34.10 Enter the artefact's find number here.

34.11 Enter the artefact's catalogue number in this field.

34.12 Description of hair: Firstly indicate whether or not the hair found is false or scalp hair, then record the colour of the hair against a Wella® Hair Colour (or similar) chart. The depth of the hair is how dark the hair is, the tone is the ash – red colouring of the hair, and the hue is the secondary tone found, if any (see **Tab. 32**). Therefore, dark golden blonde should be written as 6.3 and light ash brown as 5.1.

34.13 This section is to describe the texture of individual hairs, whether they are fine, medium or coarse. This must be ascertained with a microscope with a magnification of at least 1,000 x. The diameter of the hair must then be recorded. One micron (μm) equals 0.001 mm.

Fine   20 - 55 μm

Medium   56 - 91 μm

Coarse   92 - 130+ μm

Depth of Shade	Tone	Hue
1. Black	0. Natural	+
2. Very Dark Brown	1. Matt Ash	1 Matt Ash
3. Dark Brown	2. Ash (natural)	2 Ash (natural)
4. Medium Brown	3. Gold	3 Gold
5. Light Brown	4. Copper	4 Copper
6. Dark Blonde	5. Mahogany	5 Mahogany
7. Medium Blonde	6. Red	6 Red
8. Light Blonde	7. Beige Brown	7 Beige Brown
9. Very Light/est Blonde	8. Violet	8 Violet
10. Extra Light Blonde	------------------	------------------

Table 32: The colour depth, tone and hue numbering system.

34.14 This field is for describing the amount of hairs present per square centimetre, and again it should be done using a microscope. The average 20 year-old person has 150,000 hairs on their scalp.

Fine   <80 - 120 per square centimetre

Medium   120 - 160 per square centimetre

Thick.   160 - 200+ per square centimetre

34.15 The amount of curl of the hair must be registered in this field, along with its macroscopic shape. The circumference of straight hair has a circular section; with increasing waviness the section flattens, becoming more ovoid. In Afro-hair the section is elliptic or kidney-shaped. Wavy-straight (cynotrichous) hair also has a thicker cortex than Afro (heliotrichous) hair, and tends to survive better, because the ovoid shape of heliotrichous hair is more liable to friction and contains areas of loosely-packed keratin.

34.16 Record the maximum and minimum length of individual hairs in this field. If the hair is curly, both its curled and uncurled lengths should be recorded. If the hair is plaited, the length of the plaits should be recorded. If it is a wig, the overall dimensions should also be recorded.

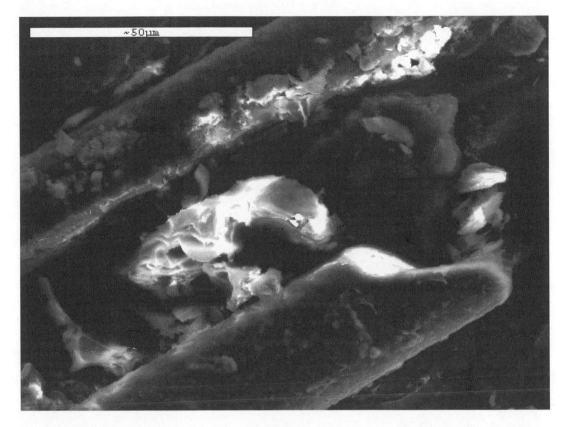

Figure 122: Scanning electron microscope (SEM) photographs at 1,100X magnification of Romano-Christian hair, *c.* 3rd century AD, Egypt. Although hair during this period could be cut using scissors leaving a blunt end, the ends of this specimen have been cut with a razor leaving a tapered end. The cortex (central part of hair) and medulla (middle segment of hair shaft) have virtually disappeared due to calcification, which can clearly be seen on the surface of the cuticles (outside layers) (photograph G. J. Tassie).

34.17 Note the percentage of grey (or white) hair present (if any), using the chart in **Fig. 85** as a guide. If there is an unequal distribution of the grey hair (i.e. mainly at the temples), this should also be indicated.

34.18 Record the style in which the hair is dressed here. There are numerous styles, but some common Egyptian variants are tripartite, gala, bob and short-curly. It must also be noted whether the hair is plaited, curled, straight or other.

34.19 Note if there is any decoration such as diadems, hairpins, etc. attached to the hair. The artefacts themselves should also be noted in the appropriate grave goods and small finds recording forms.

34.20 This field is for recording the presence of any setting or colouring agents, or any other substances applied to the hair.

Checks & description of the palaeoethnotrichological (ancient hair) remains

This section asks short but specific questions.

34.21 Record the burial context of the hair in the space provided. If it is a rock-cut tomb, a simple interment, or an offering. State whether the conditions are dry or damp.

34.22 Note any pathology here (i.e. alopecia).

34.23 The presence of a wig box or any wrapping material must be put in this field, and the artefact itself must be recorded on the appropriate finds or grave good recording form. Cross reference all sheet numbers.

34.24 Record the presence of any hair parasites such as head lice.

34.25 Note if there is any presence of natron on the hair, and if the body has been mummified this must be noted in field **34.21.** The help of a conservator may be needed to ascertain the exact nature of substances used on the hair.

34.26 The age of the individual as ascertained by the physical anthropologist must be but in the spaces provided.

34.27 Estimate the period or age of the hair.

34.28 Any other relevant information must be put in this field.

34.29 If the hair remains are a wig or postiche, describe: A) The base construction. Common variants include being made from plaited hair, being reticulated (Cox 1977), made from a central plaited core, or being stitched onto a draw-string linen bag to fasten the wig to the head. B) The manner in which the strands of hair anchored to the base. These can be knotted to the base or just looped over the base. Note how many hairs are in each mesh of hair anchored to the base. Make a scale drawing of the whole wig at 1:1, and of the base and anchoring detail at 2:1.

34.30 Describe the hair, wig or artefact, with special reference to style and arrangement.

34.31 Describe the function of the hair, (i.e. wig, natural, hair-piece or hair-offering). Also note social function if possible (see Tassie 1996; in press a). If a wig, was it used in life or just a funerary good?

34.32 Note all conservation treatments the hair has received here.

34.33 Record the manner in which the hair was excavated, lifted and stored here. A summary of any analysis carried out on the hair must also be entered here.

34.34 Note the hair's level of deterioration.

34.35 Provide a sketch of the hair *in situ*, with a blow-up of any special features (such as base construction and knotting, if a wig).

Figure 123: The construction of ancient Egyptian wig (photograph J. Johnstone),

34.36 Record the amount and numbers of any finds (bags or baskets) associated with the hair in this field.

34.37 Provide the numbers of the samples collected from the hair here. Samples of the actual hair and any parasites found on it must be taken. The hair samples can then be tested for any hair colourings and substances used as fixatives, such as bees wax and resin or used in stable isotope analysis for diet reconstruction.

34.38 The number(s) of any special finds found on or with the hair.

34.39 List the numbers of any plans, sections or any special drawings made of the hair here.

34.40 The value of the temporary bench mark or datum should be entered here, as well as the measurement from the backsight to the TBM, and the instrument height.

34.41 Insert the numbers of any photographs taken of the hair here.

34.42 Any other relevant information must be written in this field.

34.43 It is very important that the supervisor who completed the recording form signs and dates it.

34.44 The form and interpretation must be approved and counter-signed by the director or finds manager and any conflicting and differing interpretations of the same data entered.

34.45 The person that enters the data into a database must sign and date this field once the process has been completed.

35.00 Sheet Thirty-Six: Textile Recording Form: The recording of textiles requires some basic knowledge of the processes of spinning and weaving (see Jones 2008; Kemp & Vogelsang-Eastwood 2001; Vogelsang-Eastwood 2000). Spinning involves turning fibre into thread by twisting, but there are so many ways to do this that certain patterns may be characteristic of a particular time and place. These threads are joined together to create a fabric. Most textiles are made using threads which are passed around each other in such a way as to create a continuous fabric. The exception is felts, which are un-spun, unwoven fabrics created by natural stickiness of the fibres.

Most of the textiles that you will encounter will be woven. Whilst recording weaves, the weft and the warp should be considered as two separate systems, a situation which is complicated when more than one thread type is used in each system, for instance in a decorative band. The simplest way of recording the differences between warp and weft is through using the convention of a slash to separate warp and weft, in that order, so a z-spun warp with an s-spun weft is annotated as z/s. This convention differs, so always make it clear in your notes which way around it goes. The problem is of course deciding on the polarity of the warp and the weft. This is difficult unless you have a fragment which has a selvedge (edge formed by the weaving process), or you know from other sources how a particular kind of fabric was made. In general, weft selvedges have a visible return where the weaver pulls through the thread, changes the warp threads and sends the weft back in the other direction. Warp threads, however, tend to be cut off the loom, and there are many local conventions dealing with how these ends are secured. In most cases you will not be able to tell at first glance which is warp and which weft, so the rule is to be consistent, decide which will be the warp and record all the details from this premise.

At the head of the form there are boxes for the **Site Code (35.01)**, **Operational Area (35.02)**, and **Site Sub-Division (35.03)**, which should be recorded as outlined above.

35.04 Note the number of the context in which the textile remains was found.

35.05 Grid reference: Enter the grid reference here. If the context is located in just one grid square, enter the coordinates of the south-west peg of that square (i.e. 115E/205N). However if the context runs into two adjacent grid squares, it should be recorded as 115-120E/205N, or if the context runs in a north-south direction 115E/205-210N.

35.06 The category has already been filled out, as it will be a deposit.

35.07 Note the type of deposit (i.e. piece, garment).

35.08 Note the number of the feature in which the textile was found here.

35.09 Record the exact 3-D provenience of the remains in this field.

35.10 Record the artefact's find number here.

35.11 Note the artefact's catalogue number in this field.

35.12 Record the dimensions of the textile fragment.

35.13 Fibre: Distinguishing fibre types is very much a matter of practice, and is hard to do precisely in the field without access to a very high-powered microscope. Generally, however, it is relatively easy to distinguish between the main fibre types from knowledge of their modern equivalents, and the likelihood of a particular fibre being present. Fibre types can be divided into two main categories: those of plant origin and those of animal origin. Plant fibres can be broken down into three types: cotton, coarse basts, and linen. More exact identification requires a microscope. Coarse bast and linen are essentially variations in coarseness of the same fibre. Linen and bast are distinguishable from cotton by having very little fluffiness on the fibre, and having a very 'clean' appearance. Cottons have more of a felt surface quality (where warp and weft have fluffed together to make the weave structure hard to see). Fine cottons and fine linens are very hard to distinguish; the best way to do so is to research what you are most likely to find, note the qualities of the bulk of your textiles and then decide about the more unusual ones. Animal fibres are slightly easier to distinguish. The main ones you will encounter are sheep, goat and camel wool, and silk. Silk is the easiest to spot, as it is lustrous and constructed from microscopic fibres that are impossible to spot with the naked eye. Goat's wool is dark and coarse, does not felt at all, and the individual fibres are easy to distinguish. Sheep's wool has the best felt of all. To distinguish it from fluffy cotton try to pull out the fibre from a thread; if it pulls out more as if unravelling, then it is most likely to be wool, but if the fibre pulls out clean it is more likely to be cotton. Camel wool is similar to sheep's wool in that it felts, albeit not to the same extent. While high qualities may be hard to distinguish, it is generally coarser.

Construction

35.14 Thread Count: This refers to the number of warps and wefts per square centimetre within a piece of fabric. It is useful in assessing the quality of the cloth, how it was made, and also matching separate fragments into their original larger item. It is measured by placing a ruler on the fabric and counting the number of warp threads in one centimetre, then rotating the fabric 90° and counting the number of wefts.

35.15 Spin: This is a very important quality, as it can yield information on the fabric production techniques and cloth type. It involves a close examination of the warp and weft threads to determine the direction (clockwise or anti-clockwise) each was spun and plied before being made into cloth. The annotation for this is based on the use of the letters 's' and 'z'. If a thread is held vertically and the twist of the fibre starts high on the left hand side and comes down to the right hand side, rather like the middle stroke, as if writing the letter 's' in three lines, then it is 's' spun. If the reverse is true, then it is 'z' spun. If it appears not to be spun at all, then it is 'I'. In some cases these threads may be plied together, usually in the opposite direction to the original spin. So two 's' spun threads plied together would make a sZ2 cable.

35.16 Structure: It is important to record the weave structure as this can reveal information about how the textile was made and its intended purpose. There are a very wide variety of ways of making a fabric, but there are a limited number that you are likely to come across (especially in Egypt). The main ones include weaving, Coptic knitting (Nålebinding), tablet weaving, sprang and felt.

Weaves fall into two categories, tabby and twill weaves. Tabby weaves involve the weft passing under and over the warp in such a way that the next row of weft threads uses a different set of warp threads. In other words, there is no diagonal striation in the surface pattern of the fabric. Tabbies come in two varieties: a plain tabby where the weft passes under one warp over one warp, and a basket weave where the weft passes over two then under two. Twill weaves make a diagonal pattern and are recorded following the course of the weft thread. So a fabric with a weft going under two warps and over one is called a 2/1 twill.

Coptic knitting is a looping technique made with a thread and a thick needle. There are many variations, but the basic structure is a row of laterally linked loops which pierces the previous row. The technique lends itself to garments worked in the round, such as socks. Tablet weaving tends to produce long strips that are used in decorative borders and similar pieces. It is made by twisting bunches of warp threads around each other using pierced tablets or cards, and fixing these with weft threads to make a strip. The warp threads in each bunch may be different colours, which are successively brought to the front of the strip in order to make a multicoloured design. Sprang is a technique that involves twining a warp thread around its neighbour. The fabric is usually worked from both ends, as twisting at one end will create a twist at the other. The whole fabric is held together by internal tension which has to be kept in place where the two twisted ends meet in the middle. Felted fabrics are very straightforward to identify as they have no threads and thus no visible structure.

Modifications

35. 17 If the piece of textile has selvedges (edges formed by the weaving process), then you must indicate the weaving process used, giving the thread count of the warp and weft. A sketch should be put in the space provided and a scale drawing must be done on draughting film.

35.18 Colour is a straightforward quality to describe. Be as accurate as possible in your description and use a colour chart if one is available. Always note whether the fabric is a natural or dyed colour, and bear in mind points such as warp and weft being different colours, or certain colour threads decaying more rapidly than the surrounding fabric. If you know which colour was originally used, this should also be recorded.

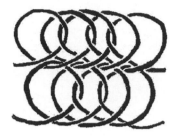

Coptic Knitting

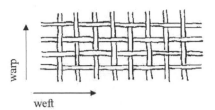

Plain Tabby

Sprang

Tablet Weaving
When finished only the
diagonal warps are visible

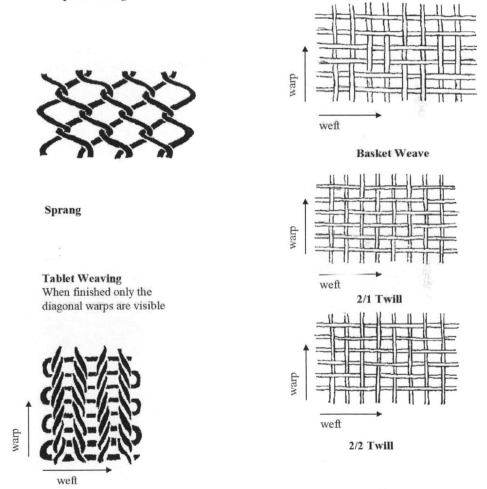

Basket Weave

2/1 Twill

2/2 Twill

Figure 124: Types of construction, textile weaving (drawings by Fiona Handley).

35.19 Sewing: Note what the sewing refers to; hems, seams, patches, darts, pockets. Is it a repair or part of the original? Examine the fabric and determine if it is of garment quality. If it may possibly be, then do a measured drawing. In terms of stitching, if you find anything more complicated than a running stitch, do a drawing, or replicate the effect using some spare fabric and a needle and thread. NB any two pieces sewn together must be recorded separately: a scale drawing must be done on draughting film.

35.20 Decoration is partially covered by colour and sewing. Any patterns on the fabric must be drawn and photographed, as must any other decoration such as embroidery. A scale drawing must be done on draughting film.

Processing

35.21 Preservation: Differentiate between the preservation of warp and the weft, and areas of particular colours or fibres. What do the damaged areas feel like? Are they crisp and friable or flexible and soapy? Are they damaged by salt encrustations? Note colour changes that are the result of exposure to the elements.

35.22 Processing: The rule is not to wash textiles, but clean with gentle strokes with a soft brush and straighten gradually in a humid atmosphere if necessary (a relaxing tent is easily created inside a large plastic bag with an internal support, containing a dish of cotton wool in water; make sure the water does not spill, or that condensation does not drip onto the textile). In exceptional instances, it may be justified to wash a piece of textile, however, this is not recommended especially if any chemical analysis is to be carried out on the fabric. All interference ultimately damages the fabric, so all interventions should be kept to a minimum. To support a piece of textile once it has been straightened, sew onto acid free tissue paper with unbleached cotton thread, taking care to pass the needle between, not through, the warp and weft of the fabric.

35.23 Storage: Each piece should be individually wrapped in acid free tissue and placed in a plastic bag which should be labelled with the textile number and the context from which it originated.

35.24 Overall description: Provide a one sentence summary of what you have just recorded, focusing on the qualities that make the textile recognisable and distinctive. This is infinitely helpful when writing up, if you have to transfer records to another recording system, or need to recognise a particular textile quickly without removing it from its packaging. An example might be: "high-quality natural coloured linen with dart in running stitch".

35.25 Note how the textile was excavated, lifted and stored (see Jones *et al.* 2007 for excavation and storage techniques). A summary of the results of any analysis must also be put here.

35.26 Provide a sketch of the textile *in situ*, along with a blow-up of any special features such as construction and sewing (if a garment). This should supplement the scale drawing, which should be done on graph paper. Usually the drawing is enlarged, indicating stitch size, or with a scale bar next to the textile. The number of threads that go to make up each section of a pattern should be indicated on both the warp and weft sides of the textile. The measurements of any repeated pattern should be indicated alongside the drawing. If the pattern repeats itself, one complete section of the pattern should suffice. When drawing warp and weft, the weft is always shown horizontal and the warp vertical. If there is selvedge, it should be shown on the left-hand side. Stitching and sewing are usually only shown in outline. Elaborate prints should have a separate drawing of the pattern drawing in black and white or line drawing (Griffiths *et al.* 1991: 48-50).

35.27 Record the amount and numbers of any finds (bags or baskets) associated with the textile in this field.

35.28 Record the numbers of the samples collected from the textile here.

35.29 Note the number(s) of any special finds found on or with the textile in this space. If the textile is attached to something else (such as leather or basketry), record this here. If the textile contains anything, either wrapped in the textile or in a pocket, record this and save it with the garment. If it is associated with any other pieces of textile or garments, their number(s) should be entered here.

35.30 List the numbers of any plans, sections or any special drawings made of the textile here.

35.31 The value of the temporary bench mark or datum should be entered here, as well as the measurement from the backsight to the TBM, and the instrument height.

35.32 Insert the numbers of any photographs taken of the textile here.

35.33 Any other relevant information must be written in this field.

35.34 It is very important that the supervisor who completed the recording form signs and dates it.

35.35 The form and interpretation must be approved and counter-signed by the director or finds manager and any conflicting and differing interpretations of the same data entered.

35.36 The person that enters the data into a database must sign and date this field once the process has been completed.

36.00 Sheet Thirty-Seven: Basketry Recording Form: Making basketry involves manipulating plant materials into rigid or semi-rigid containers. Whilst this can cover a huge range of techniques, there are four main technical categories: weaving, twining, coiling and plaiting, although there are several other techniques that are less widely practiced (including sewn plaits, looping around a core, looping/knotless netting, piercing/sewing and binding - Wendrich 2000: 256). Other objects (such as coiled pot covers and matting) made with these techniques and materials are recorded in the same way.

The basketry techniques of weaving and plaiting can also be used to make matting, so both matting and baskets can be scored using the same system. One possible area for confusion are baskets that are either stored flat or have lived beyond their storage function, and which often end up as flooring. Be aware to make the exact nature of the artefact clear at the beginning of the form, or, if you are not sure, score with a question mark.

The recording of basketry is based upon the concept of systems acting with and against one another. There are three 'systems' in a normal hair plait, and because they are all moved simultaneously to make the plait, the plait is composed of three active systems. However, if one system moves around another system which stays relatively static, the latter is said to be passive. An example of one passive and one active system is the weaving of fabric, which involves the active weft passing under and over a passive warp. The first step in analysing basketry is therefore to identify the systems, and whether they are active or passive.

This form can also be used to record wattle (and daub) structures: wattle is small woven timbers, while daub is the coating of mud-plaster used to coat the structure. The uprights are called stakes (in heavy wattle structures which are constructed *in situ*) or sails (in light wattle structures, which are portable). When recording them they must be individually numbered, the intervals between them must be noted, and they must then be described in detail on the **Timber Recording Form.** The horizontal elements (rods or weaves) should be recorded on this form, noting how the ends turn round the endsails. Extensive measurements, drawings and photographs of the wattle and daub structure must be taken, as well as samples (take a 100 mm slice sample from the thickest end of the rods and sails). The sails must be labelled with their individual context numbers, whereas the rods should take the context number of the structure. Wattle, stake and post impressions in daub and, if present keying, can provide information about the construction of buildings and as such should also be bagged. Each sample should be individually bagged, and the tag must clearly state whether it is a rod, sail or daub. The separate bags should then be bagged together in one larger bag and all the rods into another, then put these two bags into one large sample bag and complete an **Environmental Sampling Form**.

At the head of the form there are boxes for the **Site Code (36.01)**, **Operational Area (36.02)**, and **Site Sub-Division (36.03)**, which should be recorded as outlined above.

36.04 Enter the number of the context in which the basketry/matting remains was found.

36.05 Grid reference: Enter the grid reference here. If the context is located in just one grid square, enter the coordinates of the south-west peg of that square (i.e. 115E/205N). However if the context runs into two adjacent grid squares, it should be recorded as 115-120E/205N, or if the context runs in a north-south direction 115E/205-210N.

36.06 The category has already been filled out, as it will be a deposit.

36.07 Note the type of deposit (e.g. vessel, mat).

36.08 Record the number of the feature in which the basketry/matting was found here.

36.09 Record the exact 3-D provenience of the remains in this field.

36.10 Note the artefact's find number here.

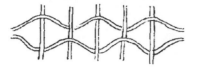 **Weaving**

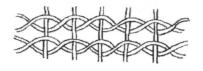 **Twining**
Two Strand 's' twining

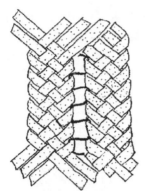 **Plaited Strips**
Two five strip plaits
showing joining cord

 **Coiling**
Centre of a coiled basket showing active
and passive system

Figure 125: Basketry construction, weaving (drawing by Fiona Handley).

36.11 Note the artefact's catalogue number field.

Overall Description

36.12 Size should be recorded in three dimensions i.e. X x Y x Z mms.

36.13 Construction techniques, see **Fig.125**.

Weaving: This uses two systems: one active system which passes under and over a passive system. It is the same technique as textile weaving.

Twining: This uses three systems, and involves one active system turning around another active system, whilst both pass around a passive system. The overall appearance is of two flexible cables twisting around each other, pierced in a perpendicular fashion by another more rigid system.

Coiling: This uses two systems. The passive system is coiled around to form the shape of the basket, and is held in place by an active system which holds them together, either by binding around or piercing through the passive system. In practice this gives an object with a very distinctive coiled appearance, usually with little of the passive system still visible.

Plaiting: Plaiting is something of a misnomer, as objects covered in this category are generally made from plaited strips sewn together rather than just being straightforwardly plaited. Plaited objects therefore consist of the systems that make the plait *and* the thread which binds it together. Both have to be recorded.

Systems

36.14 Width of the system - whether it be palm leaf, cord, or bundle of fibres - measured in centimetres.

36.15 Active or passive: Record whether the system is active or passive using the descriptions given above.

36.16 Fibre: The range of plant fibres that have been used or could be used to make basketry are endless. However in Egypt, only a few plant species have traditionally been used, and although they are not easy to identify to species by eye, they fall into general categories. Two kinds of palms have been used: the dom palm and the date palm. Both their leaf sheaths and leaves (and, in the case of the dom palm, the nut fibre) were used. A wide variety of grasses and rushes were used; note down the qualitative description of the grasses and create your own categories. A sample of each can then be taken for analysis by an archaeobotanist.

36.17 Plait systems: This section is only relevant if you are looking at a plaited object.

    a)   Number of strips: Each plait is made from strips, which must be counted. Finding the edges of the plaits is often quite difficult as they may be tightly sewn together to give the impression of a continuous sheet. However, the sewing threads leave a distinctive ridge that can usually be seen. Taking this as your marker, follow one strip to the edge with your finger, put your thumb against it, then follow its return path as it goes back across the plait, counting the number of other strips it crosses (whether under or over) until you reach the other side. Remember to include the strip you are following in the total. This is the number of strips in the plait.

b) Width of the plait.

c) Plait angle: Note the angle at which the strips cross each other at more. It will be less than, more than, or approximately 90°.

d) Structure: If the strip passes over one then under one, note it as 1/1. If it goes over two then under one, note it as 2/1; if it goes under two then over 2, this should be denoted as 2/2.

Object

36.18 Minimum diameter: Most basketry and objects made using basketry techniques are constructed in a symmetrical circular fashion; the furthest point from the centre of the object provides the minimum radius (and the diameter and circumference can thus be extrapolated) of the original object. A useful tool is a radius chart as used by ceramics specialists.

36.19 Estimate the completeness of the artefact in percentage terms.

36.20 Direction of spiral construction: This is important is determining if there is a standard local direction. Determine if the spiral goes clockwise or anti-clockwise on the **inside** of the object.

36.21 Preservation: This is a qualitative judgement, and involves deciding whether damage occurred pre- or post-deposition. Note if there are any areas of unusual wear, or if any repairs have taken place.

36.22 Decoration: Should be described and a scale drawing provided.

Attachments

36.23 Handles: These should be fully described and a scale drawing provided.

Processing

36.24 Conservation: Remove superficial layers of dirt from basketry by dry-brushing them – contact with water should be avoided. Relatively robust baskets can be relaxed and then reshaped (see textile section 35.22); be cautious with this approach to ensure that the object keeps its reformed shape.

36.25 Note how the basketry was excavated and lifted.

36.26 Storage: Three-dimensional pieces should be individually wrapped and stored in plastic boxes. Flatter pieces can be wrapped in acid free tissue paper and put in plastic bags. Larger pieces are harder to manage; fill in any unsupported areas with acid free tissue, and put into a large plastic bag. Avoid direct contact with cardboard boxes.

36.27 Description: This is interpretative to an extent but allows you to develop your own assemblage of shapes found at your site, and helps when searching for records. Your descriptions should be concise (maximum one sentence long) and must cover the important features of the object. For example: "a cup-shaped coiled pot in grass and palm fibre containing remains of cotton thread". Also note whether there are any surface coatings on the basketry, or any burn marks.

36.28 Provide a sketch of the basketry *in situ*, along with a blow-up of any special features. A sketch of the overall shape should also be provided; if there is any doubt about describing the structure, both a schematic and a representational sketch should be made.

36.29 Record the amount and numbers of any finds (bags or baskets) associated with the basketry in this field.

36.30 Note the numbers of the samples collected from the basketry here.

36.31 Record the number(s) of any special finds found in or with the basketry here

36.32 List any plans, cross sections or other drawings made of the basketry here.

36.33 The value of the temporary bench mark or datum should be entered here, as well as the measurement from the backsight to the TBM, and the instrument height.

36.34 Insert the numbers of any photographs taken of the basketry here.

36.35 Any other relevant information must be written in this field.

36.36 It is very important that the supervisor who completed the recording form signs and dates it.

36.37 The form and interpretation must be approved and counter-signed by the director or finds manager and any conflicting and differing interpretations of the same data entered.

36.38 The person that enters the data into a database must sign and date this field once the process has been completed.

37.00 *Sheet Thirty-Eight: Rope & Cordage Recording Form*: The recording of rope and cordage - and the objects made from them - involves the use of one system of description. The materials that can be scored using this system range from thick, industrial rope to everyday string, down to fine tassels used in garment decoration.

Like basketware, the recording of rope and cordage is considered in terms of systems which interact to create structure. The description of this interaction likewise permits the recording of simple spun thread to complex, multi-system objects. The basic system is the thread or cord made from the original fibres. From this, the interplay of secondary systems (themselves comprised of basic systems) can be recorded, up to the third or even fourth level. For example, a net is comprised of 's' spun thread (the basic system), which is plied with another thread (to make the secondary system) and then knotted into the form of a net (the third system).

Recording therefore starts from the basic systems, although more elaborate system structures may vary (such as a mixing of coloured fibre systems in a decorative plait). The secondary system is recorded from this point. Generally, this describes how the spun fibres are plied together to make a stronger, thicker cord. However, some objects are made directly from the most basic system.

At the head of the form there are boxes for the **Site Code (37.01)**, **Operational Area (37.02)**, and **Site Sub-Division (37.03)**, which should be recorded as outlined above.

37.04 Note the number of the context in which the rope/cordage remains was found.

37.05 Grid reference: Enter the grid reference here. If the context is located in just one grid square, enter the coordinates of the south-west peg of that square (i.e. 115E/205N). However if the context runs into two adjacent grid squares, it should be recorded as 115-120E/205N, or if the context runs in a north-south direction 115E/205-210N.

37.06 The category has already been filled out, as it will be a deposit.

37.07 Record the type of deposit (e.g. net, rope, etc.).

37.08 Note the number of the feature in which the rope/cordage was found here.

37.09 Record the exact 3-D provenience of the remains in this field.

37.10 Note the artefact's find number here.

37.11 Note the artefact's catalogue number in this field.

General Description

37.12 Write a one/two word description of the object for the purposes of instant recognition, e.g. thick rope, fishing net, plait.

37.13 Measurements: For cords, measure length and thickness of the cord in two directions; for more complex objects, measure the three dimensions.

The Basic System

37.14 Fibre: A huge range of fibres can be used to make cord and rope, so identification to species is hard and involves the use of very high-powered microscopes. The solution to this is to create your own fibre categories from which samples can be taken for subsequent analysis. As a general guide, fibres can be divided into those of animal and vegetable origin. Common animal fibres include sheep, goat and camel wool, and silk. Vegetable fibres are more varied and therefore more difficult to identify, but they can be roughly put into four categories: palm fibres, palm leaf sheaths, rushes and grasses, and fibrous linens/cottons. Palm fibres are thick and spongy, whilst palm leaf sheaths look like very broad grasses. Rushes and grasses come in a variety of qualities depending on how they have been processed; some retain their external coloured epidermi, while others have been rubbed to make long fibres that are spun together. Cottons and basts are harder to distinguish, but both produce a dense rope with very fine fibres.

37.15 Width of the system: Measuring the width of the system is important in judging quality, and also for identifying similar pieces.

37.16 Spin: The fundamental quality of cords is the spin of the base system. When fibres are processed into threads or cords, structural integrity is achieved and maintained by twisting (spinning) the fibres around each other. This is crucially important for understanding local spinning traditions and allowing the development of artefact/method typologies. The annotation for describing spin is based on the use of the letters 's' and 'z'. If you examine a thread vertically in front of you and the twist of the fibre starts high on the left hand side and comes down to the right hand side (like the middle stroke if you were writing the letter 's' in three lines) then it is 's' spun. If the reverse is true, then it is 'z' spun. If it appears not to be spun at all, it should be marked with an 'I'.

Second System

37.17 General description: If there is anything unusual about the system, note it here. Note any surface coatings or burn marks.

37.18 Construction: For describing cordage use the following guidelines:

> a) Plied: Often spun threads will be twisted together to make a thicker, plied cord. This is usually in the opposite direction to the original spin; for example, two 's' spun threads plied together make a sZ2 cable. This continues as the ropes get larger. For instance a sZ12[S]3 rope would be constructed from 12 strands of 's' thread plied in a 'z' fashion. These would be 's' plied with two other examples of the same. Note the ply and the width (in mm) of each of the systems and the angle that they cross measured in relation to the length.
>
> b) Plaited: There are two categories of plaited cord: the flat plait (i.e. three strand plaited hair), and the round plait. These are hollow, and may or may not be worked around a central cord. For both techniques you need to record the number of threads. Counting the number of threads in a round plait presents difficulties, so take some pins to act as markers between the threads as you count around. You also need to note the width of each system, and the angle that they cross measured in relation to the length.
>
> c) Sennet: 'Sennetting' is a technique which produces a solid cord, unlike round plaiting which produces a hollow cord. It is constructed by folding threads across the centre of the cord, to make a system with an exterior pattern of stitches lying parallel to the cords length. In contrast, the stitches in a plaited cord run diagonally to its length. Also record the width in millimetres of each of the systems, and the angle that they cross measured relative to the length.

If you are recording simple lengths of cord or rope, this is all the information required.

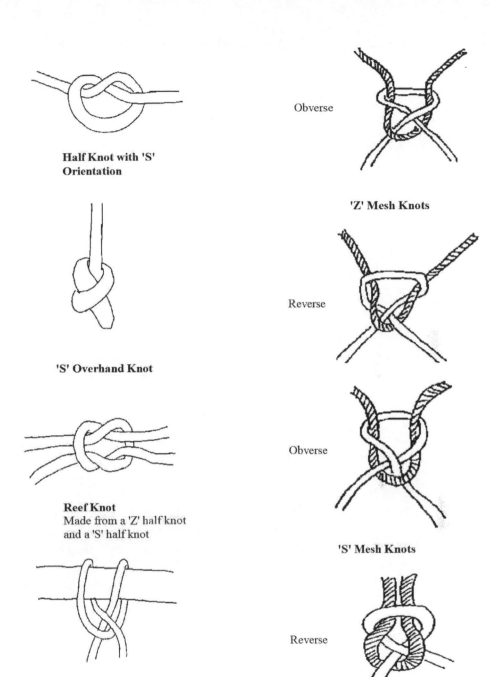

Figure 126: Knotting techniques (drawing by Fiona Handley).

Complications

Knots: There are thousands of different ways of knotting cords, and the complexities of this are compounded in an archaeological context where it is unclear whether or not the knots were made deliberately. It is best to record all those that look deliberate and/or complicated.

37.19 Type of knot: The illustrations (**Fig. 126**) provided give a rough guide to the kind of knots found. If the knot is not exactly reproduced, make a detailed drawing and a reproduction in cord. Note whether the knot is a stopper knot at the end of a length of cord, or in the middle.

37.20 Direction of knot: Some knots have a 'direction'; that is to say that the maker has to make a choice about passing the thread over or under another thread, thus making similar knots subtly different. This is often hard to decipher; see **Fig.126**.

37.21 Attachments: The function of the rope or cord is often indicated by what it is attached to (e.g. a stake). If attached to another piece of rope, the latter must be recorded separately.

Tertiary System

Nets: These cover a very wide variety of qualities and functions, from hairnets to fishing nets.

37.22 Type of net: Nets usually fall into two categories of construction: those made using reef or granny knots, the other using mesh knots.

37.23 Construction of mesh: Knot netting can be done one of several ways, and is important to establish which one as this may reveal local net-making traditions. Nets can be made either by working knots to one end of the net (then turning the net over and working a row of knots back on the reverse) or they can be made by reaching the end of the row and working back with the same side facing you. In the former instance, the mesh knot will remain the same construction (either 's' or 'z') but the reverse side of the knot will show, whilst in the latter the knot will change construction, as the other hand is used to make it.

37.24 Mesh size: This helps define the function of the net, notably in fishing nets. Measurements are carried out by measuring the four sides of the mesh aperture, taking the interior measurement.

Other Objects

37.25 Other rope-based objects must be described by this process so the materials and system can be understood. The object should be measured, photographed and drawn, and time should be taken to analyse complex objects. Two common types of complex object are shoes and tassels.

> a) Sandals: The soles of sandals are often made from plaited or plied fibres sewn into shape. As well as the systems (see above), record the size of the sole (tracing through clear plastic with an indelible pen is a good method), areas of wear, and how the edges are finished.

b) Tassels and pendants: These are often very complicated to record in terms of systems, or even through description, so the best method to record them is through a measured drawing.

Processing and Storage

37.26 Processing: As with all organics, it is best to keep cordage, etc. away from water. Cleaning can be done carefully with a dry brush, and objects can be returned to their original shape by using a relaxing tent (see **Textiles, section 35.22**). Cordage objects are fragile as well as being susceptible to damp and humidity. Consult with a conservator concerning specific requirements for the storage of particular assemblages.

37.27 Note how the cordage was excavated and lifted.

37.28 Provide a sketch of the cordage *in situ*, along with a blow-up of any special features. A sketch of the overall shape should be provided, and if there is any doubt provide both a schematic and representational sketch showing the shape/structure.

37.29 Record the amount and numbers of any finds (bags or baskets) associated with the cordage in this field.

37.30 Note the numbers of the samples collected from the cordage here.

37.31 Record the number(s) of any special finds found with or attached to the cordage in this space

37.32 List any plans, cross sections or other drawings made of the cordage here.

37.33 The value of the temporary bench mark or datum should be entered here, as well as the measurement from the backsight to the TBM, and the instrument height.

37.34 Insert the numbers of any photographs taken of the cordage here.

37.35 Any other relevant information must be written in this field.

37.36 It is very important that the supervisor who completed the recording form signs and dates it.

37.37 The form and interpretation must be approved and counter-signed by the director or finds manager and any conflicting and differing interpretations of the same data entered.

37.38 The person that enters the data into a database must sign and date this field once the process has been completed.

38.00 Sheet Thirty-Eight: Worked Stone Recording Form: This form is for recording the details about each individual worked or dressed stone, whereas the **Masonry Recording Form** is for recording the details about whole masonry context that the worked stone is a constituent of, e.g. the description of the whole wall. Masonry also includes un-worked stones and ceramic bricks, which are not recorded individually. Worked stones can be found individually, some being moved far away from their primary location and others not having moved very far, possibly deriving from a previous building nearby. Much of the information about stone has already been provided under the **Masonry Recording Form, Section 12**. Worked stone may have only constituted elements of a building, such as doorways, windows, columns, pilasters, arches, or decorative elements. The main types of worked stone are ashlars, scoinsons and moulded stones (see **Tab. 25**). Worked stone shows signs of being further finished than simply being hewn from the quarry. The casing stones of the pyramids are worked stones, whereas the majority of the fill of the pyramid are not dressed. Many worked stones, particularly those used in temples and tombs, have either raised or sunk relief on them, and also traces of paint. In these cases the relief scenes will continue over many individual worked stones, whereas in the case of an obelisk it will be only one worked stone.

At the head of the form there are boxes for the **Site Code (38.01), Operational Area (38.02), Site Sub-Division (38.03), Context (38.04), Grid References (38.05), Feature/Group Number (38.06)**, and **Number of the Worked Stone (38.07)**, all of which should be recorded as outlined above.

38.08 Type: To describe whether the worked stone is part of a building, a retaining wall or great wall, architrave, roof, a tomb wall, floor or pavement, foundation, arch, vault, dome, corbel, ventilation system, false-door, doorway, stele, stairs, column or pillar, pyramidion, facing or just a single masonry block. State the element type - base, shaft, capital, lintel, mullion, sill, coping stone, etc.

38.09 State the type of stone: ashlar, scoinson, moulded, slab, stele, etc. Is the worked stone the typestone? If yes the number of the stone is put in this field, if not put the number of the typestone that the present example is referenced to in this field. A typestone is the best preserved example of a particular type of stone. Typestones are fully recorded, whereas other examples or fragments of the same type are referenced to the appropriate typestone.

38.10 Has the stone been reused, yes or no? Has it been recut, yes or no? If the stone has been recut, the original moulding of the stone must be recorded on a separate form and given its own number, and that number entered in the space provided.

38.11 The dimensions of the individual worked stone must be recorded, giving the paired measurements of the length, width and depth.

38.12 The colour of the worked stone should be recorded using a *Munsell Colour Chart*.

38.13 If the worked stone cannot be moved from its location, the reduced level must be put here, giving the measurements of the highest and lowest points of the stone.

38.14. Type of rock is concerned with the occurrence, origin and history of rocks, and has widespread usage in archaeological analysis of building traditions, etc. Describe the stone's mineralogy, structure and texture by ticking the lithological group to which the worked stone pertains.

356

General Rock Type	Texture - Average Size of Minerals	General Colour and/or Composition -	Rock Name
Igneous Rocks - Interlocking homogenous crystalline texture - no preferred orientation to the mineral grains. Rock found as a result of the hardening of magna or lava. Examples are obsidian, basalt and rhyolite.	Extrusive, volcanic	Felsic - Light coloured	Rhyolite
		Intermediate	Andesite
		Mafic - Dark coloured	Basalt
	Medium grained -Dikes, sills, etc.	Felsic - Light coloured	_____
		Intermediate	Dacite
		Mafic - Dark coloured	Diabase
	Coarse grained -Generally intrusive	Felsic - Light coloured	Granite
		Intermediate	Diorite
		Mafic - Dark coloured	Gabbro
		Ultramafic	Peridotite
	Glassy	Dark to black – felsic (does not follow normal colour index)	Obsidian
	Frothy	Felsic - Light coloured	Pumice
		Mafic - Dark coloured	Scoria
Sedimentary Rocks - Consolidated detrital clasts, chemical precipitates, and/or biological residue. A rock composed of the bi-products of other rocks that have been eroded or dissolved. Examples of sedimentary rocks are sandstone, chalk, chert, limestone, mudstone, etc.	Coarse fragments	Rounded clasts	Conglomerate
		Angular clasts	Breccia
	Sand sized fragments	Clean quartz (w/feldspar?)	Sandstone
		Dirty w/rock fragments and clay	Greywacke
	Fine grained - cannot see individual clasts	Nonfoliated, 'clay the size'	Siltstone
		Foliated - 'clay the material'	Shale
	Chemical -fine grain *Crypto-Crystalline (CC)*	Soft - passes fizz test	Limestone
		Medium – fails fizz test. Light coloured, translucent CC fibrous quartz	Chalcedony
		Hard - fails fizz test. Compact CC (mostly from chalk) - Grey, red, black etc. Thick cortex.	Flint
		Hard - fails fizz test. Compact CC (mostly from limestone) - Yellow, brown, grey, etc. Limited cortex	Chert
	Fossiliferous	Mostly shell fragments	Coquina
Metamorphic Rocks - Interlocking non-homogenous crystalline with a preferred orientation to the mineral grains. Rock formed or changed structurally or minerologically by heat and pressure underground. Examples are marble, quartzite and slate.	Foliated, very fine grained - no visible minerals	Dull - passes 'tink test'	Slate
		Foliated, shiny due to increased size of micaceous minerals	Phyllite
	Foliated - medium to coarse grained	Individual mineral grains visible. Major mineral(s) included as name modifiers	Schist (ex. Mica Schist)
	Colour banded	Alternating layers of light (felsic) and dark (mafic) minerals	Gneiss
	Distinct layering - often highly folded and contorted	Alternating layers of felsic igneous rock (light) and mafic gneiss (dark)	Migmatite
	Non-foliated with non-oriented grains	Soft - passes fizz test	Marble
		Hard - fails fizz test	Quartzite
		Interlocking hornblende crystals	Amphibolite

Table 33: Rock types (after Kipfer 2007: 215).

38.15 The name of the rock, e.g. limestone, sandstone, granite, **Table 33** should help in this regard.

38.16 The condition of the exposed, non-exposed, internal/external (to building) surfaces of the masonry context or worked stone must be recorded. Also state whether the original surfaces are absent or present, and the colour of any paint present.

38.17 Is there any decoration on the stone? Variants include raised relief, sunk relief and painted.

38.18 The pattern code should be entered in this field; if a pattern code does not exist for the site/area, then one should be constructed.

38.19 The genre of the decoration is required here, i.e. secular or religious. Also required is the type of building that it came from, such as a temple, tomb or other type of building.

38.20 Describe the decoration and subject matter. The dimensions of the design should also be given. A translation of any writing can also be given. The decoration on the block may be part of a painted or carved scene, or may be part of a frieze or architrave. In such a case, associated block numbers must also be recorded. Further interpretation of the decoration should also be attempted, what were the reasons for its decoration, what role did the decoration or symbols fulfil?

38.21 Comment on anything interpretive or factual about the stone.

Fields 22 to 30 are only to be filled out for typestone; non-typestones go to 31 to complete form.

38.22 A list of the catalogue numbers of all the worked stones of the same type.

38.23 The state of preservation; is it complete or fragmentary.

38.24 The catalogue numbers of any typestone that were found in relation to the current worked stone.

38.25 What type of component (smallest) element is the worked stone a part of? If it is a sub-type of a component element, this name is also required.

38.26 Of what major structural element is the worked stone a component of? Although prompts are given, others such as colonnade or arcade can be put under other. If it is a sub-type of a major element, this name is also required. Note any parallel examples of this typestone in similar architectural elements.

38.27 Note any tooling marks on the exposed faces.

38.28 Are there any tooling marks on the exposed surfaces? Are the tooling marks fine strokes, diagonal strokes, scappling (marks made as a result of reducing the stone to a straight surface) or batting (striations on a surface made by a wide chisel)?

38.29 Record the kind of tool(s) used to make these marks.

38.30 A short description of the worked stone's position, giving an interpretation of its original function. Was it a part of a floor, wall, architrave, pyramid complex, tomb chapel, etc? Give any relevant context or feature numbers, and estimate the period or age of the worked stone.

38.31 Record the number(s) of the samples collected in this space. A petrological sample from a non-exposed face should be taken of each typestone. Any mortar or paint must also be sampled.

38.32 List any plans, rubbings of tooling marks or other drawings made of the worked stone here.

38.33 Insert the numbers of any photographs taken of the worked stone here.

38.34 Make epigraphic drawings of all decorated blocks; the numbers of these drawings must be listed in this field. The technique used for the epigraphy must also be given here.

38.35 Any other relevant information must be written in this field.

38.36 If the stone has been recorded *in situ* the value of the temporary bench mark or datum should be entered here, as well as the measurement from the backsight to the TBM, and the instrument height.

38.37 Provide a brief sketch of the worked stone, showing any notable aspects, and note the scale, annotate with dimensions and other useful information. A sketch of the decoration must also be made.

38.38 A list of all the foresights taken on the worked stone should be placed here. A brief sketch of the section or elevation can also be provided if necessary.

38.39 It is very important that the supervisor who completed the recording form signs and dates it.

38.40 The form and interpretation must be approved and counter-signed by the director or finds manager and any conflicting and differing interpretations of the same data entered.

38.41 The person that enters the data into a database must sign and date this field once the process has been completed.

39.00 Sheet Thirty-Nine: Building Material Recording Form: Building material is found on most settlement sites and many cemetery sites, and should be sampled and retained for further identification or used as part of a reference collection. One or two of the best examples of ceramic building materials, ceramic bricks, undressed stone, and mortar should be kept. Other types of building material need specialist recording and lifting or conservation. Decorated mosaics (*in situ* tesserae) should be retained, recorded with film and drawn. They should then be preserved *in situ* if possible or lifted by the conservator if they are about to be destroyed by modern development. The same procedure also applies to *in situ* floor tiles, with decorated floor tiles being given an individual special finds number, which must be written on the 1:20 plan (Grey 2006). If the floor tiles are plain, although make up a design due to one or more colours having been used or because of the way they have been laid, a plan of the overall design will suffice, noting the exact colours of the tiles.

At the head of the form there are boxes for the **Site Code (39.01)**, **Operational Area (39.02)**, **Site Sub-Division (39.03)**, **Context (39.04)**, **Grid References (39.05)**, and **Feature/Group Number (39.06)**, all of which should be recorded as outlined above.

39-07 Enter the period or date of the building material in this field.

39.08 Type: Describe the context where the building material came from, i.e. course of masonry, from a rubbish pit, occupation debris, etc.

39.09 Describe what the building material is made from.

39.10 Object form: The type of object, e.g. brick, tile, painted wall plaster, non-worked stone, loose tesserae, etc.

39.11 The corners of the building material as present in plan view should be described as: square, rounded, or irregular.

39.12 Record the length of the piece of building material.

39.13 Record the width of the piece of building material.

39.14 Record the thickness/depth of the piece of building material.

39.15 Note any mortar adhering to the piece of building material here.

39.16 Any comments or further description of the fragment of building material.

39.17 If the fragment of building has been catalogued, the number given is required here.

39.18 Provide any general comments and other relevant information in this field.

39.19 Selected pieces of building material should be drawn at a scale of 1:1; note their numbers and any plans showing the building material in this field.

39.20 Insert the numbers of overall, particular aspects and *in situ* photographs of the building material in this space.

39.21 Record the reference numbers of any sub-samples taken for petrology or other analysis.

39.22 It is very important that the supervisor who completed the recording form signs and dates it.

360

39.23 The form and interpretation must be approved and counter-signed by the director or finds manager and any conflicting and differing interpretations of the same data entered.

39.24 The person that enters the data into a database must sign and date this field once the process has been completed.

40.00 *Sheet Forty: Conservation Recording Form*: This is a specialist form to be filled out by conservators only. All materials and substances used in the conservation of the artefact **must** be recorded on the sheet.

41.00 *Sheet Forty-One: Object Invigilator Form*: This form is held by the finds processor and is filled out in cases where objects are given to other specialists for treatment (i.e. conservation) or analysis.

41.01 The registration number of the object.

41.02 The excavation number of the object.

41.03 The number of the feature where the object was found (i.e. grave number or structure number).

41.04 The number of the context where the object was found.

41.05 A brief description of the object, noting any distinguishing features, such as broken parts, colour or material of manufacture.

41.06 Write the name and job of the specialist to whom the object was given for special treatment.

41.07 Note the name of the finds processor (i.e. yourself).

41.08 The date that the object was sent in for treatment should be noted here.

41.09 When the object is returned to the finds processor, the person that returned the object must sign in this space. It must also be counter-signed by the finds processor who received it, and then dated with the date on which the object was returned.

41.10 Provide a sketch of the object, with its dimensions.

42.00 *Sheet Forty-Two: Object Distribution Map*: The site or feature should have been excavated by discrete contexts or lots, thus permitting all artefacts to be placed into a distribution map. This will ensure that temporally- and spatially-significant groupings of artefacts will be kept separate. For example, if excavating a rock-cut tomb by the lot system, the sieving from the matrix of each lot, shaft and chamber should be given separate area codes/names, e.g. shaft 1, chamber 1, shaft 2, chamber 2, etc.

Figure 127: Potsherd distribution

Pot No. ↓	1	2	3	4	5	6	7	1	2	3	4	5	1	2	3	4	5	6
TAD0258	Δ	Δ	Δ		Δ	Δ	Δ	Δ	Δ	Δ	Δ		Δ	Δ	Δ			Δ
TAD0095								Δ	Δ				Δ			Δ	Δ	
TAD0097								Δ		Δ	Δ							
TAD0023									Δ	Δ	Δ	Δ	Δ					
TAD0056									Δ	Δ	Δ	Δ						
TAD0325									Δ	Δ	Δ	Δ	Δ					
TAD0379								Δ	Δ	Δ	Δ	Δ						
TAD0129									Δ	Δ	Δ	Δ						
TAD0274								Δ	Δ	Δ	Δ							
TAD0197								Δ	Δ	Δ	Δ							
TAD0393														Δ	Δ	Δ		
TAD0191								Δ	Δ	Δ								
TAD0139								Δ	Δ	Δ				Δ	Δ	Δ		
TAD0349					Δ	Δ	Δ											
TAD0147																	Δ	Δ
TAD0251													Δ	Δ		Δ	Δ	
TAD0371														Δ	Δ	Δ		
TAD0296																Δ	Δ	Δ
TAD0099													Δ	Δ	Δ	Δ	Δ	Δ
Lot. No. →	1	2	3	4	5	6	7	1	2	3	4	5	1	2	3	4	5	6
Operation	Shaft 1							Chamber 1					Shaft 2					

Figure 127: Potsherd distribution (after Polz 1987: 131).

Figure 128: Numerical potsherd distribution map

Pot No. ↓	1	2	3	4	5	6	7	1	2	3	4	5	1	2	3	4	5	6
TAD0258	5	2	3		6	1	1	2	3	4	4		2	3	5			2
TAD0095								1	2				6			7	7	
TAD0097								9		8	9							
TAD0023									7	9	10	11	2					
TAD0056									12	11	9	10						
TAD0325									8	9	11	13	1					
TAD0379								4	5	6	9	10						
TAD0129									10	11	9	10						
TAD0274								9	8	15	10							
TAD0197								9	7	14	11							
TAD0393														9	8	9		
TAD0191								9	10	11								
TAD0139								1	2	3				9	11	11		
TAD0349					7	4	5											
TAD0147																	19	15
TAD0251													7	8		12	10	
TAD0371														8	10	12		
TAD0296																15	9	12
TAD0099													9	7	5	9	10	12
Lot. No. →	1	2	3	4	5	6	7	1	2	3	4	5	1	2	3	4	5	6
Operation	Shaft 1							Chamber 1					Shaft 2					

Figure 128: Numerical potsherd distribution map (after Polz 1987: 132).

During finds processing, divide the pottery into ware and shape groups, and then reconstruct as many vessels as possible. The lot or context number where the pieces of

362

each reconstructed vessel were found must be recorded and transferred onto the object distribution map (as shown in **Fig. 127**). The distribution map can be further refined by showing how many sherds of each vessel were found in each layer and putting the exact number in the space provided. This will reflect the sherd distribution pattern. Some vessels' potsherds will cluster in one or two areas (such as a single shaft or chamber) or the vessels may be spread across a wide spectrum of lots and operations. If the sherds consistently cluster in one place, then that vessel can usually be assigned as being from that area. If the vessels' sherds are dispersed over a wide area, it probably indicates that there was some form of (probably post-depositional) disturbance. A computerised format of the same method can be used to reconstruct the grave good assemblage of the original burial.

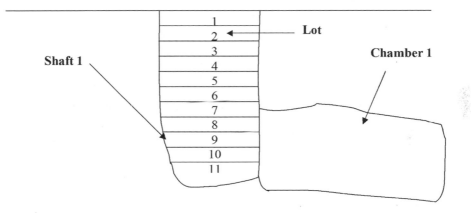

Figure 129: Excavation of a rock-cut tomb shaft with the lot system (after Polz 1987: 132).

43.00 *Sheet Forty-Three: Single Unit Inventory Form:* This form is to be used for inventorying all the different types of objects found in a single context. The various fields should either be filled out with the amount of standard sized bags of general bulk finds or the excavation numbers of special finds.

43.01 The site code is required in this field.

43.02 Name of the processor.

43.03 Date of the processing.

43.04 The context number from which the objects come.

43.05 The type of find, e.g. pottery, glass, building material, etc.

43.06 A preliminary date or period of the object(s).

43.07 Any comments about the object(s) and further description is required in this field.

43.08 The date it was sent to the relevant specialist.

44.00 *Sheet Forty-Four: Site Inventory Form*: This form is to inventory all the different types of objects found on the site. Material/industry: the substance, and the manufacturing processes to which it has been subjected

44.01 Note the site code in this field.

44.02 Note the operational area in this field.

44.03 Record the number of the context from which the object(s) came.

44.04 Note the condition of the object(s): i.e. whole, nearly complete or fragmentary.

44.05 The material: Determine if the object(s) is made from metal, stone, ceramic, pigment, vegetable or animal.

44.06 The industry: Determine which industry the object(s) belong to, e.g. bronze, tile, glass, lead white, textile or leather, etc.

44.07 Object: The type of object, e.g. sword, hand-axe, cup, paint, sandal, figurine, etc.

44.08 The number of the special find or bulk is required in this field.

44.09 A preliminary date or period for the object(s).

44.10 Any further description or comments.

Material	Industry
Metal	Any metals found as compounds.
Stone	Brick, tile, chipped stone (lithics)
Ceramics	Pottery, glass, faience
Pigments	Egyptian blue, lead white
Vegetable	Dyes, fibres, cosmetics, textile, basketry
Animal	Glue, leather, fibres, ivory, bone, horn

Table 34: Examples of material and industry.

45.00 *Sheet Forty-Five: Sex, Age and Wealth Analysis Form*: This form is to analyse the whole site, and should be filled out using the digit or tally system: (i.e. groups of five marked thus: ₩). This form was designed primarily for analysing a cemetery site, but can be used in other contexts as well. The total number of objects for each category can be added up to facilitate spatial analysis of the sites wealth distribution. As with the majority of the analytical forms, this can also be used in a computerised format.

46.00 *Sheet Forty-Six: Expenses Log*: This form is to be filled out by the director, archaeological manager, site supervisor, or finds manager as applicable, and is to record the expenditure of the field mission. All receipts and proofs of purchase concerned with the fieldwork should be saved and given to the director.

47.00 *Sheet Forty-Seven: Additional Pages*: Pre-printed additional pages that can be used with any of the previous forms.

48.00 *Sheet Forty-Eight: Drill Core Recording Form*: This form should by now be self-explanatory, and should be filled out in accordance with previously-explained conventions.

49.00 *Sheet Forty-Nine: Survey Recording Form*: This form should by now be self-explanatory, and should be filled out in accordance with previously-explained conventions.

General Points-to-Remember

These forms can be modified to meet particular requirements or different forms for particular types of objects, such a quern stones, glass vessels or clay pipes, etc. can be created using the layout of the forms provided. Points-to-remember when completing any of the forms include:

1. Give a full special finds number, etc. and put Tyvek labels on the objects themselves.

2. Fill out recording sheets right away and include all relevant sketches.

3. Follow the rules in this manual; if you are unsure, always ask the Field Supervisor.

4. It is important to note (in the sediment register) the exact position from which a sediment sample was taken. Distinguish between general sampling and those samples destined for residue analysis (i.e. from inside ceramic vessels).

5. Never use the same number twice.

6. If a question field is not applicable, either put a dash (-) or 'N/A', but **do not leave it blank**.

7. All treatments of objects must be noted, along with the names of the substances used.

Phrases for Use with the Recording Sheets

Archaeology, like most academic disciplines, is rife with jargon and technical terminology. We have therefore provided a short glossary of terms commonly used by archaeologists to describe artefacts, their condition and their conservation. A combination of these phrases will usually be sufficient to provide a reasonable record; if other descriptive comments are used their meaning must be made clear. Be consistent in your use of units, and only use standard abbreviations and symbols. If unsure about scientific terminology it is better to describe it rather than use an incorrect scientific identification or term. Be precise when describing colours, using a *Munsell Colour Chart* or *Wella Hair Colour Chart*. Always give plant and animal names according to standard taxonomic convention, underlining the Latinised systematic name, but not the English plant, animal or mineral names.

State	Term	Definition
Completeness		
	1. Complete --	Excavated find is complete (no missing pieces).
	2. Almost Complete --	Some pieces missing (over half present).
	3. Incomplete --	Most pieces missing (less than half present).
Condition		
A) Recognition	4. Unrecognisable --	Shape of object is unrecognisable on discovery.
B) Strength	5. Very Fragile --	Extremely delicate, great care required in handling.
	6. Fragile --	Delicate, requires careful handling.
	7. Fractured --	Part broken into 2-4 pieces.
	8. Fractured badly --	Part broken into over 4 pieces.
	9. Fragmentary --	Many small pieces.
	10. Fissured --	Cracks and lacunae, not necessarily fractured.
C) Surface Condition	11. Upper Side --	Side of artefact that is uppermost *in situ*.
	12. Lower side --	Side of artefact facing downwards *in situ*.
	13. Soft surface --	Usually applicable only to waterlogged materials; the surface of artefact is 'soft' to finger pressure.
	14. Powdery surface/interior --	Artefact surface/interior is dusty and powdery.
	15. Flaking --	Flakes of artefact surface become detached and fall off.

	16. Flaking visibly --	Crumbly surface that flakes to the touch.
	17. Encrusted heavily --	Thick layer of cemented sediment, grit and corrosion that adheres to the surface.
	18. Encrusted --	Surface is covered by a thin layer of a cemented sediment, grit and corrosion.
	19. Rough surface --	'Lumpy' deposits of corrosion products occur, with irregularities and uneven surfaces; areas of coarse mineralisation bonded to fine sediment and grit particles.
	20. Even compact corrosion layers --	Even, regular surface of varying thickness, but fairly uniform consistency and reasonably fine feature.
	21. Visible patina --	The surface, usually bronze or flint, is thinly coated with a very fine continuous smooth patina.
	22. Metallic surface --	Metal surface has very little to no patina, usually from anaerobic deposits.
	23. Visible detail --	Surface ornament is visible.
	24. Sediment --	Sediment is adhering to some or all of the surface.
	25. Colour (...) --	The colour as measured on the *Munsell Colour Chart*.
	26. Organic remains/fibres present --	Traces of organic materials are present on or close to an artefact.
D) Burial Condition	27. Waterlogged --	Appears waterlogged, matrix or artefact is wet.
	28. Desiccated --	The object has been preserved due to the hyper arid conditions drying the object.
	29. Anaerobic --	Oxygen free conditions.
	30. Frozen --	Appears frozen, matrix or artefact is frozen.
	31. Damp --	The artefact of matrix is moist.
	32. Burnt --	The artefact appears to have been in or near a heat source, e.g. a fire.
	33. Disturbed --	The object has been recovered from

		34. Hard packed Sediment --	Physical state of the matrix.
		35. Loose Sediment --	Physical state of the matrix.
		36. Plant roots present --	Fine roots are attached to the object.
E) Applied	**Techniques**	37. Consolidated with (…) --	The name of the consolidant used.
		38. Fungicide (…) --	The name of the fungicide used.
		39. Lifted in sediment block by (…) --	Details of block-lift.
		40. Lifted in sediment block, and / or consolidated with (…) --	Details of consolidant and block-lift.
F) Other Comments		41. Object fractured in excavation --	Damaged during discovery.
		42. Change in condition after discovery --	Describe in detail.

Table 35: Common descriptive phrases used with the recording sheets.

If there is any doubt about the condition of an artefact, place a '?' after your description.

INDIVIDUAL FIELD JOURNAL

There are two categories of journal: the individual field journal and those contained in the operational area or site folder. Each member of the team should be provided with an individual field journal so that they may keep a personal account of their daily involvement in the excavations. The journal should be hard-covered, preferably A4 size sectional books with scaled (1, 5 & 10 mm) paper on the left-hand pages and ruled feint and margin paper on the right-hand pages. *Chartwell* do a good range of student books; the laboratory books, A4-641K or A4-641C are ideal. However, if these are unavailable, any sectional or ruled feint margin book is adequate. As these journals form part of the primary site archive avoid wire-stitched books as they can rust.

If using a sectional laboratory book, fill in the boxes for the title and index as directed. The first two pages of the journal should contain the site name written out in full, the year and season of work, a table of contents, and the next three pages should contain:

Your name.

Your co-workers, including area supervisor, finds recorder and workers.

The operation and trench/unit in which you are working.

The starting date of your work in that area.

Season of work, e.g. 2009.

Trench Supervisors: Bram, Hisham, Ashraf & Mick, Workers: Mohammed, Ahmed, Ream and Hannia

First thing this morning the whole area was thoroughly cleaned with brushes to make ready for photography of Grave \1070\, photo Nos.: 9/25, 9/26, 9/27 & 9/28.

Hisham continued excavation of Grave \1070\, in trench 1, by trowel with the aid of Hania and Ream, who sieved the entire grave fill, context (979). The dimensions of the grave are now 1.1 m East-West by 1.9 m North-South.

Bram and Mohammed finished removing the matrix in the west of the trench by fas, context (920), which was a layer of sterile sand, revealing the spread of the layer (1010) across the whole trench and a new context. This new context, (1025), contains very different sedimentary material from (1010). It is a dark brown - 5yr/2.5 - alluvial sediment, with lots of calcareous inclusions, and a small amount of grit. Bram interprets this as a possible mud-cap of a large grave, although this will have to await confirmation through further excavation; it has not yet been assigned a grave number. This context's (1025) dimensions are 3.5 m East-West by 4.5 North-South.

Hisham has found the rim of a stone vessel at 91.690 m above datum in Grave \1070\, and context (979), the grave fill, although not drastically changing its matrix, has more calcareous inclusions. The Site Supervisor advised against a new context number, saying that it was still part of the same fill, just showing more leaching.

Ashraf, trowelling in the feature (1.7 m East-West by 2.2 m North-South) in the Southeast of trench 1, found a single mud-brick as he was removing context (965). Originally it was suspected that context (965) was a mud-cap for a grave, but this was unclear due to the disturbed nature of the sedimentary matrix. Ashraf will try and find the grave cut and see if there are anymore mud-bricks associated with the one already found.

1.0 PM. The lunchtime whistle has been blown, and we have dismissed the workers for lunch.

All recording forms have been completed, where appropriate.

Weather – Bright, hot, clear and sunny. First thing this morning there was a mist all over the site, this soon disappeared after half an hour.

Sediment moisture – The first 90 cm of sediment below surface was very dry, with it becoming moist at 1.50 cm, and by 2.0 m it was very wet.

Figure 130: How the right-hand page of a field journal should be filled out.

Each page should clearly state:

Its number.

The date.

The area where you are working.

Any change in the workforce.

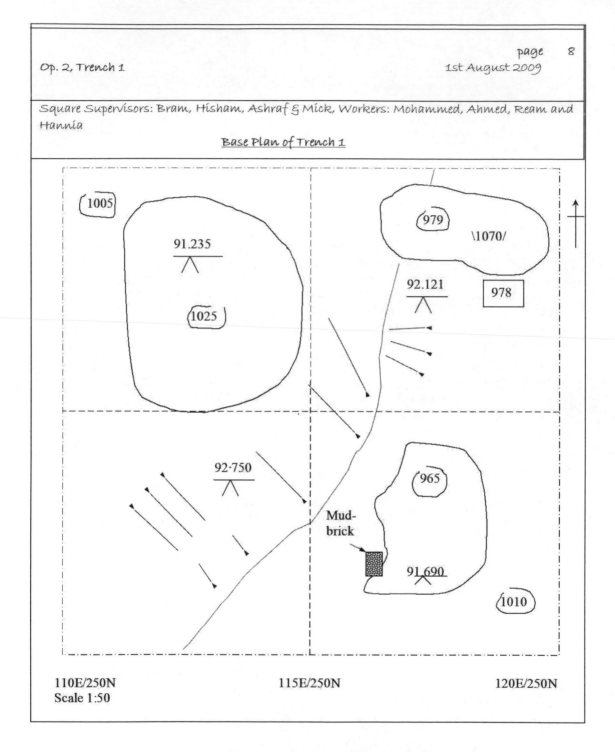

Figure 131: How the left-hand page of a field journal should be filled out.

Each time you work in a new area or return to an area that you had been working in previously, a new and clearly labelled page must be started to avoid any confusion. The operational area and sub-division of that area must be clearly shown, as must the names

370

of the people with whom you are working. The pages of the journal should contain all relevant and interesting information of the day-to-day activities. It is the place to record observations and interpretations of contexts and features as they occur to you. All pages and diagrams must be labelled clearly.

We awoke at 5.00am, and went out to site at 5.30am after having a cold shower, and surprise, surprise, another sunny day. Not all my workers were on site, I think some may have gone somewhere else, I remember the site supervisor telling me something about Susan needing some in another area.

We carried on taking down the level that we had started yesterday. Three features became apparent so we decided to take levels. The area was level at 40cm. We named these features 1, 2, & 3. We have assigned these features preliminary grave numbers 1020, 1021, & 1022. The Area Supervisor and Physical Anthropologist were busy, and could not come over at the time.

After another horrible breakfast of ful (beans) and eggs I helped Richard in his grave, I started to carefully excavate a long bone, which was 50 cm long. The body is orientated in an East West position, on its left side, facing South.

In the afternoon we took another level (4) we are now at a level 50cm below datum. The three graves are still visible, although one seems a strange shape for a grave. We will take the graves down individually tomorrow morning.

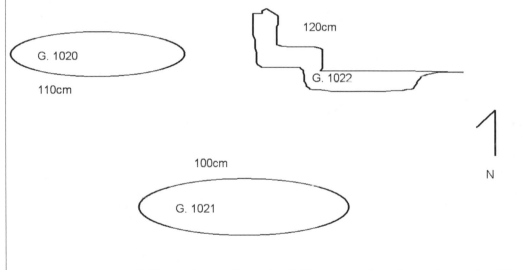

My stomach is feeling rather dodgy, I don't think I can face dinner, have left Hisham in charge of the area and I am going to lie down for a while. I will also retrieve my trowel that I think I left with Richard, and also see if he has my brush and bamboo skewers. I will try to fill out the recording sheets if I feel up to it.

Figure 132: A badly filled out journal with messy information. The diagram and writing are also both on the same page.

Figures **130** and **131** show how a journal should be written, with a sketch of the work that was carried out. The diagrams **should** be on the left-hand page, whereas the writing **should** be on the right-hand page. The diagrams can either be to scale, or measurements

371

can be shown. The diagram (**Fig. 131**) is often called a daily of base plan, which shows the process of excavation. Other diagrams to show how contexts relate to one another and specific details should also be drawn, along with sketches of sections and artefacts. Both the writing and diagrams should complement the single-context planning and recording sheets.

The diagram above is an example (**Fig. 132**) of a badly filled out journal, showing how imprecise and confusing badly-recorded information can look. The second example not only shows the wrong way to fill out a page in the journal, but also illustrates the wrong way to behave on an archaeological site.

The field journal should be used as a chronological narrative of the excavations, and to record additional information, some of which may not be recorded on the record sheets. Variables include a clear, consistent and coherent day-to-day account of work in progress, observations on areas or clusters of contexts, sketches to show artefact or context relationships, details of structures, changes in sediment, interpretations and hypotheses, methods of excavation, reasons for any changes in strategy, progress made on the project during the course of the day and light and weather conditions. It should also include as list of your team members and rough sketches of the area.

The process of excavation should be described, indicating what part of a context or feature was excavated first and why, what methodological problems were encountered, and how they were solved. Detail reasons behind any changes made to your methods or any decisions that affected the course of fieldwork and its possible outcomes (Burke & Smith 2004: 71). This allows data, interpretation and conclusions to be set within the process of archaeological enquiry, not apart from it. It should be remembered that this is not a personal journal. The information held in it will be used to write up the final report and may be used as research material by future archaeologists. Gossip and idle observations should not be recorded, as this journal will form part of the primary site archive and should be taken seriously by writer and reader alike.

SITE OR OPERATIONAL AREA FOLDER

If the site has distinct operational areas (particularly if they are separated from one another by some distance) then each will normally need a folder, although on a small or compact site a site folder should suffice. The site or operational area folder is for collating all the information pertaining to the site or that area. If there are two or more operational areas then the area supervisors maintain these folders with the help of the site supervisor, whereas if there is just one site folder the site supervisor maintains it with the help of the area supervisors. While the personal field journal moves with the person, the operational area folder stays with its area of operation and remains in use until all activities in the area have ceased. If a new area supervisor is assigned to that operational area they also take over the running of the folder. It should be noted, however, that staff transfers of this sort should be kept to a minimum. The site folder (from here on will be used but insert operational area if relevant, i.e. the site has two or more areas open) acts as the site supervisor's journal for keeping a description of the site and a record of all the activities that take place there.

The site folder is divided up into two volumes: one for the written record and one for the drawn record. The volume containing the written record should be divided into four main sections, separated by coloured section dividers. The first section is the site journal, which is an account of all activities in the area. The second is the diary of the day-to-day running of the operational area. The third is for storing the indices and registers, and the fourth is for storing the recording sheets. A separate folder should be used to store the plans, sections and other drawings pertaining to the operational area. This second volume can again be divided into sections, the first for the single-context plans, the second for the multi-context plans, the third for the sections and the fourth for other drawings.

The journal part of the operational area folder, use sectional loose-leaf pads with scale paper on the left-hand page and ruled feint margin on the right-hand page (if available). Otherwise, use a loose-leaf pad of graph paper and another of ruled feint margin A4 paper, placed in the ring binder facing one another. Plastic or cotton hole reinforcers (or adhesive tape strengtheners) should be used on the first five and last five pages of the operational area folder. If reinforcers cannot be found, then masking tape or *Sellotape* can be used instead. Plastic wallets should be used for storing the indices and recording sheets. The loose-leaf arrangement allows the addition of pages and the removal of completed sections to the site office for safe keeping.

The opening layout should follow that of the individual field journal, with the first two pages of the journal containing the site name written out in full, the year and season of work and a table of contents, and the next three pages should contain:

Your name.

The operational area and trench/units in that area.

The starting date of work in that area.

Season of work.

Each page should clearly state:

Its number.

The date.

The area in question.

(all diagrams must be clearly labelled; provide a key if necessary).

The operational area journal should follow the format of the individual field journal, containing a diary of the activities conducted in the operational area, along with descriptions, comments and interpretations of contexts, artefacts and ecofacts. If mechanical stripping is employed an explanation must be given of why, where and the results attained. The rationale behind all activities must be explained, i.e. why were trenches situated in a certain locale, what was hoped to be achieved? Provide an explanation of the relationship between the different contexts and features, and list new research questions and hypotheses generated during the course of fieldwork, or interesting ideas to follow up (Burke & Smith 2004: 71). If there is a change in sampling strategy, the reasons for this must be given. It should provide an overview of all the fieldwork, pulling all the activities in the various trenches together in a coherent narrative. Note the results of discussions with the director (site supervisor or specialists) about overall strategy or methodological problems. The stratigraphic interpretation should also be recorded. Any plans and diagrams should be drawn on the left-hand page facing the writing relating to them, recorded on the right-hand page. At the end of each day (or more frequently if the areas of excavation drastically changes) a schematic diagram of the site (or operational area) should be drawn to scale. This multi-context plan is termed the 'top plan' should be at either 1:50 or 1:100; to give greater detail top plans of each archaeological sub-unit can also be drawn at 1:20. The plans should show the location of all contexts, special finds and samples taken. The reduced levels must also be recorded on the top plan. These plans can show graphic thoughts and ideas, the location of the TBM, and any other useful information.

The second section should be a diary detailing the day-to-day management of the site or operational area. In this section the logistics of running the site or area should be detailed, such as the names of the people who are working in the operational area or on the site. This must be adjusted as personnel come and go. The **Expenses Log: Sheet 46** is for the day-to-day expenses incurred in the running of the site; all receipts must be kept and placed with the log. A record must be kept of any meetings with stakeholders, utilities staff, developers or other interested parties. Risk assessments and health and safety issues should also be detailed in this section. The placement of spoil heaps, inventory of equipment, explanation of why specialist tools were required and purchased should all be detailed here.

The third section comprises the indices for various archaeological components. These include: an index of all the photographs (**Sheet 13**), an index of all the drawings (**Sheet 14**), and a register of all the contexts (**Sheet 15**), and - where applicable - registers of all the graves, burials, structures, finds and samples. When operational areas (folders) are being used, blocks of numbers for contexts, samples, special finds, etc. should be assigned to the operational area so that the area supervisor does not have to continually consult the director or site supervisor, who in this case should keep a copy of the main registers.

The fourth section should contain all the recording forms pertaining to the operation, and must be ordered numerically and chronologically. Each sub-unit's forms should be separated into individual groups separated by coloured section dividers. Although the context forms and other recording forms may have been filled out by the actual excavators, the area supervisor must collect the completed forms at the end of each working day and store them in their proper position.

SIGNING AND CHECKING OF FORMS, JOURNALS AND PLANS

The person who filled out the recording sheets, journals and drawings must sign and date them. If there are any discrepancies or recourse to check certain points, the site supervisor or director knows whom to consult. The site supervisor can also follow up any consistent errors or flaws in the record in order to improve training (Roskams 2001: 235). The dating of forms allows the site supervisor to see if there are certain periods of excavation where the standard of recording decreased or improved, and use this to assess pressures of work or the speed at which new workers are learning core processes.

The signing-off of the forms, journals and drawings by the site supervisor or director is only done after they have been checked for errors and assessed for patterns. One part of the site may be progressing slower than others, or one area may be producing more material relevant to the research questions. The excavation strategy can then be modified as necessary.

When checking the recording forms and plans, the provenience information and the orientation/scale of the drawings must be carefully checked. All levels and symbols shown must be correct, as must the stratigraphic relationships. The completeness of the description and reasons for interpretation must also be checked. Discussions between the site supervisor or director and the various personnel involved can then rectify any problems or inconsistencies, and can highlight areas for improvement. On many of the forms there is a space entitled checked interpretation, this allows the director or site supervisor to give a differing or alternative interpretation of the context, feature or artefact.

Once the records and drawings have been checked and the finds and samples passed to the appropriate specialists, the plans and sheets should be placed in special folders and the information logged into a computer database (if one is being used on site).

SITE DIARY

The written record is complemented by the keeping of a site diary. At the end of each working day, a meeting should be held to discuss progress. Reports on the day's activities should be made by each specialist, as well as by the square assistants, area supervisors, finds processors, site supervisor and director. These meetings should also be used to discuss methodological problems, to air new hypotheses, or to discuss any interpretations. The proceedings of these meetings must be recorded, so that they can act as a check against other forms of evidence.

The daily meeting provides an opportunity for the whole team to discuss the work, and is essential for the project's success and development, providing a critical view of the project's objectives and thus enabling any adjustments to the project design to be made. It also helps to ensure that work is being carried out to the appropriate standard, and running to timetable and budget. These meetings can be held less frequently if deemed necessary (i.e. if the work is progressing slowly), and only be held once or twice a week.

At the end of the season/fieldwork there should be a debriefing, to run through all the evidence and to prepare for post-excavation analysis. All members of the team should state their methods, present their data and compare these with the original research design (Roskams 2001: 244), as this will inevitably have been amended according to evolving objectives and practicalities during fieldwork. The comparison of the original objectives with the actual results familiarises everyone with the total record and provides a good bridge to the analytical phase.

The Drawn Record

Archaeological drawings must be carefully measured to produce an objective representation that reveals technical information for use in archaeological analysis (Burke & Smith 2004: 284; Drewett 1999: 177). The drawn record consists of plans, sections, elevations, profiles and artefact drawings. Plans are the horizontal drawn record of all contexts and features, whereas sections, profiles and elevations are the vertical drawn record of contexts and features, which show the relationships of the physical layers. The drawn record exceeds the photographic record in terms of detailing quality and – as all drawings are to scale – facilitating the conversion into a complete scaled site plan. Accurate scale drawing is one of the most valuable archaeological skills, as they form a central part of the permanent record of all the contexts and features that are usually destroyed by the excavation process (Hawker 1999: 37). The visual representations in the final field report were for Petrie more important than the text, a view also held by Pitt Rivers. Petrie (1904: 115) states "the text is to show the meaning of the relation of the facts already expressed by form".

It is essential that drawing scales and draughting conventions be established and clearly stated at the start of excavation. If not using standard conventions it is essential to provide a key with all the drawings. Plans are usually drawn at a scale of 1:20, sections at 1:10, and artefacts at a scale of 1:1 (see **Tab. 38**). There are two groups of archaeological drawings: the initial in-the-field pencil drawings, which form part of the site archive, and the final inked versions, which are used in the publications. All in-the-field drawings should be made on draughting film overlaid on graph paper, using a hard-lead pencil (preferably **2H** or **4H**) as soft-lead pencils (such as **HB**) tend to smudge, thereby obscuring vital site information. Many expeditions and archaeological units now use pre-printed standard sized sheets of draughting film (i.e. Permatrace), or have all the draughting film cut to a standard size. It is vital that a record is kept of all drawings; this should be done by logging the drawings in the **Drawing Index: Sheet 14**. The final inked versions can be produced by scanning in the original pencil drawings and manipulating them in a computer programme such as *Adobe Photoshop* or *Illustrator*, or by tracing them with technical pens on draughting film.

The following nine points are to aid in the general drawing of objects, contexts and features in the field:

1. Use a drawing board of appropriate dimensions (to fit your context or feature drawing at the properly scaled-down size) and cover it with graph paper. If not using standardised draughting sheets, cut your sheet of draughting film to fit the size of your drawing board - do not fold it over the edges. Once cut to size, secure the edges of the draughting film to the board with masking tape.

2. Keep all single drawings centred on the sheet of paper/draughting film. If executing more than one drawing per sheet, draw a ruled box around each drawing.

3. Ascertain the longest measurement to be made and ensure this will fit on one sheet of draughting film at the appropriate scale. Divide your drawing up equally (ideally 50-50) if it is too large to fit on one piece of draughting film – for example, do not put ¾ of it on one piece of draughting film and a ¼ on another.

4. Work from the whole to the part, drawing the outline first, then putting in the major features and filling in the details last. Keep comparing your drawing to the actual entity. Do not overcomplicate your drawing - make it as clear as possible.

5. Coloured pencils are **never** used in archaeological draughting. If you wish to show colour or texture, use archaeological draughting conventions.

6. Keep your pencil sharp, either with a pencil sharpener, sandpaper, an emery board or on a convenient stone or rock.

7. Once the drawing is completed and registered, it should be stored in the site office for safe keeping.

8. Ensure that all equipment is kept clean, dry and tidy. Keep all the draughting supplies in one box (toolboxes and pencil cases are good) so they are always to hand.

9. Never ink-up directly on the original pencil drawing; trace the pencil drawing on to a new sheet of draughting film, as the original is part of the primary site archive. These pencil drawings may now be digitised or scanned directly into a computer, therefore avoiding the inking-up process.

Basic Equipment and Supplies

The basic equipment required for drawing objects, contexts and features in the field includes:

Draughting film, scale or graph paper, **2 H** to **7H** pencils (both wood-encased and clutch), pencil sharpener, eraser, and ruler.

Masking tape, bulldog clips, callipers, compass (or a set of spreading compasses with extension bar), protractor, isometric curve, flat or triangular scale ruler graduated at 1:5, 1:10, 1:20, 1:50, 1:100, etc.

A variety of drawing boards; A4, A3 and A2 sizes should suffice.

Six-inch (15cm) masonry nails, drawing frame, clothes pegs, builder's line, line level, 30 metre tape, 3m steel tape and plumb bob.

Rotring® pens and scalpel.

A draughting table or large flat desk, T-square, chair and angle-poise lamp (to be placed on the left), portfolio case, shelving or storage draws for finalised drawings.

Shade is essential if you are going to be sitting outside drawing for long periods in either the sun or the rain.

Scale	Size	Use
2:1	2 cm on the page = 1 cm on the object.	For enlarging small objects such as beads.
1:1	1 cm on the page = 1 cm on the object.	Normal scale for drawing artefacts.
1:2	1 cm on the page = 2 cm on the object.	For reducing large artefacts such as amphora.
1:5	1 cm on the page = 5 cm on the object or ground.	For burials or other intricate features.
1:10	1 cm on the page = 10 cm on the ground. All objects over 1 cm should be drawn	For sections, profiles and elevations.
1:20	1 cm on the page = 20 cm on the ground. All objects over 2 cm should be drawn.	For all types of plans.
1:50	1 cm on the page = 50 cm on the ground. All objects over 5 cm should be drawn	Used to compile site plans from the 1:20 area plans.
1:100	1 cm on the page = 100 cm on the ground.	Used to compile site plans from the 1:20 area plans.
1:200	1 cm on the page = 200 cm on the ground.	Used for large sites without a great amount of small detail.
1:250	1 cm on the page = 250 cm on the ground.	Used for large sites without a great amount of small detail.
1:500	1 cm on the page = 500 cm on the ground.	Used for large sites without a great amount of small detail.
1:2500	1 cm on the page = 2500 cm on the ground.	Commonly used for national and regional maps.

Table 36: Drawing scales: The scales at which different classes of archaeological features/artefacts should be drawn are presented above.

PLANS

Plans are the major method of recording the spatial dimensions of contexts and features. All plans must be surjective, clearly labelled and neatly drawn to facilitate easy interpretation by other members of the archaeological community. Although all contexts should be drawn once completely revealed, contexts that enter areas that have not yet been excavated must be clearly shown on the plan with the relevant symbols. When the new unit has been excavated, the context drawing must be completed. All plans must tie into the overall site grid. At least two points at the extremity of the plan should have coordinate points that tie into the corner of the trench, the datum, or a point already tied into the site datum.

Plans should be drawn at a scale of 1:20. At this scale anything less than 2 cm is not drawn, as it will appear as a dot on the drawing. This will prevent inaccuracies occurring during the post-excavation process. In certain cases plans with a scale of 1:5 may be required (e.g. the recording of a skeleton), while plans showing the overall layout of the site trenches may be drawn at a scale of 1: 50 or 1:100. In **all** cases the scale used in a plan **must** be clearly stated on the completed drawing. These conventions have been developed to reflect the fact that contexts often constitute barely-perceptible variations in sediment colour or texture (which may therefore merge imperceptibly into one another), and therefore convey the character of the contexts, rather than representing them as well-defined entities.

Regardless of the type of plan drawn, the following information must **always** be included on the completed drawing. A code of conventions is provided at the end of this section, however, if other symbols are used, then a key **must** be provided.

a. The site code and grid reference.

b. The date when the plan was drawn

c. A North Arrow **must** always be shown, although north should normally be at the top of the drawing (magnetic north or true north depending on the orientation of the site grid). North should be located with a compass and the North Arrow drawn in with the help of a protractor.

d. The scale of the drawing.

e. A plan number (i.e. **TAD09-67**) which is made up of site code and sequential drawing number, unless it is a single context plan, which takes the context number.

f. Context, feature, grave and artefact numbers, displayed in their correct locations with the correct conventions (see below).

g. Grid points with their coordinates **must** be shown on the drawing, especially the south-west co-ord.

h. Levels **must** be shown with the figure placed on a benchmark symbol ($\bar{\lambda}$). On sections, show the level of the datum line and nails.

i. Name of draughtsperson.

j. A stratigraphic relationship matrix.

k. An orientation grid **must** be shown on sections, indicating which section of the trench is illustrated.

There are five types of plan: the single-context plan, the multi-context plan (top or daily plan), the composite plan (multi-context phase plan), the base plan and the site plan. The type of plans used should be determined by the type of site being excavated, rather than a predetermined dogma; a mixture of the different types of plans is usually the best policy. The drawing of plans (unless they are top plans for journals) is not to record the excavation process, but to distinguish entities which actually occurred in the past; to fully and clearly record distinct stratigraphic units (Roskams 2001: 137). **Single-context plans** record just one context per sheet of draughting film, defining each context to its full extent within the 5.0 x 5.0 m grid unit (**Fig. 133**). Contexts that extend across more than one grid unit require separate sheets of draught film for each unit, with the context drawn in its true position in relation to the grid units. Plans of contexts show the surface of that deposit or cut, if the surface has no defining characteristics then an outline of the context should suffice. The actual character and type of context must be fully described in the single-context recording form. Most contexts should be planned prior to their excavation, and if required have amendments and adjustments made after excavation. A context should only be planned when its full extent, within the excavation area, is exposed. Lensing out of a context should be represented by the uncertain limit line at its maximum perceptible extent. Cuts such as graves, ditches and pits may require their own pre-excavation plan, and may need sections drawn if they are half-sectioned. Plans of cuts are done after the fill(s) are removed; there is no need to draw individual plans of the fills within pits as long as the plan of the cut defines the stratigraphic relationship of its fills and that the fills possess no significant characteristics of their own that need recording in plan (Westman 1994: 14). Complex features such as hearths or a deposit of worked stone debris may merit a pre-excavation plan, a 'during excavation plan' (to show the internal structure), a post-excavation plan, and also possibly a section. Features such as postholes will not usually receive an individual plan, but are planned on multi-context plans with the layer they cut into and any associated postholes (Hawker 1999: 51).

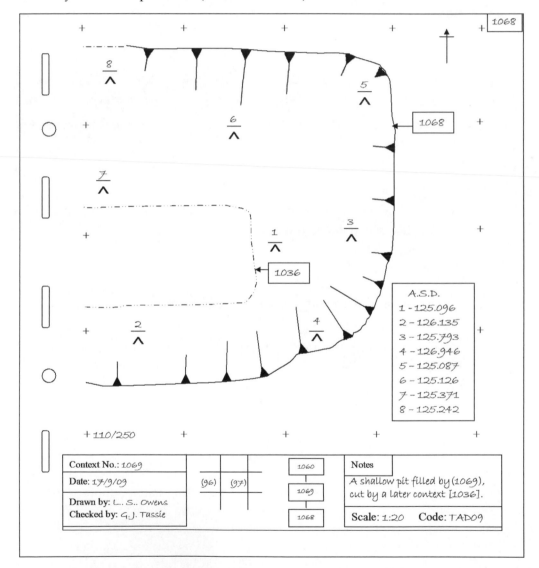

Figure 133: An example of a single-context planning sheet. Note the running matrix, and the fact that this context runs into an adjacent square to the west, shown on the matrix box grid. Although a north arrow is shown here, it is not really needed as north is always at the top of the page, the number of the modern intrusion [1036] is also not required as it will have its own plan (after Westman 1994: 13).

The rationale for single context planning is to split the site up into its component parts and record each independently (Roskams 2001: 140). The use of the running matrix helps to establish the site matrix. Each single context plan, along with its recording form and any photographs, are used to build up the site matrix and composite site phase plans, constructing a three-dimensional jigsaw (Barker 1993: 169). Using hachures to show slopes and other symbols to illustrate the nature of a context are usually sufficient to complement the information held in the recording form. However, if a surface of a context is undulating or complex, then this should graphically be shown on the plan. These types of plans are ideal for deep, highly stratified sites, such as multi-period urban or *tell* sites. This is because major surfaces are very hard to define amongst the interleaved contexts, often cutting from one surface to another. As most contexts are completely removed to aid the stratigraphic interpretation, running or cumulative sections must be drawn across the site, as well as the usual baulk section drawings (Hawker 1999: 51). The observations and interpretations of the excavator and the comments and interpretations of the area supervisor are taken into account when interpreting context relationships.

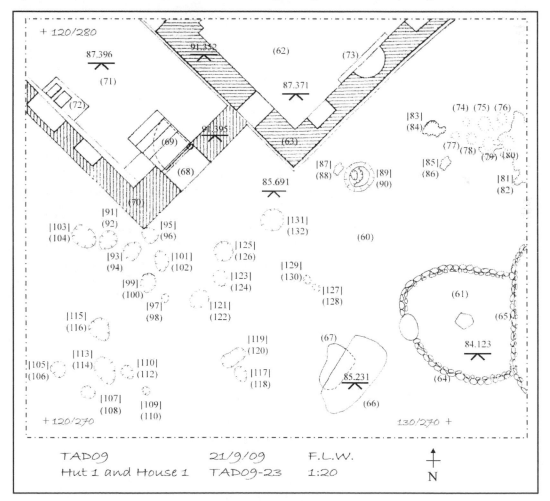

Figure 134: Multi-context plan of a single grid unit (the running matrix – as it is too complicated, and would detract from the drawing - must be shown on another piece of paper and attached).

Multi-context plans (sometimes referred to as **top plans, daily plans** or **multiple feature plans**) show the relationships of multiple contexts and features to one another (**Fig. 134**). They are done at designated points of the excavation process – end of day, week, the completion of a trench or excavation. Daily plans involve making an initial plan of the area of operation or excavation sub-unit - after the initial overburden has been stripped off – followed by area plans at the end of each working day (**top plans**). This process can be streamlined by preparing the basic outline of the plan the night before, tracing the positions of contexts and features that are not going to be removed. If an area has not changed significantly then previous plans may be added to. These plans record every context visible at any one point in the excavation process. As with all other types of plans, all context or feature numbers must be shown on the plans, as must all levels.

In multi-context plans the components drawn at a single-level (as viewed by the excavator) do not always refer to a real, existing point in historical development of the site. Indeed they may be of very different periods, and the drawing will probably only represent a surface created by the excavators, full of stratigraphically unconnected, contexts, rather than a major surface representing a single phase of activity. On a deeply stratified urban site which includes superimposed contexts, it is impossible to record the full extent of the various contexts in this manner, and as a result lacunae are likely to be embodied in the spatial record (Roskams 2001: 139). Therefore, as a record of the archaeology, the production of site plans with this method is seen as deeply unsound both methodologically and theoretically (Roskams 2001: 137). However, as a record of the excavation process these types of plans are useful to keep in the individual journals (although single context sketches should accompany them) to help the excavator understand the process and contexts in their area. As such, multi-context plans are often used to show the position of various contexts in the excavation unit.

Composite plans or **phase plans** attempt to record single surfaces, with features like walls, floors and post-holes all related to contemporary ditches and pits. They recreate a view of a surface representing a single phase of activity (Drewett 1999: 132). These types of plans are often used where several features are dug into a single geological stratum (**Fig. 135**). In such cases then all the features or contexts found in that stratum are drawn. An example of this usage - showing the relationship between various contexts - is in the illustration of a series of post-holes or group of contemporary graves. They are often published in reports, showing how a site looked during a certain period, or the relationship between various features. On single-phase sites, plans of this type can be created in the field. Composite plans are also drawn in conjunction with single-context plans to help elucidate complex stratigraphic relationships.

These types of plans suffer from many of the problems of multi-context plans, especially those concerning incompleteness of sealed or partially-sealed contexts (Roskams 2001: 139). Composite plans are less useful on deeply stratified sites and almost impossible to create in the field. Sealed or partially sealed units may not be recorded in their entirety or missed altogether as they are not visible (Roskams 2001: 139). The level of interpretation in producing phase plans in the field is a more fundamental problem, especially on multi-phase sites. The level of decision making is qualitatively greater in creating one of these types of plans than in deciding the full extent of a context; also it may not be clear if the stratigraphic sequence is fully understood until the analysis has been completed (Roskams

2001: 140). Difficulties also arise in areas containing near homogeneous strata of silt and sand, which may be imperceptible except in section.

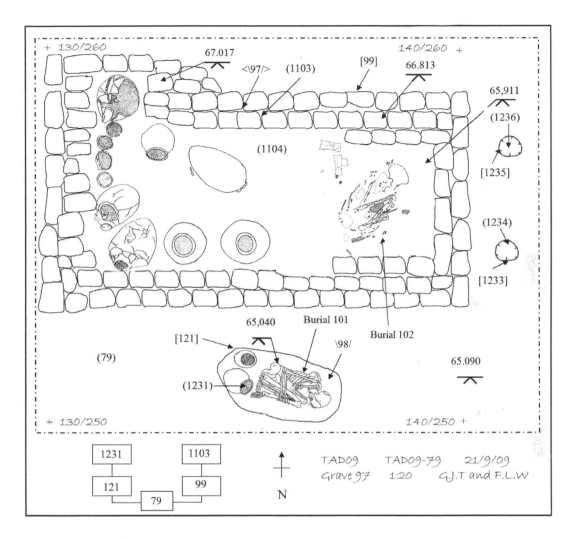

Figure 135: Composite plan of a single grid unit showing Early Dynastic remains.

Single-context planning produces a large amount of plans; to help make sense of these plans they need to be positioned in their exact provenience in a scale plan of the site. The plan on which field data are placed is called the **base plan** (see **Fig. 136**), a plan that depicts the whole site at 1:100 scale (1:20 can be used for small sites and 1:500 or more for large sites). The base plan must show the site grid, site datum, any temporary bench marks (control points), the positions of the areas of operation and trenches along with their coordinates and reference numbers and letters of any excavation sub-units. Outside the areas of operation, the base plan should also show any topographical, structural and other features on the modern landscape. As the excavation progresses and the individual unit plans are analysed, the space inside the areas of operation must be filled out with the information from the lower-scale plans, making a comprehensive **site plan** (see **Fig. 137**).

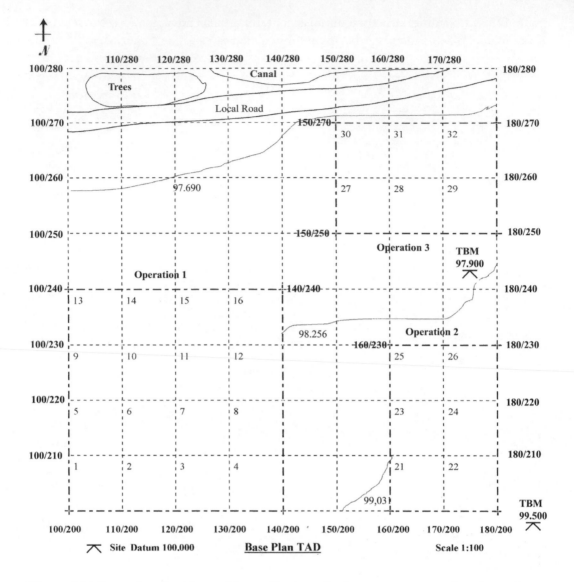

Figure 136: Base plan showing grid coordinates, site datum, temporary bench marks, site grid, excavation grid and grid units, as well as topographical features.

To be able to understand the historical growth of the site, phase plans must be reconstructed from the single-context plans during the analysis phase of the expedition. The phasing of the site should be done as the excavation progresses, with the single-context plans being overlaid to establish the stratigraphic relationships before the contexts are removed (see **Chapter 10**). However, the contexts and features are not only interpreted and phased through overlaying the individual plans onto their coordinates, but with reference to the context recording forms, section drawings, relative dating of associated artefacts, and absolute dating (processes that should also influence the building of the site matrix). Once all the contexts of the site have been phased (see **Fig. 180** and **185**) the graphic information recorded on the individual plans must be transferred into their respective trench/grid squares on the base plan. The size of the site dictates if the separate single-context plans to be transferred onto a base plan need to be scaled down or not. All context, feature, grave, structure, burial and *in situ* artefact numbers and spot heights must be shown on the site plan. Various types of site plan can then be constructed, one showing for example all contemporary contexts from the early Roman period, another all those from the Early Bronze Age period. These phased plans can be combined, using different colours or other conventions for the various periods to demonstrate the diachronic intra-site spatial patterning.

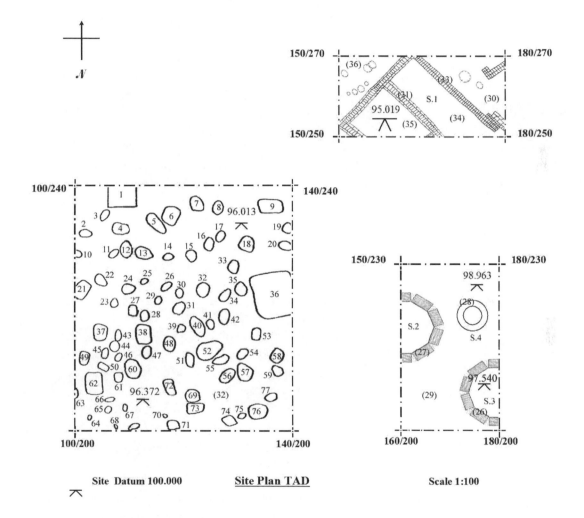

Figure 137: Site plan, showing the archaeological features excavated, corner grid coordinates of areas of operation and spot heights.

The creation of the site plan allows for clearer spatio-temporal analysis by locating the archaeological data internally, and - as all plans are geo-referenced - also locates the site within the local landscape and national grid (Westman 1994:154). It also helps the principal investigator to formulate further hypotheses, and guides the placement of future areas of operation. Reproductions of the site plan should be displayed in a prominent place such as the site office or meeting room. This will boost team morale and help workers contextualise themselves to the 'bigger picture' of the excavation.

The task of creating base plans and site plans has been made a lot more efficient and effective by the use of GIS as a spatial management tool. For placing the various components of the site, such as the trenches, into the local landscape GIS (i.e. *ArcGIS*) is the ideal tool. By digitising a map of the local landscape, using a CAD programme such as *AutoCAD* or *TurboCAD*; and plotting in the co-ordinates of the site trenches and other elements a base map can be created (Conolly & Lake 2006: 77-86). The individual single-context plans are then digitised and entered as individual layers in the GIS which can be switched on or off as required. However, if using direct digital capture equipment, such as a total station or DGPS, ArcSurvey packages extend GIS functionality to data collection, so that the digital data can be viewed and annotated in real-time on a laptop computer (Conolly & Lake 2006: 37). Entering written context and artefactual information into a related database, and digitising section drawings allows for a more holistic view of the archaeological data. Being able to quickly visualise the spatial data patterns soon after their collection facilitates the reflexive approach to archaeology, making data collection a more iterative process allowing hypotheses about data patterns and relationships to be explored quicker and more efficiently (Conolly & Lake 2006: 37).

METHODS OF DRAWING

Many planning methods have already been discussed in the section on measuring and surveying. However, two more methods are worthy of mention: the use of a drawing or planning frame, and targets. The planning frame is a metre-square wooden frame, sometimes with four legs, which is sub-divided into 20 cm squares (10 cm squares may also be used) by means of nylon string, thus dividing the planning frame into 25 segments. The strings can be attached to the frame by means of staples or nails, and the frame itself should be painted with red and white 20 cm stripes to aid in the distinguishing of the grid squares. The planning frame must be laid horizontally on the ground prior to use. If the frame has fixed legs, then rocks may be used to prop up the uneven legs until the planning frame is level (use a spirit level to ensure the frame is perfectly flat). A more efficient method is to have adjustable legs on the frame with a system of bolts and butterfly nuts, or metal legs with horizontal holes (see below). The legs should be tipped with rubber so as not to damage the archaeology (see **Fig. 138**).

At a scale of 1:20, a 1 cm square on the paper equals one of the 20 cm squares viewed through the planning frame (see **Fig. 139**). It may help to lightly outline the planning frame on your drawing, and to mark out the 1 cm points with dots. The drawing is done by eye, viewing through each of the 20 cm squares and replicating what is seen onto the paper. The head of the draughtsperson must be vertically above the square that they are drawing, using a plumb bob if necessary. It is easier to draw the outline of the larger objects first, such as the outline of the context, grave cut or large stones.

If the ground is too steep for a planning frame, the 20 cm grid can be laid out directly on the ground using string and nails. This method can cover as great an area as wished, be it a whole context or a feature. The method of drawing remains the same.

Figure 138: The adjustable planning frame.

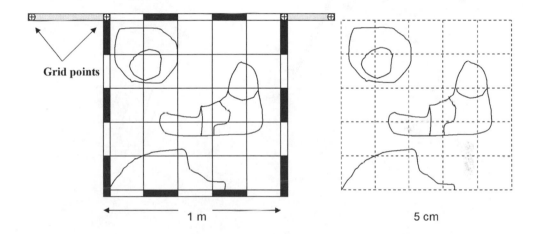

Grid points

1 m   5 cm

Figure 139: The planning frame.

In order to locate the plans drawn with a planning frame to the site grid, locate your nearest grid peg and measure down to the four corners of your drawing frame (in the same manner as locating a baseline used for off-setting to the grid coordinates), then transfer these coordinates to the plan. If you are planning a large context or feature, lay a baseline with a 30 m tape, marking its coordinates on the plan, and then move the planning frame along the 30 m tape one metre at a time.

If drawing intricate deposits such as multiple burials, the target method is a very efficient method to enable quick, accurate drawings of the feature. Initially, a temporary baseline and meridian line must be established around the feature, and these lines must be tied into the grid coordinates. Before the planning, all artefacts (etc.) must be numbered. This is done by applying paraloid and writing on it with India ink (this can be removed later, using acetone). A series of plans at a scale of 1:5 can then be drawn, one plan for each stage of the work, with the numbers of all the fragments entered on the plans. They are plotted by the triangulation method, taking measurements by tape and plumb bob from points on the baseline and meridian line. In addition to the plans, working photographs must be taken at each stage, including in the pictures small 'targets' which are placed on the freshly trowelled surfaces (see **Fig. 164**). The positions of the targets are also plotted on the working plans, and their heights determined by levelling. This makes it possible to match up plans and photographs, and to rectify the photographs using computer graphics techniques so that they fit the plans exactly and can be used to enhance the detail in the final drawings. Isometric drawings of the feature can also be created, allowing further detailed analysis of the feature. To facilitate this recording method, the excavation must be carried out in a series of horizontal 5 cm spits, going from the highest point of the context down to the lowest. This simple type of photogrammetry is a good method to use to help understand and record complex features; both digital and 35 mm photographs should be taken of the various spits.

Figure 140: Drawing with a drawing frame (photograph F. A. Hassan).

Drawing Conventions and Keys

The drawing conventions listed below are some of the most common ones used, and have been adapted from Westman (1994: 11-12) and Hawker (1999: 34-36). If an archaeological deposit is encountered that is not covered by one of the conventional symbols, invent one in consultation with the site supervisor. As long as a key explains all the conventions used, and they do not detract from the clarity of the drawing, then they are acceptable. The plans and sections should be as clear and simple as possible; colour should never be used as this makes them harder to reproduce and may blur the clarity of the drawing.

388

Plans

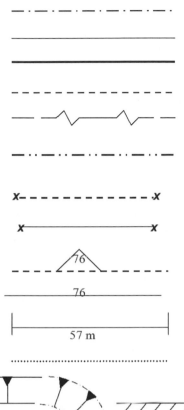

Limit of excavation.

Extent of context.

Emphasised extent of context.

Edge of context uncertain # 1

Edge of context uncertain within break of solid line # 2

Limits of later intrusion into context or feature, i.e. truncation.

Line of section showing position of nails # 1

Line of section showing position of nails # 2

Section line, labelled on side that the section is drawn # 1

Section line, labelled on side that the section is drawn # 2

Break in line, used to indicate that the two points on the line are farther apart than they are shown on the plan, with actual distance shown.

Break of slope.

The edge of layer 79 cut away obliquely.

Hachure used to denote extent of slope. The stalks go all the way to the bottom of the slope. Spaced far apart – gentle slope, close together – steep slope.

Hachure used when break of slope is unclear or for very gentle slope.

Hachure used to indicate concealed slope.

Gentle slope. The hachures run from top to bottom of the slope, as far as it can be determined.

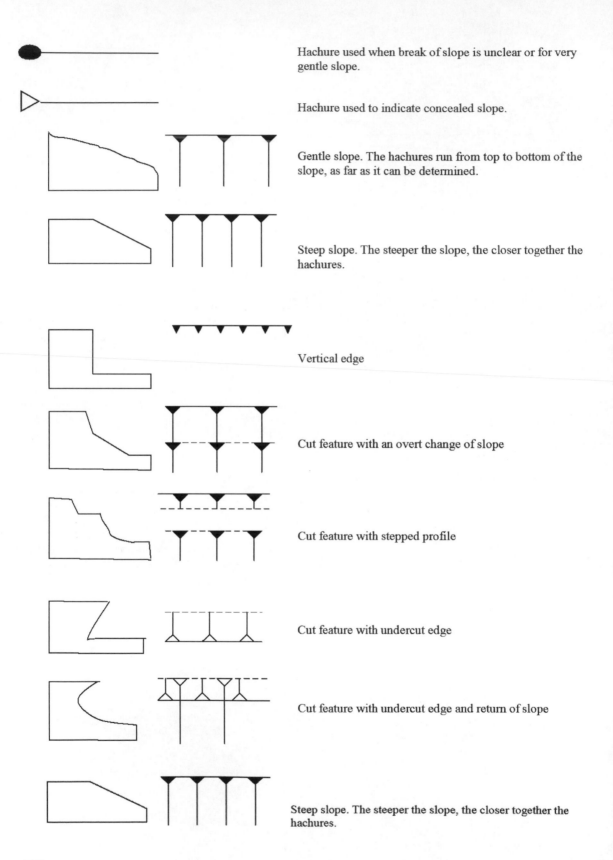

Hachure used when break of slope is unclear or for very gentle slope.

Hachure used to indicate concealed slope.

Gentle slope. The hachures run from top to bottom of the slope, as far as it can be determined.

Steep slope. The steeper the slope, the closer together the hachures.

Vertical edge

Cut feature with an overt change of slope

Cut feature with stepped profile

Cut feature with undercut edge

Cut feature with undercut edge and return of slope

Steep slope. The steeper the slope, the closer together the hachures.

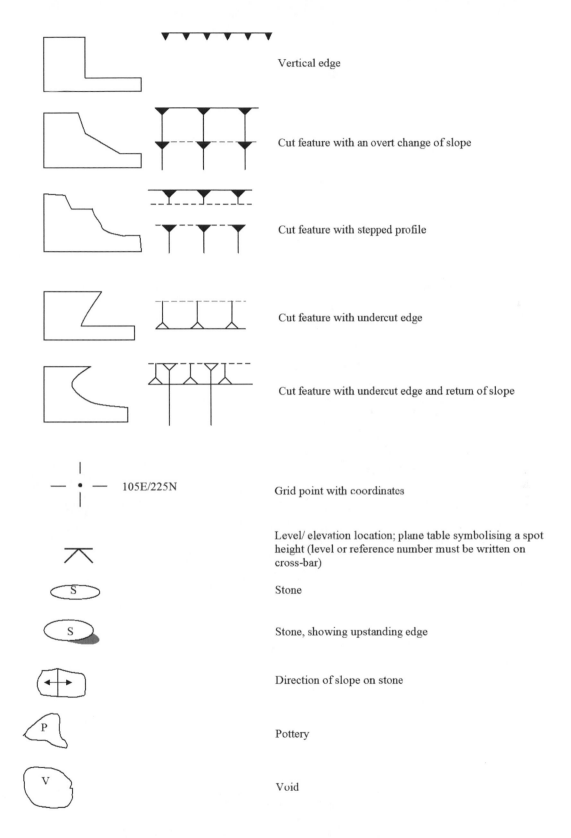

Vertical edge

Cut feature with an overt change of slope

Cut feature with stepped profile

Cut feature with undercut edge

Cut feature with undercut edge and return of slope

105E/225N — Grid point with coordinates

Level/ elevation location; plane table symbolising a spot height (level or reference number must be written on cross-bar)

Stone

Stone, showing upstanding edge

Direction of slope on stone

Pottery

Void

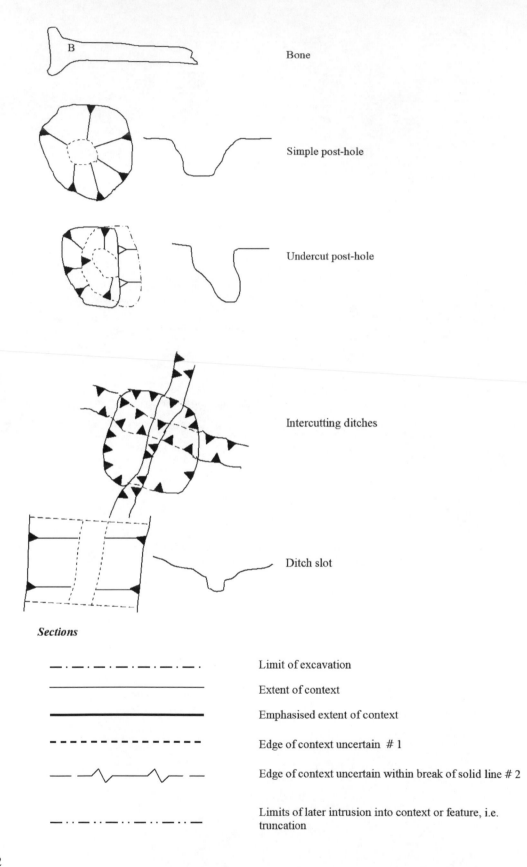

Bone

Simple post-hole

Undercut post-hole

Intercutting ditches

Ditch slot

Sections

— · — · — · — · — · — · — · — ·   Limit of excavation

——————————————   Extent of context

━━━━━━━━━━━━━━━   Emphasised extent of context

- - - - - - - - - - - - - - - - - - -   Edge of context uncertain # 1

— — ⋏⋀⋁⋀⋁⋀ — —   Edge of context uncertain within break of solid line # 2

— · · — · · — · · — · · — · ·   Limits of later intrusion into context or feature, i.e. truncation

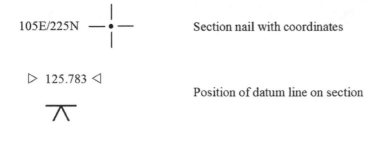 Section nail with coordinates

▷ 125.783 ◁   Position of datum line on section

Labelling Conventions for Different Types of Contexts

1069   or [1069]   Cut number

(57)   or (57)   Fill, layer or other deposit number

⟨2⟩   Artefact number

⟨9⟩   Sample number

<129> or 129̂   Structure number

\1157/   Grave number

{269}   Feature number

Symbols Representing Common Deposit Types

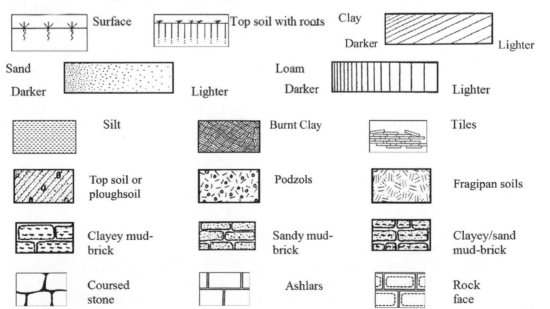

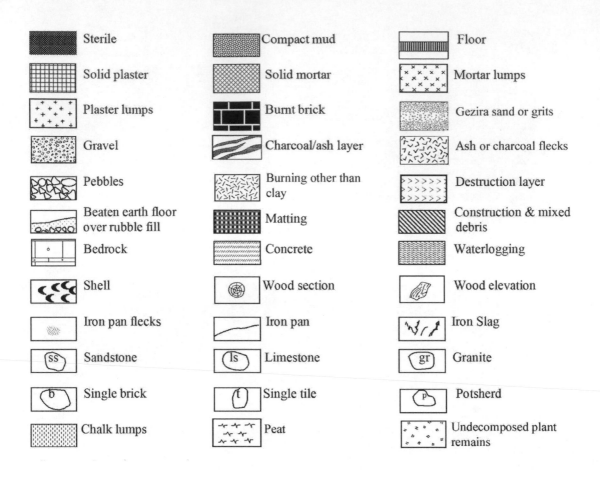

Sterile		Compact mud		Floor
Solid plaster		Solid mortar		Mortar lumps
Plaster lumps		Burnt brick		Gezira sand or grits
Gravel		Charcoal/ash layer		Ash or charcoal flecks
Pebbles		Burning other than clay		Destruction layer
Beaten earth floor over rubble fill		Matting		Construction & mixed debris
Bedrock		Concrete		Waterlogging
Shell		Wood section		Wood elevation
Iron pan flecks		Iron pan		Iron Slag
Sandstone		Limestone		Granite
Single brick		Single tile		Potsherd
Chalk lumps		Peat		Undecomposed plant remains

Table 37: Drawing conventions.

SECTIONS, PROFILES AND ELEVATIONS

Sections

Section drawing involves the graphical recording of the various contexts and features exposed in the vertical face of baulks or half sections. Sections provide the archaeologist with a view of the vertical record of the site's stratigraphic sequence, and - like plans - all sections must be surjective, covering the entire vertical profile. However, because sections cannot show the full extent of the various contexts, they can be misleading, and consequently must be compared with the plans to fully understand the site's stratigraphic sequence (Westman 1994: 11). Sections should be drawn at a scale of 1:10 to show the intricate detail of the layers.

The excavation approach used will determine the number of baulks within an area of operation. The minimum amount of baulks is four, the primary baulks. However, if using open-area excavation, it is sometimes advisable to have running sections across the site, either cutting areas of complex stratification or aligned to the four cardinal points of the compass, a north–south section and an east–west section (see below). Sections or half-sections should be drawn of features to elucidate the relationship of the different contexts (Roskams 2001: 147). If using the box-grid approach, there will be many secondary baulks dividing the individual excavation units, as well as the primary baulks around the edges of the area of operation. These secondary baulks are usually drawn using cumulative section drawings, as they are frequently removed to prevent them becoming towering structures that may endanger archaeologists working in the excavation units.

The complexity of the site's stratification dictates when to draw sections. Although primary baulks may become very tall, they should be drawn at regular intervals before they get too deep to easily reach or the shoring covers them up. They can always be added-to later as the need arises. They must be sprayed with water to help interpretation, as this brings out subtle colour differences and the differential drying can help elucidate layer boundaries. A general rule is that sections should be drawn when you have fully excavated a particularly distinctive context or stratum, so that it can be related to what preceded it (Dever & Darrel Lance 1978: 166).

Before a section drawing is made, the baulk must be cleaned up and made even by use of a trowel and a brush. The trimming of baulks is a routine job that must be carried out after the removal of each context or stratum. All baulks must be vertical and all corners must be square, and the surface must be cleaned from top to bottom. The baulks are then ready to be read. If a geoarchaeologist is on site, they may want to draw all the baulks themselves; however, as it is best for two people to draw sections – one to measure, and the other to draw – they should be assisted by an archaeologist. On rural and single-occupation sites, the stratigraphic sequence may be quite straightforward and easy to read, whereas on highly stratified urban and *tell* sites the sequence can be very complex, involving a discussion between the principal investigator, geoarchaeologist, site supervisor and area supervisors. If a section is drawn simply 'as dug' in the horizontal plane, with no further interpretation, this can perpetuate stratigraphic errors (Dever & Darrel Lance 1978: 166). Therefore, a second or third opinion from experienced stratigraphers who have no vested interest in defending a context 'as dug' in the horizontal plane can offer fresh insights (Dever & Darrel Lance 1978: 166). The sections should only be drawn after a multi-party consensus has been reached.

Sections should be drawn in a clockwise direction, with the north section being drawn first, the east second, and so on. The section should be placed at the top, in the centre of the sheet of draughting film. All sections **must** be labelled according to their location within the excavation unit, even giving a sketch of the unit showing the section drawn and a north arrow, to avoid confusion between north and north-facing section, etc (see **Figs. 141** and **143**). A north section therefore will depict the stratigraphy encountered at the north end of the excavation unit, whilst a south section will depict the stratigraphy at the south end of the unit.

Every section, profile or elevation **must** include:

a. The site code and site sub-division reference number.

b. The date when the section was drawn.

c. The scale.

d. The drawing number.

e. The drawing's name (e.g. North Section square 96).

f. Cardinal points.

g. Context and feature numbers.

h.   Coordinates (taken either from the corners of the area shown in plan or from the offset line).

i.   The level of the datum line.

j.   Levels (with figure placed on a surveying table or benchmark symbol).

k.   Name of draughtsperson.

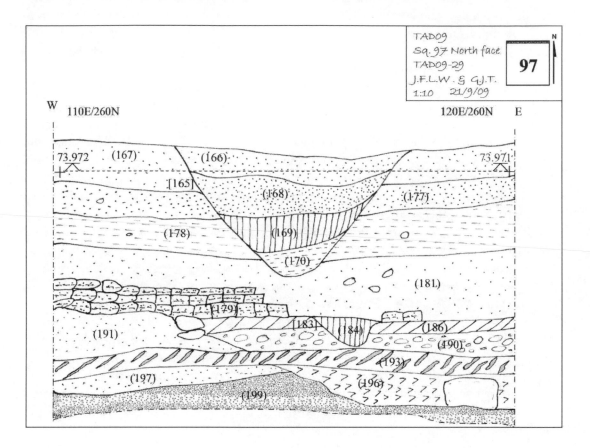

Figure 141: Section drawing.

The equipment needed to draw sections includes a builder's line (or nylon string), two 6-inch masonry nails, a plumb bob, a 30 m fibron tape, a 5 m metal hand-held tape and bulldog clips. Place the draughting film on the drawing board covered with graph paper, writing the required information on it. The masonry nails must be placed at either end of the section, 30 to 50 cm below the surface. Ideally, these nails should be at a round level above site datum (e.g. 80.000 m). Both nails must be levelled in and plotted on the section drawing with the reduced levels written beside them. The builder's line must be tied taut between the nails, and marked on the section drawing with a dotted line; this is termed the datum line. The 30 m fibron tape should then be attached to the nails with bulldog clips or clothes pegs; if necessary additional nails should be placed just under the datum line to support the tape at various points. The tape must start from the corner of the actual baulk, not the nail, which is usually placed slightly in from the corner to prevent the baulk collapsing. To achieve this drop a plumb bob down and line it up with the bottom corner of the baulk.

Before the section is drawn, the draughtsperson should place him/herself at a distance where they can see the whole baulk, with the centre at eye-level. They should then direct the measurer to measure the top, bottom, then sides of the section before filling in the detail of the main strata and features, followed by the more complex areas and smaller detail. This is done by measuring along the datum line in units of 10 centimetres, then creating a right-angle with the plumb bob, measure down with the hand-held tape to the top or bottom of each context or feature. Solid lines are used to differentiate the strata, cuts, fills, structural features and their components. Pebbles and boulders are also defined by bold pencil lines; main tip-lines and other fine detail should be put in with fainter lines (Adkins & Adkins 1989: 81).

It may take some time to learn the skill required, but this experience can be gained by assisting an experienced stratigrapher. Light flowing lines must be used to join up the dots, emulating the actual lines on the section; if a relationship is not clear, then dotted lines should be used. How much detail should be shown depends on the period and type of site, but usually all large potsherds, stones, bricks, and lumps of charcoal are plotted.

Layers, cuts and fills can be further differentiated by means of a variety of symbols; a Munsell colour number can be used to indicate the colour. If the symbols used are not conventional, then a symbol and shading key must be incorporated. The best section drawings are those that use a combination of symbols and pictorial representations. The section drawing should not be ambiguous, and be as accurate and objective as possible.

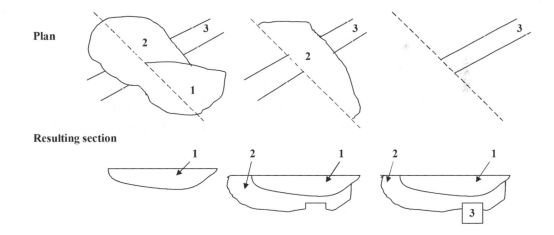

Figure 142: Running sections (after Roskams 2001: 146).

Running and **cumulative sections** are closely related. Cumulative sections are used to draw secondary baulks that are sporadically removed, so the datum line has to be regularly lowered. Therefore after every level of the cumulative section has been drawn, a new datum line for the next level must be marked just above the lower profile line. The new datum line must then be levelled to this new position when ready to draw the next level of the cumulative section. The stage at which the successive sections should be drawn can vary, but it is usually best when a distinctive stratigraphic unit is reached, or a deep or extensive horizon is uncovered (Roskams 2001: 145). Another method is to move down the section line a predetermined distance each time, such as 0.5 m.

Running sections are drawn using two wooden posts hammered into the ground at either end of the section to be drawn. The sections are drawn as the deposits are removed, thus recording the vertical section. A datum line is attached to two nails hammered into the posts at a convenient level; again, a round number is easiest. The datum line is only ever stretched across from post to post when actually drawing the section. As the excavation progresses, the post must be moved down. The new reduced level of the datum line must be marked in the section drawing, before the running section can continue (Hawker 1999: 48; Roskams 2001: 146).

These methods can be adapted to draw horizontally and vertically stepped sections, such as may be encountered in the battered or stepped sides of a deep trench (Hawker 1999: 74).

Plans and sections do not always match exactly as the two drawings record the stratigraphic sequence in different circumstances (Roskams 2001: 149). The drawback of baulk and cumulative sections is that they both cut into the stratigraphic sequence by chance, rather than intent. Therefore, they are highly unlikely to be able to portray the full stratigraphic sequence of the internal part of the feature or excavation unit. Even if these sections do cut features, the section line may be at a very oblique angle, therefore giving a distorted view. Therefore, specific or half sections are now favoured by many archaeologists to answer particular archaeological questions (Roskams 2001: 149). These half sections are placed across intercutting pits, ditches or other features to ascertain their internal configuration (see **Chapter 5**). These section drawings do not portray the whole stratigraphic sequence of an area, just of various features, so a combination of baulk, specific and cumulative sections should be used to build up the stratigraphic sequence along with the plans.

When the section drawings of the various baulks are finished, they can then be aligned by placing them on a light box. The drawings can also be aligned with the plans to check whether the various contexts and features match. The drawings of both sides of all the secondary baulks can be placed on a light box, so a continuous section drawing of the whole site can be built up. Because section drawings and plans portray the stratigraphy in different views, the contexts/strata should be independently numbered, described, and have an individual stratigraphic sequence composed. Abridged context forms should be filled out for these new contexts. The running matrix should be constructed whilst the section is still in view (Roskams 2001: 149). The assigning of the new context numbers can be from the running sequence of the site, possibly suffixed with an 'S'. In the analysis phase of the stratigraphy, it is easier to amalgamate numbers than to split them. Therefore, if a correlation is found between plans and sections which have been recorded separately, rather than them being assumed to be a single entity from the start, a better stratigraphic argument can be formulated.

Profiles

Profiles consist of only the outline of the section; they are drawn exactly the same way as section drawings, but show none of the internal details. As with section drawings, the level of the nails must be shown on the drawing. Profiles are usually used if a feature was excavated before the section was drawn, or used for features that cannot be half sectioned (such as a well) or to show the profile of the ground level (Hawker 1999: 47).

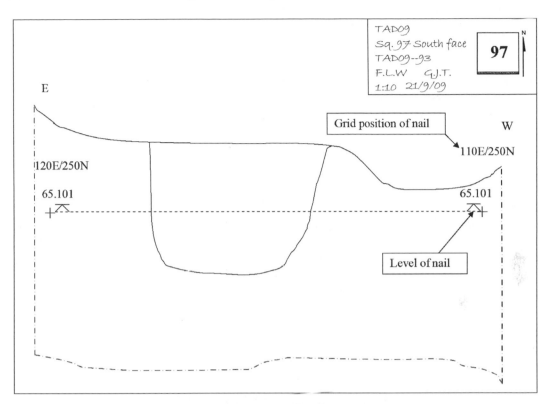

Figure 143: A profile drawing.

Elevations

Elevations are section drawings of standing structures or features, drawn using the same principles as in section drawing. Due to the nature of standing structures, ladders or scaffolding may well be required. As with section drawings, a datum line must be levelled in and perpendicular measurements taken from it, both above and below the line. However, because there may be several layers of plaster and paint on the surface of the wall, these must be differentiated (Hawker 1999: 47-8) using symbols or annotation. Any structural detail - such as rebuilding levels - must be recorded and annotated. A planning frame can also prove useful in drawing elevations.

ARTEFACT DRAWING

Archaeological illustration is a skilled art, often undertaken by highly skilled archaeological illustrators. As objects are often not allowed to be removed from an archaeological site, and definitely not from the country of origin (i.e. Egypt, Greece or Italy), all artefact illustrations have to be completed in the field. The vast amount of artefacts and other objects recovered are often too great for the site illustrator (if one is included in the personnel) to cope with, resulting in other team members drawing the easier finds. Therefore, it is essential that all archaeologists comprehend the basic methods and conventions. Unlike drawing plans and sections, the drawing of artefacts involves representing much finer detail in two-dimensions of a three-dimensional object. As with all other archaeological drawings, colour is only ever shown by conventions, never with actual colours. Two of the essential textbooks are *Drawing Archaeological Finds: A Handbook* and *The Cambridge Manual of Archaeological Illustration*.

Why should objects be drawn? An illustration can convey far more of the aesthetic character of an object, imparting information on the object's exact size, shape, form and method of manufacture, showing the thickness of walls and a number of other components far better than the photographic or written record ever can (Griffiths *et al.* 1991: 1). Drawings have another advantage over photographs in that they are cheaper to reproduce in the final publication. The intricate designs that may occur on objects can also be better portrayed in archaeological illustrations. Due to printing limitations and the nature of the different materials, fabrics and textures of the various artefacts, different conventions have been developed for outlining, in-filling and shading. Usually lines, dots and dashes of various sizes and densities are used, although cross-hatching should be used very sparingly, if at all. Drawings must be both informative and aesthetically pleasing; therefore archaeological illustration is akin to both technical scientific drawing and artistic drawing (Adkins & Adkins 1989).

The following five points are more specific guidelines for drawing of artefacts in the field:

1. The artefact must be drawn with the light source coming from the top left-hand corner of the page. This can be achieved with the use of natural light coming in from a window, a lamp, or can be nominal – imagined. With the light coming at this angle, the top left-hand corner of the object will be lightest, and the bottom right-hand corner darkest.

2. Before commencing drawing, study the artefact, consult with the finds specialist, examine the mode of manufacture, damage, extent of any decoration and any other details. Decisions should then be made as to which details to emphasise to bring out the true character of the object. Decide which is the main view of the object, the way that the artefact is normally used or most easily recognised. Subsequent views - such as plan and sections and any increased scale spotlight of detail – should be shown where necessary.

3. All drawings must be an accurate rendering of the object they represent, showing an understanding of the artefact's component parts. Although the central half-section divide should be a ruled line, all other lines should generally be drawn freehand, including the top and bottom of pottery vessels.

4. The drawing may be the only remaining representation of an artefact and its material and condition, for the artefact may subsequently be lost or degenerate so badly that its true form is lost. Therefore, all drawings should be drawn to publication standard; all drawings of objects that cannot be identified must be published.

5. When publishing drawings the scale at which they are reproduced must be put next to the objects. However, when the drawings are first drawn a 10 cm bar or line scale must be put next to the artefact, so that if they are photocopied the amount of reduction or enlargement will be shown by the size of the scale. When photocopying any drawing made on draughting film always place a sheet of white paper behind to reduce the amount of shadow.

Basic Equipment and Supplies

The basic equipment required for drawing objects in the field includes:

Desk and chair with an angle-poise lamp, T-square, a variety of drawing boards (usually A4, A3 and A2). Technical (Rotring) pens (0·2 – 1·0 mm), scalpel, hatching machine.

Draughting film, scale or graph paper, cartridge paper, acetate, tissue paper.

Wooden pencils with a range of hardness: HB, F, H (for use on cartridge paper), 2H, 3H, 4H (for use on draughting film), clutch pencil with 0·5 mm leads in the same hardness range, pencil sharpener, sandpaper, eraser - soft and fibreglass.

Ruler, masking tape, small sand bag, *Blu-Tack* or white plasticine, a set of spreading compasses with extension bar, French curves, set square, protractor, scissors, scientific magnifying glass.

Profile gauge, sliding and spreading callipers, dividers, engineer's square, radius chart.

Object	Scale drawn at	Scale reduced to for publishing
Pottery vessels	1:1	1:4
Stone vessels	1:1	1:4
Lithics	1:1	2:3
Microliths	2:1	1:1
Small finds	2:1	1:1
Finds	1:1	1:1
Large finds	1:2	1:2 or 1:4

Table 38: Artefact drawing scales for field and publication (after Griffiths *et al.* 1991).

Drawings are usually drawn on draughting film with a pencil then normally traced with a technical pen on a separate sheet of draughting film, remembering that the thinnest line that can be confidentially printed is 0.1 mm, thinner than this and the line will break-up. Therefore, due to reduction of most drawings for publication your lines will have to be proportionally thicker. When inking in:

Plans and sections, 1·0 pens are usually used for drawing the outline of contexts and features, subsequent lines are drawn with a 0·8 or 0·7 pen, no smaller than 0·5.

Small finds (drawn at 1:1) 0·3 for outline, 0·2 for detail.

Larger objects (Reduced for printing to 1:2) 0·4 for outline, 0·3 for detail

Pottery vessels (Reduced for printing to 1:4) 0·7- 0·8 for outline, 0·3 – 0·4 for detail

Conventions also exist for showing surface detail, structure, etc. Major conventions are shown in **Tab. 39**, although this list is not exhaustive. As before, new conventions can be developed where required, so long as they are adequately defined in the key.

Material	In-fill	Comment
Bone, Ivory, Antler	Smooth or polished – line Natural - stipple	Bring out character of bone with shading. Human bones use line and stipple for broken areas.
Basketry	Line showing form of weave	Some line shading to show way reeds were woven.
Faïence	Matt – stipple Glazed – fine line	
Glass	Matt – stipple Polished – fine line	Draw marks of forming, such as those formed by a core, rods, the ribbed effect left by 'mezzaforma' moulds or 'puntil' marks from blowing.
Hair	Line showing form of tresses	Some line shading to show way hair was dressed.
Leather/skin	Stipple	
Lithics	Line	Use curved line to show ripples and facets and stipple for cortex.
Masonry, bricks, tiles	Stipple	
Metal Copper, bronze, brass and lead	Stipple	Show surface as smooth even if corroded. If director wants corrosion shown, use stipple. Incised lines shown in line.
Metal Iron and steel	Line	Lines on metal get closer to show depth and shade. Uneven areas or roughness shown with more random lines. Corrosion and beaten areas shown with differential shading.

Metal Gold and silver	Fine line	Follow shape of object to show shine.
Natural polymers e.g. amber or bees wax.	Matt – stipple Shiny – fine line	
Pottery	Stipple	
Shells	Line	Lines following the natural form of the shell. Stipple on oyster shells.
Slate	Close stippling	
Statuettes, figurines	Stone, terracotta, pottery – stipple Metal – line Wood – wood grain	
Stone	Coarse grained – stipple Polished and fine grained - line	
Stone vessels	Line	
Textiles	Line showing form of weave	Some line shading to show way thread was spun.
Wood	Line	Follow direction of the wood grain. Always do a section view.

Table 39: Artefact illustration conventions.

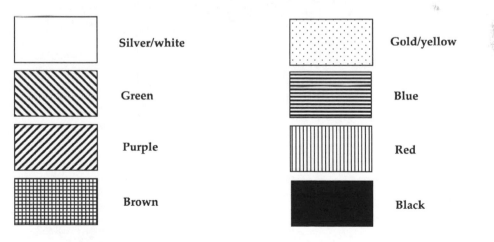

Table 40: Colour conventions for finds other than pottery.

Coins are usually photographed rather than drawn, and are usually referenced to a coin catalogue. Pottery and other hollow spherical, cylindrical and conical vessels are drawn using a system of orthographic projection, showing the elevation, plan and section (Griffiths *et al.* 1991: 56). The elevation or profile is the main view as the vessel is viewed straight on. The plan is the aerial view and the section is used for spouts, handles and for showing the thickness of vessel walls. The profile is split in two, with the section and inside view of the vessel shown on the left and the outside elevation on the right. On wheel-thrown pottery vessels the body section is shown as filled-in (solid black) whereas on hand-made vessels the body section is shown as white or un-filled in. Applied or added parts of the vessel, such as handles and spouts, are shown with close fine hatching (0·2.5) at 45° sloping from the bottom left to the top right. Therefore, if a body is wheel-thrown with applied handles and spout, then two different conventions are used to show the section. Handles are shown on the right, spouts on the left, unless there is more than one in which case they are shown where they occur. Stone vessel body sections are again shown on the left, but the section is shown with 45° hatching drawn in 0·7 or 0·8, and well spaced (see **Fig. 144**). The details of the inside of the vessel, such as rill marks, wheel thrown lines and inclusions in the actual pottery, such as shell, chaff, etc., should also shown. The wheel-thrown lines (rill marks) on Roman and later pottery may be drawn with ruled lines, while the lines on Pharaonic pottery are always drawn by hand.

The main view should be shown on the left, profile or back view on the right. Superior views are always shown on top, and inferior views on the bottom; handle sections are shown next to the handle, and with sections of circular objects such as rings, the section is shown inside the artefact. To show these different views, the object is always turned clockwise through 90°. Therefore, if three elevations of an object are being shown, the back view is on the left, the side view in the centre facing right and the front view on the right. Small lines connect the various views of the artefact, covering the middle third of the gap between the views.

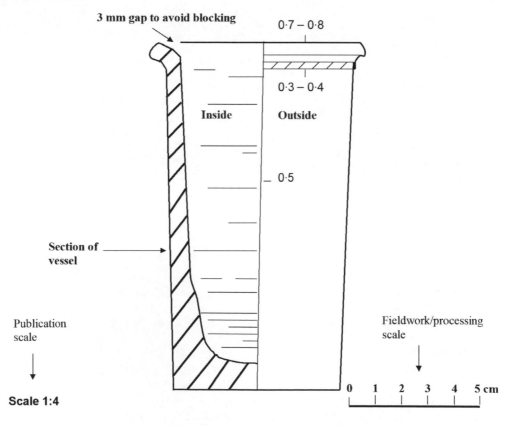

Figure 144: Stone vessel drawing conventions.

Ceramics and stone vessels are only drawn if they cannot be matched with vessels in the site corpus. To this end it is advisable to keep a photocopy of the various types of pottery and stone vessels on record cards or in a corpus reference book, which should also include written information on their fabric, temper, inclusions, decoration and typology sequence number. Each page of the corpus reference book (one book for pottery vessels, another for stone) should be given a number from 1 onwards, and then the vessels should be catalogued according to their fabric type or ware, then form, and then arranged in numerical order. Therefore, if a new vessel matches one of the vessels in the corpus reference book, it will only be necessary to record its typology number and dimensions (Griffiths *et al.* 1991: 56). However, if typology sequences are already available, then the existing typology number should be used along with the site corpus number.

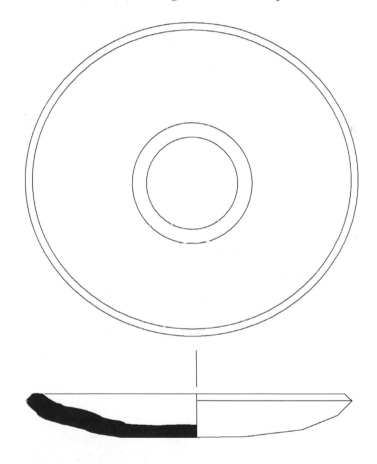

Scale 1:4

Figure 145: Plan and elevation, with half-section, of a pottery bowl.

Methods of Drawing the Artefacts

The easiest method of drawing an artefact is to trace around its outline. The object must be secured to the draughting film or cartridge paper with *Blu-Tack* or white plasticine, or if very friable, placed on a cardboard stand or crumpled acid-free tissue paper or just held in position by hand. It is preferable to use a clutch pencil, which must be held vertical

405

touching the side of the artefact with the right eye of the illustrator directly above it, moving as the pencil moves. If the pencil is not held straight, the actual outline of the artefact can be under- or overcut. The outline of the object should be checked against the actual object and the measurements taken with callipers. The internal detail of the outside of the artefact should then be measured-in; this can be done using dividers and a set square, callipers, or by tracing the detail on acetate. To trace the detail, place a square frame around the artefact, then place a sheet of glass over the top and tape a sheet of acetate to it with masking tape. The internal detail of the artefact can then be easily traced. These internal lines should be checked using callipers, remembering to take the measurements in the horizontal plane (Burke & Smith 2004: 294). This tracing can then be transferred to the drawing by placing both drawings on a light box or holding them up to the light. The shading and in-filling should then be done by eye, not forgetting that the light always comes from the top left-hand of the paper. When shading with a pencil, normal shading may be used; however, when inking-in, stipple or line must be used.

Holes that pass right through or partially through an object are shown as solid lines in section, unless the hole still has a rivet, nail or other obstruction still in it. In these cases, or if the depth is uncertain, the line of the hole is shown as a dotted line.

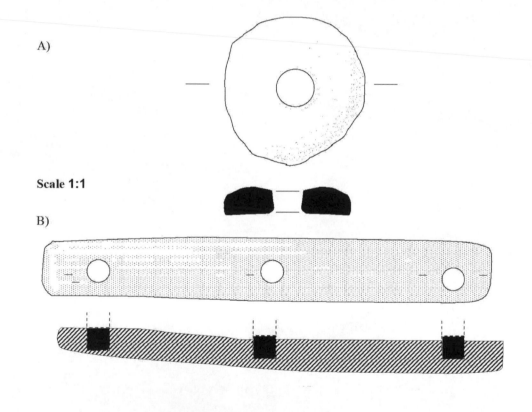

Figure 146: A) Spindle-whorl B) Plaque.

Some objects need to be either reduced or enlarged in scale. First draw the artefact at 1:1 on graph paper, and project a series of points at either double or half the distance of the original. This is done by setting up a horizontal and vertical baseline, and plotting points along these baselines (**Fig. 147**). If graph paper is not available, radiating points can be plotted from the point of the grid emanation (**Fig. 148**). As well as marking the key points (corners and changes of outline), as many other points as wished can be taken. Once drawn, check measurement accuracy with dividers against the actual object, and then erase the original 1:1 drawing.

Some objects may be too large to draw around, such as amphorae or coffins. In these situations make baselines around the actual artefact using tape measures, making sure that the tapes are at right-angles to each other (**Fig. 149**). These baselines must then be scaled down to 1:2, 1:4 or 1:10 as necessary, and drawn on the graph paper. Then use the off-setting method to take measurements along the vertical and horizontal axes and plot the scaled-down image onto the graph paper. Once the drawing is completed on the graph paper, it must be traced onto draughting film or cartridge paper.

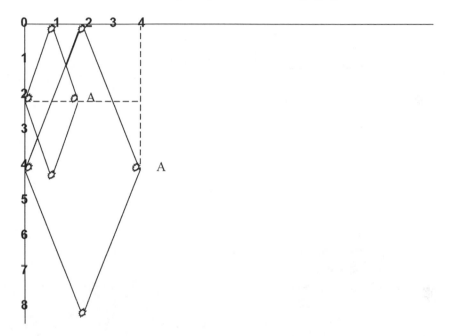

Figure 147: The double axis method of enlargement or reduction (after Griffiths *et al.* 1991: 27).

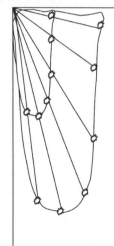

Figure 148: The radial method of enlargement or reduction (after Griffiths *et al.* 1991: 27).

407

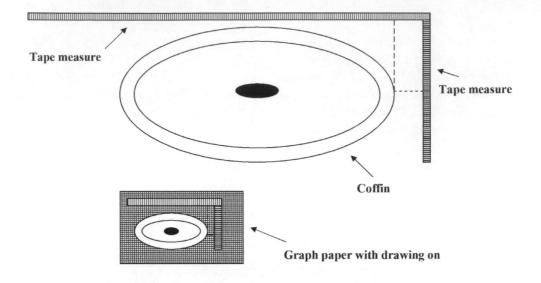

Figure 149: The off-set method of drawing artefacts.

Drawing pottery and stone vessel sherds requires a rim and base diameter chart (often termed a radius chart, see **Fig. 151**). This can be made by drawing concentric circles with a pair of compasses with pen attachment, from 4 cm - 40 cm diameter (larger if necessary), on a piece of paper or card. This should then be laminated or covered with self-adhesive clear plastic. Each circle should be 5 mm apart. To find the estimated vessel equivalents (EVES), lines must be drawn using a protractor at every 36°, marking them 0% to 100% (see **Appendix 6**). The chart can then be used to find out the rim, base and maximum diameter, as well as percentage of vessel that the sherd represents (Griffiths *et al.* 1991: 51-2).

Radius cards can also be made to measure potsherd diameters, although profile gauges can be used for this, as well as attaining profiles of pots and other artefacts. Callipers must be used to measure the thickness of - and distance between - vessel walls. Diagnostic sherds, such as rim or base sherds, the main type of sherds drawn, can be used to make a reconstruction (providing that the vessel shape is known, see **Fig. 150**). To measure potsherds on a radius chart, place the rim flat, and when no light can be seen between the rim and chart, it is at the correct angle/stance. Read off the circle measurement that best fits the curvature of the potsherd to find the rim/base diameter.

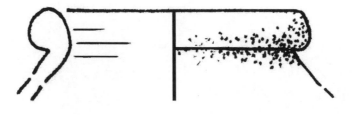

Figure 150: Drawing of a potsherd (rim).

408

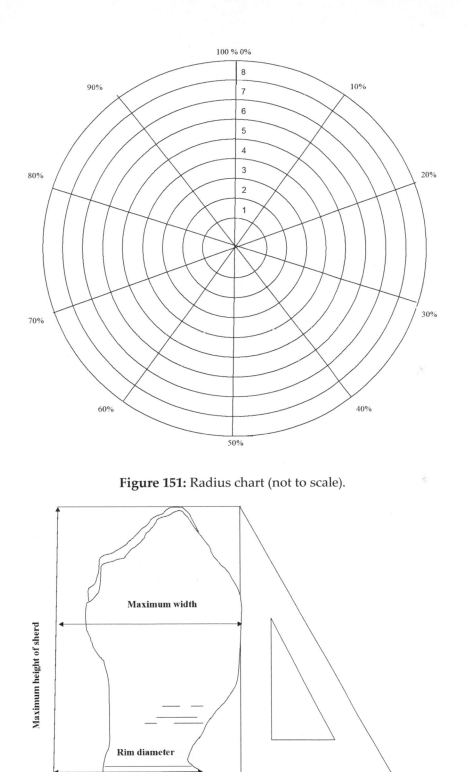

Figure 151: Radius chart (not to scale).

Figure 152: Measuring a potsherd on a radius chart with two set squares (after Griffiths *et al.* 1991: 57).

To draw a whole vessel, mark out a framework (**Fig. 153**), securing the vessel with *Blu-Tack* or little bags of sand. Then place the pot on its side and use the engineer's square or set square with weighted box attached to project down from the sides of the vessel, then plot the lines using a pencil. A special engineer's square with a pencil attached can be bought or made, as shown in **figure 154**. The thickness of the vessel's walls (as measured with the callipers) must then be drawn on the left-hand side of the drawing of the vessel (**Figs. 144-145**) (Griffiths *et al.* 1991: 60). Alternatively, use a profile gauge to make an indentation of the vessel's profile, and then draw around this impression. The hatching is best done using a T-square and a 45° set square to create equidistant lines. If a T-square is not available, then a ruler can be substituted.

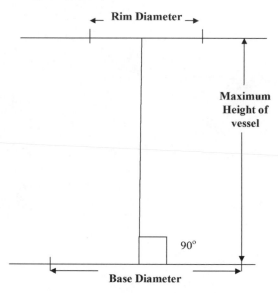

Figure 153: A framework of measurements in which to draw your vessel (after Griffiths *et al.* 1999: 60).

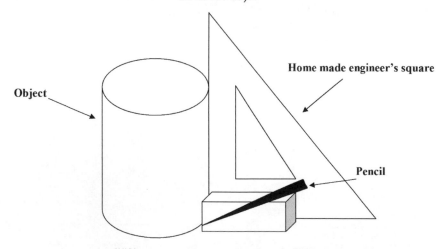

Figure 154: An engineer's square constructed with a set square, piece of wood and a pencil.

In cases of severely damaged or friable objects it is often necessary to carry out a measured scale drawing of the artefact *in situ*. If the object is severely crushed and misshapen, it is still worthwhile making a drawing and/or a profile of the vessel. *In situ* drawings can be an aid to the conservator in restoring objects, as well as forming part of the site's reference collection.

Show pot decoration in full, as though the pattern were rolled out from the pot, like a cylinder seal impression. The vessel is drawn as usual, with the inside on the left and the outside on the right, but instead of stopping at the edge of the vessel the design is rolled out to the right-hand side of the vessel (**Fig. 155**). The rolling out of the design will have the effect of 'flattening' it (compared to the 'rounded' view of how it is viewed on the vessel) where the scene is distorted and the lines at the edge of the vessel appear closer together. If the design protrudes from the vessel's surface, it may be possible to take a rubbing. Otherwise, tracing paper should be tightly wrapped around the vessel, taped at the edges with making tape, allowing the design to be traced. This can then be traced back onto your drawing of the vessel. To check the drawing is correct, take measurements at 5 mm intervals around the vessel with dividers, projecting down from the vessel to the drawing either by eye or using an engineer's square (Griffiths *et al.* 1991: 76).

Figure 155: Rollout drawing of decoration on a D-class Gerzean painted pottery vessel.

When drawing incised potmarks, potter's marks and other signs on pottery or other objects including seals and labels it is essential that the signs are accurately portrayed so that the palaeography can be studied. The epigraphic conventions for the drawing of these marks have recently been established (Bréand 2005; Jucha 2008; Tassie *et al.* 2008; Wodzińska In press). The signs must be drawn at a scale of 1:1 with the outside edge of the incised decoration followed using a 0.2 pen, with the depth of the incisions indicated with shading (see **Fig. 156**). Avoided using a single thick black line (unless the signs are painted) as it obfuscates the order in which the lines were applied, and never idealise the signs. The drawing of the vessel on which these marks are placed must show their exact position. A corpus of potmarks must also be made; this should comprise the last section of the pottery corpus reference book. Record the vessel's artefact and provenience number, the typology number, site code and placement of the potmark on the vessel.

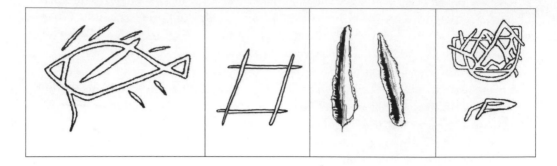

Figure 156: Conventions used for drawing potmarks, seals and other incised symbols on artefacts (not to scale), (drawn by Bram Calcoen and Anna Wodzińska).

The drawing of stone tools is a specialist art within archaeological illustration (Matingell & Saville 1988). In order to produce passable drawings of a chipped stone artefact, one should draw the ventral outline first by tracing around the outline of the tool, then establish a central axis line and trace a reversed drawing for the dorsal view. To ensure that the drawing is a correct representation, check the measurements with dividers and define the edge details if needed. The facets should then be measured in using the dividers and set square method (or by eye) and measuring-in with the dividers. The profile, proximal and distal views must then be drawn by projecting horizontal and vertical lines. There is a slight difference between the European and American system in the orientation of tools, with all lithics shown with the distal end upwards (see **Fig. 113**), this is also true in the American system, except for unmodified detached pieces that are shown with the proximal end upwards (Andrefsky 1998: 20). The direction of blow, angle and depth of the facet must all be relayed with the shading of the tools and other symbols (see **Tab. 41**); therefore, the studying of the tool is essential if an accurate representation is to be made.

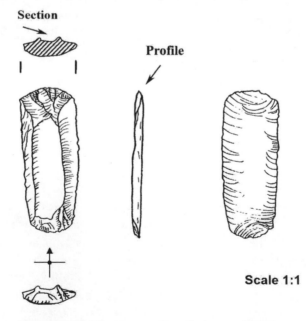

Figure 157: The conventional views of lithics.

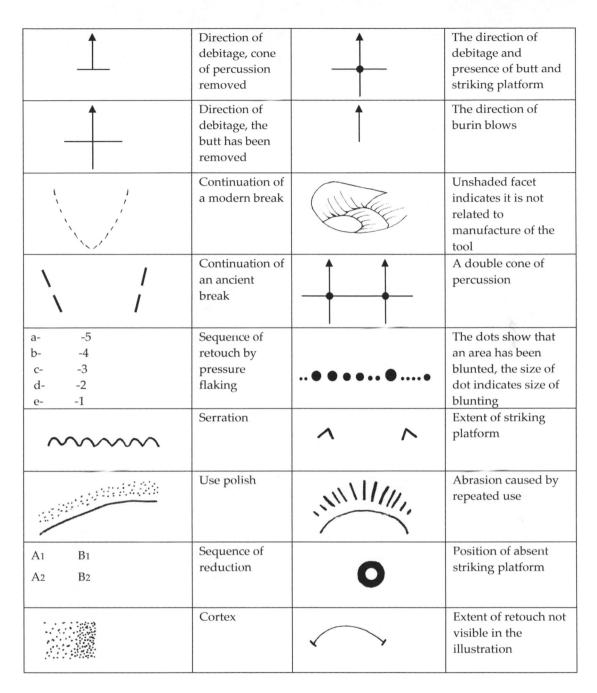

	Direction of debitage, cone of percussion removed		The direction of debitage and presence of butt and striking platform
	Direction of debitage, the butt has been removed		The direction of burin blows
	Continuation of a modern break		Unshaded facet indicates it is not related to manufacture of the tool
	Continuation of an ancient break		A double cone of percussion
a- -5 b- -4 c- -3 d- -2 e- -1	Sequence of retouch by pressure flaking		The dots show that an area has been blunted, the size of dot indicates size of blunting
	Serration		Extent of striking platform
	Use polish		Abrasion caused by repeated use
A_1 B_1 A_2 B_2	Sequence of reduction		Position of absent striking platform
	Cortex		Extent of retouch not visible in the illustration

Table 41: Symbols for use in lithic drawing (after Griffiths *et al.* 1991: 108-9).

EPIGRAPHY AND PALAEOGRAPHY

Epigraphy is the study and copying of inscriptions, scenes and general decoration in their architectural context (Dorman 2008: 77-80). Although epigraphic drawings usually record decoration on monumental structures, the technique is also applied to recording details on inscribed artefacts (i.e. ceremonial palettes), rock inscriptions and paintings/drawings. Palaeography is the study of writing and documentation, especially writing styles, types,

413

application and development, and is therefore closely linked to epigraphy. Egyptian epigraphy is not solely concerned with the recording of texts; as most hieroglyphic texts are embedded in a scene, the two being complementary halves of the whole that are designed to be read together (Bell 1987: 51). Therefore, knowledge of Egyptian hieroglyphs and iconography are essential before attempting any epigraphic work. The use of epigraphy developed not only to record Egyptian inscriptions and scenes, but those of Classical Greece, Rome and Mesopotamia (Iraq). The techniques are now widely used to record monumental inscriptions around the world, such as Aztec, Mayan and Inca in the Americas, and Indian and Chinese in Asia. However, when recording these inscriptions and scenes knowledge of the culture's writing and iconography is vital to produce accurate reproductions.

Studying the works of some of the past and current masters will be of great help, as will knowledge of some of the techniques used in the past. Four of the best Egyptological works to study are Jan Assmann's *Das Grab des Basa (Nr. 389) in der thebanischen Nekropole*, Dows Dunhan and William Kelly Simpson's *The Mastaba of Queen Meresankh III*, Hermann Junker and Eric Winter *Das Geburtshaus des Tempels der Isis in Philä* and the Oriental Institute of the University of Chicago's *Medinet Habu I-VIII.* Although studying some of these works will help, they cannot replace experience, practical knowledge, imagination, problem solving flair and artistic talent. The methodologies given below are a guideline; if another technique can be developed to fit the problem, then it should be used.

One of the earliest epigraphic missions (and still one of the most impressive achievements within the world of Egyptology) was Karl Richard Lepsius' *Denkmaeler aus Aegypten und Aethiopien.* Lepsius and his team stayed in Egypt for three years, from 1842, surveying and recording sites from Alexandria in the Mediterranean coast to Sennar on the Blue Nile. Twelve enormous folios were produced between 1849 and 1859, containing a total of 894 plates, an accomplishment unsurpassed in the field of Egyptology if not world archaeology. Some of the most beautiful coloured epigraphic work was done by Howard Carter, Nina and Norman de Garis Davies in the Theban Necropolis and Amice Calverly and Myrtle Broome at the Temple of Sety I, Abydos. These works are still masterful colour copies of the walls they portray and their methods are still in use today (Pinch-Brock 2000). Sometimes large teams of specialists are employed in epigraphic work, including drawing technicians, Egyptologists, photographers, architects and conservators. The *Epigraphic and Architectural Survey of the Oriental Institute of the University of Chicago*, established by J. H. Breasted in 1924, employs a vast array of specialists, and offers its facilities and expertise to any professional mission doing epigraphic work.

Many inscriptions and decorations are under threat of destruction from various sources - including salt efflorescence, water damage and looting – so accurate copies are essential as these may be the only records of the original in years to come (Brand 2001). If they are to stand as substitutes, they must be sufficiently detailed so as to not require recourse to the original (Bell 1987: 44). The drawings should render every significant detail of broken, weathered, discoloured and fragmentary surfaces, as well as all surviving detail of the artist's original composition. However, what is omitted by the epigrapher is also very important, therefore it is essential to discern what is extraneous damage, and what has been intentionally inflicted due to context or content (Dorman 2008: 93). Areas of active salt efflorescence, natural abrasion or weathering, discolouration (and dressing marks if not relevant to the purpose of the epigraphy) are not usually areas of human intervention, and if they do not affect the original decoration can be omitted from the final copy for the sake of clarity, but recorded in the original copying (Dorman 2008: 93). The internal details of areas of missing plaster or relief are not normally reproduced either, but the larger missing areas are indicted by a solid line around the areas of plaster or relief that are present. The remains of the depictions grid and sketch lines for the inscription should all be included (Polz 1987: 134-8). It is important to render not only the text but the adjoining decorative and architectural context. "The structural context may be indicated by including the presence of block lines and stone courses on walls, levels of floors and ceilings, and the corners of rooms" (Dorman 2008: 91). The recording of ancient and modern graffiti placed on ancient decorated surface is an area of contention, with some scholars seeing it as a vital part of the monuments biography and others as wanton vandalism. One way to record this graffiti is as an overlay, both in the copying and reproduction.

Figure 158: A section of the desert hunt from Sahure's mortuary temple, Abusir showing both reconstruction of some areas, particularly the kings legs, and the delineation of those areas of decoration that are present (after Borchardt 1913: Pl. 17).

It is important to make a dossier of all old photographs of the decoration, and any earlier published and unpublished studies. The photographs can help identify recently damaged areas, and can help guide the artist, whereas earlier epigraphic work shows what the previous epigrapher saw (or thought they saw). In the past much of the copying

415

was done with paper squeezes or impressions, although these are never used now as they can damage fragile wall surfaces (Caminos 1976). If a monument or rock inscription has never been studied before, then the epigrapher's field library should include a grammar, dictionary and a palaeography (Caminos 1976: 19). All copying must be done in front of the decorated surface and should be checked by another person.

Direct Tracing

One of the simplest methods of making an accurate one-to-one drawn record of decoration is by tracing directly on to clear sheets of acetate or draughting film. This method produces as much detail as can easily be seen. This technique works best on flat surfaces, such as painted plaster or where the relief is cut in sunk relief and the acetate can lie smooth against the surface Care must be taken if the decoration is in a fragmentary or friable state, so as not to damage it. If this is the case, a frame should be erected to keep the acetate away from the actual wall. This may cause a slight distortion, but after checking and rechecking, this can be rectified. This method is also good for curved surfaces, such as columns and areas that are difficult to access (Dorman 2008: 84). Once the initial copy is made, the technique detailed below should be followed for the pencilling-in of the drawing. It is possible to make a rubbing of high or low relief decoration, as long as it is in a good state of preservation; this type of copying is particularly employed in recording brass tomb-covers.

To help achieve accurate drawings, the wall of the tomb or small monument should first be gridded in the vertical plane, taking care not to damage the wall. The vertical grid should be tied into any extant grid and treated as elevations from the main site grid. The vertical grid on the walls must be sub-divided into 1 metre squares. If the drawing is to be scaled down, then the 1 m grid squares can be further sub-divided into 20 cm squares. Measurements should be checked with a tape measure. A base elevation (which is the same as a base plan but vertical) must be made and the individual drawings fitted onto this base elevation.

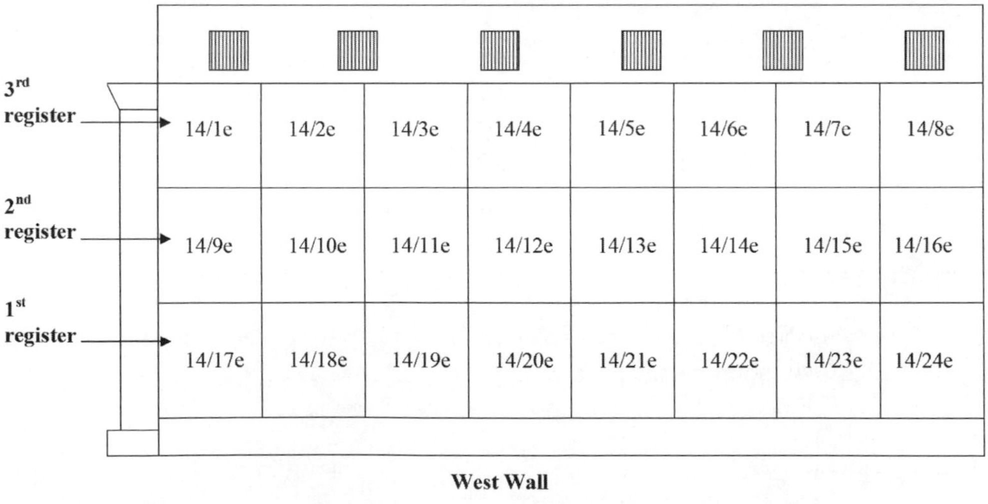

3rd register	14/1e	14/2e	14/3e	14/4e	14/5e	14/6e	14/7e	14/8e
2nd register	14/9e	14/10e	14/11e	14/12e	14/13e	14/14e	14/15e	14/16e
1st register	14/17e	14/18e	14/19e	14/20e	14/21e	14/22e	14/23e	14/24e

West Wall

Figure 159: Base elevation of a shrine.

Some of the disadvantages of this method are in the copying of raised relief that may have internal details, aspects that may not be easily copied on a flat film. One-to-one copying is also only realistic of objects of a manageable size, such as decorated artefacts, single blocks, small stelae and shrines and painted plaster tomb walls of up to 2 to 3 metres high. The larger the drawing, the more reduction is needed for publication; thus fine details may be lost. This method is not suitable for monumental buildings, and one of the following methods should be used.

Photograph Tracing

One of the least intrusive and most accurate epigraphic recording methods is that developed by Chicago House. This method (as described by Hughes 1952: 203) involves photographing a portion of the decorated surface with a large-format camera (5" x 4" or 10" x 8"). The negative is then developed and the photograph enlarged to 1:2, 1:5 or other appropriate scale. The photograph is then directly drawn on with a 4H pencil, while standing in front of the actual wall decoration. The tracing of the image in front of the actual decoration is vital as the human eye can see more detail than the photograph can show, especially if the surface is uneven or fragmentary. The lines are then inked-in with technical pens in the studio. The photographic image is then bleached out, leaving just the ink line drawing. This drawing is photocopied in order to provide a copy to check the details of the iconographic and hieroglyphic details, as well as the stylistic and general spatial arrangement and the interrelationships of various elements. Every line of the drawing is checked twice, and appropriate comments and instructions made. The instruction sheets are then given to the draughtsperson so that they can amend the preliminary drawing. Before doing this, the draughtsperson returns to the original wall decoration to check on the instructions. Once all corrections have been made and approved, the drawing is finished and can be copied onto draughting film.

Both systemic and non-systemic disturbances must be recorded, including the original gridlines and later graffiti (Polz 1987: 134), although these may not always be reproduced in the final publication for reasons of clarity. The knowledge of the Egyptologist in the principles of Egyptian art and iconography is invaluable, especially on a severely damaged wall decoration. One should of course be careful not to find what is expected or anticipated, but knowledge of iconographic systems etcetera can contribute towards the detailing of badly preserved areas (Bell 1987: 51). Chicago House holds a large catalogue of the hieroglyphs so far copied in their survey, which is of great help to the epigraphers. The finished result is the product of the combined efforts of an archaeological photographer, a draughtsperson and an Egyptologist/archaeologist. Each completed scene must then be analysed to identify its essential components, and then resynthesised in order to understand its meaning and function within the monument's structure, and within the dynamics of the ancient culture as a whole (Bell 1987: 52). This method of complete epigraphic and architectural coverage of a monument means that it takes a long time – generally around four years – for a folio to be produced. To cover the 7,000 square meters of decoration on the Great Temple of Ramesses III at Medinet Habu, eight folio volumes were produced (Bell 1987: 55). While this may seem unacceptably slow, the depredations of other techniques render it inevitable. Also, it is not always possible to take and develop photographs on site or drive to photographic studios with the means of developing large format negatives. In such cases the petroglyphs, rock-drawings, inscription, graffiti, stelae, wall painting or relief should be initially recorded by means other than photography.

Photography

As photographs can better show colour, texture and the effects of light on wall reliefs, paint layers, varying widths of brush strokes, and feathering of pigments than can the drawings, photographs are a necessary part of the epigraphic record (Bell 1998: 47; Bryan 2001: 63-72). However, to render pigments accurately in publications, the checking of proofs must ideally be done on site. Therefore, as well as collecting copies of old photographs, new photographs in colour and black and white should be taken, preferably with a large format camera. These photographs should form an essential part of the epigraphic archive and should be published along with the line drawings, notes, elevations, plans, and the report. All of this, combined with a commentary, transliteration and translation, form the basis of the final publication.

While photography is a good tool to record a monument at a specific moment of time and its state of preservation, photographs of columns produce parallax distortion. Photography usually relies on a light source, either natural or artificial, which inevitably casts shadows. The reading of these shadows and highlights causes the effects of realism for the human eye, and as such it is only rarely that all pertinent detail is captured in a single photograph (Dorman 2008: 86-7). The photograph also captures all damage to the decoration, which may create as much confusion as clarity.

Computerised Epigraphy

Computers are now being used for the recording of epigraphy. Digital epigraphy involves either the high-resolution scanning of large or medium format photographs, or the taking of high resolution digital photographs for basic 'on-screen' tracing. A computer drawing programme is then used in conjunction with a digitising tablet and cordless pen to trace the digitised photographic image and vectorise the lines on a separate layer (Der Manuelian 2000: 26). The results still have to be checked and re-checked against the actual object to verify detail and accuracy (as in the traditional methods), but this is an efficient, cost-effective technique (Der Manuelian 1998). The results of the recent application of digital epigraphy by the Giza Mastaba Project can be viewed on: http://www.manueliandesign.com and http://www.mfa.org.

Another new epigraphic innovation involves 3-D laser scanning of the monuments structure (see **Chapter 6 - High-Definition Three-Dimensional Laser Surveying**) and then a flat-bed scanner - secured to rails *c*. 12 cm from the wall - is used to record details of the decoration including the colour. These scans reproduce the wall surface itself, with all its blemishes, which in itself is of limited use. The 3-D laser scanned images are put into *Model Maker* computer software to produce facsimiles with a resolution finer than 10 microns (http://www.ideal-ist/ISTcall/Ps8thcall/actlineCPA15/ES147.htm). The epigrapher could by using a computer application cast an artificial light source over the image from different angles to obtain the basic details of the wall surface (Dorman 2008: 91).These scans after manipulation should still be checked against the actual object for confirmation of the finer details. At present this form of digital recording is primarily used for making

418

replicas of tombs and other structures (i.e. Factum arte company in the Tomb of Seti I (KV17)), although if these scans were included in with the other epigraphic documentation it may prove useful as an independent check of the reliability of the epigraphic record (Dorman 2008: 91).

Conventions

The choice of technique will usually be dictated by the type and size of object, structure or decoration to be copied, amount of personnel available, financial restrictions, time limitations, technical apparatus available, and the conception of the final publication (Dorman 2008: 91). However the copying is done, the lines must always be checked and re-checked by a different researcher at the face of the decorated wall, both by day and - especially - at night, using a movable light (Caminos 1976: 18). The decoration must be set within the architectural whole, with ground plans and elevations of the monument and base elevations to show the placement of the decoration.

Type of decoration	Line	Comment
Raised relief	Solid line	Sun and shadow used
Sunk relief	Solid line	Sun and shadow used
Flat painting	Solid line	Sun and shadow optional
Reconstruction lines	Dashed line or solid line and no internal detail	Where shape can be reconstructed from photo or documentary evidence
Deep or striking figures	Stippling	Where deep cuts have been made
Colour boundaries	Dotted line	Optional can be put in notes
Unfinished areas	Left blank	Area unfinished in antiquity
No definite carved line	Light stippling	Where lines are faint
Damaged area breaking a line	Hatching	On a figure or hieroglyph, shape uncertain
Damaged area	Stippling	Not on a figure or hieroglyph
Damaged figures where outline is still visible	Negative line shading	On a figure or hieroglyph, where shape is discernible
Modern cement or plaster	Left blank	Modern repairs
Ancient plaster	Solid line	Indicate where plaster still adheres on wall
Gouges, hacking and keying chisel marks	Stippling	Show gouged damage on the actual decoration, and the keying marks for plaster
Block-lines	Solid line	The lines of the ashlar blocks, with chipping
Ancient re-working	Stippling	Outline the area of re-working with stippling
Intentional damage to the decoration, e.g. iconoclastic	Stippling	Show the direction and shape of tool marks

Table 42: Conventions used in epigraphy.

Two-dimensional drawings can appear rather flat, so conventions are used to add three-dimensional verisimilitude. The use of imaginary light coming from the top left-hand corner of the drawing in conjunction with weighted lines can help define raised and sunken relief: these are termed sun and shadow lines - sun lines are finer, whereas shadow lines are thicker (see **Fig. 160**). In flat painted decoration, the sun and shadow convention is usually not used. Where the characters are certain, solid lines should be used; where the form is uncertain, dashed lines should be used. Where detail is missing, there is a range of conventions for showing the different types of lacunae.

The bottom chisel cut line should be followed with the pencil tracing, whether it is in raised or sunken relief. If the edges of sunken relief are not perceptibly bevelled, then split the difference between the bottom and top of the cut. Colour is not usually used in epigraphy as it tends to detract from the detail of the drawing. Colour traces, if any, should be matched to the *Munsell Colour Chart*, and the relevant code noted in the accompanying notes along with any other information that does not lend itself to graphic interpretation. The original colours should be described/matched, although this will not always be possible. It is therefore important to remark on the extent of fading.

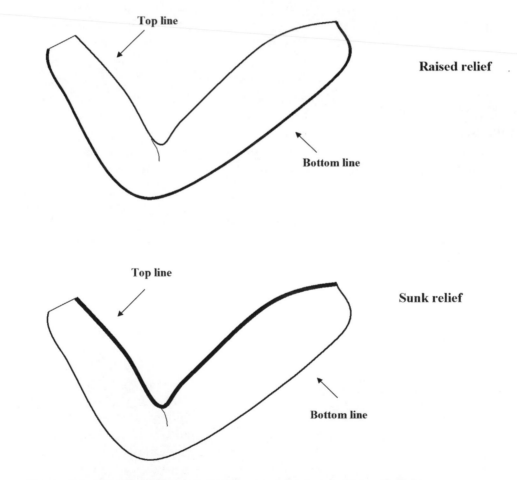

Figure 160: Showing sun and shadow on raised and sunk relief of an arm.

420

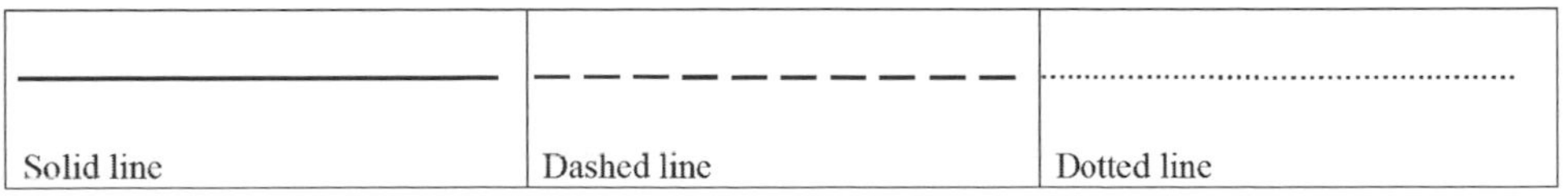

————————	— — — — — — — —	··
Solid line	Dashed line	Dotted line

Figure 161: The different types of lines used in epigraphy.

Type of Relief	Sun or shadow	Line	Technical pen size
Sunk relief outline	Shadow	Top line	1·0
Sunk relief outline	Sun	Bottom line	0·5
Sunk relief interior detail	Shadow	Top line	0·4
Sunk relief interior detail	Sun	Bottom line	0·3
Raised relief outline	Shadow	Bottom line	0·7·5
Raised relief outline	Sun	Top line	0·5
Raised relief interior detail	Shadow	Bottom line	0·4
Raised relief interior detail	Sun	Top line	0·3

Table 43: Chart of technical pen sizes for different types of relief to be published at a 1:2 scale.

ROCK ART - RUPESTRIAN ARCHAEOLOGY

Rupestrian archaeology is the subfield dedicated to the recording, scientific examination and interpretation of images made by humans on rock surfaces - rock-art sites. Sites are first located through survey and then excavated where necessary. Excavation techniques and methodology are the same as that already laid out in previous chapters; the grid may be hung from the cave ceiling rather than a hanging grid (Renfrew & Bahn 1991: 94), and the entire sedimentary matrix will usually be sieved. The majority of Egyptian rock art sites are in dry wadis in the Eastern and Western deserts (Morrow & Morrow 2001), with between one and two thousand known sites. However, rock art is known from all over Africa, with a striking range and quality in the rock art sites. Such sites are also found in the Americas, Australia, and Europe, notably the Palaeolithic cave paintings (Bahn & Vertut 1988: 26-40). Rock art can generally be defined as pictograms - made by the application of pigment to the rock surface - or petroglyphs, made by the removal of the exterior of the rock surface (Hester *et al.* 1997: 137).

The doyen of rock art recording is abbé Henri Breuil who started to copy the Palaeolithic cave paintings in Europe *c.* 1900. Although many of his methods have now been supplanted, he was hampered by the range of materials then in existence and his own preconceived ideas of what was important to record (Bahn & Vertut 1988: 41-4). As with most pioneers, the precedents that he set have been built upon and modified over the years. Rupestrian archaeology has now developed its own terminology to go with its unique place within the larger discipline of archaeology, much of which is borrowed and adapted from other disciplines (see **Tab. 44**).

Terminology	Definition
Drilling	A method of smoothing a surface.
Frottage	A method of copying rock imagery, by placing a sheet of paper over the petroglyphs and then rubbing the sheet with carbon paper, wax crayons or cobbler's wax.
Hammering, stippling and pecking	Producing stipples or peck marks, either directly by a hammer stone or indirectly, by hammering through a tool such as a chisel or punch.
Highlighting, contrast	A method used by archaeologists to make petroglyphs more visible against the natural (virgin) rock surface. One of the most effective treatments is the 'neutral method', which involves colouring the rock surface with white pigment and then staining it with lamp black to produce a bichrome effect, so all artificial and natural impressions stand out against the unmarked rock face.
Imagery	A term referring to both painted and engraved figures, thus avoiding the polemic that surrounds the term 'art'.
Petroglyph (carving, engraving or etching)	A rock image made by hammering, scratching, rubbing or drilling the rock surface.
Pictogram	Rock image made by painting pigments on the surface through a variety of means, including daubing and blowing.
Rubbing and polishing	An action used to produce smooth surfaces, possibly through use of an elongated stone.
Scratching	The production of thin lines, such as filiform figures.
Stratigraphy, overlappings, superpositions	The sequence by which layers of designs are carved or painted onto the same rock surface.
Tracing	A method of recording rock imagery, by placing sheets of clear plastic field sheets, and tracing the impressions.

Table 44: Glossary of terms used in rupestrian archaeology (after Fossati *et al.* 1990 a: 9-10).

Methods of Recording Rock Art

Although most rock art recording methods resemble those of traditional epigraphy, it is worth elucidating some of the procedures involved. The recording methods used are:

tracing, photographing, rubbing, moulding and casting, although the first two methods – being non-intrusive - are the primary techniques used.

Once the area has been surveyed, cleared, photographed and excavated (where appropriate), the area to be studied should be marked off and uncovered very carefully. Particular care should be taken when working next to the images themselves. If there are encrustations on the petroglyphs, these may need to be scrubbed off with a scrubbing brush. These encrustations can sometimes be dated, giving a *terminus ante quem* for the rock art. However, great care must be taken with pictograms when cleaning; a light brushing will usually suffice.

The next stage is to study the rock surface, to assess the state of preservation, the imposition sequence of the images, the techniques used to make the images, and variations in the patina of the engraved figures – differentiating between natural and anthropogenic wear (Fossati *et al.* 1990 a: 13). Notes should be taken, recording as much information as possible. Petroglyphs are usually best viewed in oblique light, but, if they are very unclear, they may need to be highlighted. However, this is not always necessary, as lightly touching the surface with the finger tips can usually detect subtle contours that can then be traced. Before any pigment or water is applied to the rock face, a geologist should be consulted, as coarse-grained rock can be permeated by pigments, thus damaging the substrate. Fine-grained sandstone is usually impermeable by pigments, and safe to practice highlighting on.

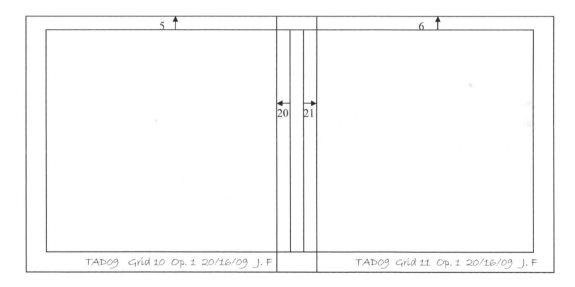

Figure 162: Example of overlapping of plastic field sheets (Fossati *et al.* 1990 a: 15).

Before recording can begin, the rock face must be gridded into 1 x 1 m grid units using the conventions given in **Chapter Two**. The plastic sheets to be used must be pliable, not too thick, allowing the texture of the rock surface to be felt through the tip of a permanent marker pen. Thicker pens are used for carvings, stippling and abraded grooves, whereas finer pens are used for filiform figures and any other fine lines (Fossati *et al.* 1990 a: 15). Three colours are used to show the various kinds of detail: black for the archaeological depictions, red for natural cracks and striations, and blue to show how the field sheets overlap (Fossati *et al.* 1990 a: 15).

The field sheets (supple plastic or acetate) should be cut to a standard size, ideally 105 x 105 cm; allowing for a 2 cm border all around them, this provides an internal area of 1.1 m². The information on the drawings should be the same as that required on any drawing: site code, operation and area numbers, grid number, sheet number, date, and the name of the draughtsperson. Any other relevant information can be noted in the border. Images are drawn as if a diffuse light is falling on to the surface, but sun and shadow are not used in rupestrian archaeology. The pen must be held at a right-angle to the drawing surface, and the draughtsperson must be careful not to smudge work already completed. A one centimetre overlap should be included of the art in the next grid square to help alignment of the drawings. When the rock surface is stable it may be possible to do direct tracing on the surface, but when either the surface or depictions themselves are likely to be damaged in this process a frame must be erected, and tracing at a distance must be practiced (Bahn & Vertut 1988: 44).

Once the field sheets are completed they should be removed from the rock face and compared with the depictions by one or more neutral observers. Once the draughtsperson and supervisor are happy with the result, the field sheets must be carefully stored for their final rendering. The rendering of the field sheets should be on draughting film; this should be carefully positioned on top of the field sheet, and the field tracing inked-in with a technical pen (Rotring). The sizes of pens should follow the normal conventions for epigraphy. Photocopies should also be made of the original field sheets, thus eliminating any deviations in the inking-in stage.

Photography must also be used to record rock art, to back up and also to contextualise field tracings. Specifically, the recorder should take pains to ensure that the photographs include both the rock imagery and the surrounding landscape, thus setting them into their context. Working shots should be taken at every stage of the fieldwork. There should be a general photograph of the whole scene, of each individual epigraphic assemblage, and individual photographs of each of the 1 m grid squares. Aerial photographs are recommended, but often financially impractical.

When photographing pictograms and petroglyphs, it is generally better to use a diffuse light rather than direct sunlight, as bright light can accentuate details of the rock surface and the resulting scatter can obscure details of the rock art (Wainwright 1990: 58). Polarising filters should be used on the lens, and also on the head of the flashlights if the light is very bright (see **Tab. 45**). Cross polarisation may be needed to give predictable and constant lighting conditions for rock paintings. The photographic tracing method outlined above (see **Epigraphy**) can also be used to record rock art (Bahn & Vertut 1988: 45-8)

Large format cameras on a sturdy tripod give the best results; however, these are so unwieldy that 35 mm cameras may be better for more routine work, or for when the rock art is not easily accessible. To bring out shallow petroglyphs, raking flashlight can be used at night, and a Wratten 38A (blue) filter will help add contrast to the photograph when shooting ochre rock paintings using black and white film (Wainwright 1990: 76). Photogrammetry may also be employed, using a camera such as a Zeiss U.M.K. 10/1318. The rules of normal archaeological photography apply to photographing rock art; for these see **Chapter Nine**. The choice of film and lens are very important, and tests should be done and the results analysed before taking the final photographic record.

Intrusive recording techniques, such as moulding with silicone rubber with a polyethylene glycol separating agent have been used in the past to record petroglyphs. However, this sort of procedure may cause damage to the rock surface, and should only be used if the moulding substance can be easily and completely removed, leaving no traces (Wainwright 1990: 76). Elastomer silicones and polyesters have proven to be quick, efficient and leave no traces on hard/solid rock faces. These faithful replicas turn parietal art into portable art. Casts of the originals can then be produced and treated with water and ink, which is then wiped away so that the engraved lines stand out more clearly (Bahn & Vertut 1988: 44).

It should be noted that rock art, while potentially invaluable for examining social dynamics of past populations, is prone to certain analytical problems. Notable amongst these is the fact that they cannot reliably be dated as they have very limited organic properties, and are not therefore suited to standard scientific dating techniques. The dating from associated artefacts (if present) is not always possible, as association with the rock art is often assumed. Taçon & Chippendale (1998: 6) suggest that the minute traces of carbon, blood or plant fibres present in the pigments may be equated to the 'art event' and as such the rock art can be reliably AMS radiocarbon dated. The use of AMS radiocarbon dating has also been used to date the calcite layers, calcareous accretions, and oxalate deposits that can build up on the surface of the images (Renfrew & Bahn 2004: 162). However, as the association of events is often equivocal it is usually necessary to rely upon indirect dating methods, which fall into four general categories:

1. Faunal and floral identity

2. Calibrated relative dating: cation-ratio (patination) and chlorine 36 dating

3. Relative dating against other types of artefacts

4. Contextual and stylistic dating

1. Variations in climate can cause significant changes in both the floral and faunal population patterns, such as those that occurred in Egypt between 6,000 and 7,000 BP (Hassan 1988). Savannah game virtually disappeared from the Nile Valley north of Aswan by the beginning of the Old Kingdom (Butzer 1976: 26). As much of the rock art depicts the changing fauna and flora, it is theoretically possible to assign rock art manifestations to broad temporal phases according to the flora and fauna they depict (Renfrew & Bahn 1991: 200-1). A good example of this is the faunal groups in Europe's Ice-Age cave paintings from Spain and Southern France or the African cave of fishers, or Saharan hippopotamus depictions.

2. In desert conditions, a 'varnish' forms on rock surfaces exposed to the desert dust, and this patina can now be directly dated using cation-ratio dating (Renfrew & Bahn 2004: 161-2). The varnish or patina includes clay minerals, oxides, hydroxides of manganese and iron, minor and trace elements, and a small amount of organic matter. The method relies upon the fact that cations of certain element are more soluble than others, and leach out at different rates. However, unlike radiocarbon and other absolute dating techniques, there is not a fixed rate of decay; the method must be calibrated for each region (Renfrew & Bahn 2004: 161-2). Chlorine-36 dating

allows the surface of rocks to be dated after it has been exposed to cosmic radiation. Like cation-ratio, this technique is imprecise and gives huge time ranges for an event (Renfrew & Bahn 2004: 162-3). The analysis of the pigments and binding applied to the rock surface is another area where much recent work has been conducted. The presence or absence of certain elements or substances within the pigments and binding agents can also help to determine the timing of execution of different paintings, and this can be contextualised using superimposition and stylistic data (Renfrew & Bahn 1991: 284).

3. The comparison of artefacts shown in rock art with finds from securely dated deposits is one of the most common methods of dating rock imagery. For example, the depicting of boats or beaked women with up-raised hands can be seen both on the Naqada vessels and in the rock art – this has led to the assumption that the artworks and the ceramics are contemporary. Even if absolute specifics cannot be matched, it is usually possible to assign artworks to general periods.

4. On multi-period sites it has been posited that the earliest work will have utilised the best rock face, whereas the later work will either have been forced to use lesser rock faces or may be superimposed over earlier imagery (Morrow & Morrow 2001). There may be diverse sociological reasons for the use of certain surfaces – or perhaps for overpainting more ancient depictions – and such reasons would by no means be universal. This technique is therefore usually used in association with stylistic dating methods. This has been attempted by Winkler (1938; 1939) and Cervicek (1974) for Egypt and Nubia and Leroi-Gourhan (1971) for Europe, and while a comprehensive stylistic dating method has not been found, certain advances have been made. Winkler looked at the styles of boats, humans and people depicted on Naqada wear, and tried to match them with the rock art. This line of enquiry may also prove fruitful in other parts of the world.

In scientific photography it is essential to know the size, sharpness, and how accurate the chroma, value and hue are. An indication of the severity of distortion can be obtained by checking the colour distortion on a scale photographed with the art. The IFRAO Standard Scale was developed not only to check for colour distortion in new photographs, but also to act as a calibration tool for fading of old photographs and the actual paintings. The Scale must never be placed over any part of the rock art. Preferably it should not be attached to the rock face. The use of small double-sided adhesive pads should be considered only where definitely undecorated and structurally sound rock surface is available. The scale should be positioned parallel to the predominant plane of the rock art motif, and at a consistent distance from the camera lens. Ensure that the scale does not directly reflect the lighting source. One scale should be used for distances of up to 1.5 m. Between 1.5 and 4.5 m, two scales are required. The scale cannot be used with precision at distances exceeding 4.5 m, using lenses of standard focal length. Best results will be achieved at distances of under 1 m. Where artificial lighting is required, place the scale on upper left corner and light the image from the same direction. However, natural lighting is preferred to artificial. The small scale on the left-hand end of the IFRAO scale is intended for close-up photography. The IFRAO scale can be used in any type of scientific photography where colour is an important element, such as recording of wall-paintings, painted pottery vessels, anthropoid coffins, or indeed any artefact.

Figure 163: The International Federation of Rock Art Organisations (IFRAO) Standard Scale. The IFRAO Standard Scale is distributed free from the IFRAO Convener's Office, P.O. Box 216, Caulfield South, Victoria, 3162, Australia (http://mc2.vicnet.net.au/home/record/web/scale.html).

The Photographic Record

While photographs often do not convey as much information as the drawn record, they are nonetheless indispensable to the archaeological team. Photography is also, in many senses, the hardest medium to master. To produce good, clear, unambiguous archaeological photographs takes time, technique, and the right equipment. To produce excellent photographs is more dependent on the skill and flair of the photographer. Many site photographs are ruined by bad composition, allowing a stray foot or head to creep into the photograph, or not removing an unsightly bucket or shovel. This chapter is not designed to explain the full technicalities of archaeological photography - for there are many excellent books for that purpose (such as Peter Dorrell's *Photography in Archaeology and Conservation*) – but will give a brief overview of the main aspects of archaeological site and finds photography.

Photography is not a cheap process, but if sturdy well-made products are bought they can last for many years. Ideally a specialist archaeological photographer should be present at all times, who will usually have their own equipment, thus saving the expense of purchasing hardware other than film. If a specialist photographer is not available, a photographic enthusiast should be appointed to this position; roles must thus be combined. It is better for the archaeologist to direct the photographer on what should be photographed, than for a photographically untrained archaeologist to take unpublishable site photographs. It may be worthwhile asking a student from a photographic college to take the site photographs as part of a college project or in their holidays. Professional photographers may also be willing to give up their spare time. It is important that only one person takes the photographs and is in charge of the equipment, therefore insuring consistency and reducing the risk of loss or error (Drewett 1999: 138).

The following nine points are essential guidelines for archaeological photography in the field:

1. The main objective of archaeological photography is to record the site and objects found in a clear and accurate manner for documentation and illustration. Do not use dramatic lighting or anything that distracts from the archaeology; use diffuse light where possible.

2. Remember that the foreground appears larger and the background smaller, therefore distorting the scale of objects. If the image being photographed is all on one plane, the centre will appear smaller and the edges larger. If photographing a building, stand well back to take the photograph. Blank areas can be cut out during the printing process.

3. Choose the time of day with some care, especially when taking panoramic views. The sun's light in the early morning and late afternoon is at an oblique angle and casts shadows which add contrast to your photographs. This may help in bringing out the contours of various features.

4. Develop your photographs as soon as practically possible, allowing for re-taking or replication of pictures not of sufficiently high quality. Copy all digital images to a mass storage device at the end of each day; if your computer crashes and you lose all the stored information, it means that only one day's photography is lost.

5. Always shoot three exposures; one on the settings dictated by the meter, one under- and one over-exposed. Do this by changing the shutter speed dial to give faster and slower speeds. Do not do it by altering aperture, or your depth-of-field will change with each shot.

6. Use a tripod for most shots, particularly on long exposures, close-up photography or when using a small aperture. Use a cable release or self-timer to avoid camera shake.

7. Keep a log of shots, so you know what has been photographed. Note technical information, i.e. the exposure and direction, etc. This must be done immediately after the photograph has been taken and not left to the end of the day, for details may be forgotten.

8. All equipment must be kept clean and dry, free of sand, and tidy. Keep the photographic equipment all in one place, with the cameras and lenses in a camera bag or cool box for protection. Store the film in a dry cool place, in a fridge if possible, and in humid conditions place silica gel in the film container.

9. It is essential that you choose the appropriate background when photographing objects. This does not always have to be artificial, such as a cloth or paper background; sand can work just as well in many instances. It is essential that the background does not impair the clarity of the object being photographed; therefore, bright colours and patterned surfaces should be avoided.

Basic Equipment and Supplies

The basic equipment required for photography in the field includes:

Two sturdy 35 mm single-lens reflex (SLR) camera bodies, with cable releases and flash units. Zoom, 28 mm, 50 mm and 200 mm and macro lenses. Note that prime (fixed focal length) lenses generally give better results than zoom lenses. Hand-held exposure meter. Extra batteries if required.

Polarising and blue (see below) filters for colour film; red, yellow and green filters for black and white film. UV (skylight) filters should be fitted to all lenses as this will protect them from damage.

Panchromatic medium-speed black and white film, 100-125 ISO, Kodachrome medium-speed colour slide film: 25, 64, 100 up to 200 ISO, Kodak Ultra medium-speed colour print film: 100 or 200 ISO. If shooting indoors ISO 400-800 should be sufficient

Camera bag and film containers, camel's hair lens brush, air bulb, photographic lens tissue and lens-cleaning fluid. Wet wipes to clean the photographer's hands before handling the equipment.

A sturdy tripod with adjustable legs is essential; monopod, bipod, quadripod and tripod towers are optional.

Reflectors and shaders (a survival blanket is a useful shader and reflector that folds up into a small bundle). Photographic lamps are essential if one intends to carry out photography indoors.

Letterboard, north arrow, 1 cm, 5 cm, 10 cm, 25 cm, 50 cm and 1 m scales and a dark and light coloured cotton cloth for photography of small finds. Two metre-long ranging poles for buildings.

Camcorders, digital cameras and large/medium format cameras are desirable but not indispensable.

CAMERAS

It is important that the camera bodies be as sturdy as possible, preferably made of metal, for working in the frequently harsh conditions often encountered on archaeological sites (modern polycarbonate camera bodies are also very hard-wearing). Cameras can be manual, semi-automatic or fully automatic; experienced photographers will usually prefer a manual camera, but you should use the latter two types if you lack extensive inexperience. For general archaeological work, a semi-automatic SLR with built-in metering and manual override is the best choice. It is preferable to have two cameras of the same make, so that they can use the same lenses. Ideally one of the two bodies will be loaded with black and white film, the other with colour (slide) film.

The range of lenses should include a short zoom (35-70 mm or 28-80 mm) plus a longer lens (e.g. a 135 mm or a long zoom, 80-200 mm). Separate prime lenses can be used as well if you wish. For close-up work the best lens would be a 'macro lens', which is specifically designed for close-up work (see **Tab. 46**). A cheaper alternative is a standard lens and set of extension tubes that fit between the camera body and lens. For very small objects, a set of bellows – an accessory used in the same general manner as the extension tubes – can be utilised. The short focal length of wide-angle lenses makes them unsuitable for most archaeological photography; longer lenses are generally preferable as these avoid distortion. To create an image close to what the human eye sees (45°), use a standard lens (35-50 mm).

Camera stability is essential, as any movement can spoil the shot. Slow-medium speed films, which are usually recommended for archaeological photography (e.g. Kodachrome 64; Ilford Delta 100) demand long exposure times in order to obtain high-range f-stops (i.e. large depth-of-field). Because slower film speeds (lower ISO number) are finer-grained, they are better for enlargement for use in publications or posters (Smith & Burke 2004: 268). The tripod should be the kind that allows you take out the central column and put the tripod head upside down between the legs, allowing the camera to be attached pointing vertically downwards. This is useful for vertical photography of small features, *in situ* finds and 'macro photography' (Barker 1993: 181). A cable release will allow you to trigger the shutter without actually touching the camera, therefore eliminating camera motion.

Thirty-five mm cameras provide unacceptable distortion when photographing buildings and long narrow trenches, although shift lenses are available to correct converging diagonals. Such features should be photographed using large format (5 x 4 inches / 12.5 x 10 cm) or medium format cameras (2 ¼ x 2 ¼ inches / 6 x 6 cm) with shift lenses (Dorrell 1994: 20-24). These cameras are more expensive to buy, and to load with film. One sheet of film (one shot) for a large format camera can cost twenty times the amount of one frame of 35 mm film, but the quality is far superior (Dorrell 1994: 20-24). The general rule of photography is: the larger the negative, the better the quality of photograph and the sharper the image. Large format cameras also come in 9 x 7 inch (23 x 18 cm) and 10 x 8 inch (25 x 20 cm), but these larger formats are extortionately expensive and their advantage over the 5 x 4 inch is minimal in archaeological terms (Dorrell 1994: 20). Large and medium format cameras are also ideal for close-up photography, such as photographing artefacts (Dorrell 1994). Medium format cameras take 120 film with up to 15 frames per roll; the cost of these films is comparable to a roll of 35 mm film (albeit with fewer exposures). Medium format is more economical than large format, and is sufficient for most archaeological sites. When photographing iconographic images, inscriptions on monumental buildings or rock engravings, large format cameras should always be used. The Chicago House Epigraphic Survey has over 13,000 large format negatives of tomb and temple scenes. The fact that some of these negatives are the only surviving record of monumental inscriptions underscores the absolute necessity of making accurate recording. Emulate their example by using the best photographic materials and high-quality accompanying notes and drawings.

Although many professional photographers disapprove of using zoom (compact) cameras, reasonable quality photographs can be produced by using top-of-the-range models. Optical quality varies; cameras made by companies such as *Canon, Nikon, Olympus* and *Pentax* can produce optical quality comparable with some SLR cameras if due care is taken with their usage. These cameras come with an array of additional features, such as macro lenses and built-in timer.

Polaroid cameras, although useful for taking photographs for quick reference, cannot produce photographs of publishable quality. However, **digital photography** is now becoming increasingly sophisticated, and while it will probably never completely replace traditional chemical-based photography, it has its own unique niche within archaeological photography. What digital cameras lack in image quality they make up for in convenience. They have the advantage in producing instantly – viewable images which can be manipulated in the computer, rather than having to scan traditional photographs and digitise them. Furthermore, when producing the interim report on site, digital photographs can be more easily imported into the document. Although digital photography is constantly advancing, lower-end cameras should be avoided as they tend to produce pixellated images. It is worth investing in a good mid-range to top-end digital camera, avoiding models that take images of less than 6 megapixels. Some top-of-the-range digital SLR cameras can accept traditional lenses, thus vastly improving the quality of the images taken through them. It is essential to have a sturdy, preferably weatherproof camera, such as the *Pentax* K-7 (which has 126 weatherproof seals) when working in the often harsh field conditions of bright sunlight, sand and/or rain. Digital backs are also available for some of the new range of large format cameras, producing digital images of exceptional quality. The size of the memory card should be at least 1 GB or higher for working in the field, as it may not always be possible to download the images when needed, particularly if out surveying. The images should originally be taken in RAW or TIFF (high quality and long lasting) formats rather than JPEG to keep the quality as high as possible and allow further manipulation. When downloading your photographs onto a computer for storage, it is essential that back-up copies are made at the end of each day on to a CD-ROM, flash-drive or other mass storage device. This minimises the loss of your digital record to just one day's photography if the computer unexpectedly crashes. The photographs should be named as soon as possible after download. Computer programmes such as *Adobe Photoshop* can be used to manipulate the photographs (both digital and digitised), crop, sharpen, brighten and generally enhance the quality of the images or save them in various formats, such as JPEG (compressed) or BITMAP. Colour calibration can also be done in software packages such as *VIPS*, available for free from www.vips.ecs. soton.ac.uk/index.php?title=VIPS (Scharff 2007: 34). Most publications require a resolution of at least 300 dots per inch (dpi) for photographs and 600 dpi for line drawings (slides should be scanned at 2400 dpi). Digital images are quick and easy to insert into programmes such as *Microsoft PowerPoint*, for use in illustrating lectures.

Video is another medium becoming increasingly popular on archaeological sites, as it can be used as a visual site diary to show how a site was excavated. This can help in writing the report and can be used as an archival record of the site's excavation. Video footage can be used to show edited highlights of the excavation, while webcams can be positioned around the site to relay pictures to a website. An exciting new development is digital video ('DV'), which produces digitised images so there is no image quality loss as there is with analogue video when digitised. The quality of the best DV camcorders is comparable with professional television cameras, so that near broadcast quality videos can be shot and edited (using programmes such as *Radius Edit DV*) and used for broadcast on national television. The other exciting possibility with DV is that camcorders can take up to 500 still images on one 60 minute tape, which can be loaded into applications (such as *Quicktime VR*) thus permitting 3D manipulation of images and the generation of a virtual reality tour of the site. In this increasingly media-based world, photography and digital technology are likely to play a large part in assisting with scholarly publications, as well as presenting the results of research to the public in an exciting yet informative manner.

The main photographic record of the site should still be black and white photographs, both vertical and oblique. Colour transparencies should be used for publication purposes and illustrating lectures, with colour prints used as a temporary record and for exhibitions. Regardless of medium, however, all should be taken to publication standard, as all constitute the site photographic record (Barker 1993: 181; Drewett 1999: 138).

WHAT TO TAKE AND FRAME COMPOSITION

Photographs should be taken of the excavation area and surrounding landscape before digging commences. If any archaeological features are visible, detailed photographs should be taken of them. To take **panoramic photographs** it is usually best to set-up on a high vantage point; avoid the midday sun as this will have the effect of 'flattening' the landscape (Drewett 1999: 74). Photographing the site within the landscape shows the how the site fits in to the local topography and geology, and helps to place the site in context. Panoramas of a site should be shot with a standard lens, to avoid the possible edge distortion of a wide-angle lens. The camera should be mounted on a tripod and rotated slightly after each shot. If the tripod has no degree scale marked, you will have to judge the movement of the camera by eye. This will then produce a complete photographic record of the site's surroundings and show the placement of the various areas of operation. A polarising filter can be used to reduce haze in both BW and colour photography, while yellow or orange filters can be used for black and white film. Polarising filters enhance contrast and sharpen distant images by cutting out reflected light and atmospheric hazing (Drewett 1999: 74; Dorrell 1994: 48). Although there is little point in putting scales in panoramic views (as the foreground inevitable appears larger and the background smaller), including a building or a human figure may help to aid perspective. It is also advisable to take a shot of the grid after it has been laid out but before any excavation has taken place, to show the grid's location in the landscape. It is essential that you keep a record of your photographs in the **Photographic Index: Sheet 13**. When the photographs are received back from developing the rolls should be put in numerical order and the numbers on the negatives should be compared to those on the **Photographic Index** (and other recording sheets). If there are any discrepancies the numbers should be amended as applicable so that there is accord in the record (Burke & Smith 2004: 305). Photographs that do not have information such as place, date, and subject on them lose their archival value, so this information should be written on their backs as-soon-as-possible. Digital photographs can be stored in cataloguing software; this software acts like a card index and allows you to search for images using key words such as date, location or subject (Burke & Smith 2004: 305-6).

Photograph each stage of the excavation in both black and white and colour, including **details within a context**, such as *in situ* artefacts or ecofacts. This will help pinpoint the position and status of a find in relation to its associated deposit (Roskams 2001: 121). Conservators and finds processors must photograph artefacts and ecofacts as part of the finds-processing procedure, over and above the *in situ* shots. The *in situ* photographs must be of the artefact or ecofact on the surface in which it originated, so if the top of an artefact first appears in one context, but actually lies on a surface below, it should be photographed on the surface on which it lies (Dorrell 1994: 149). Artefacts must be photographed in relation to their surroundings, showing their association with other artefacts and the feature in which they were found.

Each context needs to be photographed separately, before, during and after excavation. The choice of viewpoints is of great importance; usually the front-to-back depth of the context or feature should be visible. It is important that the surface details of each context are recorded photographically, as drawings usually only show the smaller details schematically (Roskams 2001: 122). It is important to photograph the **physical relationships** of contexts, thus clarifying stratigraphic relationships (Roskams 2001: 122). When photographing structures, the walls' and floors' shape, size, construction, surface texture, tone and colour must be recorded, as must their relationships – how a wall meets a floor, how a wall abuts another wall, etc., to give some idea of the sequence in which they were built (Dorrell 1994: 126). View the building from all sides and all possible elevations before choosing the best viewpoints to relay the overall shape and setting (Dorrell 1994: 126). As choosing what relationships to photograph involves some degree of interpretation; a general rule is photograph those relationships that are believed to be important, either because of the nature of the specific feature or as a result of the research design (Roskams 2001: 122). However, some relationships are very difficult to determine;

in this case it is better to record the area as fully as possible (Roskams 2001: 124). Strong sunlight is bad for this kind of photography, but strong side-lighting by the sun can bring out the detail of mud-brick, masonry work, etc.

When photographing a skeleton in a grave, two types of photograph should be taken - vertical and oblique. Vertical photographs can be enlarged to the scale of the site plan and traced off on to it if wished, whereas the oblique photographs should show the complete rim of the grave from the surface into which it was cut, the cut or walls of the grave, and the completely uncovered skeleton on the floor of the grave (Dorrell 1994: 132). As with other complex contexts, photographs should be taken before, during and after excavation; close-ups should also be taken of the skeleton and any associated artefacts.

Filter	Wratten No.	Darkens	Lightens
Blue	38A	Red, yellow	Blue
Green	54	Red. Orange	Green
Deep yellow	15	Blue	Yellow, orange
Red	25	Blue. Green	Red, orange

Table 45: The effects of some of the popular filters (after Dorrell 1994: 46).

Multi-context and composite shots should be taken to show the relationship of contexts and features. This type of photography can help in deducing what set of features go together, possibly clarifying a whole period of the site's formation. Filtration can be used to highlight detail; if, for example you have a green stain in brown/red earth, putting a green filter over the lens will make it lighter than the earth around it (see **Tab. 45**). Photographs of the whole trench should be taken at least once a day or whenever there is a major change. A series of both vertical and horizontal photographs should be taken of tombs, although working in the often dark confines of tombs and caves present problems, which can be overcome by consideration of the viewpoints and lighting. **Working shots** should also be taken, as these can make good images to use in articles or as instructional shots or just for showing at lectures. To make shots of people working more interesting, do not have too many people in the scene; try and have different activities going on, ideally at differing levels or various distances, making sure that their faces and what they are doing can be seen (Dorrell 1994 152). Photographs of any VIPs visiting the site may be a valuable asset in publicity material, as are general shots. Good photographs can be a powerful incentive to sponsors and may help generate further funding for the project (Roskams 2001: 126). Photographs must also be taken of the final levels at the end of season; these are usually taken from photographic towers or step ladders (see below).

It is essential when composing the shot to ensure that the area that you are photographing is clean and tidy. As archaeological sites are working environments special preparation is required for the taking of photographs, even working shots. Certain objects should not be seen in the photograph, such as spoil heaps, loose sand, buckets, tools, clothes and people. Although working shots will of course have people in then, it is still best to remove clutter. Area preparation also includes cleaning. On a horizontal surface this is best done by brushing the surface, moving from one side to the other with a stiff brush, followed by a gentle trowelling or hoeing. On vertical surfaces, the cleaning must always be from top to bottom; sloping surfaces must be cleaned from highest to lowest. Clean back from the top of baulks, not into the trench. This will usually be sufficient for most surfaces, although masonry and mud-brick will usually only need brushing with a stiff brush, being careful not to dislodge any mortar. On sites that are entirely of stone, hosing down the area to be photographed with either air or water hoses cuts down the time involved in cleaning (Dorrell 1994: 149). If just brushing is used on sedimentary surfaces, the various contexts are liable to blur into one another. Do not cut lines around or between contexts or strata in the section, as if hinders reinterpretation of the contexts when studying the photographs. Photographs of sections or elevations should be taken square-on with as long a lens as space permits, in order to fill the frame and avoid distortion (Dorrell 1994: 129). If further detail is required, use filters or dampen the sediment with a fine mist from a garden spray. Once the area has been cleaned, stand back to examine the area or asking another opinion of the area, in case anything has been overlooked.

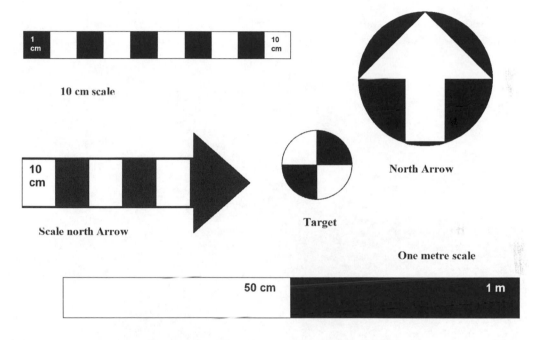

Figure 164: Different scales used on archaeological sites.

Reflectors are used to reflect light into shadowed areas, whereas shaders or diffusers are used to shade areas from direct sunlight. In areas up to 2 m square, light can successfully be reflected into shaded areas such as deep pits, trenches or behind walls, using the dull side of silver foil, polystyrene tiles or white bed-sheets (Dorrell 1994: 128). Shade can also be arranged by means of flysheets or blankets (see **Fig. 165**). Blocking or including light should equalise the amount of light and shade in an area, thus avoiding solid black shadows or burnt-out areas of bright sunlight. Sometimes diffused or oblique sunlight is desirable in the scene, casting soft shadows to give depth to structures (Dorrell 1994: 128). This sort of light is normally only available in thick cloud cover or in the early morning or late afternoon.

Once the area has been cleaned and the viewpoint/target chosen, information about the context must be placed in the shot. All archaeological photographs must include a scale, although if this is going to be intrusive, duplicate shots with and without the scale should be taken. For the photography of small objects, thin white card scales of 20, 10, 5, 3 and 1 cm should be used, divided into centimetre sections. For close-up photography and small finds such as coins, use 1 cm scales divided into millimetres. Larger scales should be used for buildings, contexts and large artefacts. These should include 25 cm to 1 m scales made of hard wood, 4 x 2 cm for the 1 m scale and 2.5 x 0.5 for the 25 cm scale (Dorrell 1994: 53). The 25 cm scale can be divided up into 1 or 5 cm segments, the 50 cm scale into 10 or 25 cm centimetre segments, and the 1 m scale into 50 cm or 20 cm segments. The divisions should be painted black and white, or red and white. The length of one of the white sections must be painted on and the total length of the scale must also be indicated (Dorrell 1994: 51). The scale should match the size of the object being photographed, so a 20 cm pottery vessel should include a 10 cm scale next to it, whereas a 1 metre grave should include a 50 cm scale. For buildings, a ranging pole can be used as a scale; if the building has some depth, two should be used, one in the foreground and another in the background. The scale should be placed upright or horizontal in the frame, and checked using the camera's viewfinder. Never have the scale leaning, at an angle, or obscuring features or artefacts (Dorrell 1994: 51).

Figure 165: Shading the area to be photographed (photograph B. Calcoen).

A north arrow must be placed, indicating the direction of north. The scale and north arrow can be combined in one scale; however, north may not be in a convenient direction, and it is better to use a separate scale and north arrow (see **Fig. 167**). If taking a photograph of a section, the arrow should point upwards if it is a north section and downwards if a south section (Dorrell 1994: 52). The last piece of information required in the photograph is the information or letter board (**Fig. 166**). Some excavation directors prefer not to use this as they feel that it clutters the frame too much. In these cases they prefer to rely on the information contained in the **Photographic Index** and careful cataloguing and storing of the photographs, writing the information on the back of prints and on the frames of slides. The best policy is to take **two** photographs, one with the information board, and another without. The latter can be used for publication and lecturing purposes.

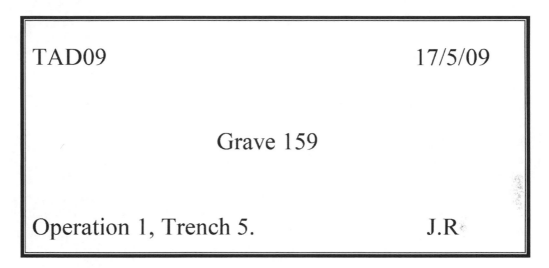

Figure 166: The layout of the information board.

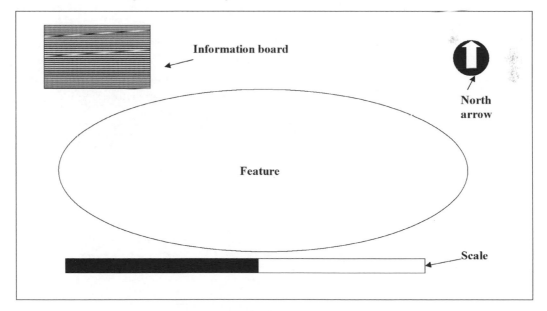

Figure 167: The composition of a typical archaeological photograph.

The information boards should be about 20 x 30 cm, and should be black with white letters (white boards are more likely to affect the exposure time because of the glare they cause). Magnetic letters on metal boards or plastic letters that fit into slots on a board are ideal. The information required includes the site code, date, context, grave or structure number, operation number and site sub-division (trench), lot or level (if relevant) and the initials of the area supervisor (see **Fig. 166**). Graves do not always need a scale as the skeleton itself acts as a scale by proxy. However, a north arrow is essential to show the orientation, as is the information board with the at least the number of the grave on it.

VERTICAL PHOTOGRAPHY

The height of the camera above the ground will depend upon the size of the feature you intend to photograph. If you are taking a vertical photograph of a pottery vessel or a small grave, a tripod with a reversible central pole may be sufficient. If taking photographs of horizontal engravings a 2-3 m long monopod should suffice to create a collage. However, for larger features and taking vertical photographs of the whole site, a bigger apparatus should be used.

Although there are various methods for suspending a camera vertically over a feature or site (including balloons with remote control cameras, or putting the camera on the end of a boom) the most common are large stepladders and mobile scaffold towers. Any apparatus that safely lifts the photographer above the ground can be used, including the bucket of a bulldozer. The apparatus used should be easily movable across the site, and light enough to not damage the archaeology (Barker 1993: 181). A quadripod made of light metal (aluminium) legs braced with wooden slats and a cradle to hold the camera is another option. If the camera is placed so that the four legs bound the photograph frame, whatever the quadripod encloses will be photographed. The camera is placed in a cradle and raised and lowered by means of a pulley device; the photograph is taken by means of a shutter release cable (Barker 1993:182). A 35 mm camera with a 35 mm lens will take a vertical picture of a grave measuring 2.1 m x 1.7 m if the quadripod is at a height of 2.25 m (Dorrell 1994: 145). Distortion at the edges of the photograph can be cut down by using a longer focal length, but this will entail raising the camera. A basic formula for working out relationship of camera height, focal length and area covered is presented below:

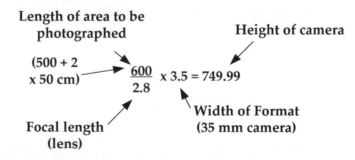

Figure 168: The formula for working out the height needed to raise your camera (after Dorrell 1994: 140).

The height of the camera in **Figure 168** was 7.50 metres above the 5 metre square unit of excavation, in order to have the whole square and a 50cm overlap in sharp focus (500 cm + 2 x 50 cm = 600 cm). A helium balloon with a camera in a cradle, with the shutter fired by the pneumatic cable release, can be used to attain heights of over 20 metres. As long as the cable release is not in the picture, this will usually produce a good vertical photograph. If a

438

motordrive is fitted or it already has automatic drive facilities, the camera will not have to be brought down in order to wind on the film.

Vertical photography can show size, texture and layout in a way that oblique photography can rarely match. Vertical photographs give a less distorted view of features and contexts than oblique photography, and a photographic plan of the site can be made using a mosaic of overlapping photographs. Stereoscopic photography can be blown-up to a 1:20 scale, published as a photographic mosaic of the site, used in photogrammetry or - better still - incorporated into a Geographic Information System (GIS) to be manipulated on the computer along with site plans and other data (Conolly & Lake 2006: 74-5). If taking an interim large-scale photograph of the whole site, all areas should roughly be at the same stage of excavation (Roskams 2001). Overall vertical photographs of a site should be taken at the end of each season of a multi-season project, both to show the progress and to help assess the strategy for the next season's work. As well as overall vertical photographs, overall oblique photographs should be taken. Vertical photographs of features or specific contexts (such as graves) can be stitched together in a computer programme and using applications such as *Adobe Illustrator* these can be traced and the weight of individual lines chosen and adjusted as wished to produce a good scale drawing with the help of a digitising tablet.

OBLIQUE PHOTOGRAPHY

Oblique photography is basically defined as any photograph taken where the camera is not held directly over the subject being photographed. This is usually done by standing to one side of the feature or context, and taking a variety of shots from various angles to capture the true nature of the feature. Most of the photography discussed previously pertains to oblique photography. It is useful to find a high viewpoint to take oblique photographs, such as a nearby building, hill or sand dune. These three-quarter views can illustrate structural details of features and structures better then vertical photographs or oblique photographs taken at the same ground level as the feature. If possible, it is advisable to take a series of overlapping shots of the site. Many aerial photographs are also taken at an oblique angle to capture the shadows, vegetation, and soil patterns and textures, which can then be rectified for mapping with computer programmes such as *AirPhoto* included in the Bonn Archaeological Statistics Package (Dorrell 1994: 145-7; Conolly & Lake 2006: 67-9)

OBJECT PHOTOGRAPHY

Object photography can be done in the open-air, in a shaded location (to avoid strong cross lighting or unwanted shadows), or in a studio. Studio photographs should have one light coming from the top left and another from the same height as - and slightly right of - the camera. Good backgrounds include black velvet and light opaque Perspex that should be two stops brighter than the light on the object. Coloured backgrounds can also be used, but not those that would dominate the photograph. Creases in the material can be avoided by ironing. Always ensure that there is no dirt on the background cloth by brushing it between shots.

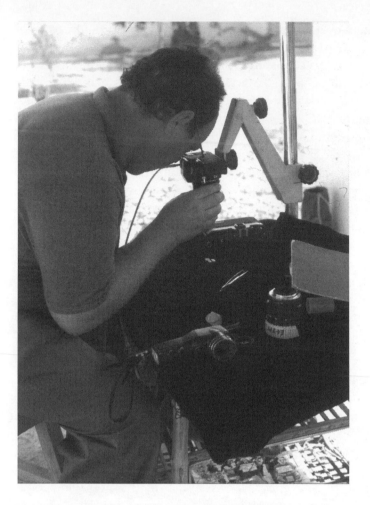

Figure 169: Close-up photography of shells (photograph J. van Wetering).

Focus the camera on the scale, which should be placed vertically, next to the artefact. The scale should be a third back from the front of the artefact; by focusing on it with a small aperture everything in the frame should be in focus. For close-up photography, place the scale half way up the object. The catalogue number (printed from the computer) should be placed in the photograph next to the scale. Therefore, at least two photographs should be taken: one with information, and one without. Ensure that the object is in the centre of the frame and that the whole composition fills the frame. Keep the plane of the film/camera as close as possible to horizontal or vertical to avoid any distortion (Burke & Smith 2004: 283).When photographing a pottery or stone vessel, you should be a little above it, looking down so that the inside of the rim is shown as a shallow eclipse (Dorrell 1994: 209). If the pot has a handle, position it on the right to avoid deep shadows. Take your exposure reading with an 'incident' or 'spot' meter. Generally the placing of objects follows the conventions for drawing objects: the light source from the top left, spouts of vessels to the left and handles on the right. However, the lighting may need to be adjusted if the directional lighting is distorting the detail on the artefact: soft all-over lighting may solve the problem (Dorrell 1994: 209). Bowls will need both elevation and plan photographs. If unsure as to what views to take, follow the drawing conventions or ask the site director. If excavating a cemetery, photographs of the complete artefactual assemblage from each grave should also be taken once they have been removed and conserved. Graves

440

with large artefactual assemblages may require a series of photographs to be taken. As the objects are often crushed or obscured when photographs are take of them in the graves, this allows for easier interpretation of the grave good assemblage and provides an excellent image for use in publications and lectures. Taking photographs through a microscope will need a special camera attachment; these are often supplied with the microscope or can be bought separately. The rules for close-up photography should then be followed, making sure that there is correct lighting, scale in the frame, the magnification is recorded and that the correct focal length is set (see **Tab. 46**). Image processing software, such as *Scion Image* can be used to process and analyse digital macro- and microscopic images. These programmes can also be used for measuring areas, perimeters, path lengths and angles and can be downloaded from www.scioncorp.com (Scharff 2007: 35).

When taking photographs of inscriptions it is important that the light source comes from the top left. Large format cameras are ideal for this type of photography, as they produce more detail than 35 mm. It is important to not only take photographs of the inscription, but also to show the inscription's setting if it is still *in situ,* and from the original viewpoint of the inscription (Dorrell 1994: 229).This oblique lighting technique is also a good method to use when photographing rock art. This should be done in the evening or where there are dark conditions, such as in a cave. The use of reflectors is another good means of bringing light into dark areas to illuminate faint images.

Magnification	Focal Length
50 x	2 mm
100 x	1 mm
200 x	500 μm
500 x	200 μm

Table 46: Focal lengths when taking photographs through a microscopic.

When taking overlapping images of a large rock art panel, fresco, or inscription, distortions can occur at the outer portions of the images if using anything greater than a 50 mm lens. This distortion is particularly noticeable when the overlapping images are put together to form a collage of the parietal art. If using a digital camera to capture overlapping images of parietal art, place targets (see **Fig. 164**) in an unobtrusive part of the art's surface to ensure that the photographic images can be positioned correctly when stitching together and manipulating in a photographic computer programme (McDonald 2006: 64-5).

Large epigraphic drawings are often difficult to reduce in size on a photocopier or scanner. Photographing these is an economical method to produce accurate scaled-down images. This is best done in a photographic studio, but a make-shift one can be easily assembled in the research centre. To photograph these large tracings a white wall that is evenly lit from behind the tracing is essential, this can be done with floodlights. Suspend the tracing from the ceiling with ropes and pulleys about 2.5 metres from the wall, weighting the bottom of the tracing and making sure that there is a scale next to it. Then place your camera a further 2.5 metres away, facing the tracing and beyond that the white wall. These images can then be manipulated in photographic computer programmes and printed out at a precise scale. If wished these photos can be traced again to produce exact scale copies of the parietal art (McDonald 2006: 68-9).

Human skeletal remains should be photographed with the head at the top of the frame. If photographing *in situ* skeletal remains, two lights (or one light and a reflector) should be used at a low enough angle to bring out the roundness of the bones (Dorrell 1994: 236). Moving light should be used to avoid deep shadows in the eye orbits. If taking photographs in natural sunlight, it is best to use the low sunlight of early morning or late afternoon. For mummified remains, slightly diffused lighting is best for bringing out the details. This can be achieved artificially with lights directed on or through a wall of white paper encircling the body (Dorrell 1994: 232).

When excavated, long bones should be photographed the right way up both front and back and side - anterior, posterior and lateral views (Dorrell 1994: 236). The innominate, scapula and other bones should be placed in anatomical position, and be shot in anterior, posterior and lateral views. Human skulls should be photographed using the 'Frankfurt Plane', which draws a horizontal line between the superior edge of the auditory meatus and the interior edge of the eye orbit. Five standard views should be taken: from the left side (*norma lateralis*), from the top (*norma verticalis*), from the front (*norma frontalis*), from the back (*norma occipitalis*) and from below (*norma basilaris*). The mandible should be photographed in the occlusal plane and from the side to show the shape of the mandibular body and the biting surfaces of the teeth (Dorrell 1994: 236).

SETTING THE EXPOSURE

There are disadvantages in using the camera's internal exposure meter as it is likely to be 'centre weighted' and thus take an average of tones, assuming that they demonstrate average reflectance, or 'mid tone'. The best way of setting the exposure is to use a separate exposure meter to assess reflected and incident light, ideally in conjunction with a 'grey card' which will give the meter precisely what it needs for a perfect exposure. Reflected light is the light that is bounced back from the subject, whereas incident light is the light shining onto the subject (e.g. sunlight). Of the two, incident light is usually the safest reading, unless you have a spotmeter which reads reflected light in a very narrow field.

To read incident light, place the white dome supplied with the light meter over the photoelectric cell and take the reading whilst pointing the dome towards the camera. To read with a spot meter, point the spot meter at the lightest part of the subject (e.g. the matrix) and take a reading. Then, point the spotmeter at the darkest part of the subject (e.g. a dark pottery vessel) and take a reading. Add the two readings together and divide by two to find the correct reading.

All exposure meters will give a choice of combinations of shutter speed and aperture. The aperture is the size of the hole (which is adjustable) that lets light through the lens to the film, while the shutter speed is the time that the aperture is open to expose the film to the light. The shutter speed and aperture of the diaphragm have an inverse relationship, so that if one is moved then the other has to be moved the corresponding stops in the opposite direction. If the aperture size is increased (i.e. from f 18 to f 2.8), the shutter speed needs to be decreased correspondingly. Always use as small an aperture (i.e. larger number) as you safely can in order to provide a good depth-of-field, while remembering that smaller apertures slow the camera down, possibly resulting in camera shake. The aperture **increases** in size the smaller the number used – so f 2.8 is a far larger aperture than f 22; the former will provide a sharply focused main section, and the foreground/background will be blurred out. The latter, however, will be focused through the range. The slower the shutter speed the more a tripod is needed. To gain a greater depth-of-field (f 16, f 22 or f 32) will require a slower shutter speed (⅛, ¼ or ½ a second) and thus use of a tripod (Burke & Smith 2004: 266-7). There is a trade-off, for most lenses give a better overall definition in the mid-range of apertures (e.g. f 8 and f 11). These two apertures (especially f 11) will give more than adequate depth-of-field for most field archaeology. However, for object photography you should expect to use at least f 16, and for close-up or macro photography f 22 or f 32. A good rule is to focus the camera **one-third** of the way into your composition, as the depth-of-field extends from one-third in front of the point of focus to two-thirds behind. This means that all of your composition will be sharp (Burke & Smith 2004: 270).

USE OF ARTIFICIAL LIGHT

It may be necessary to add artificial light when taking a photograph. The main uses of flash in archaeology are to: 1. to add a light from one side to skim across the surface of an inscription in order to bring out the details. 2. to light areas that are in darkness or where light levels are very low. 3. to employ a fill-in flash for general low-key illuminations.

To bring out details such as inscriptions, connect a flash-gun to the camera by a remote cable so it can still be triggered by the camera shutter. Place the flash-gun so that the flash will skim across the surface from top left to bottom right (Dorrell 1994: 229). Check the exposure with a flash meter if you are going to do this in a dark area because the flash will supply the main light for the exposure. In daylight, wait for a time of the day when the sunlight skims across the surface, and then measure that light reading.

To use flash in dark areas such as caves and tombs, measure the power of the flash with a flash meter and set your f-stop accordingly. If you do not have a flash meter, you can use the scale usually printed on the back of flash-guns to decide on the right f-stop. If you have a large, dark area to photograph, use multiple flashes. To do this you should set the camera up on a tripod and use a torch to focus and set the f-stop. Then lock the camera shutter open by setting the shutter speed dial on 'B' and firing it with a cable release that is locked open. You are then free to walk around and fire the flash-gun several times by hand in the direction of the area you want to photograph. Ensure you are behind the flash, otherwise you will appear several times in the photograph! Alternatively you can use two flash-guns and bounce the flash off the walls. However, if the rock is sandstone, filters may have to be used to avoid a yellowish tint (Dorrell 1994: 134). When working in tombs and caves, you must work quickly, as the opening of the tomb can change the atmosphere and start irreversible changes (Dorrell 1994: 133). Often there is not a lot of room to work, or there is not enough light to focus through the viewfinder. In such a situation, all that can be done is to focus the lens and rely on the depth-of-field. If a 28 mm lens is set to 2 m at f 16, it will yield a fairly sharp picture from 2 m to infinity (Dorrell 1994: 133).

Fill-in flash can be used to equalise light and shadow. The flash gun must be on the camera, but instead of using the flash exposure scale given on the back, use it as if the film you are using in the camera is one stop faster than it actually is. For example if you have a 100 ISO speed film in the camera, use the flash scale as if there were a 200 ISO speed film. This will provide just enough flash to fill-in and not dominate the shot (Dorrell 1994: 59).

Artificial light (e.g. floodlights) may be useful, but as these large lights tend to be powered by mains electricity, their use is rather restricted on archaeological sites. Exposure can be worked out with a normal exposure meter for floodlights, but ensure you compensate for colour temperature. Tungsten bulbs normally give off a more yellow light (3,200 or 3,400 degrees Kelvin) than sunlight (5,500 degrees Kelvin). While we cannot see this difference, film can detect it (Dorrell 1994: 74). This is not important for black and white film, but to achieve true colours for daylight slide film, you will have to use a light blue filter (80A) to compensate. This also means that uncorrected light from floodlights and sunlight do not mix, as the colour temperatures are different. Flash, by contrast, has the same colour temperature as sunlight or daylight, so can therefore be mixed with either.

CHAPTER TEN

The Stratigraphic Record

The principal of stratification is fundamental to the understanding of any archaeological site (Barker 1982: 200). If one deposit or object can be shown to overlay another, then the lower context or object must have been deposited before the upper context (Barker 1982: 200). This will give a relative chronology for the site using the law of superposition and context. The purpose of studying stratification (stratigraphy) is to establish the position of strata and objects in space and time. In a simply stratified site, each stratum or context can be peeled off one at a time, the youngest first and the oldest last. However, sites are normally much more complex, made up of many cuts and deposits, which have been transformed due to site formation processes. As well as cultural strata, sites also consist of natural strata to a greater or lesser degree. These sediments were laid down by various natural forces, such as wind, water or volcanic action. In conjunction with sedimentary analysis and an absolute dating programme, stratigraphy as well as giving relative lengths of time over which cultural events happened, can provide information about the environment at the time of deposition. Stratigraphy can be used to reconstruct the shape of the landscape at the time of occupation(s), as the shape influences people's choice of location for particular activities, and can illuminate how humans modified the landscape (Balme & Paterson 2006: 98).

The rates of sedimentary deposition vary according to the process that created it. For example, in an area of sand dunes, a period of strong winds can deposit a thick layer of sand on their surface, with a gentle wind depositing a thin layer. If sediment has been deposited for a long time without additional depositional episodes, vegetation may grow and the mixing of the dead vegetation may cause soils to form (Balme & Paterson 2006: 98-9). Rivers may deposit thick layers of alluvium over large distances or move boulders many thousands of miles (Butzer 1976). The same processes that caused the deposition of sediments can also cause their erosion. The sediments can be scoured, mixed and redeposited elsewhere due to wind or water forces. Certain parts of a deposit can be eroded away and replaced by different sediments.

Cultural contexts can also form quickly or slowly, be the result of a longer or shorter event. The cut of a pit may take a matter of a few minutes, whereas the cut of a large grave can take several days or even weeks. The length of time needed to create a cultural context may therefore be representative of its size. A context's size however, is not necessarily a reflection of the length of its use-life. The destruction layer resulting from the collapse of a building may be the result of a quick event such as an earthquake or take several decades. Alternatively, a wall may be in use for several hundred years, whereas a hearth may only be used for a matter of hours. Unlike natural strata that can be reversed if they are solid, cultural strata cannot have a reverse stratigraphic sequence. If a pit has been excavated and the sediment put in a pile on the nearby surface, although the earliest objects from the digging of the pit may occur at the top of this pile, it will generally be a pile of mixed sediments from the different strata that the pit cut through, and as such a new deposit not reversed stratification. The infilling of the pit with the same pile of sediment will also

445

result in a new deposit, albeit with artefacts of different periods mixed through it (Harris 1989: 45).

The principals of archaeological stratification were developed out of those used by geologists. Ed Harris was the principal advocate of designating new laws of archaeological stratification as he argued that cultural formation processes were unlike natural ones, and so required an adjustment of the laws of natural stratification (Harris 1979). The five main principals (Harris 1979; 1989) of archaeological stratification are:

1. *The Law of Superposition*: This refers to the layering effect. Providing there has been no subsequent disturbance, deeper stratigraphic layers are older than those overlaying them. Each layer must have been deposited on, or created by the removal of, a pre-existing mass of material.

2. *The Law of Association*: Providing that there has been no disturbance, materials in the same stratigraphic layer are associated with each other. However, because some stratigraphic layers represent vastly greater time periods than others, the usefulness of this law varies.

3. *The Law of Original Horizontal Deposition*: Any layer deposited in an unconsolidated for will tend toward the horizontal. This means that strata found with tilted surfaces were either created that way or lie over the contours of previous basins or depositions. The shape of cultural layers will not necessarily be horizontal but, rather will be determined by the people that created them.

4. *The Law of Original Continuity*: A deposit will either be bounded by a basin of deposition or end in a feathered edge. Therefore, if it is not bounded or feathered edge, its original extent has been destroyed or altered. Its continuity must be sought or absence explained.

5. *The Law of Stratigraphical Succession*: A unit of archaeological stratification takes its place in the stratigraphic sequence of a site from its position between the undermost (or earliest) of the units which lie above it and the uppermost (or latest) of all the units which lie below it and with which the unit has a physical contact, all other superpositional relationships being redundant.

These laws have been slightly modified through time, but still generally remain true. However, the caveat 'providing there has been no subsequent disturbance' is important. Most stratigraphic successions on archaeological sites will have been disturbed by one means or another. The site formation processes outlined in **Chapter 4** cover the many different cultural and natural processes. These processes make the understanding of how a site formed more difficult, and as such it is important to identify these processes while excavating. It is important to understand when and how these disturbances took place in relation to the original deposition in order to gain a true understanding of the stratigraphic sequence, and as such the chronological succession of the site. Due to the dynamic nature of the natural and cultural processes involved in creating and altering the stratigraphic complexity of an archaeological site, the stratigraphic analysis should be done in stages rather than being left to a 'post-excavation' analysis stage. To make this task faster and easier the initial stages must begin as the excavation of the individual contexts proceeds. The understanding of this process is helped by the building of a Harris Matrix. The Harris Matrix was designed to graphically show the vertical and horizontal stratigraphy, and is a diagrammatic representation of the site designed to help interpretation (Harris 1975; 1979). This matrix relationships go from top to bottom, so should be read this way.

THE RUNNING MATRIX

Knowing the physical relationship of contexts can help in understanding the truncation of certain contexts, how environmental or artefactual samples may have been contaminated and help in understanding the manner in which structures were built. Some of the recording sheets have boxes for recording a context's physical relationship with others, termed the **Physical Stratigraphic Relationship**, and uses words to describe the physical association. Relationships are recorded using four terms: abutted by, bonded with, abutting and uncertain. A modern pit may cut through many contexts, and therefore will have many physical relationships of the cuts variety. However, these are not direct stratigraphic relationships, and should only appear stratigraphically as being directly above the layer it was first cut into. It will consequently appear on more than one of the context recording forms, not as a stratigraphic relationship but as a physical relationship placed in the **Context Boundary Interface** or description fields. Many of the recording forms provide spaces to record a context's stratigraphic relationships; these are plotted in the **Running Matrix** (**Fig. 170**). As each context is a defined event, the stratigraphic relationship is not concerned with which context touches another, but with the chronological sequence in which the contexts were constructed; creating a record of the order in which the deposition of successive units occurred (Roskams 2001: 155). The stratigraphic relationship is the type that is of most importance for understanding how the site fits together chronologically.

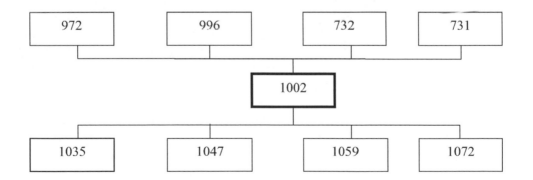

Figure 170: The Running Matrix (horizontal) allows you to show which contexts lie directly above and below the current context. If more context boxes are required, they should be drawn in accordingly.

The relationship that is recorded in the running matrix is a stratigraphic relationship where a context is either earlier or later than another. The running matrix is a compilation of the contexts after they have been removed over the whole area of the excavation unit or trench, and recorded on the recording forms in the order in which they were removed. At the end of the day the site supervisor must check all running matrices for accuracy and to build up a larger-scale trench running matrix. Harris (1989: 36) suggests that purely stratigraphic relationships can take three forms: 1) have no direct stratigraphic connection, 2) be in superposition, or 3) be correlated as parts of a once-whole deposit or feature interface.

1. If two contexts have no proven link to each other, they can be seen as being 'potentially contemporary', or 'floating with respect of each other'.

2. If a context is in superposition to another, it is (stratigraphically) later than the other.

3. If two contexts are physically separated (i.e. by a wall), they are thought to have once been the same unit due to their physical characteristics, surface level and date of finds.

Unlike operational area and site matrices (which are compiled at the excavation centre), the running matrix is compiled in the field by the excavators. It is kept to aid clear thinking, to help understand and clarify stratigraphic relationships, and to guide the excavation process. It is also a good way of displaying the stratigraphy in a graphic form, and making sure that apparently insignificant contexts are considered in the site formation process. Filling-out the running matrix is not as simple as it may appear. The number of the context currently being worked on must be placed in the central box, and the context(s) which overlaid it in the box(es) above. The box(es) below must not be filled out until the current, and contexts below have been fully excavated. This may be easy to do on shallow sites with limited horizontal stratigraphy and extensive layers, but is more difficult, on deep, complex or/and urban or *tell* sites.

Overlaying Single-Context Planning Sheets to Construct a Grid Square Running Matrix

Either pre-printed or cut to size single context draughting sheets contain the drawing of a context in a single grid square, these sheets of draughting film can be overlain to establish the stratigraphic relationship (**Figs. 171-76**). In order to establish a context's (A) stratigraphic position on the running matrix, compare the current plan with those of other contexts that may overlie it by vertically 'stacking' the plans. If there is an overlap between them, the new context must be earlier. This process will allow you to fill out the central box and the top box(es) of the running matrix on the sheets and plans. To be able to fill out the lowest box, you must fully excavate context A, which may subsequently reveal contexts B and C. Both these contexts must be fully revealed and planned, and then the overlaying process can begin again. By seeing which contexts A overlays, you will be able to fill out the lowest box of the running matrix. In this way, a matrix can be built up for the 5.0 m grid square, which in turn can be built into the larger trench and site matrices.

The first (uppermost) context is recorded, planned and excavated, and its context number shown on the stratigraphic relation matrix in the following manner:

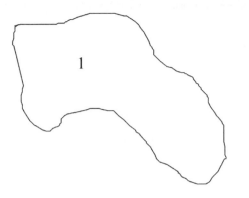

Figure 171: Context 1 planned and recorded in the matrix (after Westman 1994: 8).

Figure 172: The plan of context 2 is placed over context one for comparison and the relationship noted on the matrix thus (after Westman 1994: 9).

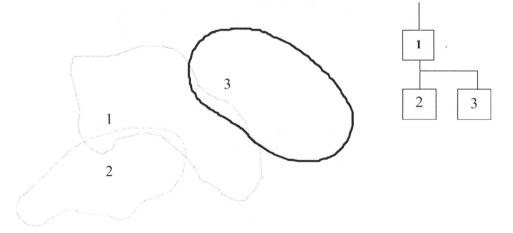

Figure 173: After the third context is excavated, it is noted that it has a direct relationship with context 1 and an indirect relationship with context 2, and that both have a relationship with context 1. It is shown on the matrix thus (after Westman 1994:10).

449

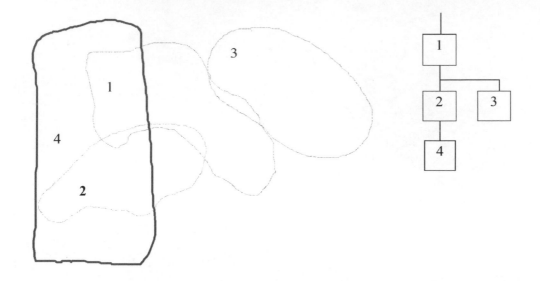

Figure 174: The establishing of the stratigraphic relationship between the contexts carries on as the excavation deepens. In the above figure there is a stratigraphic relationship between context 4 and 2 and 3, but not context 1 (after Westman 1994: 10).

The planned context sheets continue to be placed over one another, with each new context sheet being placed on the ones above it, leading to a full running matrix. The overlaying process should start as soon as possible to ascertain the stratigraphic relationships and enable any planning inaccuracies to be quickly recognised and corrected. It is therefore best done when the plan has just been drawn, but before any of the context has been removed (Roskams 2001: 163-5).

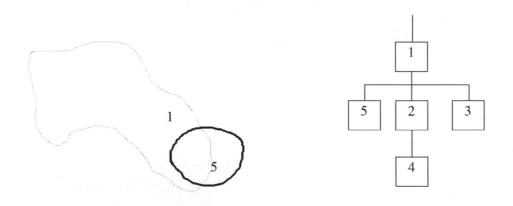

Figure 175: This running matrix shows no stratigraphic relationships between 2, 3 & 4 and context 5, which only has a relationship with context 1 (after Westman 1994: 11).

450

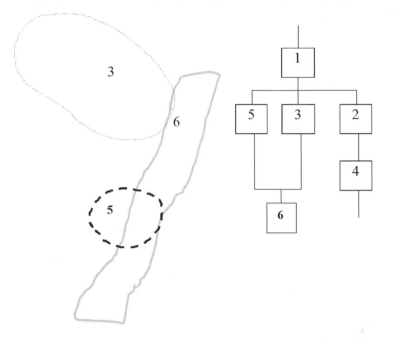

Figure 176: This is the complete stratigraphic sequence for the area; the earlier contexts are not shown, so as to avoid confusion. There are no stratigraphic relationships between 2, 3 and 4; context 5 and 3 overlay context 6 (after Westman 1994).

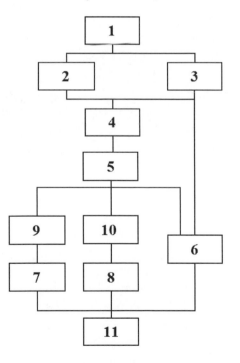

Figure. 177: A common error in building a matrix.

A common error in building a matrix is to insert physical relationships as well as the stratigraphic relationships. The matrix shown in **Fig. 177** is from the lower section in **Fig. 183**. Although (3) physically overlies (6), the stratigraphic relationship goes through (4) and (5), and the correct matrix showing this relationship is shown in **Fig. 183**. Another common error is to merge threads when there is no proven relationship between contexts. In **Fig. 178** (3) underlies (2) and (4), as (4) overlays (3) and (5), but is not overlain by (2) the strands must not be merged as it would indicate a relationship between (2) and (5) that does not exist. Also, as (5) does not overlay (6) the strand must enter under (6) rather than above.

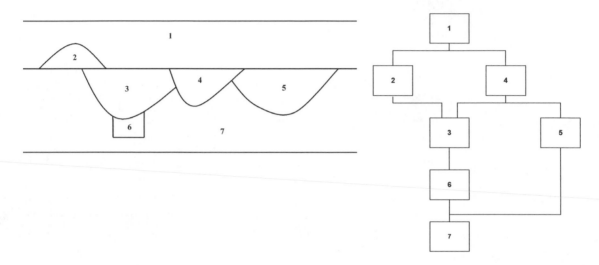

Figure 178: Unmerged threads to indicate no stratigraphic relationship.

As the running matrix is constantly evolving, with the relationships between all previously excavated contexts already being recorded on the matrix, it is best to start the overlaying process with the plans that hang at the base of one of the matrix's strands. If no overlap can be found with any of the contexts at the base of one of the strands, then overlaps must be looked for further up the strands. If no overlap can be found at all, the context can float to the top of the matrix until underlying contexts have been excavated and it can be pulled into the sequence (Roskams 2001: 165). Therefore, the diagram of the grid unit matrix is added to as the excavation progresses. A reading of the baulks should also be made to help verify the accuracy of the running matrix. This should be a separate matrix containing just the contexts seen in the baulks (see **Fig. 181**).

If using pre-printed single-context planning draughting film the stratigraphic relationship is shown using the **Stratigraphic Relation Matrix**, the current context being placed in the central box, with the context directly stratigraphically above it in the grid unit being placed in the box above, and the context directly below in the lower box (**Fig. 179**). Only contexts that have been excavated and planned in the same grid unit must be included in the stratigraphic relation matrix. This is helpful in identify the stratigraphic relationship of the various contexts within a grid unit when overlaying single-context plans. There is also a grid shown on the recording forms and planning sheets: this is the **Context Location Box**, and is designed to show the other grid units/squares into which a context may physically run to the north, east, west, or south (**Fig. 179**). The context location box can be filled out in two different ways. A cross should be placed in the central box to indicate the grid unit of the context just planned, subsequent crosses are placed in any adjacent box to indicate other grid units the context extends into. If the grid units are numbered, then the numbers of the grid squares should be used instead of crosses. Therefore, if the part of context 929 that lies in square 97 has just been planned, 97 is placed in the central box, and as context 929 extends into square 96 to the west, this is a written in the context location box on the left (see **Fig. 179**). This system facilitates the quick location of the adjacent grid squares that may be holding the rest of a context. As single-context planning sheets are often filed per grid unit, it is essential to know the other grid units that any given context may run into to aid quick location of those plans. If the stratigraphic relation matrix and context location box are not already pre-printed on the draughting film, then you **must** draw them on yourself.

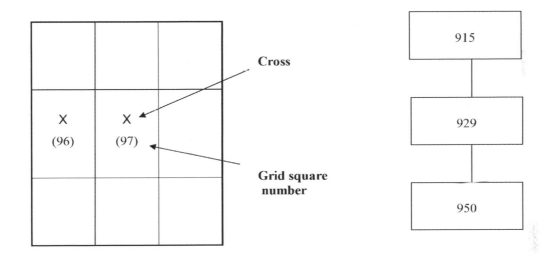

Figure 179: Context Location Box and Stratigraphic Relation Matrix, A) is for showing which plans adjoin the current plan, and which adjacent grid square the current context runs into; B) is for indication which single-context plan lies directly above or below the current context plan.

BUILDING A RUNNING MATRIX FOR A TRENCH

Before constructing the trench matrix the matrices from the individual grid units within the trench should be built (see **Fig. 180C**). This is done in the manner outlined above, although these should be checked at regular intervals by the supervisors and director. If a context lies entirely within one grid unit, it can only overlap with other contexts in that grid unit. These individual grid matrices must then be amalgamated to make the trench matrix; if a certain context lies within more than one grid unit, they will appear on several grid matrices (see **Fig. 180D**). Plans will only need to be overlaid if there is some doubt whether certain contexts are in superposition or can be correlated as parts of a once-whole deposit or feature interface. If a plan is wholly in one grid unit it cannot overlay another context wholly in a different grid unit, although there may be a correlation (this will need to be checked from the single context forms and associated artefacts). The amalgamation of the running matrices of the grid squares should be checked from the bottom up. The relationships deduced in each of the grid matrices must be added together, so that of Sq. 95 is added to Sq. 96, these are added to Sq. 97 and so forth. Many of the relationships will simply confirm the deductions of the first square matrix, others may be additional relationships. Some relationships may be shown to be true relationships, but irrelevant as they are superseded by more critical relationships in other grid units. Once the grid unit matrices have been amalgamated, and the true-but-irrelevant ones removed, the results can be entered on the recording sheets and then go on to form part of the site or operational area matrix (Roskams 2001: 166).

A) **Plan of Trench**

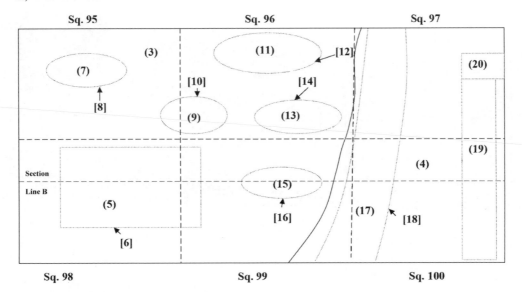

B) Section of Plan A

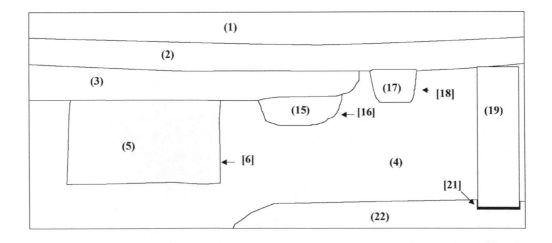

C)

The individual matrices for:

Sq. 95

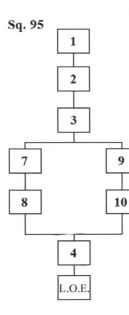

Sq. 96

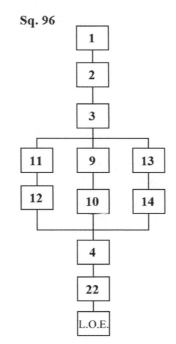

Sq. 97

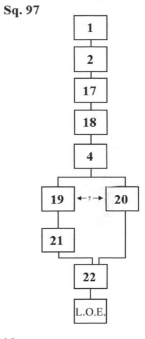

Sq. 98

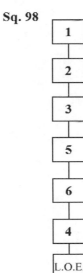

Sq. 99

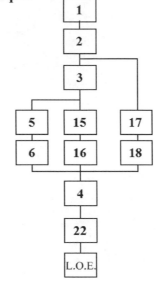

Sq.100

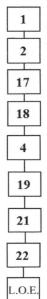

The threads above (4) have been merged in squares 95, 96, and 99, whereas those above (22) in square 97 have been left unmerged (**Fig. 180C**), although this may seem personal preference, this is not the case, for in certain circumstances it can represent false relationships, so the merging of threads should only be done where it is a true reflection of the stratigraphic relationships (see **Fig. 178**). The double headed arrow between (19) and (20) indicates that the chronological sequence between the two needs to have further information from dating analysis to resolve the relationship of which wall abuts the other; this should be done during further analytical phases. The resolved trench matrix (**Fig. 180D**) shows that the graves, contexts 5 to 16 were dug into the same matrix (4), which in turn is overlain by (3). Although the ditch (17) and [18] was also dug into (4), as it was not overlain by (3), which seals all the graves, it can be demonstrated to be stratigraphically later than the graves.

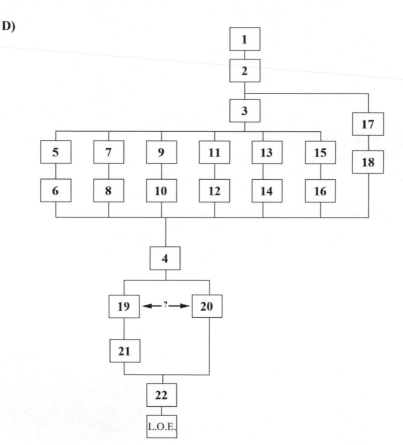

Figure 180: The resolved trench matrix: A) plan view of trench showing levels 1 and 2 removed; B) section across matrix; C) individual grid square matrices; D) the resolved trench matrix.

No grid boxes should ever be left empty; if need be two acronyms can be used: LOE = limit of excavations, and NFE = no further excavation (or Nor Fully Excavated).This also allows for any grid boxes left hanging in the air to be identified as errors and their relationship to be revisited and tied into the sequence before the matrix can be considered completed (Roskams 2001: 159).

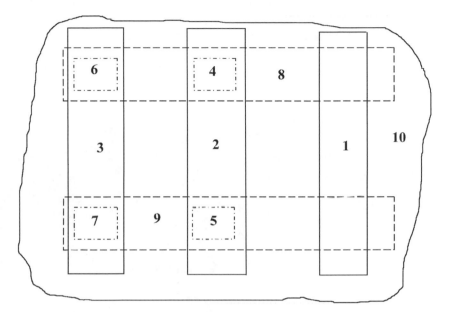

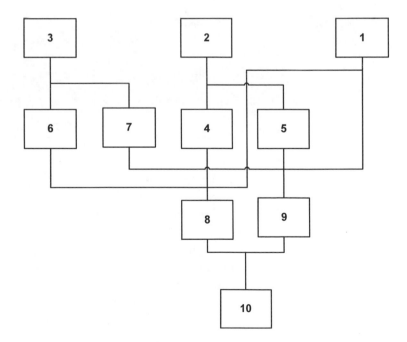

Figure 181: Bridges across stratigraphic threads (after Roskams 2001: 158).

Another practical point is the use of arched 'bridges' over threads, this indicates that there is no stratigraphic relationship between certain overlapping threads and so the line jumps over the thread (**Fig. 181**). It is best to try and avoid these if possible, but in certain circumstances they are unavoidable. These bridges can make the diagram look messy, but if they cannot be removed easily by placing the matrix boxes in different places, it is best they are left in. In **Fig. 181** a rubble foundation (10) is overlain by timber sills (8) and (9), capped with levelling tiles (4), (5), (6) and (7). These tiles were themselves overlain with further timbers (2) and (3). When a further timber (1) is added that overlays sills (8) and (9) its position cannot be shown accurately without bridges, otherwise false relationships would be implied. The relationship between context (7) and (9) also cannot be shown accurately without bridges (Roskams 2001: 158-9).

Figure 182: Measuring the stratigraphy in a section (photograph G. J. Tassie).

In **Figure 183** the section and plan matrices of a 5.0 x 5.0 m trench are combined to make an amalgamated trench matrix. The plans are shown as combined single-context plans for diagrammatic reasons, but the matrix should be compiled from stacking the single-context plans. Multi-context plans should not be relied on to generate a matrix as many of the relationships are assumed as apposed to being proved. The contexts have been analysed and correlated and the numbers amalgamated. As the contexts in plan and section are numbered separately, this should only be done in the analysis phase in preparation for publication and clarity, otherwise the combined contexts should be indicated with an = sign (see below). As sections and plans show the stratigraphic sequence in different circumstances, looking for correlations between the two is best done on site in front of the sections with the plans, recording sheets, and other data to hand. Once this has been completed it allows for a fuller interpretation of the stratigraphic record and the building of the full trench matrix. However, this is usually only possible once all the dating information has been gathered from the specialists (see below). These contexts can then be grouped into higher order blocks of contexts that correlate with phases of the house's life

458

(see below on grouping contexts). The blocks illustrate changes from action to activity: building to living, destruction to re-building.

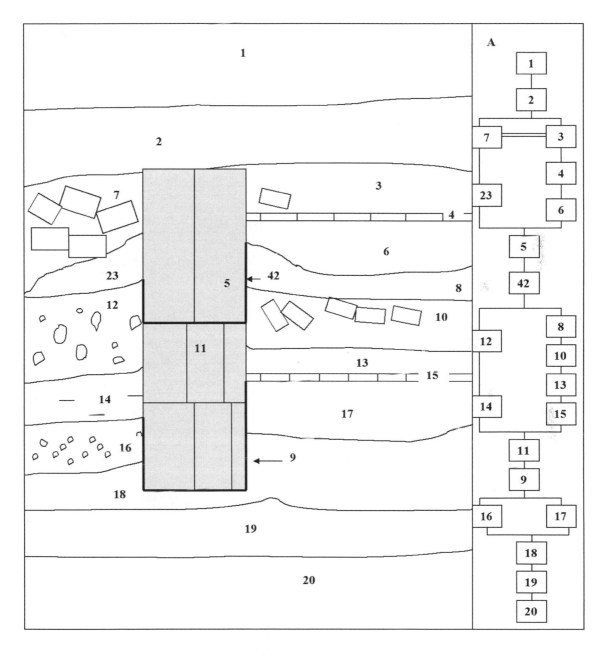

North Section

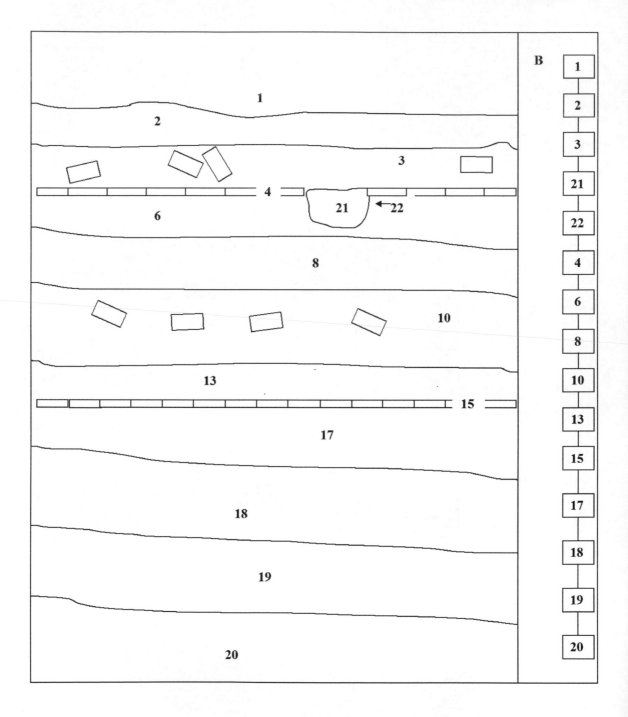

East Section

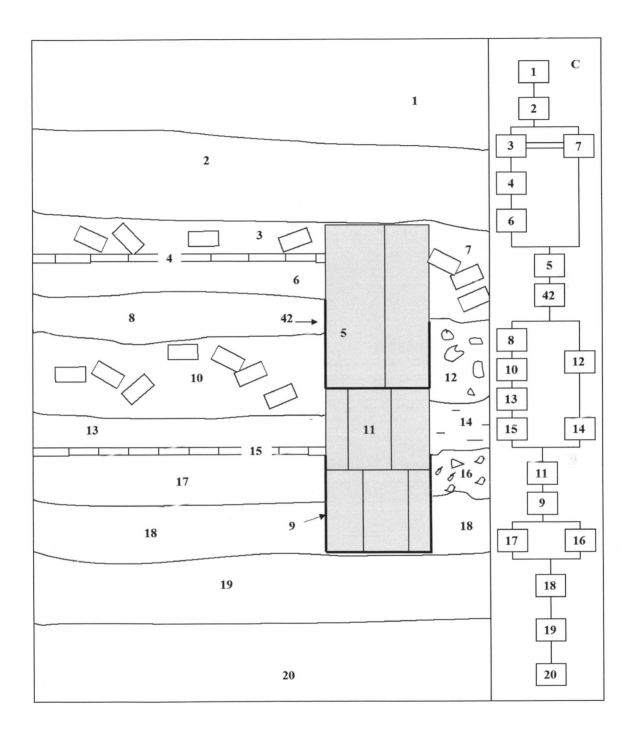

South Section

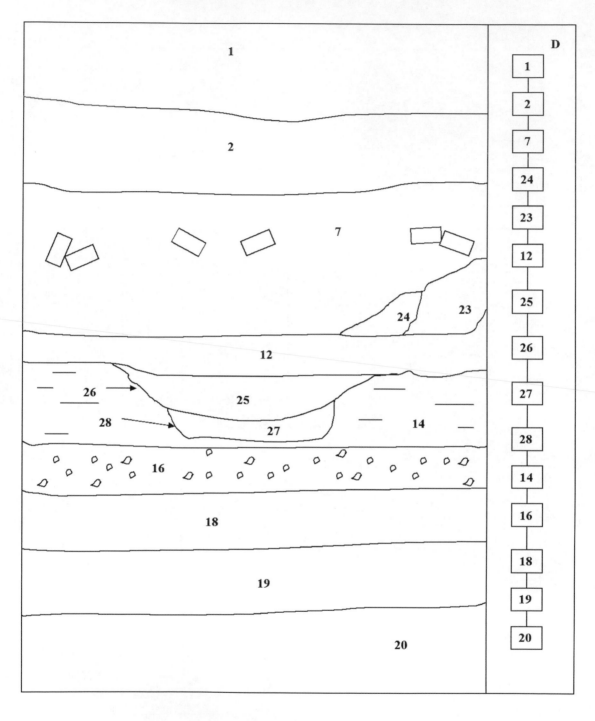

West Section

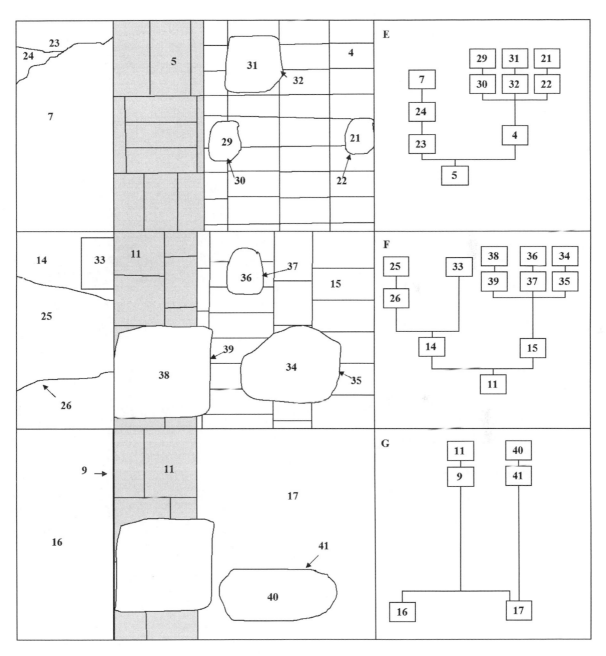

Plans

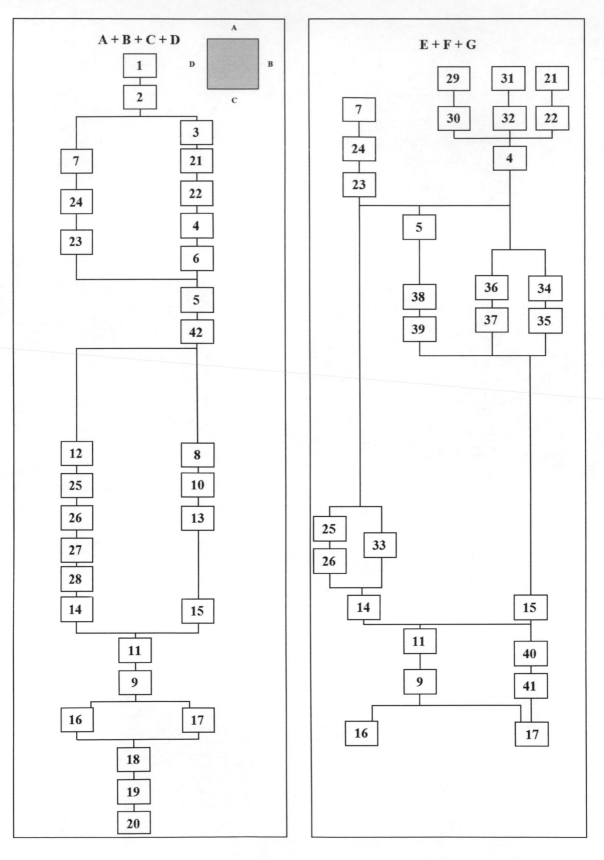

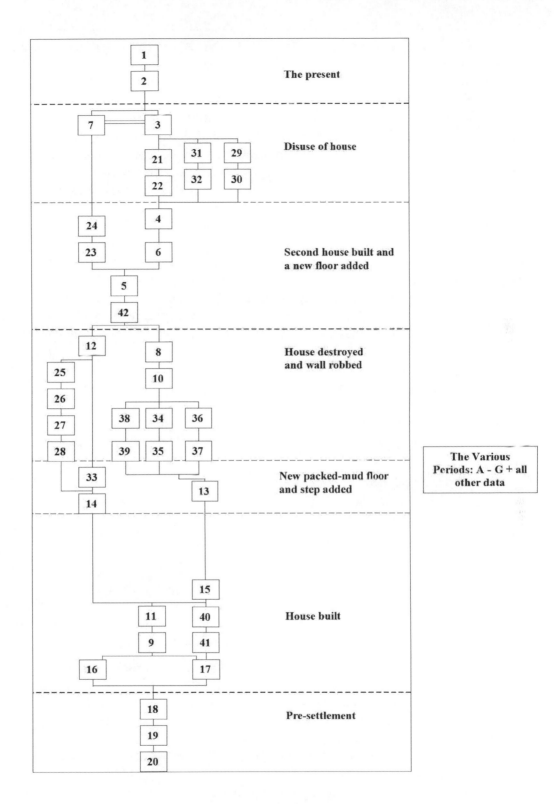

Figure 183: The Harris matrix compiled from both plans and sections (after Harris 1989). The section drawings are simplified, shown without drawing conventions (symbols) for clarity of interpretation.

STRATIGRAPHIC ANALYSIS AND CONSTRUCTING AN OPERATIONAL AREA OR SITE MATRIX

The various areas of an archaeological site must be inter-correlated, and the sequence in one operational area or trench has to be correlated with those in all the others. It may be necessary in certain circumstances (particularly on prehistoric sites) for a geoarchaeologist to examine the microstratigraphy and sedimentology before correlations can be made. Either during or after the fieldwork season, the stratigraphic, photographic, written and drawn records will have to be analysed in order to enable the phasing of the site and the assigning of function to the various contexts. Rather than having just a graph of the context numbers, the numbers must be grouped into contexts relating to a specific feature, such as a building or grave. Where possible, dating evidence of the features or groups of contexts should also be indicated (Barker 1982: 202). However, there are two diametrically opposing views on when data should be interpreted, namely: 1) when the archaeology is in front of you, and 2) after all the data has been collected and collated. Both these views have their advocates and critics; however, a third way is advocated here, the holistic method, encompassing both views. Roskams (2001: 247) suggests that interpretation of the function of a context or feature should be part of the on-site excavation process, which can then be built upon during the analytical phase. On-site interpretation can usefully influence notions of site formation processes and functions of contexts and features, whereas correlations between separate stratigraphic units are best done during the analytically-based, post-excavation phase. The two activities are inter-linked, and both can be modified in post-excavation work from ideas originally generated in the field. The stratigraphic sequence is best interpreted from the bottom up, from the earliest to the latest (Roskams 2001: 247). The sequence is as follows:

1. Make horizontal links across the sequence.

2. Block the units together vertically and create a phasing structure for these blocks.

3. Make decisions as to the function of a context or group of contexts on ever increasing hierarchy of interpretation -feature 70 is interpreted first as 'occupation debris', then as 'an accumulation of mud-bricks' and finally as 'east wall of the southern magazine of the Horus Temple'.

Because the matrix is evolving and being recorded as the excavation progresses, not all the previous plans need to be overlaid (Roskams 2001: 165). As each context comes up for analysis, possible contextual links must be considered. The primary interpretation should be arrived at through study of the in-field archaeology, plans, sections and photographs. In the stratigraphic analysis phase, the running matrices must be checked for missing relationships by cross-referencing other records. It may not be possible to build a complete site matrix if the operational areas are in different geographical locations, e.g. tombs in the low desert or mountains and settlement on the flood plane. Therefore, two operational area matrices may have to be constructed for the site.

This sequence of planned matrices can also be recorded from the vertical profile.

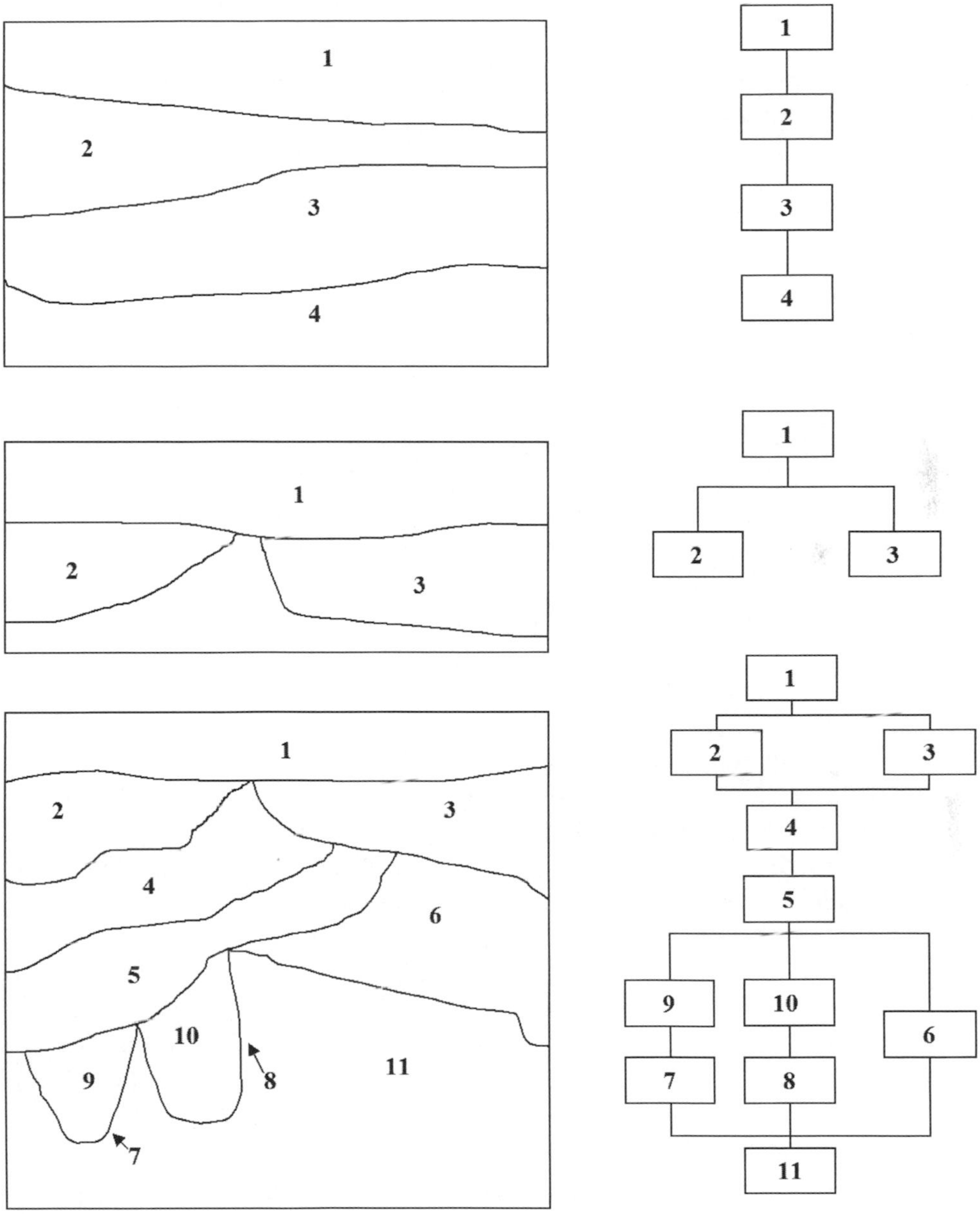

Figure 184: The top section shows a simple stratigraphy, whereas the second section shows a slightly more complicated stratigraphy where no relationship can be directly demonstrated between contexts 2 and 3. The last section shows a yet more complicated stratigraphy (after Baker 1982: 201). The section drawings are simplified, shown without drawing conventions so as to maximise clarity.

After all the running matrices have been completed and submitted for analysis, each context must be fitted into a higher-order group. Only after this has been done can one be sure that all the stratigraphic evidence has been thoroughly considered (Roskams 2001: 249). The first step is to seek correlations across the sequence and to see if any two contexts can be amalgamated. If two contexts are found to be one-and-the-same, possibly cut by a pit, then correlations must be made and the two can be amalgamated. This is particularly relevant when the operational area or/and site matrix is being constructed from both section and plan matrices. To make a correlation between contexts it is important to analyse sedimentary composition and form from the written record and samples. It should be noted, however, that it may be very difficult to distinguish contexts, and that variability in recording of contexts by different excavators may affect the results. It is therefore best to avoid having to make horizontal correlations during the analysis phase, by taking great care when recording in the field, and making any 'simple' horizontal correlations in the field when the archaeology in front of you and any relationships are less speculative. However, on large sites or where there are single contexts covering a large surface area this may be impossible, and the horizontal correlation may only be possible in the analysis phase.

After making the connections across the sequence (horizontal), based on their specific properties and conception of the whole sequence, associations of successive contexts must be made in the vertical sequence. This entails the blocking/grouping of contexts based on their functional similarities (e.g. walls and floors of a building or fills of a pit). Contexts represent single actions, whereas context blocks represent longer-term groups of activities. Plans, recording sheets, sections and photographs must all be consulted, as must the artefactual and ecofactual records. When blocking contexts it is not simply enough to observe similarities in structure - there must be a common function. The function of contexts will of course incorporate decisions made on site formation processes. Therefore, it is important to consult the recording sheets for the interpretation reached in the field. This interpretation must be correlated with the artefactual, ecofactual, environmental and other scientific data. The creation of context blocks, therefore, has a dynamic relationship with decisions made about site formation processes (Roskams 2001: 251).

Finds (especially pottery) can be used as dating evidence; however, finds can also be used to elucidate site function, and either general or specific activities associated with a feature. Although finds may be analysed in isolation or by stratigraphic unit, the assemblages must be examined in sequence, and sometimes grouped together in order to reach meaningful connections and obtain stratigraphically significant results. As all the various components of the site are mutually interactive, it is important to assess the site record as a whole. The analysis of the site stratigraphy is the first step in processing the site record, and a necessary prerequisite for the integration of specialist data (Roskams 2001: 240). If a lot of intrusive pottery is found in a context, the excavator should be asked to re-evaluate the context. This errant pottery may indicate that the excavator has missed a pit that should have been assigned a new context number. The place from whence the pottery came is then assigned a new context number, if this is found to be the case, and the pottery's context is then subsequently corrected. If this same late pottery is found in a pit that lies physically beneath this deposit, it is probable that the pit was actually cut from a ground surface in the upper layer and not actually recognised until the lower level. It could also be that bioturbation caused the movement of the pottery (Dever & Darrel Lance 1978).

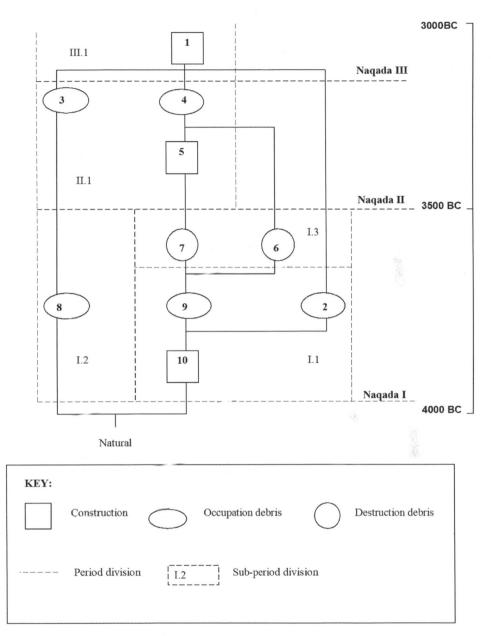

Figure 185: Matrix showing the different time periods, with phasing imposed on the sequence (after Roskams 2001: 265).

Blocks can then be grouped and put into the higher-order interpretation of 'periods' (see **Fig. 185**), so that a line can be drawn across the whole range of the sequence. No block of contexts or a single context can belong to more than one period. Moreover, it is more likely to find a site-wide period on a small, shallow site, with limited stratigraphy, than on a large, deeply stratified site (Roskams 2001: 251).

CHECKING THE SITE MATRIX THROUGH NODES AND CRITICAL PATHS

When checking the site matrix, it is vital that it is built from the bottom up using these three principles to follow, as outlined by:

1. Only the basic stratigraphic relationships should be used when first examining the strata.

2. The time to consider any individual, floating stratigraphic unit, is just before examining the one above it.

3. If there is a long sequence and a short sequence to be correlated, then always choose the long sequence to analyse as it is more likely to elucidate the shorter sequence than *vice versa* (Roskams 2001: 253).

Figure 186: Stratigraphic nodes. The shaded contexts 5, 12 and 31 are the nodes from which strands of contexts hang. Context 31 is a sub-node of 5 as it is overlain by 5 much higher up the sequence.

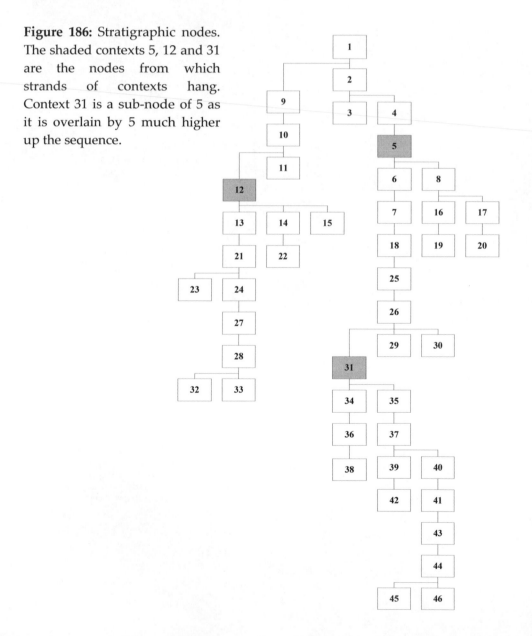

These principles allow a route through the sequence to be established, not relying on any preconceived notions of links worked out previously. This is particularly relevant in complex matrices involving a thousand or more units as it can be a very time-consuming exercise. On a complex site there will be many strands, and each will have to be checked individually. Therefore, when dealing with large matrices, it is often prudent to define nodal points; these are defined as single units which draw together many other units underneath or above it (Roskams 2001: 154). The node unit (context), with the units below it, can then be lifted out of the site matrix, and this smaller sub-matrix sequence can then be analysed and ordered in the manner outlined above. This process can be repeated for other nodal groups, some of which may be separate from one another, others successive. An order for the groups and a route between them can then be found, no matter how complex the site matrix. Alternatively, define the longest sequence, and then fit all the floating units into it. However, it must be remembered that the longest sequence of context units does not necessarily represent the longest temporal sequence of development on site (Roskams 2001: 254). Computer software packages such as the *Bonn Archaeological Programme*™, *ArchEd* and *Stratify* can be used to build large site matrices.

THE VARIOUS MEANS OF PRESENTING STRATIGRAPHIC INTERPRETATIONS AS A MATRIX

As the traditional Harris Matrix uses rectangular boxes to portray the stratigraphic units diagrammatically, it cannot show all the intricacies of the stratigraphic record. To solve this problem, circles, ovals, triangles and units with staggered edges can also be used (Brown & Harris 1993). **Figures 187** and **188** show various methods of portraying the site matrix. The boxes can also be stretched to indicate relative time. This can be achieved by assessing how long it took for an overlying unit to come into play or in respect of adjacent components in the stratigraphic sequence (Dalland 1984; Lowe 1993). A wall may have a whole series of floors or there may be a long pottery sequence in the context (Carver 1979). In addition to showing features such as destruction, construction, debris (**Fig. 187**), further interpretive labels such as feature numbers and use can be added (i.e. F.3, cesspit). Internal and external contexts can also be indicated illustrating different types of land use. The strengths of correlation between contexts can be shown by the types of horizontal lines used to connect the boxes (see **Fig. 187**). A = B indicates that the two contexts were originally one entity, whereas, A---B indicates that the two contexts have similar interpretations and formed roughly at the same time, and A opposite B suggests that the two are not strongly connected, but that circumstantial evidence suggests that they are probably contemporary (Roskams 2001: 262). Uncertainties in boundaries can also be illustrated with zigzags on the boundary that is uncertain (**Fig. 188**). These types of matrices can help specialists, such as ceramicists to understand the pottery assemblage. However, interpretative matrix units must only be used in the full site sequence, as equal weight must be given to the contexts in the previous matrices to avoid making inappropriate interpretative or qualitative judgements prior to the elucidation of the full site sequence. As well as using various shaped boxes to indicate the different classes of contexts, colours can be used to indicate cuts, walls, possible walls, floor levels, destruction debris, plaster, natural deposits, cultural fills, etc.

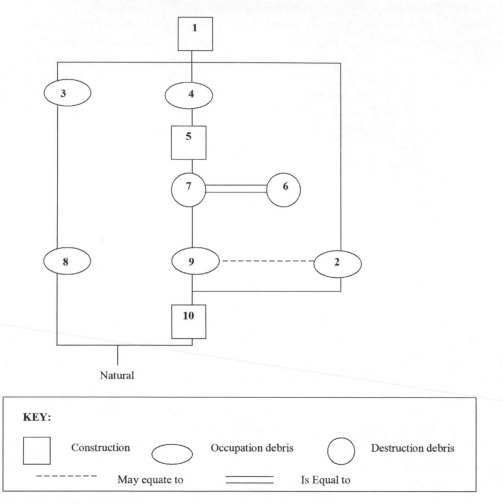

Figure 187: Various unit shapes on the matrix showing different interpretations of context and different strengths of linkage (after Roskams 2001: 263).

Ghost context boxes can be added to the matrix if a context that was once there, but has been destroyed is essential to understanding the chronological sequence. This is a higher level of interpretation than is generally required when generating the matrix and should only be done if the archaeologist is absolutely sure of the position of the missing context. An example of the necessity of a ghost context is when one burial totally recuts and removes an earlier primary burial. The recognition of the primary burial may take the form of disarticulated elements from the original skeleton being redeposited with the second skeleton in the recut burial pit. Grave goods from the primary burial may also be found in with the second burial. To record this sequence of events on the matrix, it is necessary to create 'ghost' contexts representing the original burial pit, though little trace of this may have survived (Chadwick 1998). This information could be coded onto the matrix in a different manner to the main stratigraphic elements, or it could be recorded on a different set of matrices altogether, which would perhaps be similar to trait or attribute matrices (Adams 1991; 1992; Harris *et al.* 1993).

Although the rules laid down by Harris were one of the major steps forward in archaeology, sites do not always conform to these stratigraphic rules. Stratigraphic conundrums such as fills that build up in much earlier capped drains, or pits that were dug through deposits whilst the latter were still forming, later tunnels dug beneath earlier remains are to be found on many sites (Matthews 1993). Matrices can be adapted and transformed to meet such challenges, although it may be necessary to supplement the stratigraphic matrix with other forms of graphic display to illustrate the full dynamic character of a site (Adams 1992; Lucas 2001).

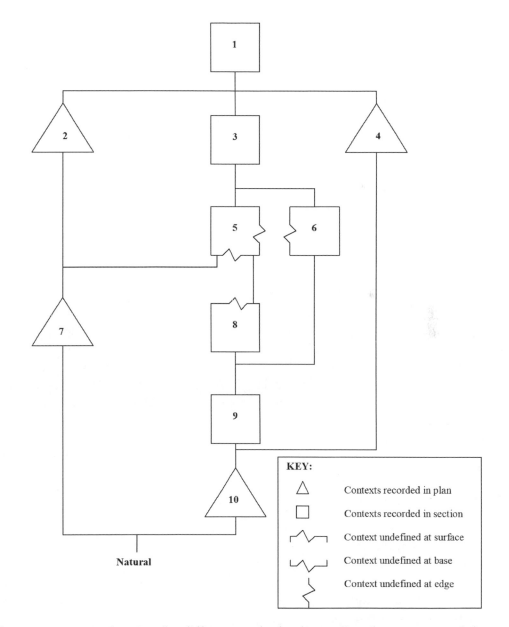

Figure 188: Matrix showing the different methods of recording the contexts and the meeting of the edges (after Roskams 2001: 256).

473

Finds Processing

Finds processing involves retrieving, sorting, cleaning, labelling, logging, quantifying, cataloguing and – where necessary – conserving material remains (see **Fig. 190**), before classifying, analysis and interpretation takes place (IFA 2001a: 2; Shopland 2006). Most of the finds retrieved on site are artefacts. While the vast majority of these (on sites dating to the Neolithic and later) are likely to be ceramic, all artefacts, ecofacts, building material, environmental material, biological remains (including human remains) and decay products constitute finds (IFA 2002a: 2). The purpose of finds processing is to produce an ordered, stable and accessible archive and report(s), which act as a resource for current and future research. Whereas, their analysis aims to provide an understanding of societies and their environments on the local, regional, national and international scale (IFA 2002a: 2). It can occur during a watching brief, evaluation, excavation, as a post-excavation process as part of a research programme, within the context of interpretation and presentation of finds to the public, or as an analysis of collections in long-term storage (IFA 2002a: 2). During the planning stage of the archaeological project it is essential to budget for the type and quantity of finds likely to be encountered, using variables such as preservation rate, period and site type. It is also important to budget time and personnel for processing along with any materials required for packaging, storage, conservation and documentation (IFA 2002a: 7).

Preliminary finds processing and classification should run alongside fieldwork. This allows for data evaluation, so that working hypotheses can be modified and strategies can be adapted to best suit the requirements of the record and the finds it contains (Sharer & Ashmore 1987: 281). If all the finds processing is left until after the fieldwork has finished, you will lose the recovered data's potential to guide the excavation. Finds processing or post-excavation **must** therefore be concurrent with the fieldwork, so that preliminary interpretations of the finds can be fed back into the fieldwork plan (see **Fig. 190**). Finds managers must therefore be involved in the planning aspects of the research design. Aspects of finds work will continue after the fieldwork has ceased, including specialist/advanced analysis and conservation, and finer detailed archiving and accessioning (Shopland 2006).

Most finds will have undergone some form of processing and classification in the field during their retrieval, including – if necessary – extensive *in situ* recording. The majority of finds processing, however, is carried out in the field research centre; which is used for processing finds before they are moved to more secure facilities. At the end of each working session, all finds that have finished being recorded in the field should be brought back to the field research centre for further processing. Copies of the fieldwork recording forms should accompany the objects to the processing areas and laboratories; their excavational, provenience and contextual information must be logged into the database, allowing the system to expand as the analytical process continues (Sharer & Ashmore 1987: 281). The excavators and finds processors should exchange information to allow each better understanding of the material remains.

Ideally, the field research centre should be divided into a central area for sorting and other communal activities, and a series of specialised laboratories for human remains, ceramics, environmental analysis, conservation or other specialist activities. The size of the centre will ultimately depend on the size of the project, although there should always be enough space for processing and short-term storage of the amount of data being generated. This centre may take the form of standing buildings, tents, covered areas and other makeshift laboratories. The structure must comply with health and safety regulations, have adequate lighting, heating and water resources (preferably using renewable energy and water), and must also be secure and furnished with the necessary equipment, materials and furniture. When building the field and research centre, think about the future use of the building, for it can be converted into a visitor centre or on-site museum after the project has finished. An example of an archaeological field complex is presented in **Figure 189**. Detailed finds processing should be done as soon as possible after the data is recovered from the field, thus assisting with hypothesis development and also minimising the risk of errors and loss of labels from the finds (Sharer & Ashmore 1987: 282).

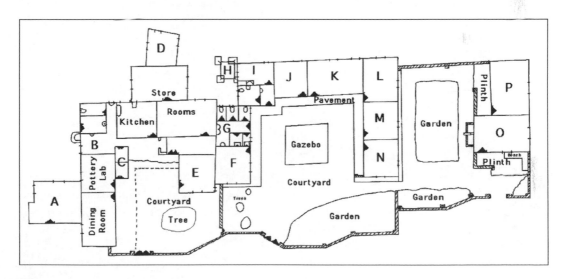

KEY:

A. Conservation lab
B. Environmental lab and outside toilets
C. Store cupboards
D. Unfinished extension to storerooms
E. Bedroom
F. Bedroom
G. Bathroom
H. Watertower
I. Office
J. Osteology lab
K. Bedroom
L. Draughting and equipment room
M. Bedroom.
N. Bedroom
O. Lecture and meeting room
P. Storeroom
Gazebo – Processing area
Courtyards - Processing areas

Figure 189: The Kafr Hassan Dawood Field Research Centre, East Delta, Egypt (drawn by G. J. Tassie, J. M. Rowland and J. F. L. van Wetering).

This section does not cover the higher analysis, classification and interpretation of finds, as these are specialist activities (see **Bibliography and Recommended Reading**). Rather, it allows the archaeologist to prepare finds for these further processes by cleaning, basic classification, quantification description, provenience, retrieval information and contextual integrity. The processing work is made easier by the use of *pro forma* recording sheets and the use of laptop computers. Certain aspects of the assemblage's potential to contribute to the project's aims will only become fully apparent during specialist analysis, i.e. under a scanning electron microscope or stable isotope analysis. It is the excavator's responsibility to ensure the integrity of the collections and their organisation, so they can always serve specialist reinterpretation regardless of schools of thought or scoring standards.

The following seven points are essential guidelines for the processing of finds:

1. The main objective is to prepare finds in as ordered a manner and stable state as possible for further classification, analysis, and interpretation.

2. It is essential that provenience information stays with the finds at all times and is written clearly. When writing it on the actual object it must be placed in as unobtrusive a place as possible.

3. Finds processing areas must be well-shaded if outdoors, and well ventilated and lit if indoors. Sufficient space must be available for washing and drying of objects and for their initial storage. If storing artefacts on-site, the magazine must be secure, although extremely valuable finds, should be recorded as quickly and fully as possibly and then sent straight to the local museum for safe keeping.

4. When storing and transporting finds, ensure that heavy items - such as building material - are crated or boxed separately and not placed on top of the more fragile objects in order to avoid damage to these more vulnerable materials.

5. Keeping the site inventory up-to-date is essential, and should be done as fieldwork progresses. The use of electronic databases facilitates cataloguing of finds, making data retrieval easier and more efficient.

6. Ensure that special finds are stored in acid-free boxes surrounded with acid-free tissue, or in Stewart tubs away from the bulk materials. The storage magazine should be equipped with metal shelving; enamel finished metal is preferred for its durability. The boxes should be stacked on these shelves by categories or context.

7. The trench and area supervisors should always know where all the finds from their areas or trenches are. They should constantly update their context sheets as processing proceeds, noting processing drawing and photograph numbers.

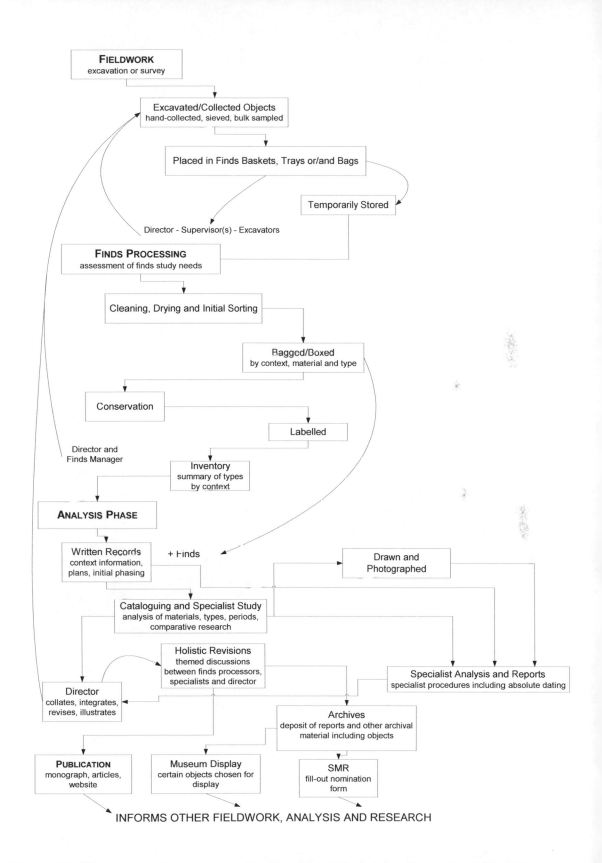

Figure 190: The stages in the treatment of archaeological finds (after Hurcombe 2007: 16-7).

Basic Equipment and Supplies

The basic equipment required for finds processing in the field and research centre includes:

A tent or room with floor space of at least 5.0 x 7.0 metres. This room should contain a sink with drainer and with hot and cold water supply, power points for table lamps, heaters, microscopes, computers, printers, etc., and windows for natural light and ventilation. The room should also be furnished with tables, chairs, and drying shelves. These comprise slatted wooden shelving fitted against the walls approximately 2.0 m high and 0.70 m deep, with shelves about 0.17 m apart.

An outdoor mains water supply, a hose, buckets, washing-up bowls, a drain for the waste water, toothbrushes, fingernail brushes, sponges, scrubbing brushes, and a skip or area for dumping the sludge from finds washing.

A secure magazine furnished with enamel finished metal shelving with shelves at ground level as no finds must be stored on the floor. Enough shelving should be installed to allow the temporary storage of the anticipated finds in boxes. If storing skeletal material; acid-free boxes and tissue paper should be used. Adult skeleton boxes should be no smaller than 68 cm long, 27 cm wide and 24 cm tall. Some shelving should be found that could also hold large finds, such as a mummy, coffin or stone blocks (wide shelves without vertical supports required). Always install more shelving than you think you need.

Purchase polythene bags - 4"x 6" (102 x 153 mm), 6"x 9" (153 x 230 mm), 8"x 12" (204 x 306 mm), 12"x18" (306 x 459 mm), 18"x 24" (459 x 612 mm) and 24"x 36" (612 x 918 mm), preferably zip-seal. Spun bonded polyethylene (Tyvek®) labels, acid-free tissue paper, acid-free boxes, an assortment of *Stewart*® tubs or other seal-fresh storers, bags of silica gel incorporating a humidity indicator strip, plastic tanks (in case of larger waterlogged finds), masking tape, *Sellotape*®, double-sided adhesive tape, aluminium foil, Plaster of Paris, gypsum, and gardening gloves (for handling heavy items like stone).

Microscopes, magnifying-glass, scientific sieves, tweezers, Petri dishes, glass or plastic beakers, liquid measures, scalpels, barbecue/cocktail sticks/skewers, wooden spatulas, dental probes, wire, saws, rubber gloves, seed trays, bread crates, weighing scales. Specialist equipment for the measuring of skeletal material: anthropometer (for certain measurements of long bones) and an osteometric board, and dental putty for casting teeth and cutmarks.

Glue (HMG cellulose nitrate adhesive), alcohol, Primal WS24 (acrylic colloidal dispersion), diluted to a 15% v/v solution in tap water, Paraloid B72 diluted to a 10-15% v/v solution in acetone, epoxy for imbedding thin sections, micro-balloons for filling.

CLEANING AND SORTING

Some directors disapprove of finds washing, whereas others see it as a standard procedure. Between these two extremes is a more flexible policy where status of the finds is the criterion which determines whether or not a find should be cleaned. Therefore, before cleaning can begin, objects must be assessed as to their need and suitability for cleaning. Three factors should be considered before commencing any cleaning activity:

1. The type of matrix from which the object was extracted.

2. The state of preservation of the object.

3. What information will be lost if the object is cleaned?

Some types of matrix – such as clay/soil – adhere very strongly to artefacts/ecofacts, whereas sand can usually be brushed off. If the object can be identified and examined merely by brushing, then there is generally no need to wash it. The next factor to consider is that of friability – how delicate is the object? Can the fabric of the object survive washing or even brushing? If not, then it should not be cleaned. Lastly, what other kinds of information besides shape, form, and type may be damaged by overly-enthusiastic cleaning? Microscopic and residue analysis techniques can elucidate the function of the object in subsistence patterns, food preparation, craft production, weaponry and other activities (Fullagar 2006: 207-234), so if you intend to do useware analysis or chemical analyses for pigments, plant remains or animal remains the artefacts (generally stone artefacts and pottery) should not be washed. If there is any doubt about any of these points, a conservator should be consulted (White & Page 1992).

Most ecofacts will not require cleaning. However, if they are in need of cleaning, it must be carried out by a conservator or environmentalist (flotation notwithstanding). Human remains should only be cleaned under the supervision of a physical anthropologist, as they may be deceptively fragile, or may lose valuable chemical/pathological evidence through unskilled washing. Any artefact requiring special conservation treatment must be isolated and passed to the conservator before the cleaning process begins.

If deemed necessary, washing is normally done in a bucket of water with a stiff washing-up, nail- or toothbrush, removing the sediment until the artefact feels free of grease, taking care not to erode or scratch the surface of the artefact. Particularly robust finds may be hose washed (i.e. bulk pottery and large fragments of building material). The artefacts are then left to dry on drying trays, which can be compartmentalised if the artefacts have separate numbers, purpose-built drying shelves or in seed trays lined with paper. The most commonly washed artefacts - potsherds - must be bagged, washed and dried by context: their information label must be kept with them throughout their move from field to processing centre. Compartmentalised drying trays are only required if artefacts from mixed contexts are being dried together. Special finds must be washed separately from the bulk of potsherds and other objects. Finds must be **thoroughly** dry before bagging, as mould may grow in damp bags, necessitating rewashing (Grey 2006: 22). In a cold climate heaters and de-humidifiers may be needed to help the objects dry. Plastic (polythene) bags may be used to store bones, but they should be punctured several times with small holes to allow some air transfer.

Particular groups of artefacts, such those from a grave, floor of rubbish pit, or room of a house should be placed together and a preliminary list made of the assemblage. The initial sorting of potsherds should also be done at this stage, by separating diagnostic sherds from body sherds. Washed diagnostic (rim, base, handle, spout and decorated) sherds should be put in a separate compartment of the drying tray to the body (non-diagnostic) sherds. If only brushed, the diagnostic sherds should be put into a smaller bag within the larger bag of potsherds from the same context. If this procedure is not done during cleaning, then it should be done during labelling. If metal staples have been used to seal the bags during excavation, they should be removed (as they may rust) and the dry finds put in perforated zip-seal polythene bags with their provenience information on a label.

Intact pottery, glass, and stone vessels should not be cleaned, and sent straight to the conservator to have their contents removed. They can be analysed for remains of ancient food (and its production) or other substances in order to ascertain the function of the object. Pots with ink inscriptions or friable pigments on the surface should also go straight to the conservator for treatment. Other categories of artefact that should not be washed include leather, metal or wooden objects, papyri and make-up palettes, as these are either too delicate or may retain some food/pigment remnant that can be identified using scientific methods. To this list you may add other categories of artefacts as appropriate to the site and period you are excavating. The golden rule should be: **IF IN DOUBT, DO NOT WASH.**

Figure 191: Communal potwashing (photograph G. J. Tassie).

In certain circumstances, an artefact may need to go through desalination. Because of the length of time of the process, the objects chosen for desalinisation will usually be those with surface decoration, such as incised potmarks or painted detail that has become obscured by soluble salt encrustations. This is likely to happen in places where there is a high water-table, and the objects have been exposed to the water, such as the Nile Delta, the Nile Valley floodplain or coastal sites. Although usually done by conservators, desalination can also be done by the finds processors. It involves placing the artefact (stone/ceramic only) in trays or buckets of distilled or deionised water. If distilled water is not readily available, then fresh drinking water can be used, but not well water as this is likely to be highly saline. The water must be changed once or twice a day for between 7-20 days, but potentially up to 40 days. The process is carried out until all the salt has been dissolved into the clean water. To test if the artefact is desalinated fully a conductivity meter should be used regularly to test the salinity of the water; when the salinity level ceases to fall any further, the object should be removed. However, the length of time of the desalinisation process is often determined by the length of time left available on the expedition; more often than not a very important artefact is excavated in the last week of the expedition. If desalinisation must be speeded up or there is serious calcite encrustation, the artefact can be placed in a 5-15% solution of *Calgon®* (vinegar or muriatic acid can be substituted) in distilled water; this will usually produce results in 2 to 3 days. In really serious cases a 10% solution of acetic (CH_3COOH) or 5% nitric acid (HNO_3) in distilled water may be used after pre-soaking for two hours in distilled water (Hester *et al*. 1997: 155). This process should only be used if the fabric of the artefact is solid enough to withstand the use of acid; if in doubt, test the solution on specimen sherds first.

Ideally, (human) bones should not be washed. However, if it cannot be avoided, wash well-preserved remains with warm water, using soft brushes and sponges. Do not soak the bones as their structure may be compromised. It is best to wash the bones over a fine sieve to catch any fragments that may be washed off. Wash only one skeleton at a time and change the water after each one is finished. Take great care with the delicate areas of the skeleton (the vertebrae, facial bones etc), and those of high importance (such as the pubis and auricular surface of the pelvis). Pathological bone is usually very fragile and should be given to the physical anthropologist for cleaning. Skeletal material must be allowed to dry completely at room temperature, and out of direct sunlight. Mummified material must never be washed, although it may be lightly brushed if necessary. Poorly preserved skeletal material should be cleaned in the laboratory using wood and bamboo tools, remembering to sieve all sediment that is extracted from the skeletal material. If you break an element, you may repair it, however do not try to assemble whole elements. Use HMG cellulose nitrate adhesive (or UHU Hart if HMG is not available) and dry in a drying tray filled with sand or similar. Do **not** stick teeth into their sockets. The sediment in the inside of the skull **must** be removed; otherwise it will harden, shrink and crush the bone. Bag skeletal remains as they were lifted – usually by limb/thorax etc – ensuring that their context labels remain with them at all times. Plastic (polythene) bags may be used to store small bones, but they should be punctured several times with small holes to allow some air transfer. These bags should then be put in acid-free boxes and stored on metal shelving.

CONSERVATION

The conserving of objects is the job of a professional conservator, who will be in charge of the repair, consolidation, stabilisation, cleaning and packaging of objects. The basic ideology of modern conservation is to intervene as little as possible beyond stabilising the object's disintegration. In certain environments preservation may be near perfect, especially if the sediments are frozen (i.e. Siberia) desiccated (i.e. Egypt/Chile/Gobi), salt rich (i.e. Iran) or anaerobic (i.e. Scandinavian bogs). In these settings, even organic materials are likely to be found in a good state of preservation. These organic artefacts are often very fragile, and will need immediate conservation treatment. Therefore, if you expect to recover such fragile objects on your site it is best to employ the services of a skilled conservator. Basic guidelines are presented below.

Artefacts and structures undergo a major environmental change when they are excavated, and can experience considerable shock and deteriorate rapidly when removed from their relatively moist sediment and exposed to the bright sunlight. In the case of stone artefacts the deterioration is hardly perceptible and may not be detected for many years, while fragile organic material may deteriorate at such a fast rate that the artefact turns to dust in a matter of minutes. Many countries have extreme environmental conditions, with high temperatures, winds and hot sun by day and cold temperatures with heavy dew formation at night. High daytime temperatures increase the rate of drying with exposed features - such as burials - acting as a wick for the watertable beneath. This 'wick-action' is particularly exacerbated by 'pedestalling', as this moves the freshly-excavated objects into the evaporation zone. Salts in solution will then be continually pulled up through the pedestals in the form of ground water to the surface, where the solution evaporates, allowing integral salts to crystallise in the top of the pedestal and any material in it. Artefacts thus exposed would be subject to not only the usual post-excavation changes, but a secondary form of continuing saline damage. Therefore, pedestalling is not recommended, and should be avoided if at all possible. These post-excavation changes are often compounded if objects are left *in situ* longer than is required for their recording, so fast and efficient removal is required in order to combat adverse environmental effects. Fragile objects will need special lifting techniques in the field, possibly including some of the surrounding sedimentary matrix (see section on **Lifting in the Field**). Large finds, such as statues, may require the use of winches and pulleys. Before the lifting straps are put around the object a separating agent, such as a blanket should be wrapped around the object to protect the often fragile surfaces.

Conservators try to limit the change in an object's environment, first during the excavation process and later in long-term storage. Therefore, it is essential to stabilise objects with as little intervention with the archaeological evidence as possible (Corr 2000; Cronyn 1990; Pye 2001; Rogers 2004). If a conservator is not present on-site, some general rules for the basic stabilisation and conservation of different categories of materials are listed below (**Tab. 47**). Those artefacts that are not already in boxes should be placed in a suitably-sized plastic, wooden or cardboard box, with appropriate wrapping of acid free tissue, bubble wrap or silica gel. The golden rules are to interfere as little as possible, and maintain finds in an approximate environment to that from which they were removed. If in doubt do not clean immediately, do not do or use anything that cannot be reversed, and keep accurate records of any actions taken to clean or preserve an artefact (Banning 2000: 129; Westman 1994: 106). Damp object should be left to dry out slowly in a shaded place. It is also essential to remember that certain adhesives and consolidants have relatively low glass transition temperatures (Tg), e.g. Paraloid B 72 has a Tg of 40° C, and therefore its use in places such as Egypt and other countries where temperatures regularly exceed that are limited. Therefore, always check the Tg of your consolidants, HMG cellulose nitrate adhesive or UHU Hart have much higher Tgs and are suitable for use as an adhesive for ceramics in hot countries.

Material	Treatment	Packaging
Metal from dry sites	Do not clean	Place in perforated sample bag. Store in a 'Dry box' containing silica gel.
Metal from wet sites	Do not clean	Firstly, dry at room temperature. Then as for metal from dry sites
Ceramic Stone / mortar Wall plaster	If material is delicate, lift using extra support.	Place in a sample bag. Support articulated sections.
Amber Shale Lapis-lazuli Ochre	Do not clean. Keep damp, if already damp.	Place in a doubled sample bag. Store in a 'Damp box' if found damp.
Glass	If plain and in a good state of preservation place in a dry sample bag. If decorated or painted, bag wet.	Store fragile and decorated glass in a 'Damp box'. Ensure that all glass is stored separately from large finds.
Organics (leather, wood, worked bone, fibre, horn, basketry, papyrus, antler, ivory, shell, textiles, hair)	Do not clean and keep damp if found damp. If material is delicate, lift using extra support and wrap in acid free tissue.	Place in a doubled sample bag or 'Dry box'. Store in a 'Damp box' if found damp, & add a 1% fungicide solution.

Table 47: First aid for finds (after Westman 1994: 107-8).

LABELLING

The moment when artefacts or ecofacts are removed from their labelled bags or containers is the moment when they are most likely to become permanently – and disastrously – separated from one another. Therefore, great care must be taken by the finds processors and conservators when cleaning and repairing objects to **always** keep labels with their objects whilst out of their containers. The labels should be made of spun bonded polyethylene and be written on with a spirit-based marker pen before being pinned or **tied** to containers, or **pushed** inside complete artefacts. The **Object Invigilator Form: Sheet 41**, has been designed to act as a secondary control to keep a track of the whereabouts of artefacts going to other specialists for treatment. To prevent loss of provenience during further stages of processing, objects need to be directly labelled. This involves painting a little strip of clear nail varnish or acetone (3 x 1 cm) on an inconspicuous part of the object, such as the base or inside. After the nail varnish has dried, the provenience number should be written on the strip of nail varnish. This must be done with a mapping pen and indelible ink, such as black India ink (e.g. that made by Winsor and Newton), although white ink may be preferable on darker artefacts (Sharer & Ashmore 1987: 286). When the ink is dry another dab of clear nail varnish or acetone will seal and protect the number. Do **not** place a label on the decorated surface of an object or on the cutting edge of a blade, on or near the articular surfaces of joints (or any pathological lesions) on bones or any other surface that may be useful in later analysis. Metal objects should **never** have their provenience number written on them. The labelling of artefacts allows them to be split up, which is the genesis of classification.

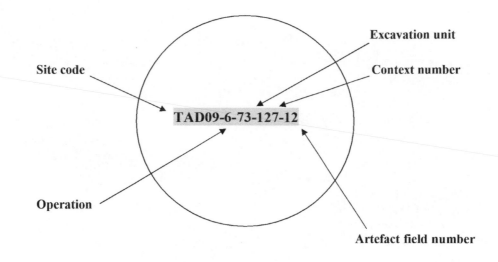

Figure 192: Example of how to mark objects with their provenience number.

The provenience numbering system should include the site code (TAD09), the operational area number (6) followed by the excavation trench unit or square number (73). If operational area and/or trench numbers are not used, the coordinates should be recorded here instead. The last set of numbers denotes the location where the object was found, its context, and individual object identification number. Therefore, the twelfth special find excavated at the site and found in context 127 would be recorded as 127-12 (see **Fig. 192**). However, the site code, context number and sequential find number should suffice in most instances for the find's provenience to be identifiable.

INVENTORY

Creating the inventory involves recording the quantity of artefacts within each industry (Sharer & Ashmore 1987: 286), following a set of standard procedures. The initial stage is a gross classification into material (the substance from which the object is made) and technology (the manufacturing technique). Some materials are used in their natural or slightly modified state; these include tools and rough stone that have only been minimally modified (Banning 2000: 35-72; Herz & Garrison 1998: 195; Hurcombe 2007: 18-22). The material itself can be classified into 'organic' and 'inorganic'. These combined criteria produce two gross categories of classification – 'manufactured' (such as smelted metal or ceramic) and 'natural' (such as antlers, hides or ochre).

	Material	Naturally Occurring	Technology
Inorganic	Metals	*Ferrous –* Iron *Non-ferrous –* Gold Silver Tin Lead Copper	All metals found as compounds (sulphides, oxides, carbonates, etc.), such as bronze. All metals that have been extracted or smelted. Waste or debris, such as slags. Artefacts, including jewellery, tools, and vessels.
	Stone	Limestone Sandstone Granite Basalt Diorite Jade Porphyry Alabaster Flint Chert	Chipped stone, such as flint knives or microliths. Ground stone, such as tools, jewellery, and vessels. Small worked and shaped stone, querns, mortars, millstones, weights, and tesserae. Large worked and shaped stone, building stones, megalithic blocks. Carved stone, statues and figurines.
	Ceramic	Clay Sand Obsidian	Pottery, faïence, glass, made into figurines, beads, vessels, tiles, bricks, and musical instruments.
Organic	Pigments	Ochre	Paint, cosmetics, dyes
	Vegetable	Wood / Reeds Resin/Gum Waxes Flax / Cotton / Silk	Dyes, textiles, cosmetics, basketry, papyri, boardwork, food
	Animal	Shell / Bone / Ivory / Horn Hide Hair Feathers	Glue, leather, fibres, figurines, dyes, food

Table 48: Materials and industries (after Herz & Garrison 1998: 195).

The inventory is annotated by entering the numerical totals of each natural or industrial category found in a given context into **The Inventory Logs**, forms 43 and 44. This quantitative information can be entered straight into the computerised database or used straight from the hard copy to analyse the objects and their spatial patterning.

All human remains must be inventoried by a bioarchaeologist, initially in the field recording burial information *in situ*, and the second following laboratory analyses. The first form (**Sheet Seven**) includes a diagram of the human skeleton; the bone 'blanks' are to be shaded to indicate presence or absence. The second set of forms (found in publications such as Buikstra and Ubelaker (1994) details specific bones, which are scored according to presence and completeness. The standard frame of reference for osteological analyses is the Standardized Osteological Database (SOD), although recording systems and methods have evolved dramatically since the 'standard' work on the subject (Buikstra and Ubelaker 1994). The SOD comprises 12 tables of skeletal data and 11 tables of dental data. The SOD ensures that the maximum amount of skeletal information is obtained in a format that facilitates comparison with other data for future osteological analyses. Space is provided for recording pathological lesions (infection, degeneration, nutritional disorders and trauma), skeletal anomalies and antemortem and postmortem modifications. Special consideration is given to the identification of primary reactions, secondary and healing lesions. Initial observations should be made during the inventory process, while subsequent discoveries will be added during later phases of analysis.

Once the bones have been labelled and an inventory made, they should be packed into a sturdy-lidded acid-free cardboard box. The bones should be wrapped in acid free tissue and bagged following the procedure outlined in **Chapter 5**. The code/name of the site and the contents of the box must be written on the lid and on one end of the box. Use plentiful acid-free tissue to provide extra padding for the skeletal remains.

REGISTERING AND CATALOGUING FINDS

The individual finds now need to be described and recorded in detail. The recording forms required include the Pottery Recording Form, Lithic Tools Recording Form, Special finds Recording Form, Micro Faunal Recording Form, Archaeobotanical Analysis Form, Coffin Recording Form, Stone Vessel Recording Form, Worked Stone Recording Form, Building Material Recording Form, Hair Recording Form, Textile Recording Form, Basketry Recording Form and the Rope and Cordage Recording Form. When compiling the catalogue, it is advisable to have all the finds forms relating to that object to hand, so the information can be easily cross-checked. The finds processor should coordinate with the area supervisors to ensure information accuracy. The registration forms should detail the material used, the colour, decoration, form, function, method of use, method and technique of manufacture, dating (if known) and provenience information (Joukowsky 1980: 228). Object descriptions must be consistent, using the same terminology when describing objects of the same types. The main purpose of cataloguing artefacts is: 1) to determine the extent of the corpus of artefacts; 2) to sub-divide the site's corpus of artefacts into individual industry corpora; 3) to produce an accurate description of each artefact and 4) to present information in a systematic manner for the site publication (Banning 2000: 35-72; Joukowsky 1980: 228).

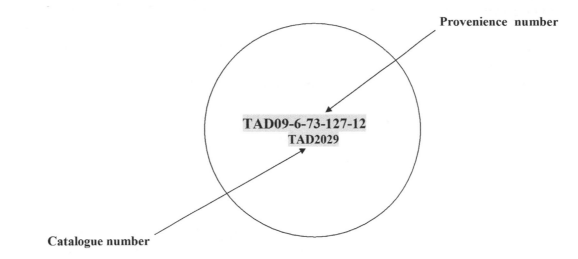

Provenience number

TAD09-6-73-127-12
TAD2029

Catalogue number

Figure 193: The full registration number of an object will include the provenience number and the catalogue number.

The object is given a catalogue number, and is recorded in both the area supervisors' records and on the objects catalogue form or/and database. The number is also applied to the actual object, and is executed in the same manner as the provenience label; both numbers are noted on the registration form and constitute the registration number. In this system (see **Fig. 193**), all finds have a four-digit number preceded by the site code (e.g. TAD for Tell Abu Dawood). If much larger amounts of artefacts are expected on site, then the numbers can run from 00001-09999, then 10000-19999, 20000-29999, etc. The first prefix number signifies the type of finds (0 = pottery vessels, 1 = potsherds, 2 = stone vessels, 3 = small finds, 4 = potmarks, 5 = building material, 6 = lithics). These are only guidelines for a numbering system; the precise details depend on the number of different categories and objects within those categories recovered on site. The sequential numbering of the objects is carried over from season to season; therefore, if the last pottery vessel recorded in the 2009 season was TAD0257, then the first vessel to be recorded in the 2010 season will be TAD0258, and so on. The last number should be referenced from the on-site catalogue or database.

It is also necessary to make a scale drawing (usually 1:1 or, for larger objects, 1:2) on draughting film; a black and white and colour photograph must also be taken, to include the registration number, provenience information, and a scale. The numbers of these drawings and photographs should be recorded on the relevant forms. The recording of this information in the three different media is a time consuming process, meaning that bulk artefacts such as potsherds cannot normally be afforded their own individual catalogue number. Potsherds and other bulk items should receive a bulk context registration number, with only diagnostic sherds of the different types of pots being individually registered.

The objects will either be deposited in the on-site storage magazine to await fuller classification or scientific tests, or will be transported to an off-site place of storage such as a museum. The further analysis of the finds is dependent on the type of find and research questions (for analytical techniques see Balme & Paterson 2006; Banning 2000; Hurcombe

2007; Renfrew & Bahn 2004). Artefact associations can be further examined and typologies/chemical analyses made (Drewett 1999: 147). The storage location of each object must also be annotated in the catalogue of finds, and the finds catalogue kept in triplicate. The original copy should be kept by the principal investigator (director), another retained at the site for year-to-year reference, and a third should accompany the objects to their final repository (Joukowsky 1980:234-5).

SITE FINDS BOOK

A site finds book should be compiled, collating all the drawings, photographs and written description of the objects. On some sites, reference or index cards are compiled with this information. However, placing this information in a book makes referencing the artefacts a much easier task. This book should comprise several sections: pottery (sub-divided into whole vessels and diagnostic sherds), stone vessels, small finds, lithics, etc. The drawings of the ceramic and stone vessels are usually reduced to a 1:4 scale, whereas small finds are shown at 1:1 or 1:2. The scale by which the drawings have been reduced must be clearly indicated. Each drawing must be accompanied by catalogue information and a photograph. This will facilitate the construction of a site assemblage and pottery corpus, allowing further analysis to proceed.

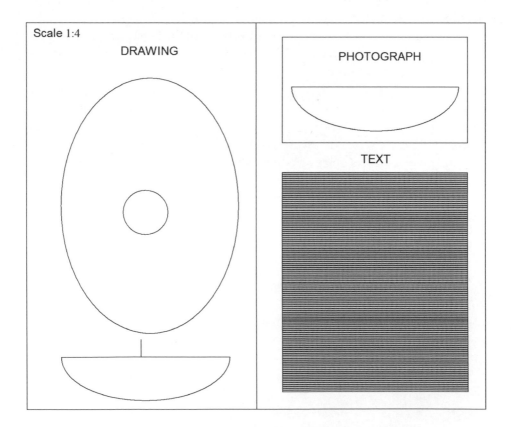

Figure 194: Finds book showing drawing on the left and the written description and provenience information and photograph on the right.

488

This type of recording can be adapted to place the assemblage from each feature in order, using one page or a double page-spread per feature. When doing this only the feature (e.g. grave or structure) number is recorded at the top of the page, also showing the drawings of each find retrieved from that feature.

ARCHIVING

Field survey, evaluation, watching briefs, building recording, and excavation will always result in an archive. The analytical process will also create its own archives of paper and digital data. Finally, the artefacts and environmental samples collected from the site will also need to be catalogued and stored in an appropriate repository (Cohen In press). Archives are the contemporary transactional records of the activity. One of the major aims of undertaking an archaeological project is to produce a comprehensive site archive that is properly curated and stored so that it can be consulted in the future (Ferguson & Murray 1997). There are two major types of archaeological archives: site archives and research archives (in addition to the minor archives produced during planning and assessment phases). The site or primary archive is simply a record of all data collected, whereas the research or derived archive is the data in amended format with artefactual and environmental reports and an interpretation and history of the site (Drewett 1999: 176). What constitutes a site archive and where it should be stored are normally governed by the principal investigator, the institution running the excavation, and the local or national archaeological authority. Therefore, as archive formats vary considerably; the current recording system has been designed to comply with the requirements of most archives.

During the planning stage – desk-based assessments, geophysical and other forms of prospecting – where field work has taken place, archives will have been created. The type of material that is likely to have been generated are reports, site definition and location data, site drawings, hand-written logs and notebooks, terrain-modelling and other survey data, photographs and correspondence. The fieldwork part of a project – fieldwalking, watching briefs, test-pitting or trial trenching, standing building recording and excavation – will also produce a large amount of archival material. The original site records must be stored in a proper site archive, so that they are safe and accessible and in a regulated state for transferral to regional or central archive repositories (Grew 1998). According to Grew (1998) a site archive normally consists of:

Primary Records

- Site definition and location - site code, base plan at 1:100 or 1:50, map at 1:2500. The base plan must contain the following information:

    1. The site code and title

    2. The investigation area

    3. The maximum extent of areas of excavation

    4. Selected points of reference on the site grid

    5. Relationship of the site grid with the national grid

6. Location of sections and elevations

7. Location of any other fieldwork (e.g. test pits or drill core locations)

8. Location and value of datum and control points (temporary bench marks)

- Survey data – the data relating to the laying out of the site grid and its relationship to the national grid, providing two 'x, y' coordinates and their UTM WGS84 longitude and latitude equivalent for the placement of each trench. The manner in which the grid was located in the landscape must also be stated (e.g. a run of levels from a bench mark, GPS or topographic).

- Levels data – information relating to the establishment of the site datum and levels taken from it and other control points. The increasing use of total stations will mean that much of this data is in digital form.

- Site notebooks, area folders, and diaries – a photocopy or original note books and digital forms should be provided.

- Recording sheets – the information required on the recording sheets is detailed in 'how to fill out the recording sheets'. The sheets must not be stapled or taped together.

- Registers and indices – the data required on these is also detailed in 'how to fill out the recording sheets'. The sheets must not be stapled or taped together.

- Original photographs – the context and locational data should appear either in the image or be written on the back of hard copies. An images register must accompany all photographic records. With digital photographs the image name must relate to the photographic register.

- Plans and context drawings – the data required on plans is detailed in 'the drawn record'. The draughting film sheets must not be stapled or taped together.

- Section drawings – the data required on section drawings is detailed in 'the drawn record'. The draughting film sheets must not be stapled or taped together.

- Object drawings – the data required on object drawings is detailed in 'the drawn record'. The draughting film sheets must not be stapled or taped together.

- Original environmental sample records, including dating catalogues, drill core, geophysical and other documentary data.

- Context matrix – a definitive stratigraphic context matrix or matrices for the site. The matrix must be marked with the site code and title; if continuing sheets are used their relationship must be clearly marked.

- Original skeleton records – the original recording forms and analysis records.

- Skeletal material – the skeletal remains.

- Artefacts and ecofacts – the actual artefacts and ecofacts, including bulk finds.

The skeletal material, artefacts and ecofacts must stay in the designated museum, state or local magazine, whereas the rest of the site archive will usually go to the institution of the principal investigator. A duplicate of the site archive should stay with the material in

490

the museum or magazine in which it is deposited, and relevant entries made in the sites and monuments records detailing the site and whereabouts of the site archive.

If not using a computerised recording system the indices should be typed-up and cross-referenced. These form the basis of a site catalogue along with the site and artefact drawings and photographs, human skeletal records, sampling data and analytical reports on artefacts, structures, stratigraphy, environmental data, records of conservation and x-rays undertaken during fieldwork. Digital material must also be placed in the archive; such records may be text documents, artefact and context databases, CAD, GIS and survey data, images, matrices and analytical data. The formats used should be standardised, preferably using programmes such *Microsoft Office, Adobe, AutoDesk, Oracle*, and the data should be stored on media such as memory sticks, removable hard-drives, CDs and DVDs, along with hardcopy printouts of the material contained on the discs. GIS files should be stored in DXF + DWG formats, database files in ASCII delimited text and DBF formats. Images should be stored as TIFF files as they do not lose any image quality, whereas JPEGS although enabling more compression, lose some image quality. A log containing all the metadata should be kept when creating digital records. This should include different variables and codes used in the database, the original scale of any paper maps that were digitised and the increments used, what exactly it contains, anything deliberately not included. This log should be put into a manual and included with the site archive, suitable category divisions are project title, history of the project, creators and other personnel on the larger project, content, information about methods, details of source materials used to create the dataset, content and structure of the dataset, metadata records, details of how the dataset relates to other archives and publications, and intellectual property rights. The ordering of the data should enable a preliminary report to be compiled before further analysis and classification is carried out for the final report. It is desirable to keep a preliminary report with the archive material, and submit this report to a national or international digest of fieldwork.

Once the finds have been analysed and interpreted, all finds should be prepared for long-term storage (Hurcombe 2007: 109 *ff*). The packaging and storage conditions of the archaeological material should be uniform. Most museums and magazines will stipulate what size and type of packaging and containers are required and the museum curator should be consulted before and during the project for practical advice on handling and storage of the archive. The on-site magazine should consist of sturdy metal shelving and drawers; the objects should be stored by context and material in wooden, plastic or strong cardboard boxes with sealable lids. These containers should be ordered in rows in a logical order with labels on the end of the container facing out, so they can be easily read. The three basic categories of artefacts are A (the most unstable materials, such as metals and organic material, which should be kept in their own micro-environment [sealed containers]); B (less sensitive objects such as bone, which are more sturdy but need to be protected from breakage, fungus, damp and pests) and C (robust material such as pottery and lithics) (UKIC Archaeological Section 1982). Small objects should be stored in polythene containers within the larger storage box, which should be clearly labelled with the site code, context numbers and types of material (Drewett 1999: 175). Pottery and stone objects should be loosely packed to prevent breakage; sherds should be put in linen or plastic bags with air holes punched in them. Bone and glass should be wrapped in acid-free tissue paper and put in strong cardboard boxes. Metals should be kept in polythene boxes packed with silica gel to remove excess moisture, preferably with a humidity indicator strip (Banning 2000:132-3; Drewett 1999: 175). Plans should be stored flat in acid-free card folders or polyester packets with the drawing numbers written on the front so that they can be found easily; the written record should also be stored in acid-free boxes, avoiding metal paper clips and staples and tape; use plastic paper clips if required (Drewett 999: 176). Negatives should be stored in acid-free negative strip folders, avoiding mylar, polyester and polyethylene plastic folders, the printed photographs should be stored, not in 'sticky backed' albums, but in mylar envelopes separated by acid-free tissue paper (Burke & Smith 2004: 305). Every photographic print should be individually labelled on the back stating the roll and negative number, the site name, date and the subject (Burke & Smith 2004: 307). Drawings, documentation, objects and photographs are best stored in the dark, in a temperature range of 13° – 20° and a relative humidity of 45-50%, maintaining an environment that is moderate and stable (Drewett 1999: 176). Guidelines for computerised data archives are published by the International Standards Organisation (ISO), the Open Archival Information (OASIS) and the International Council of Archives Committee on Electronic Records across the globe (ADS 2001; Roskams 2001: 82).

Any materials used for the long- or short-term storing and packaging of archaeological material must be as chemically inert as possible. Archaeological materials may remain in their initial packaging for years. The artefacts' survivorship is in large part defined by the quality of their packing materials (see **Tab. 49**).

Towards the end of project, assessment archives will also be generated. The principal components of these archives will be the report, including recommendations and specialised assessments of the site, plans, interpretative drawings, deposit models, site matrix and diagrams.

The research archive comprises of the published monograph, general reports (including all articles relating to the project), additional interpretive drawings, specialist reports, photographs, and a full bibliography of the site, including previous research. This archive contains all the analytical data often grouped into tables and diagrams and interpretive material relating to the site or area, as well as all the catalogues of the finds and environmental material. This archive is an invaluable resource for future investigators and - along with the site archive - constitutes the core of the archival material.

Derived Information

- Site abstract – The site abstract should be no more than 500 words and should:

    1. Summarise the project design and strategy,

    2. Describe the type of work conducted,

    3. Detail the main phases of building or site occupation,

    4. Draw attention to key artefacts and environmental evidence,

    5. Relate the site to previous research, such as other similar sites,

- Preliminary report – a copy of the preliminary report or reports.

- Publications – include copies of all published material about the site, including monographs and articles.

- Sites and Monuments Record – a copy of the filled-out SMRs form(s), e.g. EAIS and CultNat entry forms.

- Archive bibliography – a list of all reports that comprise the archive, together with details of any publications.

- Specialist reports – reports made by the various specialists on artefacts, ecofacts, human remains, environmental material, and geology.

	Do Use	Do Not Use	Reason for Not Using
Boxes	Acid-free document storage boxes R-Kive storage 'Bankers Boxes' Good quality new cardboard boxes for storing climate insensitive materials Clear polystyrene 'crystal' boxes Polypropylene plastic containers Polyethylene plastic containers with snap on lids	Grocery or cigar boxes Boxes that have already been used, with labels crossed out	Unstable materials, potential insect infestation from previous contents and storage conditions Difficult to read through the old crossing out.
Pockets & Folders	Acid-free card folders Fiche jackets Polyester Pockets and sleeves Polyester suspension files Acid-free envelopes	Paper or card folders Ordinary paper envelopes or paper	Chemically unstable, contains impurities and are not durable Chemically unstable, contains impurities and are not durable
Padding	Non-buffered acid-free tissue Cotton or polyester batting in plastic or muslin bags	Buffered acid free tissue Paper tissues or kitchen towels or toilet paper News papers or printed material Loose cotton Excelsior Vermiculite Bubble-pak or air-cap	By placing the object in an alkaline condition it could affect results of chemical analysis Chemically unstable, contains impurities and are not durable Very acidic; the ink can smear and stain objects surface Can easily snag brittle and fragile objects, and can transfer lint to object Acidic Generates dust that is difficult to remove from objects, and is a health hazard May contain polyvinylidene chloride

	Recommended	Avoid	Reason
Bags	Resealable polyethylene bags (Ziploc®, Baggies®, Whirl-pak®, zip sealed bags) Polythene bags Tyvek ® (spun polyethylene bags)	Lunch bags, waxed paper, envelopes or paper bags	Unstable; waxed paper can transfer wax to objects. Also no visual accessibility
Plastic Foams	Ethafoam 220®; polyethylene closed-cell foam (white only) Jiffy® foam; polythene closed-cell foam Microfoam®; low density, closed-cell polypropylene Sentinel® Foam; polyethylene Extruded polystyrene Plastozote®; polyethylene closed-cell foam Volara®; cross-linked polyethylene foam	Blue Ethafoam (fire retardant) Pink Ethafoam (anti-static) Any chlorinated or nitrated plastic (e.g. PVC-polyvinyl chloride Polyurethane plastics, sheet or foam Ethylene vinyl / acetate (EVA)	Fire-retardant additives may creep into the objects. Absorbs water from the air and can become soapy Out gases hydrogen chloride; can produce hydrochloric acid Unstable, possibility of off-gassing harmful products Can cause yellow staining, and is more elastic than polyethylene
Plastic Sheets	Mylar®; polyethylene terephthalate clear polyester Mellnex®; polyester film Film-O-Wrap 7750®; clear polyester and fluorocarbon laminate Scotchpak®; clear polyester / polyolefin laminate	Saran-Wrap® or Cling-Film® (polyvinylidene chloride) Cellophane	Unstable chlorinated plastic Acidic by-products caused by sulphuric acid used in manufacturing process
Padded Sheets	Archival corrugated board Acid-free Fome-Cor®; extruded polystyrene core covered with acid free paper Art-Cor®; extruded polystyrene with polystyrene skin Honeycomb boards, e.g. Tycore®; acid-free rigid paperboard Fluted polypropylene boards, e.g. Cor-X® Double-walled polycarbonate, e.g. Lexan Thermoclear®	Regular cardboard	Acidic

Table 49: Recommended storage materials (after Verner, Johnson & Horgan 1979).

Many regional and national archives make catalogues, databases and other material available on 'live' systems for reworking by future researchers. If any new interpretations result, these should be added to the archive as appropriate (Grew 1998: 17). Abstracts of the archive may also be made available on-line for research purposes along with an index of archive content for each individual project. It is essential that all archives are kept as accessible as possible and any digital data is migrated to keep it in a usable format. Many archive repositories still insist on the microfilming of paper archives as this is a highly stable means of keeping a duplicate copy (Cohen In press).

SITES AND MONUMENTS RECORDS

It is important to log your findings with the local equivalent of the central Sites and Monuments Records (SMRs), Heritage Environmental Records or a National Register. SMRs are a database of all archaeological sites and monuments within a country, recorded in a standardised manner (Larson 1992). The majority of SMRs are now computerised and have an integrated GIS to graphically show site distribution and other information. The details of each site or monument usually include cross-references to maps, publications, satellite images and aerial photographs, and also store information on the periods of site occupation, size, form, function, condition, location, finds, present status of archaeological protection, history of archaeological investigation, and incident threats. The keeping of SMRs allows continuous monitoring and protection of sites and monuments by defining the amount, distribution and types of cultural properties, therefore making it much easier to assess the implications of planning and development, as the information is readily available to all stakeholders and interested parties. Nominations for inclusion on a SMR are made on standardised forms, in a manual or electronic format provided by national or local organisations. In Egypt, two fledgling organisations exist for this purpose; they are the National Center for Documentation of Cultural and Natural Heritage (CultNat [www.cultnat.org]) and the Egyptian Antiquities Information System (EAIS [www.eais.org.eg]). The ordering of archaeological and related data into a common administrative and research unit facilitates further research and enables more efficient cultural heritage management (Tassie & Hassan 2009).

Figure 195: The regional SMR office in Cornwall (photograph G. J. Tassie).

Absolute Dating Age determination based on a specific time scale, as in years before present (B.P.). It is also referred to as chronometric dating, and includes such dating methods as radiocarbon and thermoluminescence dating (compare this type of dating with relative dating).

Aceramic A period, site or feature that has no pottery or other ceramics.

Aeolian Sand or loess that has been deposited by the action of the wind, also called windblown sand or loess.

Aerial Photography A photographic recording technique involving aerial reconnaissance to record the terrain in the hope of discovering buried archaeological sites, using either vertical or oblique photography. The examination of the contours, shadows, soilmarks and cropmarks in the terrain can reveal buried features.

Alluvium Sediments deposited by running water on the floodplain usually consisting of minerogenic silty loam.

Ambit A set of points within a given distance of a given or set point, used to lay out a grid. This ambit may be the points of the main site grid, or a set of points plotted in over a particular feature. The points within the ambit can either be plotted in using a multi-station or dumpy level, or by triangulation and off-sets. The points must be an exact distance from a standard reference point (such as a bench mark, temporary bench mark or datum point).

Anthropology The study of humanity and its physical and culture characteristics.

Archaeobotany The study of ancient plant remains. This usually constitutes the analysis of vegetable materials that humans used for food, fuel, fibres, constructional material for tools, houses, vehicles, etc. Organic matter usually only survives due to desiccation, waterlogging or charring.

Archaeological Site A place bearing significant traces of human activity, where artefacts, ecofacts, features and layers are found together in association.

Archaeological Assessment An archaeological assessment is a statement concerning the potential for a development project to encounter and impact on archaeological remains. An assessment can be conducted on its own or as part of an environmental impact assessment and can range from an initial investigation that draws on an archaeologist's knowledge of the area, to a detailed, thoroughly researched and well-sampled investigation based on empirical data.

Archaeology The study of the human past through its material remains and effects on the landscape (see **Introduction**).

Archaeomalacology The scientific study of shells and molluscs to reconstruct past environments or modes of social behaviour.

Archaeometallurgy The scientific study of ancient production, purification and properties of metals and their applications. The examination of metal ores, artefacts and waste products from extraction and processing to investigate the materials and technology used to make artefacts.

Artefact Any portable object modified by humans, including pottery, stone tools and vessels, glass, ivory, plastic, jewellery, wood and metal objects.

Ashlar A large squared-off worked stone, sometimes polished.

Assemblage A group of associated finds from one context, feature or the group of finds from one site, forming a reference collection and representing the sum of human activities carried out at that feature or site.

Association The co-occurrence of an artefact/ecofact/feature with other finds or features.

Attribute A minimal characteristic of an artefact that cannot be further sub-divided. Attributes commonly studied include aspects of form, style, decoration, colour and raw material.

Augering A method of sub-surface detection using a soil-boring tool (drill or auger) turned manually to extract a drill-core. The drill-core can reveal the depth and characteristics of archaeological or natural deposits.

Backfill The sediment used to deliberately fill in a feature or site.

Backfilling The action of filling a feature or site with sediment.

Barrow Run A specially-prepared path along which wheelbarrows are pushed en route to the spoil heap.

Base Map A small-scale map of the study area (1:50 or 1:100) used for recording basic data, such as the position of the site grid in relationship to permanent features on the landscape. The map shows topographical features of the local landscape and should be used for analysing basic spatial relationships and presenting archaeological and geographical data. Although duplicates of the base map may be made, the only map that should be called the base map is the one on detailing the actual field data.

Baulk A primary baulk is each of the vertical sides of the trench; a secondary baulk is a linear section of matrix left between excavation units for purposes of section drawing.

Bioarchaeology An alliance of forensic anthropology and physical anthropology, dedicated to answering archaeological questions about physical attributes, lifestyle and activities in past human populations. See 'physical anthropology'.

Bioturbation Disturbance caused by plants or animals.

Break of Slope The point at which the angle of a slope changes direction, such as the bottom of a pit, ditch or hill.

Brunton Brunton are manufacturer's of compasses, the most famous being the pocket transit, but they produce a whole range of surveying and orienteering equipment at varying prices capable of many functions, the full range can be viewed at: www.brunton.com.

Brushing A form of surface treatment used in pottery production. It is characterised by a series of overlapping, uneven lines created by a brush constructed from reed fibre, quills, stone, or shell.

Ceramic Building Material (CBM) Ceramic building material, often shortened to CBM, is a term used for any kind of building material made from ceramics such as brick, roof tile, floor tile, tesserae, etc. Another common acronym is BM, used for building materials such as stone, plaster, wood, etc.

Ceramics Artefacts made from fired or

heated clay. Although pottery vessels are usually termed as ceramics, glass and faience are also included in the broader ceramic term.

Chronometric Dating Absolute dating based upon regular and measurable clocks, such as the rate of decay of radioactive isotopes.

Clasts This is a geological term for fragmentary inclusions in the main matrix, usually comprising up to 10% of the sample. As well as rocks and minerals, weathered artefacts can be included and treated in the same manner as the rocks to understand the formation process of sedimentary matrix.

Colluvium Sediments from hill tops that have moved down the slope into a valley.

Constructed Feature A built feature such as a wall, house or tomb.

A Context A cultural or geological deposit that comprises a discrete unit of archaeological record, usually defined stratigraphically; it is any single action which leaves either a positive or negative record within the stratigraphic sequence. It is the smallest entity (other than a removable object) about which useful data may be recorded. Features can be made up of various contexts. For example, a pit will have a context number for the cut and other numbers for the fills. 'Context' is the term used to describe and give meaning to the various elements of stratification that make up an archaeological site.

The Context The context of an artefact or feature consists of the following three elements: matrix, provenience and association. The primary context is where these three elements have not been disturbed since the original deposition. Looted artefacts lose their context and thus their ability to give meaning to an archaeological site. The primary context helps archaeologists to evaluate the behavioural and transformation processes that were conducted to produce that particular piece of archaeological data. A secondary context is where the primary context has been wholly or partially altered after the original deposition.

Context Number The number given to a single context; no two contexts can have the same number. The context should be labelled on site with a Tyvek label, so that the excavators can identify it without having to refer to the context register and plans.

Contract Archaeology Archaeological work conducted under governmental legislation, often in advance of major construction or development projects. Construction companies are legally obliged to pay archaeological units to conduct research, including watching briefs and full-scale excavation if necessary. This type of archaeological research was developed to protect national and world heritage from urban development and associated destruction.

Coordinates The grid reference of a single point on an excavation, site or national grid.

Coprolites Fossilised faeces, which contain food residue that can be used to reconstruct past diet and subsistence.

Coring A subsurface method of surveying using a hollow metal tube driven into the ground to extract a column of sediment for stratigraphic and environmental analysis.

Cropmark The outline of an archaeological site revealed by variations in crop growth. These usually manifest themselves as shadows.

Cross-Dating The use of artefacts of known date to establish the age of undated contexts or assemblages; this dating may be used to date other artefacts of undefined date.

Cultural Heritage/Resource Management (CHM or CRM) An umbrella term for the research, location, conservation, protection, management and selective investigation of ancient sites and materials. This includes rescue archaeology, the development of means to mitigate damage by tourism, the prevention of looting and vandalism, the encouragement of cultural tourism, the enhancement of public awareness and appreciation of a nation's cultural heritage, and the development of legislation to safeguard the past.

Cumulative Feature A feature without signs of deliberate construction, such as a midden.

Curvilinear A narrow, curved feature.

Data Structure Report A report comprising a narrative account of field interpretations and questions which may be answered by post-excavation analysis. This narrative report is supported by full lists of contexts, finds, samples and records (including plans, artefact drawings, photographs and digital media).

Daub Clay or clay with inclusions used to cover walls (which are often made of *wattle*).

Debitage Fragments of flint discarded during flint knapping.

De´capage Excavation of contexts where the artefacts are left in place until an entire surface is uncovered, they are then planned and photographed as an assemblage.

Dendrochronology The study of tree ring growth, which reflect a continuous chronological sequence that can be used for dating. Ideal sample sizes are 50+ rings preferably with bark to be sent to the laboratory.

Deposit A sedimentary layer or fill.

Diachronic Literally meaning "through time". Archaeology is a diachronic discipline in that it studies people through time.

Diatom A plant microfossil, the remains of a unicellular alga that has silica cell walls. These cell walls are very durable, and are found in great quantities at the bottom of any body of water. Their forms are highly diagnostic; identifying them allows for the assessment of a body of water's salinity, alkalinity, and nutrient status, and to determine what the immediate environment was like at different periods.

Downwash Sediments washed down a slope by water.

Dry Box A plastic container with a tight-fitting lid and a handle that keeps the objects inside dry (see wet box).

Ecofact Any organic/environmental non-artefactual material that has been modified by humans - such as felled trees, food remains, shellfish middens, animal bones, cereal grains, coprolites and teeth - but not used as artefacts.

Epi-Palaeolithic A term used for the Middle Stone Age primarily in North Africa and Southwest Asia. It is the period after the last ice age when mobile hunter-gatherer societies began to adopt new subsistence and settlement strategies in the new environment. The tool kit was mainly microlithic and a semi-sedentary and village life occurred as did manipulation, but not cultivation of plants.

Ethnoarchaeology The ethnographic study of contemporary peoples from traditional societies, with a focus on material culture and the formation processes that create archaeological deposits.

Evaluation The examination of a site to reveal its archaeological potential; to assess whether or not it is worthy of full-scale excavation and/or survey.

Experimental Archaeology The simulation or replication of ancient activities, structures and artefacts to study their performance, with carefully designed scientific observation, recording and controls.

Ex Situ Not found in the original place where it was deposited; literally 'out of place'.

Feature A non-portable artefact or disturbance that has been modified by humans, such as post holes, graves, hearths, architectural elements, ditches, or stains. This is a useful neutral term used in the initial stages before more precise higher levels of interpretation are given.

Fieldwalking A systematic walk across a gridded area, searching for and recording any surface clues - such as artefacts - to judge the likely types of archaeology in a particular area.

Fire-Cracked Stones cracked by exposure to a flame or heat.

Fissures Linear, natural faults in the natural sediments or rocks.

Flot The organic and other remains retrieved in a single action of flotation.

Fluvial Deposits Materials that have been deposited by flowing water.

Foundation Trench The ditch dug for the foundations of a wall.

Geomatics This discipline integrates the acquisition, modelling, analysis, and management of spatially referenced data, i.e. data identified according to their locations. It is based on the scientific framework of geodesy, and uses terrestrial, marine, airborne, and satellite-based sensors to acquire spatial and other data. It incorporates the process of transforming spatially referenced data from different sources into common information systems with well-defined accuracy characteristics. It includes the tools and techniques used in land surveying (cadastral, cartographic, engineering, hydrographic, photogrammetic, topographic), remote sensing (aerial photographs, satellites), Geographic Information Systems (GIS), Global Navigation Satellite Systems (COMPASS, GALILEO, GLONASS, and GPS), and related forms of earth mapping. It is often used to establish the site grid and temporary bench marks (and as such all archaeological features and artefacts) and spatially relate them to the world-grid (i.e. WS84).

Geophysical Surveying Sub-surface survey using instruments including ground penetrating radar (short radio pulses), resistivity meter (electrical conductivity), and magnetometer (magnetic field) to locate positive and negative anomalies or features buried beneath the ground.

GIS: (Geographical Information System(s)) A range of techniques using graphic capabilities combined with database facilities of computers for an integrated spatial analysis of maps, images, sites and finds.

Grid The grid is the visible or invisible lines set up between the points of an ambit. The grid usually refers to the main site grid, although smaller sub-grids may be set up within the main grid. There are three main types of archaeological grid. The first type is where lines of string connect all the points within the ambit making a solid grid; this type is usually used in box-trenching. The second is where only the outline of the ambit is marked out with string, and the internal points of the ambit marked with flags. This type is usually used in open area excavation. The third type of grid is an electronic grid that is invisible except for the base-line pegs; it connects the points of the ambit by means of a multi-station or EDM. This type of grid is often employed when a site has been excavated over a long period of time by different archaeological units with different grid systems; it is thus a means to correlate these systems.

Grid Reference or Co-ordinates The site grid comprises individual (5m) squares, the point where these grid squares meet, the ambit points, are given grid reference numbers, such as 115E/200N. These are the distances east and north from the zero point or grid datum. Grid references are used to record an artefact's or feature's provenience.

Harris Matrix A system designed by Ed Harris to help understand the stratigraphy of an archaeological site. Stratigraphic layers are represented by boxes; the placement of the boxes relative to each other corresponds to their superpositional relationships. The relationship of the strata with one another is shown by connecting lines.

Heat-Affected Any material that has changed colour, shape or texture by exposure to heat (especially fire).

Hoard A group of 10 or more coins or other artefacts found together deposited in the ground. There can be a personal hoard, stored to keep the personal belongings of an individual safe. A votive hoard found in a shrine, temple, cave may have been deposited over a long period of time as a religious offering. Merchant's and founder's hoards will have artefacts just made and awaiting sale in the former case, and raw material, obsolete or worn out objects awaiting melting down and recasting in the latter.

Hominin Any member of the *Hominini* tribe, part of the *Hominidae* family of the *Primutes* order. Hominid palaeontology is an ultra-specialised area of research, which has undergone systematic revolutions since the 1970s as a host of new species have been uncovered. Hominin ancestors are known back more than 20 million years. The hominin phylogeny now stretches back to *Sahelanthropus tchadenis* (7–6 mya) and *Orrorin tugenensis* (*c.* 6 mya), before evolving into *Ardipithecus ramidus* (5-4.4 mya), which probably evolved into *Australopithecus anamensis* (4.2-3.9).

Hominin Toolmakers The first decedents of the early hominins to make tools were probably *Australopithecus afarensis* (4-3 mya) and *Australopithecus africanus* (3-2 mya), although tools have not been found directly associated with their remains. The earliest direct evidence of tool making (c. 2.6 mya) is associated with *Australopithecus aethiopicus* (2.8-2.2 mya), *Australopithecus garhi* (2.5 mya), *Australopithecus boisei* (2.8-2.2 mya), *Early Homo* sp. Indet. (2.4-2.3 mya), *Homo rudolfensis* (2.3-1.8 mya), *Australopithecus sediba* (2.0-1.8 mya), *Homo habilis* (1.9-1.6 mya), *Australopithecus robustus* (1.8-1.0 mya),

Homo ergaster (1.8-0.6 mya), and *Homo erectus* (1.6-0.05 mya [from 0.6 mya it developed into evolved *Homo erectus*]). These Hominins all lived in Africa (apart from *Homo erectus*, a descendent of *Homo ergaster* that moved out-of-Africa *c*. 1.6 mya and who lived in the Far East) and seem to have developed tool-making by about 2.6 mya in the Oldowan tradition. By 1.65 mya *Homo ergaster* had developed the Acheulian tradition (Foley & Lahr 2003: 118-120; Klein 2007: 94). The first toolmaker in Europe was *Homo ergaster*, where finds at the Dmanisi site in Georgia dating to between 1.7 to 1.2 mya indicate an Oldowan tradition (Klein 2007: 102-5). However, like *Homo antecessor*, another Oldowan tradition using Hominin found at Sierra de Atapuerca in Spain, they were unsuccessful in colonising Europe. The first successful colonisers of Europe were *Homo heidelbergensis* who brought with them Acheulian tradition handaxes *c*. 0.4 mya (Foley & Lahr 2003: 118-120; Klein 2007: 94). Mode 3 industries are primarily associated with *Homo neanderthalensis*, but it seems probably that *Homo helmei* (an early form of *Homo sapiens*) originally developed this form of tool making (Foley & Lahr 2003: 120). Modes 4 and 5 were developed by *Homo sapiens* (Foley & Lahr 2003: 120). In terms of the evolutionary process, technologies seem to change during the course of a lineage's existence, and that some of the descendents persisted in using that mode of tool making (Foley & Lahr 2003: 120).

Hunter-foragers These are small mobile groups whose subsistence is based on hunting and foraging for wild plants, fruits and nuts, practicing residential mobility by moving the entire social unit from one resource patch to another.

Hunter-gatherers These are small groups that hunt wild animals and collect plants

and apply logistic mobility by moving resources to the group that is based in long-term residential camps.

Hyper-Spectral This is an image similar to multispectral satellite imagery, but with many more bands. The data is captured by hyper-spectral scanners such as Hyspex (with more than 300 bands and a ground-resolution of 0.4 cm) flown in transects over the area in an aeroplane. This gives a high-resolution of Quaternary geological and botanical mapping as well as mineral prospection. Other environmental parameters can also be mapped in this way and allows the location of archaeological sites.

Inclusions Natural material (i.e. grits) or archaeological material (i.e. pottery fragments) that constitutes less than 10% of the sedimentary matrix.

In Situ Found in the original place where it was deposited. The exact spot in a cultural deposit in which an artefact was found. Literally 'in place'.

Interfaces The junction between two or more contexts. All contexts have at least three interfaces: one above, one below and at least one to the sides. A good example of an interface are objects dropped on a flooring surface, for they are neither part of the floor construction, and neither do they belong to the layers above, but are actually in the interface. All buried surfaces have interfaces. There are also negative interfaces, such as cuts into pre-existing contexts, such as grave pits, post-holes or ditches where there is an interface between the cut, the contexts that fill it, and the contexts that it is dug into. Although all contexts have interfaces, it is only deposits and cuts that receive a context number, as it would be too time-consuming and technically unrewarding to record every interface.

Isometric Drawing A three-dimensional rendering of a site, feature or artefact, to show how the object would originally have looked.

Kubiena Box A five-sided metal box (10 x 10 x 50 cm) with two removable sections used to take environmental samples from a section. Related to monolith boxes that have no removable sections. The box is pushed into the side of the section and when extracted is full of the sedimentary matrix from that section, which is then taken to the laboratory for analysis.

Kom The term *kôm* is colloquial Egyptian Arabic for Classical Arabic *kawm* 'pile', 'heap', and is used to describe an accumulated mound of debris from ancient settlement remains, and although related to the word *tell*, it is probably a better term to use when describing Egyptian settlement mounds than *tell* (see *tell*).

Lacustrine Sediments Sediments that have been deposited on a lake bed.

Large Finds These are finds, such as statues, millstones or other not easily portable objects.

Lens A thin layer of sediment contained within a different larger deposit, or between deposits.

Levels Depth measurements taken from a temporary benchmark (TBM) or datum. The recording of levels is one of the most important controlling factors of an archaeological excavation, and denotes the spatio-temporal order of the archaeological units. The level of an object allows it to be precisely associated with other artefacts, ecofacts and features, therefore allowing the digital recreation of the site.

Line Level A small spirit level that can be attached to a piece of string, used to take vertical measurements or to set up section lines.

Living/Occupation Surface Any surface where past human activity has taken place, such as a floor, street or threshing floor.

Locus A unit of stratigraphy - deriving from the Latin for 'place' - that refers to an archaeological or geological deposit or layer, a single phase of a multi-phase wall, a pit lining, pit fill, a surface such as a floor, destruction debris or any stratum than can be meaningfully isolated (see Introduction). In practice, a locus is assigned when it becomes necessary to distinguish one locus from another, or to refer to it apart from a feature. Each locus is recorded separately along with its level. Loci are primarily excavation units designed to help the ceramicist date phases or strata. Everything excavated belongs to one locus or another. The locus numbers in an operational area will normally be numbered starting with the number of the operation. Therefore in operation 9 the first locus number will be 9000, the next 9001, and so on. Sometimes letters will be affixed onto a locus number; for example, this is done if a wall is found to have a second phase of building, so if the first phase of the wall is 9029, the second will be 9029A and if a third phase is uncovered it is given the locus number 9029B, and so on. If a whole pit is found on a surface it is treated as a discrete locus, but rather than giving it a whole new context number, a 'P' is added after the locus number of the surface on which it was found. If pottery is found 10 cm below one surface embedded into another surface, this material is given a .1 of the locus above this surface.

Therefore one surface can have three locus numbers, 7035, 7035P and 7035.1, indicating the surface, the material found on that surface, and material found 10 cm below that surface that has been trodden into surfaces below it. These conventions are to assist the ceramicist in identifying those loci that are likely to contain pottery of a phase or stratum.

Locus Pottery Basket Each locus is assigned a pottery basket (although other objects are put in bags and placed within the basket). The sequential numbering of the baskets forms the basic framework of the field notebook. If a lot of intrusive pottery is found, the basket is split by the ceramicist and the excavator is asked to re-evaluate the locus. This errant pottery may indicate that the excavator has missed a pit that should have been assigned a new locus number. The place from whence the pottery came is then assigned a new locus number, if this is found to be the case, and the basket is then subsequently corrected in post-excavation.

Lot This is an American term used for a unit of excavation called a 'spit' in Europe. It can be an arbitrary level of 5 cm, 10 cm or 20 cm, each of which receives its own lot number (although, if a distinct stratum appears, a new lot is assigned immediately). However, if excavation is proceeding following the natural strata (the more favoured and accurate method), then each separate stratum gets its own number. If a pit or other kind of discrete feature appears, it is defined, segregated and given its own set of lot numbers. The exact horizontal and vertical dimensions of each lot must be recorded.

Magnetometer A piece of equipment used in subsurface survey to measure minor variations in the earth's magnetic field. Archaeological features often show up as magnetic anomalies.

Material Remains A blanket term used for architectural and artefactual material found on an archaeological site.

Matrix The medium in which archaeological artefacts, ecofacts, contexts, and features are found. The substance that immediately surrounds archaeological data; usually some sort of sediment such as gravel, sand, or clay.

Mesolithic The Middle Stone Age, characterised by the use of microlithic tools. A term usually used to describe the transitional period from the Palaeolithic hunting gathering way of life to the new environment created after the retreat of the ice sheets, particularly in Europe.

Microlith A type of stone tool, usually less than 5 mm long. Often hafted singly on the tip of an instrument, or arranged in sequence along a bone/wood handle to form a composite cutting edge.

Microwear Analysis The analysis of wear patterns on the edges of stone tools to reveal how they were used.

Midden The accumulation of debris built up from human activities, often as the result of disposal away from the area of manufacture. The disposal of shellfish shells over a long period of time often resulted in a shell midden.

MNI This abbreviation stands for minimum number of individuals, and is a method of assessing the smallest number of animals or humans necessary to account for all the fragments present in the assemblage.

Munsell Colour Book A book of soil colour charts used to identify the colour of soil.

Natural The original sediment of the site; non-anthropogenic sediments.

Neolithic The New Stone Age, a period characterised by the adoption of domesticated plants and animals, but still relying on lithic technology. Polished and ground stone tools and the adoption of ceramics are characteristic of this period, although some regions and cultures adopted agriculture before pottery (i.e. the Levant), whilst others adopted pottery before agriculture (i.e. Mali and Japan).

NISP The abbreviation for the number of identified species, used in zooarchaeology to quantify the species found in the faunal assemblage.

Occupation Layer A layer of sediment created by human activity, usually found on top of a floor, road or similar surface.

Operational Area A defined area where work is carried out. It may be preferable to divide the site up into different areas, which are excavated in order to address specific questions. If possible, divide the site by functional area, such as the cemetery or settlement parts of a site. These areas of operation may be separated by great distances. Teams of archaeologists are usually assigned to an operational area; therefore it is primarily a way of organising the work force in the most efficient way to excavate the site to answer the research questions.

Ostracon (pl. Ostreaca) Potsherds or limestone flakes bearing inscriptions, drawings, personal jottings, letters, sketches or exercises of scribes.

Overburden The archaeologically sterile sediment or vegetation covering archaeological deposits, which is usually removed by mechanical means. Overburden is also sometimes called plus, and given + as the context number.

Palaeoentomology The study of insects from archaeological contexts. Insect remains are highly durable and - owing to insects' sensitivity to climatic change - are good indicators of ancient climate.

Palaeoethnotrichology The area of archaeological research concerned with the cultural and scientific study of ancient hair. Hair is analysed both artistically and scientifically, analysing false hair, natural body hair, and loose hair, as well as iconography or texts concerning hairstyles and related issues. Chemical examinations can also be carried out. These examinations can provide information about ancient people's general state of health, diet, social status and even profession.

Palaeolithic The Old Stone Age, which is sub-divided into the Lower, Middle and Upper Palaeolithic. The period begins about 2.6 mya with the advent of stone tool manufacture and continues to about 12 kya depending on the region.

Palaeontology The study of fossil remains of animals (i.e. dinosaurs) or hominins (*Homo erectus*).

Palimpsest A manuscript on which the original writing has been imperfectly erased to make way for other writing. In spite of the over-writing, however, the original can often be identified.

Palynology The identification, study and analysis of ancient fossilised pollen, used to aid the reconstruction of past ecological conditions.

Patination A weathering reaction that coats the surface of minerals, metals, ceramics and wood.

Physical Anthropology or Bioanthropology The study of ancient human remains with a view to understanding the biological characteristics of past populations. Related to 'bioarchaeology'.

Phytoliths These are microscopic parts of plants made from silica, which derive from individual plant cells. These can survive, especially in ash layers, hearths or pottery, long after the plant has decomposed. Phytoliths of different species have distinct shapes and sizes, and can be used to gain information about plant use, and to help build up a picture of the environment.

Plumb Bob A piece of metal (often conical) on a piece of string, used for establishing a true vertical. Often used for placing a tripod directly above the datum.

Primary Discard Artefacts and ecofacts that are in their original place of deposition. These objects must be 3-D recorded and individually lifted; they are kept separate from the other general finds (see 'secondary discard').

Provenance The specific geographical and/or cultural origin of an artefact or material.

Provenience The horizontal and vertical position of an artefact, feature or ecofact within the site matrix, judged in reference to a datum, grid corner or other landmark.

Public Archaeology The involvement and education of the public in archaeology and archaeological projects. This can take the form of holding open days at the site for visitors who are given guided tours, or building a visitor centre where various means of communicating the results to the public are held, such as re-enactments of various activities such as craftwork, a recreation of the actual site, and provide visual displays and offer brochures and other publications.

Rectilinear A long, thin rectangular feature.

Reference Collection A collection of dated and identified archaeological remains against which freshly excavated material can be compared.

Relationship The connections of a single context with other contexts; either above, below or to the side of it.

Relative Dating The determining of a chronological sequence without reference to a fixed time-scale. Items or deposits are older/younger than those above/below them (see 'absolute dating').

Remote Sensing Method of locating and determining the nature and extent of features or whole sites by non-invasive reconnaissance and surface survey, including geophysics and use of aerial or satellite imaging.

Rescue (or Salvage) Archaeology The excavation and recording of sites in advance of urban development or other projects. This is usually done under great time-pressure from the developers.

Resistivity Meter A piece of equipment used in sub-surface survey to measure fluctuations in the earth's conductivity of electrical current. These differences are then used to identify sites and features.

Retent The stony remnants of a flotated sedimentary sample.

Satellite Imagery An image of the earth's surface taken from a satellite used to study regional patterns of land use and other resources. The method's basis is that the creation of human sites generally involves the local accumulation of foreign minerals which can be traced chemically after thousand of years. In a settlement the accumulation of bones from game will for instance create a concentration of Iron (Fe) that typically will be one of the elements that makes such sites visible as 'anomalies' in multispectral satellite images. Old roads and mounds, that are today invisible on the surface, can also be distinguished in this way. The major types of multi-spectral satellite image are called QuickBird, SPOT, Corona, LANDSAT, IKONOS and ASTER, which have varying qualities of resolution. To be able to distinguish small features it is necessary to use the higher-resolution satellite-images such as IKONOS with a resolution of 4 m in the multispectral part (four bands) and 1 m in the panchromatic part – or – QuickBird with a resolution of 2.6 m in the multispectral part (four bands) and 0.6 m in the panchromatic part. The thermal bands in the ASTER data have a resolution down to 15 m. That allows recognition of larger anomalies covered by up to 60 cm of sand if the recordings are from the evening when the covering sediments are cooling down. The study of these images makes it possible to locate buried sites, examine the effects of climatic change, alterations in riverine regimes, coastal expansion, loss of archaeological sites, and changes in floral and faunal resources over time. These results need to be ground truthed (fieldwalked) and used in conjunction with existing archaeological survey data and maps.

Schnitt (or Slice) Method A method of excavation used primarily in Central Europe to excavate timber buildings. It involves cleaning a square area using hoes and shovels, therefore producing a horizontal section where the posts of the wooden house can be identified as rows of dark circles in the sandy matrix. The site is recorded as a set of horizontal and vertical sections, which are used together to provide a controllable model. This method is limited to shallow deposits as this method may cut through structures if they are concealed by deep deposits.

Secondary Discard Artefacts and ecofacts that are not in their original place of deposition. These redeposited objects are normally grouped together and collected in context-specific finds bags (see 'primary discard').

Seriation A process first developed by Petrie to understand the sequence of 'development' of Predynastic Egypt. It is a relative dating method which uses the attributes of artefacts that changed slowly over time to cluster assemblages into time periods. Also termed 'sequence dating'.

Single-Context Recording In this system, each context is planned separately on draughting film, and recorded on a single-context recording sheet. The context planning sheets are overlain to help build the site matrix.

Site Code The acronym of the site usually an alphanumeric code comprising of an abbreviated form of the name of the site, the year, and if relevant the season of fieldwork, i.e. TAD09 for Tell Abu Dawood (site), 2009 (year), and TAD09-2 for the second season in the same year (season of fieldwork).

Site Catchment Analysis The analysis of the area around the archaeological site within which it is assumed that the contents of the site have been derived. It can be a full inventory of the site's artefactual and non-artefactual remains and their sources.

Site Exploitation Territory This is a method of achieving a fairly standardised assessment of the area habitually used by the site's past inhabitants.

Skeuomorph An object, which in shape or decoration copies the form it had when made from a different substance or by a different technique.

Slag The material residue of metal smelting.

Small Finds Portable artefacts that can usually fit in a finds bag or small container.

Spit An arbitrary excavation unit of 5 cm, 10 cm or 20 cm which receives its own number. This method of excavation is usually employed when distinct contexts or deposits cannot be identified. This is equal to the US 'lot'.

Sondage A test pit placed to preview the site for evaluation purposes.

Stable Isotopes Hydrogen, carbon, nitrogen, oxygen and sulphur possess two or more naturally occurring isotopes that can be used in characterisation studies of raw materials and for detecting variations in diet from bones. Unstable isotopes decay to form a different element, and are fundamental to several radiometric dating techniques including radiocarbon, potassium-argon and uranium series.

Station A point of known height and location used in surveying by a total station to locate itself and the archaeology.

Stele (pl. stelae) A free standing stone, wooden or clay carved monument. These will usually have writing and iconographic scenes on them.

Stratification The arrangement of layers or strata of sediments, often called deposits, one upon the other. It is also the arrangement of contexts on a time line. The study of stratification should give a relative chronological sequence of events, with the earliest at the bottom and latest at the top.

Stratigraphy Stratigraphy - a modern compound of ancient Greek words, meaning literally 'layerwriting' - is the study and validation of stratification.

Synchronic Literally 'at the same time', comprising studies of people living at the same time.

***Talatat* Blocks** Small stone blocks (27 x 27 x 54 cm) used in the Amarna Period to construct monumental buildings, usually laid as a series of headers and stretchers. These limestone or sandstone blocks were usually decorated with relief. Their small size and lightness allowed the Amarna Period building projects progress speedily.

Taphonomy The study of processes that have affected organic materials after death, and the 'behaviour'' of artefacts after they have been deposited. It also involves the analysis of tooth or cut marks to assess the effects of butchery and scavenging.

Tell The Arabic word for mound, used to describe a mound of accumulated debris from a long lived settlement, usually superimposed phases of mud-brick buildings. Domestic refuge combined with the mud-brick can create huge mounds of 30 metres or higher. *Tells* can have very deep stratigraphy covering many periods of occupation and great periods of time. Many Western Asian and Egyptian toponyms have incorporated the word in their title. Alternative words used in the Near East are *tepe* (Iran) *hüyük* (Turkey) and *kôm* (Egypt).

Temper Inclusions in the clay of pottery (such as straw or sand) which act as fillers to the clay to add strength and workability and also to counteract any shrinkage or cracking during the firing process.

Terminus ante quem The date before which a certain context or feature cannot have been created; gives the date before which earlier context were deposited.

Terminus post quem The date after which a context or feature cannot have been created; gives the date on or after which a context was deposited.

Thin Section A prepared slice of stone or ceramic, about 0.03 mm thick, which is placed under a microscope and analysed to distinguish constituents of the material and thus identify the place where the material was quarried or manufactured.

Three-Dimensional Plotting The measuring and recording of objects in both the vertical and horizontal planes.

Tip Lines Lines of stones or other inclusions in a fill, showing how the deposit was tipped into a pit or ditch.

Trace Element Analysis Chemical methods - such as neutron activation analysis or X-ray fluorescence spectrometry - used to determine the occurrence of trace elements in rocks and minerals, and thus to identify the source of the raw material.

Truncation This is a term used to describe the cutting away of an archaeological deposit or structure. A layer can be truncated by a later pit. Truncation to archaeological deposits can have occurred either in antiquity or the modern era and refers to any kind of cutting event.

Unstratified and Stratified These are terms used to describe whether an object was found within undisturbed stratified layers or features that it was originally laid down in, or has been disturbed and moved around. Where disturbance, such as ploughing, has taken place an object will be unstratified and whilst interesting for its own sake it contributes little to the dating, or understanding, of an archaeological site. Objects found in stratified layers provide evidence of what happened and the date at which that event occurred.

Upcast The sediment removed from pits, ditches and post-holes.

Use-Wear Striations, polish and other abrasions on lithic tools, associated with particular tasks (see 'microwear').

Vienna System A visual classification system used to identify different pottery fabrics. It defines the major groups into which the fabrics may be placed (i.e. Nile A-E and Marl A-E) and gives sub-divisions of these groups. It was conceived as a guide as to how fabrics may be described in the field. It is not designed to be used with post-New Kingdom pottery, when profound changes in pottery technology and organisation begin to take place.

Watching Brief A commission given to an archaeologist to observe and record any archaeological remains revealed during construction projects.

Waterlogged Deposit Sedimentary deposits that lie beneath the water table or in water-retaining contexts, and which are likely to contain well preserved organic remains.

Wattle Woven twigs that form panels and walls, often coated with daub.

Wet Box A plastic container with a tight-fitting lid and a handle that holds a centimetre or more of water in the bottom to keep the objects inside damp. A small amount of water is usually placed inside the finds bags as well. The water used must be clean, such as drinking water (see dry box).

Zooarchaeology The identification and analysis of faunal species from archaeological sites, to reconstruct past human diets and also to gain an understanding of the ancient environment.

Appendix 1: The Code of Ethics of the Egyptian Cultural Heritage Organisation

The Egyptian Cultural Heritage Organisation (ECHO) is dedicated to the greater understanding, protection and preservation of Egypt's cultural heritage and the dissemination of archaeological knowledge to the academic and wider public audience. ECHO recognises that archaeologists, specialist consultants and cultural heritage managers have a responsibility to practice a moral and professional code of ethics to the cultural material of the past, the public and their colleagues.

I) The Responsibility to the Cultural Heritage:

1. ECHO condemns the looting and destruction of archaeological property and are supporters of: the 1954 UNESCO *Convention for the Protection of Cultural Property in the Event of Armed Conflict*; the 1956 UNESCO *Recommendation on International Principles Applicable to Archaeological Excavations*, the 1964 ICOMOS *International Charter for the Conservation and Restoration of Monuments and Sites*; the 1970 UNESCO *Convention on the Means of Prohibiting and Preventing the Illicit Import, Export and Transfer of Ownership of Cultural Property*; the 1972 UNESCO *Convention Concerning Protection of the World Cultural and Natural Heritage,* the 1990 ICOMOS International Committee on Archaeological Heritage Management (ICAHM) *Charter for the Protection and Management of the Archaeological Heritage*; the 1995 UNIDROIT *Convention on Stolen or Illegally Exported Cultural Objects*; the 2001 UNESCO *Convention on the Protection of the Underwater Cultural Heritage*; the 2001 UNESCO *Universal Declaration on Cultural Diversity*; the 2003 UNESCO *Convention for the Safeguarding of the Intangible Cultural Heritage*, and the 2005 UNESCO *Convention on the Protection and Promotion of the Diversity of Cultural Expressions*. All members must acquaint themselves with these legislative documents, and comply with their legal requirements. All members should also make themselves familiar with Egyptian law governing archaeology and the antiquities trade, and abide by these laws, especially Law no. 215 (31st October 1951) on the *Protection of Antiquities*, revised by laws no. 529 of 1953, no. 24 of 1965 and no. 117 of 1983.

2. All archaeologists, scientists, art historians or other archaeological specialists, must refrain from giving credence to stolen or looted artefacts, by refusing to study, evaluate or examine them in any manner whatsoever, unless it is to verify that the artefacts in question are indeed stolen or looted, and as such must be reported to the appropriate authorities. These experts must also not consciously contribute any scholarly knowledge to an exhibition that knowingly allows artefacts illegally acquired after 30th December 1970 to be shown in their displays. An artefact may be considered illicit if:

    a) The person in possession of it cannot produce good title to it under the applicable law.
    b) An object has been acquired in - or exported from - its country of origin in violation of that country's laws.

c) The object was imported or acquired illegally from an official excavation or monument, or originated from an unofficial, illegal or clandestine dig.

3. Archaeologists must undertake to report any dishonest or unethical behaviour, especially that which threatens any cultural materiality, such as breaches of the UNESCO, ICOMOS or UNIDROIT agreements, to the proper legal authorities.

4. Members must not engage in any illegal or unethical conduct involving archaeological material or knowingly permit the use of their name in support of any illegal or unethical activity involving archaeological matters, including, theft, fraud, deceit or misrepresentation.

5. Archaeologists and archaeological specialists should refrain from authentication and testing for any objects not curated in a public institution or where they are not open to scientific study, interpretation or display, such as those held by private individuals, salesrooms or commercial galleries.

6. The principal investigator or director must ensure that all governmental permits and necessary permissions from landowners and other persons are obtained and that the site and personnel conform to all legal requirements.

7. The principal investigator or director should include adequate plans for conservation, preservation, storage receptacles and materials and archives in their project design, and should secure funds for such purposes from the outset.

8. The principal investigator or director must ensure that experimental design, recording, and sampling procedures are adequate for the project being undertaken.

9. The principal investigator or director of a project must before any archaeological work is undertaken, carefully consider the purpose and consequences of the intended research. The methods and approaches chosen must be the most suitable for not only extracting the maximum amount of information from the archaeological material, but for creating the least amount of damage to the local or regional environment. Less intrusive methods of archaeological investigation - such as survey - should always be sought first before resorting to excavation. The objectives of the research should be adequate justification for the destruction of archaeological evidence which it will entail.

10. The recording and collecting of archaeological material must retain their provenience and identification throughout the whole archaeological process of retrieval, conservation and analysis.

11. The archaeologist shall ensure that resultant records of an investigation, along with the methods and results of any analysis, must be fully described, recorded and archived in an intelligible, readily usable and durable manner, it must be maintained in good condition and the full archive - including any artefacts and

specimens - eventually deposited where it can receive adequate curatorial care and storage conditions and be readily available for study and examination.

12. The recovery and study of archaeological material must be conducted only by - or under the guidance - of fully qualified professional personnel.

13. The principal investigator or director must develop a project digest that specifies the project objectives and takes into account all previous work and relevant research.

14. The principal investigator or director must ensure the availability of adequate and qualified personnel and facilities to carry the project through to completion. The archaeologist shall not undertake any work for which he or she is not adequately qualified and shall try to ensure to the best of their ability that all members of the team undertaking archaeological work are adequately qualified. The principal investigator or director should arrange for specialists to be contacted in the event of unforeseen archaeological issues, which they can recommend to their employers, funders or clients.

15. Archaeologists must keep themselves informed about developments in their field of specialisation.

16. When cultural heritage is under a direct threat, such as human induced - war zone or building of a dam or a natural threat such as earthquake or flooding, it is the archaeologists duty to try and protect/rescue as much of the threatened heritage as possible. Participation in a rescue project in a country where the current regime has low human rights, is corrupt, brutal, illegitimate or has UN sanctions against it, does not imply that the archaeologists working in that country support the regime as long as they do not:

    a) Offer support for the regime, either privately or publicly.
    b) Produce literature or other media proclaiming the rights of the regime.
    c) Oppress or exploit any of the people in the country or are partisan in anyway.
    d) Directly receive money from - or give money to - the regime for the work they are doing in the country. UNESCO money being channelled through the regime is, however, permissible.
    e) Participate in any political activities that support the regime.

    Therefore, as long as the rescuing (surveying, excavating, conserving) of the cultural heritage and objective report writing of the analysis of the material is the goal of the project it is ethically and morally acceptable to salvage the cultural heritage within that country. The archaeological record is finite, whereas modern political regimes are transient; therefore it is the archaeologist's duty to record as an objective view of history as possible.

17. If the country or regime where a human or naturally induced threat is occurring or about to occur cannot safely and effectively look after the artefacts, monuments and other objects of cultural heritage that are salvaged from an archaeological rescue project and as a consequence offers to share these objects with the agencies participating in the project, then these objects must be:

    a) Deposited with a national or local museum or within a teaching collection of a university on a fixed term renewable, and revisable loan. It must be understood and stated that the objects/material (archives) are recognised as belonging to the country of origin and that the intention is to eventually repatriate the objects to that country.

Objects may not be

    b) Sold to any person.
    c) Deposited in private collections not accessible by the public and scholarly research.
    d) Kept by the archaeologist or funding agency.

II) The Responsibilities to the Public

1. When the principal investigator or director is planning a project, due consideration must be given to the overall impact that the project may have on the local population.

2. All archaeological personnel must respect the cultural norms and dignity of the local population. Archaeologists should take into account legitimate concerns of groups whose material past may be the subject of archaeological investigation.

3. The principal investigator or director should hold consultations with the appropriate representatives of the local community during the planning stage of the project, and invite local participation in the project, giving the local population regular updates of the progress being made.

4. The project personnel should actively engage in outreach programmes through lecturing, popular writing, school education programmes, site tours, and other educational initiatives.

5. Archaeologists must present archaeology and its results in a responsible manner, to avoid and discourage exaggerated, misleading or unwarranted statements about archaeological practice.

6. The principal investigator or director must make adequate provision for continued site management at the planning stage of the project if the site is to be opened to the public.

7.   An archaeologist must not offer advice, make a public statement, or give legal testimony about archaeological matters without being as fully informed about such matters as is reasonably possible.

III) The Responsibilities to Colleagues

1.   ECHO is an equal opportunities organisation. Members of ECHO must not practice discrimination or harassment based on age, sex, religion, colour, national origin, disability or sexual preference.

2.   The principal investigator or director of a project must provide acceptable standards of health, hygiene and safety on site and give due regard to the requirements of employment legislation. Archaeologists must ensure that adequate insurance cover is maintained for all personnel and property that may be affected by archaeological activities.

3.   All archaeologists must adhere to the highest standards of ethical and responsible behaviour in the conduct of archaeological affairs, and shall conduct himself or herself in a manner that will not bring archaeology or their institution into disrepute.

4.   Those in authority on a project must behave with consideration and courtesy to those under their authority, while all team members should reciprocate and strive to promote the success of the project.

5.   Archaeologists should strive to make public the record and results of their research in a timely manner providing evidence to others. Yearly interim reports should be submitted to reputable journals to disseminate the latest findings, and a final report must be published.

6.   The principal investigator or director is responsible for the analysis and publication of data derived from his or her investigations. If publication is not completed within 5 years of completion of a project then, a waiver of the rights of primacy shall be judged and evidence should be made available to researchers upon request for analysis and publication. Extenuating circumstances shall be considered by interested parties.

7.   Archaeologists should communicate and cooperate with colleagues with similar interests, giving due respect to colleagues' interests in - and rights to - information about sites, areas, collections or data where there is a shared field of concern, be it active or potential.

8.   Archaeologists must give due regard and appropriate support to the training and development of all personnel to enable them to execute their duties.

9.   All personnel must give the appropriate credit for work done by other archaeologists and specialist consultants.

10. All personnel must give reasonable consideration to cumulative service and proven experience of employees, colleagues or helpers when deciding rates of pay and other employment benefits.

11. Requests from colleagues or students for information on the results of research or projects should be honoured by the archaeologist if it is consistent with his or her prior rights to publication and other archaeological responsibilities.

12. Archaeologists must not commit plagiarism in electronic, written (hard copy) or oral communication.

13. An archaeologist shall not reveal confidential information unless required by law, nor use any confidential or privileged information to his or her own advantage or that of a third party.

Appendix 2: Recording Forms

The Recording Forms (see the CD attached to the back cover and available from the ECHO website: www.e-c-h-o.org) should be printed double-sided on A4 sized paper.

Appendix 3: Examples of Filled Out Recording Forms

Sheet One

Excavation (Context) Recording Form

1. SITE CODE	2. OPERATIONAL AREA	3. SITE SUB-DIVISION	4. CONTEXT NO.
TAD09	3	T3	1023

5. GRID REFS.		6. FEATURE/ GROUP NO.	7. TYPE
115E/220N		N/A	FILL

8. REDUCED LEVEL	9. LENGTH	10. WIDTH	11. THICKNESS/DEPTH
MAX. 94.267	MAX. 3.21 M	MAX. 2.37 M	MAX. N 0.27 M
MIN. 94.270	MIN. 3.15 M	MIN. 2.21 M	MIN. S 0.22 M

DEPOSIT	12. COLOUR	13. COMPOSITION / TEXTURE / GRAIN SIZE
	10YR 6/4 (MOIST)	SANDY SILT, MODERATELY SORTED, SUB-ANGULAR DISK SHAPED.

14. COMPACTION / CONSOLIDATION	15. STRUCTURE
WEAK COHESION WITH FLECKS OF CARBONATES.	EVIDENCE OF BIOTURBATION AND WATER LEVEL MARKS. THE TIP LINE RUNS FROM THE SOUTH TO NORTH.

16. COARSE ARCHAEOLOGICAL COMPONENTS	17. COARSE NATURAL COMPONENTS
THERE IS 5% OF POTTERY AND 1% OF BONES.	OPEN PACKED, INTERSPERSED GRITS (25%) AND STONES (5%).

18. FILL OF	19. CONTEXT BOUNDARY INTERFACES
FILL OF CONTEXT [972].	THE TIP LINE IS FROM THE SOUTH TO NORTH.

CUT	20. TOP OF CUT IN PLAN	21. CORNERS
	N/A	N/A

22. BREAK OF SLOPE - LIP	23. SIDES	24. BREAK OF SLOPE – BASE
N/A	N/A	N/A

25. BASE	26. ORIENTATION	27. INCLINATION OF AXIS
N/A	N/A	N/A

28. TRUNCATED	29. FILL NOS.	30. OTHER COMMENTS
N/A	N/A	N/A

31. DISCUSSION, COMMENTS & DESCRIPTIVE TEXT OF CONTEXT: INTERNAL   EXTERNAL ✓ STRUCTURAL   OTHER

THIS IS THE MIDDLE FILL OF THE RUBBISH PIT [972].

32. CONTEXT INTERPRETATION AND OTHER INFORMATION

THIS SEEMS TO BE A RUBBISH FILL OF PIT [972]. IT IS DISTINCT FROM THE ORIGINAL FILL (1096) AND LATER FILL (973) AS IT HAS A DIFFERENT COMPOSITION AND COMPACTION, AS WELL AS BEING DARKER IN COLOUR.

SAME AS CONTEXT: ASSOCIATED CONTEXTS: 973, 972, 1096

33. METHOD OF EXCAVATION (SIEVED/Un-Sieved)	34. WEATHER CONDITIONS, TIME OF DAY
EXCAVATED WITH A FAZ AND TROWEL, THE MATRIX WAS SIEVED.	DRY AND SUNNY WEATHER, 9.30 AM.

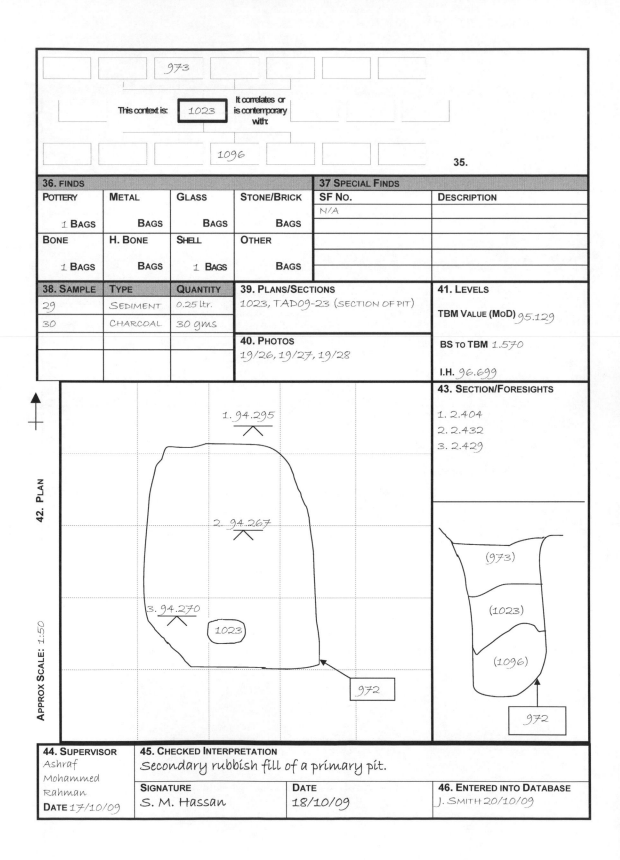

973

This context is: 1023   It correlates or is contemporary with:

1096

35.

36. FINDS				**37** SPECIAL FINDS	
POTTERY	METAL	GLASS	STONE/BRICK	SF No.	DESCRIPTION
1 BAGS	BAGS	BAGS	BAGS	N/A	
BONE	H. BONE	SHELL	OTHER		
1 BAGS	BAGS	1 BAGS	BAGS		

38. SAMPLE	TYPE	QUANTITY
29	SEDIMENT	0.25 ltr.
30	CHARCOAL	30 gms

39. PLANS/SECTIONS
1023, TAD09-23 (SECTION OF PIT)

40. PHOTOS
19/26, 19/27, 19/28

41. LEVELS

TBM VALUE (MOD) 95.129

BS TO TBM 1.570

I.H. 96.699

42. PLAN

APPROX SCALE: 1:50

1. 94.295

2. 94.267

3. 94.270

1023

972

43. SECTION/FORESIGHTS

1. 2.404
2. 2.432
3. 2.429

(973)

(1023)

(1096)

972

44. SUPERVISOR Ashraf Mohammed Rahman DATE 17/10/09	**45.** CHECKED INTERPRETATION Secondary rubbish fill of a primary pit.		
	SIGNATURE S. M. Hassan	DATE 18/10/09	**46.** ENTERED INTO DATABASE J. SMITH 20/10/09

Arbitrary Lot Recording Form

1. SITE CODE	2. OPERATIONAL AREA	3. SUB-DIVISION	4. CONTEXT NO.
TAD09	1	97	105

5. GRID REF.	6. LOT NO.	7. THICKNESS OF LOT	8. TYPE
150E/270N	105-5	10 cm	Deposit/layer

9. TBM VALUE (MOD) 100.000 M   **BS TO TBM** 1.590 **I.H.** 101.590

10. REDUCED LEVEL	11. DIMENSIONS
FROM _93.60_ CM TO _93.50_ CM	L _4.5 M_ W _4.5 M_

12. MATRIX

THE MATRIX IS A SILTY SAND WITH INCLUSIONS OF GRITS AND GRAVELS, FRIABLE (SEE CONTEXT RECORDING FORM 105/1/1).

13. CONTAINS

THE MAIN MATRIX IS CONTEXT (105), WHICH CONTAINS THREE OTHER CONTEXTS (357), (369), (391). THESE ARE PROBABLY GRAVES.

14. METHOD OF EXCAVATION AND REMARKS

THE LOT WAS EXCAVATED WITH A FAZAND SHOVEL. THE EXCAVATION WILL NOW BE CONDUCTED WITH TROWELS IN THE FEATURES.

15. FINDS				16. SPECIAL FINDS	
POTTERY	STONE	WOOD	H. BONE	SF NO.	DESCRIPTION
1 BAGS	BAGS	BAGS	BAGS	NONE	
BONE	METAL	SHELL	OTHER		
1 BAGS	BAGS	BAGS	BAGS		

17. SAMPLE	TYPE	QUANTITY	18. PLANS/SECTIONS	19. PHOTOS
165	SEDIMENT	0.25 ltr.	TAD09-75	11/1, 11/2

20. OTHER N/A

93.50

(357) (391) (105) (369)

Baulk

21.

73 96 105

Supervisor
Andy Smith

Checked by
S. M. Hassan

Date
17/06/09

MANUAL LEVEL LOG SHEET

SITE CODE: _TAD09_   OPERATIONAL AREA: _2_   SUB-DIVISION: _91_

CONTEXT NO.: _929_   GRID REFS.: _155E/265N_

DATUM: _100.000 M_   TBM OR CENTRAL DATUM: _93.000 M_

[_____4.5M_____]

```
4                                                    1 ┌ ─ ─ ─ ┐
                                                       │       │
                                                       │ Datum │
                                                       │       │
                         8                           2 └ ─ ─ ─ ┘ 3




                         7




5                                                                6
```

1) True North must be indicated.

2} Only finished levels to be recorded in the log, <u>not</u> intermediate ones.

3) The string secured to the peg in the centre of the central datum is usually placed 0.10 m above ground level. A couple of grooves cut in the wooden post will help secure the string in place and stop it moving up and down. When recording levels, the +0.10 m above ground level must be subtracted first, i.e. the measure will show 0.20 m, when the +0.10 m is subtracted the actual level will be 0.10 m below ground level, this is what must be entered in the log.

4) Contexts that are taken down in non-stratigraphically related lots or spits, are removed in 0.10 m levels, unless otherwise stated. It is these levels that are recorded on this form.

5) Each context has its own unique number; this must be indicated on the sheet.

SUPERVISOR: _M. NOUR EL-DIN_   CHECKED BY: _S. HASSAN_   DATE: _9/4/09_

Location Number	Datum	Reduced level	Lot No.	New Lot No.
1	+0.10 m	0.10 m		C.929
2	+0.10 m	0.11 m	929/2-1	
3	+0.10 m	0.12 m	929/2-1	
4	+0.10 m	0.10 m	929/2-1	
5	+0.10 m	0.11 m	929/2-1	
6	+0.10 m	0.10 m	929/2-1	
7	+0.10 m	0.12 m	929/2-1	
8	+0.10 m	0.10 m	929/2-1	
1	+0.10 m	0.19 m		929/2-2
2	+0.10 m	0.20 m	929/2-2	
3	+0.10 m	0.20 m	929/2-2	
4	+0.10 m	0.21 m	929/2-2	
5	+0.10 m	0.20 m	929/2-2	
6	+0.10 m	0.22 m	929/2-2	
7	+0.10 m	0.21 m	929/2-2	
8	+0.10 m	0.20 m	929/2-2	
1	+0.10 m	0.30 m		929/2-3
2	+0.10 m	0.29 m	929/2-3	
3	+0.10 m	0.30 m	929/2-3	
4	+0.10 m	0.32 m	929/2-3	
5	+0.10 m	0.30 m	929/2-3	
6	+0.10 m	0.31 m	929/2-3	
7	+0.10 m	0.30 m	929/2-3	
8	+0.10 m	0.30 m	929/2-3	
1	+0.10 m	0.40 m		929/2-4
2	+0.10 m	0.42 m	929/2-4	
3	+0.10 m	0.40 m	929/2-4	
4	+0.10 m	0.41 m	929/2-4	
5	+0.10 m	0.40 m	929/2-4	
6	+0.10 m	0.42 m	929/2-4	
7	+0.10 m	0.40 m	929/2-4	
8	+0.10 m	0.41 m	929/2-4	
1	+0.10 m	0.50 m		929/2-5
2	+0.10 m	0.50 m	929/2-5	
3	+0.10 m	0.52 m	929/2-5	
4	+0.10 m	0.50 m	929/2-5	
5	+0.10 m	0.49 m	929/2-5	
6	+0.10 m	0.50 m	929/2-5	
7	+0.10 m	0.51 m	929/2-5	
8	+0.10 m	0.50 m	929/2-5	
1				
2				
3				
4				
5				
6				
7				
8				

FINDS REGISTER

SITE CODE: ___TAD09_____

FIND NO.	CONTEXT	DESCRIPTION	IN SITU	AREA	DATE & INITIALS
1	(1022)	A SMALL POTTERY VESSEL, FOUND IN THE NORTH WEST OF THE CONTEXT	YES/~~No~~	T3	J.M. 17/06/09
2	(1023)	A SMALL FAIENCE BOWL FOUND NEAR THE TOP, BUT NOT IN GRAVE {923}.	YES/~~No~~	T3	J.M. 17/06/09
3	(1037)	A COPPER CHISEL FOUND DURING SIEVING	~~YES~~/No	T3	J.M. 17/06/09
4	(1071)	TWO SMALL CARNELIAN BEADS FOUND DURING SIEVING.	~~YES~~/No	T3	J.M. 17/06/09
5	(1060)	A SMALL GREEK COIN FOUND DURING SIEVING.	~~YES~~/No	T3	J.M. 17/06/09
6	(1015)	A SMALL STONE VESSEL FOUND IN THE SOUTH WEST OF THE CONTEXT.	YES/~~No~~	T5	M.H. 18/06/09
7	(1072)	A PIECE OF WORKED STONE, FOUND NOT ASSOCIATED WITH ANY OTHER STONES	~~YES~~/No	T5	M.H. 18/06/09
8	(993)	POTTERY VESSEL FROM SW OF G. 971	YES/~~No~~	T1	B.T. 19/06/09
9	(993)	POTTERY VESSEL FROM SW OF G. 971	YES/~~No~~	T1	B.T. 19/06/09
10	(993)	POTTERY VESSEL FROM SW OF G. 971	YES/~~No~~	T1	B.T. 19/06/09
11	(993)	POTTERY VESSEL FROM SW OF G. 971	YES/~~No~~	T1	B.T. 19/06/09
12	(993)	POTTERY VESSEL FROM SW OF G. 971	YES/~~No~~	T1	B.T. 19/06/09
13	(993)	POTTERY VESSEL FROM SW OF G. 971	YES/~~No~~	T1	B.T. 19/06/09
14	(993)	POTTERY VESSEL FROM NW OF G. 971	YES/~~No~~	T1	B.T. 19/06/09
15	(993)	POTTERY VESSEL FROM NW OF G. 971	YES/~~No~~	T1	B.T. 19/06/09
16	(993)	POTTERY VESSEL FROM SE OF G. 971	YES/~~No~~	T1	B.T. 19/06/09
17	(993)	STONE VESSEL FROM NE OF G. 971	YES/~~No~~	T1	B.T. 19/06/09
18	(993)	STONE VESSEL FROM NE OF G. 971	YES/~~No~~	T1	B.T. 19/06/09
19	(1077)	FIGURINE FOUND DURING SIEVING	~~YES~~/No	T6	A.S. 20/06/09
			YES/No		
			YES/No		
			YES/No		
			YES/No		

Sediment Sampling Form

1. SITE CODE		**2. OPERATIONAL AREA**		**3. SITE SUB-DIVISION**		**4. CONTEXT NO.**
TAD09		3		T3		1023

5. GRID REFERENCE	**6. FEATURE/GROUP NO.**	**7. SAMPLE NO.**	**8. CATEGORY = DEPOSIT**
115E/220N	N/A	29	**9. TYPE** SANDY SILT PIT FILL

10. COORDINATES OF SAMPLE	**11. CONDITION**		**12. CONTAMINATION**			
X. 117.5 E	DRY	✔	ROOT ACTION	✔	ANIMAL ACTION	
Y. 222.5 N	MOIST		OVER-BURDEN		DECAY	
Z. 94.267 D	WET		HUMAN ( )		OTHER	

13. MATRIX SANDY SILT, MODERATELY SORTED, SUB-ANGULAR DISK SHAPED. WEAK COHESION WITH FLECKS OF CARBONATES. THERE IS EVIDENCE OF BIOTURBATION AND WATER LEVEL MARKS.	**INCLUSIONS** THERE IS 5% OF POTTERY AND 1% OF BONE ARCHAEOLOGICAL INCLUSIONS. OPEN PACKED, INTERSPERSED GRITS (25%) AND STONES (5%).

14. MASS OF SAMPLE 1 15 X 7.5CM FINDS BAG	**15. SAMPLE SIZE**
	<5% ✔ **5-20%** **20-40%** **40-60%** **60-80%** **90-100%**

16. REASON FOR SAMPLING STANDARD SEDIMENT SAMPLE, ALTHOUGH THERE MAY BE SOME BOTANICAL REMAINS PRESENT.	**17. QUESTIONS TO BE ASKED OF SAMPLE** ALTHOUGH THIS IS A STANDARD SEDIMENT SAMPLE, FURTHER TESTING OF THE BOTANICAL REMAINS MAY SUGGEST IF THEY ARE ANCIENT OR MODERN, AND THEREFORE WHAT WAS DUMPED IN THE PIT.

18. SKETCH OF FEATURE IN PLAN & SECTION, SHOWING SAMPLES PROVENIENCE

(1023)

● = SAMPLE

[1096]

	973			
	This context is:	1023	It correlates or is contemporary with:	
		1096		**19.**

20. TBM VALUE (MOD) 95.129	**BS TO TBM** 1.570	**I.H.** 96.699

21. METHOD OF SAMPLING TROWEL AND ZIP SEAL BAG		

22. FINDS 1 BAG POTTERY, 1 BAG BONE AND 1 BAG SHELL	**23. PLANS/SECTIONS** 1023, TAD09-23 (SECTION OF PIT)	**24. PHOTOS** 19/26, 19/27, 19/28

25. ASSOCIATED SAMPLES YES, 30 CHARCOAL	**26. SUB-SAMPLES REQUIRED** NO

27. NAME/DATE A. M. Rahman 17/06/09	**CHECKED BY/DATE** S. M. HASSAN 17/06/09

1. SITE CODE TAD09	2. OPERATIONAL AREA 3	3. SUB-DIVISION T3	4. CONTEXT NO. 1019
5. GRID REFERENCE 115E/220N	6. BURIAL NO. B. 569	7. GRAVE NO. G. 601	8. CO-ORD B 116E/222.1N
			9. CO-ORD A 116.2E/223N

10. Colour-in bones present and show any truncation

95% of skeleton remaining

11. BURIAL STATISTICS	a LENGTH 0.9 M	b WIDTH 0.6 M	c DEPTH 0.17 M
1 (skull) 96.137	**2 (Sacrum)** 96.127		**3 (feet)** 96.112

12. TYPE OF BURIAL	STANDARD FLEXED BURIAL WITH NO SIGNS OF MUMMIFICATION.

CHECKS	DESCRIPTION
13. ORIENTATION	HEAD NORTH FACE WEST SIDE RIGHT
14. LAYOUT OF BODY	FLEXED _✓_ SEMI-FLEXED ___ EXTENDED ___ OTHER ___
15. POSITION OF LIMBS	HANDS H.10(A. r 30, l 32); (B. r 45, l 40) FEET F.8(A. r 10, l20); (B. r 10, l 21).
16. ARTICULATED	FULLY ARTICULATED
17. MAJOR MISSING BONES	THE PHALANGES OF THE HANDS AND FEET ARE MISSING
18. COLOUR OF BONES AND SKIN	Munsell colour 8/N
19. CONDITION OF BONES	Good, approximately 95% of the skeletal material preserved.
20. TAPHONOMY	COMPRESSION OF BONES DUE TO PRESSURE OF GRAVE MUD CAP
21. CULTURAL MODIFICATIONS	NONE
22. PATHOLOGIES	NONE
23. TREPANATION / CUT-MARKS	NONE
24. EPIPHYSES	FUSED
25. INFANT, CHILD OR ADULT	ADULT: 17-25
26. GENDER	FEMALE
27. BURNING	NONE
28. SECONDARY OR PRIMARY	PRIMARY
29. MULTIPLE INHUMATION	SINGLE
30. FURTHER COMMENTS	BURIAL APPEARS TO HAVE BEEN TIGHTLY BOUND.

31. DENTAL RECORD																

| | | | C | | C | | A | | C | | | | | | | |

Extreme dental attrition in the anterior dentition with mesiodistally directed flat notched occlusal surface and extensive caries.

⑧ 7 6 5 4 3 2 1 | 1 2 3 4 5 6 7 ⑧

8 7 6 5 4 3 2 1 | 1 2 3 4 5 6 7 8

C C C   C   C   C

---

32. SPECIALIST TREATMENT: YES / ~~No~~

SKELETAL REMAINS CONSOLIDATED WITH PRIMAL W.S40

---

33. METHOD OF EXCAVATION (SIEVED/~~UN-SIEVED~~): EXCAVATED WITH BAMBOO STICKS AND SMALL BRUSHES. BLOCK-LIFTED IN FOAM BY CONSERVATOR.	34. WEATHER CONDITIONS, TIME OF DAY SUNNY, 8.30 AM.

35. BURIAL DESCRIPTION AND INTERPRETATION

The legs of the burial were extremely flexed in the South of the burial, directly below the burial. The distal extremity of the right tibia and fibula were touching the proximal right femur and were placed across the proximal left femur. This indicates that the burials must have been tightly bound or perhaps the skeleton was defleshed prior to burial; however there is no evidence of cut marks or other evidence for deliberate removal of flesh. The left hand of the burial was placed at the face and the right hand was under an ivory pendant /5\ touching the left radius.

36. PLANS, SECTIONS AND OTHER DRAWINGS TAD09-2	37. PHOTOS 23/25, 23/26, 23/27, 23/28	38. FINDS N/A
39. SPECIAL FINDS (INC. COFFIN & WIGS) 1, 2, 3, 4, 5	40. SAMPLES 1, 2, 3, 4, 5, 6	41. OTHER N/A

42. TBM VALUE (MOD) 95.129	BS TO TBM 1.570	I.H. 96.699

43. SKETCH

|1019]

/3\   /4\   /5\   (965)

/2\

/1\   (1020)   96.112   96.165

44. SUPERVISOR M. Zabecki	45. CHECKED INTERPRETATION POSSIBLE TRAUMA TO RIGHT FEMUR, NEEDS FURTHER EXAMINATION.		
DATE 11/06/09	SIGNATURE L. S. OWENS	DATE 11/06/09	46. ENTERED INTO DATABASE J. SMITH 12/06/09

1. SITE CODE	4. OPERATIONAL AREA	3. SUB-DIVISION	4. GRID REF.
TAD09	3	T3	115E/220N

5. CONTEXT NOS.		6. GRAVE NO.	7. SKELETON NO.
1055. 1049, 1050, 1051, 1052, 1053, 1054		G.972	B.991

8. COFFIN NO.	9. MATRIX
NONE	COMPACT MUD WITH CALCAREOUS INCLUSIONS

REDUCED LEVELS	10. TOP	11. BOTTOM
	89.111	88.311

12. TBM VALUE (MOD) 95.129	BS TO TBM 1.570	I.H. 96.699

GRAVE STATISTICS	13. LENGTH	14. WIDTH	15. DEPTH	16. GRAVE VOLUME
	TOP 6.0 M	TOP 4.0 M	0.8 M	19.2 M³
	BOT. 5.6 M	BOT. 3.8 M		

SUPERSTRUCTURE	17. TYPE	18. MATERIAL
	TUMULUS/MOUND (1049)	SILT. SAND, MUD.

19. LENGTH	20. WIDTH	21. HEIGHT	22. NO. ROOMS	23. SPECIAL FEATURES
7.0 M	5.0 M	0.5 M	NONE	COMPACT MUD RAMP TO SOUTH

CUT	24. TRUNCATED	25. TOP OF CUT IN PLAN	26. CORNERS
	NO	RECTANGULAR	SQUARE

27. BREAK OF SLOPE - LIP	28. SIDES	29. BREAK OF SLOPE - BASE
SHARP	STRAIGHT	SHARP

30. BASE	31. ORIENTATION	32. ENTRANCE
FLAT	E BY W	NONE

33. LINING	34. ROOFING
MUD-BRICK, A2 BONDING CORPUS, FIVE COURSES THICK.	WOODEN BEAMS LAID ACROSS THE WIDTH OF THE GRAVE, COVERED WITH MUD COATED MATTING

35. NO. CHAMBERS	36. FILL NOS.
FOUR	1051, 1052, 1053, 1054

37. TYPE OF GRAVE & COMMENTS & DESCRIPTIVE TEXT OF GRAVE: G.6

THE WALLS OF THE GRAVE ARE MADE FROM A SINGLE ROW OF MUD BRICKS AND THE FLOOR OF THE GRAVE IS LINED WITH REED MATTING COATED WITH MUD. THE CENTRAL CHAMBER IS THE BURIAL CHAMBER WITH SUBSIDIARY CHAMBERS TO THE EAST (1) AND WEST OF IT (2).

38. GRAVE INTERPRETATION AND OTHER INFORMATION

THIS GRAVE IS IN THE CENTRE OF THE CEMETERY, IT IS THE LARGEST GRAVE EXCAVATED TO DATE. THIS GRAVE MAY HAVE BELONGED TO A LOCAL CHIEF, ONE OF THE WINE JARS BEARS A SEREKH OF KING NARMER AND SOME OF THE POTTERY VESSELS ARE IMPORT WARES FROM THE LEVANT. THE GRAVES AROUND IT ARE ALL SMALL AND OVAL IN SHAPE.

39. SPECIALIST TREATMENT: YES / NO NONE

NOTES ON SPECIALIST TREATMENT

NONE

40. METHOD OF EXCAVATION (SIEVED/~~UN-SIEVED~~): TROWEL AND BRUSH. A DEDICATED GRID WAS PLACED OVER THE GRAVE AND TEAMS OF EXCAVATORS EXCAVATED THE QUADRANTS USING TROWELS AND BRUSHES.	41. WEATHER CONDITIONS, TIME OF DAY SUNNY, EXCAVATED OVER A THREE WEEK PERIOD.

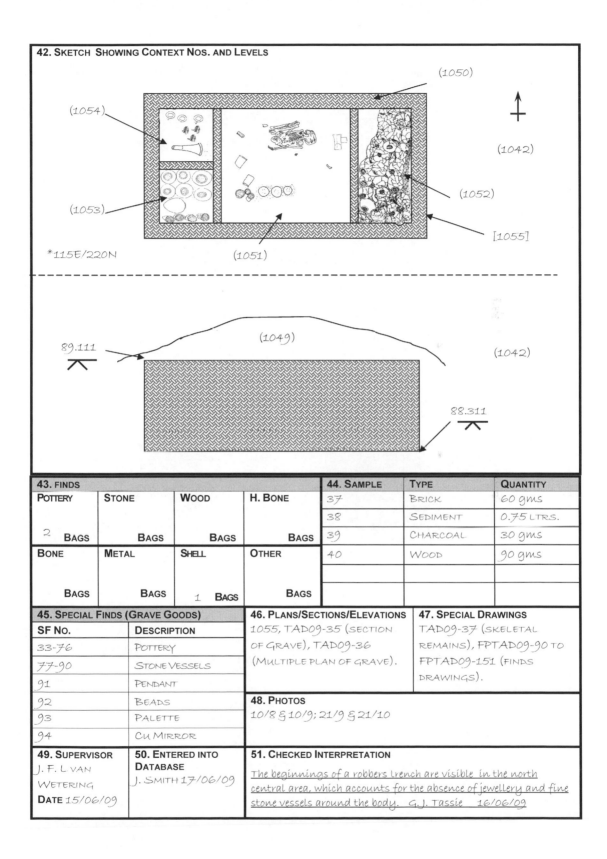

42. SKETCH SHOWING CONTEXT NOS. AND LEVELS

(1050)

(1054)

(1042)

(1053)

(1052)

[1055]

*115E/220N

(1051)

89.111

(1049)

(1042)

88.311

43. FINDS				44. SAMPLE	TYPE	QUANTITY
POTTERY	STONE	WOOD	H. BONE	37	BRICK	60 gms
				38	SEDIMENT	0.75 LTRS.
2 BAGS	BAGS	BAGS	BAGS	39	CHARCOAL	30 gms
BONE	METAL	SHELL	OTHER	40	WOOD	90 gms
BAGS	BAGS	1 BAGS	BAGS			

45. SPECIAL FINDS (GRAVE GOODS)		46. PLANS/SECTIONS/ELEVATIONS	47. SPECIAL DRAWINGS
SF No.	**DESCRIPTION**	1055, TAD09-35 (SECTION	TAD09-37 (SKELETAL
33-76	POTTERY	OF GRAVE), TAD09-36	REMAINS), FPTAD09-90 TO
77-90	STONE VESSELS	(MULTIPLE PLAN OF GRAVE).	FPTAD09-151 (FINDS
91	PENDANT		DRAWINGS).
92	BEADS	**48. PHOTOS**	
93	PALETTE	10/8 & 10/9; 21/9 & 21/10	
94	CU MIRROR		

49. SUPERVISOR	50. ENTERED INTO DATABASE	51. CHECKED INTERPRETATION
J. F. L VAN WETERING **DATE** 15/06/09	J. SMITH 17/06/09	The beginnings of a robbers trench are visible in the north central area, which accounts for the absence of jewellery and fine stone vessels around the body. G. J. Tassie 16/06/09

527

SPECIAL FINDS RECORDING FORM

PROVENIENCE AND CONTEXT	**1A. CATALOGUE NO.** TAD3150		**1B. EXCAVATION NO.** 93

2. SITE CODE TAD09	**3. OPERATIONAL AREA** 3	**4. SITE SUB-DIVISION** T3	**5. CONTEXT NO.** 1051

6. GRID REFERENCE 115E/220N	**7. CATEGORY** DEPOSIT	**8. TYPE** GRAVE 972

9. COORDINATES OF ARTEFACT X. 119.9 E Y. 223.3 N Z. 88.391 D	**10. ASSOC. FINDS** 33-94	**11. DRAWING NO.** FPTAD09-90	**12. PHOTO NO.** 22/1

13. DESCRIPTION AND INTERPRETATION	**13A. MATERIAL** STONE - SILTSTONE

THIS MAKE-UP PALETTE WAS FOUND NEAR THE BODY OF THE DECEASED WITH A CACHE OF STONE VESSELS IN THE CENTRAL CHAMBER OF THE GRAVE, CONTEXT (1051). IT WAS LYING FLAT ON THE FLOOR OF THE TOMB. THE PALETTE IS A RECTANGULAR WITH CONCAVE FACSE AND THREE INCISED LINES DECORATING THE EDGE.

13B. INDUSTRY GROUND STONE

13C. OBJECT MAKE-UP PALETTE

14. PERIOD OF ARTEFACT NAQADA IIIC, DYNASTY I

15. LENGTH 250 MM	**16. WIDTH** 150 MM	**17. DIAMETER** N/A	**18. THICKNESS** 9 MM	**19. HEIGHT/DEPTH** N/A

TECHNOLOGICAL INFORMATION

20. MATERIAL OF CONSTRUCTION SILTSTONE **COLOUR** 1 GLEY-4/5GY	NATURALLY OCCURING, FOUND IN THE LOCAL REGION OF MEMPHIS.

21. FORMING TECHNIQUE AND USE WEAR	The palette was originally roughly shaped by chipping and then ground down. In the centre of the palette, on the obverse side are signs of wear in the form of a concave depression and mineral residues. Both sides were very slightly convex.

22. DECORATION **COLOUR** N/A	THREE INCISED LINES RUNNING AROUND THE EDGE OF THE PALETTE, 5 MM FROM THE EDGE.

OTHER FEATURES	**23. RESIDUES** Traces of bright red ochre.	**24. FILL DESCRIPTION** N/A

25. ANCIENT REPAIRS N/A		**26. DRILL HOLES** N/A	**27. OTHER** N/A

ARTEFACT RELATIONSHIPS	**28. ABOVE** N/A	**29. BELOW** N/A
30. FILLED WITH N/A	**31. CONTAINS** N/A	**32. WITHIN** N/A

STATE OF PRESERVATION

33. WHOLE YES	**34. BROKEN NO. OF FRAGMENTS** N/A	**35. SOLUBLE SALT EFFLORESCENCE** NONE	**36. ENCRUSTATIONS** NONE

37. STRESS CRACKS	38. FLAKING/ POWDERING	39. FRIABILITY	40. CONSERVATION THE VESSEL WAS
N/A	N/A	SOLID	EXAMINED UNDER THE MICROSCOPE AND USE WEAR SCRATCHES WERE FOUND IN CENTRE OF PALETTE.

41. SAMPLES TAKEN	42. METHOD OF LIFTING	BY HAND, THE ENTIRE GRAVE FILL HAS BEEN SIEVED.
SAMPLE NO.102 WAS TAKEN OF PIGMENTS ON THE SURFACE.		

43. SKETCH TO SHOW RELATED ARTEFACTS (INCLUDING NOS.) / ADDITIONAL MATRIX

93   - 0.25 M -

77

79

78

0.90 M

44. DRAWING OF SPECIAL FIND

45. SUPERVISOR	46. CHECKED INTERPRETATION		
N. FINNERAN	S. KOROLNIK		
DATE			
16/16/09	**SIGNATURE**	**DATE**	**47. ENTERED INTO DATABASE**
	M. A. SALEH	17/06/09	J. SMITH 19/06/09

1. SITE CODE	2. OPERATIONAL AREA	2. SITE SUB-DIVISION	4. STRUCTURE NO.
TAD09	5	SQ.106-107	S.3

5. GRID REFERENCE	6. TYPE	7. ROOM NOS.	8. ANCIENT GROUND LEVEL
190E/260N	SHRINE	3A,3B,3C, 3D, 3E & 3F (6 ROOMS)	75.932 TO 75,997

9. GENERAL LOCATION	10. NO. OF STOREYS	11. DATE
NORTH-WEST AREA OF SITE	1	OLD KINGDOM

12. LENGTH	13. WIDTH	14. HEIGHT / DEPTH
55.0 M	30.0 M	12.0 M

15. COMPLEX	16. AREA OF BUILDING	17. GENERAL SHAPE
PYRAMID COMPLEX 2	500 M²	RECTILINEAR

18. INTERPRETATION AND FUNCTION

THE BUILDING APPEARS TO BE A SHRINE OR TEMPLE FOR HATHOR, INDICATED BY THE HIEROGLYPHIC INSCRIPTIONS AND STATUARY IN MAIN CHAPEL.

19. WALLS NO. OF WALLS 10 **STRUCTURE** LIMESTONE	**FINISHES** THE OUTSIDE OF THE WALLS ARE DRESSED, THE INTERNAL SURFACES ARE PLASTERED AND HAVE HIEROGLYPHIC AND ICONOGRAPHIC RELIEFS.
PERCENTAGE OF WALLS LEFT STANDING 50%	**HEIGHT** MIN H. 5.0 M, MAX. H. 12.0 M.

20. FLOOR AND PAVEMENTS NO. OF FLOORS 5 **STRUCTURE** LIMESTONE	**FINISHES** IRREGULAR SIZED AND SHAPED PAVING STONES LAID IN A PATCHWORK MANNER.

PERCENTAGE OF FLOOR LEFT IN SITU
70 %

21. ROOF NO. OF ROOFS 1 **STRUCTURE** GRANITE	**FINISHES** THE RECTANGULAR ROOFING SLABS ARE SUPPORTED BY ARCHITRAVES RESTING ON COLUMNS. THE SLABS ARE EACH 3.0 X 1.0 M

PERCENTAGE OF ROOF LEFT IN SITU
30%

22. WINDOWS	23. DOORWAYS	24. OBELISKS	25. COURTYARDS
NUMBER NONE	NUMBER 6	NUMBER NONE	NUMBER NONE
LOCATIONS	LOCATIONS NORTH, SANCTUARY & SIDECHAMBERS	LOCATIONS	LOCATIONS
TYPE MONUMENTAL	TYPE MONUMENTAL	TYPE	TYPE
DIMENSIONS 2 X 1 X 0.5 M	DIMENSIONS 0.8 M WIDE, 10 M HIGH, SC 0.5M WIDE, 10 M HIGH	DIMENSIONS	DIMENSIONS
MATERIALS LIMESTONE	MATERIALS LIMESTONE	MATERIALS	MATERIALS
FURNITURE NONE	FURNITURE	DETAILS	DETAILS
DETAILS	DETAILS		

26. COLUMNS	27. STAIRS	28. PYLONS	29. ARCHES
NUMBER 8	NUMBER NONE	NUMBER NONE	NUMBER NONE
LOCATIONS CENTRAL ROOM, SANCTUARY	LOCATIONS	LOCATIONS	LOCATIONS
TYPE PAPYRIFORM	TYPE	TYPE	TYPE
DIMENSIONS 10 M HIGH, 3.5 DIAM	DIMENSIONS	DIMENSIONS	DIMENSIONS
MATERIALS LIMESTONE	MATERIALS	MATERIALS	MATERIALS
DETAILS	DETAILS	DETAILS	DETAILS

30. FOUNDATIONS

ONE LEVEL OF BLOCKS RECEESSED TO THE ANCIENT GROUND LEVEL.

31. FACING, SCULPTING, PAINTING

THE EXTERNAL SURFACES OF THE BUILDING ARE OF DRESSED STONE. THE INTERNAL WALLS ALL HAVE GYPSUM PLASTER, AND HAVE PAINTED RELIEFS AND HIROGLYPHIC INSCRIPTIONS.

32. FIXTURES AND FITTINGS

GUTTERS CUT INTO THE ROOFING SLABS TO CHANNEL AWAY THE RAIN.

33. FINDS	34. PLANS/ELEVATIONS/EPIGRAPHY	35. PHOTOS
90 TO 180, 201 TO 240, 253 TO 270	TAD09-100 TO 132 AND CONTEXT SHEETS 1235 TO 90, 12790 TO 1350, 1352	15/8 TO 15/29, 14/1 TO 14/30

36. TBM VALUE (MOD) 97.129	BS TO TBM 1.412	I.H. 98.531

37. SKETCH	38. SECTION / DETAIL

37. SKETCH

86.935

3a

3c

3e

75.932

3b

3d

3f

90.932

75.997

38. SECTION / DETAIL

N/A

39. Supervisor: Ashraf Mohammed Rahman **Checked By** S. M. Hassan **Date** 21/06/09

1. SITE CODE TAD09	2. OPERATIONAL AREA 5	3. SITE SUB-DIVISION SQ.106	4. ROOM NO. 3D
5. GRID REFERENCE 190E/260N	6. TYPE SANCTUARY	7. STRUCTURE NO. S.3	8. ANCIENT GROUND LEVEL 75,997

9. MATERIALS LIMESTONE, WOOD, LIMESTONE PLASTER, PAINT	10. GENERAL LOCATION IN BUILDING SOUTH CENTRAL AREA OF BUILDING

DIMENSIONS & DESCRIPTION	11. AREA OF ROOM 15 M²	12. GENERAL SHAPE RECTILINEAR

13. OVERALL DIMENSIONS OF ROOM

L. 5 M   W. 3 M   H. 12 M

14. WALLS STRUCTURE LIMESTONE & PLASTER, STRENGTHENED BY WOODEN BEAMS	FINISHES THE OUTSIDE OF THE WALLS ARE DRESSED, THE INTERNAL SURFACES ARE PLASTERED AND HAVE HIEROGLYPHIC AND ICONOGRAPHIC RELIEFS.

PERCENTAGE OF WALLS LEFT STANDING 60 %	HEIGHT 12 M

NO. OF COURSES 24	LENGTH / WIDTH 5 X 3 M	THICKNESS 1 M

15. FLOOR STRUCTURE LIMESTONE	FINISHES IRREGULAR SIZED AND SHAPED PAVING STONES LAID IN A PATCHWORK MANNER.

PERCENTAGE OF FLOOR LEFT IN SITU
80 %

NO. OF RELAYS 1	LENGTH / WIDTH 5 X 3 M	THICKNESS 0.3 M

16. CEILING STRUCTURE GRANITE	FINISHES THE RECTANGULAR ROOFING SLABS ARE DECORATED WITH A SUNK RELIEF OF STARS. PAINTED BLUE BACKGROUND AND YELLOW STARS.

PERCENTAGE OF CEILING LEFT IN SITU
50 %

NO. OF COURSES 1	LENGTH / WIDTH 2.5 X 3 M	THICKNESS 0.5 M

17. WINDOWS NUMBER None LOCATIONS TYPE DIMENSIONS MATERIALS FURNITURE DETAILS	18. DOORS NUMBER 1 LOCATIONS North TYPE Monumental DIMENSIONS 0.8 M WIDE, 10 M HIGH MATERIALS Limestone FURNITURE DETAILS

19. COLUMNS

NUMBER 2

LOCATIONS CENTRE OF ROOM

TYPE PAPYRIFORM **BASE** ROUND **SHAFT** PAPYRUS **CAPITAL** OPEN PAPYRUS

DIMENSIONS 10.0 M HIGH, DIAM: SHAFT 3.5, CAPITAL 4.0 M, BASE 4.5 M

MATERIALS LIMESTONE, BASE GRANITE

DETAILS

20. FACING, SCULPTING, PAINTING (DECORATION)

THE WALLS HAVE RAISED RELIEF AND ARE COATED WITH PLASTED. TRACES OF PAINT STILL REMAIN. OFFERING SCENE TO THE GODDESS HATHOR.

21. FIXTURES AND FITTINGS

UPPER ANS LOWER DOOR SOCKETS. NAOS IN CENTRE OF ROOM

22. INTERPRETATION / ROOM FUNCTION

THIS ROOM IS THE SANCTUARY HOUSING THE NAOS WHERE THE BARK OF THE GODDESS ONCE STOOD. THIS IS THE HEART AND FOCUS OF THE SHRINE.

23. FINDS	**24. PLANS/ELEVATIONS/EPIGRAPHY**	**25. PHOTOS**
253 TO 270	TAD09-123 TO 132 AND CONTEXT SHEETS 1257 TO 90	COLOUR 9/8 & 9/9

26. SAMPLES COLLECTED	**PETROLOGICAL**	**MORTAR**	**BRICK**
	73	74 TO 75	76

27. TBM VALUE (MOD) 97.129	**BS TO TBM** 1.412	**I.H.** 98.531

28. SKETCH

29. SECTION / DETAIL

N/A

30. Supervisor: _M. A. Nor el Din_   **Checked By:** _A. Smith_   **Date:** _17/8/09_

MUD-BRICK RECORDING FORM

1. SITE CODE	2. OPERATIONAL AREA	3. SITE SUB-DIVISION	4. CONTEXT NO.
TAD09	3	SQ.97	109

5. GRID REFERENCE	6. FEATURE/GROUP NO.	7. TYPE
110E/250N	S.5	RETAINING WALL IN RECTILINEAR BUILDING

8. REDUCED LEVEL	9. LENGTH	10. WIDTH	11. HEIGHT/THICKNESS/DEPTH
MAX. 89.021	MAX. 6.5 M	MAX. 4.7 M	MAX. 1.20 M
MIN. 90.132	MIN. 6.47 M	MIN. 4.65 M	MIN. 0.09 M

MATERIALS & CONSTRUCTION

12. COLOUR
10YR-5/4

13. COMPOSITION OF BRICKS (BURNT / UNBURNT)	14. COARSE COMPONENTS
SUN DRIED MUD-BRICK. 80% NILE MUD (MEDIUM TO HIGH PERCENTAGE OF CLAY IN THE ALLUVIUM), 15% SAND AND 5% STRAW.	A SMALL PERCENTAGE (1 %) OF GRAVEL IN THE BRICKS.

15. DIMENSIONS OF THE BRICKS

X 0.24 M X 0.25 M	Y 0.12 M X 0.14 M	Z 0.60 M X 0.65 M	16. SHAPE OF BRICKS
			RECTANGULAR

17. COURSING / BOND	18. REED MATTING, TIMBER OR STONE
THE BOND IS A3 (5.5) NUMBER OF COURSES 15	THERE IS EVIDENCE OF REED MATTING IN BETWEEN EVERY 6 COURSES. IT SEEMS TO BE THE WIDTH OF THE WALL, AND EACH STRIP OF MATTING IS 1.0 M LONG.

19. PLASTER (CONTEXT NO.)	20. BONDING MATERIAL: FORM WEATHERED
THE OUTSIDE AND INSIDE WALLS HAVE A THIN COAT OF GREY-BROWN MUD PLASTER WITH PATCHES OF GYPSUM PLASTER STILL ADHEREING.	THE BRICKS ARE BONDED WITH ROUGHLY APPLIED MUD MORTAR. SIZE OF HORIZONTAL BEDS 9 MM SIZE OF VERTICAL BEDS 8 MM

21. OCCURRENCE OF STAMPED BRICKS	22. SPECIAL USAGE OR FORMS OF BRICKS
NO STAMP BRICKS.	NO SPECIAL BRICKS.

23. EVIDENCE OF BOTANICAL REMAINS

THERE ARE SOME PLANT REMAINS, POSSIBLY EMMER WHEAT, AND A SAMPLE HAS BEEN TAKEN FOR PALYNOLOGICAL ANALYSIS. 109/6/4.

24. DESCRIPTION OF FORM: INTERNAL ✔ EXTERNAL OTHER

FIFTEEN COURSES OF BUILDING 5, THE FACES OF THE BRICKS ARE NORTH. THERE ARE TWO WALLS THAT WALL (109) IS ABUTTING (110) & (111) AND THREE WALLS IT IS BUTTED BY (115), (120) & (127). THE WALL RESTS ON THE FLOOR (1056).

25. CONTEXT INTERPRETATION AND OTHER INFORMATION

THIS CONTEXT IS THE NORTH WALL OF A LARGE BUILDING, POSSIBLY AN ADMINISTRATIVE BUILDING WITH 4 ROOMS ON ITS INTERIOR.

26. METHOD OF EXCAVATION (SIEVED/UN-SIEVED)	27. WEATHER CONDITIONS, TIME OF DAY
FAZ AND TROWEL.	THE WEATHER WAS SUNNY. SEVERAL DAYS.

PHYSICAL STRATIGRAPHIC RELATIONSHIPS

EARLIER THAN	CONTEMPORARY WITH	LATER THAN
28. BUTTED BY 115, 120, 127	29. BONDED WITH	30. ABUTTING 110, 111

31. UNCERTAIN/ASSOCIATED CONTEXTS/FOOTINGS/FOUNDATIONS

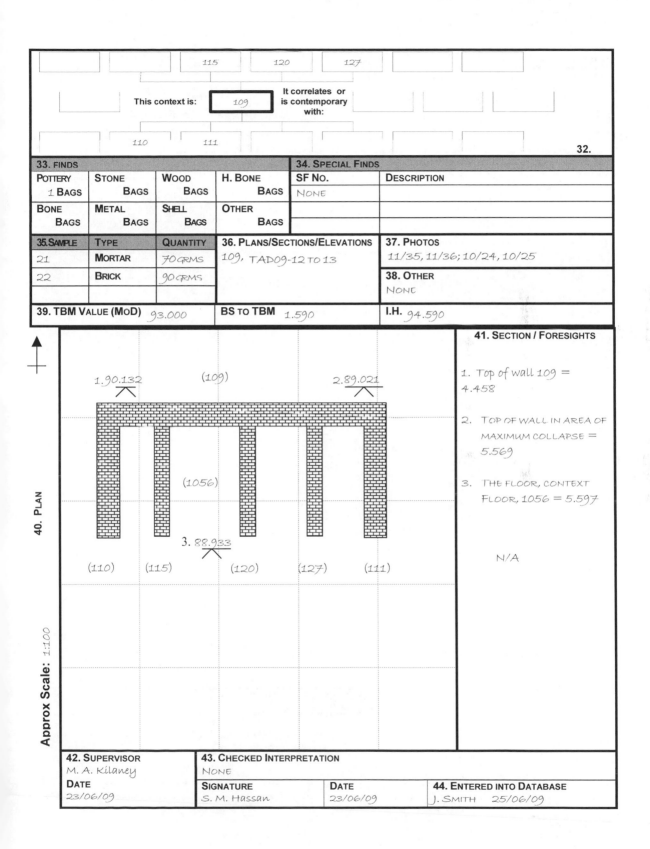

| | | 115 | 120 | 127 | | |

This context is: **109**

It correlates or is contemporary with:

| | 110 | 111 | | | | |

32.

33. FINDS				**34. SPECIAL FINDS**	
POTTERY 1 **BAGS**	**STONE** **BAGS**	**WOOD** **BAGS**	**H. BONE** **BAGS**	**SF NO.** NONE	**DESCRIPTION**
BONE **BAGS**	**METAL** **BAGS**	**SHELL** **BAGS**	**OTHER** **BAGS**		

35. SAMPLE	**TYPE**	**QUANTITY**	**36. PLANS/SECTIONS/ELEVATIONS** 109, TAD09-12 TO 13	**37. PHOTOS** 11/35, 11/36; 10/24, 10/25
21	**MORTAR**	70 GRMS		
22	**BRICK**	90 GRMS		**38. OTHER** NONE

39. TBM VALUE (MOD) 93.000	**BS TO TBM** 1.590	**I.H.** 94.590

40. PLAN

Approx Scale: 1:1:00

1.90.132 (109)   2.89.021

(1056)

3. 88.933

(110)   (115)   (120)   (127)   (111)

41. SECTION / FORESIGHTS

1. Top of wall 109 = 4.458

2. TOP OF WALL IN AREA OF MAXIMUM COLLAPSE = 5.569

3. THE FLOOR, CONTEXT FLOOR, 1056 = 5.597

N/A

42. SUPERVISOR M. A. Kilaney **DATE** 23/06/09	**43. CHECKED INTERPRETATION** NONE		
	SIGNATURE S. M. Hassan	**DATE** 23/06/09	**44. ENTERED INTO DATABASE** J. SMITH 25/06/09

535

MASONRY RECORDING FORM

1. SITE CODE	2. OPERATIONAL AREA	3. SITE SUB-DIVISION	4. CONTEXT NO.
TAD09	4	SQ.100-102	521

5. GRID REFERENCE	6. FEATURE/GROUP NO.	7. NO. OF WORKED STONE	8. TYPE/COMPONENT
150E/240N	S.1	17	CASING OF RETAINING WALL

9. DIMENSIONS					
	OVERALL MAX.	L. 29.5 M	W. 1.5 M	H. 3.0 M	
	OVERALL MIN.	L. 29.47 M	W. 1.45 M	H. 2.9 M	
	X 1.6 M BY 1.57 M	Y 0.90 M BY 0.93 M	Z 1.1 M BY 1.15 M		
	X 0.6 M BY 0.5 M	Y 0.30 M BY 0.29 M	Z 0.4 M BY 0.35 M		

10. COLOUR	5YR-2/3
11. REDUCED LEVELS	MAXIMUM 97.025 MINIMUM 97.123
12. CONDITION	

13. MATERIALS	CERAMIC BRICK	ROCK ✔	MORTAR ✔	OTHER

14. MATERIALS DESCRIPTION

THE STONE BLOCKS ARE ALL CUT FROM LIMESTONE WIRTH NO REUSE OF EARLIER BUILDING MATERIAL.

15. FINISH OF STONES OR BRICKS ALL BUT THE INSIDE FACE ARE DRESSED. THE LOWER COURSE OF THE MASONRY CONTEXT ALSO HAS THE BOSS LEFT ON THE OUTSIDE FACE. THE FIELDSTONE BLOCKS ARE ROUGHLY HEWN.	16. SHAPE OF STONES OR BRICKS ASHLAR AND IRREGULAR ROUGHLY HEWN STONES.	17. COURSING / BOND MEGALITHIC MASONARY B4, REGULAR ASHLAR OF A C2 RETAINING WALL. NUMBER OF COURSES 7

18. DIRECTION OF FACES

INSIDE FACE IS NORTH

OUTSIDE FACE IS SOUTH

19. BONDING MATERIAL: FORM FLUSH

THICK LIME MORTAR APPLIED TO THE HORIZONTAL BEDDING JOINTS.

SIZE OF HORIZONTAL BEDS 5 MM   SIZE OF VERTICAL BEDS N/A

20. SHAPING, TOOL MARKS	21. REUSED, RECUT
THERE ARE CHISEL MARKS ON ALL SURFACES OF THE BLOCKS.	N/A

22. DESCRIPTION OF FORM: INTERNAL   EXTERNAL   OTHER

Seven courses of masonry surrounding a fieldstone (rubble) core of structure <1> laid on flagstone footings (573), which is laid in a shallow foundation trench filled with clean sand (535).

23. CONTEXT INTERPRETATION AND OTHER INFORMATION

Casing of retaining wall of structure <1>, the partially destroyed south pylon of the Hathor temple.

24. METHOD OF EXCAVATION (SIEVED/UN-SIEVED)	25. WEATHER CONDITIONS, TIME OF DAY
FAS AND TROWEL WITH DRY SIEVING.	THE WEATHER WAS SUNNY. SEVERAL DAYS.

PHYSICAL STRATIGRAPHIC RELATIONSHIPS

EARLIER THAN	CONTEMPORARY WITH	LATER THAN
26. BUTTED BY	27. BONDED WITH	28. ABUTTING

29. UNCERTAIN / ASSOCIATED CONTEXTS

30. FOOTINGS, BASE COURSE, FOUNDATIONS

A LAYER OF CLAEN SAND (535) WITH FLAGSTONE (573) PLACED AS FOOTINGS/BASE FOR THE WALL.

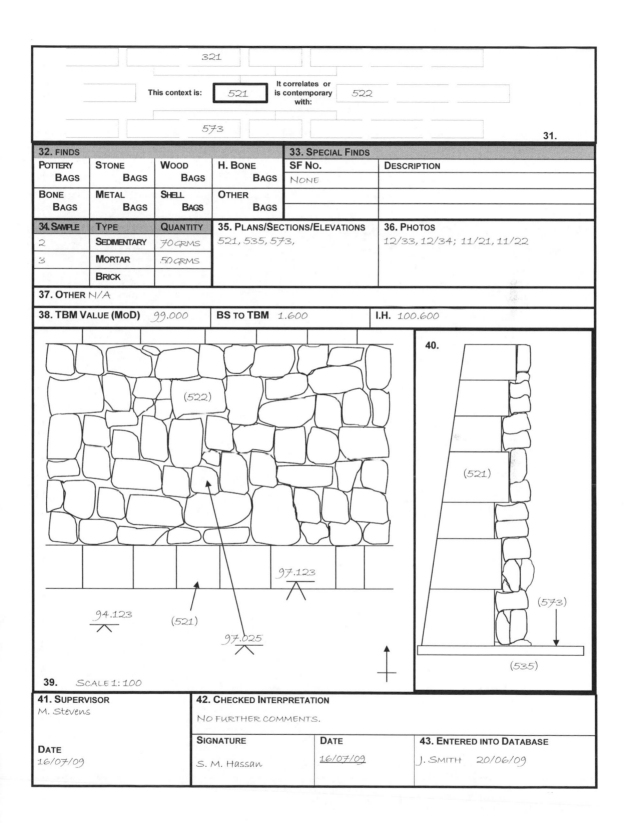

		321			
	This context is: **521**	It correlates or is contemporary with:	522		
		573			**31.**

32. FINDS

POTTERY BAGS	STONE BAGS	WOOD BAGS	H. BONE BAGS
BONE BAGS	METAL BAGS	SHELL BAGS	OTHER BAGS

33. SPECIAL FINDS

SF NO.	DESCRIPTION
NONE	

34. SAMPLE

SAMPLE	TYPE	QUANTITY
2	SEDIMENTARY	70 GRMS
3	MORTAR	.50 GRMS
	BRICK	

35. PLANS/SECTIONS/ELEVATIONS
521, 535, 573,

36. PHOTOS
12/33, 12/34; 11/21, 11/22

37. OTHER N/A

38. TBM VALUE (MOD) 99.000   BS TO TBM 1.600   I.H. 100.600

40.

(522)

97.123

94.123   (521)   97.025

(521)

(573)

(535)

39. SCALE 1:100

41. SUPERVISOR M. Stevens	**42.** CHECKED INTERPRETATION NO FURTHER COMMENTS.		
DATE 16/07/09	SIGNATURE S. M. Hassan	DATE 16/07/09	**43.** ENTERED INTO DATABASE J. SMITH 20/06/09

537

1. SITE CODE	2. OPERATIONAL AREA	2. SITE SUB-DIVISION	4. CONTEXT NO.
TAD09	4	SQ.110	696

5. GRID REFERENCE	6. REDUCED LEVEL	7. STRUCTURE NO.	8. TYPE
150E/240N	MAX. 96.113 MIN. 96.131	G.505	TIMBER ROOF SUPPORT BEAM

DIMENSIONS OF TIMBER	9. OVERALL LENGTH	OVERALL WIDTH	OVERALL THICKNESS
	MAX. 3.9 M	MAX. 1.7 M	MAX. 0.3 M
	MIN. 3.8 M	MIN. 1.6 M	MIN. 0.25 M

10. X	1.7 M BY	1.71 M	Y	0.31 M BY	0.30 M	Z	0.3 M BY	0.3 M

MATERIALS & CONSTRUCTION

11. COLOUR
10YR-5/3

12. TYPE OF WOOD	13. TYPE OF TIMBER
ACACIA (A. NILOTICA).	ROOFING SUPPORT BEAM..

14. SETTING	1. ORIENTATION
HORIZONTAL, IN ORIGINAL POSITION.	THE TRUNKS ARE LAID EAST/WEST.

16. FITTINGS	12. CONVERSION
NONE.	WHOLE.

13. CROSS-SECTION (SEE NO. 41)	19. TOOL MARKS
ROUND OF HEARTWOOD, SAP WOOD AND BARK..	PULLSAW MARKS.

18. INTENTIONAL MARKS	19. SURFACE TREATMENT
NONE.	MUD PLASTER APPLIED TO SURFACE.

22. JOINTS AND FIXINGS	23. DECORATION AND OTHER COMMENTS
THE TRUNKS WERE BOUND TOGETHER WITH TWINE.	THE ENDS OF THE TRUNKS WERE SET INTO THE SUPERSTRUCTURE, IN NICHES FORMED IN THE MUDBRICK WALLS.

24. CONDITION
WHOLE, SLIGHTLY DECAYED IN THE NORTHEAST CORNER OF THE CONTEXT.

25. DESCRIPTION OF FORM
THIS CONTEXT IS PART OF THE SUPERSTRUCTURE OF TOMB {505}, THE CONTEXT (TREE TRUNKS) IS LAID OVER THE ENTRANCE STAIRWAY TO TOMB {505}.

26. CONTEXT INTERPRETATION AND OTHER INFORMATION
TIMBER ROOFING OVER THE ENTERANCE STAIRWAY TO TOMB {505}. THIS IS SIMILAR TO THE ROOFING BEAMS USED TO COVER THE ENTRANCE TO TOMB 3506 AT SAQQARA.

REUSED: NO

27. METHOD OF EXCAVATION	28. WEATHER CONDITIONS, TIME OF DAY
TROWEL, UN-SIEVED.	SUNNY, SEVERAL DAYS.

PHYSICAL STRATIGRAPHIC RELATIONSHIPS

EARLIER THAN	CONTEMPORARY WITH	LATER THAN
29. BUTTED BY	30. BONDED WITH	31. ABUTTING 671
32. UNCERTAIN / ASSOCIATED CONTEXTS		

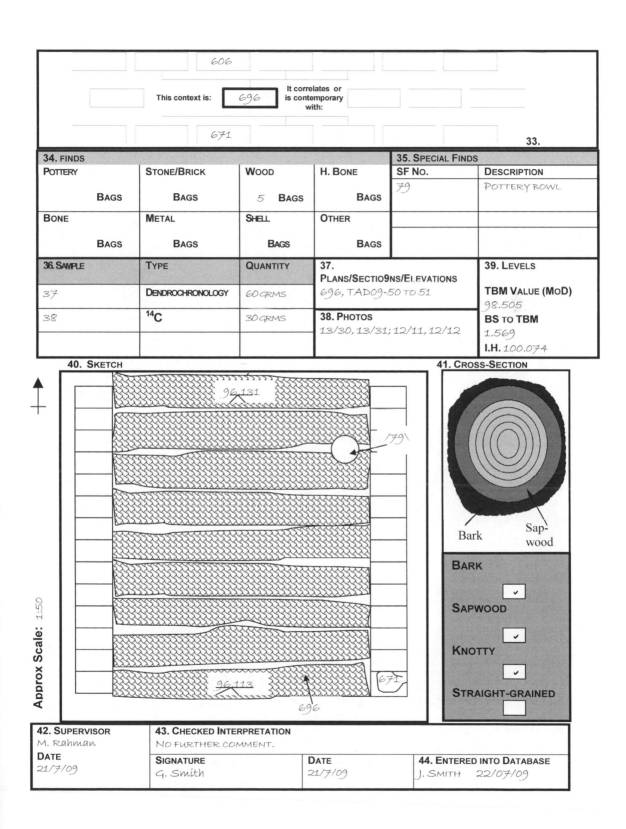

	606			
	This context is: **696**	It correlates or is contemporary with:		
	671			**33.**

34. FINDS				**35.** SPECIAL FINDS	
POTTERY	STONE/BRICK	WOOD	H. BONE	SF NO.	DESCRIPTION
BAGS	BAGS	5 BAGS	BAGS	79	POTTERY BOWL
BONE	METAL	SHELL	OTHER		
BAGS	BAGS	BAGS	BAGS		

36. SAMPLE	TYPE	QUANTITY	**37.** PLANS/SECTIO9NS/ELEVATIONS	**39.** LEVELS
37	DENDROCHRONOLOGY	60 GRMS	696, TAD09-50 TO 51	**TBM VALUE (MOD)** 98.505
38	¹⁴C	30 GRMS	**38.** PHOTOS 13/30, 13/31; 12/11, 12/12	**BS TO TBM** 1.569
				I.H. 100.074

40. SKETCH

Approx Scale: 1:50

96.131

/79\

96.113

671

696

41. CROSS-SECTION

Bark   Sap-wood

BARK	
☑	
SAPWOOD	☑
KNOTTY	☑
STRAIGHT-GRAINED	☐

42. SUPERVISOR M. Rahman **DATE** 21/7/09	**43.** CHECKED INTERPRETATION NO FURTHER COMMENT.		
	SIGNATURE G. Smith	DATE 21/7/09	**44.** ENTERED INTO DATABASE J. SMITH 22/07/09

| | | | | **POTTERY RECORDING FORM**

1. SITE CODE TAD09	**2. OPERATIONAL AREA** 3	**3. SITE SUB-DIVISION** T3	**4. CONTEXT NO.** 1052

5. GRID REFERENCE 115E/220N		**6. CATEGORY** DEPOSIT	**7. TYPE** GRAVE FILL

8. FEATURE/GROUP NO. G.972	**9. CO-ORDS** **X** 115.9 E	**Y** 221.3 N	**Z** 88.391 D	**10. S.F. No.** 69 **11. Artefact No.** TAD1051

12. COMPLETENESS	**COMPLETE**	**YES** > ✓	**NUMBER OF SHERDS** 26	**WEIGHT** 4 KILOGRAMS
	NO >	**NUMBER OF SHERDS**	**EXTENT OF SHERDS**	**WEIGHT**

13. DIMENSIONS	**RIM DIAMITER** MIN. 120 MM MAX. 198 MM	**BASE DIAMETER** MIN. 52 MM MAX. 88 MM	**GIRTH** SHOULDER 236 MM MAX. 340 MM

THICKNESS RIM 20 MM BODY 16 MM BASE 24 MM	**RIM** 100 %	**BASE** 100 %	**HEIGHT** MAX. 852 MM SHOULD. 788 MM NECK 20 MM

14. FABRIC TYPE	**NAME** Alluvial Silt Fabric Type B	**FIRING CONDITIONS** Incompletely oxidised

FIRING	**EXT. SURF.** OXIDISED	**EXT. MARGIN** OXIDISED	**CORE** REDUCED	**INT. MARGIN** OXIDISED	**INT. SURF.** OXIDISED
COLOUR	**EXT. SURF.** 2.5YR5/8	**EXT. MARGIN** 2.5YR5/6	**CORE** 2.5YR3/2	**INT. MARGIN** 2.5YR5/6	**INT. SURF.** 2.5YR5/6
HARDNESS	**SOFT**	**HARD** ✓	**VERY HARD**	**MOHS SCALE** 2.5	
TEXTURE	**SMOOTH**	**SOAPY**	**SANDY** ✓	**VERY SANDY**	**GRANULAR**

FRACTURE	**CONCHOIDAL**	**FINE**	**HACKLY**
	SMOOTH	**IRREGULAR** ✓	**LAMINATED**

INCLUSIONS	**FREQUENCY**	**SORTING**	**ROUNDING**	**SPHERICITY**	**SIZE**	**TYPE**
Chaff	5%	Poor	Angular	Low	1.5 mm	Temper
Limestone	1%	Fair	Very Angular	Low	2.0 mm	Temper
Mica	1%	Good	Sub-rounded	High	0.5 mm	Natural
Quartz	2%	Good	Rounded	High	0.7 mm	Temper

15. SOURCE OF INCLUSIONS Local	**16. SOURCE OF CLAY** Local	**17. POROSITY** Elongated pores	**18. PETROLOGY** SEE REPORT BY PROF. HAMDEN

19. COMMENTS

Only a small amount of temper present within the fabric. Nearest Vienna-system comparison is - Nile A. The majority of the large storage jars are made of this fabric. See Spreadsheet for distribution of this fabric.

CROSS REFERENCED TO: Saqqara, Minshat Abu Omar, Tell Ibrahim Awad, Tell el-Farkha (see bibliography).

20. CONSTRUCTION	**NON-RADIAL** Pounding with paddle & anvil	**FREE-RADIAL**	**CENTRAL RADIAL**

VESSEL FORM, TYPE & ELEMENTS	**21. VESSEL FORM** JAR	**22. VESSEL TYPE** STORAGE	**23. FUNCTION** WINE

24. RIM SHAPE THICKENED	**25. RIM STANCE** EVERTED	**26. RIM EDGE** CUSP	**27. RIM EMBELLISHMENT** None	**28. BASE SHAPE** Knobbed

29. BASE EMBELLISHMENT Cordage	**30. BODY SHAPE** Elongated ovoid	**31. NECK SHAPE** Indefinable	**32. NECK HEIGHT** Short	**33. NECK GIRTH** Medium-narrow

34. NO. HANDLES N/A	**35. HANDLE TYPE** N/A	**36. HANDLE PLACEMENT** N/A	**37. NO. SPOUTS** N/A

38. SPOUT TYPE	39. SPOUT PLACEMENT	40. FOOT TYPE	41. LID TYPE
N/A	N/A	N/A	N/A

42. KNOBS	43. PERFORATION TYPE	44. PERFORATION PLACEMENT	45. OTHER
N/A	N/A	N/A	N/A

46. SURFACE TREATMENT	METHOD	INTERIOR	EXTERIOR	BOTH	TOOL		COLOUR
	SLIP		✓		Brush		2.5YR5/8

47. DECORATION	LOCATION		TECHNIQUE
	Below shoulder and another mid body		Applied, pinched

ELEMENTS		COLOUR	DRYNESS WHEN APPLIED
Two bands - ring hatching		N/A	Plastic

48. POTMARKS	SIGNS	WRITING	POTTERS MARKS	OTHER
	A group of lines			

49. RESIDUES Possible food residue (sent to lab).	50. USE WEAR	51. CONDITION OF SHERDS	52. REUSE
	N/A	Slight abrasion	N/A

53. COMMENTS: CROSS-CONTEXT JOINTS N/A

THIS WINE JAR WAS FOUND IN A CACHE OF POTTERY VESSELS IN THE EASTERN CHAMBER OF THE GRAVE, CONTEXT (1052). IT WAS LYING AT AN ANGLE OF 45 DEGREES UPON OTHER WINE JARS. THE JAR WAS CRUSHED, ALTHOUGH THE WHOLE VESSEL APPEARS TO BE PRESENT. THE RESIDUE IN THE BOTTOM OF THE VESSEL MAY INDICATE IT ONCE HELD SOME FORM OF OFFERING (WINE OR OIL?). THIS IS A COMMON TYPE OF VESSEL FOUND IN MANY GRAVES AT THE SITE AND ALSO AT SITES SUCH AS MINSHAT ABU OMAR AND SAQQARA.

PRELIMINARY DATE/PERIOD <u>NAQADA IIIC, DYNASTY I</u>

54 . SAMPLE	TYPE	QUANTITY	55. PLANS/DRAWINGS	56. PHOTOS
78	FABRIC	30 GRMS	TAD09-91	35/36, 35/37; 36/1, 36/2
	PAINT			
79	RESIDUE	0.25 LTR		

57. SKETCH

58. DECORATION, MARKS

POTMARK 1: 1

59. SUPERVISOR	60. CHECKED INTERPRETATION
C. smith	The interpretation of the residue will have to await the results of the lab analysis before any
DATE	conclusions can be drawn.
28/06/09	

	SIGNATURE	DATE	61. ENTERED INTO DATABASE
	A. Senoussi	29/06/09	J. SMITH 30/06/09

1. SITE CODE TAD09	2. OPERATIONAL AREA 3	3. SUB-DIVISION T3	4. CONTEXT NO. 1060	5. FINDS NO. 173
6. CATEGORY **DEPOSIT**	7. TYPE **COFFIN**	8. GRAVE NO. G. 973	9. SKELETON NO. B. 992	

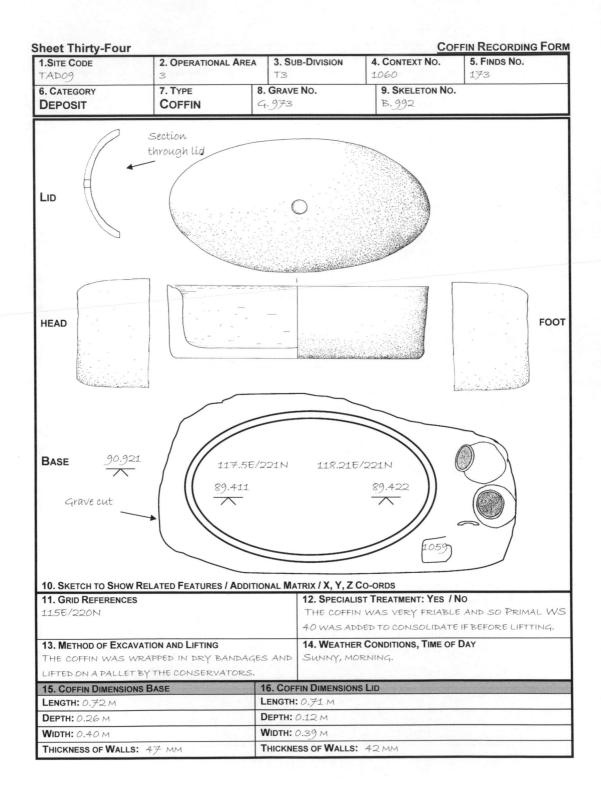

LID

Section through lid

HEAD

FOOT

BASE

90.921

117.5E/221N   118.21E/221N

89.411   89.422

Grave cut

1059

10. SKETCH TO SHOW RELATED FEATURES / ADDITIONAL MATRIX / X, Y, Z CO-ORDS

11. GRID REFERENCES 115E/220N	12. SPECIALIST TREATMENT: YES / NO THE COFFIN WAS VERY FRIABLE AND SO PRIMAL WS 40 WAS ADDED TO CONSOLIDATE IF BEFORE LIFTING.
13. METHOD OF EXCAVATION AND LIFTING THE COFFIN WAS WRAPPED IN DRY BANDAGES AND LIFTED ON A PALLET BY THE CONSERVATORS.	14. WEATHER CONDITIONS, TIME OF DAY SUNNY, MORNING.

15. COFFIN DIMENSIONS BASE	16. COFFIN DIMENSIONS LID
LENGTH: 0.72 M	LENGTH: 0.71 M
DEPTH: 0.26 M	DEPTH: 0.12 M
WIDTH: 0.40 M	WIDTH: 0.39 M
THICKNESS OF WALLS: 47 MM	THICKNESS OF WALLS: 42 MM

17. PRESERVATION	18. FABRIC: POTTERY, ALLUVIAL	19. HEAD LEVEL	20. FOOT LEVEL
FAIR	SILT FABRIC TYPE C	BASE 89.411	BASE 89.422
		LID 89.602	LID 89.611

21. DECORATION AND / OR FURNITURE

THERE IS A HOLE IN THE CENTRE OF THE LID.

22. COFFIN TYPE & DESCRIPTION

TYPE AND SHAPE: C1, OVAL

THE COFFIN IS FRIABLE, ALTHOUGH ABLE TO BE EXCAVATED VIRTUALLY COMPLETE. THE LID HAS BEEN CRUSHED INTO THE COFFIN AND IS IN 20 PIECES (POTSHERDS), WHEREAS THE BASE ONLY HAS A FEW CRACKS ON IT. IT IS AN OVAL CERAMIC COFFIN WITH A 10 CM DIAMETRE HOLE IN THE CENTRE OF THE LID. THERE ARE NO OTHER DECORATIVE FEATURES EXCEPT THE RIM OF THE BASE WHICH IS INDENTED TO ACCEPT THE LID.

23. YOUR INTERPRETATION / DISCUSSION

THE COFFIN IS THAT FOR THE SKELETON 992, AND WAS MEANT FOR ONLY A SINGLE INHUMATION. THERE IS A SINGLE POTSHERD OF A DIFFERENT FABRIC INSIDE THE COFFIN, SO PROBABLY A SYMBOLIC POTSHERD. SEVERAL CARNELIAN BEADS WERE FOUND, PROBABLY MADE INTO A JEWELLERY NECKLACE, ALSO PRESENT WAS A BLACK STONE BRACLETE, BUT NO OTHER GRAVE GOODS WERE FOUND INSIDE THE COFFIN. ———— PRELIMINARY DATE/PERIOD 1ST DYNASTY

24. FINDS				25. SAMPLE	TYPE	QUANTITY
POTTERY	STONE/BRICK	WOOD	H. BONE	153	FABRIC	60 GRMS
BAGS	BAGS	BAGS	BAGS	154	POTSHERD	10 GRMS
BONE	METAL	SHELL	OTHER			
BAGS	BAGS	BAGS	BAGS			

26. SPECIAL FINDS		27. PLANS/SECTIONS/ELEVATIONS
SF NO.	DESCRIPTION	TAD09-72 TO 73
109	39 CARNELIAN BEADS	
110	1 STONE BRACLET	
111	POTSHERD	**28. PHOTOS**
		9/25 & 9/29; 12/8 & 12/9

29. LEVELS	30. SUPERVISOR
TBM VALUE (MoD) 95.129	
BS TO TBM 1.570	B. JONES
I.H. 96.699	DATE 17/7/09

31. CHECKED INTERPRETATION

NO OTHER COMMENTS.

SIGNATURE	DATE	32. ENTERED INTO DATABASE
M. A. RAHMAN	16/7/09	J. SMITH 20/07/09

Sheet Forty-Three

SINGLE UNIT INVENTORY FORM

SITE CODE: TAD09   PROCESSOR: A. D. WALSIQ   DATE: 1/6/09

	Bag 6	Bag 5	Bag 4	Bag 3	Bag 2	Bag 1	CONTEXT / #
	(997)	(997)	(997)	(997)	(997)	(997)	
AREA	T1	T1	T1	T1	T1	T1	
POTTERY						✓	
STONE							
A. BONE		✓					
H. BONE							
SHELL					✓		
METAL							
GLASS							
WOOD							
LEATHER							
IVORY			✓				
PLASTIC							
ORGANIC							
FLINT				✓			
TEXTILES	✓						
BUILD. MAT.							
OTHER							
PERIOD	NAQ III	NAQ III	NAQ III	NAQ III	NAQ III	NAQ III	
FIELD COMMENTS	POSSIBLE PIECE OF MUMMY WRAPPINGS.	A SINGLE PIECE OF CATTLE BONE.	A FRAGMENT OF HIPPOPOTIMUS IVORY.	POORLY MADE LITHIC TOOLS.	MOLLUSC SHELLS, BOTH UNI AND BIVALVE, MOSTLY FRESHWATER SPECIES.	POTSHERDS, WITH A FEW DIAGNOSTIC ONES. FOUND THROUGHOUT CONTEXT.	
TO LAB	1/6/09	1/6/09	1/6/09	1/6/09	1/6/09	1/6/09	

Site Code: TAD09

Area	Context	Condition		Material	Industry	Object	Find No.	Period	Comments
T1	906	Whole	~~Frag.~~	STONE CARNELIAN	GROUND STONE	Discoidal BEAD	SF. 1	NAQ III	NO OTHERS ASSOCIATED
T1	906	~~Whole~~	Frag.	CERAMIC	POTTERY	VESSEL SHERDS	BULK, B. 1	NAQ III	MAINLY DIAGNOSTICS
T1	906	Whole	~~Frag.~~	STONE PORPHYRY	GROUND STONE	SMALL BOWL	SF. 2	NAQ III	FOUND IN GRAVE 56
T2	1026	Whole	~~Frag.~~	CERAMIC	POTTERY	BEER JAR	SF. 3	NAQ III	FOUND IN GRAVE 59
T2	1025	~~Whole~~	Frag.	CERAMIC	POTTERY	BUILDING MATERIAL	BULK, B. 1	PTOLEMAIC	FLOOR TILES
T3	1021	Whole	~~Frag.~~	METAL	BRONZE	FIGURINE	SF. 4	PTOLEMAIC	ISIS
T3	1020	Whole	~~Frag.~~	~~VEGETABLE~~	REEDS	BASKETRY	SF. 5	NAQ III	FOUND IN GRAVE 29
T3	1020	Whole	~~Frag.~~	STONE CHERT	CHIPPED STONE	BLADE	SF. 6	NAQ III	SICKLE GLOSS ON SURFACE
T3	1021	~~Whole~~	Frag.	CERAMIC	POTTERY	WINE JAR	SF. 7	NAQ III	FOUND IN GRAVE 19
T4	1035	Whole	~~Frag.~~	METAL	SILVER	COIN	SF. 8	PTOLEMAIC	PTOLEMY I TETRARACHM
T4	1037	~~Whole~~	Frag.	ANIMAL	BONE	ANIMAL BONE	BULK, B. 3	PTOLEMAIC	——————
T5	1057	~~Whole~~	Frag.	CERAMIC	GLASS	KOHL POT	SF. 9	LATE PERIOD	BLUE, WHITE AND YELLOW
T6	1076	Whole	~~Frag.~~	METAL	COPPER	ADZE	SF. 10	NAQ III	CORRODED
T6	1079	~~Whole~~	Frag.	STONE LIMESTONE	S. WORKED STONE	QUERN	SF. 11	NAQ III	RESIDUES ON SURFACE
		Whole	Frag.						
		Whole	Frag.						
		Whole	Frag.						
		Whole	Frag.						
		Whole	Frag.						
		Whole	Frag.						

PROCESSOR A. D. WALSIQ   **CHECKED BY** T. D. MALEK   **DATE** 15/6/09

Appendix 4: Guidelines for Report Writing and Publication

There are various levels of publication: the first level is the site itself, which may be the target for long-term conservation and site management, as it still contains unrealised information. The second level describes the records made on site or *Field Records*, the first-hand account of what the archaeologists observed, the graphic, written, photographic and digital records, and the finds and samples. Level three consists of the archaeologists' first analysis and synthesis, the stratigraphic matrix, the site plans and base plans, artefact distribution maps, site notebooks/diaries and interim reports. Levels two and three are stored in the site archive for future reference and as a research tool for other researchers and should try to present the facts as objectively and clearly as possible. Level four is the *Research Report*, which contextualises the findings; this consists of selected data and research results presented for future researchers to study. Publication may also be aimed at the public (level five) and the media (level six). A website can also be built and maintained (level seven) that gives an overview of the project, with monthly or seasonal updates allowing for more non-linear, interactive texts to be produced. Having these various levels of publication allows interest in the project to be raised from a new audience at each stage, while still retaining the primacy of the encounter in the field and the thoughts of the excavators (Carver 2005: 109). The materialising of archaeology from level two up validates the archaeological interpretation and enables the archaeological record to be subjected to repeated investigations, creating the possibility of iterability (Lucas 2001: 213-4). The site monograph will be the main primary resource that many researchers consult, and should follow certain guidelines (IFA 2001b; English Heritage 1991). However, when writing the research report try to avoid compartmentalisation by integrating artefactual, contextual, and visual information within the text, adding some form of personalised, humanised narrative, and acknowledge complexity and multivocality (Hamilton 1996; Hodder 1992; Shanks 1992; Tilley 1993).

The Research Report *should contain the following information:*

Non-Technical Summary

- Overview of project.
- Overview of results.
- Overview of significance.
- Overview of recommendations.

Table of Contents

Table of Figures

Table of Tables

Acknowledgements

- Acknowledgement of all people and institutions that help make the project function.

Introduction

- A brief description of the scope of the project.
- Where the project was located (i.e. nearest towns or geological features), including a location map with borders of the study area.

- When fieldwork, analysis and report writing was undertaken.
- A list of all personnel involved in the project along with their roles in data collection, analysis and report writing.
- The methodologies used to retrieve the data.
- Any constraints placed upon the project, such as bad weather, time limitations, financial restrictions, negative attitudes of landowners or institutional restrictions.
- Circumstances and organisation of the work and the date(s) it was undertaken.

Site Description

- A general description of study area (i.e. size, present land use, access, etc.).
- General description of the environment (i.e. geographical location, geology/geomorphology, topography, water resources, extant flora and fauna, relevant raw material sources, etc.).

Background Information and Previous Research

- Previous impacts on the study area (i.e. ploughing, mining, building, erosion, etc.).
- Description of any proposed development and associated works.
- Any relevant past archaeological projects, historical studies, ethnographic or oral studies, along with a summary of their findings.

Aims and Objectives

- These should reflect the aims and objectives of the original research design.

Methods

- Research strategy and aims.
- Detailed description of fieldwork methods for all stages of the project, an outline of the equipment, techniques, and approaches used to implement the strategy along with the recording methods, sampling and collection methods, storage of artefacts, and methods of analysis.
- A discussion of any problems that arose during fieldwork, analysis or report writing.
- Description of any decisions made in the field or laboratory that changed the original strategy or hypothesis.

Presentation of Results

- A summary of what was found or achieved (i.e. quantities, types, distribution).
- Presentation of the results in graphic, photographic and written form.
- Description of findings based on the recording forms and field notes, with excavation and stratigraphic narratives.
- Relevant tabulations and graphs of the data.

Analysis and Interpretation

- Summary of points of interest or major research problems arising from the study.
- Discussion of the evidence in local, regional, national and international contexts.

- Implications of the findings for future research.
- A description of the development and function of the site through time.

Assessment of Significance

- Statement of the significance of the study area in local, regional, national and international contexts.
- An assessment of its archaeological, historical, and technical significance in terms of setting, origin purpose, form, function, status.

Recommendations

- General and specific management recommendations.
- Recommendations for further research in the study area or wider region.

Conclusions

- A summary of the results and interpretations.

Appendices

- A glossary of any technical terms.
- Essential technical details.
- A summary of the site archive, its current location and how it may be accessed.
- Any relevant additional information.

Bibliography

Index

When writing up the results of a project consideration should be given to the following criteria:

- The report should present information in a well-balanced, logical, accessible and well-structured manner. It should present the plans, photographs and assemblages of the various features and overall assemblage and site layout in an intelligible and usable manner.

- The report should reflect the importance of the results and examine the site's social, political, economic, and historical importance in a local, regional, national and international context.

- Site interpretation must be justified by the evidence presented. Any ambiguities in the data should be discussed; if more than one interpretation is possible, other interpretations should be summarised.

- State the extent to which the aims and objectives of the project have been fulfilled, including a presentation and critical assessment of the methodologies used. It is important that the report is written clearly and concisely, making appropriate use of tables, diagrams, graphs and photographs.

- Specialist reports should never be relegated to appendices; they and their supporting data should be incorporated in the main report and given their proper value.

- All the components of the report (text, figures, tables, photographs) should be adequately cross-referenced. This enables the reader to find their way around the report without difficulty.

- Any recommendations for future research should be presented, stating the limitations of the present research and how these might be overcome in future work.

The following considerations must be given to producing figures and typescript for the publishers:

- Write carefully and concisely then thoroughly edit the text before submitting to the publisher, as accuracy at this stage avoids extra correction stages.

- Use graphical visual representations, such as graphs and data-sets, to communicate complex ideas with clarity, precision and efficiency. Integrate visuals with statistics and text, not as appendices. Show the data at different levels of detail.

- Choose the types of visual representations carefully to show spatial attributes (i.e. maps, plans, sections, elevations, spatial database graphics, distribution maps, reconstruction drawings, and photographs), chronological attributes (i.e. time-lines, Harris matrices, bar charts, battleship graphs, and time charts), diagnostic attributes (i.e. percentage of types tables, selection of properties, database tables, photographs, relational graphics, conceptual graphics, and 3-D scans) and quantitative attributes (i.e. tables, stem and leaf graphs, bubble charts, pie charts, bar charts, and histograms).

- High resolution, clear black and white and colour images for plates should be selected at an early stage, and must be made available to the publishers with the draft report.

- Consistent line drawings must be made available to the publishers along with the text and photographs.

- All illustration captions must be prepared ready for the draft stage.

- A complete bibliography of all references cited must be prepared in the publisher's designated house style.

- The nature of the refereeing policy must be established at an early stage so that any differences with refereeing requirements of the sponsoring institute and publishers can be resolved at an early stage.

- The precise format and presentation of material must be agreed with the publishers at an early stage.

- The production of an index is a specialist skill best preformed by a trained professional, and many publishers will have in-house indexers.

Appendix 5: Measurement Conversions

To change the scale of your drawing on a photocopier it may be necessary to scale up or down more than once. Remember that the photocopier can distort the drawing, so measure between distances on the final scaled-down or -up drawing to make sure that the distance is correct. The drawing must be centred on the copier before starting. It may be necessary to then trace the photocopied drawing as the photocopied version may not show the lines at the correct thickness.

Scaling From	First at	Then at	Then at	Then at
1:10 to 1:20	>50%	___	___	___
1:10 to 1:4	<200%	<125%	___	___
1:20 to 1:50	>50%	>80%	___	___
1:20 to 1:100	>50%	>50%	>80%	___
1:20 to 1:200	>50%	>50%	>80%	>50%
1:50 to 1:20	<200%	<125%	___	___
1:50 to 1:100	>50%	___	___	___
1:50 to 1:200	>50%	>50%	___	___
1:100 to 1:200	>50%	___	___	___
1:10,000 to 1:25,000	>50%	>80%	___	___
1:25,000 to 1:10,000	<200%	<125%	___	___

To Convert Temperature

From degrees F to C: subtract 32, multiply by 5, divide by 9

From degrees C to F: multiple by 9, divide by 5, add 32

To Change	To	Multiply by	To Change	To	Multiply by
Acres	hectares	0.4047	Litres	quarts (dry)	0.9081
Acres	square feet	43,560	Litres	quarts (liquid)	1.0567
Acres	square miles	0.001562	Metres	feet	3.2808
Atmospheres	cms of mercury	76	Metres	miles	0.0006214
Btu/hour	horsepower	0.0003930	Metres	yards	1.0936
Btu	kilowatt-hour	0.0002931	Metric tonnes	tons (long)	0.9842
Bto/hour	watts	0.2931	Metric tonnes	tons (short)	1.1023
Bushels (US)	hectolitres	0.3524	Miles	kilometres	1.6093
Centimetres	inches	0.3937	Miles	feet	5,280
Centimetres	feet	0.03281	Miles (nautical)	miles (statute)	1.1516
Cubic feet	cubic metres	0.0283	Miles (statute)	miles (nautical)	0.8684
Cubic meters	cubic feet	35.3145	Miles/hour	feet/minute	88
Cubic meters	cubic yards	1.3079	Millimetres	inches	0.0394
Cubic yards	cubic meters	0.7646	Ounces (avdp)	grams	28.3495
Degrees	radians	0.01745	Ounces	pounds	0.0625
Fathoms	feet	6.0	Ounces (troy)	ounces (avdp)	1.09714
Feddans	acres	1.0385	Pints (dry)	litres	0.5506
Feddans	hectares	0.4202	Pints (liquid)	litres	0.4732
Feet	metres	0.3048	Pounds (ap or troy)	kilograms	0.3782
Feet	miles (nautical)	0.0001645	Pounds (avdp)	kilograms	0.4536
Feet	miles (statute)	0.0001894	Pounds	ounces	16
Feet/second	miles/hour	0.6818	Quarts (dry)	litres	1.1012
Gallons (US)	litres	3.7853	Quarts (liquid)	litres	0.9463
Grains	grams	0.0648	Radians	degrees	57.30
Grams	grains	15.4324	Rods	meters	5.029
Grams	ounces (avdp)	0.0353	Rods	feet	16.5
Grams	pounds	0.002205	Square feet	square meters	0.0929
Hectares	acres	2.4710	Sq. kilometres	square miles	0.3861
Horsepower	watts	745.7	Square meters	square yards	1.1960
Horsepower	Btu/hour	2,547	Square miles	sq. kilometres	2.5900
Hours	days	0.04167	Square yards	square metres	0.8361
Inches	millimetres	25.4000	Tons (long)	metric tonnes	1.016
Inches	centimetres	2.5400	Tons (short)	metric tonnes	0.9072
Kilograms	pounds (avdp or troy)	2.2046	Tons (long)	pounds	2,240
Kilometres	miles	0.6214	Tons (short)	pounds	2,000
Kilowatt-hour	Btu	3,412	Watts	Btu/hour	3.4121
Litres	gallons (US)	0.2642	Watts	horsepower	0.001341
Litres	pints (dry)	1.8162	Yards	meters	0.9144
Litres	pints (liquid)	2.1134	Yards	miles	0.0005682

Appendix 6: The Rim and Base Diameter Chart

The Rim and Base Diameter Chart (see the CD attached to the back cover and available from the ECHO website: www.e-c-h-o.org) must be printed out on A3 sized paper. If an A3 printer is not available print out on A4 and photocopy at 200%. After photocopying check to make sure the measurements are correct. A form of plastic paper (i.e. Tyvek) is best for the chart, as this can be wiped down after use.

Appendix 7: Abridged Recording Guidelines of *Standards of Archaeological Excavation*

The Abridged Guidelines (see the CD attached to the back cover and available from the ECHO website: www.e-c-h-o.org) are for filling out the single context recording forms. These guidelines can be printed out on A4 paper and laminated, then ring bound to form a sturdy, water resistant guide for excavation that can be taken into the muddiest of trenches.

BIBLIOGRAPHY & RECOMMENDED READING

Adams, B. 1984. *Predynastic Egypt.* Princes Risborough: Shire Publications Ltd.

Adams, B., and Cialowicz, K. M. 1997. *Protodynastic Egypt.* Princes Risborough: Shire Publications Ltd.

Adams, M. 1991. A logic of archaeological inference, *Journal of Theoretical Archaeology,* 2: 1-11.

Adams, M. 1992. Stratigraphy after Harris: some questions, in K. Steane (ed.) *Interpretation of Stratigraphy: A Review of the Art.* Proceedings of the 1st Stratigraphy Conference, Lincoln. Lincoln: City of Lincoln Archaeology Unit, pp.13-16

Adams, M. and Brooke, C. 1995. Unmanaging the past: truth, data and the human being, *Norwegian Archaeological Review* 28(2): 93-104.

Adkins, L. & Adkins, R. A. 1982. How to construct a grid frame for drawing plans on site, *The London Archaeologist* 4(9): 214-16.

Adkins, L. & Adkins, R. A. 1989. *Archaeological Illustration.* Cambridge: Cambridge University Press.

ADS 2001. Digital archives from excavation and fieldwork, *Guide to Good Practice,* 2nd Edition. (http://ads.ahds.ac.uk/project/goodguides/excavation/).

Aitken, M. 1990. *Science-based Dating in Archaeology.* London: Longman.

Alcock, S. E. & Cherry, J. F. (eds.) 2004. *Side-by-Side Survey: Comparative Regional Studies in the Mediterranean World.* Oxford: Oxbow.

Alexander, A. 1970. *The Directing of Archaeological Excavations.* London: John Baker Publishers Ltd.

Allchin, B. & Allchin, R. 1982. *The Rise of Civilization in India.* Cambridge: Cambridge University Press.

Allen, J. L. & Holt, A. St. John. 1986. *Health and Safety in Field Archaeology.* S.C.A.U.M.

Allison, P. (ed.) 1999. *The Archaeology of Household Activities.* London: Routledge.

Ammerman, A. J. 1981. Surveys and archaeological research, *Annual Review of Anthropology* 10: 63-88.

Anderson, H. 1994. PENMAP: applications in archaeological surveying, *Graphic Archaeology: Journal of the Association of Archaeological Illustrators and Surveyors*: 30-4.

Anderson, M. J. & Mikhail, E. M. 1998. *Surveying: Theory and Practice,* 7th Edition. New York: McGraw Hill.

Anderson, S. & Boyle, K. (eds.) 1997. *Computing and Statistics in-Osteology: Proceedings of the Second Meeting of the Osteoarchaeological Research Group Held in London on 8th April 1995.* Oxford: Oxbow Books.

Anderson-Gerfaud, P. 1988. Using prehistoric stone tools to harvest cultivated wild cereals: preliminary observations of traces and impact, in S. Beyries (ed.) *Industrie Lithiques: Tracéologie et Technologie.* Oxford: BAR, pp. 175-195.

Andrefsky, A., Jr. 1998. *Lithics: Microscopic Approaches to Analysis.* Cambridge: Cambridge University Press.

Arnold, Di. 1991. *Building in Egypt: Pharaonic Stone Masonry.* New York: Oxford University Press.

Arnold, D. 1981. *Studien zur altägyptischen Keramik.* Mainz am Rhein: Philipp van Zabern.

Arnold, D. & Bourriau, J. 1993. *An Introduction to Ancient Egyptian Pottery.* Mainz am Rhein: P. von Zabern.

Arnold, D. E. 1981. A model for the identification of non-local ceramic distribution: a view from the present, in H. Howard & E. L. Morris (eds.) *Production and Distribution: a Ceramic Viewpoint.* Oxford: BAR, pp. 31-44.

Ashmore, W. & Sharer, R. J. 2000. *Discovering Our Past: A Brief Introduction to Archaeology.* Third Edition. Mountain View: Mayfield Publishing Co.

Aston, B. G. 1994. *Ancient Egyptian Stone Vessels: Materials & Forms.* Heidelberg: Heidelberger Orientverlag.

Aston, B. G., Harrell, J. A. & Shaw, I. 2000. Stone, in P. Nicholson & I. Shaw (eds.) *Ancient Egyptian Materials and Technology.* Cambridge: Cambridge University Press, pp. 5-77.

Aston, D. 1996. *Egyptian Pottery of the Late New Kingdom and Third Intermediate Period (Twelfth - Seventh Centuries BC).* Heidelberg: Heidelberger Orientverlag.

Aufderheide, A. C. *The Scientific Study of Mummies.* Cambridge: Cambridge University Press.

Ayyad, S. 1991. Mudbrick as a bearer of agricultural information: an archeaopalynological study, *Norwegian Archaeological Review* 24(2): 77-91.

Bachmann, H-G. 1981. *The Identification of Slags from Archaeological Sites.* London: Occasional Publication 6, Institute of Archaeology.

Bachmann, K. (ed.) 1992. *Conservation Concerns: A Guide for Collectors and Curators.* Washington: Smithsonian Institution Press.

Bahn, P. G. & Vertut, G. 1988. *Images of the Ice Age.* Leicester: Windward.

Bailey, G. & Thomas, G. 1987. The use of percussion drilling to obtain core samples from rock shelter deposits, *Antiquity* 61: 433-9.

Balme, J. & Paterson, A. 2006. Stratigraphy, in J. Balme and A Paterson (eds.) *Archaeology in Practice: A Student's Guide to Archaeological Analysis.* Oxford: Blackwell, pp. 97-116.

Balme, J. & Paterson, A. (eds.) 2006. *Archaeology in Practice: A Student's Guide to Archaeological Analysis.* Oxford: Blackwell.

Balssse, M. 2002. Reconstructing dietary and environmental history from enamel isotopic analysis: time resolution and intra tooth sequential sampling, *International Journal of Osteoarchaeology* 12: 155-65.

Band, P. 2001. Rescue epigraphy in the Hypostyle Hall at Karnak, *Egyptian Archaeology* 19: 11-13.

Banning, E. B. 2000. *The Archaeologist's Laboratory: The Analysis of Archaeological Data: Manuals in Archaeological Method, Theory and Technique.* New York: Kluwer Academic/Plenum Publishers.

Banning, E. B. 2002. *Archaeological Survey: Manuals in Archaeological Method, Theory and Technique.* New York: Kluwer Academic/Plenum Publishers.

Barber, D., & Mills, J. 2001. Redefining the three Rs, *Surveying World.* June: 33-35.

Barber, D., Mills, J., & Bryan, P. G. 2001. Laser Scanning and Photogrammetry - 21st Century Metrology, *The Proceedings of the XVIII CIPA 2001 International Symposium: Surveying and Documentation of Historic Buildings, Monuments, Sites - Traditional and Modern Methods.* Potsdam: University of Potsdam. (http://cipa.icomos.org/fileadmin/papers/potsdam/2001-07-db02.pdf).

Bard, K. A. 2008. *An Introduction to the Archaeology of Ancient Egypt.* Oxford: Blackwell.

Barich, B. E., Hassan, F. A. & Mahmoud, A-M. A. 1991. From settlement to site: formation and transformation of archaeological traces, *Scienze Dell'Antichita, Storia Archeologia Anthropologia* 5: 33-62.

Barker, P. 1986. *Understanding Archaeological Excavation.* London: Batsford.

Barker, P. 1993. *Techniques of Archaeological Excavation,* Third Edition. London: Batsford.

Bar-Yosef, O. 1992. Middle Palaeolithic chronology and the transition to the Upper Palaeolithic in Southwest Asia, in C. Brauer & F. H. Smith (eds.), 1992. *Continuity or Replacement? Controversies in Homo sapiens Evolution*. Rotterdam: Balkema, pp. 261-72.

Bar-Yosef, O. 1994. The Lower Palaeolithic of the Near East, *Journal of World Prehistory* 8: 211-65.

Bass, W. M. 2005. *Human Osteology: A Laboratory & Field Manual*. Sixth Edition. Special Publication No.2. Columbia: Missouri Archaeological Society.

Beck, M. E., Skibo, J. M., Hally, D. J. & Yang, P. 2002. Sample selection for ceramic use-alteration analysis: the effects of abrasion on soot, *Journal of Archaeological Science* 29(1): 1-15.

Bell, L. 1987. The Epigraphic Survey: The Philosophy of Egyptian Epigraphy After Sixty Years' Practical Experience, in J. Assmann, G. Burkard & V. Davies *Problems and Priorities in Egyptian Archaeology*. London: KPI, pp. 43-55.

Bellwood, P. 2004. *First Farmers: The Origins of Agricultural Societies*. Oxford: Wiley-Blackwell

Bennett, K. 1993. *A Field Guide for Human Skeletal Identification*. Springfield, IL: Charles C. Thomas.

Bentley, R. A., Price, T. D., Lüning, J. Gronenborn, D. Wahl, J. & Fullagar, P. D. 2002. Human migration in early Neolithic Europe, *Current Anthropology* 43: 799-804.

Bentley, R. A., Price, T. D. & Chikhi, L. 2003a. Comparing broad scale genetic and local scale isotopic evidence for the spread of agriculture into Europe, *Antiquity* 77: 63-66.

Bentley, R. A., Krause, R., Price, T. D. & Kaufmann, B. 2003b. Human mobility at the early Neolithic settlement of Vaihingen, Germany: evidence from strontium isotope analysis, *Archaeometry* 45: 471-486.

Bentley, R. A., Price, T. D., & Stephan, E. 2004. Determining the local87Sr/86Sr range for archaeological skeletons: a case study from Neolithic Europe, *Journal of Archaeological Science* 31: 365-375.

Bentley, R. A., Pietrusewsky, M., Douglas, M. T. & Atkinson, T. C. (n.d.). Skeletal-isotopic evidence for matrilocality during the prehistoric transition to agriculture in Thailand. Submitted to *Antiquity*.

Bettess, F. 1998. *Surveying for Archaeologists*, 3rd Edition. Cleadon: Penshaw Press, University of Durham.

Bietak, M. 1979. The present state of Egyptian archaeology, *Journal of Egyptian Archaeology* 65: 156-160.

Binford, L. R. 1972. *An Archaeological Perspective*. New York: Seminar Press.

Binford, L. R. 1983. *In Pursuit of the Past: Decoding the Archaeological Record*. London: Thames & Hudson.

Birkeland, P. W. 1999. *Soils and Geomorphology*, Third Edition. New York: Oxford University Press.

Boismier, W. A. 1997. *Modelling the Effects of Tillage Processes on Artefact Distribution in the Plough Zone*. Oxford: BAR 259.

Borchardt, L. 1913. *Das Grabdenkmal des Königs Sahu-re II: Die Wandbilder*. Leipzig: J. C. Hinrichs.

Bordes, F. 1961. *Typologie du Paléolithique Anchen et Moyen*. Bordeaux: Delmas.

Bordes, F. 1968. *Old Stone Age*. London: World University Library.

Bowden, M. (ed.) 1999. *Unravelling the Landscape: an Inquisitive Approach to Archaeology*. Stroud: RCHME/Tempus.

Bowden, M. 2002. *With Alidade and Tape: Graphical and Plane Table survey of Archaeological Earthworks*. London: English Heritage.

Bowman, D. L. & Givens, D. R. 1996. Stratigraphic excavations: the first 'New Archaeology', *American Anthropologist* 98: 80-95.

Box, P. 1999. *GIS and Cultural Resource Management: A Manual for Heritage Managers*. Bangkok: UNESCO.

Bréand, G. 2005. Les marques et graffiti sur poteries de l'Egypte pré- et protodynastique. Perspectives de recherches à partir de l'exemple d'Adaïma, *Archéo-Nil* 15: 17-30.

Brennan, L. A. 1975. *Artifacts of Prehistoric America*. New York: Sackpole Books.

Bretschneider, J. Dreissen, J. & van Lerberghe, K. (eds.) 2007. *Power and Architecture: Monumental Public Architecture in the Bronze Age Near East and Aegean: Proceedings of the International Conference 'Power and Architecture' organized by the Katholieke Universiteit Leuven, the Université Catholique de Louvain and the Westfälischen Wilhelms-Universität Münster on the 21st and 22nd of November 2002*. Dudley, Mass.: Peeters, Orientalia Lovaniensia analecta 156.

Brickley, M. & McKinley, J. I. (eds.) 2004. *Guidelines to the Standards for Recording Human Remains*. IFA Paper No. 7. Reading: BABAO, Department of Archaeology, University of Southampton & the Institute of Field Archaeologists,

Brink, E. C. M. van den (ed.) 1988. *The Archaeology of the Nile Delta: Problems and Priorities*. Proceedings of the Seminar Held in Cairo 19th-22nd October 1986 at the Netherlands Institute of Archaeology and Arabic Studies in Cairo. Amsterdam: Netherlands Foundation for Archaeological Research in Egypt.

Brink, E. C. M. van den (ed.) 1992. *The Nile Delta in Transition: 4th-3rd Millennium BC*. Proceedings of the Seminar Held in Cairo 21st-24th October 1990 at the Netherlands Institute of Archaeology and Arabic Studies in Cairo. Tel Aviv: R. Pinklas.

Brothwell, D. 1981. *Digging up Bones: the Excavation, Treatment, and Study of Human Skeletal Remains*, Third Edition. New York: Cornell University Press.

Brown, A. G. 1997. *Alluvial Geoarchaeology: Floodplain Archaeology and Environmental Change*. Cambridge: Cambridge Uversity Press.

Brown, D.H. 1994. Contexts, their contents and residuality, in L. Shepherd (ed.) *Interpreting Stratigraphy*. Proceedings of the 5th Stratigraphy Conference, Norwich. Norwich: Norfolk Archaeological Unit, pp.1-8

Brown, G. A. & Brown K. A. 1992. Ancient DNA and the archaeologist, *Antiquity* 66: 10-23.

Brown, K. A. 1998. Keeping it clean: the collection and storage of ancient DNA samples from the field, *The Archaeologist* 33: 16-7.

Brown, M. R. and Harris, E.C. 1993. Interfaces in archaeological stratigraphy, in E. C. Harris, M. R. Brown III and G. J. Brown (eds.) *Practices Of Archaeological Stratigraphy*. London: Academic Press, pp. 7-22

Bryan, B. 2001. Painting techniques and artisan organization in the tomb of Suemniwet, Theban Tomb 92, in W. V. Davies (ed.) *Colour and Painting in Ancient Egypt*. London: British Museum Press, pp. 62-72.

Buikstra, J. E. & Ubelaker, D. H. (eds.) (1994) *Standards for Data Collection from Human Skeletal Remains: Proceedings of a Seminar at The Field Museum of Natural History*. Arkansas: Arkansas Archaeological Survey Research Series No. 44.

Burke, H. & Smith, C. 2004. *The Archaeologist's Field Handbook*. Sydney: Allen & Unwin.

Butler, C. 2008. *Prehistoric Flintwork*. Stroud: Tempus Press.

Butzer, K. 1976. *Early Hydraulic Civilization in Egypt: A Study in Cultural Ecology*. Chicago: University of Chicago Press.

Caminos. R. A. 1976. The Recording of Inscriptions and Scenes in Tombs and Temples, in *Ancient Egyptian Epigraphy and Palaeography*. New York: The Metropolitan Museum of Art Press: 3-25.

Caminos, R. A. 1987. Epigraphy in the Field, in J. Assmann, G. Burkard & V. Davies (eds.) *Problems and Priorities in Egyptian Archaeology*. London: KPI, pp. 57-67.

Camps, C., G. Delibrias & Thommeret, J. 1973. Chronologie des civilisatioris préhistoriques du Nord de l'Afrique d'apres Ie radiocarbone, *Libyaz* 21: 65-89.

Canti, M. & Meddens, F. 1998. Mechanical coring as an aid to archaeological projects, *Journal of Field Archaeology* 25: 97-105.

Carver, M. 1979. Notes on some general principles for the analysis of excavated data, *Science and Archaeology* 35(7): 1-14.

Carver, M. 2005. Key ideas in excavation, in C. Renfrew & P. Bahn (eds.) *Archaeology: Key Concepts*. London: Routledge, pp. 106-110.

Cather, S. (ed.) 1991. *The Conservation of Wall Paintings: Proceedings of a Symposium Organized by the Courtauld Institute of Art and the Getty Conservation Institute, London, July 13-16, 1987*. Marina del Rey, CA: Getty Conservation Institute.

Cauvin, J. 2000. *The Birth of the Gods and the Origins of Agriculture*. (English translation by T. Watkins). Cambridge: Cambridge University Press.

Cervicek, P. 1974. *Felsbilder des Nord-Ethbia, Oberagypten und Unternubiens*. Wiesbaden: Steiner.

Chadwick, A. 1998. Archaeology at the edge of chaos: further towards reflexive excavation methodologies, *Assemblage* 3 (http://www.assemblage.group.shef.ac.uk/3/3chadbib.htm#bibliog).

Chen, T. & Zhang, Y. 1991. Palaeolithic chronology and possible co-existence of *Homo erectus* and *Homo sapiens* in China, *World Archaeology* 23: 147-54.

Cherry, J. F. 2003. Archaeology beyond the site: regional survey and its future, in J. K. Papadopoulos & R. M. Leventhal (eds.) *Theory and Practice in Mediterranean Archaeology: Old and New World Perspectives*. Los Angeles: The Costen Institute of Archaeology at UCLA, pp. 137=59.

Chiotasso, L., Chiotasso, P., Pedrini, L., Rigoni, G., Sarnelli, C. 1992. La Parruca di Merit, in *VI Congresso Internazionale di Egittologia - Atti.I.* Rome, pp. 99-105.

Clark, A. 1996 *Seeing Beneath the Soil: Prospecting Methods in Archaeology*, New Edition. London: Batsford.

Clark, J. D. 1934. The classification of a microlithic culture: the Tardenoisian of Horsham, *Archaeological Journal* 90: 52-7.

Clark, J. D. 1951. *The Prehistoric Cultures of the Horn of Africa*. Cambridge: Cambridge University Press.

Clark, J. G. D. 1968. *World Prehistory: A New Outline*, Second Edition. Cambridge: Cambridge University Press.

Clarke, S. & Engelbach, R. 1990. *Ancient Egyptian Construction and Architecture*. New York: Dover Publications, Inc.

Claassen, C. 1998. *Shells*. Cambridge: Cambridge University Press.

Cochran, W. G. 1977. *Sampling Theory*, Third Edition. New York: John Wiley.

Cohen, N. In Press. Creating perfect paperwork; creating Egyptian archaeological archives, in F. A. Hassan, G. J. Tassie, A. De Trafford & L. Owens (eds.) *Management of Egypt's Cultural Heritage*, Volume 2. London: Golden House Publications.

Coiner, M & Bruno, A. 2001. 3D Laser Scanning for Common Surveying Applications. *Cyrax Application White Paper*. London.

Collis, J. 2001. *Digging Up the Past: An Introduction to Archaeological Excavation*. Far Thrupp Stroud: Alan Sutton Publishing.

Conolly, J. & Lake, M. 2006. *Geographical Information Systems in Archaeology*. Cambridge: Cambridge University Press.

Cooper, M. A., *et al.* (eds.) 1995. *Managing Archaeology*. London: Routledge.

Corbishley, M. J. 2004. *Aerial Photography*. London: English Heritage, Education on Site.

Corr, S. 2000. *Caring for Collections: A Manual of Preventive Conservation*. Dublin: Heritage Council of Ireland; Institute for the Conservation of Artistic and Historic Works in Ireland.

Courboin, E. 2009. Lithic knapped tools in a Naqadian context, *I-Medjat* 3: 12-14.

Coutts, P. 1977. Old buildings tell tales, *World Archaeology* 9(2): 200-219.

Cox, C. 1992. Satellite imagery, aerial photography and wetland archaeology, *World Archaeology* 24(2): 249-67.

Cox, J. S. 1977. The construction of an ancient Egyptian wig (*c.* 1400) in the British Museum, *Journal of Egyptian Archaeology* 63: 67-70.

Cox, M. & Keeler, P. 2002. *Crypt Archaeology: An Approach*. IFA Paper No. 3, Birmingham: Institute of Field Archaeologists.

Crawford, H. E. W. 1977. *The Architecture of Iraq in the Third Millennium B.C.* Copenhagen: Akademisk Forlag.

Cronyn, J. 1990. *The Elements of Archaeological Conservation*. London: Routledge.

Curtis, J. W. 1926. *Coinage in Pharaonic Egypt*. Chicago: Ares Publications.

Dalland, M. 1984. A procedure for use in stratigraphical analysis. *Scottish Archaeological Review:* 116-127

Dancey, W. 1987. *Archaeological Field Methods: An Introduction*. Minneapolis: Burgess.

Darnell, D. 2000a. Predynastic and Pharaonic activity in Kharga Oasis and beyond: new ceramic evidence from desert routes, in Z. Hawass and A. M. Jones (eds.) *Abstracts of Papers for the Eighth International Congress of Egyptologists*. Cairo: American University in Cairo Press, pp. 46-7.

Darnell, J. 2000b. The pony express and the origins of the alphabet in the Egyptian Western Desert, in Z. Hawass and A. M. Jones (eds.) *Abstracts of Papers for the Eighth International Congress of Egyptologists*. Cairo: American University in Cairo Press, pp. 47-8.

David, A. 1995. *Geophysical Survey in Archaeological Field Evaluation*. London: English Heritage, Ancient Monuments Laboratory.

David, A. 2001. Overview –the role and practice of archaeological prospection, in D. R. Brothwell & A. M. Pollard (eds.) *Handbook of Archaeological Sciences*. Chichester: John wiley & Sons, pp. 521-7.

David, R. & Tapp, E. (eds.) 1984. *Evidence Embalmed: Modern Medicine and the Mummies of Ancient Egypt*. Manchester: Manchester Museum.

David, R. & Tapp, E. (eds.) 1992. *The Mummy's Tale: The Scientific and Medical Investigations of Nefer-Amun, Priest in the Temple at Karnak*. London: Routledge.

Davis, V. & Friedman, R. 1998. *Egypt*. London: British Museum Press.

Dean, M., Ferrari, B., Oxley, I., Redknap, M. & Watson, K. (eds.) 1995. *Archaeology Underwater: The NAS Guide to Principles and Practice*. London: Nautical Archaeological Society & Archetype Books.

Der Manuelan, P. 1998. Digital epigraphy: an approach to streamlining Egyptological epigraphic method, *Journal of the American Research Center Egypt* 35: 97-113.

Der Manuelan. P. 2000. Digital epigraphy at Giza, *Egyptian Archaeology* 17: 25-27.

Dever, W. G. & Darrel Lance, H. 1978. *A Manual of Field Excavation: Handbook for Field Archaeologists.* Cincinnati: Hebrew Union College, Jewish Institute of Religion.

Dillon, B. D. (ed.) 1993. *Practical Archaeology: Field and Laboratory Techniques and Archaeological Logistics,* Third Edition. Los Angeles: UCLA Institute of Archaeology, Archaeological Research Tools 2.

Dincauze, D. F. 2000. *Environmental Archaeology: Principles and Practice.* New York: Cambridge University Press.

Dodson, A. 1991. *Egyptian Rock-Cut Tombs.* Princes Risborough: Shire Publications Ltd.

Donoghue, D. 2001. Remote sensing, in D. R. Brothwell & A. M. Pollard (eds.) *Handbook of Archaeological Sciences.* Chichester: John Wiley & Sons, pp. 555-63.

Dorman, P. F. 2008. Epigraphy and recording, in R. H. Wilkinson (ed.) *Egyptology Today.* Cambridge: Cambridge University Press, pp. 77-97.

Dorrell, P. 1994. *Photography in Archaeology and Conservation.* Cambridge: Cambridge University Press.

Drennan, R. D. 1996. *Statistics for Archaeologists: A Commonsense Approach.* New York: Plenum.

Drewett, P. L. 1999. *Field Archaeology: An Introduction.* London: UCL Press.

Driesch, A. von den. 1976. *A Guide to the Measurements of Animal Bones from Archaeological Sites: As Developed by the Institut Für Palaeoanatomie, Domestikationsforsung und Geschichte der Tiermedizin of the University of Munich.* Boston: Peabody Museum of Archaeology and Ethnology, Harvard University, Peabody Museum Bulletin No. 1.

Dugdale, R. H. 1980. *Surveying.* London: George Godwin Ltd.

Dunnel, R. & Simek, J. 1995. Artifact size and plowzone process, *Journal of Field Archaeology* 22: 305-19

Eidt, R. C. 1984. *Advances in Abandoned Settlement Analysis: Application to Prehistoric Anthrosoils in Columbia, South America.* Milwaukee: The Center for Latin America, University of Wisconsin.

Eiteljorg, H. II & Limp, W. F. 2007. *Archaeological Computing.* Bryn Mawr, PA: Center for the Study of Architecture.

El Daly, O. 2005. *Egyptology: The Missing Millennium. Ancient Egypt in Medieval Arabic Writings.* London: UCL Press.

El-Khouli, A. A. R. H. 1978. *Egyptian Stone Vessels: Predynastic to Third Dynasty, Vols. I-III.* Mainz/Rhein: Verlag Philipp von Zabern.

Ellis, L. 1982. *Laboratory Techniques in Archaeology: A Guide to the Literature, 1920-1980.* New York: Garland Publishers.

Emery, W. B. 1971. *Archaic Egypt: Culture and Civilization in Egypt 5,000 Years Ago.* London: Penguin.

Empereur, J-Y. 2000. Alexandria rising, in C. Jacob & F. de Polignac (eds.) *Alexandria, Third Century BC: The Knowledge of the World in a Single City.* Alexandria: Harpocrates, pp. 188-205.

English Heritage. 1991. *Management of Archaeological Projects.* London: English Heritage.

English Heritage 1995. *Geophysical Survey in Archaeological Field Evaluation.* (Research & Professional Guidelines 1). London: English Heritage.

English Heritage. 2001. *Centre for Archaeology Guidelines: Archaeometallurgy.* London: English Heritage.

English Heritage. 2002a. *Centre for Archaeology Guidelines: Environmental Archaeology: A Guide to the Theory and Practice of Methods, from Sampling and Recovery to Post-Excavation.* London: English Heritage.

English Heritage. 2002b. *Centre for Archaeology Guidelines: Human bones from Archaeological Sites: Guidelines for Producing Assessment Documents and Analytical Reports.* London: English Heritage.

English Heritage. 2003. *Where on Earth Are We? The Global Positioning System (GPS) in Archaeological Field Survey.* London: English Heritage.

English Heritage. 2004. *Geoarchaeology: Using Earth Sciences to Understand the Archaeological Record.* London: English Heritage.

Evans, J. & O'Connor, T. 1999. *Environmental Archaeology: Principles and Methods.* Far Thrupp Stroud: Alan Sutton Publishing.

Eve, S. & Hunt, G. In Press. ARK: a development framework for archaeological recording, *Layers of Perception: Advanced Technology Means to illuminate Our Past, Proceedings of the 35th Computer Applications Quantitative Methods in Archaeology (CAA) Conference, April 2-6 2007, Berlin.*

Fagan, B. M. 2001. *In the Beginning: An Introduction to Archaeology,* Tenth Edition. Upper Saddle River: Prentice Hall.

Fairgrieve, S. I. & Oost, T. S. 2001. *Human Skeletal Anatomy: Laboratory Manual and Workbook.* Springfield, Ill.: Charles C Thomas.

Fangi, G., Fiori, F., Gagliardini, G., & Malinverni, E. 2001. Fast and Accurate Close Range 3D Modelling by Laser Scanning System, *The Proceedings of the XVIII CIPA 2001 International Symposium: Surveying and Documentation of Historic Buildings, Monuments, Sites - Traditional and Modern Methods.* Poisdam: University of Potsdam. (http://cipa.icomos.org/fileadmin/papers/potsdam/2001-21-gf01.pdf).

Farrar, R. 1987. *Surveying by Prismatic Compass.* Practical Handbooks in Archaeology 2. London: Council for British Archaeology.

Fasham P. J. 1984. *Groundwater Pumping Techniques for Excavation.* IFA Technical Paper 1. Birmingham: Institute of Field Archaeologists.

Fasham, P. J. *et al.* 1980. *Fieldwalking for Archaeologists.* Andover: Hampshire Field Club & Archaeological Society.

Ferguson, L. M. & Murray, D. M. 1997. *Archaeological Documentary Archives: Preparation, Curation and Storage.* IFA Paper No. 1. Birmingham: Institute of Field Archaeologists.

Fischer, H. G. 1976. Archaeological aspects of epigraphy and palaeography, in *Ancient Egyptian Epigraphy and Palaeography.* New York: The Metropolitan Museum of Art Press, pp. 29-50.

Flannery, K. V. (ed.) 1976. *The Early Mesoamerican Village.* New York: Academic.

Fletcher, A. J. 2000. Hair, in P. Nicholson & I. Shaw (eds.) *Ancient Egyptian Materials and Technology.* Cambridge: Cambridge University Press, pp. 495-504.

Fogel, M. L. & Tuross, N. 2002. Extending the limits of paleodiversity studies of humans with compound specific carbon isotope analysis of amino acids, *Journal of Archaeological Science* 99: 1-11.

Foley, R. & Lahr, M. M. 2003. On stony ground: ground lithic technology, human evolution, and the emergence of culture, *Evolutionary Anthropology* 12: 109-122.

Fossati, A., Jaffe, L. & de Abreu, M. S. (eds.) 1990 a. *Rupestrian Archaeology: Techniques and Terminology, A Methodological Approach: Petroglyphs.* Vol. 1. Val Camonica (Brescia): Cooperativa Archeologica.

Fossati, A., Jaffe, L. & de Abreu, M. S. (eds.) 1990 b. *Rupestrian Archaeology: Techniques and Terminology, A Methodological Approach: Rock-Paintings.* Vol. 2. Val Camonica (Brescia): Cooperativa Archeologica.

Friedman, F. D. 1998. *Gifts of the Nile: Ancient Egyptian Faience.* London: Thames & Hudson.

Friedman R. & Adams, B. (eds.) 1992. *Followers of Horus: Studies in Honour of Michael A. Hoffman.* Oxford: Egyptian Studies Publication No. 2. Oxbow Monograph 20.

Fuchs, G. 1991. Petroglyphs in the Eastern Desert: new finds in the Wadi el-Barramiys, *Sahara* 4: 19-29.

Fullagar, R. 2006. Residues and usewear, in J. & A. Paterson (eds.) *Archaeology in Practice: A Student Guide to Archaeological Analyses.* Oxford: Blackwell Publishing, pp. 207-234.

Furguson, L. M. & Murray, D. M. 1997. *Archaeological Documentary Archives: Preparation, Curation and Storage.* IFA Paper No 1. Birmingham: Institute of Field Archaeologists.

Fryer, D. H. 1971. *Surveying for Archaeologists.* Durham: University of Durham Press.

Gaffney, V., Gaffney, C. & Corney, M. 1998. Changing the Roman landscape: the role of geophysics and remote sensing, in J. Bailey (ed.) *Science in Archaeology: An Agenda for the Future.* London: English Heritage, pp. 145-56.

Gaffney, C. & Gater, J. with Ovenden, S. 1991. *The Use of Geophysical Techniques in Archaeological Interpretations.* IFA Technical Paper No. 9. Birmingham: Institute of Field Archaeologists.

Gale, R., Gasson, P., Hepper, N. & Killen, G. 2000. Wood, in P. Nicholson & I. Shaw (eds.) *Ancient Egyptian Materials and Technology.* Cambridge: Cambridge University Press, pp. 334-371.

Ganderton, P. 1981. *Environmental Archaeology: Site Methods and Interpretation.* (Vorda Research Series 2). Highworth: Vorda.

Garlake, P. S. 2002. *Early Art and Architecture of Africa.* Oxford: Oxford University Press.

Gé, T., Courty, M. A., Matthews, W. & Wattez, J. 1993. Sedimentary formation processes of occupation surfaces, in P. Goldberg, D. T. Nash & M. D. Petraglia (eds.) *Formation Processes in Archaeological Contexts.* Madison WI: Prehistory Press, pp. 149-163.

Ghilani, C. D. & Wolf, P. R. 2008. *Elementary Surveying. An Introduction to Geomatics,* 12th Edition. Upper Saddle River, NJ: Prentice Hall.

Giddy, L. 1999. The present state of Egyptian archaeology: 1997 update, in A. Leahy & J. Tait (eds.) *Studies on Ancient Egypt in Honour of H. S. Smith.* London: Egypt Exploration Society, pp. 109-113.

Gilbert, B. M. 1990. *Mammalian Osteology,* Reprint Edition. Columbia: Missouri Archaeological Society.

Goldberg, H. E. 2001. Scan Your World With 3D Lasers, *Cadalyst.* (http://www.cadalyst.com/features/0201cyra/index.htm).

Goldberg, P. & Macphail, R. I. 2006. *Practical and Theoretical Geoarchaeology.* Oxford: Blackwell.

Goldberg, P., Holliday, V. T. & Ferring, C. R. (eds.) 1994. *Earth Science and Archaeology.* New York: Kluwer Academic/Plenum Publishers.

Greene, B. 1989. *Ancient Egyptian Stone Vessels: Materials and Forms.* Berkeley: U.M.I.

Greene, K. 2002. *Archaeology: An Introduction,* Fourth Edition. Philadelphia: University of Pennsylvania Press.

Grew, F (ed.) 1998. *General Standards for the Preparation of Archaeological Archives Deposited with the Museum of London.* London: Museum of London.

Grey, A. 2006. *Archaeological Finds Procedures Manual.* Unpublished. London: Museum of London Specialist Services.

Griffiths, N., Jenner, A., & Wilson, C. 1991. *Drawing Archaeological Finds: A Handbook.* London: Archetype Publications Ltd.

Grimal, N. 1992. *A History of Ancient Egypt.* (English translation by Ian Shaw). London: Blackwell.

Grinsell, L., Rahtz, P. & Warhurst, A. 1976. *The Preparation of Archaeological Reports.* London: John Baker Publishers Ltd.

Guksch, C. H. 1991. Ethnological models and processes of state formation – chiefdom survivals in the Old Kingdom, *Göttinger Miszellen* 125: 37-50.

Gumerman, G. IV & Umemoto, B. S. 1987. The siphon technique: an addition to the flotation process, *American Antiquity* 52(2): 330-335.

Gupta, S. P. 1980. *The Roots of Indian Art: a Detailed Study of the Formative Period of Indian Art and Architecture, Third and Second Centuries B.C., Mauryan and Late Mauryan.* Delhi: B.R. Pub. Corp.

Gurney, D. 1985. *Phosphate Analysis of Soils: A Guide for Field Archaeologists.* IFA Technical Paper 3. Birmingham: Institute of Field Archaeologists.

Hafford, W. 2006. The taste of a dig: cooking up successful fieldwork, *Expedition* 44(3): 7-8.

Hally, D. J. 1983. Use alteration of pottery vessel surfaces: an important source of information of vessel function, *North American Archaeologist* 4: 3-26.

Hally, D. J. 1986. The identification of vessel function: a case study from northwest Georgia, *American Antiquity* 51: 267-95.

Hamilton, S. D. 1996. Reassessing archaeological illustrations: breaking the mould, *Graphic Archaeology* 5, Newsletter of the Association of Archaeological Illustrators & Surveyors: 20-27.

Harris, D. R. & Thomas, K. (eds.) 1991. *Modelling Ecological Change.* London: Institute of Archaeology.

Harris, E. C. 1975. The stratigraphic sequence: a question of time, *World Archaeology* 7(1): 109-21.

Harris, E. C. 1979. *Principals of Archaeological Stratigraphy.* London: Academic Press Ltd.

Harris, E. C. 1989. *Principals of Archaeological Stratigraphy*, 2nd Edition. London: Academic Press Ltd.

Harris, E. C., Brown, M. R., III, & Brown, G. J. 1993. *Practices of Archaeological Stratigraphy.* London: Academic Press Ltd.

Haselgrove, C., Millet, M. & Smith, I. (eds.) 1985. *Archaeology from the Ploughsoil: Studies in the Collection of Interpretation of Field Survey Data.* Sheffield: University of Sheffield.

Hassan, F. A. 1978. Sediments in archaeology: methods and implications for palaeoenvironmental and cultural analysis, *Journal of Field Archaeology* 5: 197-213.

Hassan, F. A. 1981. Rapid quantitative determination of phosphate in archaeological sediments, *Journal of Field Archaeology* 8: 384-7.

Hassan, F. A. 1984. *A Brief Guide to Field Description of Sediments.* Washington: Washington State University Press.

Hassan, F. A. 1987. Re-forming archaeology: a forward to natural formation processes and the archaeological record, in D. T. Nash & M. D. Petraglia (eds.) *Natural Formation Processes and the Archaeological Record.* Oxford: BAR, International Series 352, pp. 2-9.

Hassan, F. A. 1988. The Predynastic of Egypt, *Journal of World Prehistory* 2(2): 135-185.

Hassan, F. A. 1993. Rock art: cognitive schemata and symbolic interpretation, in G. Calegari (ed.) *L'Arte d l'Ambiente del Sahara prehistorico: dati e interpretazioni.* Milano: Memorie della Societa Italiana di Scienze Naturali s del Museo Civico di Storia Naturale di Milano, pp. 269-282.

Hassan, F. A., Jiménez Serrano, A., & Tassie, G. J. 2007. The sequence and chronology of the Protodynastic and Dynasty I rulers, in M. Chlodnicki, K. Kroeper & M. Kobusiewicz (eds.) *Archaeology of Northeast Africa: Studies in Memory of Lech Krzyżaniak.* Poznań: Archaeological Museum, pp. 687-722.

Hatt, G. 1957. Nørre Fjand, an Early Iron Age village in West Jutland, *Arkaeol. Kunsthist, Skr. Dan, Selsk.* 2(2) Copenhagen.

Hawker, J. M. 1999. *A Manual of Archaeological Field Drawing.* Edinburgh: J. M. Hawker.

Hawker, J. M. 1999a. *A Manual of Archaeological Field Recording.* Edinburgh: J. M. Hawker.

Hayden, B. (ed.) 1979. *Lithic Usewear Analysis.* New York: Academic Press.

Hendrickx, S. 1996. The relative chronology of the Naqada Culture: problems and possibilities, in J. Spencer (ed.) *Aspects of Early Egypt.* London: British Museum Press, pp. 36-69.

Hendrickx, S. 1999. La chronologie de la préhistoire tardive et des débuts de l'histoire de l'Egypte, *Archéo-Nil* 9: 13-81, 99-107.

Hendrickx, S., Faltings, D., Beck, L. Op de., Raue, D. & Michiels, C. 2002. Milk, beer and bread technology during the Early Dynastic Period, *Mitteilungen des Deutschen Archäologischen Instituts, Abteilung, Kairo* 58: 277-304.

Hendrickx S., Friedman R. F., Cialowicz K. M., Chlodnicki M. (eds.) 2004. *Egypt at its Origins: Studies in Memory of Barbara Adams: Proceedings of the International Conference "Origin of the State, Predynastic and Early Dynastic Egypt", Kraków, 28th August-1st September 2002.* Leuven: Uitgeverij Peeters en Departement Oosterse Studies.

Heron, C. & Pollard, A. M. 1988. The analysis of natural resinous materials from Roman amphora, in E. A. Slatter & J. O. Tait (eds.) *Science and Archaeology Glasgow 1987.* Oxford: BAR, pp. 429-47.

Hertz, N. & Garrison, E. G. 1998. *Geological Methods for Archaeology.* Oxford: Oxford University Press.

Hester, T. R., Shafer, H. J. & Feder, K. L. 1997. *Field Methods in Archaeology,* Seventh Edition. Mountain View: Mayfield Publishing.

Higham, T. 1999. The 14C Method, *C14 Dating , Com.* www.c14.com

Hill, J. D. 1995. *Ritual and Rubbish in the Iron Age of Wessex.* Oxford: BAR, British Series 242.

Hillman, G. C. 1989. Late Palaeolithic plant foods from Wadi Kubbaniya in Upper Egypt: dietary diversity, infant weaning, and seasonality in a riverine environment, in D. R. Harris & G. C. Hillman (eds.) *Foraging and Farming: The Evolution of Plant Exploitation.* London: One World Archaeology, Unwin Hyman, pp. 207-239.

Hillson, S. 1986. *Teeth.* Cambridge: Cambridge University Press.

Hillson, S. 1996. *Dental Anthropology.* Cambridge: Cambridge University Press

Hodder, I. 1992. *Theory and Practice in Archaeology.* London: Routledge.

Hodder, I. 1999. *The Archaeological Process.* Oxford: Blackwell.

Hodder, I. (ed.) 2000. *Towards Reflexive Method in Archaeology: the Example at Çatalhöyük.* Cambridge: BIAA.

Hodges, H. W. M. (ed.) 1987. *In Situ Archaeological Conservation.* Los Angeles: Getty Conservation Institute.

Hoffman, M. 1991. *Egypt Before the Pharaohs: The Prehistoric Foundations of Egyptian Civilization,* Second Edition. Austin: University of Texas Press.

Hogg, A. H. A. 1980. *Surveying for Archaeologists and Other Fieldworkers.* London: Croom Helm.

Holdaway, S. 2006. Absolute dating, in J. Balme & A. Paterson (eds.) *Archaeology in Practice: A Student Guide to Archaeological Analyses.* Oxford: Blackwell Publishing, pp. 117-158.

Holliday, V. T. (ed.) 1992. *Soils in Archaeology: Landscape Evolution and Human Occupation.* Washington: Smithsonian Institution Press.

Holmes, D. L. 1989. *The Predynastic Lithic Industries of Upper Egypt: A Comparative Study of the Lithic Traditions of Badari, Naqada and Hierakonpolis.* Oxford: BAR.

Hooft, P. M. van't, Raven, M. J., Rooij, E. H. C. van, & Vogelsang-Eastwood, G. M. 1994. *Pharaonic and Early Medieval Egyptian Textiles.* Leiden: Rijksmuseuym van Oudheden.

Howard, P. 2007. *Archaeological Surveying and Mapping: Recording and Depicting the Landscape.* London: Routledge.

Huckleberry, G. 2006. Sediments, in J. Balme & A. Paterson (eds.) *Archaeology in Practice: A Student Guide to Archaeological Analyses.* Oxford: Blackwell Publishing, pp. 338-361.

Hughes, G. R. 1952. Recording Egypt's ancient documents, *Archaeology* 5: 201-4.

Hughes, P. 1999. Archaeological drawings are in black and white, *Association of Archaeological Illustrators and Surveyors Newsletter.* Bradford: Thornton & Pearson.

Hunter, J. & Ralton, J. (eds.) 1993. *Archaeological Resource Management in the U.K.* Far Thrupp Stroud: Alan Sutton Publishing

Hunter, J. Roberts, C. & Martin, A. 1996. *Studies in Crime: An Introduction to Forensic Archaeology.* London: Routledge.

Hutton, B. 1986. *Recording Standing Buildings.* Sheffield: Sheffield University Press.

Ikram, S. & Dodson, A. 1998. *The Mummy in Ancient Egypt: Equipping the Dead for Eternity.* London: Thames & Hudson.

Inizan, M-L, Reduron-Ballinger, M., Roche, H. and Tixier, J. 1999. *Technology and Terminology of Knapped Stone,* followed by a multilingual vocabulary in Arabic, English, French, German, Greek, Italian, Portuguese, and Spanish. Meudon: Cercle de Recherches et d'Etudes Préhistoire.

Institute of Field Archaeologists. 1993. *Uses of Arial Photography in Archaeological Evaluations.* (Technical Paper No. 12). Birmingham: Institute of Field Archaeologists.

Institute of Field Archaeologists. 1996. *Standard and Guidance for the Archaeological Investigations and Recording of Standing Buildings or Structures.* Birmingham: Institute of Field Archaeologists.

Institute of Field Archaeologists. 1999a. *Standard and Guidance for Archaeological* Desk-Based Assessment. Birmingham: Institute of Field Archaeologists.

Institute of Field Archaeologists. 1999b. *Standard and Guidance for an Archaeological* Watching Brief. Birmingham: Institute of Field Archaeologists.

Institute of Field Archaeologists. 1999c. *Standard and Guidance for Archaeological* Field Evaluation. Birmingham: Institute of Field Archaeologists.

Institute of Field Archaeologists. 1999d. *Standard and Guidance for Archaeological* Excavations. Birmingham: Institute of Field Archaeologists.

Institute of Field Archaeologists. 1999e. *Standard and Guidance for Archaeological* By-Laws Code of Approved Practice. Birmingham: Institute of Field Archaeologists.

Institute of Field Archaeologists. 1999f. *Standard and Guidance for Archaeological* By-Laws: Code of Conduct. Birmingham: Institute of Field Archaeologists.

Institute of Field Archaeologists. 2001a. *Standard and Guidance* for the Collection, Documentation, Conservation and research of Archaeological Materials. Birmingham: Institute of Field Archaeologists.

Institute of Field Archaeologists. 2001b.*Standard and Guidance* Appendices. Birmingham: Institute of Field Archaeologists.

Internet Archaeology. 1999-2005. (http://intarch.ac.uk/journal.html).

Jacobi, R. 1978. The Mesolithic of Sussex, in P. L. Drewett (ed.) *Archaeology in Sussex to AD 1500.* London: CBA Research Report 29.

James, T. G. H. 1982. *Excavating in Egypt: The Egypt Exploration Society 1882-1982.* London: British Museum Press.

Jia, L. & Huang, W. 1985. The late Palaeolithic in China, in R. Wu & W. Olsen (eds.) *Palaeoanthropology and Palaeolithic Archaeology in the People's Republic of China.* Orlando (FL): Academic Press, pp. 211-23.

Johnson, C., Anderson, A., Dallimore, J. Winser, S. & Warrell, D. A. 2008. *Oxford Handbook of Expedition and Wilderness Medicine.* Oxford: Oxford University Press.

Johnson, D. In Press. Architectural drafting standards in archaeological computer modeling: Reconstructions from drawings and surveys of the Metropolitan Museum of Art Egyptian Expedition, *Layers of Perception: Advanced Technology Means to illuminate Our Past, Proceedings of the 35th Computer Applications Quantitative Methods in Archaeology (CAA) Conference, April 2-6 2007, Berlin.*

Jones, J. 2008. Pre- and Early Dynastic textiles: technology, specialisation and administration during the process of state formation, in B. Midant-Reynes, Y. Trisant, S. Hendrickx & J. Rowland (eds.) *Egypt at its Origins 2: Proceedings of the Conference on Predynastic and Early Dynastic Egypt: Origin of the State, Toulouse – 5th – 8th Sept. 2005.* Leuven: Peeters, pp. 99-132.

Jones, J., Unrub, J., Knaller, R., Skals, I., Raeder-Knudsen, L., Jordan-Fahrbach, E. & Mumfor, L. 2007. Guidelines for the excavation of archaeological textiles, in C. Gills & M-L. B. Nosch (eds.) *First Aid for the Excavation of Archaeological Textiles.* Oxford: Oxbow Books, pp. 5-29.

Jones, M. 2004. Archaeology and the genetic revolution, in J. Bintliff (ed.) *A Companion to Archaeology.* Oxford: Blackwell Publishing, pp. 39-51.

Joukowsky, M. J. 1980. *A Complete Manual of Field Archaeology: Tools And Techniques of Field Work for Archaeologists.* New Jersey: Prentice-Hall Inc.

Jucha, M. A. 2008. The corpus of "potmarks" from the graves at Tell el-Farkha, in B. Midant-Reynes, Y. Trisant, S. Hendrickx & J. Rowland (eds.) *Egypt at its Origins 2: Proceedings of the Conference on Predynastic and Early Dynastic Egypt: Origin of the State, Toulouse 5th – 8th Sept. 2005.* Leuven: Peeters, pp. 133-150.

Kaiser, W. 1957. Zur inneren chronologies der Naqadakultur, *Archaeologia Geographica* 6: 69-77.

Keeley, H., & MacPhail, R. 1981. *A Soil Handbook for Archaeologists.* London: University of London

Kelly, A. L. 1976. *The Pottery of Ancient Egypt: Dynasty I to Roman Times.* Ontario: Royal Ontario Museum.

Kemp, B. J. 1991. *Ancient Egypt: Anatomy of a Civilization.* London: Routledge.

Kemp, B. J. 2000. Soil (including mud-brick architecture), in P. Nicholson. & I. Shaw (eds.) *Ancient Egyptian Materials and Technology.* Cambridge: Cambridge University Press, pp. 78-103.

Kemp, B. J. & Vogelsang-Eastwood, G. 2001. *The Ancient Textile Industry at Amarna.* London: Egypt Exploration Society.

Kenyon, K. M. 1952. *Beginning in Archaeology.* London: Phoenix House.

Killen, G. 1994. *Egyptian Woodworking and Furniture.* Princes Risborough: Shire Publications Ltd.

Kintigh, K. 1988. The effectiveness of subsurface testing: a simulation approach, *American Antiquity* 53: 686-707.

Kipfer, B. A. 2007. *The Archaeologist's Fieldwork Companion.* Oxford: Blackwell Publishing.

Klein, R. G. 2007. Hominin dispersals in the old World, in C. Scarre (ed.) *The Human Past: World Prehistory and the Development of Human Societies.* London: Thames & Hudson, pp. 84-123.

Klemm, R. & Klemm, D. D. 2008. *Stones and Quarries in Ancient Egypt,* Second Edition. London: British Museum Press.

Köhler, E. C. & Smythe, J. C. 2004. Early Dynastic pottery from Helwan – Establishing a ceramic corpus of the Naqada III Period, *Cahiers de la Céramique Égyptienne* 7: 123-143.

Kondo, J. 1997. The re-use of the private tombs on the Western Bank of Thebes and its chronological problem: the cases of the Tomb of Hnsw (no. 31) and the Tomb of Wsr-h3t (no. 51), *Orient* 32: 50-68.

Kooyman, B. P. 2000. *Understanding Stone Tools and Archaeological Sites.* Calgary: University of Calgary Press.

Kunow, J., Giesler, J., Gechter, M., Gaitzsch, W., Fullmann-Schulz, A & von Brandt, D. 1986. *Suggestions for the Systematic Recording of Pottery.* Cologne: Rheinland Verlag.

Lamb, L. 1999. Visualising past landscapes, *Association of Archaeological Illustrators and Surveyors Newsletter.* Bradford: Thornton & Pearson.

Lamotta, V. M. & Schiffer, M. B. 2005. Archaeological formation processes, in C. Renfrew & P. Bahn (eds.) *Archaeology: Key Concepts.* London: Routledge, pp. 121-127.

Lapp, P. W. 1975. *The Tale of the Tell.* Pittsburgh: The Pickwick Press.

Larson, C. S. 1997. *Bioarchaeology: Interpreting Behaviour from the Human Skeleton.* Cambridge: Cambridge University Press.

Larson, C. U. (ed.) 1992. *Sites and Monuments: National Archaeological Records.* Copenhagen: Museum of Denmark, DKC.

Leach, P. E. 1994. *Surveying of Archaeological Sites,* Second Edition. London: Institute of Archaeology Publications.

Lehner, M. 1997. *The Complete Pyramids.* London: Thames & Hudson.

Lemmens, M. & Heuval, F. van den 2001. 3D Close-Range Laser Mapping Systems. *GIM International* 15(1): 30-31.

Leroi-Gourhan, A. 1971. *Préhistoire de l'Art Occidental,* Second Edition. Paris: Mazenod.

Léva, C. (ed.) 1990. *Aerial Photography and Geophysical Prospection in Archaeology: Proceedings of the Second International Symposium, Brussels 8-XI-1986.* Brussels: C.I.R.A.-I.C.L.

Lloyd, S., Müller, Müller H. W. & Martin, R. 1974. *Ancient Architecture: Mesopotamia, Egypt, Crete, Greece.* New York: Abrams, History of World Architecture.

Locke, G. & Stančič, Z. (eds.) 1995. *Archaeology and Geographic Information Systems: A European Perspective.* London: Taylor & Francis Ltd.

Lovell, N. C. 2001. The 1995 excavations of the cemetery at Kafr Hassan Daud, Wadi Tumilat; in: *Journal of the Society for the Study of Egyptian Antiquities*: 34-41.

Lowe, C.E. 1993. Data washing, the database and the Dalland Matrix, in J.W. Barber (ed.) *Interpreting Stratigraphy.* Proceedings of the 2nd Stratigraphy Conference, Edinburgh. Edinburgh: AOC Scotland Ltd, pp.23-25

Lucas, A. 1989. *Ancient Egyptian Materials and Industries.* (4th edition revised by J. R. Harris). London: Histories & Mysteries of Man Ltd.

Lucas, G. 2001. *Critical Approaches to Fieldwork: Contemporary and Historical Archaeological Practice.* London: Routledge.

Luciani, M. 2007. Archaeological field training for a variety of different types of archaeological sites: from the Near Eastern tell to the prehistoric settlement camp, in P. Ucko, Q. Ling & J. Hubert (eds.) *From Concepts of the Past to Practical Strategies: The Teaching of Archaeological Field Techniques.* London: Saffron, pp. 149-164.

Luedtke, B. E. 1992. *An Archaeologist's Guide to Chert and Flint.* Los Angeles: Archaeological Research Tools 7, University of California.

Lyman, R. L. 1994. *Vertebrate Taphonomy.* Cambridge: Cambridge University Press.

Marks, A. E. 1990. The Middle and Upper Palaeolithic of the Near East and the Nile Valley: the problem of cultural transformations, in P. Metiars (ed.) *The Emergence of Modern Humans.* Ithaca (NY): Cornell University Press, pp. 56-80.

Maschner, H. D. G. & Chippindale, C. (eds.) 2005 *Handbook of Archaeological Methods.* Walnut Creek: Altamira Press.

Maspero, G. 1895. *Manual of Egyptian Archaeology: And Guide to the Study of Antiquities in Egypt; For the Use of Students and Travellers,* Fourth Edition. (Translated by Amelia B. Edwards). London: Grevel.

Matingell, H. & Saville, A. 1988. *The Illustration of Lithic Artefacts: A Guide to Drawing Stone Tools for Specialist Reports.* Technical Paper 9. The Lithic Studies Society Occasional Paper 3 & Association of Archaeological Illustrators and Surveyors.

Matthews, K. 1993. A futile occupation? Archaeological meanings and occupation deposits, in J.W. Barber (ed.) *Interpreting Stratigraphy.* Proceedings of the 2nd Stratigraphy Conference, Edinburgh. Edinburgh: AOC Scotland Ltd, pp.55-61.

Matthews, R. 2003. *The Archaeology of Mesopotamia: Theories and Approaches.* London: Routledge.

Mays, S. 1998. *The Archaeology of Bones.* London: Routledge.

McBurney, C. B. M. 1960. *The Stone Age of Northern Africa.* London: William Clowes & Sons Ltd.

McBurney, C. B. M. 1967. *Haua Fteah and the Stone Age of the Southeast Mediterranean.* Cambridge: Cambridge University Press.

McCarter, S. F. 2007. *Neolithic.* London: Routledge.

McDonald, J. 2006. Rock-art, in J. Balme and A Paterson (eds.) *Archaeology in Practice: A Student's Guide to Archaeological Analysis.* Oxford: Blackwell, pp. 59-96.

McKinley, J, & Roberts, C. 1993. *Excavation and Post-excavation Treatment of Cremated and Inhumated Human Remains.* IFA Technical Paper 13. Birmingham: Institute of Field Archaeologists.

McManamon, F. 1984. Discovering sites unseen, in M. Schiffer (ed.) *Advances in Archaeological Method and Theory* 7: 223-92.

McMillon, W. 1991. *The Archaeology Handbook.* Chichester: John Wiley & Sons Ltd.

McPherron, S. P. & Dibble, H. L. 2003 Using computers in adverse field conditions: tales from the Egyptian desert, *SAA Archaeological Record* 3(5): 28-32.

McPherron, S. P., Gernat, T., & Hublin, J-J. 2009. Structured light scanning for high-resolution documentation of *in situ* archaeological finds, *Journal of Archaeological Science* 36: 19-24.

McPherron, S. P. Dibble, H. L. & Olzsewski, D. In Press. A mapping and on-site data collection system applied to the high desert locality of Abydos, Egypt, *Layers of Perception: Advanced Technology Means to illuminate Our Past, Proceedings of the 35th*

Computer Applications Quantitative Methods in Archaeology (CAA) Conference, April 2-6 2007, Berlin.

Medieval Pottery Research Group. 1998. *A Guide to the Classification of Medieval Ceramic Forms.* Over Wallop: Occasional Paper 1, BAS Printers.

Melville, K. E. M. 1981. *Stay Alive in the Desert.* London: Roger Lascelles, Cartographical and Travel Publishers.

Mesika, N. 1999. Real time, *in situ*: computerised graphic documentation in archaeological excavation, in J. Barceló, J. Briz & A. Vila (eds.) *New Techniques for Old Times: CAA98.* Oxford: British Archaeological Reports International Series, 757, Archaeopress, pp. 81-3.

Meyer, C. 1992. *Glass from Quseir Al-Qadim and the Indian Ocean Trade.* Chicago: University of Chicago Press.

Midant-Reynes, B. 2000. *The Prehistory of Egypt: From the First Egyptians to the First Pharaohs.* (English translation by Ian Shaw). Oxford: Blackwell.

Miksicek, C. H. 1987. Formation processes of the archaeobotanical record, in M. B. Schiffer (ed.) *Advances in Archaeological Method and Theory* 10: 211-42.

Miller-Rosen, A. 1986. *Cities of Clay: The Geoarchaeology of Tells.* Chicago: University of Chicago Press.

Miller-Rosen, A. 2007. *Civilizing Climate: Social Responses to Climatic Change in the Ancient Near East.* New York: Altamira Press.

Moffitt, F. H. & Bouchard, H. 1992. *Surveying,* 9th edition. New York: Harper and Row.

MoLas. 2001. *Health and Safety Policy: Operational Procedures.* London: MoLas.

Molyneaux, B. L. (ed.) 1997. *The Cultural Life of Images: Visual Representations in Archaeology.* London: Routledge.

Monmonier, M. 1991. *How to Lie with Maps.* Chicago: University of Chicago Press.

Mora, P., Mora, L. & Philippoi, P. 1984. *Conservation of Wall Paintings.* London: Butterworths.

Morrow, M & Morrow, M. 2001. Ships of the desert, *Followers of Horus.* (http://www.nunki.net/PerMin/Followers/Morrow2.html).

Moser, S. 2007. On disciplinary culture: archaeology as fieldwork and its gendered associations, *Journal of Archaeological Method and Theory* 14: 235–263.

Mountjoy, P. 1993. *Mycenaean Pottery: An Introduction.* Oxford: Oxford University Press.

Moussa, A., Dolphin, L. T. & Mokhtar, G. 1977. *Applications of Modern Sensing Techniques to Egyptology.* Washington: National Science Foundation.

Murphy, P. & Wiltshire, P. 1994. A guide to sampling archaeological deposits for environmental analysis, (unpublished - teaching collection no. 1178, Institute of Archaeology, University College London).

Murray, B. 1994. *Ceramic Production in Predynastic Egypt: A Preliminary Reassessment of a Predynastic Industry.* New York: U.M.I.

Muzzolini, A. 1995. *Les images Rupstres du Sahara.* Toulouse.

Muzzolini, A. 2000. Livestock in Saharan rock art, in R. M. Blench and K. C. MacDonald (eds.) *The Origins and Development of African Livestock: Archaeology, Genetics, Linguistics and Ethnography,* London: UCL Press, pp. 87-110.

Needhan, S. P. & Evans, J. 1987. Honey and dripping: Neolithic food residues from Runnymede B ridge, *Oxford Journal of Archaeology* 6: 21-8.

Needham, S. P. & Spence, T. 1997. Refuse and the formation of middens, *Antiquity* 71: 77-90.

Neumann, T. W. & Sanford, R. M. 2001a. *Cultural Resources Archaeology: An Introduction.* Walnut Creek: Altamira Press.

Neumann, T. W. & Sanford, R. M. 2001b. *Practicing Archaeology: An Introduction to Cultural Resources Archaeology.* A Training Manual. Walnut Creek: Altamira Press.

Newberry, P. E. 1905. *Scarabs in Ancient Egypt.* Chicago: Ares Publications.

Nicholson, P. T. & Shaw, I. (eds.) 2000. *Ancient Egyptian Materials and Technology.* Cambridge: Cambridge University Press.

O'Connell, T. C. & Hedges, R. E. M. 2000. Human diet and the isotopic values of hair keratin, in V. I. Molodin (ed.) *The Phenomenon of the Altai Mummies.* Novosibirsk: Russian Academy of Sciences, pp. 234-236.

Odell, G. H. 2004. *Lithic Analysis.* New York: Kluwer.

O'Keefe, P. & Prott, L. 1984. *Law and the Cultural Heritage.* Abingdon: Professional Books.

Ortner, D. J. & Thomas, W. G. J. 1981. *Identification of Pathological Conditions in Human Skeletal Remains.* Washington D. C.: Smithsonian Institution Press.

Orton, C. 1980. *Mathematics in Archaeology.* Cambridge: Cambridge University Press.

Orton, C. 1993. How many pots make five? – An historical review of pottery quantifications, *Archaeometry* 35(2): 169-84.

Orton, C. 2000. *Sampling in Archaeology.* Cambridge: Cambridge University Press.

Orton, C., Tyers, P. & Vince, A. 1993. *Pottery in Archaeology.* Cambridge: Cambridge University Press.

Paice, P. 1997. *The Pottery of Daily Life in Ancient Egypt.* Mississauga: Out Beneben Publications.

Parcak, S. H. 2009. *Satellite Remote Sensing for Archaeology.* London: Routledge.

Parker Pearson, M. 1999. *The Archaeology of Death and Burial.* Stroud: Sutton.

Patrik, L. 1985. Is there an archaeological record? *Advances in Archaeological Method and Theory* 8: 27-62.

Payton, R. (ed.), 1992. *Retrieval of Objects from Archaeological Sites.* London: Archetype Books.

Peacock, D. P. S. 1977. *Pottery and Early Commerce.* London: Academic Press.

Pelletier, A 1989. *L'Archeologie et des Methods.* Horvath: Le Coteau.

Peterson, B. N. 1987. Stable isotopes in ecosystem studies, *Annual Review of Ecology and Systematics* 18: 293-320.

Petrie, W. M. F. 1904. *Methods and Aims in Archaeology.* London: Macmillan.

Petrie, W. M. F. 1920. *Prehistoric Egypt.* London: British School of Archaeology in Egypt.

Phillips, J. P. 2002. *The Columns of Egypt.* Manchester: Peartree Publishing.

Phillips, P., Ford, J. A., & Griffin, J. B. 1951. *Archaeological Survey in the Lower Mississippi Valley, 1940-1947,* Papers of the Peabody Museum of Archaeology and Ethnology No. 25. Cambridge Mass.: Harvard University Press.

Philo, C. & Swann, A. 1992. *Preparation of Artwork for Publication.* AAIS & IFA Technical Paper 10. Birmingham: Institute of Field Archaeologists.

Pinch-Brock, L. 2000. In the footsteps of Nina and Norman de Garis Davies, *Egyptian Archaeology* 17: 18-20.

Polz, D. 1987. Excavation and recording of a Theban tomb: some remarks on recording methods, in J. Assmann, G. Burkard & V. Davies (eds.) *Problems and Priorities in Egyptian Archaeology.* London: KPI, pp. 119-140.

Prehistoric Ceramics Research Group. 1992. *The Study of Later Prehistoric Pottery: Guidelines for Analysis and Publication.* Oxford: Occasional Paper No. 2, Prehistoric Ceramics Research Group.

Price, T. D., Bentley, R. A., Gronenborn, D., Lüning, J. & Wahl, J. 2001. Human migration in the Linearbandkeramik of Central Europe, *Antiquity* 75: 593-603.

Price, T. D., Burton, J. H. & Bentley, R. A. 2002. The characterisation of biologically-available strontium isotope ratios for investigation of prehistoric migration, *Archaeometry* 44: 117-135.

Privat, K. & Schneeweiss, J. 2002. Palaeodietary research with the stable nitrogen analysis of bone collagen, Northern Eurasia in the Bronze Age (proceedings of the conference held in Barnaul, Russia, in October 2002), *Barnaul: Izdatel'stvo Altaiskogo Univeriteta* (in English and Russian): 187-195.

Pusch, E. B. 2000. Further steps towards a map of Pi-Ramesses, in Z. Hawass and A. M. Jones (eds.) *Abstracts of Papers for the Eighth International Congress of Egyptologists.* Cairo: American University in Cairo Press, pp. 145-6.

Pye, E. 2001. *Caring for the Past: Issues in Conservation for Archaeology and Museums.* London: James & James.

Rains, M. 2007. *Integrated Archaeological Database.* (http://www.iadb.org.uk/).

Rapp, G. & Hill, C. L. 1998. *Geoarchaeology: The Earth-Science Approach to Archaeological Interpretation.* New Haven: Yale University Press.

Read, D. W. 2007. *Artifact Classification: A Conceptual and Methodological Approach.* Dubai: International Publishing Services Ltd.

Rehren, T. von & Pusch, E. B. 2000. Glass and glass making at Qantir-Pi-Ramesses and beyond, *Ägypten und Levante* 9: 171-179.

Reid, D. M. 1984. Indigenous Egyptology: the decolonization of a profession, *Journal of the American Oriental Society.* 105: 233-246.

Reid, D. M. 2002. *Whose Pharaohs? Archaeology, Museums and Egyptian National Identity from Napoleon to World War I.* Cairo: American University in Cairo Press.

Reisner, G. 1936. *The Development of the Egyptian Tomb Down to the Accession Cheops.* Cambridge MA: Harvard University Press.

Reisner, G. 1942. *A History of the Giza Necropolis, Vol. 1.* Cambridge MA: Harvard University Press.

Reitz, E. J. & Wing, E. S. 1999. *Zooarchaeology.* Cambridge, Cambridge University Press.

Renfrew, C. & Bahn, P. 1991. *Archaeology: Theories, Methods and Practice,* First Edition. London: Thames & Hudson.

Renfrew, C. & Bahn, P. 2004. *Archaeology: Theories, Methods and Practice,* Fourth Edition. London: Thames & Hudson.

Resch, W. 1967. *Die Felsbilder Nubiens.* Akademische Druke-und Verlagsanstalt.

Rice, P. M. 1987. *Pottery Analysis: A Sourcebook.* Chicago: University of Chicago Press.

Rick, J. W. 1996. Interface: total stations in archaeology, *Society of American Archaeologists Bulletin* 14(4) (http://www.saa.org/publications/SAAbulletin/14-4/SAA16.html).

Riley, D. 1987. *Air Photography and Archaeology.* London: Duckworth.

Ring, L. In Press. ArchaeoCAD, ArchaeoMAP and ArchaeoDATA 2007, on the comprehensive digital recording of excavations using a combination of tacheometry, CAD and databases, *Layers of Perception: Advanced Technology Means to illuminate Our Past, Proceedings of the 35th Computer Applications Quantitative Methods in Archaeology (CAA) Conference, April 2-6 2007, Berlin.*

Rogers, B. A. 2004. *The Archaeologist's Manual for Conservation: A Guide to Non-Toxic, Minimal Intervention Artifact Stabilization.* New York: Kluwer Academic/Plenum Publishers.

Rose, J. C. 1997. *The Bioarchaeology of Ancient Egypt and Nubia: A Bibliography.* British Museum Occasional Paper 112, London: British Museum Press.

Roskams, S. 2001. *Excavation.* Cambridge: Cambridge University Press.

Ryan, N., Pascoe, J. & Morse, D. 1999. Fieldnote: extending a GIS into the field, in J. Barceló, J. Briz & A. Vila (eds.) *New Techniques for Old Times: CAA98.* Oxford: British Archaeological Reports International Series, 757, Archaeopress, pp. 127-131.

Rye, O. S. 1981. *Pottery Technology: Principles and Reconstruction.* Washington D. C.: Manuals on Archaeology 4, Taraxacum Press.

Said, R. 1993. *The River Nile: Geology, Hydrology and Utilization.* New York: Pergamon Press.

Sauneron, S. 1968. *L'Egyptologie.* Paris: Que Sais-Je? Series.

Savage, S. 1990. GIS in archaeological research, in K. Allen, S. Green & E. Zubrow (eds.) *Interpreting Space: GIS and Archaeology.* London: Taylor & Francis, pp. 22-32.

Scarre, C. (ed.) 2007. *The Human Past: World Prehistory and the Development of Human Societies.* London: Thames & Hudson.

S.C.A.U.M. 1997. *Recording Information About Archaeological Fieldwork.* Standing Conference of Unit Managers

Scharff, A. B. 2007. Use of a digital camera for documentation of textiles, in C. Gills & M-L. B. Nosch (eds.) *First Aid for the Excavation of Archaeological Textiles.* Oxford: Oxbow Books, pp. 31-40.

Schiffer, M. B. 1995. *Behavioural Archaeology: First Principles.* Salt Lake City: University of Utah Press.

Schiffer, M. B. 1996. *Formation Process of the Archaeological Record.* Salt Lake City: University of Utah Press.

Scollar, I., Tabbagh, A., Hesse, A. & Herzog, I. 1990. *Archaeological Sensing and Remote Sensing.* Cambridge: Cambridge University Press.

Sear, D. R. 1978. *Greek Coins and Their Values: Volume 1 Europe.* London: Seaby.

Sear, D. R. 1979. *Greek Coins and Their Values: Volume 2 Asia and North Africa.* London: Seaby.

Sease, C. 1994. *A Conservation Manual for the Field Archaeologist,* Third Edition. Los Angeles: UCLA Institute of Archaeology, Archaeological Research Tools, No. 4.

Seiler-Baldinger, A. 1994. *Textiles: A Classification of Techniques.* Bathurst: Crawford House Press.

Shaffer, B. S. 1992. Quarter-inch screening: understanding biases in recovery of vertebrate faunal remains, *American Antiquity* 57(1): 129-136.

Shakley, M. L. 1975. *Archaeological Sediments: A Survey of Analytical Methods.* New York: Wiley.

Shanks, M. 1992. *Experiencing the Past.* London: Routledge.

Shanks, M. and Tilley, C. 1987. *Re-Constructing Archaeology. Theory and Practice.* Cambridge: Cambridge University Press.

Sharer, R. J. & Ashmore, W. 1993. *Archaeology: Discovering Our Past,* Second Edition. California: Mayfield Publishing Co.

Shaw, I. (ed.) 2000. *The Oxford History of Ancient Egypt.* Oxford: Oxford University Press.

Shennan, I & Donoghue, D. 1992. Remote sensing in archaeological research, in A. M. Pollard (ed.) *New Developments in Archaeological Science.* Oxford: Clarendon Press, pp. 223-32.

Shennan, S. 1988. *Quantifying Archaeology.* Edinburgh: Edinburgh University Press.

Shira, N. 2005. Walking with herdsmen: In search of the material evidence for the diffusion of agriculture from the Levant to Egypt, *Neo-lithics, The Newsletter* of *Southwest Asian Neolithic Research* 1/05: 12-17.

Shira, N. 2007. Origins and development of bifacial stone tools and their implications for the beginning of animal herding in the Egyptian Western Desert, in M. Chlodnicki, K. Kroeper & M. Kobusiewicz (eds.) *Archaeology of Northeast Africa: Studies in Memory of Lech Krzyżaniak.* Poznań: Archaeological Museum, pp. 355-374.

Shopland, N. 2005. *Archaeological Finds: A Guide to Identification*. Stroud: Tempus Publishing.

Shopland, N. 2006. *A Finds Manual: Excavating, Processing and Storage*. Stroud: Tempus.

Shortland, A., Freestone, I. C. & Rehren, T. (eds.) 2009. *From Mine to Microscope: Advances in the Study of Ancient Technology*. Oxford: Oxbow Books.

Shott, M. 1987. Feature discovery and the sampling requirements of archaeological evaluations, *Journal of Field Archaeology* 14: 359-71.

Shott, M. 1995. Reliability of archaeological records on cultivated surfaces: a Michigan case-study, *Journal of Field Archaeology* 22: 475-90.

Sickman, L. C. S. 1956. *The Art and Architecture of China*. Harmondsworth: Penguin.

Sievert, A. K. 1992. *Maya Ceremonial Specialisation: Lithic Tools from the Sacred Cenote at Chichen Itza, Yucatan*. Madison, Wisconsin: Prehistory Press.

Skibo, J. M. 1992. *Pottery Function: A Use-Alteration Perspective*. New York: Plenum Press.

Smardz, K. and Smith, S. 2000. *The Archaeology Education Handbook*. Walnut Creek: Altimira Press.

Smith, L. 1985. *Investigating Old Buildings*. London: Batsford.

Spencer, A. J. 1979. *Brick Architecture in Ancient Egypt*. Warminster: Aris & Phillips Ltd.

Spencer, A. J. 1994. Mud brick: Its decay and detection in Upper and Lower Egypt, in C. Eyre, A. Leahy & L. Montagno Leahy (eds.) *The Unbroken Reed: Studies in the Culture and Heritage of Ancient Egypt in Honour of A. F. Shore*. London: Occasional Publications 11, Egypt Exploration Society, pp. 315-320

Steensberg, A. 1968. *Atlas Over Borups Agre*. Copenhagen: Munksgaard.

Steensberg, A. 1975. *Store Valby*. Copenhagen: Munksgaard.

Stein, J. K. 1987. Deposits for archaeologists, in M. B. Schiffer (ed.) *Advances in Archaeological Method and Theory* 11: 337-93.

Stein, J. K. & Farrand, W. R. (eds.) 1994. *Sediments in Archaeological Context*. Salt Lake City: University of Utah Press.

Steinberg, J. M. 1996. Ploughzone sampling in Denmark: isolating and interpreting site signals from disturbed contexts, *Antiquity* 70 (286): 268-292.

Steinbock, R. T. 1979. *Paleopathological Diagnosis and Interpretation*. Springfield, IL: C.C. Thomas.

Sundstrom, L. 1993. A simple mathematical procedure for estimating the adequacy of site survey strategies, *Journal of Field Archaeology* 20: 91-6.

Sutton, M. Q. & Arkush, B. S. 1998. *Archaeological Laboratory Methods: An Introduction*. Dubuque: Kendall/Hunt.

Taçon, P. S. C. & Chippendale, C. 1998. An archaeology of rock-art through informed methods and formal methods, in C. Chippendale & P. S. C. Taçon (eds.) *The Archaeology of Rock-Art*. Cambridge: Cambridge University Press, pp. 1-10.

Tassie, G. J. 1996. Hair-offerings: an enigmatic Egyptian custom, *Papers from the Institute of Archaeology* 7: 59-67.

Tassie, G. J. 2002. Ancient Egyptian wigs in the Cairo and other museums, in M. Eldamaty & M. Trad (eds.) *Egyptian Museum Collections around the World*, Volume Two. Cairo, Supreme Council of Antiquities / AUC Press, pp. 1141-1153.

Tassie, G. J. 2005. Egyptian cultural heritage: Let's work together, in N. Finneran (ed.) *Safeguarding Africa's Archaeological Past: Selected Papers from a Workshop Held at the School of Oriental and African Studies, University of London, 2001*. Oxford: Cambridge Monographs in African Archaeology 65, BAR International Series, Vol. 1454, Tempus Reparatsm, pp. 47-54.

Tassie, G. J. 2007. Have we dug ourselves into a hole? Reappraising excavation methodology and approaches in Egyptian archaeology (part two): Kafr Hassan Dawood, a case study, in J-C. Goyon & C. Cardin (eds.) *Proceedings of the Ninth International Congress of Egyptologists*. Leuven: Peeters, Orientalia Lovaniensia Analecta 150, pp. 1769-1782.

Tassie, G. J. In Press a.   What your hair says about you: changes in hairstyles as an indicator of state formation processes, in R. Friedman and L. McNamara (eds.) *Egypt at its Origins 3: Proceedings of the International Conference "Origin of the State. Predynastic to Early Dynastic Egypt", London (UK), 27th July-1st August 2008.* Leuven/Paris/Dudley: Orientalia Lovaniensia Analecta, Peeters.

Tassie, G. J. In Press b. Single-Context Recording in the context of archaeological fieldwork in Egypt, part one, in F. A. Hassan, G. J. Tassie, A. De Trafford, & L. Owens (eds.) *Management of Egypt's Cultural Heritage,* Volume 2. London: Golden House Publications.

Tassie, G. J. & Hassan, F. A. 2009. Sites and Monuments Records (SMRs) and cultural heritage management (CHM), in F. A. Hassan, G. J. Tassie, A De Trafford, L. S. Owens & J. van Wetering (eds.) *Managing Egypt's Cultural Heritage: Proceedings of the First Egyptian Cultural Heritage Organisation Conference on Egyptian Cultural Heritage Management.* London: Golden House Publications, pp.191-205.

Tassie, G. J., Hassan, F. A., van Wetering, J. & Calcoen, B. 2008. Potmarks from the Protodynastic to Early Dynastic cemetery at Kafr Hassan Dawood, Wadi Tumilat, East Delta, Egypt, in B. Midant-Reynes, Y. Trisant, S. Hendrickx & J. Rowland (eds.) *Egypt at its Origins 2: Proceedings of the Conference on Predynastic and Early Dynastic Egypt: Origin of the State, Toulouse – 5th – 8th Sept. 2005.* Leuven: Peeters, pp. 201-34.

Tassie, G. J., Rowland, J. M. & de Trafford, A. 2000. The 8th International Congress of Egyptologists, Cairo, 28th March - 3rd April 2000, *Papers From the Institute of Archaeology* 11: 98-109.

Taylor, J. H. 1989. *Egyptian Coffins*. Princes Risborough: Shire Publications Ltd.

Tilley, C. 1993. Interpretation and a poetics of the past, in C. Tilley (ed.) *Interpretative Archaeology*. Oxford: Berg, pp.1-27.

Tixier, J. 1963. *Typologie de l'épipaléolithique du Maghreb*. Paris: Arts et Métiers Graphiques.

Tixier, J. 1974. *Glossary for the Description of Stone Tools: with Special Reference to the Epipalaeolithic of the Maghreb*. Trans. M. H. Newcomer. London: Newsletter of Lithic Technology: Special Edition Number 1.

Trigger, B. G., Kemp. B. J., O'Connor, D. & Lloyd, A. B. 1983. *Ancient Egypt: A Social History*. Cambridge: Cambridge University Press.

Tyers, P. & Vince, A. G. 1983. *Pottery Archive Users Handbook*. London: Museum of London.

Ucko, P., Ling, Q. & Hubert, J. 2007. *From Concepts of the Past to Practical Strategies: The Teaching of Archaeological Field Techniques*. London: Saffron.

UKIC Archaeology Section 1993. *Packing and Storage of Freshly-Excavated Artefacts from Archaeological Sites.* London: Guidelines 2, United Kingdom Institute for Conservation.

Uren J., & Price W.F. 2005. *Surveying For Engineers*, 4th Edition. London: Palgrave Macmillan.

Verner Johnson, E. & Hogan, J. C. 1979. *Museum Collection and Storage*. Paris: UNESCO.

Vogelsang-Eastwood, G. 1993. *Pharaonic Egyptian Clothing*. Leiden: E. J. Brill.

Vogelsang-Eastwood, G. 2000. Textiles, in P. Nicholson & I. Shaw (eds.) *Ancient Egyptian Materials and Technology*. Cambridge: Cambridge University Press, pp. 268-298.

Wainwright, I. N. M. 1990. Rock painting and petroglyph recording projects in Canada, *Association for Preservation Technology Bulletin* 22(1/2): 55-84.

Waldron, T. 2001. *Shadows in the Soil: Human Bones and Archaeology.* Stroud: Tempus.

Walker, W. H. 1998. Where are the witches of prehistory? *Journal of Archaeological Method and Theory* 5: 245-308,

Walton, P. & Eastwood, G. 1995. *A Brief Guide to the Cataloguing of Archaeological Textiles.* Leiden: Brill.

Ward, C. 2006. Boat-building and its social context in Early Egypt: interpretations from the First Dynasty boat-grave cemetery at Abydos, *Antiquity* 80: 118–129

Wass, S. 1992. *The Amateur Archaeologist.* London: Batsford.

Watkins, S. A. & Brown, C. E. 1988. *Conservation of Ancient Egyptian Materials.* London: Institute of Archaeology Publications.

Watkinson, D. & Neal V. (ed.) 1998. *First Aid for Finds.* Hertford: The British Archaeology Trust.

Watson, P. 1987. *Egyptian Pyramids and Mastabas Tombs.* Princes Risborough: Shire Publications Ltd.

Webster, G. 1974. *Practical Archaeology: An Introduction to Field Archaeological Field-work and Excavation.* London: Adam & Charles Black.

Weeks, K. 2008. Archaeology and Egyptology, in R. H. Wilkinson (ed.) *Egyptology Today.* Cambridge: Cambridge University Press, pp. 7-22.

Wendrich, W. Z. 1994. *Who is Afraid of Basketry: A Guide to Recording Basketry and Cordage for Archaeologists and Ethnographers.* Leiden: Research School CNWS.

Wendrich, W. Z. 2000. Basketry, in P. Nicholson. & I. Shaw (eds.) *Ancient Egyptian Materials and Technology.* Cambridge: Cambridge University Press, pp. 254-267.

Wengrow, D. 2006. *The Archaeology of Early Egypt: Social Transformations in North-East Africa, 10,000 to 2,650 BC.* Cambridge: Cambridge University Press.

Wenke, R. J. 2009. *The Ancient Egyptian State: The Origins of Egyptian Culture (c. 8000-2000 BC).* Cambridge: Cambridge University Press.

Westman, C., (ed.) 1994. *Archaeological Site Manual: Museum of London Archaeological Service, Third Edition.* Hampshire: Museum of London, BAS Printers ltd, Over Wallop.

Wheeler, M. 1954. *Archaeology from the Earth.* Oxford: Oxford University Press.

White, R. & Page, H. (eds.) 1992. *Organic Residues in Archaeology: Their Identification and Analysis: Proceedings of the Conference Organised by the United Kingdom Institute for Conservation, Archaeology Section, Held at York, May 10th 1990.* London: United Kingdom Institute for Conservation, Archaeology Section.

White, T. D. 1991. *Human Osteology.* New York: Elsevier, Academic Press.

White, T. D. & Folkens, P. A. 2005. *The Human Bone Manual.* New York: Elsevier, Academic Press.

Whitley, D. S. (ed.) 2001. *Handbook of Rock Art Research.* Walnut Creek: Altamira Press.

Whittaker, J. C. 1994. *Flintknapping: Making and Understanding Stone Tools.* Houston: Texas University Press.

Wholey, J. S., Hatry, H. P., & Newcomer, K. E. (eds.) 2000. *Handbook of Practical Program Evaluation.* San Francisco: Jossey-Bass.

Wilkinson, R. H. (ed.) 2008. *Egyptology Today.* Cambridge: Cambridge University Press.

Wilkinson, T. A. H. 1999. *Early Dynastic Egypt.* London: Routledge.

Wilkinson, T. A. H. 2001. Rock drawings of the Eastern Desert, *Followers of Horus.* (http://www.nunki.net/PerMin/Followers/Wilkinson.html).

Wilson, D. R. 1982. *Air Photo Interpretation for Archaeology*. London: Batsford.

Wilson, K., Smith, C., Kacyra, B., Dimsdale, J., & Zayhowski, J. 1998. CYRAX: A portable Three-Dimensional Laser-Mapping and Imaging System, *Physics Division Progress Report*. London: 76-79.

Wilson R. (ed.) 1987. *Rescue Archaeology: Proceedings of the Second New World Conference on Rescue Archaeology*. Dallas: Southern Methodist University Press.

Winkler, H. 1938. *Rock Drawings of Southern Upper Egypt*. Vol. 1. Oxford: Oxford University Press.

Winkler, H. 1939. *Rock Drawings of Southern Upper Egypt*. Vol. 2. Oxford: Oxford University Press.

Wodzińska, A. 2009a. *Manual of Egyptian Pottery, Volume 1: Fayum A – Lower Egyptian Culture*. Brighton [MA]: Ancient Egypt Research Associates.

Wodzińska, A. 2009b. *Manual of Egyptian Pottery, Volume 2: Naqada III – Middle Kingdom*. Brighton [MA]: Ancient Egypt Research Associates.

Wodzińska, A. 2009c. *Manual of Egyptian Pottery, Volume 3: Second Intermediate through Late Period*. Brighton [MA]: Ancient Egypt Research Associates.

Wodzińska, A. 2009d. *Manual of Egyptian Pottery, Volume 4: Ptolemaic through Modern Period*. Brighton [MA]: Ancient Egypt Research Associates.

Wodzińska, A. In Press. Potmarks of Early Dynastic Buto and Old Kingdom Giza, their occurrence and economic significance, in R. Friedman & L. McNamara (eds.) *Egypt at its Origins 3: Proceedings of the Conference on Predynastic and Early Dynastic Egypt: Origin of the State, London 27th July – 1st Sept, 2008*. Leuven: Peeters.

Wood, W. R. & Johnson, D. L. 1978. A survey of disturbance processes in archaeological site formation, in M. B. Schiffer (ed.) *Advances in Archaeological Method and Theory. Selections for Students from Volumes 1 Through 4*. New York: Academic Press.

Wright, L. Schwarcz, H. P. 1998. Stable carbon and oxygen isotopes in human tooth enamel: identifying breastfeeding and weaning in prehistory, *American Journal of Physical Anthropology* 106: 1-18.

Wylie, A. 1992. The interplay of evidential constraints and political interests: recent archaeological research on gender, *American Antiquity* 57 (1): 15-35.

Wymer, J. 1984. *The Palaeolithic Age*. London: Croom Helm.

Yang, D. Y. & Watt, K. 2005. Contamination controls when preparing archaeological remains for ancient DNA analysis, *Journal of Archaeological Science* 32: 331-6.

Yarrow, T. 2008, In context: meaning, materiality and agency in the process of archaeological recording, in C. Knappett & L. Malafouris (eds.) *Material Agency: Towards a Non-Anthropocentric Approach*. New York: Springer, pp.121-137.

Zdziebłowski, S. 2008a. Some remarks on the earliest settlement mudbrick structures in Egypt, *Göttinger Miszellen* 217: 111-122.

Zdziebłowski, S. 2008b. Predynastic and Protodynastic mudbrick settlement architecture: an overview and new interpretation in the light of recent research, in V. Gashe & J. Finch (eds.) *Current Research in Egyptology 2008: Proceedings of the Ninth Symposium*. Bolton: Rutherford Press Limited, pp.139-150.

Ziebart, M., Holder, N. & Dare, P. 2003. Field digital data acquisition (FDA) using total station and pencomputer: a working methodology, in D. Wheatley, G. Earl & S. Poppy (eds.) *Contemporary Themes in Archaeological Computing*. Oxford: Oxbow Books, University of Southampton Department of Archaeology Monograph No. 3, pp. 58-64.

Zimmerman, L. J. (ed.) 2003. *The Archaeologist's Toolkit*. Walnut Creek: Altamira Press.